Why Do You Need this New Edition?

1. **Forty-two brand new readings**—many written within the last five years—address the controversial topics of today. Subjects range from Chapter 11's new coverage of the changing nature of gender in contemporary society to Chapter 12's look at the way the U.S. is perceived abroad and how terrorism and the war in Iraq continue to shape America's national identity.

2. **A new Chapter 13, In God We Trust?,** explores the complex debate over evolution and takes a look at the ever changing relationship between church and state.

3. **A new Chapter 14, Campus Experience,** addresses the value of a college education and personal rights on campus while inviting you to rethink the role of the university.

4. **Reading the Visual** segments encourage you to consider how graphs, charts, cartoons, ads, and photographs can be used to persuade and influence.

5. **New "Blog It" feature** allows you to read a real blog, related to each chapter's theme. This feature invites you to experience each topic from the perspective of the blogger and see how these increasingly popular online diaries blur the lines between journalism and opinion.

6. New sections on **Narrative Argument** and **Interpreting Evidence**—featured in the updated rhetoric chapters—encourage you to engage in discussion and understanding rather than confrontation and dispute. Fresh study and discussion questions and new sample readings with analysis help you develop effective arguments of your own.

7. The **updated Documentation Guide for MLA and APA** features expanded coverage on using electronic sources and includes two annotated and fully documented student essays. These examples, each incorporating visual devices, show you how your peers have tackled the important task of documentation in their college courses.

PEA
Long

Dialogues

An Argument Rhetoric and Reader

GARY GOSHGARIAN
Northeastern University

KATHLEEN KRUEGER

PEARSON
Longman

New York Boston San Francisco
London Toronto Sydney Tokyo Singapore Madrid
Mexico City Munich Paris Cape Town Hong Kong Montreal

Executive Editor: Suzanne Phelps Chambers
Senior Sponsoring Editor: Virginia L. Blanford
Editorial Assistant: Erica Schweitzer
Senior Marketing Manager: Sandra McGuire
Senior Supplements Editor: Donna Campion
Production Manager: Stacey Kulig
Project Coordination, Text Design, and Electronic Page Makeup: Pre-Press PMG
Cover Design Manager: John Callahan
Cover Designer: Maria Ilardi
Cover Images: (top) courtesy of Robert Llewellyn/ImageState/Alamy; (middle) courtesy of Banana Stock/SuperStock; (bottom) courtesy of David Young-Wolff/PhotoEdit Inc.
Photo Researcher: Chris Pullo
Senior Manufacturing Buyer: Alfred C. Dorsey
Printer and Binder: R.R. Donnelley and Sons
Cover Printer: Phoenix Color Graphics

For permission to use copyrighted material, grateful acknowledgment is made to the copyright holders on pp. 772–777, which are hereby made part of this copyright page.

Library of Congress Cataloging-in-Publication Data

Dialogues: an argument rhetoric and reader / [edited by] Gary
    Goshgarian; Kathleen Krueger. — 6th ed.
        p.   cm.
    Includes index.
    ISBN-13: 978-0-205-64276-2
    ISBN-10: 0-205-64276-4
    1. English language—Rhetoric.   2. Persuasion (Rhetoric)

3. College readers.   I. Goshgarian, Gary.   II. Krueger, Kathleen.

PE1431.D53   2009
808'.0427—dc22   2008014453

Please visit us at www.ablongman.com

ISBN 13: 978-0-205-64276-2
ISBN 10:   0-205-64276-4

1 2 3 4 5 6 7 8 9 10—DOC—11 10 09 08

Contents

PART TWO Essays and Readings 327

CHAPTER 10 Advertising and Consumerism 329

Hooking the Consumer 330

Targeting a New World 330

Joseph Turow

"With budgets that add up to hundreds of billions of dollars, the [advertising] industry exceeds the church and the school in its ability to promote images about our place in society—where we belong, why, and how we should act toward others."

Buy This 24-Year-Old and Get All His Friends Absolutely Free 335

Jean Kilbourne

"Although we like to think of advertising as unimportant, it is in fact the most important aspect of the mass media. It is the point."

Consumer Angst 343

Paul Lutus

"Consumerism is one of religion's modern replacements, and, like religion, it actively encourages, then exploits, dissatisfaction with everyday reality."

Which One of These Sneakers Is Me? 353

Doug Rushkoff

"The battle in which our children are engaged seems to pass beneath our radar screens, in a language we don't understand. But we see the confusion and despair that results. How did we get in this predicament, and is there a way out?"

CHAPTER 11 Gender Matters 424

Fitting In 425

ourselves to the gradual erosion of freedoms that have defined the Western spirit, or do we decide to live with terrorism on our terms — and not theirs?

CHAPTER 14   Campus Experience   625

Preface

Dialogues: *An Argument Rhetoric and Reader* focuses on promoting meaningful discussion, that is, the effective exchange of opinions and ideas. In this book, we move away from traditional models of confrontation and dispute and, instead, promote ways to create dialogue by examining different points of view with an open mind. This exploration of multiple perspectives on an issue helps students reach informed positions and develop their own compelling cases. While dialogue and consensus are encouraged, we realize that not all arguments can be resolved to everyone's satisfaction. However, understanding the principles of persuasive writing and the techniques of argument provides students with the tools to engage productively in negotiation. And although students may not always reach a consensus of opinion, they will be able to discuss diverse issues in a thoughtful and productive way.

Organization of the Book

As the title indicates, this book is divided into two parts. The rhetoric section consists of nine chapters explaining the strategies of reading and writing arguments. The reader section consists of seven thematic units containing over 100 essays that present a challenging collection of thought-provoking contemporary arguments.

Part One: The Rhetoric

Part One of the book is designed to stimulate critical thinking, reading, and writing, and to introduce students to research skills. It explores how issues are argued while emphasizing the actual process of persuasive writing, from brainstorming exercises to shaping the final product. Each of the nine chapters in *Part One* focuses on a particular facet or principle of persuasive writing, including a new visuals chapter that addresses how visuals can act as arguments in and of themselves, or as auxiliary support for written arguments.

Chapter 1 offers an overview of argumentation, clarifies key terminology, and introduces the processes of debate, dialogue, and deliberation. Chapter 2 focuses on critical reading, presenting a series of activities designed to help students evaluate arguments and recognize their primary components. An extensive section on testing arguments for logical fallacies ends the chapter. Chapter 3 discusses how to begin writing arguments. It helps students find worthwhile and interesting topics to write about by demonstrating techniques for brainstorming, limiting topics, and formulating claims. Chapter 4 examines the presence of audience, encouraging students to think about the different kinds of readers they may have to address.

This chapter suggests ways to evaluate readers' concerns and strategies to reach different audiences.

Chapter 5 focuses on the organization of the argument essay by analyzing two basic types of arguments—position and proposal. Outlining is reviewed as a tool to ensure effective organization. Chapter 6 considers the importance of evidence. We demonstrate that the effectiveness of a writer's argument largely depends on how well the writer uses evidence—facts, testimony, statistics, and observations—to support his or her ideas. Chapter 7 introduces the socially constructed Toulmin model of logic as a way of testing the premises of the writer's argument.

Chapter 8 explores the principles of visual argument in art, advertisements, editorial cartoons, photographs, and ancillary graphics such as charts and tables. Focusing on developing visual literacy skills, the chapter shows students how to apply the tools of critical analysis to the many visual arguments they encounter every day. Finally, Chapter 9 discusses research strategies, including locating and evaluating print and electronic sources, note-taking, and drafting and revising argument essays. The Documentation Guide provides documentation formats and annotated sample student papers for both MLA and APA styles.

Part Two: The Readings

With over 100 contemporary essays and visuals, the readings offer a wide range of challenging and stimulating issues that we think will be of interest both to students and instructors. The topics are selected to encourage discussion, and attempt to represent the diversity of opinion connected to the controversial issues we face today.

The first six chapters of *Part Two* examine broad themes, including consumerism, gender, immigration, race, religion, personal rights, and relationships. Each of these chapters is divided into two or three subtopics that take a closer look at the multiple viewpoints surrounding an issue. Reflective of current cultural trends, a new "Blog It" feature presents opinions through the medium of the blog and invites students to add their own viewpoints.

Study Apparatus

The study apparatus of the book is designed to help students thoughtfully consider the issues, their own opinions on these issues, and how they might engage in meaningful dialogue. Questions encourage critical thinking about each article's content and style. Each chapter in Part Two features an introduction to the chapter theme and its subsections. A brief headnote to each reading provides students with context and pertinent information regarding the reading, as well as biographical information about the author of the piece. "Before You Read" and "As You Read" questions help frame the reading. Following each reading are "Questions for Analysis and Discussion" that stimulate thinking on the content, argument, and writing strategies of the author. Some questions ask students to consider how other authors in the section would respond to a particular essay's argument or evidence, encouraging critical thinking across the theme or chapter. "Writing Assignments" follow the end of each subsection of readings, helping students to synthesize the information they have read and their own opinions.

New to This Edition

The sixth edition reflects the efforts of the previous edition to teach students how to create effective arguments. At the same time, we continue to encourage discussion and understanding rather than confrontation and dispute. For this edition we have incorporated the insights and suggestions of many instructors who used the last edition. Some changes to this edition include:

The Rhetoric

Most of the rhetoric chapters have been revised and updated, and they include new study and discussion questions and expanded apparatus. Furthermore, we have added new sample readings with analyses and replaced others in these chapters. Likewise, we have refreshed some examples and discussion in the visuals chapter. Finally, the examples of documentation using electronic sources have been updated and expanded in the "Documentation Guide: MLA and APA Styles," which concludes with two annotated and fully documented sample student essays, each incorporating visual devices.

The Reader

Part Two contains over 100 essays and visuals, many of which are new to this edition, and written or created within the last five years. We extensively revised several chapters, including "Gender Matters," "Spotlight on America," and "Race and Ethnicity." New chapters include, "Campus Experience," and "In God We Trust?" "Reading the Visual" segments encourage students to consider how visuals—graphs, charts, cartoons, ads, and photographs—can be used to persuade and influence.

In addition to magazines and journals, today's students increasingly find their information online. Online networks such as Facebook and MySpace have created online communities through which students connect and share information. Blogs, which operate as online diaries, present viewpoints and invite others to discuss ideas and experiences. This edition includes a new "Blog It" feature that presents a real blog reading related to the chapter's theme or subtheme.

Writing assignments that follow each section encourage students to address issues further, prompting them to formulate critical responses to the different points of view expressed in the section. Some questions include suggestions for using the Internet to explore a topic more fully and to aid research.

Supplements

MyCompLab

MyCompLab provides multimedia resources for students and teachers on one easy-to-use site. Students will find guided assistance through each step of the writing process; Exchange, Longman's online peer-review program; the "Avoiding Plagiarism" tutorial; diagnostic grammar tests and more than 2,500 practice exercises; and Research Navigator™, a database with thousands of magazines and academic journals, the subject-search archive of the *New York Times*, "Link Library," library guides, and more. Tour the site at http:// www.mycomplab.com.

Instructor's Manual

The Instructor's Manual has been updated to assist and guide instructors as they teach each chapter. In addition to summarizing how instructors might teach each chapter, the manual provides answers to all the questions in the textbook. Questions from each reading that are particularly appropriate for class discussion are indicated in boldface, with suggestions on how instructors might use specific questions to stimulate class dialogue.

Acknowledgments

Many people behind the scenes deserve much acknowledgment and gratitude. It would be impossible to thank all of them, but there are some for whose help we are particularly grateful. First, we would like to thank all the instructors and students who used the first five editions of *Dialogues*. Their continued support has made this latest edition possible. Also, we would like to thank those instructors who spent hours answering lengthy questionnaires on the effectiveness of the essays and who supplied many helpful comments and suggestions in the preparation of this new edition: Patricia R. Campbell, Lake Sumter Community College; James Matthews, Fairmont State University; James R. Sodon, St. Louis Community College at Florissant Valley; Jeffrey Foster, Naugatuck Valley Community College; Jay L. Gordon, Youngstown State University; and RoseAnn Morgan, Middlesex County College.

A very special thanks goes to Kathryn Goodfellow, for her extraordinary contribution in locating articles and writing the study apparatus for Part Two, as well as for her considerable work creating the Instructor's Manual. We would also like to thank Kristine Perlmutter for her assistance in formulating some of the questions in Part Two, and Amy Trumbull for her help in securing permissions.

Finally, our thanks to the people at Longman Publishers, especially our former editor, Virginia L. Blanford and her ever-efficient editorial assistant, Rebecca Gilpin, as well as our new editor, Suzanne Phelps Chambers and her editorial assistant, Erica Schweitzer. We are very appreciative of their fine help.

Gary Goshgarian
Kathleen Krueger

PART ONE

Strategies for Reading and Writing Arguments

CHAPTER 1

Understanding Persuasion

Thinking Like a Negotiator

Think of all the times in the course of a week when someone tries to convince you of something. You listen to the radio on the way to school or work and are relentlessly bombarded by advertisements urging you to buy vitamins, watch a particular television show, or eat at the new Mexican restaurant in town. You open a newspaper and read about the latest proposals to lower the drinking age, raise the age for retirement, and provide tax relief for the poor. The phone rings and the caller tries to sell you a magazine subscription or to convince you to vote for candidate X. There's a knock on your bedroom door and your sister wants to borrow a CD and the keys to your car. Whether the issue is as small as a CD or as important as taxes, everywhere you turn you find yourself called on to make a decision and to exercise a choice.

If you think about all these instances, you'll discover that each decision you finally do make is heavily influenced by the ability of others to persuade you. People who have mastered the art of argument are able to influence the thoughts and actions of others. Your ability to understand how argument works and how to use it effectively will help you become aware of the ways in which you are influenced by the arguments of others, as well as become more persuasive yourself. Anyone can learn to argue effectively by learning the techniques needed to create successful arguments.

This book is designed to help you achieve two goals: (1) to think critically about the power of other people's arguments and (2) to become persuasive in your own arguments.

Argument

Broadly speaking, *persuasion* means influencing someone to do something. It can take many forms: fast-paced glittering ads, high-flying promises from salespeople, emotional appeals from charity groups—even physical threats. What will concern us in this book is *argument*—the form of persuasion that relies on reasoning and logical thought to convince people. While glitter, promises, emotional appeals, and even veiled threats may work, the real power of argument comes from the arguer's ability to convince others through language.

3

Because this is a book about writing, we will concentrate on the aspects of persuasion that most apply in writing, as opposed to those that work best in other forms (advertisements or oral appeals, for instance). Although written arguments can be passionate, emotional, or even hurtful, a good one demonstrates a firm foundation of clear thinking, logical development, and solid supporting evidence to persuade a reader that the view expressed is worth hearing. The ultimate goal might be to convince readers to change their thinking on an issue, but that does not always happen. A more realistic goal might be to have your listeners seriously consider your point of view and to win their respect through the logic and skill of your argument.

Most of what you write in college and beyond will attempt to persuade someone that what you have to say is worthy of consideration, whether it's a paper stating your views on immigration laws, an analysis of "madness" in *King Lear,* a letter to the editor of your school newspaper regarding women's varsity basketball, or a lab report on the solubility of salt. The same demands of persuasion and argument will carry over into your professional life. Such writing might be in the form of progress reports on students or colleagues, legal briefs, business reports, medical evaluations, memos to colleagues, results of a technical study or scientific experiment, proposals, maybe even a sales speech. In searching for a job or career, you might have to sell yourself in letters of inquiry.

The success or failure of those attempts will strongly depend on how well you argue your case. Therefore, it's important that as a college student you learn the skills of writing persuasive arguments. Even if you never write another argument, you will read, hear, and make them the rest of your life.

What Makes an Argument?

Arguments, in a sense, underlie nearly all forms of writing. Whenever you express ideas, you are attempting to persuade somebody to agree with you. However, not every matter can be formally argued. Nor are some things worth the effort. So, before we go on to discuss the different strategies, we should make clear which subjects do and do not lend themselves to argument.

Facts Are Not Arguable

Because facts are readily verifiable, they can't be argued. Of course, people might dispute a fact. For instance, you might disagree with a friend's claim that Thomas Jefferson was the second president of the United States. But to settle your dispute, all you have to do is consult an encyclopedia. What makes a fact a fact and, thus, inarguable, is that it has only one answer. It occurs in time and space and cannot be disputed. A fact either *is* or *is not* something. Thomas Jefferson was the third president of the United States, not the second. John Adams was the second. Those are facts. So are the following statements:

- The distance between Boston and New York City is 214 miles.
- Martin Luther King, Jr.'s birthday is now celebrated in all 50 states.
- I got a 91 on my math test.
- The Washington Monument is 555 feet high.

- The Japanese smoke more cigarettes per capita than any other people on earth.
- My dog Fred died a year ago.
- Canada borders the United States to the north.

All that is required to prove or disprove any of these statements is to check with some authority for the right answer. Sometimes facts are not easily verifiable, for instance, "Yesterday, 1,212,031 babies were born in the world" or "More people have black hair than any other color." These statements may be true, but it would be a daunting, if not impossible, challenge to prove them. And what would be the point?

Opinions Based on Personal Taste or Preference Are Not Arguable

Differing opinions are the basis of all argument. However, you must be careful to distinguish between opinions based on personal taste and opinions based on judgments. Someone who asks your "opinion" about which color shoes to buy is simply seeking your color preference—black versus brown, say. If someone asks your "opinion" of a certain movie, the matter could be more complicated.

Beyond whether or not you liked it, what might be sought is your aesthetic evaluation of the film: a judgment about the quality of acting, directing, cinematography, set design—all measured by critical standards you've developed over years of movie-going. Should you be asked your "opinion" of voluntary euthanasia, your response would probably focus on moral and ethical questions: Is the quality of life more important than the duration of life? What, if any, circumstances justify the taking of a life? Who should make so weighty a decision—the patient, the patient's family, the attending physician, a health team?

The word *opinion* is commonly used to mean different things. As just illustrated, depending on the context, opinion can refer to personal preference, a reaction to or analysis of something, or an evaluation, belief, or judgment, all of which are different. In this text, we categorize all these different possibilities as either opinions of taste or opinions of judgment.

Opinions of taste come down to personal preferences, based on subjective and, ultimately, unverifiable judgments. Each of the following statements is an opinion of taste:

- George looks good in blue.
- Pizza is my favorite food.
- Brian May of the group Queen is the greatest living rock guitarist.
- Video games are a waste of time.

Each of these statements is inarguable. Let's consider the first: "George looks good in blue." Is it a fact? Not really, since there is no objective way to measure its validity. You might like George in blue, whereas someone else might prefer him in red. Is the statement then debatable? No. Even if someone retorts, "George does *not* look good in blue," what would be the basis of argument but personal preference? And where would the counterargument go? Nowhere.

Even if a particular preference were backed by strong feelings, it would not be worth debating, nor might you sway someone to your opinion. For instance, let's say you make the statement that you never eat hamburger. You offer the following as reasons:

1. You're turned off by the sight of ground-up red meat.
2. When the meat is cooked, its smell disgusts you.
3. Hamburgers remind you of the terrible argument that broke out at a family barbecue some years ago.
4. You once got very sick after eating meatloaf.
5. You think beef cattle are the dirtiest of farm animals.

Even with all these "reasons" to support your point of view, you have not constructed an argument that goes beyond your own personal preference. In fact, the "reasons" you cite are themselves grounded in personal preferences. They amount to explanations rather than an argument. The same is true of the statements about pizza, musicians, and video games.

Opinions Based on Judgments Are Arguable

An *opinion of judgment* is one that weighs the pros and cons of an issue and determines their relative worth. That "something" might be a book, a song, or a public issue, such as capital punishment. Such an opinion represents a position on an issue that is measured against standards other than those of personal taste—standards that are rooted in values and beliefs of our culture: what's true and false, right and wrong, good and bad, better and worse. Consequently, such an opinion is arguable.

In other words, personal opinions or personal preferences can be transformed into bona fide arguments. Let's return to the example of hamburger. Suppose you want to turn your own dislike for ground meat into a paper persuading others to give up eating beef. You can take several approaches to make a convincing argument. For one, you can take a health slant, arguing that vegetarians have lower mortality rates than people whose diets are high in animal fat and cholesterol or that the ingestion of all the hormones in beef increases the risk of cancer. You might even take an environmental approach, pointing out that the more beef we eat, the more we encourage the conversion of woodlands and rain forests into grazing land, thus destroying countless animals and their habitats. You can even take an ethical stand, arguing from an animal-rights point of view that intensive farming practices create inhumane treatment of animals—that is, crowding, force-feeding, and force-breeding. You might also argue that the killing of animals is morally wrong.

The point is that personal opinions can be starting points for viable arguments. But those opinions must be developed according to recognized standards of values and beliefs.

The Uses of Argument

Many arguments center on issues that are controversial. Controversial issues, by definition, create disagreement and debate because people hold opposing positions about them. And, most of the time, there are more than two sides. Depending on the issue, there may be multiple opinions and perspectives. Because these views are often strongly held, we tend to view argument only in the form of a *debate,* an encounter between two or more adversaries who battle with each other over who is right. The media does much to contribute to the way we picture argument, particularly in the area of politics.

Every four years or so, the image returns to our television screens. Two candidates, dark-suited and conservatively dressed, hands tightly gripping their respective podiums, face off for all of America to watch. Each argues passionately for his or her solution to poverty, educational failings, high taxes, and countless other social and economic problems. Each tries desperately to undermine the arguments of the opponent in an effort to capture the votes of those watching. It's a winner-take-all debate, and it's often the image we see in our minds when we think of argument.

Argument *is* a form of persuasion that seeks to convince others to do what the arguer wants. Argument allows us to present our views and the reasons behind those views clearly and strongly. Yet argument can serve more productive purposes than the above illustration. Although argument can be a debate between two or more opponents who will never see eye-to-eye, in the world outside presidential debates and television sound bites argument can also begin a *dialogue* between opposing sides. It can enable them to listen to each other's concerns and to respond to them in a thoughtful way. Rather than attempt to demolish their opponent's arguments, these negotiators can often arrive at positions that are more valuable because they try to reconcile conflicting viewpoints by understanding and dealing directly with their opponent's concerns. Through the practice of *debate, dialogue,* and *deliberation,* real change can happen. In this chapter, we explore these three essential elements of argument and explain how they will enable you to be more effective when you write to persuade others.

Debate

Think for a moment of all the associations the word *debate* suggests to you: winning, losing, taking sides, opposition, and competition. Debate is how we traditionally think of argument. It is a situation in which individuals or groups present their views as forcefully and persuasively as possible, often referring to their opponents' arguments only to attack or deride them. Practiced with just this goal in mind, debate can serve the purpose of presenting your position clearly in contrast to your opposition's, but it does little to resolve controversial issues. Focusing too much on the adversarial qualities of debate can prevent you from listening and considering other viewpoints. You can become so preoccupied with defeating opposing arguments that you fail to recognize the legitimacy of other opinions. This may lead you to ignore them as you fashion your own argument.

Consider the last time you debated an issue with someone. Perhaps it was an informal occasion in which you attempted to convince the other person of your point of view. It may have been about a job opportunity or the best place to spend spring break or what movie to see next weekend. Your aim was to persuade the other person to "see it your way," and, if it was a typical debate, you were successful only if the other individual acquiesced. Debates are traditionally won or lost, and losers often feel frustrated and disappointed. Even more important, reasonable concerns on the losing side are often overlooked or not addressed. Debate does not provide a mechanism for compromise. It is not intended to provide a path toward common ground or a resolution in which all parties achieve a degree of success and positive change is made. Although some issues are so highly contentious that true consensus can never be achieved, an effective argument must acknowledge and respond to opposition in a thoughtful and productive manner.

But debate is an important way to develop your arguments because it allows you to explore their strengths and weaknesses. It can be a starting point for argument rather than a conclusion. Debate contains some of the essential elements of argument: Someone with a strong opinion tries to demonstrate the effectiveness of that view, hoping to persuade others to change positions or to take a particular course of action. When we debate, we have two objectives: to state our views clearly and persuasively and to distinguish our views from those of our opponents. Debate can help us develop our arguments because it encourages us to *formulate a claim, create reasons to support it,* and *anticipate opposition.*

Formulating Claims

The claim is the heart of your argument. Whether you hope to protest a decision, change your readers' minds, or motivate your audience to take action, somewhere in your argument must be the assertion you hope to prove. In an argument essay, this assertion or claim functions as the *thesis* of the paper, and it is vital to the argument. The claim states precisely what you believe. It is the *position* or opinion you want your readers to accept or the action you want them to take. Thus, it's very important to state your claim as clearly as possible. It will form the basis for the rest of your argument.

Claims often take the form of a single declarative statement. For example, a claim in an argument essay about homelessness might look like this:

> If we look further into the causes of homelessness, we will discover that in many cases it is not the homeless individual who is at fault but rather conditions that exist in our society that victimize certain individuals.

A claim for an essay about teen pregnancy might be stated even more simply:

> The current rhetoric, which maintains that the sexual references in the lyrics of popular music are to blame for the rise in teenage parenthood in the United States, ignores several crucial realities.

Sometimes writers signal their claims to their readers by certain words: *therefore, consequently, the real question is, the point is, it follows that, my suggestion is.* Here's an example:

> Therefore, I believe that scientists can find other effective ways to test new medicines and surgical techniques other than relying on helpless laboratory animals.

Because some arguments make recommendations for solving problems, your claim might be framed as a conditional statement that indicates both the problem and the solution. This can be accomplished with split phrases such as *either . . . or, neither . . . nor, if . . . then.* For example,

> If we continue to support a system of welfare that discourages its recipients from finding employment, then the result will be a permanent class of unemployed citizens who lack the skills and incentives to participate fully for their own economic benefit.

Claims must have support to convince a reader, so they are often followed by "because" statements—that is, statements that justify a claim by explaining why something is true or recommended or beneficial:

> Outlawing assisted suicide is wrong because it deprives individuals of their basic human right to die with dignity.

Formulating your claim when you debate is a first step for three basic reasons:

1. It establishes the subject of your argument.
2. It solidifies your own stand or position about the issue.
3. It sets up a strategy on which your argument can be structured.

There are no hard-and-fast rules for the location of your claim. It can appear anywhere in your essay: as your opening sentence, in the middle, or as your conclusion. However, many writers state their claim early in the essay to let their readers know their position and to use it as a basis for all the supporting reasons that follow. In later chapters, we will look at strategies for arriving at a claim and ways to organize your reasons to support it effectively.

Creating Reasons

We have all seen a building under construction. Before the roof can be laid or the walls painted or the flooring installed, the support beams must be carefully placed and stabilized. Reasons are the support beams of an argument essay. Whether your claim will be considered correct, insightful, or reasonable will depend on the strength and persuasiveness of your reasons.

Reasons answer some basic questions about your claim:

1. Why do you believe your claim to be true?
2. On what information or assumptions do you base your claim?
3. What evidence can you supply to support your claim?
4. Do any authorities or experts concur with your claim?

You can derive reasons from personal experience, readings, and research. Your choices will depend on your claim and the information and evidence you need to make your reasons convincing. Let's use one of the examples from our discussion about claims to demonstrate what we mean:

> **Your Claim:** Outlawing assisted suicide is wrong because it deprives individuals of the basic human right to die with dignity.
>
> **Question 1:** Why do you believe your claim to be true?

Response: When individuals are terminally ill, they suffer many indignities: They can lose control of their bodily functions and must be dependent on others for their care. A prolonged illness with no hope of recovery causes the individual and family members to suffer needlessly. When death is imminent, individuals should be given the right to decide when and how to end their lives.

Question 2: On what information or assumptions do you base your claim?

Response: I believe that no individual wants to suffer more than necessary. No one wants to lose his or her independence and have to rely on others. Everyone wants to be remembered as a whole human being, not as a dying invalid.

Question 3: What evidence can you supply to support your claim?

Response: This is based on personal examples and on readings about how terminal illness is dealt with in hospitals and clinics.

Question 4: Do any authorities or experts concur with your claim?

Response: Yes, many authorities in the field of medicine agree with my claim. I can use their statements and research to support it.

By examining the responses to the questions, you can see how reasons can be created to support your claim. The answer to the first question suggests several reasons why you might be opposed to outlawing assisted suicide: the indignities suffered by the terminally ill, unnecessary suffering, the right to control one's own fate. Question 2 explores your assumptions about what the terminally ill might experience and provides additional reasons to support your claim. The third and fourth questions suggest ways to support your claim through personal examples, references to ideas and examples found in readings related to your topic, and the support of experts in the field.

Credibility is an essential element in creating reasons. To be a successful debater, you must be believable; you must convince your audience that you are knowledgeable about your subject and that the facts, statistics, anecdotes, and whatever else you use to support your reasons are accurate and up-to-date. This means constructing your reasons through research and careful analysis of all the information available. For example, if you argue in an essay that there are better ways to run the U.S. welfare system, you will need to understand and explain how the current system operates. You can use the facts and statistics that you uncover in your research to analyze existing problems and to support your ideas for change. Being thoroughly informed helps you present and use your knowledge persuasively. Acquainting yourself with the necessary information will make you appear believable and competent. In later chapters, we will discuss how to formulate reasons to support your claim and how to evaluate evidence and use it effectively.

Another way to achieve credibility is to avoid logical fallacies, which will undermine the logic or persuasiveness of your argument. *Logical fallacies,* a term derived from the Latin *fallere,* meaning "to deceive," are unintentional errors in logic or deliberate attempts to mislead the reader by exaggerating evidence or using methods of argument that appeal to prejudice or bias. In Chapter 2, we will review the most common forms of logical fallacies so you can recognize them in the arguments of others and avoid them in your own writing.

Anticipating Opposition

Because debate anticipates opposition, you need to be certain that your reasons can withstand the challenges that are sure to come. Your goal as a successful debater is not only to present your reasons clearly and persuasively but also to be prepared for the ways in which those individuals holding other views will respond to them. For instance, in an essay on discrimination in women's collegiate sports, you may state that the operating budget of the women's varsity basketball team at your school is a fraction of that for the men's team. As evidence, you might point to the comparative lack of advertising, lower attendance at games, and lesser coverage than for the men's team. Unless you anticipate other perspectives on your issue, however, your argument could fall apart should someone suggest that women's basketball teams have lower budgets simply because they have smaller paying audiences. Not anticipating such a rebuttal would weaken your position. Had you been prepared, you could have acknowledged that opposing point and then responded to it by reasoning that the low budget is the cause of the problem, not the result of it. Putting more money into advertising and coverage could boost attendance and, thus, revenue.

In short, it is not enough simply to present your own reasons, no matter how effectively you support them. Unless you are aware of and familiar with opposing reasons, you leave yourself open to being undermined. To make your case as effective as possible, you must acknowledge and respond to the strongest reasons that challenge your own. To present only the weakest points of those who disagree with you or to do so in a poor light would likely backfire on your own credibility.

The following are strategies we recommend to help you become more aware of views that are different from your own and ways you might respond to them.

"Yes, but . . ." Exchanges

One way to be aware of the reasons on the other side is to study and research your topic carefully. After you've done some reading, a useful method to explore the way others might respond to your ideas is to engage in a "Yes, but . . ." exchange. Imagine you are face-to-face with someone holding a different position and, as you run down the list of your own reasons, his or her response is "Yes, but . . . [something]." What might that "something" be? Your task is first to acknowledge the validity of the other individual's viewpoint, and then to respond to that idea with reasons of your own. Consider, for instance, how a debate about affirmative action programs might proceed. You begin:

> Affirmative action programs discriminate against white males by denying them employment for which they are qualified.

From what you've heard and read, your opponent might respond this way:

> Yes, there are probably instances in which white males have lost employment opportunities because of affirmative action programs, but without these programs

minority candidates would never be considered for some job openings regardless of their qualifications.

Another reason might be:

Race and gender should not be considerations when hiring an applicant for a job.

From your readings, you may uncover this opposing reason:

Yes, in an ideal society race and gender would never be factors for employers, but since we don't live in such a society, affirmative action programs ensure that race and gender don't become negative considerations when an individual applies for a job.

Imagining your debate in a "Yes, but . . ." exchange will help you work through a number of possibilities to strengthen your reasons in the light of opposition and to become more aware of other viewpoints.

Pro/Con Checklists

Another method to help you become more aware of opposing viewpoints is to create a pro/con checklist. Making a pro/con checklist is useful for several reasons. First, it helps you solidify your own stand on the issue. It puts you in the position of having to formulate points on which to construct an argument. Second, by anticipating counterpoints you can better test the validity and strength of your points. By listing potential resistance you can determine the weak spots in your argument. Third, tabulating your own points will help you decide how to organize your reasons—which points to

Sample Pro/Con Checklist

CLAIM: Human cloning should be outlawed because it is unnecessary and unethical.

PRO	CON
Human cloning is unnecessary because we have better ways to treat infertility.	Current fertility treatments are very expensive and are often unsuccessful.
Because we have too many unwanted children in the world already, we should not create more.	People have a right to have their own children.
Cloning is an unnatural process.	It is no more unnatural than many of the ways we currently treat infertility.
Human cloning will devalue the uniqueness of each individual.	A clone will still be a unique and separate human being.

put at the beginning of your paper and which to put in the conclusion. Depending on the issue, you may decide for the sake of impact to begin with the strongest point and end with the weakest. This is the strategy of most advertisers—hitting the potential customer right off with the biggest sales pitch. Or you may decide to use a climactic effect by beginning with the weakest point and building to the strongest and most dramatic. Last, by ordering your key points you can create a potential framework for constructing your argument. Page 12 shows an example of a pro/con checklist.

Moving from Debate to Dialogue

Debate is an important step in constructing an argument. It propels us to find a strong position and to argue that position as effectively as possible. But if we define argument as only debate, we limit the potential power of argument in our society. One common misconception is that all arguments are won or lost. This may be true in formalized debates, but in real life few arguments are decided so clearly, and when they are, the conflicting issues that lie at the heart of the debate can persist and continue to create dissent among individuals and groups. The prolonged tensions and sometimes violent confrontations that surround the issue of abortion may be the outcome of a debate that supposedly was resolved by a Supreme Court decision, *Roe* v. *Wade,* but remains a continuing problem because the debate did not engender a dialogue in which conflicting sides listened to each other and reconsidered their views from a more informed perspective. Argument must do more than provide an opportunity to present one's views against those of an opponent. We need to use it as a vehicle to explore other views as well and to help us shape a process in which change can happen and endure.

Dialogue

Take another moment to consider words that come to mind when you think of *dialogue:* discussion, listening, interaction, and understanding. By definition, a dialogue includes more than one voice, and those voices are responsive to each other. When we have a dialogue with someone, we don't simply present our own views. We may disagree, but we take turns so that no one voice monopolizes the conversation. The object of a dialogue is not to win or lose; the object is to communicate our ideas and to listen to what the other person has to say in response.

For example, you may find a policy in a particular class regarding make-ups unfair. Since your instructor seems to be a reasonable person, you visit her office to discuss your objections. Your dialogue might proceed like this:

You: Professor, your syllabus states that if a student misses a test, there are no make-ups. I think that this is unfair because if a student is genuinely ill or has an important conflict, the student will be penalized.

Professor: I can understand your concern, but I have that policy because some students use make-ups to gain extra time to study. And, by asking other students about the questions on the test, they gain an advantage over students who take the test when it's scheduled. I don't think that's fair.

You: I hadn't thought of that. That's a good reason, but I'm still worried that even if I have a legitimate excuse for missing a test, my grade in the course will suffer. What can I do if that happens?

Professor: Let me think about your problem. Perhaps there's a way that I can be fair to you and still not jeopardize the integrity of my exams.

You: What if a student provides a physician's note in case of illness or a few days' advance notice in case of a conflict? Would you be able to provide an alternative testing day if that should happen?

Professor: That might be a good way to deal with the problem, as long as the make-up could be scheduled soon after. I'm going to give this more thought before I decide. I appreciate your suggestions. Stop by tomorrow and we can come to an agreement.

This hypothetical dialogue works because each participant listens and responds to the ideas of the other. Each has an important stake in the issue, but both focus on finding constructive ways to deal with it rather than trying to prove that the other is wrong. As a result, a compromise can be reached, and each person will have made a contribution to the solution.

When we move from debate to dialogue, we move from an arbitrary stance to one that allows for change and modification. Dialogue requires that both sides of the debate do more than simply present and react to each other's views in an adversarial fashion; it demands that each side respond to the other's points by attempting to understand them and the concerns they express. Often it is difficult for those participating in a debate to take this important step. In such cases, it will be your task, as a student of argument, to create the dialogue between opposing sides that will enable you to recognize common concerns and, if possible, to achieve a middle ground.

Creating a dialogue between two arguments involves identifying the writers' claims and key reasons. This is a skill we discuss in Chapter 2, when we look at strategies for reading and analyzing argument essays.

Deliberation

Deliberate is a verb that we don't use very much and we probably don't practice enough. It means to consider our reasons for and against something carefully and fully before making up our minds. We often speak of a jury deliberating about its verdict. Jury members must methodically weigh all the evidence and testimony that have been presented and then reach a judgment. Deliberation is not a quick process. It takes time to become informed, to explore all the alternatives, and to feel comfortable with a decision.

Deliberation plays an important part in the process of developing arguments. *Debate* focuses our attention on opposition and the points on which we disagree. *Dialogue* creates an opportunity to listen to and explore the arguments that conflict with our own. Deliberation, the careful consideration of all that we have learned through debate and dialogue, enables us to reach our own informed position on the conflict. Because we have participated in both debate and dialogue, we have a more complete understanding of the opposing arguments, as well as the common ground they may share. We are able to take the concerns of all sides into account.

Deliberation does not always resolve an issue in a way that is pleasing to all sides. Some issues remain contentious and irreconcilable, so that the parties are unable to move beyond debate. And, just as a jury sometimes reaches a verdict that is not what either the defense or the prosecution desires, deliberation does not ensure that all concerns or arguments will be considered equally valid. However, deliberation does ensure that you have given the arguments of all sides careful attention. And, unlike a jury, you have much broader parameters to determine your position. You do not have to decide *for* or *against* one side or the other. Your deliberations may result in an entirely new way of viewing a particular issue or solving a problem.

Review: Basic Terminology

Argument Essay

An essay that attempts to convince or persuade others through reason, logic, and evidence to do what the writer wants or believe as the writer wishes.

Claim

The statement in your essay that expresses your position or stand on a particular issue. The claim states precisely what you believe. It is the viewpoint you want your readers to accept or the action you want them to take.

Reasons

The explanation or justification behind your claim. To be effective, reasons must be supported by evidence and examples.

Debate

The act of presenting your claim and reasons, and challenging and being challenged by someone who holds a different viewpoint. Debate often focuses on differences between opponents rather than shared concerns and values.

Dialogue

The act of listening and responding to those who hold viewpoints that are different from your own on a particular issue. The object of a dialogue is to find common ground by trying to understand other viewpoints while sharing your own. It is intended to reduce conflict rather than promote it.

Deliberation

The careful and informed consideration of all sides of an issue before reaching a conclusion or position on it. Deliberation can result in the resolution of a contentious issue.

Consider, for example, a debate about whether a new football stadium should be built in a city experiencing economic problems, such as high unemployment and a failing public school system. One side of the debate may argue that a new stadium would result in additional jobs and revenue for the city from the influx of people who would come to watch the games. Another side may argue that the millions of dollars intended to subsidize a new stadium would be better spent creating job-training programs and promoting remedial education for schoolchildren. Your deliberation would involve several steps:

1. Becoming informed about the issue by reading and researching the information available
2. Creating a dialogue by listening to the arguments of all sides in the debate and trying to understand the reasons behind their claims
3. Weighing all the arguments and information carefully
4. Determining your own position on the issue

Your position might agree with one side or the other, or it might propose an entirely different response to the situation—say, a smaller stadium with the extra funds available to the schools, or a delay in the construction of a stadium until the unemployment problem is solved, or an additional tax to fund both, and so on. It would then be your task to convince all sides of the value of your position.

Deliberation enables you to use argument productively. It allows you to consider all sides of a problem or issue and to use your own critical analysis to find a way to respond.

As you learn more about writing your own arguments, you'll find that debate, dialogue, and deliberation can help you identify different perspectives, search for shared concerns, and develop your own position on an issue.

Taking a "War of Words" Too Literally
Deborah Tannen

The following essay provides important insights into the ways in which we often approach argument in our society. This article by Deborah Tannen appeared in the weekly edition of the *Washington Post* on March 23, 1998. It is adapted from her book, *The Argument Culture: Moving from Debate to Dialogue,* which explores how U.S. culture promotes a warlike, adversarial approach to problem-solving. Tannen is a professor of linguistics at Georgetown University. She is the author of the bestsellers *You Just Don't Understand: Women and Men in Conversation* and *Talking from 9 to 5: Women and Men in the Workplace.* As you read Tannen's article, think about whether you have had experiences similar to those Tannen describes, when disagreements could have been settled more successfully through dialogue and thoughtful deliberation than through conflict.

1   I was waiting to go on a television talk show a few years ago for a discussion about how men and women communicate, when a man walked in wearing a shirt and tie and a floor-length skirt, the top of which was brushed by his waist-length red hair.

He politely introduced himself and told me that he'd read and liked my book *You Just Don't Understand*, which had just been published. Then he added, "When I get out there, I'm going to attack you. But don't take it personally. That's why they invite me on, so that's what I'm going to do."

2   We went on the set and the show began. I had hardly managed to finish a sentence or two before the man threw his arms out in gestures of anger, and began shrieking—briefly hurling accusations at me, and then railing at length against women. The strangest thing about his hysterical outburst was how the studio audience reacted: They turned vicious—not attacking me (I hadn't said anything substantive yet) or him (who wants to tangle with someone who screams at you?) but the other guests: women who had come to talk about problems they had communicating with their spouses.

3   My antagonist was nothing more than a dependable provocateur, brought on to ensure a lively show. The incident has stayed with me not because it was typical of the talk shows I have appeared on—it wasn't, I'm happy to say—but because it exemplifies the ritual nature of much of the opposition that pervades our public dialogue.

4   Everywhere we turn, there is evidence that, in public discourse, we prize contentiousness and aggression more than cooperation and conciliation. Headlines blare about the Starr Wars, the Mommy Wars, the Baby Wars, the Mammography Wars; everything is posed in terms of battles and duels, winners and losers, conflicts and disputes. Biographies have metamorphosed into demonographies whose authors don't just portray their subjects warts and all, but set out to dig up as much dirt as possible, as if the story of a person's life is contained in the warts, only the warts, and nothing but the warts.

5   It's all part of what I call the argument culture, which rests on the assumption that opposition is the best way to get anything done: The best way to discuss an idea is to set up a debate. The best way to cover news is to find people who express the most extreme views and present them as "both sides." The best way to begin an essay is to attack someone. The best way to show you're really thoughtful is to criticize. The best way to settle disputes is to litigate them.

6   It is the automatic nature of this response that I am calling into question. This is not to say that passionate opposition and strong verbal attacks are never appropriate. In the words of Yugoslavian-born poet Charles Simic, "There are moments in life when true invective is called for, when it becomes an absolute necessity, out of a deep sense of justice, to denounce, mock, vituperate, lash out, in the strongest possible language." What I'm questioning is the ubiquity, the knee-jerk nature of approaching almost any issue, problem or public person in an adversarial way.

7   Smashing heads does not open minds. In this as in so many things, results are also causes, looping back and entrapping us. The pervasiveness of warlike formats and language grows out of, but also gives rise to, an ethic of aggression: We come to value aggressive tactics for their own sake—for the sake of argument. Compromise becomes a dirty word, and we often feel guilty if we are conciliatory rather than confrontational—even if we achieve the result we're seeking.

8   Here's one example. A woman called another talk show on which I was a guest. She told the following story: "I was in a place where a man was smoking, and there

was a no-smoking sign. Instead of saying 'You aren't allowed to smoke in here. Put that out!' I said, 'I'm awfully sorry, but I have asthma, so your smoking makes it hard for me to breathe. Would you mind terribly not smoking?' When I said this, the man was extremely polite and solicitous, and he put his cigarette out, and I said, 'Oh, thank you, thank you!' as if he'd done a wonderful thing for me. Why did I do that?"

9 I think the woman expected me—the communications expert—to say she needs assertiveness training to confront smokers in a more aggressive manner. Instead, I told her that her approach was just fine. If she had tried to alter his behavior by reminding him of the rules, he might well have rebelled: "Who made you the enforcer? Mind your own business!" She had given the smoker a face-saving way of doing what she wanted, one that allowed him to feel chivalrous rather than chastised. This was kinder to him, but it was also kinder to herself, since it was more likely to lead to the result she desired.

10 Another caller disagreed with me, saying the first caller's style was "self-abasing." I persisted: There was nothing necessarily destructive about the way the woman handled the smoker. The mistake the second caller was making—a mistake many of us make—was to confuse ritual self-effacement with the literal kind. All human relations require us to find ways to get what we want from others without seeming to dominate them.

11 The opinions expressed by the two callers encapsulate the ethic of aggression that has us by our throats, particularly in public arenas such as politics and law. Issues are routinely approached by having two sides stake out opposing positions and do battle. This sometimes drives people to take positions that are more adversarial than they feel—and can get in the way of reaching a possible resolution. . . .

12 The same spirit drives the public discourse of politics and the press, which are increasingly being given over to ritual attacks. On Jan. 18, 1994, retired admiral Bobby Ray Inman withdrew as nominee for Secretary of Defense after several news stories raised questions about his business dealings and his finances. Inman, who had held high public office in both Democratic and Republican administrations, explained that he did not wish to serve again because of changes in the political climate—changes that resulted in public figures being subjected to relentless attack. Inman said he was told by one editor, "Bobby, you've just got to get thicker skin. We have to write a bad story about you every day. That's our job."

13 Everyone seemed to agree that Inman would have been confirmed. The news accounts about his withdrawal used words such as "bizarre," "mystified" and "extraordinary." A *New York Times* editorial reflected the news media's befuddlement: "In fact, with the exception of a few columns, . . . a few editorials and one or two news stories, the selection of Mr. Inman had been unusually well received in Washington." This evaluation dramatizes how run-of-the-mill systematic attacks have become. With a wave of a subordinate clause ("a few editorials . . ."), attacking someone personally and (from his point of view) distorting his record are dismissed as so insignificant as to be unworthy of notice.

14   The idea that all public figures should expect to be criticized ruthlessly testifies to the ritualized nature of such attack: It is not sparked by specific wrongdoing but is triggered automatically.

15   I once asked a reporter about the common journalistic practice of challenging interviewees by repeating criticism to them. She told me it was the hardest part of her job. "It makes me uncomfortable," she said. "I tell myself I'm someone else and force myself to do it." But, she said she had no trouble being combative if she felt someone was guilty of behavior she considered wrong. And that is the crucial difference between ritual fighting and literal fighting: opposition of the heart.

16   It is easy to find examples throughout history of journalistic attacks that make today's rhetoric seem tame. But in the past such vituperation was motivated by true political passion, in contrast with today's automatic, ritualized attacks—which seem to grow out of a belief that conflict is high-minded and good, a required and superior form of discourse.

17   The roots of our love for ritualized opposition lie in the educational system that we all pass through.

18   Here's a typical scene: The teacher sits at the head of the classroom, pleased with herself and her class. The students are engaged in a heated debate. The very noise level reassures the teacher that the students are participating. Learning is going on. The class is a success.

19   But look again, cautions Patricia Rosof, a high school history teacher who admits to having experienced just such a wave of satisfaction. On closer inspection, you notice that only a few students are participating in the debate; the majority of the class is sitting silently. And the students who are arguing are not addressing subtleties, nuances or complexities of the points they are making or disputing. They don't have that luxury because they want to win the argument—so they must go for the most dramatic statements they can muster. They will not concede an opponent's point—even if they see its validity—because that would weaken their position.

20   This aggressive intellectual style is cultivated and rewarded in our colleges and universities. The standard way to write an academic paper is to position your work in opposition to someone else's. This creates a need to prove others wrong, which is quite different from reading something with an open mind and discovering that you disagree with it. Graduate students learn that they must disprove others' arguments in order to be original, make a contribution and demonstrate intellectual ability. The temptation is great to oversimplify at best, and at worst to distort or even misrepresent other positions, the better to refute them.

21   I caught a glimpse of this when I put the question to someone who I felt had misrepresented my own work: "Why do you need to make others wrong for you to be right?" Her response: "It's an argument!" Aha, I thought, that explains it. If you're having an argument, you use every tactic you can think of—including distorting what your opponent just said—in order to win.

22   Staging everything in terms of polarized opposition limits the information we get rather than broadening it.

23   For one thing, when a certain kind of interaction is the norm, those who feel comfortable with that type of interaction are drawn to participate, and those who do not feel comfortable with it recoil and go elsewhere. If public discourse included a broad range of types, we would be making room for individuals with different temperaments. But when opposition and fights overwhelmingly predominate, only those who enjoy verbal sparring are likely to take part. Those who cannot comfortably take part in oppositional discourse—or choose not to—are likely to opt out.

24   But perhaps the most dangerous harvest of the ethic of aggression and ritual fighting is—as with the audience response to the screaming man on the television talk show—an atmosphere of animosity that spreads like a fever. In extreme forms, it rears its head in road rage and workplace shooting sprees. In more common forms, it leads to what is being decried everywhere as a lack of civility. It erodes our sense of human connection to those in public life—and to the strangers who cross our paths and people our private lives.

QUESTIONS FOR DISCUSSION AND WRITING

1. Do you agree with Tannen's assertion that our public discussions about controversial issues have been turned into "battles and duels" by the media? Explain why or why not. Look through several current newspapers or newsmagazines to see if you can find evidence of this trend. Do other forms of media, such as television and radio, also encourage this outlook?

2. How has the "argument culture" affected our ability to resolve controversial issues? Can you think of any examples of current controversies that have been negatively affected by the tendency of those involved to defend their own "turf" rather than listen and respond constructively to the ideas of others who hold differing views?

3. Tannen cites the example of a woman who called in to a talk show and questioned whether her conciliatory approach to a potential conflict was the best course of action (paragraphs 8 and 9). In your journal, discuss some of your own experiences in confronting someone else about behavior you find unacceptable. What approaches have been successful for you? Do you agree with Tannen that the woman was wise to avoid conflict?

4. In your own experience, have you found that schools and teachers promote and reward students who engage in heated debate with other students, as Tannen contends in paragraphs 18 to 20? Do you think this style of communication discourages students who may not be as comfortable with this confrontational behavior? Have you found that a "winner-take-all" approach to argument is a productive way to solve problems or disagreements? What problems can arise from this approach? Are there any benefits?

SAMPLE ARGUMENTS FOR ANALYSIS

Read the following two essays to find the basic components in writing arguments and to practice debate, dialogue, and deliberation. After you have read each essay carefully, respond to these questions about them:

1. Identify each writer's claim and restate it in your own words. What do you think is the writer's purpose in writing the essay?
2. What reasons does each writer use to support his claim? Make a list of the reasons you find in each essay. Are the reasons convincing?
3. Find examples of the ways each writer supports those reasons. How convincing is the evidence he presents? Is it pertinent? reliable? sufficient? Is it slanted or biased?
4. Does the writer acknowledge views about the subject that are different from his own? Where does he do this? What is the writer's attitude toward those who hold different views? Does he try to understand those views or does he respond only negatively toward them?
5. Using debate, dialogue, and deliberation, complete the following activities individually or in small groups:
   a. To become acquainted with opposing reasons, write a "yes, but . . ." exchange or a pro/con checklist.
   b. Using your checklist or exchange, create a dialogue between two or more opposing sides on the issue that attempts to find points of disagreement as well as common ground or shared concerns among them. Look for opportunities for each side to listen and respond constructively to the other.
   c. Deliberate. Review the reasons and examples from a number of perspectives. What reasons on either side do you find the most compelling? What concerns have particular merit? How can you balance the interests of all sides of the issue? Formulate a claim that takes into account what you have learned from listening and considering several perspectives and provide reasons to support it.

The Case Against Tipping
Michael Lewis

> Many people have strong views about tipping. Some consider it an optional act of kindness to express appreciation for good service, an additional expense over what they have already paid. For others, it is an essential part of their day's wages, and thus their income. The following essay by Michael Lewis explores this dichotomy. Lewis, a journalist, writes about economics, politics, international economic relations, and society. As you read this article, which appeared in the *New York Times Magazine* on September 23, 1997, think about your own attitudes toward the practice of tipping. What motivates a tip? If you have ever been on

the receiving end, did you find that relying on others' generosity for your income left you vulnerable to their whims?

1   No lawful behavior in the marketplace is as disturbing to me as the growing appeals for gratuities. Every gentle consumer of cappuccinos will know what I'm getting at: Just as you hand your money over to the man behind the counter, you notice a plastic beggar's cup beside the cash register. "We Appreciate Your Tips," it reads in blue ink scrawled across the side with calculated indifference. The young man or woman behind the counter has performed no especially noteworthy service. He or she has merely handed you a $2 muffin and perhaps a ruinous cup of coffee and then rung them up on the register. Yet the plastic cup waits impatiently for an expression of your gratitude. A dollar bill or two juts suggestively over the rim—no doubt placed there by the person behind the counter. Who would tip someone a dollar or more for pouring them a cup of coffee? But you can never be sure. The greenbacks might have been placed there by people who are more generous than yourself. People whose hearts are not made of flint.

2   If you are like most people (or at any rate like me), you are of two minds about this plastic cup. On the one hand, you do grasp the notion that people who serve you are more likely to do it well and promptly if they believe they will be rewarded for it. The prospect of a tip is, in theory at least, an important incentive for the person working behind the counter of the coffee bar. Surely, you don't want to be one of those people who benefit from the certain hop to the worker's step that the prospect of a tip has arguably induced without paying your fair share of the cost. You do not wish to be thought of as not doing your share, you cheapskate.

3   And these feelings of guilt are only compounded by the niggling suspicion that the men who run the corporation that runs the coffee shops might be figuring on a certain level of tipping per hour when they decide how generous a wage they should extend to the folks toiling at the counters. That is, if you fail to tip the person getting you that coffee, you may be directing and even substantially affecting that person's level of income.

4   That said, we are talking here about someone who has spent all of 40 seconds retrieving for you a hot drink and a muffin. When you agreed to buy the drink and the muffin you did not take into account the plastic-cup shakedown. In short, you can't help but feel you are being had.

5   There in a nutshell is the first problem with tipping: the more discretion you have in the matter the more unpleasant it is. Tipping is an aristocratic conceit—"There you go, my good man, buy your starving family a loaf"—best left to an aristocratic age. The practicing democrat would rather be told what he owes right up front. Offensively rich people may delight in peeling off hundred-dollar bills and tossing them out to groveling servants. But no sane, well-adjusted human being cares to sit around and evaluate the performance of some beleaguered coffee vendor.

6   This admirable reticence means that, in our democratic age at least, gratuities are inexorably transformed into something else. On most occasions where they might be conferred—at restaurants, hotels and the like—tips are as good as obligatory. "Tipping is customary," reads the sign in the back of a New York City taxi, and

if anything, that is an understatement. Once, a long time ago, I tried to penalize a cabdriver for bad service and he rolled alongside me for two crowded city blocks, shouting obscenities through his car window. A friend of mine who undertipped had the message drummed home more perfectly: a few seconds after she stepped out of the cab, the cab knocked her over. She suffered a fracture in her right leg. But it could have been worse. She could have been killed for . . . undertipping! (The driver claimed it was an accident. Sure it was.)

7   There, in a nutshell, is the second problem with tipping: the less discretion you have in the matter, the more useless it is as an economic incentive. Our natural and admirable reluctance to enter into the spirit of the thing causes the thing to lose whatever value it had in the first place. It is no accident that the rudest and most inept service people in America—New York City cabdrivers—are also those most likely to receive their full 15 percent. A tip that isn't a sure thing is socially awkward. But a tip that is a sure thing is no longer a tip really. It's more like a tax.

8   Once you understand the impossibility of tipping in our culture, the plastic cup on the coffee-bar counter can be seen for what it is: a custom in the making. How long can it be before the side of the coffee cup reads "Tipping Is Customary"? I called Starbucks to talk this over, and a pleasant spokeswoman told me that this chain of coffee bars, at least, has no such designs on American mores. The official Starbucks line on their Plexiglas container is that it wasn't their idea but that of their customers. "People were leaving loose change on the counter to show their gratitude," she said. "And so in 1990 it was decided to put a tasteful and discreet cup on the counter. It's a way for our customers to say thanks to our partners." (Partners are what Starbucks calls its employees.)

9   Perhaps. But you can be sure that our society will not long tolerate the uncertainty of the cup. People will demand to know what is expected of them, one way or the other. Either the dollar in the cup will become a routine that all civilized coffee buyers will endure. Or the tasteful and discreet cup will disappear altogether, in deference to the straightforward price hike.

10   A small matter, you might say. But if the person at the coffee-bar counter feels entitled to a tip for grabbing you a coffee and muffin, who won't eventually? I feel we are creeping slowly toward a kind of baksheesh economy in which everyone expects to be showered with coins simply for doing what they've already been paid to do. Let's band together and ignore the cup. And who knows? Someday, we may live in a world where a New York City cabdriver simply thanks you for paying what it says on the meter.

QUESTIONS FOR DISCUSSION AND WRITING

1. Do you think Lewis has had much experience in a job that relies on tips? What evidence can you find to demonstrate this?
2. Do you agree with Lewis? In your journal, respond to Lewis's ideas by exploring your own views on tipping. What is your position on this topic? What experiences have you had that support your own view?

Some Lessons I Learned on the Assembly

Andrew Braaksma

Most college students would probably agree that the most desirable job would be one that demands the least amount of work and provides the most fun. Whether the job is waitperson at a beachside restaurant or resort, caddying at a flossy golf club, or mindlessly folding T-shirts at the Gap, the job is simply a means to an end—increased funds for future school expenses. Typically, a summer job offers reprieve from the onerous demands of study and exams. As a junior at the University of Michigan, Andrew Braaksma took a different approach: Instead of working at a beach resort or trendy mall shop, he chose a grueling factory job with hard-earned wages. In this essay, originally published in the "My Turn" column of *Newsweek*, Braaksma explains how a demanding blue-collar job taught him to value the privilege of education.

Braaksma wrote this winning essay for a contest entitled "Back to School," sponsored by *Newsweek* magazine, where this piece appeared in the September 12, 2005, issue.

1   Last June, as I stood behind the bright orange guard door of the machine, listening to the crackling hiss of the automatic welders, I thought about how different my life had been just a few weeks earlier. Then, I was writing an essay about French literature to complete my last exam of the spring semester at college. Now I stood in an automotive plant in southwest Michigan, making subassemblies for a car manufacturer.

2   I have worked as a temp in the factories surrounding my hometown every summer since I graduated from high school, but making the transition between school and full-time blue-collar work during the break never gets any easier. For a student like me who considers any class before noon to be uncivilized, getting to a factory by 6 o'clock each morning, where rows of hulking, spark-showering machines have replaced the lush campus and cavernous lecture halls of college life, is torture. There my time is spent stamping, cutting, welding, moving or assembling parts, the rigid work schedules and quotas of the plant making days spent studying and watching "SportsCenter" seem like a million years ago.

3   I chose to do this work, rather than bus tables or fold sweatshirts at the Gap, for the overtime pay and because living at home is infinitely cheaper than living on campus for the summer. My friends who take easier, part-time jobs never seem to understand why I'm so relieved to be back at school in the fall or that my summer vacation has been anything but a vacation.

4   There are few things as cocksure as a college student who has never been out in the real world, and people my age always seem to overestimate the value of their time and knowledge. After a particularly exhausting string of 12-hour days at a plastics factory, I remember being shocked at how small my check seemed. I couldn't believe how little I was taking home after all the hours I spent on the sweltering production floor. And all the classes in the world could not have prepared me for my battles with the machine I ran in the plant, which would jam whenever I absentmindedly put in a part backward or upside down.

5   As frustrating as the work can be, the most stressful thing about blue-collar life is knowing your job could disappear overnight. Issues like downsizing and overseas relocation had always seemed distant to me until my co-workers at one factory told me that the unit I was working in would be shut down within six months and moved to Mexico, where people would work for 60 cents an hour.

6   Factory life has shown me what my future might have been like had I never gone to college in the first place. For me, and probably many of my fellow students, higher education always seemed like a foregone conclusion: I never questioned if I was going to college, just where. No other options ever occurred to me.

7   After working 12-hour shifts in a factory, the other options have become brutally clear. When I'm back at the university, skipping classes and turning in lazy rewrites seems like a cop-out after seeing what I would be doing without school. All the advice and public-service announcements about the value of an education that used to sound trite now ring true.

8   These lessons I am learning, however valuable, are always tinged with a sense of guilt. Many people pass their lives in the places I briefly work, spending 30 years where I spend only two months at a time. When fall comes around, I get to go back to a sunny and beautiful campus, while work in the factories continues. At times I feel almost voyeuristic, like a tourist dropping in where other people make their livelihoods. My lessons about education are learned at the expense of those who weren't fortunate enough to receive one. "This job pays well, but it's hell on the body," said one co-worker. "Study hard and keep reading," she added, nodding at the copy of Jack Kerouac's "On the Road" I had wedged into the space next to my machine so I could read discreetly when the line went down.

9   My experiences will stay with me long after I head back to school and spend my wages on books and beer. The things that factory work has taught me—how lucky I am to get an education, how to work hard, how easy it is to lose that work once you have it—are by no means earth-shattering. Everyone has to come to grips with them at some point. How and when I learned these lessons, however, has inspired me to make the most of my college years before I enter the real world for good. Until then, the summer months I spend in the factories will be long, tiring and every bit as educational as a French-lit class.

QUESTIONS FOR DISCUSSION AND WRITING ───────

1. Describe a summer job you recently had. What, if anything, did you learn from the job? Did you take the job for reasons of finances? experience? recreation? some other reason or combination of reasons? Having read this essay, do you take a different view of your employment plans for next summer?

2. Consider how contrast is the organizing principle of this essay—that is, the material is organized by showing the differences between two matters. How does contrast figure in the opening paragraphs of this essay? What does the author contrast and for what effect?

3. An essay is often an opportunity for exploration, for discovering new ways of looking at things, for seeing parts of the world in new ways. What does Braaksma learn about "blue-collar" life? Given your knowledge of the world, do you agree with Braaksma's conclusions about blue-collar life? Does he undervalue or fail to recognize any of the positive attributes of a blue-collar lifestyle? What might a blue-collar worker say about Braaksma's analysis of factory life? about Braaksma's study of French literature?

4. Explain what Braaksma means when he says, "These lessons I am learning, however valuable, are always tinged with a sense of guilt." Have you had similar revelations about the value of education as a result of summer employment?

5. After studying the various points Braaksma makes, create a dialogue in your journal that might transpire between a worker in the factory Braaksma describes and a college student working at the Gap for the summer.

EXERCISES

1. Try to determine from the following list which subjects are arguable and which are not.
   a. Letter grades in all college courses should be replaced by pass/fail grades.
   b. Sororities and fraternities are responsible for binge drinking among college students.
   c. Lobster is my favorite seafood.
   d. Professor Greene is one of the best professors on campus.
   e. Children are better off if they are raised in a traditional nuclear family.
   f. Advertisements now often appear in commercial films using a strategy called product placement.
   g. Minorities make up only 9 percent of upper management positions in corporate America.
   h. The earth's population will be 7.3 billion by the year 2010.
   i. Juveniles who commit serious crimes should be sent to adult prisons.
   j. Last night's sunset over the mountains was spectacular.
   k. Advertisers often mislead the public about the benefits of their products.
   l. AIDS testing for health care workers should be mandatory.
   m. Bilingual education programs fail to help non-English-speaking children become part of mainstream society.
   n. Scenes of the nativity often displayed at Christmastime should not be allowed on public property.
   o. The tsunami that struck Asia in December of 2004 is the worst natural disaster in recorded history.
   p. Couples should have to get a license before having children.
   q. Given all the billions of galaxies and billions of stars in each galaxy, there must be life elsewhere.
   r. Secondhand smoke causes cancer.

2. In your argument notebook, create a pro/con checklist for the following topics. Make two columns: pro on one side, con on the other. If possible, team up with other students to brainstorm opposing points on each issue. Try to come up with five or six solid points and counterpoints.
   a. I think women are better listeners than men.
   b. If a juvenile is charged with a serious crime and his/her parents are found to be negligent, the parents should be charged with the crime as well.
   c. "Hard" sciences such as math are more difficult than "soft" sciences such as sociology.
   d. There should be a mandatory nationwide ban of cigarette smoking in all places of work including office buildings, restaurants, bars, and clubs.
   e. The university should reduce tuition for those students who maintained an A average during the previous year.
   f. ROTC should be made available to all students in U.S. colleges and universities.
   g. The majority of American people support prayer in school.
   h. Mandatory national ID cards would reduce the threat of terrorism in this country.

3. Use one of these topics to construct a dialogue in which the object is not to oppose the other side but to respond constructively to its concerns. As a first step, analyze the reasons provided by both sides and make a list of their concerns, noting whether any are shared. Then create a dialogue that might take place between the two.

4. Write about a recent experience in which you tried to convince someone of something. What reasons did you use to make your claim convincing? Which were most successful? What were the opposing reasons? How did you respond?

Reading Arguments

Thinking Like a Critic

We read for a variety of purposes. Sometimes it's to find information about when a particular event will take place, or to check on the progress of a political candidate, or to learn how to assemble a piece of furniture. Other times we read to be entertained by a favorite newspaper columnist, or to discover the secrets behind making a pot of really good chili. But if you've ever picked up a book, a magazine article, a newspaper editorial, or a piece of advertising and found yourself questioning the ideas and claims of the authors, then you've engaged in a special kind of reading called *critical reading*. When you look beyond the surface of words and thoughts to think about the ideas and their meaning and significance, you are reading critically.

Critical reading is active reading. It involves asking questions and not necessarily accepting the writer's statements at face value. Critical readers ask questions of authors such as these:

- What do you mean by that phrase?
- Can you support that statement?
- How do you define that term?
- Why is this observation important?
- How did you arrive at that conclusion?
- Do other experts agree with you?
- Is this evidence up-to-date?

By asking such questions, you are weighing the writer's claims, asking for definitions, evaluating information, looking for proof, questioning assumptions, and making judgments. In short, you are actively engaged in thinking like a critic.

Why Read Critically?

When you read critically, you think critically. Instead of passively accepting what's written on a page, you separate yourself from the text and decide what is convincing to you and what is not. Critical reading is a process of discovery. You discover where

28

an author stands on an issue, and you discover the strengths and weaknesses of an author's argument. The result is that you have a better understanding of the issue. By asking questions of the author, by analyzing where the author stands with respect to others' views on the issue, you become more knowledgeable about the issue and more able to develop your own informed viewpoint on the subject.

Critical reading not only sharpens your focus on an issue, it also heightens your ability to construct and evaluate your own arguments. That will lead you to become a better writer because critical reading is the first step to critical writing. Good writers look at the written word the way a carpenter looks at a house—they study the fine details and how those details connect to create the whole. It's the same with critical reading. The better you become at analyzing and reacting to another's written work, the better you are at analyzing and reacting to your own, by asking: Is it logical? Are my points clearly stated? Do my examples really support my ideas? Have I explained this term clearly? Is my conclusion persuasive? In other words, critical reading will help you use that same critical eye with your own writing, making you both a better reader and a better writer.

Additionally, as you sharpen your skills as a reader and a writer, you will also develop your critical skills as an interpreter of arguments embodied not in words but in visual images. As you will see in Chapter 8, argumentation is not limited to verbal presentation. Photographs, political cartoons, and advertisements, among others, express potent and persuasive arguments in visual imagery.

Even though you may already employ many of the strategies of critical reading, we'd like to offer some suggestions and techniques to make you an even better critical reader.

Preview the Reading

Even before you begin reading, you can look for clues that may reveal valuable information about the subject of the article, the writer's attitude about the subject, the audience the writer is addressing, and the purpose of the article. As a prereading strategy, try to answer the following questions:

1. *Who is the writer?* Information about the writer is sometimes provided in a short biographical note on the first or last page of the reading. The writer's age, education, current profession, and professional background can tell you about his or her experience and perspective on the subject. For instance, a physician who is writing about assisted suicide may have a very different attitude toward that subject than an individual who has a degree in divinity. A writer who has held a high-ranking position in a government agency or a political appointment will bring that experience to bear in a discussion of a political issue. A writer's background and professional training can provide knowledge and credibility; you may be more inclined to believe an expert in a field than someone with little or no experience. However, direct experience can also limit the writer's perspective. A review of this information before you read can help you better evaluate the writer as an authority.

2. *Where was the article originally published?* Often the publication in which the article originally appeared will indicate the writer's audience and purpose. Some publications, such as scholarly journals, are intended to be read by other professionals in a particular field. Writers for such a journal assume that readers are familiar with the terminology of that profession and possess a certain level of education and experience. For example, an author writing about cancer research in a scholarly medical journal such as the *Journal of the American Medical Association (JAMA)* would assume a high degree of medical expertise on the part of the readers. An author writing about the same cancer research in *Newsweek* would provide a greatly simplified version with little medical terminology. Popular magazines you see at newsstands are designed to communicate to a larger, more general audience. Writers make an effort to explain difficult concepts in terms an inexperienced reader can understand. Knowing where the article was originally published will prepare you for the demands of the reading. It may also prepare you for the writer's point of view. Publications are usually designed for a specific audience. The *Wall Street Journal,* for example, has a readership largely comprising people interested in the economy, business, or investments. The articles in it reflect the concerns and interests of the business community. In contrast, an article appearing in *High Times,* a publication that endorses the use and legalization of marijuana, has a very different set of readers. By familiarizing yourself with the publication in which the article originally appeared, you can learn much about the writer's likely political and professional opinions, knowledge you can use to judge the credibility of his or her argument.

3. *When was the article originally published?* The date of publication can also provide background about what was happening when the article was published. It will indicate factors that might have influenced the writer and whether the evidence used in the reading is current or historical. For instance, an article written about the economy during an earlier time of economic recession would be strongly influenced by factors of high unemployment and business failures. The writer's argument might not be as convincing during a period of growth and stability. Some readings are timeless in their consideration of basic truths about people and life; others can be challenged about whether their arguments still apply to current circumstances.

4. *What does the title reveal about the subject and the author's attitude toward it?* The title of an article often indicates both the subject of the article and the writer's attitude toward it. After you have identified the subject, look carefully at the words the writer has used to describe it. Are their connotations negative or positive? What other words do you associate with them? Does the title make reference to another written work or to a well-known slogan or familiar saying? Sometimes writers use their titles to suggest a parallel between their subject and a similar situation in recent times or a particular event in history. An article about the possibility of an annihilating nuclear attack in 2020 might be titled "Hiroshima in the Twenty-First Century." These choices are deliberate ways to inform readers about a writer's views and ideas on a subject. By considering the language in the title, you will be more aware of the writer's intent.

Let's try a preview of the first reading in this chapter. By carefully reading the introductory paragraph, you can learn the following information:

Preview Question 1: Who is the writer? As the introduction tells us, Henry Wechsler is the director of the College Alcohol Studies Program at the Harvard School of Public Health. His professional title suggests that he is knowledgeable about alcohol use, particularly at the college level, because he directs a program that studies this area. You are about to read an essay, then, written by an expert in the field of alcohol research.

Preview Question 2: Where was the article originally published? By reading further in the paragraph, you find that the article was originally published in the *Boston Globe*. This is a widely circulated newspaper located in a major American city. The writer would expect the article to be read by a large cross-section of people with diverse economic and educational backgrounds. Because Boston is the city where Harvard and many other colleges are located, readers might have a special interest in issues that affect the college community.

Preview Question 3: When was the article originally published? The introduction tells you that the article first appeared on October 2, 1997. Although this was written some 11 years ago, the topic is still relevant to current concerns.

Preview Question 4: What does the title reveal about the subject and the author's attitude toward it? The title of the article, "Binge Drinking Must Be Stopped," suggests an emphatic and nonnegotiable attitude on the part of the author.

As you can see, your preview of the article has provided much valuable information that will help prepare you to begin the critical reading process.

Skim the Reading

Just as an athlete would never participate in a competitive event without first stretching his or her muscles and thoroughly warming up, you will find that successful critical reading is a process that benefits from a series of activities aimed at increasing your understanding of the writer's ideas. The first time through, you may wish to skim the reading to get a general idea of its subject and intent. Further readings should be slower and more thoughtful so that each reason presented can be analyzed and evaluated and each idea judged and considered. Now that you have previewed the material about the author, the original publication and date, and the title, you are ready to skim the reading to find its basic features.

When you skim a reading, you are trying to discover the topic and the claim. Start by reading the first one or two paragraphs and the last paragraph. If the reading is a relatively short newspaper article, such as the following sample essay, this may be enough to give you a general idea of the writer's topic and point of view. If the reading is longer and more complex, you will also need to examine the first sentence or two of each paragraph to get a better sense of the writer's ideas.

SAMPLE ARGUMENT FOR ANALYSIS

For practice, let's skim the first reading in this chapter. To organize your impressions from skimming the reading, it's a good idea to write down some of them in your journal.

Binge Drinking Must Be Stopped
Henry Wechsler

"Binge" drinking is a problem on many college campuses. Away from home for the first time, many freshmen celebrate their new freedom by abusing alcohol at parties. But this behavior is not only confined to freshmen, as Henry Wechsler's research indicates. Henry Wechsler is the director of the College Alcohol Studies Program at the Harvard School of Public Health. He completed a survey focusing on the binge drinking practices of students at 140 colleges and universities. The survey revealed a high rate of binge drinking and a wide range of problems associated with this behavior, especially when connected to fraternity life. He wrote the following article in response to the death of MIT freshman Scott Krueger who died of alcohol poisoning after participating in binge drinking during a fraternity party. This essay was originally published in the *Boston Globe* on October 2, 1997.

1   We should be saddened and outraged by the tragic death of a young man just starting to fulfill his life promise.

2   This week's death from alcohol overdose of Scott Krueger, a freshman at the Massachusetts Institute of Technology, is an extreme and unfortunate consequence of a style of drinking that is deeply entrenched and widespread in American colleges. Binge drinking is a reality of college life in America and perhaps the central focus of fraternity house life.

3   Since the Harvard School of Public Health study on college binge drinking was released almost three years ago, colleges have been deluged with reports on alcohol abuse. Even before our results became public, it was inconceivable that college administrators were unaware of the existence of alcohol problems at their institutions.

4   A quick ride in a security van on a Thursday, Friday, or Saturday night could provide all the information needed. A conversation with the chief of security could easily reveal where the binge drinking takes place and which students, fraternities, and alcohol outlets are violating college rules or local ordinances.

5   An incoming freshman learns during the first week of school where the alcohol and parties are and often has a binge drinking experience even before purchasing a textbook. If students can find it so easily, so can college administrators. It is not that complicated: Drunken parties are usually at certain fraternity houses and housing complexes just off campus. The heaviest drinking most likely takes place in a few bars near campus where large quantities of alcohol are sold cheaply.

6   If we know so much about the problem, why is it that we have not been able to do much about it? First, because colleges, like problem drinkers, do not recognize that they have a problem. It has been there for so long that they have adapted to it. They are lulled into complacency as long as the problem does not seem to increase or a tragedy does not occur.

7   Second, the solutions that are offered are usually only partial: a lecture, an awareness day, a new regulation in the dorms. The root of the problem is seldom touched. The supply of large quantities of cheap alcohol is viewed as outside the purview of college officials. "It's off campus" is a euphemism for "that's not my job." The bar or liquor store may be off campus, but it is controlled by licensing boards that city officials and colleges can substantially influence. The fraternity house may be off campus and not owned by the college, but it is affiliated with and depends on the college for its existence. Many colleges and universities simply wink at the activities of the fraternities and claim no responsibility.

8   Third, when new policies are established, they are often assumed to be in effect without proper verification. It is easy to say there is no drinking allowed in a dormitory or a fraternity, but enforcement is necessary to put the policy into effect. Legally, no alcohol can be sold to people under age 21, but 86 percent of college students drink.

9   We can no longer be shocked at what is happening on many college campuses and in many fraternities. This is no longer a time merely to form a committee to study the situation. It is time to act.

10   Action needs to be taken on many fronts: the college president's office, the fraternity and sorority system, the athletics department, community licensing boards, and foremost, those students who are sick of the drinking they see around them.

11   Parents who pay for college tuitions should demand a safe environment for their children. Binge drinking need not remain an integral part of college life. University presidents must make it their responsibility to produce change.

After skimming "Binge Drinking Must Be Stopped," you might record the following (we indicate in parentheses the paragraphs in which we found our ideas):

> Wechsler starts off with a reference to a young man who died from an alcohol overdose. He says we should be saddened and outraged by this. Then he suggests that binge drinking has become very common on college campuses, particularly in fraternities (*paragraphs 1 and 2*). Wechsler believes parents should insist that colleges provide a safe environment for their children by finding solutions for binge drinking. University presidents must take responsibility for solving this problem (*paragraph 11*).

By skimming the article, you now have some sense of what the reading will be about and the writer's position. Before beginning a closer reading of the text, you will want to take one additional step to prepare yourself to be an active and responsive reader: Consider your experience with the topic.

Consider Your Own Experience

Your next step in the reading process is to consider your own experience. Critical reading brings your own perspective, experience, education, and personal values to your reading. Sometimes you begin with very little knowledge about the subject of your reading. It may be a topic that you haven't given much thought or one that is unfamiliar and new. Other times you may start with some of your own ideas and opinions about the subject. By taking the time to consider what you know and how your own experiences and values relate to the author's ideas, you can add a dimension to your reading that enables you to question, analyze, and understand the writer's ideas more effectively. You will be a more active critical reader because you can respond to the writer's ideas with ideas of your own.

Before beginning a close reading, take the time to reflect on these questions:

• What do I know about this subject?
• What have I heard or read about it recently?
• What attitudes or opinions do I have about the subject?

Exploring what you already know or think about a subject can have several benefits: You can use your knowledge to better understand the situation or issue described in the reading; you can compare your own experience with that of the writer; you can formulate questions to keep in mind as you read; and you can become more aware of your own opinions about the subject. For instance, you may be reading an article about the benefits of the proposed plan for improving your state's welfare system. If you have some knowledge about this proposal from reading news stories or hearing discussions about it, you will begin your reading with some understanding of the issue. If you have had actual experience with the welfare system or know of others' experiences, you can provide examples of your own to challenge or support those of the writer. If you have taken the time to consider questions you have about the proposed plan, you will be actively seeking answers as you read. And, by exploring your own views on the subject before you read, you will find that the ideas in the article will enrich, inform, and possibly change your opinion.

After previewing and skimming the reading, John, a freshman composition student, wrote the following reflection on the topic of binge drinking in his journal:

> It would be hard to be a student at college and not notice the heavy drinking that goes on every weekend. Some people just can't have fun unless they drink too much. It's a fact of college life—for some people. And if you live in a small college community, sometimes that's all there is to do on Saturday night. I've seen some kids really ruin their lives with too much partying. They forget why they came to college in the first place—or maybe that is why they came. But not everybody drinks to excess. Most of us just like to get a little buzz and socialize and have fun. Most of us will just go just so far and stop, but there's always a few who can't seem to stop until they pass out or puke their guts out on the sidewalk. Yeah, we've all been told the dangers of drinking too much, but some people aren't mature enough to see that they're hurting themselves. Binge drinking happens every weekend around here. It's not a pretty sight, but I'm not sure how the college president or anybody else could stop it. College students have always partied to relieve

tension and to socialize. It's been going on for years. Why is college drinking suddenly such a big issue? And, if the drinking takes place outside of campus, how can the college stop it? If students want to get alcohol, even if they're underage, they'll find a way. Why should the college tell us whether we can drink or not?

John clearly has considerable experience with the topic and some strong opinions of his own. By considering them before he begins a close reading of the article, he is ready to explore and challenge the ideas he encounters in the reading.

Annotate the Reading

Annotating the text is the next stage of critical reading to help you become a thoughtful and careful reader. *Annotating* is responding to the ideas in the reading right on the pages of your text. (If you don't own the publication the essay appears in, make a photocopy.) There are many different ways to annotate a reading, but many readers use the following methods:

- Highlight or underline passages that you consider significant.
- Write questions in the margins that respond to the writer's ideas or that you wish to follow up with further investigation.
- Circle words or phrases that need to be defined or made clearer.
- Add comments or brief examples of your own that support or challenge the writer's.
- Draw lines between related ideas.
- Note the writer's use of transitions and qualifiers that subtly shade meaning.
- Point out with arrows or asterisks particularly persuasive examples.
- Mark difficult-to-understand sections of the text that need a closer look.

Annotation is a way to create an active dialogue between you and the writer by responding in writing to individual points in the reading. Your annotations become a personal record of your thoughts, questions, objections, comments, and agreements with the writer. Annotation can help you read like a critic because it makes you slow down and pay attention to each idea as you read. As an additional benefit, your written comments in the margin will serve as a reminder of your response to the ideas in the essay when you read it again. Figure 2.1 on pages 35–37 is an example of some of the ways you might annotate "Binge Drinking Must Be Stopped."

Binge Drinking Must Be Stopped

1 We should be saddened and outraged by the tragic death of a young man just starting to fulfill his life promise.

2 This week's death from alcohol overdose of Scott Krueger, a freshman at the Massachusetts Institute of Technology, is an extreme and unfortunate consequence of a style of drinking that is deeply entrenched and widespread in American colleges. Binge drinking is a reality of college life in America and perhaps the central focus of fraternity house life.

Does everyone at college drink?

claim

3   Since the Harvard School of Public Health study on college binge drinking was released almost three years ago, colleges have been deluged with reports on alcohol abuse. Even before our results became public, it was inconceivable that college administrators were unaware of the existence of alcohol problems at their institutions.

Find out more info on this.

flooded

4   A quick ride in a security van on a Thursday, Friday, or Saturday night could provide all the information needed. A conversation with the chief of security could easily reveal where the binge drinking takes place and which students, fraternities, and alcohol outlets are violating college rules or local ordinances.

Is this the job of college administrators?

5   An incoming freshman learns during the first week of school where the alcohol and parties are and often has a binge drinking experience even before purchasing a textbook. If students can find it so easily, so can college administrators. It is not that complicated: Drunken parties are usually at certain fraternity houses and housing complexes just off campus. The heaviest drinking most likely takes place in a few bars near campus where large quantities of alcohol are sold cheaply.

qualifier

How does he know this?

qualifier

who is "we"?

6   If we know so much about the problem, why is it that we have not been able to do much about it? First, because colleges, like problem drinkers, do not recognize that they have a problem. It has been there for so long that they have adapted to it. They are lulled into complacency as long as the problem does not seem to increase or a tragedy does not occur. *smug self-satisfaction*

Is this contradicted by the next ¶? Don't colleges try to do something about binge drinking?

7   Second, the solutions that are offered are usually only partial: a lecture, an awareness day, a new regulation in the dorms. The root of the problem is seldom touched. The supply of large quantities of cheap alcohol is viewed as outside the purview of college officials. "It's off campus" is a euphemism for "that's not my job." The bar or liquor store may be off campus, but it is controlled by licensing boards that city officials and colleges can substantially influence. The fraternity house may be off campus and not owned by the college, but it is affiliated with and depends on the college for its existence. Many colleges and universities simply wink at the activities of the fraternities and claim no responsibility.

Agreed. These don't change behavior much.

less offensive substitute word

What does he mean?

8   Third, when new policies are established, they are often assumed to be in effect without proper verification. It is easy to say there is no drinking allowed in a dormitory or a fraternity, but enforcement is necessary to put the policy into effect. Legally, no alcohol can be sold to people under age 21, but 86 percent of college students drink.

proven to be true

Impressive statistic.

9   We can no longer be shocked at what is happening on many college campuses and in many fraternities. This is no longer a time merely to form a committee to study the situation. It is time to act.

Who is "we"? Has it changed?

10   Action needs to be taken on many fronts: the college pres- *his solution*
ident's office, the fraternity and sorority system, the athletics *What should*
department, community licensing boards, and foremost, those *they do?*
students who are sick of the drinking they see around them.

11   Parents who pay for college tuitions should demand a safe   *Who is*
environment for their (children.) Binge drinking need not remain *responsible?*
an (integral) part of college life. University presidents must make *Don't the*
it their responsibility to produce change.   *drinkers*
        essential   *Are college students*   *have some*
                              "children"?   *responsibility?*

Figure 2.1

Summarize the Reading

Before you can begin to analyze and evaluate what you read, it's important to understand clearly what the writer is saying. *Summarizing* is a type of writing used to capture the essential meaning of a reading by focusing only on the writer's main points.
When you summarize, you "tell back," in a straightforward way, the writer's main
ideas. Although summaries can vary in length depending on the length of the original
reading, all summaries share these qualities:

- **A summary is considerably shorter than the original.**   Because a summary
  is concerned only with the writer's main ideas, supporting details and examples
  are usually omitted. The length of a summary will vary depending on your purpose and the length and content of the original.
- **A summary is written in your own words.**   Although it may be necessary to
  use certain of the writer's words for which there are no substitutes, a summary
  is written in your own words. If you find it necessary to include a short phrase
  from the original, then quotation marks must be used to set it off. (In Chapter 9,
  we discuss ways to use summary in a researched argument paper and the need
  to document the ideas in your summary with a citation.)
- **A summary is objective.**   When you summarize, your job is to "tell back" the
  writer's main ideas with no comments or personal opinions of your own. Of
  course, once you have completed your summary, you are free to respond to it in
  any way you wish.
- **A summary is accurate.**   It's a good idea to reread several times before you attempt to summarize a reading because it's important that you truly understand what
  the writer means. Sometimes it takes many tries to capture that exact meaning.
- **A summary is thorough.**   Even though a summary is, as we've explained, much
  shorter than the original, a good summary contains each of the writer's main points.

Summarizing is an important step in critical reading because you need to understand a writer's ideas thoroughly before you can explain them, in writing, to others.
Don't be discouraged when you first try to summarize a reading. Over time and with
practice you will feel more comfortable writing summaries.

A good method to begin summarizing a reading is to write a one-sentence summary of the ideas in each paragraph. (Brief paragraphs that elaborate the same point can be summarized together.) By considering each paragraph separately, you will be sure to cover all the main ideas in the reading and be able to see at a glance how the ideas in the essay are connected to each other and how the writer has chosen to sequence them.

Let's go back to the essay "Binge Drinking Must Be Stopped" and try a one-sentence summary of each paragraph (we combine short paragraphs that are about the same idea):

Paragraphs 1 and 2: The recent death of an MIT student was a terrible event that was caused by excessive drinking practices that are common on college campuses.

Paragraph 3: Colleges should be aware of the problem of excessive drinking among their students because studies have been released about it.

Paragraph 4: By speaking with law enforcement professionals in their own communities, colleges could become aware of where alcohol laws are being broken.

Paragraph 5: Freshmen learn where to find alcohol when they first arrive on campus: fraternities, student housing, and bars close to campus.

Paragraph 6: Colleges aren't doing anything about the problem because they have accepted it and don't want to admit it exists.

Paragraph 7: Because the cause of the problem is the availability of alcohol off campus, colleges don't think it is their responsibility to act even though they could exercise a strong influence over the places that sell alcohol to students.

Paragraph 8: Colleges don't check to see whether their own alcohol policies are being enforced.

Paragraphs 9 and 10: Rather than just talk about this problem, we need to do something about it at many different levels within the college and the community.

Paragraph 11: College presidents need to take responsibility for reducing the practice of excessive drinking at their colleges to provide a safe place for students.

Your one-sentence summary of each paragraph should reveal the essential parts of the essay: the claim and the main reasons the writer uses to support the claim. Once you have identified these important elements, you are ready to begin your summary. It might look something like this (note that we've added the name of the writer and the title of the article):

In his essay "Binge Drinking Must Be Stopped," Henry Wechsler expresses his concern about the common practice of excessive drinking on college campuses. He suggests that colleges are failing in their responsibility to deal with this problem adequately. Although colleges should be informed about the problem, they won't acknowledge its seriousness. Because it doesn't happen on their campuses, they don't feel that it is their responsibility. Wechsler thinks that colleges could exercise their influence off campus in ways that would help to solve the problem. And, even when colleges do have alcohol policies to restrict drinking, they don't check to see if their policies are being enforced. The problem of binge drinking needs to be dealt with now at many different levels within the college and the community. Wechsler thinks that college presidents need to take responsibility for dealing with binge drinking so that it is no longer an important part of college life.

In looking over this summary, you'll notice that we begin with a general sentence that presents the writer's topic and claim. Then, after reviewing our one-sentence paragraph summaries, we have chosen the writer's main reasons to include in the rest of our paragraph. We have tried to eliminate any ideas that are repeated in more than one paragraph, so we can focus on only the major points.

Summarizing a reading means taking all the separate ideas the writer presents, deciding which ones are important, and weaving them together to create a whole. Our next step in the critical reading process is to consider the ways in which the writer has presented those ideas.

Analyze and Evaluate the Reading

To *analyze* something means to break it down into its separate parts, examine those parts closely, and evaluate their significance and how they work together as a whole. You already began this process when you summarized the main idea in each paragraph of your reading. But analysis goes beyond identifying the ideas in the essay. When we analyze, we consider how each part of the essay functions. We are discovering and evaluating the assumptions and intentions of the writer, which lie below the surface of the writing and which we consider separately from the meaning of the essay itself. Analysis helps us consider how successfully and effectively the writer has argued.

Although there is no set formula for analyzing an argument, we can offer some specific questions you should explore when reading an essay that is meant to persuade you:

- What are the writer's assumptions? What does the writer take for granted about the readers' values, beliefs, or knowledge? What does the writer assume about the subject of the essay or the facts involved?
- What kind of audience is the writer addressing?
- What are the writer's purpose and intention?
- How well does the writer accomplish those purposes?
- What kinds of evidence has the writer used—personal experience or scientific data or outside authorities?
- How convincing is the evidence presented? Is it relevant? Is it reliable? Is it specific enough? Is it sufficient? Is it slanted or dated?
- Does the writer's logic seem reasonable?
- Did the writer address opposing views?
- Is the writer persuasive?

For the sake of illustration, let's apply these questions to our reading:

- *What are the writer's assumptions?*

  The writer assumes that the death of the MIT student indicates a widespread problem of binge drinking on college campuses. He thinks that colleges have a responsibility to control the behavior of their students. He assumes that college students will continue to binge drink without any such controls.

- *What kind of audience is the writer addressing?*

  He seems to be addressing college administrators, parents of college students, and readers who have a special interest in college life.

- *What are the writer's purpose and intention?*

  He wants to make his readers aware that a problem exists and that colleges are not effectively dealing with it.

- *How well does the writer accomplish this purpose?*

  He makes a strong argument that colleges refuse to acknowledge that there's a problem.

- *What kinds of evidence has the writer used?*

  He refers to a study by the Harvard School of Public Health and uses examples of student hangouts that he has heard about but not experienced personally. He seems familiar with college programs on alcohol awareness. He implies that he consulted with the campus security chief for some of his information.

- *How convincing is the evidence?*

  Wechsler mentions a scientific study in paragraph 3 but never offers any details from it. Wechsler could provide more solid evidence that the problem is widespread. His examples of places where students can find alcohol seem convincing.

- *Does the writer's logic seem reasonable?*

  Wechsler effectively links the evidence he presents to his claim that excessive drinking on college campuses is being ignored by college administrators.

- *Did the writer address opposing views?*

  No. We never hear how college administrators respond to this criticism. We also don't know if college students agree with the description of their behavior.

- *Is the writer persuasive?*

  The writer is persuasive if we assume that the problem is widespread and that colleges can have a major impact on students' behavior when they are not on campus.

Argue with the Reading

Asking questions and challenging assumptions are important ways to read critically. Although you may not feel qualified to pass judgment on a writer's views, especially if the writer is a professional or an expert on a particular subject, you should keep in mind that as a part of the writer's audience, you have every right to determine whether an argument is sound, logical, and convincing. Your questions about and objections to the writer's ideas will help you evaluate the effectiveness of his or her argument and form your own judgment about the issue.

You may wish to record some of these thoughts in your annotations in the margins of the text. However, a good strategy for beginning writers is to respond at greater length in a journal. You might start by jotting down any points in the essay that contradict your own experience or personal views. Note anything you are skeptical about. Write down any questions you have about the claims, reasons, or evidence. If some point or conclusion seems forced or unfounded, record it and briefly explain why. The more skeptical and questioning you are, the more closely you are reading the text and analyzing its ideas. In particular, be on the lookout for logical fallacies, those instances in which the writer—whether unintentionally or purposefully—distorts or exaggerates evidence or relies on faulty logic to make a point. We discuss these fallacies extensively later in this chapter.

Likewise, make note of the features of the text that impress you—powerful points, interesting wording, original insights, clever or amusing phrases or allusions, well-chosen references, or the general structure of the essay. If you have heard or read different views on the issue, you might wish to record them as well.

As an example, let's consider some questions, challenges, and features that might have impressed you in our sample essay:

- Wechsler claims that binge drinking is a common practice at colleges across America. Is that true? Does binge drinking take place at all colleges or only on certain campuses? Do all students engage in this practice, or is it more common among certain age groups, gender, fraternity members as opposed to nonmembers, residential students? Do college students drink more than noncollege students in the same age group?
- The statistic about the percentage of college students who drink (paragraph 8) is convincing.
- Colleges exist to educate students. Are they responsible for monitoring students' behavior when they are not attending classes or socializing off campus? Is it realistic to expect colleges to do this?
- Are colleges really denying that the problem exists? Don't they have counseling services to help students with drinking problems? What else can they do?
- Wechsler's points about the influence that colleges have in their communities (paragraph 7) are persuasive.
- Mentioning the concerns of students who don't drink and the parents of college students is a clever strategy Wechsler uses to expand his audience and pressure colleges to act.

Create a Debate and Dialogue Between Two or More Readings

Few of us would expect to be experts on tennis or golf after watching one match or tournament. We know that it takes time and effort to really begin to understand even the fundamentals of a sport. Reading a single article on a particular subject is the first step in becoming educated about the issues at stake, but a single essay provides us with only one perspective on that subject. As we continue to read about the subject, each new article will offer a new perspective and new evidence to support that view. The more we read, the more complex and thorough our knowledge about the subject becomes. Creating a dialogue between two or more readings is the next step in the process of critical reading.

When you annotate a reading in the earlier stages of critical reading, you begin a dialogue between yourself and the writer. When you create a dialogue between two or more readings, you go one step further: You look at the ideas you find in them to see how they compare and contrast with each other, how they are interrelated, and how the information from one reading informs you as you read the next. By creating a dialogue between the ideas you encounter in several readings, you will be able to consider multiple viewpoints about the same subject.

SAMPLE ARGUMENT FOR ANALYSIS

Begin reading this second selection on binge drinking by following the steps we've outlined in this chapter:

1. Preview the information about the author, where the article first appeared, the date of publication, and the title.
2. Skim the reading to discover the writer's topic and claim.
3. Consider your own experience, values, and knowledge about the subject.
4. Annotate the reading.
5. Summarize the essay.
6. Analyze and evaluate the effectiveness of the reading.
7. Argue with the reading.

Stop Babysitting College Students
Froma Harrop

> Froma Harrop presents another viewpoint on the subject of binge drinking and college students in the following essay, which appeared in the *Tampa Tribune.* Harrop, an editorial writer and columnist for the *Providence Journal,* argues that college students should be the ones held responsible for their behavior, not businesses and educational institutions.

1 Anyone suspicious that the American university experience has become a four-year extension of childhood need look no farther than the colleges' latest response to the binge-drinking "problem." Now, in a grown-up world, college administrators would tell students who down four or five stiff drinks in a row that they are jerks.

2 If they commit violent acts as a result, the police get called. If they drive after drinking, they go to the slammer. If they die from alcohol poisoning, they have nothing but their own stupidity to blame.

3 But if they can drink responsibly, then let them have a good time.

4 Forget about hearing any such counsel, for that would turn students into self-directing adults. Better to blame the problem on all-purpose "cultural attitudes" and "societal pressures" abetted by the villainous alcohol industry.

5   Thus, demands grow for better policing of off-campus liquor outlets. That is, turn local businesses into babysitters. There are calls to ban sponsorship of college events by companies selling alcohol or the marketing of such beverages on campus. That is, protect their charges from evil influences and trample on free speech. (What should colleges do with the frequent references in Western literature to the glories of drink? Rabelais, for example, said, "There are more old drunkards than old physicians.")

6   One former college official has suggested that universities stop serving champagne at parents' weekend brunches or at fundraising events. Remove the bad example for the sake of the children. (Somehow it is hard to believe that a college with any sense of self-preservation would insist that its big-check writers remain cold sober.)

7   The truth is, most Americans can drink without a problem. Careful use of alcohol relaxes and warms the drinker with a sense of well-being. Winston Churchill and Franklin Roosevelt saved Western civilization without ever missing a cocktail hour. Students have long enjoyed their own drinking traditions. Brahms' Academic Overture, the stately piece heard over and over again at college commencements, took its melody from a student drinking song.

8   Where is there a campus drinking crisis, anyway? Six college students have supposedly died this year from excessive drinking. These cases are lamentable, but many more college students died from sports-related injuries or car accidents.

9   An even more interesting question is: How many noncollege people in their late teens or early 20s have died from alcohol poisoning? Take note that no one is memorizing this particular statistic—even though the majority of high school students do not go on to college. That number is not etched on our national worry list for the following strange reason: Our society considers the 19-year-old who has a job an adult, while universities see the 19-year-old pre-law student as a child. Working people who cause trouble because they drink are punished. College students are given others to blame.

10   College administrators should know that, from a purely practical point of view, playing hide-the-bottle does no good when dealing with an alcoholic. Indeed, anyone who has hung around Alcoholics Anonymous or Al-Anon can immediately identify such behavior as "enabling." Rather than allow the problem drinker to sink into the mire of his addiction until he can no longer stand it and takes steps to straighten out, the enabler tries to save him. Rest assured that students interested in getting smashed for the night will find the booze.

11   Let us end here with yet another proposition: that binge drinking is more about binge than drinking. It would seem that someone who gulps five glasses of Jim Beam in five minutes is not looking for a pleasant high. Binge drinking is a stunt that has more in common with diving off bridges or swallowing goldfish than the quest for inebriation.

12   What any increase in binge drinking probably indicates is that the students really don't know how to drink. Binging may just be the latest evidence of decline in our nation's table arts. Instead of savoring wine and spirits in the course of a civilized meal, young people are administering them. The colleges' response is to put condoms on bottles.

Construct a Debate

Now that you have a good understanding of Froma Harrop's views on college students' binge drinking, you are ready to consider the ideas in both the essays you read. Our first step will be to consider the differences between these two writers by constructing a debate. From your summaries of the readings, select the main ideas that seem directly opposed to each other. To highlight those differences, create two columns, one for each writer. Here are a few of the ideas Wechsler and Harrop debate in their essays:

Wechsler	*Harrop*
Binge drinking is a major problem on college campuses: A student has died.	Binge drinking is not a major problem on campuses: Few students have died.
Colleges have a responsibility to take action about this problem.	Students are responsible for their own drinking.
Colleges should prevent off-campus suppliers of alcohol from selling it to college students.	Colleges should not "police" off-campus suppliers of alcohol.
Colleges should provide a safe environment for students.	College students are adults and should take care of themselves.
Binge drinking continues because colleges aren't treating it as an important problem.	Binge drinking happens because some college students haven't learned to drink responsibly.

These are just a sampling of the many ideas that might be debated by these writers. You should be able to come up with several more.

By considering differences, you can see at a glance the ways in which these writers oppose each other. Your next step is to find the ideas they have in common. This may take more searching, but it's an important step in creating a dialogue between them. To get you started, we'll list a few of the ideas we found. See if you can come up with a few more:

1. Both writers acknowledge that drinking takes place on college campuses.
2. Both writers indicate that binge drinking can be a problem and that students have died as a result.
3. Both writers agree that colleges are aware that binge drinking takes place off campus.

Now that you have found both differences and common ideas, you are ready to create a dialogue. When you create a dialogue between two readings, you find ways for the writers to speak to each other that recognize their differences and points of agreement.

Your dialogue will reveal how the ideas in both readings interrelate. Let's try to create a dialogue using some of the ideas we found:

Wechsler: Binge drinking is a serious problem on college campuses. It's an activity that has become commonplace.

Harrop: I agree that college students engage in binge drinking, but six deaths this year don't necessarily indicate that this is a crisis.

Wechsler: Just because more students haven't died doesn't mean that it isn't a dangerous activity and should be ignored. Colleges need to take steps to ensure that more students aren't harmed by this common practice.

Harrop: It's unfortunate that students have died, but why should we think it is the college's responsibility to police student drinking? College students are adults and should suffer the consequences of their behavior. It's their choice whether to drink and how much.

Wechsler: Colleges are responsible for their students. They need to find ways to prevent students from getting alcohol. They are responsible to the parents who pay the tuition and to the other students who have to tolerate excessive drinking among their peers.

Harrop: Practically speaking, colleges can't prevent students from drinking. Students who want to drink will find a way because they are adults with drinking problems, not children in need of supervision.

Complete this dialogue by finding additional ways in which the writers' ideas speak to each other.

As you can see, the dialogue helps us explore the readings in far greater depth than if we had read both essays in isolation. Each writer's ideas help us to evaluate the ideas of the other. By interrelating them in a dialogue, we can better appreciate how the perspective of each writer changes the way similar facts and information are interpreted. For instance, Henry Wechsler is outraged by the death of one MIT student from a binge-drinking episode; in contrast, Froma Harrop does not find the deaths of six college students from excessive drinking an alarming statistic when she compares it with the number of college students who have died from other accidental causes. It is up to us as readers to decide which writer's interpretation is more persuasive.

SAMPLE ARGUMENTS FOR ANALYSIS

To practice creating your own dialogue between readings, read the following two letters to the editor, which appeared in two newspapers before and after Henry Wechsler's article. Read them critically, going through the steps we outlined in this chapter, and add them to the dialogue already created between Wechsler and Harrop. We think you'll find that your understanding of the issue will increase and that you'll feel more confident about forming your own position on the question of college binge drinking.

Letter from the *Washington Post*

To the Editor:

1   When we saw the headline "Party Hardly" and the revolting picture of four bare-chested, probably underage fraternity brothers guzzling cheap beer, we thought, "Finally! Your paper is tackling an issue that affects every college student." Much to our chagrin, however, the article wasted two pages of newsprint glorifying drunkenness and poor study habits.

2   Perhaps you need to be aware of some ugly facts before your next article on college drinking: One out of every four student deaths is related to alcohol use (research shows that as many as 360,000 of the nation's 12 million undergraduates will die as a result of alcohol abuse); alcohol is a factor in 66 percent of student suicides and 60 percent of all sexually transmitted diseases; studies show that between 33 percent and 59 percent of drinking college students drive while intoxicated at least once a year (with as many as 30 percent driving impaired three to 10 times per year); and alcohol consumption was a factor in at least half of the cases of a study of college women who had been raped by an acquaintance.

3   Alcohol affects not only those who drink it: Those students who do not drink are affected by their classmates or roommates who do. Students at schools with high levels of binge drinking are three times more likely to be pushed, hit or sexually assaulted than are students at schools with less drinking. Students who live with people who drink heavily often are kept awake by obnoxious behavior or the sound of their roommates vomiting in the trash can.

4   The shame does not lie solely with your paper, however. *The Princeton Review,* which ranks "party schools" based on how much students use alcohol and drugs, how few hours students study every day and the popularity of fraternities and sororities, should focus on what most feel is the real purpose of a college education: to learn—not to learn how to party.

Kathryn Stewart
Corina Sole

Letter from the *Times-Picayune*

To the Editor:

1   The entire nation is justifiably concerned about recent tragic deaths caused by alcohol abuse on our college campuses. College students everywhere know where to procure alcohol and where to consume it without being "hassled."

2   Public dialogue asks if institutions are doing enough to control the situation. Unfortunately, it must be stated that colleges and universities are doing all they can.

3   A typical university fosters an alcohol awareness program, provides the services of a substance abuse coordinator, disciplines students for infractions and provides an atmosphere in which young people can grow responsibly.

4 There is more that must be done. Parents at one time held their sons and daughters accountable for the company they kept. A student who deliberately associates with a group known for its excesses, or who joins an organization suspended or expelled by the institution, is choosing bad company. Peer pressure does the rest.

5 The courts restrict the ability of colleges to discipline students for off-campus behavior unless the activity in question has a fairly direct relationship with institutional mission.

6 They require due process, including confrontation by witnesses, for any disciplinary action. Peer pressures in the college-age group are so strong that testimony of witnesses is frequently difficult to obtain.

7 Until we return to a system in which colleges can function, at least in part, in loco parent is (in place of the parent), other agencies of society will have to step in.

8 To be fully effective, a college would need the ability to impose severe sanctions, including dismissal, on the base of reasonable proof of misbehavior or association with bad elements. Advocates of unrestrained constitutional rights will have difficulty with this, but the student enters a contractual relationship with a college to pursue an education.

9 The educators, not the legal system, should do the educating. Colleges exist to form good citizens, conscious of their own rights and the rights of others. Colleges and universities should be evaluated on the basis of the results of their educational work.

James C. Carter, S.J.
Chancellor,
Loyola University,
New Orleans

Deliberate About the Readings

As we explained in Chapter 1, deliberation is a way to arrive at your own position on a particular issue. You can't begin deliberation until you have really listened to and reflected on the complexities each issue involves. Once you have engaged in all the steps in the process of critical reading, you are ready to deliberate.

In your deliberation, first consider each of the writer's claims and main points. Then, thinking like a critic, find a way to respond that defines your own position on the issue. Using the four readings in this chapter, a deliberation in your journal about college binge drinking might look like this:

All the writers see binge drinking as a problem, although they differ about where they place the blame and how they plan to solve the problem. Wechsler thinks that binge drinking among college students occurs because colleges are indifferent to it and refuse to recognize its seriousness. He urges colleges to use their influence and power to prevent students from obtaining alcohol. He doesn't seem to think that the students who engage in binge drinking have a lot of control over their behavior. Carter, Sole, and Stewart all agree with Wechsler about the seriousness of the problem; however, they disagree about where to place the blame. Carter thinks that colleges are doing all they can and should be given more legal power to discipline students who binge drink. Sole and Stewart suggest that the media is to blame by endorsing values that encourage students to drink and party rather than concentrate on their studies. Only Harrop places the blame squarely on the shoulders of the binge drinkers themselves. She feels strongly that students need to be treated as adults with drinking problems and suffer the consequences of their actions.

After reading these writings, I am convinced that binge drinking is a problem worthy of our attention. The statistics that Wechsler, Stewart, and Sole cite are convincing and impressive. I also know from my own experience that many students drink excessively, and I think that six deaths are too many for us to ignore. I also think that binge drinking is a problem that affects the entire college community, not just the drinkers, as Stewart and Sole point out. However, I tend to agree with Harrop that students must be held responsible for their own actions. I disagree with Carter that schools should act like parents. College is about becoming an adult in all areas of our lives, not just academics.

Any solution to the problem of binge drinking needs to include the students who abuse alcohol. Unless those students also see their drinking habits as a problem, nothing the college or legal system can impose will affect their behavior. Perhaps a combination of actions, including broader and stronger efforts to educate students about alcohol abuse, greater enforcement and harsher penalties for underage drinking by the legal system, and efforts by colleges to restrict alcohol availability in the community and on the campus, would make a significant dent in this problem.

Now try writing your own deliberation, in which you consider the points you find most important in each reading, to arrive at your own position on the issue of binge drinking.

Look for Logical Fallacies

When you read the arguments of others, you need to pay attention to the writer's strategies, assertions, and logic to decide if the argument is reasonable. Like the cross-examining attorney in a court case, you must examine the logical connections between the claim, the reasons, and the evidence to reveal the strengths and weaknesses of the writer's argument.

Sometimes writers make errors in logic. Such errors are called **logical fallacies,** a term derived from the Latin *fallere,* meaning "to deceive." Used unintentionally, these fallacies deceive writers into feeling that their arguments are more persuasive than they are. Even though an argument may be well developed and contain convincing evidence, a fallacy creates a flaw in the logic of an argument, thereby weakening its structure and persuasiveness.

Not all logical fallacies are unintentional. Sometimes a fallacy is deliberately employed—for example, when the writer's goal has more to do with persuading than with arriving at the truth. Every day we are confronted with fallacies in media commercials and advertisements. Likewise, every election year the airwaves are full

Preview: Logical Fallacies

- Ad hominem argument
- Ad misericordiam argument
- Ad populum argument
- Bandwagon appeal
- Begging the question
- Circular reasoning
- Dicto simpliciter
- False analogy
- False dilemma
- Faulty use of authority
- Hasty generalization
- Non sequitur
- Post hoc, ergo propter hoc
- Red herring
- Slippery slope
- Stacking the deck
- Straw man

of candidates' bloated claims and pronouncements rife with logical fallacies of all kinds.

Recognizing logical fallacies when they occur in a reading is an important step in assessing the effectiveness of the writer's argument. This final section of our chapter will acquaint you with some of the most common logical fallacies.

Ad Hominem Argument

From the Latin "to the man," the **ad hominem** argument is a personal attack on an opponent rather than on the opponent's views. Certainly the integrity of an opponent may be important to readers. Nonetheless, writers are usually more persuasive and credible when they focus on issues rather than character flaws. If, for instance, you are reading a paper against the use of animals in medical research and the writer refers to the opposition as "cold-hearted scientists only interested in fame and fortune," you might question whether the writer objects to the scientists' views or to their personal prosperity. Name-calling and character assassination should make you suspicious of the writer's real motives or balanced judgment. Personal criticisms, even if true, can be overemphasized and, therefore, undercut the writer's credibility.

However, there may be cases in which an ad hominem argument is a legitimate rhetorical tool. When the special interests or associations of an individual or group appear to have a direct impact on their position on an issue, it is fair to raise questions about their lack of objectivity on that basis. For example, the organizer of a petition to build a state-supported recycling center may seem reasonably suspect if it is revealed that he owns the land on which the proposed recycling center would be built. While the property owner may be motivated by sincere environmental concerns, the direct relationship between his position and his personal life makes this fair game for a challenge.

Examples of Ad Hominem Arguments

- How could Tom accuse her of being careless? He's such a slob.
- Of course he doesn't see anything wrong with violent movies. The guy's a warmonger.
- We cannot expect Ms. Lucas to know what it means to feel oppressed; she is the president of a large bank.

Ad Misericordiam Argument

Its name also derived from Latin, the **ad misericordiam** argument is the appeal "to pity." This appeal to our emotions need not be fallacious or faulty. A writer, having argued several solid points logically, may make an emotional appeal for extra support. Your local Humane Society, for instance, might ask you to donate money so it can expand its facilities for abandoned animals. To convince you, the society might point out how, over the last few years, the number of strays and unwanted pets has tripled. And because of budget constraints, the society has been forced to appeal to the public. It may claim that a donation of $25 would house and feed a stray animal for a month. Any amount you give, they explain, will ultimately aid the construction of a new pet "dormitory" wing. To bolster the appeal, the Humane Society literature might then describe how the adorable puppy and kitten in the enclosed photo will have to be put to death unless the overcrowding of the society's facilities is relieved by donations such as yours.

When an argument is based solely on the exploitation of the reader's pity, however, the issue gets lost. There's an old joke about a man who murdered his parents and appealed to the court for leniency because he was an orphan. It's funny because it ludicrously illustrates how pity has nothing to do with murder. Let's take a more realistic example. If you were a lawyer whose client was charged with bank embezzlement, you would not get very far basing your defense solely on the fact that the defendant was abused as a child. Yes, you may touch the hearts of the jurors, even move them to pity. Yet that would not exonerate your client. The abuse the defendant suffered as a child, as woeful as it is, has nothing to do with his or her crime as an adult. Any intelligent prosecutor would point out the attempt to manipulate the court with a sob story while distracting it from more important factors such as justice.

> ## Examples of Ad Misericordiam Arguments
>
> - It makes no difference if he was guilty of Nazi war crimes. The man is 85 years old and in frail health, so he should not be made to stand trial.
> - Paula is 14 years old and lives on welfare with her mother; she suffers serious depression and functions like a child half her age. She should not be sent to adult court, where she will be tried for armed robbery, so she can spend her formative years behind bars.

Ad Populum Argument

From the Latin "to the people," an **ad populum** argument is just that—an argument aimed at appealing to the supposed prejudices and emotions of the masses. Writers attempt to manipulate readers by using emotional and provocative language to add appeal to their claims. The problem with the ad populum argument, however, is that such language sometimes functions as a smoke screen hiding the lack of ideas in the argument. You'll find examples of this fallacy on the editorial pages of your local newspaper—for example, the letter from parents raising a furor because they don't want their child or the children of their friends and neighbors taught by teachers with foreign accents; or the columnist who makes the ad populum case against capital punishment by inflating the number of innocent people wrongfully executed by the state; or the writer who argues that if gays and lesbians are allowed to serve in the military, our national defense will be jeopardized by "sex maniacs."

> ## Examples of Ad Populum Arguments
>
> - High-school students don't learn anything these days. Today's teachers are academically underprepared.
> - If you want to see the crime rate drop, tell Hollywood to stop making movies that glorify violence.
> - Doctors oppose health reform because it will reduce their large incomes.

Bandwagon Appeal

This familiar strategy makes the claim that everybody is doing this and thinking that. If we don't want to be left out, we had better get on the **bandwagon** and do and think the same things. The basic appeal in this argument is that of belonging to the group, behaving like the majority. It plays on our fears of being different, of being excluded. Of course, the appeal is fallacious inasmuch as we are asked to "get with it" without weighing the evidence of what is being promoted: "Smart shoppers shop at Sears"; "America reads Danielle Steel."

Examples of Bandwagon Appeals
• Everybody's going to the System of a Down concert. • Nobody will go along with that proposal. • The majority of the American people want a constitutional amendment outlawing flag burning.

Begging the Question

Similar to circular reasoning, **begging the question** passes off as true an assumption that needs to be proven. For instance, to say that the defendant is innocent because he passed a polygraph test begs the question: Does passing a polygraph test mean somebody is innocent? Sometimes the begged question is itself loaded in a bigger question: "Are you ever going to act like you are equal and pay for one of our dates?" The begged question here is whether paying the costs of a date is a measure of sexual equality.

Examples of Begging the Question
• That foolish law should be repealed. • She is compassionate because she's a woman. • If you haven't written short stories, you shouldn't be criticizing them.

Circular Reasoning

Circular reasoning is another common fallacy into which many writers fall. In it, the conclusion of a deductive argument is hidden in the premise of that argument. Thus, the argument goes around in a circle. For instance: "Steroids are dangerous because they ruin your health." This translates: Steroids are dangerous because they are dangerous. Sometimes the circularity gets camouflaged in a tangle of words: "The high cost of living in today's America is a direct consequence of the exorbitant prices manufacturers and retailers are placing on their products and services." Cut away the excess, and this translates: The high cost of living is due to the high cost of living. Repetition of key terms or ideas is not evidence. Nor does it prove anything. Instead of simply restating your premise, find solid evidence to support it.

Examples of Circular Reasoning
• People who are happy with their work are cheerful because they enjoy what they're doing. • Smoking is bad for you because it ruins your health. • Bank robbers should be punished because they broke the law.

Dicto Simpliciter

The fallacy known as **dicto simpliciter** comes from the Latin *dicto simpliciter ad dictum secundum quid,* which roughly translates as "from a general truth to a specific case regardless of the qualifications of the latter." In its briefer form, it means "spoken simply" and refers to a sweeping generalization that doesn't always apply. A dicto simpliciter argument makes the logical fallacy of exploiting an overly simplistic or unqualified "rule of thumb" while disregarding exceptions to that rule. For example, it's generally understood that birds fly. We know that at the local zoo Kiki the kiwi is a bird and is housed in the aviary. But to conclude that because she's a bird Kiki can therefore fly is fallacious reasoning. And the reason is that the kiwi bird is an exception—one of the few types of birds that are flightless.

Here's another more familiar matter where dicto simpliciter arguments might be heard. It is generally accepted that men are physically stronger than women. However, it would be a fallacious claim that women shouldn't be allowed in military combat since they aren't strong enough to carry weapons. This statement is a logical fallacy since it does not account for the exceptions to the rule—women who are stronger than the average. In other words, this argument exploits a stereotype.

Examples of Dicto Simpliciter Arguments
• If torture can save the lives of those who would be killed by terrorists, then the government should employ torture as a preemptive measure of protection.   • Exercise is good for people. Now that Bob is out of the hospital, he should get back to the treadmill.   • Guns kill. So we cannot allow the average citizen to possess a weapon.

False Analogy

An analogy compares two things that are alike in one or more ways. In any form of writing, analogies are very useful, as they expand meaning and demonstrate imagination. In arguments, they can be wonderful tools for persuasion. Unfortunately, they can also lead the writer astray and make his or her argument vulnerable to attack.

The problem with **false analogies** arises when the two things compared do not match up feature for feature, and ideas being compared do not logically connect or are pressed beyond legitimacy. The result is a false analogy. For instance, a candidate for a high-powered job may ask to be employed because of his extraordinary heroics during the Persian Gulf War. He may even claim that being a CEO is like fighting a battle: He needs to be brave, tough in mind and body, and willing to take and deal out punishment. Although the argument might sound appealing, running a company involves more than combat skills. Certainly it is important for a corporate executive to be strong and tough-minded. However, an office full of five-star generals might not be expert at dealing with economic recession or product liability. The fallacy is an imperfect analogy: Business and soldiering overlap minimally.

A sound analogy will clarify a difficult or unfamiliar concept by comparing it with something easily understood or familiar.

Examples of False Analogy
• The Ship of State is about to wreck on the rocks of recession; we need a new pilot.
• This whole gun control issue is polarizing the nation the way slavery did people living above and below the Mason-Dixon line. Do we want another Civil War?
• Letting emerging nations have nuclear weapons is like giving loaded guns to children.

False Dilemma

A **false dilemma** involves the simplification of complex issues into an either/or choice. For example, "Either we legalize abortion or we send young women to back-alley butchers," "Love America or leave it," "Either we keep gun ownership legal or only criminals will have guns." Such sloganizing ultimatums, although full of dramatic impact, unfortunately appeal to people's ignorance and prejudices.

Examples of False Dilemma
• English should be the official language of the United States, and anybody who doesn't like it can leave.
• Movies today are full of either violence or sex.
• Either we put warning labels on records and compact discs, or we'll see more and more teenage girls having babies.

Faulty Use of Authority

The **faulty use of authority** occurs when someone who is an expert in one area is used as an authority for another unrelated area. For instance, the opinions of a four-star general about the use of force against an uncooperative foreign tyrant carry great weight in a discussion of U.S. foreign policy options. However, the opinions of that same individual about the Supreme Court's ruling on the question of assisted suicide are less compelling. His military expertise does not guarantee that his views on euthanasia are particularly valuable.

Advertisers frequently resort to the faulty use of authority to promote their products. Celebrities are asked to endorse products they may have no special knowledge about or any interest in aside from the sizable check they will receive for their services. Another example occurs when well-known popular figures rely on their achievements in one area to lend credibility to their views in another. For instance, the late Benjamin Spock, famous for his work on child development, became a spokesperson for the nuclear disarmament movement. Because of his reputation, people were willing to listen more closely to his views than to others who were less well known, yet his expertise in child-rearing gave him no more authority in this area than any other well-educated person. While Dr. Spock may, indeed, have been knowledgeable about nuclear arms, his expertise in that area would have to be demonstrated before he could be used as an effective authority on the subject.

Examples of Faulty Use of Authority

- You should buy these vitamins because Larry King recommended them on television last night.
- The American Bar Association states that secondhand smoke is a serious cancer threat to nonsmokers.
- Americans shouldn't find hunting objectionable because one of our most popular presidents, Theodore Roosevelt, was an avid hunter.

Hasty Generalization

As the name indicates, the **hasty generalization** occurs when a writer arrives at a conclusion based on too little evidence. It's one of the most frequently found fallacies. If the local newspaper's restaurant critic is served underdone chicken at Buster's Diner during her first and only visit, she would be making a hasty generalization to conclude that Buster's serves terrible food. Although this may be true, one visit is not enough to draw that conclusion. If, however, after three visits she is still dissatisfied with the food, she is entitled to warn her readers about eating at Buster's.

Hasty generalizations can also occur when the writer relies on evidence that is not factual or substantiated. A generalization can only be as sound as its supporting evidence. Writers should provide multiple and credible examples to support their points. Be wary of sweeping, uncritical statements and words such as *always, all, none, never, only,* and *most.* Note whether the writer qualifies the claim with words that are limiting, such as *many, some, often,* and *seldom.*

Examples of Hasty Generalizations

- That shopping mall is unsafe because there was a robbery there two weeks ago.
- I'm failing organic chemistry because the teaching assistant doesn't speak English well.
- This book was written by a Stanford professor, so it must be good.

Non Sequitur

From the Latin for "does not follow," a **non sequitur** draws a conclusion that does not follow logically from the premise. For instance, suppose you heard a classmate make the following claim: "Ms. Marshall is such a good teacher; it's hard to believe she wears such ugly clothes." The statement would be fallacious because the ability to teach has nothing to do with taste in clothing. Some of the worst teachers might be the best dressers. Although you might want to believe a good teacher would be a good dresser, there is no reason to think so. Writers must establish a clear connection between the premise and the conclusion. And unless one is made through well-reasoned explanations, readers will not accept the cause-and-effect relationship.

Political campaigns are notorious for non sequiturs: "Candidate Jones will be a great senator because she's been married for twenty years." Or, "Don't vote for Candidate Jones because she is rich and lives in an expensive neighborhood." Whether the voters decide to vote for Candidate Jones should not depend on the length of her marriage or the neighborhood in which she lives—neither qualifies her for or disqualifies her from public office. The non sequiturs attempt to suggest a relationship between her ability to be a successful senator and unrelated facts about her life.

Examples of Non Sequitur
<ul><li>Mr. Thompson has such bad breath that it's a wonder he sings so well.</li><li>She's so pretty; she must not be smart.</li><li>I supported his candidacy for president because his campaign was so efficiently run.</li></ul>

Post Hoc, Ergo Propter Hoc

The Latin **post hoc, ergo propter hoc** is translated as "after this, therefore because of this." A post hoc, ergo propter hoc argument is one that establishes a questionable cause-and-effect relationship between events. In other words, because event *Y* follows event *X,* event *X* causes event *Y.* For instance, you would be making a post hoc argument if you claimed, "Every time my brother Bill accompanies me to Jacobs Field, the Cleveland Indians lose." The reasoning here is fallacious because we all know that although the Indians lose whenever Bill joins you at Jacobs Field, his presence does not cause the team to lose. Experience tells us that there simply is no link between the two events. The only explanation is coincidence.

Our conversations are littered with these dubious claims: "Every time I plan a pool party, it rains"; "Whenever I drive to Chicago, I get a flat tire"; "Every movie that Harry recommends turns out to be a dud." What they underscore is our pessimism or dismay, rather than any belief in the truth of such statements.

It's not surprising that post hoc reasoning is often found in arguments made by people prone to superstition—people looking for big, simple explanations. You would be committing such a fallacy if, for instance, you claimed that you got a C on your math test because a black cat crossed your path that morning or because you broke a mirror the night before. Post hoc fallacies are also practiced by those bent on proving conspiracies. Following the assassination of President Kennedy in 1963, there was considerable effort by some to link the deaths of many people involved in the investigation to a government cover-up, even though the evidence was scanty. Today, we hear Democrats protest that America goes to war every time Republicans are in office and Republicans protest that America gets poorer when Democrats are in office.

You might also have heard people argue that since the women's liberation movement, the number of latchkey children has risen sharply. The claim essentially says that the women's movement is directly responsible for the rise in working mothers over the last 30 years. While it is true that the women's movement has made it more acceptable for mothers to return to the workforce, the prime reason is particular to the individual. For some, it is simple economics; for others, personal fulfillment; for others still, a combination of the two. The feminist movement is one among many factors linked with women in the workforce and the consequent rise in latchkey children.

Examples of Post Hoc, Ergo Propter Hoc Arguments

- Just two weeks after they raised the speed limit, three people were killed on that road.
- I saw Ralph in the courthouse; he must have been arrested.
- It's no wonder the crime rate has shot up. The state legislature voted to lower the drinking age.

Red Herring

A **red herring,** as the name suggests, is evidence that is fallaciously used to distract the audience from the true issues of an argument. The term is derived from the practice of using the scent of a red herring to throw hunting dogs off the trail of their real prey. In modern life, this fallacy is more often used to confuse the audience by providing irrelevant information or evidence. For instance, when the head coach of a major league team was accused of using team funds on personal expenses, he defended himself by pointing to the team's winning record under his leadership. While the team had undeniably performed well during this period, his response was irrelevant to the charges made against him. He had hoped to distract his accusers from the real issue, which involved his lack of honesty and abuse of power. A red herring may distract the audience momentarily, but once it is discovered, it indicates that the individual has little or no effective reasons or evidence to support his or her position.

Examples of Red Herrings

- Even though that hockey player was convicted of vehicular homicide, he shouldn't go to jail because he is such a great athlete.
- Susan didn't hire John for the job because his wife is always late for meetings.
- The teacher gave me an F in the course because she doesn't like me.

Slippery Slope

The **slippery slope** presumes one event will inevitably lead to a chain of other events that end in a catastrophe—as one slip on a mountaintop will cause a climber to tumble down and bring with him or her all those in tow. This domino-effect reasoning is fallacious because it depends more on presumption than hard evidence: "Censorship of obscene material will spell the end to freedom of the press"; "A ban on ethnic slurs will mean no more freedom of speech"; "If assault rifles are outlawed, handguns will be next." America's involvement in Vietnam was the result of a slippery slope argument: "If Vietnam falls to the Communists, all of Southeast Asia, and eventually India and its neighbors, will fall under the sway of communism." Even though Vietnam did fall, the result has not been the widespread rise of communism in the region; on the contrary, communism has fallen on hard times.

Examples of Slippery Slope Arguments

- Legalized abortion is a step toward creating an antilife society.
- A ban on ethnic slurs will mean no more freedom of speech.
- If we let them build those condos, the lake will end up polluted, the wildlife will die off, and the landscape will be scarred forever.

Stacking the Deck

When writers give only the evidence that supports their premise, while disregarding or withholding contrary evidence, they are **stacking the deck**. (Science students may know this as "data beautification," the habit of recording only those results that match what an experiment is expected to predict.) A meat-packing manufacturer may advertise that its all-beef hot dogs "now contain 10 percent less fat." Although that may sound like good news, what we are not being told is that the hot dogs still contain 30 percent fat.

This stacking-the-deck fallacy is common not only in advertising but also in debates of controversial matters. The faculty of a college, for instance, may petition for the firing of its president for failing to grant needed raises while an expensive new football stadium is being built. The complaint would not be fair, however, if the faculty ignored mentioning that the stadium funds were specifically earmarked for athletic improvement by a billionaire benefactor. Also, if the complaint left unrecognized the many accomplishments of the president, such as the successful capital campaign, the plans for a new library, and the influx of notable scholars, it would be an example of stacking the deck.

As you progress through the chapters in this book, you will find that thinking like a critic is the key to understanding and responding to arguments. It will make you a stronger reader and a more effective writer. In the next chapter, we explore ways that you can think like a writer to find and develop topics for your own argument essays.

Examples of Stacking the Deck

- Parents should realize that private schools simply encourage elitism in young people.
- We cannot take four more years of her in office, given the way she voted against the death penalty.
- Dickens's *Bleak House* is six hundred pages of boring prose.

Straw Man

A **straw man** literally refers to a straw-stuffed dummy in the shape of a man and dressed in clothes: a scarecrow, for instance, or an effigy for burning or target practice. Metaphorically, the term refers to something less than a real person, or a weak or ineffective substitute. As a rhetorical term, the straw man (or straw person) refers to a strategy of refuting another person's actual position by substituting an exaggerated or distorted version of that position. What makes it a fallacy is that the user declares the opponent's conclusion to be wrong because of flaws in another, lesser argument: The straw man user presents a fictitious or misrepresented version of the opponent's argument, and refutes that. In short, it's a setup of the opponent, a deliberate misstatement or overstatement of his or her position. And it is easier to refute somebody whose real ideas have been pushed to the extreme—reduced to a dismissible straw man.

It's no surprise that the straw man argument is a familiar strategy in politics, as candidates will attack opponents on positions often much weaker than their best arguments. Consider, for example, this statement: "Senator Jane Smith claims that we should not fund the superbomber program. Do we really want her to leave our country defenseless?" In reality, Smith may be opposed to the superbomber program for technical, economic, or even strategic reasons, or she may be in favor of an alternative defense system. However, like a red herring, the opponent tries to refute Senator Smith's position by attacking a position that Smith doesn't hold—that she wants to leave the country defenseless. In short, the arguer arrives at a conclusion that easily dismisses the "straw man" he has set up while disregarding Smith's real arguments.

Examples of Straw Man Arguments

- Home schooling is dangerous because it keeps kids isolated from society.
- Discrimination in hiring is *not* unfair. An employer has to discriminate between competent and incompetent, good and bad workers. Otherwise, we'd be hiring people least qualified for the job.
- People who are opposed to urbanization just want to go back to living in caves.

EXERCISES

1. In your journal, list examples of logical fallacies you find in essays, news articles, editorials, advertising, junk mail, and other persuasive materials that you confront on a daily basis. Based on the information you and other group members collect, draw some hypotheses about which fallacies are most prevalent today and why. If your instructor asks you to do so, convert those hypotheses into an outline of an argument essay for your campus newspaper.

2. Explain the faulty logic of the following statements. Of what fallacy (or fallacies) is each an example?
   a. When did you stop hiring other people to take your exams for you?
   b. He's too smart to play football; besides, he broke his leg ten years ago.
   c. If we don't stop the publication of this X-rated material now, it won't be long before our children will be reading it at school.
   d. Karen must be depressed; she wore dark clothes all weekend.
   e. How can you accuse me of being late? You're such a slowpoke.
   f. Rap music isn't music because it's just noise and words.
   g. He's at least 6 feet 6 inches tall, so he must be a terrific basketball player.
   h. WGBB is the most popular radio station on campus because it has more listeners than any other station.
   i. Indians living on reservations get the necessities of life at government expense, so they have no worries.
   j. Take Tummy Tops laxatives instead of Mellow Malt, because Tummy Tops contains calcium while Mellow Malt has aluminum and magnesium.
   k. Lite Cheese Popcorn contains 34 percent fewer calories!
   l. Any decent person will agree that Nazism has no place in modern society.

CHAPTER 3

Finding Arguments

Thinking Like a Writer

When confronted with an issue we feel strongly about, most of us have no trouble offering an energetically delivered opinion. Yet when we're asked to *write* an argument, we feel paralyzed. To express our ideas in written form forces us to commit ourselves to some position or to endorse a particular action. We have to take a risk and make a public statement about what we think and feel and believe. Our written words can be scrutinized. That makes us vulnerable, and nobody likes to feel exposed.

It is helpful to think of writing an argument as one way to explore our ideas about a subject or issue. As such, writing can be a means of growth and discovery. Exploring new ideas can be intimidating, but it's also challenging. This chapter will demonstrate how writers begin the process of exploring their ideas to write argument essays. As novelist E. M. Forster explained, "How will I know what I think until I've seen what I've said?"

Exploration, of course, takes time. We're not recommending a writing process that begins an hour before a paper is due; rather, we're recommending what successful writers do: Take time to think your writing through. This means starting assignments early, working through all the stages, and allowing time to revise and polish your work before you submit it. Learning to write well is the same as learning to perform any other skilled activity. You have to practice your strokes or your scales to be a good tennis player or pianist; likewise, you have to practice your craft to be a good writer. As you gain more experience, some of the stages of the writing process will go more quickly for you on most projects. Even when you become a polished logician, however, you may find yourself writing about a topic that requires you to work out the assumptions in your argument slowly and painstakingly. That's okay. All writers do that.

The Writing Process

Many rhetorical theorists have tried to describe the writing process, but that's a little like describing snowflakes: Each one is different. Each person has a different way of writing, especially depending on the job. Think about it. You can dash off a note to your roommate in a second; if you're writing a job application letter, you'll probably take a great deal more time. If you have only 20 minutes to answer an essay question on a history exam, you'll get it done somehow; but give you an entire semester to write a term paper on the same subject, and you'll probably spend several weeks (if not months) doing the job. The scope and length of the assignment dictate a different writing process.

What most people studying the writing process agree on is that almost everyone goes through four distinct stages when writing: prewriting, drafting, rewriting, and editing.

Prewriting

When something prompts you to write (your instructor gives you an assignment, your boss tells you to write a report, a letter requires an answer, you feel strongly about a controversy and want to write a letter to the editor), you spend time either mentally or physically preparing to respond. You may make notes, go to the library, interview someone, or just stare out the window. This is the *prewriting* stage in which you're letting the ideas you'll use begin to incubate, to take form. In this chapter, we provide strategies you can use to make this early stage of writing work for you.

Drafting

In the second stage, you begin, however haltingly, to put words to paper. Some people make an outline; others write a bare-bones rough draft in an attempt to get some ideas down on paper. Many people like to start by sketching out their conclusions so that they can see where their writing must take them. Others prefer the linear, start-with-the-introduction system that moves them through the task. The first goal in the drafting stage is to get the framework of the writing in place so you can start adding material to fill it out. At some point in the process you also take your potential readers into account in order to get some idea of their expectations and receptivity.

Rewriting

Once you have a rough draft framed, you're ready to do the hard work of writing: *rewriting*. At this stage, you may move parts of your paper around, or make a new outline, or add or cut material to fill in gaps or eliminate imbalances. You'll have your readers much more clearly in mind because your goal is to persuade them; what you know about their background, experiences, and values will help you decide on a final shape for your paper, even if it means throwing away a lot of what went into the rough draft. (A bad paper that's finished is still a bad paper; that's why you need to allow time for flexibility. Writers who are pressed for time sometimes have to polish something that's not good and hope their readers won't notice, a technique that doesn't usually work.) All writing is rewriting. So at this stage, most good writers turn to other writers for feedback—a sense of what prospective readers will think of their writing. In a classroom, this is done by exchanging drafts with classmates or having conferences with your instructor.

Editing

To maximize your chance of persuading readers, your writing needs to be as readable as possible. That's why, after you've rewritten it, you need to work on your sentence structure so that words "flow" smoothly. Or you may need to change words here and there to heighten their impact. If others have read your paper and offered feedback, you may wish to act on some of their suggestions for improvement. You always need to edit and proofread what you've written so that careless errors don't distract your readers from getting the message you're trying to convey.

In a nutshell, that's the writing process. Now let's look at how you might exploit the features of that process when you start writing arguments.

Finding Topics to Argue

Every writer knows the experience of being blocked—of having a topic but not knowing what to say about it, or of having only one point to make about an issue. Even worse is having an assignment but no topic. To help generate ideas, writers need to tap both internal and external resources.

In Your Immediate Vicinity

The world around you is full of arguments; you just need to take a moment to see them. Look at the front page and editorial pages of your campus newspaper, for instance. What's going on? Look at billboards and bulletin boards. What are people having meetings about? What changes are coming up? Listen to the conversations of people on the bus, or waiting in line at the bookstore, or in the library. What's up? What have you been reading for a class that gets you thinking? You might want to know how a theory for the origin of the universe was derived, or what the results of a recent study of employment success for former welfare recipients were based on, or even why two experts in the field of early childhood learning draw different conclusions from the same evidence. The reading you do for your own enjoyment may also provide some interesting ideas. A science fiction novel may make you wonder about the plausibility of alien life. Reading a murder mystery may make you think about the value of forensic anthropology. Look through the magazines in your room, or at the ads on television, or at the junk mail that fills your mailbox. Even casually reading magazines and newspapers on a daily or weekly basis will turn up issues and controversies. What claims are people making? What are people asking you to do, or think, or wear, or look like, or support? These are sources of potential arguments; all you have to do is become aware of them. As Thoreau put it, "Only that day dawns to which we are awake."

In Your Larger Worlds

Don't limit yourself to campus. Often there are debates and discussions going on in your workplace, in your place of worship, on your block, in your town. You belong to a number of communities; each has its issues of interest, and in those issues you can find plenty to write about. And those environments aren't the only places you'll find sources for arguments; the world turns on proposals, positions, and controversies. It's almost impossible to turn on the radio or television today without seeing someone presenting an opinion. Your computer (or the one available on your campus) can connect you to a global community engaged in debate and dialogue on every issue imaginable. On the Internet, you can participate in a number of discussions about controversial issues through listservs, Usenet newsgroups, Web logs, and chat rooms. Make a list of the issues that interest you. What are the headlines in the newspaper? What's Congress voting on? What are the hot spots around the globe (or in the larger universe)? Don't stick to the familiar; there is much experimental territory just waiting to be explored.

Keeping a Journal

You've probably noticed that we encourage recording ideas and observations in a journal, a technique used by many professional writers. The journal doesn't have to be fancy; the cheap supermarket variety works just as well as the $2,000 laptop. (If you're comfortable at a keyboard, a computer disk makes a great notebook and fits in your shirt pocket, too—although you might want to keep a backup copy.)

Writers use journals as portable file cabinets of ideas. In a journal, we record anything in language that interests us, not just materials for current projects. We may copy down a word or phrase or sentence we hear that we like, or photocopy and staple in a piece by a writer we admire, or even add things that infuriate or amuse us. A journal becomes a supermarket of ideas and strategies, but there's something very positive about the simple act of copying words. Somehow, physically writing or typing them makes them yours; you learn something about technique in doing the physical work of copying. (That's why we don't recommend making too many photocopies; you don't mentally store the information in the same way you do when you copy a passage yourself.)

For the novice argument writer, a journal is invaluable. You can use yours to include notes on possible topics; examples of good introductions and conclusions; catchy words, phrases, and titles; examples of logical fallacies—just about anything a writer might need. A journal is also particularly helpful for creating *dialogues,* the voices and opinions of others who may hold views that are different from your own on particular issues. By keeping a record or notes on what people have to say in newspapers, magazine articles, television talk shows, and casual conversation about various controversial issues, you'll have a ready resource to consult when you begin to deliberate about your position on a particular issue.

When you begin keeping the journal, set yourself a formal goal: for example, adding 100 words a day or writing five days out of the week. Then *stick to it.* Journals don't fill themselves. It takes discipline to keep a journal, and discipline is a characteristic of good writers. If you don't do the groundwork, your creativity won't break through. Throughout this text, we've scattered suggestions and exercises for using journals; if you want to master the power of argument fully, we encourage you to *do* the exercises. Don't just read them. Write!

Developing Argumentative Topics

Topics alone aren't arguments, and many inexperienced writers have trouble making the jump from subject to argument. For example, you may be interested in heavy metal music. That's a subject—a big one. What can you argue about it? You could ask yourself, "What are the facts about heavy metal? When did it start? How can it be defined? What differentiates it from the mainstream rock played on most commercial radio stations? Why are some groups played, it seems, once an hour, and others almost totally ignored?" You can ask functional questions, such as "Who is the most influential figure in heavy metal music? Is heavy metal more relevant than, say, techno music?" You might ask aesthetic questions about the importance of melody or lyrics or harmony, or ethical questions such as whether the music industry should put parental advisory labels on albums. You could even consider moral questions such as whether heavy metal music videos encourage sexism or violence. In recognizing the multiple possibilities of issues, you may find you have more to say on a topic than you think.

Getting Started

Sometimes getting started can be the most difficult step in the writing process. Where do I begin? What should I include? What ideas will work best? How shall I organize it all? You may have a hundred ideas in your head about the topic or—even worse—none at all. When this happens, there are a number of tried-and-true techniques that professional writers use to redirect those anxious questions and concerns into productive writing. While you may not need to use all the strategies each time you begin to write, you'll find that trying out each one of them will help you discover what works best for you.

Brainstorming

Brainstorming can help you get your ideas on paper in an informal and unstructured way. When you brainstorm, you write down as many ideas as you can about your subject, usually in short phrases, questions, or single words. Don't worry about placing them in any special order or even about making complete sense. The one rule to observe while you're brainstorming is not to judge the ideas that pop into your head and spill out onto your paper. When you give yourself permission to write down anything that seems related to your subject, you'll be surprised at the number of ideas that will occur to you. By not rejecting anything, you'll find that one idea will naturally lead to another. Even an idea that you may throw out later can lead you to an idea that may be a real gem. And the more ideas you record in your brainstorm, the more choices you will have to consider later as you sift through this record of your thoughts and decide what is and is not useful.

After reading the essays in Chapter 2 of this text, John, our first-year composition student, decided to write his first paper on college binge drinking. The topic was in the news because a student at another college in his state had died as the result of excessive drinking at a fraternity party. John began his prewriting preparation by brainstorming about the subject. Here's what he came up with:

binge drinking	want to forget all about the week
drinking until you feel sick	makes us feel grown up
getting together with friends for a good time	nothing better to do on Saturday night
partying after a tough week at school	why does the college care?
so many bars, so little time	people can really hurt themselves
half the people underage	prevention—how?
whose responsibility is it?	part of the college experience
nobody checks anyway	ignore it—will it go away?
feeling terrible the next morning	trying to act cool
smelling like a beer can	what starts as fun can lead to death
role of the college administration	definition of an adult
rite of passage	do other cultures experience this?
impact of peer pressure	why drink to excess?

As you can see, John had many different ideas about binge drinking, and the more he brainstormed, the more he discovered what they were. After looking over his brainstorm, John chose a few of the ideas that especially interested him to explore further.

John was lucky to have a subject before he began brainstorming. But what happens if you don't have a particular topic in mind or your instructor doesn't assign one? You may find it difficult to come up with a topic, and you're not alone. Students often comment that the hardest part of writing is deciding what to write about.

Finding Ideas Worth Writing About

Let's suppose you're not assigned a specific paper topic and are left on your own to come up with an issue worth arguing about. That can be daunting, of course. When asked where he gets the ideas for his stories, best-selling author Stephen King's joke response was "Utica"—as if there were an idea shop in that New York town. Other writers respond with the tongue-in-cheek claim that there's a post office box in, say, Madison, Wisconsin, where you can write for ideas, but to qualify you need to be published. The point is that ideas for fiction as well as nonfiction are all around us. You just have to know where to look.

Again, one of the most useful prewriting strategies for coming up with an idea is brainstorming—just as you might do if you had a topic to expand upon. Take out a piece of paper and jot down whatever comes to mind in response to these questions:

- What issues in print or TV news interest you?
- What issues make you angry?

- What problems in your dorm/on campus/in your town/in your country concern you?
- What political issue concerns you most?
- What aspects about the environment worry you?
- If you were a professor, dean, college president/mayor/governor/senator/president, what would be the first thing you'd do?
- What policies/practices/regulations/laws would you like to see changed?
- What do you talk about or argue over with friends or classmates?
- What ideas from books or articles have challenged your thinking?
- What books/movies/music/fashions/art do you like, and why?
- What television shows do you like/hate, and why?
- What personalities in politics/show business/the media/academia do you have strong feelings about?

Here's a quick brainstorming list one student developed:

Issues That Interest Me
1. The war on terrorism
2. Excessive salaries for athletes
3. People who protest movie violence but oppose bans on assault rifles
4. The benefits of stem cell research
5. Reality TV
6. Social messages in rap music
7. Environmentally unfriendly vehicles
8. Immigration policies
9. Smoking bans
10. Movies

Another strategy is to brainstorm these items in a group of classmates. Begin by choosing a subject in the day's news, then play free-association with it. Say the subject is *sports* and you begin saying the word. The next student then says the first word that comes to mind; then the next student responds with a new word, et cetera, et cetera. For instance: sports; baseball; St. Louis Cardinals; World Series; the latest player trades. And maybe eventually you and the group will generate ideas worth debating—the need for better coaching; salary caps; the use of steroids; team loyalty, or the lack thereof; the designated hitter rule.

Once you have brainstormed a list, organize the issues according to categories—for example, sports, politics, social issues, environment, the media, television, education, and so on. Then transfer the list to your journal. Now, whenever an assignment comes up, you'll have a database of ideas worth writing about.

Next try to focus these ideas by deciding the following:

- Which subjects do I know something about?
- Have I had personal experiences with any particular subject?
- How do I feel about the subject? (angry? glad? sad? neutral?)
- What is my stand on the subject? Should I defend it? argue against it? Do I feel strongly enough to make suggestions for changes?

- Would this be a subject I'd want to do more research on?
- Who would be my audience—friends? instructor? parents? And how much does he, she, or they know about the topic?

In subsequent chapters, we'll discuss how to frame an argument on a topic, the ways of approaching your audience, the kinds of evidence to present, and so forth. But at this point, we're simply interested in helping you come up with a checklist of arguable subjects worth writing about. Whatever you come up with in your checklist, each topic should have three basic things:

1. It should be interesting.
2. It should appeal to readers.
3. It should have a specific slant.

Clustering

Some writers find that visualizing their ideas on a page helps them explore their subject in new ways. Clustering[1] is a technique you can use to do that. It involves choosing a key word, phrase, or even a short sentence, and placing it in the center of a blank page with a circle around it. Next you try to think of ideas, words, or other short phrases that you can associate or relate to your key word or phrase. As you do, write them in the blank area surrounding the center and circle them and draw lines linking them to your center circled word or phrase. As you accumulate more and more clusters, the words and phrases within them will generate ideas on their own; these can be linked to the words that inspired them. When you have exhausted your cluster, you will have a complex network of ideas that should provide many ways to begin to explore your subject. By choosing any one or a combination of these words or ideas as a starting point, you can move to freewriting to find ways of developing these ideas further.

Figure 3.1 shows how John used clustering to find new ways of thinking about binge drinking, the topic he had chosen for his paper. When John examined his cluster, he found a map of the many ideas he might explore further:

- Should colleges play the role of in loco parentis and regulate student drinking or is drinking a matter of personal responsibility?
- What role does peer pressure play in binge drinking?
- Are print ads and television commercials for beer partly responsible for binge drinking among young people?
- Is the extent of binge drinking on college campuses exaggerated or overstated?
- If a student violates campus drinking rules, what should the consequences be?

John's cluster revealed the complexity of the issue and became a starting point for him to investigate the subject in greater depth.

---

[1]Clustering is a technique explored by Gabriele L. Rico in her book *Writing the Natural Way: Using Right Brain Techniques to Release Your Expressive Powers* (Los Angeles: J. P. Tarcher, 1983).

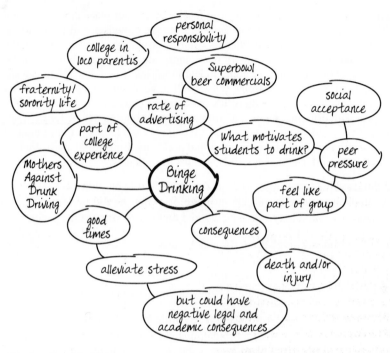

Figure 3.1 Sample Cluster

Freewriting

The next step is freewriting, which goes one step beyond brainstorming and which helps get a focus on the subject while developing things to say about it. Instead of simply listing phrases, questions, and words related to your subject, freewriting involves writing freely, and without stopping, whatever thoughts and ideas you have about your subject, without worrying about sentence structure, spelling, or grammar. As in brainstorming, when you freewrite, it's important not to censor your ideas. Your aim is to discover what you know about your subject, and the best way you can do that is by giving your mind permission to go wherever it pleases. Freewriting isn't intended to be a finished part of your paper; instead, it's a way to generate the ideas and focus that you can use later as you begin to draft the paper itself.

Freewriting can begin with anything: your topic, a particularly interesting idea you've read about, or an experience that you can connect with your subject. If you have used brainstorming or clustering before freewriting, these activities can provide you with a key word or phrase to get you started. For instance, John found a good idea from his brainstorm to begin his freewriting:

> Getting together with friends for a good time. That's what everyone looks forward to every weekend. Throw away the books, get out of the dorm and party. Four, five, sometimes more drinks. Feeling no pain. Binge drinking just seems to happen. It isn't something you plan to do. When you're having a good time, you don't think about how terrible you're going to feel the next day or about all the stupid things you're doing. It's easy to get alcohol in town. Nobody ever

checks for proof and if they do, you just go to another place down the street. It's so easy to get phony proof anyway. And the crowds are so large, no one looks carefully. If college students want to drink, who's to say they can't? We're old enough to vote, die for our country, sign a contract. Why not drinking? And how are you ever going to learn to drink if you don't? College students drink for lots of reasons. Why? Well, it gets them in a party mood. It's fun. It makes us feel like adults. It's so cool. Everyone does it. There's nothing wrong with drinking, but is it a problem if you drink too much? Every weekend. I've heard about students who have died. They let it get out of control. Drunk driving, alcohol poisoning, stupid accidents. Binge drinking is drinking gone overboard. Guess that's all I can think of right now.

John used his freewriting to think on paper. While he didn't come up with any conclusions about how he felt about binge drinking, he did produce a number of ideas that he explored later, when he worked on the first draft of his paper:

- College students binge drink for many reasons.
- Binge drinking can be a problem.
- Drinking is related to feeling adult.
- Binge drinking is not a planned behavior, but it can get to be a habit.

One of the best reasons for using freewriting before you begin the first draft of your paper is to avoid the most intimidating sight a writer can see: a blank page. Unfortunately, sometimes that blank page is the result of a blank mind and undue concern about how your writing and ideas will appear to others. When you freewrite, you write for yourself alone. It is a way to make your ideas flow. Freewriting generates ideas that will help you begin to think about your subject before worrying about polishing your writing for an audience.

Asking Questions

Once you have a subject in mind, a good strategy for generating ideas is to make a list of questions you have about the subject. Your questions can cover areas in which you need more information, as well as questions you might like to answer as you think and write about your topic. For instance, John tried this strategy for his topic of college binge drinking and came up with the following questions:

Why do college students binge drink?

How many college students actually binge drink?

Is binge drinking a result of peer pressure?

Do students binge drink to show they are adults?

Do most college students find binge drinking acceptable?

Is binge drinking strictly a college student activity or do other age and economic groups do this as well?

Do college students stop binge drinking once they leave college?

Who should be responsible for binge drinking? the drinkers? the college? the law?

Why do college administrations feel that they must respond to the problem of drinking if it's off campus?

Do colleges have a legal responsibility to protect their students?

Are the alcohol prevention programs on campus effective?

It's easy to see how one question can lead to another. By choosing one question or several related ones, John had real direction for exploring his topic and focusing his paper as he began his research and his first draft.

Engaging in Dialogue with Others

Talking to other people is a great source of ideas. None of the techniques we've discussed so far have to be lonely activities. By sharing your ideas and listening to the responses of others, you will find a wealth of new ideas and perspectives. In fact, you'll be engaging in the kind of *dialogue* we discussed in Chapter 1. You can do this in a number of ways: participate in either small peer groups in your class or larger class discussions; speak individually with your instructor; seek out members of your community, on campus or outside your school; share ideas with others electronically through Internet chat rooms, e-mail, or listservs; or talk with family and friends. As Larry King and other talk show hosts prove every day, people love to talk. So, take advantage of it—and take notes.

Refining Topics

Once you have found—through the strategies we've discussed—subjects that strike you as interesting, you have to begin narrowing down your topic to a manageable size. The next step, then, is to look over your list and reduce it to those topics that are legitimately arguable. (See Chapter 1 for a refresher.)

Reducing Your Options

Your first step is to determine whether your subject is manageable. You don't want a subject that is too broad or unwieldy or that requires prohibitive amounts of research. For example, you would not want to argue that "welfare needs to be reformed." You could write a book about that if you had time to do all the research. To write a short paper, you have to narrow your subject. "The only people who should be eligible for welfare support should be disabled people and mothers of preschool children" is a manageable reduction of your first idea, and one that you can handle in an average-length paper (see Figure 3.2). The more narrow your topic, the more you restrict your research and tighten the focus of your argument.

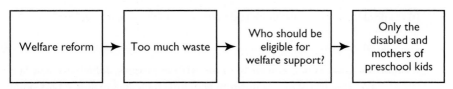

Figure 3.2 "Reducing Your Options" Diagram

Avoiding Overspecialized Topics

Don't pick a topic that requires extensive specialized knowledge, however, such as how to reduce the trade deficit or the problems inherent in thermonuclear fusion. The issue you choose should be one you know a little something about and, to keep you interested, about which you have strong convictions. Also, it should be an issue you are willing to spend a reasonable amount of time exploring on your own or perhaps in the library. Aside from writing a convincing argument, a parallel goal of any project you research is to become better informed and more appreciative of the complexity of the issue. Therefore, select a topic on which you wish to be well informed and that you are willing to investigate and reflect on.

Formulating a Working Claim

Once you have decided on your topic and used some of the strategies we've discussed, you are ready to create a working claim. As we explained in Chapter 1, the claim is the heart of your essay. It functions as a thesis statement. It states what you believe or what action you'd like your readers to take. In Chapter 1, we provided examples of the different ways you can state your claim. However, at this early stage of your writing, it would be difficult to create a claim that would be perfect for the paper you have yet to research and write. It's too early in the game to commit yourself. After all, your research may yield some surprising results, and you want to be open to all sides of the issue. At best, you can create a working claim—that is, a statement of your opinion or position on your topic that you can use temporarily to help you focus and organize your paper and limit your research.

After John, our first-year composition student, considered his subject of binge drinking by brainstorming, clustering, freewriting, asking questions about the topic, and engaging in dialogue with others, he realized what an enormous and complex topic it was and that he needed to narrow it. He began by asking questions about binge drinking. How prevalent is binge drinking? Who should be responsible for the regulation of student drinking? Are students themselves solely responsible? Should a college or university act in loco parentis? What are the consequences of ignoring the problem of binge drinking? What is the role of peer pressure in binge drinking? How can binge drinking be discouraged or controlled? What role does advertising play?

As John thought about the answers to these questions, he began to narrow the focus of his broad topic to one that he could explore in a paper of reasonable length. He decided that he would focus only on the issue of how to control or eliminate binge drinking on college campuses.

John's next step was to formulate a *working claim* for his paper on binge drinking. When he sat down to create his working claim, he examined and reflected on his topic and decided on the following *working claim*:

> Binge drinking is a serious problem on college campuses, and if we continue to ignore it or treat it as normal and acceptable student behavior, no one will ever find an effective way to eliminate it.

By creating a working claim early in his writing process, John benefited in a number of ways. He clearly took a position about his topic and expressed his point of view. While he had the opportunity to change his viewpoint as he thought further about his topic, his working claim served as a baseline. John's working claim also helped him organize the reasons he needed to support his position.

Let's take a look at John's working claim to see how it is organized. His claim can be divided into three parts:

1. Binge drinking is a problem on college campuses.
2. It is ignored or simply accepted as normal student behavior.
3. No one has yet found an effective way to solve this problem.

All these statements are arguable because, as we discussed in Chapter 1, they are based on judgment and interpretation, not on indisputable facts or personal opinion. As he developed his paper, John needed to decide on reasons to effectively convince his readers that these three parts of his working claim are true.

In addition, John's working claim helped him decide what he needed to investigate further. As John researched and became more knowledgeable about his topic, he revised his working claim to better reflect what he had learned. But at this stage of his paper, his working claim provided him with several specific areas that he needed to investigate in order to argue persuasively about them:

1. Is binge drinking really a problem on college campuses? How significant is it?
2. How is binge drinking ignored and by whom?
3. Is binge drinking regarded as normal student behavior and by whom?
4. What has been done to eliminate binge drinking?
5. What are some ways this problem can be dealt with?

In Chapter 9, we look at a number of ways available to John to research his topic. By using the questions suggested by his working claim as a guide, John had plenty of avenues to explore.

Thinking like a writer will help you make the jump from simply having an opinion on a subject to finding ways to express that opinion in an argument essay. In the next chapter, we look at the way in which audience influences and affects the choices we make about what to include in an argument essay and how to present our arguments.

SAMPLE STUDENT ARGUMENT FOR ANALYSIS

Stephanie Bower, a student majoring in English Literature, was interested in the subject of television news reporting. She realized what a complicated and multifaceted topic it is and that she needed to focus on a particular aspect of broadcast news. She began refining her topic by asking questions about TV news reporting. What does the viewing audience expect of television news? What is the responsibility of news broadcast? Are the when, where, why, what, and how enough? What are the qualities of a newscast that satisfy my expectations for good news coverage? Which news programming do I find inadequate? What differences exist between national and local news coverage? What is the state of reporting on my local news channels? What are the strengths and weaknesses of those channels? What role does advertising

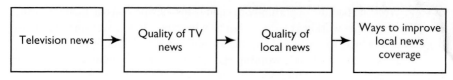

Figure 3.3 Stephanie's "Reducing Options" Diagram

play in a broadcast? How can local television news be improved? What are critics of the television news industry saying about the caliber of local news? What would I discover if I were to examine the quality of local news on a minute-by-minute basis? What recommendations could be made to improve the news?

As Stephanie thought about the answers, she realized that although each question poses an interesting issue to explore, she had to narrow the topic to one that she could cover in a paper of reasonable length. She thought back to some recent local news stories that had interested her, discovering to her dismay how complicated social issues had been pressed into just a few seconds. Worse, she was stunned to discover that extended coverage was given to a story about an abandoned dog. Reflecting on this, Stephanie realized she had material for a specific topic: local news—what was wrong with it, and how it might be improved. The box diagram in Figure 3.3 reflects her thought process as she narrowed down her topic.

Her working claim, then, both limited the range of her topic and very clearly expressed her point of view about it:

> Local television news is known for its bare-bones coverage and journalistic mediocrity. Now, competing with the convenience of Internet news sources and the far more in-depth coverage available in newspapers, local television news must reconsider its responsibilities and its approach.

```
                                            Bower 1

        Stephanie Bower
        Professor Van Zandt
        English 111
        December 4, 2006
                     What's the Rush?
              Speed Yields Mediocrity in Local
                    Television News
           Down to the second, time is a factor in
        television. Though national television news has
        outlets for lengthy reports and analysis in
        hour-long news magazines like Dateline and panel
```

Bower 2

discussions like Meet the Press, local news is
rendered almost exclusively in a "short story"
format. Most local TV news stories are just
twenty or thirty seconds long. These stories
succeed in stating the basic facts, but they
simply do not have time to do more. Though
television newscasts operate in minutes and
seconds, the brevity of local news stories is
not just a natural feature of the medium.
Rather, these stories are often the result of
local news stations that lack resources and
reporters, or that lack effort and enterprise.
Local television news is known for its bare-
bones coverage and journalistic mediocrity.
Now, competing with the convenience of Internet
news sources and the far more in-depth coverage
available in newspapers, local television news
must reconsider its responsibilities and
its approach.

Local news gives people the opportunity to
see and hear the news that is specifically
relevant to their communities. Local stations
have the potential to reach large regional
audiences interested in excellent coverage of
issues affecting their towns and cities. Joe
Barnes, former News Director of KOMO-TV in
Seattle, says most people aren't watching local
news because it isn't relevant to their lives.
In order to survive, says Barnes, "We must cover
news that affects the lives of our viewers. We
must have investigative stories that push for
positive changes in the community."

A Columbia Journalism Review study showed
that viewers appreciate investigative reporting,
and they "like stations that air more long
stories and minimize the number of very short
stories" (Rosenthiel, Gottlieb and Brady). Not

Bower 3

all news stories demand a great deal of time and depth, but many stories require more than the thirty or sixty seconds they are allotted during a newscast. A news story that runs for one minute and thirty seconds can tell viewers the who, what, when, where, and how of a story, but it cannot delve into an analysis of a situation or its contextual significance. The <u>Columbia Journalism Review</u>'s research indicates that longer, more contextualized stories improve station quality and, ultimately, station ratings.

4   If more in-depth stories improve news quality and help stations gain loyal viewers, then why don't more stations air them? The answer seems to come down to money matters. In the world of corporate-owned and advertiser-dependent media, it becomes unclear whether local journalism outlets are impartial civic informers or cogs in the machinery of big business. During sweeps weeks, local stations engage in a high-stakes war to see who wins the important time slots. Stations suddenly run costly "Special Reports" and exclusive interviews that are rarely seen at other times, many because they are so expensive to produce. Sean Treglia writes that "large corporate owners seek to increase profits quickly, putting local stations under great pressure to generate revenues through their news stations." These stations, says Treglia, are "forced to reduce newsroom costs, seriously undermining their ability to cover local news." Therefore, local market stations cannot spend money consistently on the equipment, resources, and manpower required to do investigative or in-depth

reporting. These resources are only available during sweeps weeks.

Deborah Potter, Executive Director of NewsLab, cites severely understaffed local news teams as a primary cause of low-quality coverage. She says the majority of local station budgets are spent on equipment and anchor salaries, and there is simply not enough left over to pay for reporters and photographers to go out in the field. Potter says this shortage is the reason why there is "so little enterprise, so much cheap-to-cover crime, and so little depth on the air. Most television reporters have a simple mission every day: Get out there and scratch the surface" ("The Body Count").

Because there are not enough reporters to fill the time, stations become heavily dependent on news wires and video feeds. It is cheaper to get video from the satellite feeds than to send a photographer and reporter out in the field, and it is faster to rephrase a story taken from the news wires than to research and report on an original story. However, CJR reporters warn that "using more out-of-town feeds is a business model that bows to short-term gain rather than building long-term audience loyalty" (Rosenthiel, Gottlieb and Brady). They report that over half of all local news stories are either taken from feeds or are covered using video and no reporter. Stories taken from wire copy or satellite video feeds account for many of the "quick-hit" twenty or twenty-five second pieces seen during local newscasts.

On February 18, 2006, I examined the story line-ups for the local 11 p.m. newscast at WHDH-TV, Boston's NBC affiliate station. Excluding

commercials, the full air-time given to WHDH for
this newscast was twenty-three minutes. From this
twenty-three minutes, two minutes were spent on
leads for upcoming stories and promotional spots
for future newscasts. Three minutes and forty
seconds were given to weather, and four minutes
were given to sports. This left only thirteen
minutes for local news coverage. Six of the local
news stories were allotted two minutes of
coverage each, and seven of the stories were
allotted twenty or thirty seconds. Even the time
given to the longest piece of local news coverage
was significantly shorter than the time given to
sports or to weather. Clearly, these news stories
could do little more than highlight key facts and
perhaps include a sound bite or two. Stations are
forced to select stories that can be told quickly
and that require little background or context.
The top local stories in WHDH's newscast, for
example, covered a woman who was attacked at
work, an apartment flood, and a boy recovering
from a sledding accident.

8

  If more time is given to news, it naturally
must be taken from coverage of something else.
So what has to go? Stations could take the time
back from the promotional graphics that devour
precious seconds with useless visuals, or they
could have less repetition of stories in back-
to-back newscasts. Another option is to take the
time from the twenty-second wire or "quick hit"
stories, particularly those that are covering
national news stories. Of course these stories
are news and they are of interest to viewers,
but if viewers want the national news tidbits,
then isn't national network news the place to
find them? According to both <u>CJR</u> and NewsLab's
studies, viewers want local news above all else.

9   Another possible solution is to take the
time back from the teases that remind viewers of
what stories are coming up later in the newscast.
Potter says that many viewers are turned off by
local news because "they're annoyed by the tricks
and gimmicks stations use to try to make them
watch" ("Stemming the Losses"). Boston's ABC
affiliate station, WCVB-TV, runs one-and-a-half
to two minutes of tease video per half-hour
newscast. This time, in addition to the time
spent on promotional station graphics, branding
slogans and music, adds up to a significant
amount of seconds that could be spent expanding
on news stories. Teases do work, and it is
valuable for busy viewers to know what is coming
up in case a story may be of particular interest
to them. But stations should not underestimate
their audiences by assuming they need to be lured
in and continually reminded of what's coming up.
A NewsLab research report showed that people were
annoyed with the number of teases in a typical
newscast, and many were "angry and frustrated
with stations that promote a story throughout a
newscast only to have it turn out to be a
throwaway" ("The Savvy Audience for Local TV
News"). The story is what the viewers really
want; it is what they are watching and waiting
for. Teases have no journalistic value and take
time away from the journalists and their pieces.

10   Because of the time constraints imposed on
television news, it can never provide the in-
depth coverage available in newspapers, despite
the countless graphics and brandings promising
"I-teams" and "in-depth coverage." Dane Claussen
notes that "the entire transcript of a half-hour
local television news broadcast will fit onto
less than one page of a newspaper," and argues

that the content of television news "has become
so poor that many consumers can no longer deny
that newspapers are higher quality news media
than television news broadcasts" ("Cognitive
Dissonance"). Stephanie Ebbert, City Hall Bureau
Chief at the Boston Globe, says that local TV
news is best-suited for "quick-hit" news:

> For more sophisticated, involved
> coverage, the consumer really has
> to turn to either a lengthier
> discussion of an event on a TV
> news magazine, or to radio or
> print media, which devote more
> resources to individual stories.
> That's not to say it can't be done
> on TV; it simply often isn't. The
> very subtleties that make some
> stories interesting and newsworthy
> are often difficult to crystallize
> in a minute and a half or to make
> friendly to viewers who are
> believed to be so very impatient.
> (personal interview)

Ebbert questions the idea that modern Americans,
with their busy lifestyles and MTV-influenced
visual perceptions, cannot pay attention long
enough to ingest longer, more sophisticated TV
news stories.

11   Local news affiliates may not have the
financial resources or tremendous market sizes
of their parent networks, but they still provide
the important service of informing communities
about their local schools, governments,
citizens, and breaking news. Surely, it must be
frustrating for professional television
journalists to abandon insightful analysis and
instead package the facts into a minute and

Bower 8

thirty seconds of lead, soundbite, and tag.
Current research indicates that viewers want in-
depth local news stories that are relevant to
their lives and their communities. The question
is whether local news stations will risk
altering standard formats to give reporters the
space to tell these stories.

Bower 9

Works Cited

Barnes, Joe. "How Can We Change Local TV to
     Bring Viewers Back?" Editorial. NewsLab 10
     Sept. 2004. <http://www.newslab.org/
     articles/changetv.htm>.

Claussen, Dane S. "Cognitive Dissonance, Media
     Illiteracy, and Public Opinion on the News."
     American Behavioral Scientist 48.2 (2004):
     212.

Ebbert, Stephanie. Personal Interview. 12 Dec,
     2004.

Potter, Deborah. "Stemming the Losses: How Can
     TV News Win Back Viewers?" American
     Journalism Review 22.12 (2000): 48.

---. "The Body Count." American Journalism
     Review 24.6 (2002): 60.

Rosenthiel, Tom, with Carl Gottlieb and Lee Ann
     Brady. "Time of Peril for TV News." Columbia
     Journalism Review Nov.-Dec. 2000: 84.

"The Savvy Audience for Local TV News: Are
     Stations Turning Viewers Off?" Newslab 10
     Sept. 2004. <http://www.newslab.org>.

```
                                        Bower 10
Treglia, Sean P. "Changing Channels: How the
    Nonprofit Sector Can Help Improve Local
    Television News." National Civic Review
    91.2 (2002): 185.
```

QUESTIONS FOR DISCUSSION AND WRITING

1. Where does Stephanie Bower state her claim? Do you agree with Stephanie's working claim here? Did you have a strong opinion about local TV news before you read Stephanie's piece? Did reading her paper change your mind, or reinforce your thinking?

2. Did Stephanie sufficiently narrow her topic? Is her evidence convincing? Considering that some of her evidence is from leading critics of the world of journalism, did she make their information accessible to you and relevant to her claim?

3. Examine two instances in which Stephanie cites quotations from experts in the field to develop her argument. Comment on the way she incorporated the quotations into the text. Was it done successfully or awkwardly?

4. What two factors, according to Stephanie, account for mediocrity in local news? Do you agree? disagree?

5. What are some of the brandings such as "I-Team" or "Storm Center" or "in-depth coverage" your local stations use? How do these brandings affect you? Do they earn your respect, your curiosity, or even your disdain? Explain your reaction.

6. What suggestions does Stephanie offer to improve the quality of local TV news? Which suggestions do you think could be realistically implemented? Which are obstacles too great to control in your opinion?

7. In your journal, select a local TV newscast, one that is broadcast nightly at the same time. Watch it every day if you can, or at least three times. Like Stephanie, break down the content of the newscast recording the length of time in minutes and seconds of the story, the topic of the story, and the depth of the story. Evaluate the content.

8. How do you respond to Stephanie's question, "Is journalism an impartial civic informer or a big business?" To shape your answer, use some of the evidence Stephanie presented in her paper and find some of your own.

EXERCISES

1. Get together with a small group of students in your class and brainstorm possible topics for an argument essay concerning a controversial issue on your campus or in your community. Try to think of at least ten topics that are current and that most people in your group find interesting and arguable.

2. Make a visit to the periodicals section of your college library and look through current issues of periodicals and newspapers on the shelves to find out what issues and subjects are being debated in America and around the world. Find one or more topics that interest you and make copies of those articles for further reading and response in your journal.

3. Take some time to explore the Internet by doing a keyword search using a Web search engine. In your journal, describe the results of your search. How many different sites devoted to your topic did you locate? What did you find surprising about the comments and opinions expressed by the participants?

4. Engage in a dialogue with other students, family members, friends, or people in the community who might have some interest and opinions on a potential topic. In your journal, record and respond to their diverse views.

5. Choose a topic that you might wish to investigate for an argument essay and use some of the strategies suggested in this chapter to get started: brainstorm, cluster, freewrite, question.

6. Formulate a list of questions about your potential topic.

7. After you have followed some of the strategies for exploring your topic, formulate a working claim. In your journal, identify which parts of your claim will need to be supported by reasons in your essay. Which parts of your claim will need to be investigated further?

Addressing Audiences

Thinking Like a Reader

As we've discussed in previous chapters, the purpose of writing an argument is to prompt your listeners to consider seriously your point of view and for you to win their respect through the logic and skill of your thinking. When used productively, argument can be a way to resolve conflict and achieve common ground among adversaries. Thus, one of the primary ways to measure the success of your argument is to gauge how effectively it reaches and appeals to your audience. Knowing something about your audience will enable you to use that knowledge to make your arguments most effective.

Creating an argument would be a simple task if you could be guaranteed an audience of readers just like yourself. If everyone shared your cultural, educational, religious, and practical experiences, persuading them to accept your point of view would require very little effort. Clearly, however, this is not the case. A quick look around your classroom will reveal the many differences that make argument a challenging activity. Is everyone the same age? race? gender? ethnicity? Do you all listen to the same music? dress alike? live in the same neighborhood? vote for the same candidates? attend the same place of worship? Unless you attend a very unusual school, the answer to most of these questions will be a resounding "no." People are different; what interests you may bore the person behind you, whereas what puts you to sleep may inspire someone else to passionate activism. And what you see on the surface isn't the whole story about your classmates, either. That rough-looking guy who works as a mechanic may write poetry in his spare time; that conservatively dressed woman may spend her weekends touring the countryside on a motorcycle. It's too easy to make assumptions about people's values and beliefs just by looking at them. If you want to persuade these people, you're going to have to assess them very carefully.

Knowing your audience will help you determine almost every aspect of the presentation of your case: the kind of language you use; the writing style (casual or formal, humorous or serious, technical or philosophical); the particular slant you take (appealing to the reader's reason, emotions, or ethics, or a combination of these); what emphasis to give the argument; the type of evidence you offer; and the kinds of authorities you cite. Also, this knowledge will let you better anticipate any objections to your position. In short, knowing your audience lets you adjust the shape of your argument the way you would refocus a camera after each photo you shoot.

If, for instance, you're writing for your economics professor, you would use technical vocabulary you would not use with your English professor. Likewise, in a newspaper article condemning alcohol abusers, you would have to keep in mind that some of your readers or their family members might be recovering alcoholics; they may take exception to your opinions. A travel piece for an upscale international magazine would need to have a completely different slant and voice than an article for the travel section of a small local newspaper.

Knowing your audience might make the difference between a convincing argument and a failing argument. Suppose, for instance, you decide to write an editorial for the student newspaper opposing a recently announced tuition hike. Chances are you would have a sympathetic audience in the student body because you share age, educational status, and interests. Most students do not like the idea of a higher tuition bill. That commonality might justify the blunt language and emotional slant of your appeal. It might even allow a few sarcastic comments directed at the administration. That same argument addressed to your school's board of trustees, however, would probably not win a round of applause. With them it would be wiser to adopt a more formal tone in painting a sympathetic picture of your financial strain; it's always smart to demonstrate an understanding of the opposition's needs, maybe even a compromise solution. In this case, your appeal to the trustees would be more credible if you acknowledged the university's plight while recommending alternative money-saving measures such as a new fund-raising program.

Or suppose you write an article with a religious thrust arguing against capital punishment. You argue that even in the case of confessed murderers, state execution is an immoral practice running counter to Christian doctrine; for supporting evidence you offer direct quotations from the New Testament. Were you to submit your article to a religious publication, your reliance on the authority of the scriptures would probably appeal to the editors. However, were you to submit that same article to the "My Turn" column for *Newsweek,* chances are it would be turned down, no matter how well written. The editors aren't necessarily an ungodly lot, but *Newsweek,* like most other large-circulation magazines, is published for an audience made up of people of every religious persuasion, as well as agnostics and atheists. *Newsweek* editors are not in the business of publishing material that excludes a large segment of its audience. Knowing your readers works in two ways: It helps you decide what materials to put into your argument, and it helps you decide where to publish your argument, whether it be on an electronic bulletin board, in a local paper, or on the op-ed page of the *Wall Street Journal.*

The Target Audience

The essays in this book come from a variety of publications, many of them magazines addressed to the "general" American readership. Others, however, come from publications directed to men or women, the political right or left, or from publications for people of particular ethnic, racial, and cultural identities. They're written for *target audiences.* When writers have a "target" audience in mind, particularly readers who share the same interests, opinions, and prejudices, they can take shortcuts with little risk of alienating anybody, because writer and readers have so many things in common. Consider the following excerpts concerning the use of animal testing in scientific research:

> Contrary to prevailing misperception, in vitro tests need not replace existing in vivo test procedures in order to be useful. They can contribute to chemical-safety evaluation right now. In vitro tests, for example, can be incorporated into the earliest stages of the risk-assessment process; they can be used to identify chemicals having the lowest probability of toxicity so that animals need be exposed only to less noxious chemicals.

It is clear from the technical terminology (e.g., *in vitro, in vivo, toxicity*), professional jargon *(test procedures, chemical-safety evaluation, risk-assessment process)*, and the formal, detached tone that the piece was intended for a scientifically educated readership. Not surprisingly, the article, "Alternatives to Animals in Toxicity Testing," was authored by two research scientists, Alan M. Goldberg and John M. Frazier, and published in *Scientific American* (August 1989). Contrast it with another approach to the topic:

> Almost 30 years ago, Queen had been a child herself, not quite two years old, living in Thailand under the care of her mother and another female elephant, the two who had tended to her needs every day since her birth. They taught her how to use her trunk, in work and play, and had given her a sense of family loyalty. But then Queen was captured, and her life was changed irrevocably by men with whips and guns. One man herded Queen by whipping and shouting at her while another shot her mother, who struggled after her baby until more bullets pulled her down forever.

What distinguishes this excerpt is the emotional appeal. This is not the kind of article you would find in *Scientific American* or most other scientific journals. Nor would you expect to see this kind of emotional appeal in a newsmagazine such as *Newsweek* or *Time,* or a general interest publication such as the Sunday magazine of many newspapers. The excerpt comes from an animal rights newsletter published by PETA, People for the Ethical Treatment of Animals. Given that particular audience, the writer safely assumes immediate audience sympathy with the plight of elephants. There is no need for the author to qualify or apologize for such sentimentalizing statements as "Queen had been a child herself" and "They taught her how to use her trunk, in work and play, and had given her a sense of family loyalty." In fact, given the context, the author is probably more interested in reminding readers of a shared cause rather than winning converts to the cause of animal rights.

Sometimes targeting a sympathetic audience is intended to move people to action—to get people to attend a rally or to contribute money to a cause or to vote for a particular political candidate. During the 2004 presidential campaign, fund-raising letters went out asking for donations to one particular candidate who pledged to fight the high cost of health care. In one of several Web logs ("blogs") supporting that candidate, the pharmaceutical industry was portrayed as a "greedy goliath" that was no different than "illegal drug cartels, extorting money from hapless consumers." As used in this blog, the strategy in appealing to a target audience is to streamline the issue into an "us-versus-them" conflict—in this case, the consumer as innocent victim and the manufacturers as bad guys. The blogger went on to argue that drug manufacturers inflate their prices astronomically, citing as evidence how company CEOs enjoy incomes in the tens of millions of dollars. "The pharmaceutical industry exists for the sole purpose of preying upon Americans who are sick, unhealthy, in discomfort and injured," said the blogger. "Their goal is to insure [sic] that only your symptoms are treated." Crackling with charged language, the blog invited voters to join the effort to change a system that exploited the taxpaying consumer and bloated company profits.

While pharmaceutical companies may indeed inflate the cost of their products, the campaign blog was a one-way argument, addressed to people already sympathetic to the cause. But the blog lacked perspectives from the other side. Nothing was said about the billions of dollars spent by pharmaceutical companies to develop and bring to market a new drug, or the fact that only a small percentage of drugs that reach the market ever turns a profit. Nor was there mention of the fact that the FDA is funded by the pharmaceutical companies and not taxpayer dollars, or the fact that the time frame for turning a profit is a limited number of years, after which patents expire, allowing the generic makers to market the same product at reduced costs. In short, the function of the campaign letters and blogs was not to plumb the depths of the issue and offer a balanced argument. On the contrary, most of the target audience was already sold on the cause. The basic intention was to convert conviction into money and votes. And the means was charged, motivational rhetoric.

The General Audience

Unless you're convinced that your readers are in total agreement with you or share your philosophical or professional interests, you may have some trouble picturing just whom you are persuading. It's tempting to say you're writing for a "general" audience; but, as we said at the beginning of this chapter, general audiences may include very different people with different backgrounds, expectations, and standards. Writing for such audiences, then, may put additional pressure on you.

In reality, of course, most of your college writing will be for your professors. This can be a little confusing because you may find yourself trying to determine just what audience your professor represents. You may even wonder why professors expect you to explain material with which they are familiar. You may feel that defining technical terms to your psychology instructor who covered them in class the week before, or summarizing a poem that you know your English professor can probably recite, is a waste of time. But they have a good reason: They assume the role of an uninformed audience to let you show how much *you* know.

Of course, if you are arguing controversial issues you may find yourself in the awkward position of trying to second-guess your instructor's stand on an issue.

You may even be tempted to tone down your presentation so as not to risk offense and, thus, an undesirable grade. However, most instructors try not to let their biases affect their evaluation of a student's work. Their main concern is how well a student argues a position.

For some assignments, your instructor may specify an audience for you: members of the city council, the readers of the campus newspaper, Rush Limbaugh's radio listeners, and so on. But if no audience is specified, one of your earliest decisions about writing should be in choosing an audience. If you pick "readers of *The National Review,*" for instance, you'll know you're writing for mostly male, conservative, middle-aged, middle-class whites; the expectations of these readers are very different than for readers of *Jet* or *Vibe.* If you are constrained to (or want the challenge of) writing for the so-called general audience, construct a mental picture of who those people are so you'll be able to shape your argument accordingly. Here are some of the characteristics we think you might include in your definition.

The "general" audience includes those people who read *Newsweek, Time,* and your local newspaper. That means people whose average age is about 35, whose educational level is high school plus two years of college, who make up the vast middle class of America, who politically stand in the middle of the road, and whose racial and ethnic origins span the world. You can assume that they read the daily newspaper and watch the evening news and are generally informed about what is going on in the country. You can assume a good comprehension of language nuances and a sense of humor. They are people who recognize who Shakespeare was, though they may not be able to quote passages or name ten of his plays. Nor will they necessarily be experts in the latest theory of black holes or be able to explain how photo emulsions work. However, you can expect them to be open to technical explanations and willing to listen to arguments on birth control, gun control, weight control, and the issues of women and gays in the military. More importantly, you can look upon your audience members as people willing to hear what you have to say.

Guidelines for Knowing Your Audience

Before sitting down to write, think about your audience. Ask yourself the following questions: Will I be addressing other college students, or people from another generation? Will my audience be of a particular political persuasion, or strongly identified with a specific cultural background? How might the age of my readers and their educational background influence the way they think about a given issue? On what criteria will they make their decisions about this issue? A good example of profiling your audience was evident in the 2004 presidential election. On the one hand, the Republicans gambled that "moral leadership" and "trust" were the chief criteria for voters. The Democrats, on the other hand, focused on a need for change. As the election results showed, the Republicans assessed their audience more accurately than did the Democrats.

As the example above illustrates, an effective argument essay takes into account the values, beliefs, interests, and experiences of its audience. If you simply choose to argue what you feel is important without regard to your audience, the only person you persuade may be yourself! An effective argument tries to establish common ground with the audience. While this may be difficult at times, recognizing what you have in common with your audience will enable you to argue most persuasively.

Audience Checklist

1. Who are the readers I will be addressing?
   a. What age group?
   b. Are they male, female, or both?
   c. What educational background?
   d. What socioeconomic status?
   e. What are their political, religious, occupational, or other affiliations?
   f. What values, assumptions, and prejudices do they have about life?
2. Where do my readers stand on the issue?
   a. Do they know anything about it?
   b. If so, how might they have learned about it?
   c. How do they interpret the issue?
   d. How does the issue affect them personally?
   e. Are they hostile to my stand on the issue?
3. How do I want my readers to view the issue?
   a. If they are hostile to my view, how can I persuade them to listen to me?
   b. If they are neutral, how can I persuade them to consider my viewpoint?
   c. If they are sympathetic to my views, what new light can I shed on the issue? How can I reinspire them to take action?
4. What do I have in common with my readers?
   a. What beliefs and values do we share?
   b. What concerns about the issue do we have in common?
   c. What common life experiences have we had?
   d. How can I make my readers aware of our connection?

Before you can do this, however, you will need to create a profile of your audience. You may find the audience checklist above helpful in assessing an audience. If you like visual prompts, write the answers to these questions on a card or a slip of paper that you can hang over your desk or display in a window on your computer screen while you're working on your argument. Looking at these questions and answers occasionally will remind you to focus your arguments on these particular people.

Using Debate and Dialogue

Debate and dialogue, two of the methods of developing arguments discussed in Chapter 1, can also be used to sharpen your awareness of audience. For an example of how this can happen, let's revisit John, our first-year composition student who had decided to write his argument essay on the topic of binge drinking. After reading critically in his subject area (Chapter 2) and formulating a working claim (Chapter 3), John turned his attention to the question of audience. He found that using debate and dialogue helped him answer some of the questions in the audience checklist and provided essential information about how his audience might respond to his ideas.

John decided that his audience would be a general one composed of people of all ages. He anticipated that most people in his audience would not endorse excessive drinking, but with such a diverse group of people he was unsure whether they would have similar reasons for their concern and how strongly they would agree or disagree with his reasons. John found that using two strategies, a "Yes, but . . ." exchange and creating a dialogue between different perspectives, helped to answer questions 2 and 3 on the audience checklist: Where do my readers stand on the issue? and How do I want my readers to view the issue? He used this information to develop ways to engage his readers in the essay.

Working with classmates in small peer groups, John found that a "Yes, but . . ." exchange revealed specific points that his audience might use to oppose his reasons. For instance, John began with the following statement:

College administrators have a responsibility to deter binge drinking by their students.

He received several responses from his peer group:

Yes, college administrators have a responsibility to their students, but that responsibility should be limited to academic matters.

Yes, binge drinking by students should be a concern to college administrators, but college administrators shouldn't interfere with the private lives or habits of their students.

Yes, college administrators should try to deter binge drinking by students, but they will be ineffective unless they receive support from the community and parents.

Although each of John's classmates agreed that college administrators had a valid interest in student binge drinking, there was considerable disagreement over how far that interest should extend and how effective any action taken by administrators would be. The "Yes, but . . ." exchange gave John greater insight into the ways others might respond to his ideas. As he developed his argument, he was able to acknowledge and address such concerns by his potential audience.

In a similar fashion, John used dialogue to gain insight into question 4 on the audience checklist: What do I have in common with my readers? In particular, John wanted to discover any shared concerns and values between himself and those who took different positions on solving the problem of binge drinking. To create a dialogue, John interviewed several of his classmates, his teachers, members of his family, and a few individuals from the community; he also read articles by health professionals concerned with alcohol abuse and young adults. His goal was to listen to a wide spectrum of views on the subject and to keep an open mind as he listened. He used his journal to record their comments and his own impressions. What emerged from this dialogue were several areas of shared concerns: Most agreed that binge drinking was an unhealthy practice that should be discouraged, and while there were many different suggestions about the measures that should be taken to eliminate it, all agreed that the students who engaged in binge drinking must ultimately accept responsibility for ending it. No solution would work, all agreed, unless the drinkers themselves were willing to stop. John found this information helpful because he knew that his audience would be more willing to listen to his argument if he could identify these shared values and concerns.

By engaging in both debate and dialogue, John gained knowledge that enabled him to appeal to his audience more effectively.

Adapting to Your Readers' Attitudes

Writing for a general audience is a challenge because in that faceless mass are three kinds of readers you'll be addressing:

1. people who agree with you
2. people who are neutral—those who are unconvinced or uninformed on the issue
3. people who don't share your views, and who might even be hostile to them

Each of these different subgroups will have different expectations of you and give you different obligations to meet if you are to present a convincing argument. Even readers sympathetic to your cause might not be familiar with special vocabulary, the latest developments around the issue, or some of the more subtle arguments from the opposition. Those hostile to your cause might be so committed to their own viewpoints that they might not take the time to discover that you share common concerns. And those neutral to the cause might simply need to be filled in on the issue and its background. If you're going to persuade your readers, you'll have to tailor your approach to suit their attitudes.

When addressing an audience, whether general or one of a particular persuasion, you must try to put yourself in its place. You must try to imagine the different needs and expectations these readers bring to your writing, always asking yourself what new information you can pass on and what new ways of viewing you can find for addressing the issue you're arguing. Let's look at some of the strategies you, as a writer, might use, depending on whether you anticipate a neutral, friendly, or unfriendly group of readers.

Addressing a Neutral Audience

Some writers think a neutral audience is the easiest to write for, but many others find this the most challenging group of readers. After all, they're *neutral*; you don't know which way they're leaning, or what may make them commit to your position. Your best role is the conveyor of knowledge: The information you bring, and the ways in which you present it, are the means by which you hope to persuade a neutral audience. Here are some of the ways to convey that information.

Fill in the Background

There are some issues about which few people are neutral: abortion, capital punishment, drug legalization, same-sex marriage, gun control. However, there are other issues about which some readers have not given a thought or made up their minds, or they may simply be uninformed. For instance, if you're part of a farming community, your concern about preserving good farmland might make you feel some urgency about unchecked industrial development in your area. To make a convincing case for readers from, say, Chicago or New York City, you first would have to tell them a little about the shortage of prime land for agriculture and why it is crucial to maintain the existing land. Similarly, as a resident of a large town, you might need to explain to readers from rural Vermont or Iowa why you think their community should be concerned with mandatory recycling in large cities. In both cases, your task would be to provide your readers with the information they need to evaluate the issue by relating some of the history and background behind the controversy. All the while, you need to encourage them to weigh with an open mind the evidence you present.

Present a Balanced Picture

Part of educating a neutral audience about your position involves presenting a balanced picture of the issue by presenting multiple perspectives about the issue, not just one. Even though you are trying to help your readers understand why your position has value, you will be more persuasive if you treat *all* views fairly, including opposing views. You should clearly and accurately lay out the key arguments of all sides; then demonstrate why your position is superior. Your readers need to feel that you have looked at the total picture and reached your position after carefully weighing all views, a process you hope your readers will engage in as well. Let your readers make their decisions based on their own analysis of the information you have provided. Don't be guilty of stacking the deck, a logical fallacy we discussed in Chapter 2. Not representing the other sides at all, or representing them unfairly and inaccurately, can leave you open to criticisms of distortion, and it may make your readers feel that you're misleading them.

Personalize the Issues

One sure way of gaining readers' attention is to speak their language—that is, address their personal needs, hopes, and fears. (It's what skillful politicians do all the time on the campaign trail.) If you want to engage your readers' attention, demonstrate how the problem will affect them personally. On the matter of farmland, explain why if nothing is done to prevent its loss, the prices of corn and beans will triple over the next three years. On the recycling issue, explain how unrestricted trash dumping will mean that city dwellers will try to dump more trash in rural areas. However, although personalizing the issue is an effective way to make your readers aware of the importance of your issue, you should avoid creating an ad misericordiam argument. To be fully credible, you should be certain that the reasons and evidence you present to your readers are anchored in fact rather than emotion.

Show Respect

When you're an informed person talking about an issue to people with less knowledge than you, there's a dangerous tendency to speak down to them. Think how you feel when someone "talks down" to you. Do you like it? How persuasive do you think you can be if your readers think you're talking down to them? Don't condescend to or patronize them. Try not to simplify a complex issue so much that it is reduced to a false dilemma: "If we don't increase school taxes immediately, our children will no longer receive a quality education." Don't assume that your audience is so ill informed that it cannot envision a middle ground between the two alternatives. On the contrary, treat your readers as people who want to know what you know about the issue and who want you to demonstrate to them clearly and accurately why you think they should agree with you. Invite them into the discussion, encouraging them with sound reasons and strong evidence to consider the merits of your side. Although your audience may not be as informed as you, they are willing to listen and deserve respect.

Addressing a Friendly Audience

Writing an argument for the already converted is much easier than writing for a neutral audience or one that is hostile. In a sense, half the battle is won because no minds have to be changed. You need not brace yourself for opposing views or refutations. Your role is simply to provide readers with new information and to renew enthusiasm for and commitment to your shared position. Nonetheless, there are still steps you should take.

Avoid Appealing to Prejudices

One of the risks of addressing a sympathetic audience is appealing to prejudices rather than reasons and facts. Although it might be tempting to mock those who don't agree with you or to demean their views, don't. Stooping to that level only diminishes your own authority and undermines your credibility. Two of the logical fallacies we discussed in Chapter 2 address this problem. The first, an ad hominem argument, is a personal attack on those who disagree with your position. Unfortunately, this approach will reflect negatively on *you*. Use reason and hard evidence instead of insults and ridicule to underscore the weakness of other arguments while you make your readers aware of your mutual concerns. The second fallacy is an ad populum argument and involves using the presumed prejudices of your audience members to manipulate their responses to your argument. Once again, this approach will make you appear unreasonable and biased and may backfire if your audience does not share your prejudices. Instead, encourage your readers to respect different viewpoints, recognizing the merits of their arguments even though you ultimately disagree. It's simply a more reasonable approach, one that allows you and your readers to share informed agreement, and it will win the respect of friends and foes alike.

Offer New Information About the Issue

Even when your readers agree with you, they may need to have their memories refreshed regarding the history of the issue. In addition, you should provide readers with important new information on the issue. Such new developments might involve recent judiciary decisions, newly enacted legislation, or new scientific data that could serve to strengthen your position and their agreement or require a reconsideration of your views. Unless you are absolutely up-to-date about the progress of your issue, you will appear to be either ill informed or deliberately withholding information, seriously undermining your credibility with your audience, even a friendly one. Your willingness to share and educate your audience will enhance the persuasiveness of your views.

Addressing an Unfriendly Audience

As difficult as it may be to accept, some readers will be totally at odds with your views, even hostile to them. Writing for such a readership, of course, is especially challenging—far more than for neutral readers. So how do you present your argument to people you have little chance of winning over?

Seek Common Ground and Remind Your Audience About It

In this argumentative strategy, recommended by psychologist Carl Rogers, your goal is to find ways to connect with your audience through empathy and common experiences. For instance, let's say you are trying to persuade a group of senior citizens to support a tax increase to fund local schools. After analyzing your audience, you might conclude that many are living on limited incomes and are concerned about the financial burden of additional taxes. This factor might make them a hostile audience, one not easily receptive to your position. A good strategy, then, to begin your argument might be to let them know that you are well acquainted with the difficulties of living on limited means. You might even refer to relatives or friends who are in a similar position. If you let your audience know that you empathize with and understand their difficulties, they will be more willing to listen to you.

Remind your audience of the beliefs and values you have in common. While it is unlikely that many of the senior citizens still have children attending the local schools, nonetheless, they may value education and understand its importance. You can let them know that you share this value, one that underlies your support for additional public school funding.

Recognize the concerns of your audience as legitimate and worthy of attention; you will demonstrate that you are aware of and respect their views. This means, of course, finding out what their concerns are. For instance, if you are trying to persuade your audience to support a tax increase to fund new programs in the public schools in your district, do some reading to find out the reasons why people would choose not to support the tax increase. By addressing those concerns, you will make your audience aware that you understand their position. This may make them more receptive to listening to yours.

Review: Addressing Audiences

A Neutral Audience
- Fill in the background
- Present a balanced picture
- Personalize the issues
- Show respect for your readers

A Friendly Audience
- Avoid appealing to prejudices
- Offer new information about the issue

An Unfriendly Audience
- Seek common ground
- Convey a positive attitude
- Remember the Golden Rule

To Improve Your Credibility with Your Audience, Avoid These Fallacies

Ad hominem argument	Leveling a personal attack against an opponent. A reliance on ad hominem arguments undercuts your credibility and may make you appear mean-spirited and desperate. Focus instead on the substance of an opponent's claim.
Ad misericordiam argument	Attempting to exploit the audience's emotions rather than appealing to logic and reason. Avoid using arguments that rely only on wrenching the reader's heart strings rather than logic and real evidence.
Ad populum argument	Appealing to the audience's presumed prejudices rather than proven facts. Even if you know the prejudices of your audience, such an appeal at best only persuades those already convinced. Rely on the force of logic and supporting evidence rather than bias and stereotyping.
Stacking the deck	Presenting only evidence that supports your points and withholding contrary evidence. Instead, acknowledge that conflicting evidence exists and respond to it.
False dilemma	Presenting an issue as an either–or choice and ignoring the possibility of a middle ground. Treat your audience as intelligent equals who are aware that at least several thoughtful alternatives are likely to exist.

Convey a Positive Attitude

Whether or not they know it, your audience will benefit from seeing the issue from another side. In other words, approach a hostile audience as someone who can shed a different light on the problem. View them as people who are potentially interested in learning something new. Without being defensive, arrogant, or apologetic, make your claim, enumerate your reasons, and lay out the evidence for your readers to evaluate on their own. Regard them as intelligent people capable of drawing their own conclusions. You may not win converts, but you might at least lead some to recognize the merits of your side. You might even convince a few people to reconsider their views.

Remember the Golden Rule

Even though they may not agree with you, treat the opposition with respect. Look upon them as reasonable people who just happen to disagree with you. Demonstrate your understanding of their side of the issue. Show that you have made the effort to research the opposition. Give credit where credit is due. If some of their counterpoints make sense, say so. In short, treat those from the other side and their views as you would want to be treated. You may just win a few converts.

SAMPLE ARGUMENTS FOR ANALYSIS

How a writer appeals to his or her audience can have a positive or a negative effect on the way the writer's message is received. The following four articles—three by professionals and one by a student—are concerned with the controversy regarding regulations on smoking and the resulting treatment of smokers. In major U.S. cities, notably Boston and New York City, legislation banning smoking at all indoor workplaces including bars, restaurants, and nightclubs was passed in 2003. Some nonsmokers as well as smokers approve of these new laws and look forward to smoke-free environments. However, many smokers protest what they feel is an infringement of their individual rights. Tackling this important health issue, the writers address the audience in notably different ways. For the first essay, by C. Everett Koop, we have used annotations to illustrate some of the strategies he uses to appeal to his audience and the assumptions he makes about them. As a class exercise, read each of these essays and then consider the following questions:

1. Locate the claim or thesis statement and summarize the main ideas in each essay.
2. What kind of audience is each writer addressing? neutral? friendly? hostile? What evidence can you find to support this?
3. Which writers attempt to present a balanced picture to the audience? Provide examples.
4. Do the writers convey a positive attitude toward the audience? Do any of the writers antagonize the audience? How is this done?
5. Have these writers committed any of the logical fallacies we've discussed? Where do these errors occur, and how would you correct them?

6. How well does each writer establish common ground with the audience?
7. What is the purpose of each essay? How effectively does each writer accomplish this purpose?

Don't Forget the Smokers
C. Everett Koop

> Dr. C. Everett Koop served as Surgeon General of the United States from 1981 until 1989. His duties in office were to advise the public on matters such as smoking, diet and nutrition, environmental health hazards, and disease prevention. Since leaving office, Dr. Koop has been a spokesperson and activist on issues of public health. This article appeared in the *Washington Post* on March 8, 1998.

1   To date, most of the tobacco control efforts of this administration have focused on preventing young people from taking up smoking. Everyone can agree that teenagers and younger children should not smoke. Even the tobacco industry can safely join in that refrain, and frequently does, with characteristic and clamorous hypocrisy as it turns its marketing machines loose on the young. But at exactly what age does the plight of American smokers lose its poignancy?   *Establishes common ground, shared views charged language*

2   One-third of teenagers who experiment casually with cigarettes will become regular smokers, with one-half of these trying to quit, but failing, by age 18. In fact, the vast majority of current smokers were hooked in their teens or earlier. During the '80s, the tobacco industry mounted a public relations campaign maintaining that smoking was "an adult decision." It was a model of reverse psychology, tempting teens at the same time it offered false reassurance to their elders. The vast majority of smokers are captive to their addiction, so that most who "decide" to quit cannot—not without help or years of repeated tries.   *Assumes media-savvy reader familiar with ad campaigns*

3   If we pretend that adult smoking is a consumer choice like any other, we fall prey to the trap laid by Big Tobacco. Addiction makes the very notion of choice moot. Who would freely choose sickness and suffering, lost productivity or 50 percent chance of premature death? Yet cigarette smokers of all ages continue to die prematurely at the rate of more than 400,000 per year. If not one single young person started smoking from this day forward, these losses would still continue unabated for 30 years. Imagine 1,000 jumbo jets emblazoned   *Allusion to Big Brother assumes reader has literary background*

with Marlboro and Winston and Camel insignia crashing each year for the next three decades. <u>Should we accept such dramatic losses as par for the course?</u>

Rhetorical question involves reader

4   <u>We must not focus our efforts so narrowly on preventing tobacco use by youth that we send smokers the message that we have abandoned them</u>—that their addiction is their own fault and that we don't care about them. This is exactly what the tobacco industry wants them to hear. Forget quitting, hedge the health bets instead. Responding to founded fears, tobacco companies unleashed so-called "low-tar" brands in an effort to hold on to their smokers and reduce the concerns of the uninitiated. But in their attempt to avoid becoming yet another statistic, smokers have only changed the form of their resultant lung cancers from the squamous cell cancers of the upper lung to the adenocarcinomas of the lower lung as they inhaled more deeply to extract the nicotine their bodies craved from such cigarettes. There is an alternative. We can combine tobacco prevention initiatives with efforts to ensure that those who are hooked can obtain effective treatments.

Addresses readers as adults who have power to shape public attitudes

Assumes readers are comfortable with medical terms

5   The facts are that quitting smoking at any age reduces the risk of premature death; current treatments can substantially increase the odds of quitting. It therefore seems logical that each decision to smoke should present an equal opportunity not to smoke and an equal opportunity to get help. The Food and Drug Administration's actions in 1996 to restrict tobacco marketing to minors and to approve over-the-counter marketing of nicotine gum and patches for adults were pioneering steps in the right direction. So are several pieces of congressional legislation currently under discussion that include provisions for tobacco addiction treatments.

Uses facts and reasons, not emotions

Assumes broad general knowledge

6   Nevertheless, much remains to be done if our nation is to make tobacco dependence treatment as acceptable and as readily available as tobacco itself. <u>We must evaluate and approve potentially life-saving treatments</u> for tobacco dependence at the level of priority we assign to treatments for diseases such as AIDS and cancer. Signaling such a course could help empower the private sector to meet these challenges in a way that will contribute to the health of our nation in the short and long run.

Suggests readers are in decision-making positions

7   Currently, the tobacco industry is lobbying Congress for its own solution to the needs of smokers. Under the guise of the new-found concern for the health of their consumers, these companies want incentives to market products that they claim will reduce the dangers of smoking. We do not want to stifle development of such products. Indeed, we should require reduced

Tone: serious

Sketches opposition's plan and shows weaknesses

toxicity of tobacco products, as we now understand that they are unnecessarily dangerous and addictive. But such a course should not enable tobacco companies to undermine our efforts to reduce overall tobacco use by allowing them to advertise their products with claims such as "low tar" or "reduced delivery." *Makes a direct appeal to knowledgeable readers* Legitimate concern for the health of tobacco users should balance efforts to reduce the toxicity of tobacco products with the means to expedite the development of new treatments for those who are addicted. Under its existing authorities, including its designation of cigarettes and smokeless tobacco products as combination drug and device products, the FDA has many regulatory tools at its disposal to accomplish its goal of reducing the risk of death and disease in tobacco-addicted Americans. Congressional legislation that weakens the FDA's authority over tobacco reduces its ability to serve the public health.

8   I strongly encourage any forthcoming congressional legislation or executive actions to strengthen, if not leave alone, the FDA's authority over tobacco, and to support the FDA's ability to evaluate new treatments and treatment approaches in a manner that is consistent with the devastation wrought by unremitting tobacco use. Moreover, in our battle with Big Tobacco, we should not hide behind our children. Instead, as we take every action to save our children from the ravages of tobacco, we should demonstrate our commitment to those who are already addicted, and those who will yet become addicted, will never expire. *Forceful language* *Plays on connotation and denotation of word*

What the Antismoking Zealots Really Crave
Jeff Jacoby

> Jeff Jacoby, a founding director of the Pioneer Institute, a conservative public-policy think tank in Boston, writes a regular column for the *Boston Globe*, where this piece appeared on March 24, 1998.

1   A question for antitobacco militants: Why do you draw the line at private homes?

2   To protect nonsmokers, especially young ones, you've made it illegal to smoke in more and more places. You have banished smoking from tens of millions of private workplaces; from airplanes and buses; from most government buildings. You have gotten hundreds of cities—Boston is your latest conquest—to ban smoking in restaurants altogether. In California, you've even driven smokers from bars.

3   But smoking at home is OK.

4   Curious, no? You militants routinely justify your crusade by claiming to act for "the kids," yet in the one place a kid is likeliest to encounter cigarettes, smoking is wholly unregulated. Why? It can't be because you respect the rights of private property owners. After all, restaurants and bars are private property. And it can't be because the state never interferes in the way parents raise their children—the state interferes in everything from the commercials children see on television to the paint that goes on their walls. So why aren't you clamoring to take away parents' freedom to smoke at home?

5   Granted, that would just about outlaw *all* smoking. But isn't that what you want?

6   One of the nation's foremost antismoking activists, Stanton Glantz, compares cigarette manufacturers to Timothy McVeigh, the mass murderer of Oklahoma City. A *New York Times* reporter likens tobacco employees to "the guards and doctors in the Nazi death camps." Over a decade ago, the *Journal of the American Medical Association* was calling for "a declaration of all-out war" against the perpetrators of "the tobaccoism holocaust."

7   Such murderous rhetoric is typical. On taxpayer-funded billboards in California, a man about to light up asks, "Mind if I smoke?" The woman replies: "Care if I die?" Elizabeth Whelan of the American Council on Science and Health says smoking kills more people than "if every single day two filled-to-capacity jumbo jets crashed, killing all on board." A former director of the Centers for Disease Control has predicted that "the annual global death toll of tobacco will equal the total death toll of the Holocaust in Nazi Germany."

8   Such hysteria is more than repugnant, it is false. In *For Your Own Good* (Free Press), a lucid and superbly researched new book on the antitobacco jihad, journalist Jacob Sullum pinpoints the deceit:

9   "The rhetoric of tobacco's opponents implies a rough equivalence between a 65-year-old smoker who dies of lung cancer and a 40-year-old businessman killed in a plane crash, a 19-year-old soldier shot in the trenches of World War I, or a child murdered by the Nazis at Auschwitz. But there is a big difference between someone who dies suddenly at the hands of another person or in an accident and someone who dies as a result of a long-term, voluntarily assumed risk."

10   Maybe so, you antismoking activists might say, but the harm caused by smoking isn't limited to the smoker. His smoke poisons everyone he comes into contact with. They shouldn't be made to suffer because of his vile habit. Nonsmokers have a right to a smoke-free society.

11   In fact, the danger of secondhand smoke is more myth than science. Most epidemiological studies have found no statistically significant link between lung cancer and secondhand smoke. Exposure to cigarette fumes may not be *good* for your health, but the medical fact is that secondhand smoke is not likely to do lasting harm to anyone.

12   Still—what about those kids growing up in smokers' homes? How can you sworn enemies of tobacco be so intent on criminalizing the smoke in smoky jazz bars, yet do nothing about the millions of children whose parents light up with abandon?

Why don't you demand that cigarettes be outlawed in any house with kids? In other words, why don't you demand that cigarettes be outlawed—period!

13   Maybe the answer is that even zealots like you realize it wouldn't work. Alcohol Prohibition in the 1920s was a hideous failure, drenching the country in corruption, crime, and oceans of impure alcohol. In a nation with 45 million smokers, Tobacco Prohibition would be no less a disaster and most of you know it.

14   Or maybe the answer is that you couldn't *afford* to end smoking entirely. Ban all tobacco, and there'd be no tobacco taxes or (legal) tobacco profits. No profits or taxes, no hundreds of billions of dollars to fund a settlement. No gusher of dollars for new "health care" programs. No bonanza for plaintiffs' lawyers. No lavish budgets for all your antitobacco outfits. No goose. No golden eggs.

15   But I think the real answer is that you don't think you can get away with it—yet. Already some of you *are* targeting smokers' homes. At least one law review article has claimed that parents who expose their children to tobacco smoke "should be viewed as committing child abuse." A Pennsylvania legislator has proposed a ban on smoking in any vehicle carrying a minor. More intrusion is on its way.

16   Nicotine may be pleasurable, but it's nothing like the high of forcing others to behave the way you want them to. Power over other people's pleasures is very addicting, isn't it? "The true nature of the crusade for a smoke-free society," Sullum writes, is "an attempt by one group of people to impose their tastes and preferences on another." It's illiberal, it's vindictive, it's intolerant. It's you.

Media Have Fallen for Misguided Antismoking Campaign

Robert J. Samuelson

Robert J. Samuelson, the recipient of numerous journalism awards, is a nationally known columnist who focuses on political, economic, and social issues. This article was published in the *Boston Globe* on September 30, 1997.

1   The media are deeply sensitive to the rights of those we consider minorities: the poor, the disabled, blacks, gays, and immigrants, among others. But there is one minority much larger than any of these (at least 25 percent of the population) whose rights we deny or ignore: smokers. The debate over cigarettes has been framed as if smokers are the unwitting victims of the tobacco industry. They lack free will and, therefore, their apparent desires and interests don't count. They are to be pitied and saved, not respected.

2   This is pack journalism run amok. We media types fancy ourselves independent thinkers. Just the opposite is often true: We're patsies for the latest crusade or fad. In this case, the major media have adopted the view of the public health community,

which sees smoking as a scourge to be eradicated. The "story" is the crusade; the villain is the tobacco industry. Lost are issues that ought to inform this debate.

3   The simplest is whether, in trying to make Americans better off, the antismoking crusade would make many Americans worse off. Smokers would clearly suffer from huge price and tax increases. The cost of the $368.5 billion agreement between the tobacco industry and the state attorneys general is estimated at 62 cents a pack. President Clinton suggests raising that to $1.50 a pack—about six times today's federal tax (24 cents). The cost would hit the poor hardest. They smoke more than the rich.

4   Consider. About half (53 percent) of today's cigarette tax is paid by taxpayers with incomes of less than $30,000, estimates the congressional Joint Committee on Taxation. Higher prices will deter some people from smoking. But for the rest, would siphoning billions away from poorer people be good policy? Or fair?

5   The antismoking crusaders try to seem fair by arguing: (1) smoking has been increasing among teenagers who, once they try cigarettes, may become addicted for life; (2) tobacco ads cause much teenage smoking—teenagers are, therefore, victims; and (3) passive smoking (nonsmokers inhaling smoke) in public places is a serious health threat, justifying action against smokers. These assumptions permeate media coverage, but the first two are open to question and the third is untrue.

6   Start with teenage smoking. One survey from the University of Michigan does show a rise. In 1996, 34 percent of 12th-graders reported smoking in the past month—the highest since 1979 (34.4 percent). But the government's survey on drug abuse suggests the opposite: In 1996, only 18.3 percent of teenagers between 12 and 17 had smoked in the past month, the lowest since 1985 (29 percent). It's hard to know which survey to believe, but neither depicts runaway teenage smoking.

7   As for ads, teenagers do a lot of dangerous things (drugs, early sex) that aren't advertised and are often illegal. The tobacco industry no doubt targets teenagers, but the ads may affect brand choices more than they do the decision to smoke. A new, comprehensive study—financed by the National Institutes of Health—suggests that teenagers' home environment is more important in determining who smokes. "Children who report feeling connected to a parent are protected against many different kinds of health risks including . . . cigarette, alcohol, and marijuana use," it says.

8   And even teenagers who smoke do not necessarily become lifetime smokers. Among 12th-graders, the percentage of those who once smoked (63 percent) is about twice as high as for those who currently do. The "addiction" isn't so great that millions haven't broken it.

9   Finally, passive smoking isn't a big public health risk, as many stories imply. The latest example of misreporting involved a study from Harvard Medical School. It purported to show that passive smoking doubled the risk of heart attacks, indicating a huge public health problem. That's how both the *New York Times* and *Washington Post* reported it. In fact, the study—at most—showed that passive smoking doubles a very tiny risk.

10   Here's why. The study followed 32,046 nonsmoking nurses between 1982 and 1992. Of these, four-fifths said they were exposed to passive smoking. But there were only 152 heart attacks (127 nonfatal) among all the nurses: a small number.

Many heart attacks would have occurred even if no one was exposed to smoke. And most exposure to passive smoke is now private or voluntary, because public smoking has been barred in so many places. Will we outlaw husbands smoking in front of their wives—or vice versa?

11   You don't hear much of all this, because the press has an antismoking bias. The crusaders do have a case. Smoking is highly risky for smokers. But lots of things are risky, and don't smokers have a right to engage in behavior whose pleasures and pains are mainly theirs without being punished by the rest of society?

12   There is almost no one to make the smokers' case. They have been abandoned by the tobacco industry, politicians, and the press. Do smokers have rights? Apparently not.

Smoking: Offended by the Numbers

Danise Cavallaro

> Danise Cavallaro is an English major, and it's clear from her word choice, tone, and the slant she takes that she is addressing her peers. As she mentions in her essay, many college students smoke, even if only at parties. In this essay, Cavallaro wonders why anyone would ever want to smoke at all.

Cavallaro 1

Danise Cavallaro

Professor Mitrani

English 102

October 13, 2007

Smoking: Offended by the Numbers

1   I majored in English because I hate mathematics and numbers. I hate these numbers too, but at least they are non-mathematically interesting. 11; 445; 1,200; 50,000.

• Eleven is the number of chemical compounds found in cigarettes that are known to cause cancer.

• Four hundred forty-five is the number of people per day who are diagnosed with smoking-related lung cancer.

Cavallaro 2

- One thousand two hundred is the number of people who die every day from tobacco.
- Fifty thousand is the number of people who die every year from secondhand smoke. (www. thetruth. com)

2   I thought that I would defy the rules of journalism and write out those numbers again in longhand, because they seem awfully small on the page when I looked at them numerically. I thought if they looked bigger on the page, they might hold a little more meaning. They're even larger when they're not written in longhand. Yankee Stadium, filled, holds just over 57,000 people. That's roughly all the people who die from secondhand smoke per year, plus about five-and-a-half days' worth of the daily death toll from firsthand smoke. Keep thinking about Yankee Stadium. If you were at a baseball game, who would you be there with? Your parents or your family? Your boyfriend or girlfriend, your best friends, your roommate from college? Don't forget about yourself. Now imagine them hooked up on an oxygen tank, struggling to do something as simple as breathe, unable to pull enough air into their lungs to cheer a run or a tag-out at home. They're living, still very much medically alive, but think of their quality of life: struggling to breathe, severely limited activity, and feigned happiness at most things.

3   In 21 years of being alive, I have never once felt the urge to light a cigarette. However, I have a lot of friends and family who have. I'm still struggling to understand what makes cigarettes appealing. Kissing my ex fresh after he squashed his cigarette underneath his heel tasted similar to what I'd imagine licking

Cavallaro 3

an ashtray would be like. My best friend lives
in Manhattan, complains to no end about how
expensive things are, but has no problem forking
over nearly $10 for a pack of cigarettes. Her
parents give her a hard time about it every
time she's home and she usually retorts with,
"At least my cigarettes are safer than the
unfiltered ones you rolled in the Army!" My
uncle watched my grandfather slowly lose a two-
year battle with lung cancer caused by working
with asbestos and smoking unfiltered cigarettes
for more than 40 years, but he would still take
smoke breaks while visiting him in the hospital.
He still smokes today. It makes me sick.

4   With all this firsthand knowledge, such as
the statistics I cited above, along with the
deluge of widely available facts and help
(Aren't we living in the Information Age?) and
as smart as these select people are, how could
anyone not be motivated to quit by the numbers
alone? The anti-smoking ad campaigns are not
strong enough, and, for whatever silly economic
reason, cigarettes are marketed as cool. Yet
people still buy them even though they're a
waste of money and smoke them even though they
carry a high mortality rate, all in the name of
being able to exercise their rights as an
autonomous American.

5   I wonder if smokers still think in that
hard-headed American way when they're gasping
for breath as they walk up the stairs. It's no
secret that nicotine is an extremely addictive
drug, and one of the hardest to give up. As with
many things, if quitting were easy more people
would do it; and Mount Everest would be as
popular as Disneyland if it were just a hill.

Cavallaro 4

6   To help lower the numbers in America, I
propose a national anti-smoking campaign much
like "Scared Straight," a program for to-be
juvenile offenders that worked well as it
showed exactly what the troubled youths would
become in their future if they kept to the path
they were on. The popular anti-drug website,
"thetruth.com," famous for its silently-shocking
TV commercials depicting nonviolent boycotts of
tobacco companies, is a good start. Certainly,
more can be done. It starts with the youth
of today.

7   Bring in a cancer-ravaged lung to a high
school health class. Consider the postmortem
donation as a gift to science—the science of
staying alive. Black and white X-rays of lungs
filled with malignant growths don't shock and
revolt nearly as much as once-live flesh does,
or ever will. While nicotine-yellowed teeth are
becoming increasingly easier to whiten with do-
it-yourself kits, it's impossible to peek at the
inside of your own lungs to see the damage
that's been done. Plaster huge pictures of
cancer- or emphysema-ravaged lungs across
billboards along I-95. Realize that not being
politically correct, not being afraid to offend,
may actually save your life, your friends'
lives, your children's lives. Grossing out the
populace could be a highly effective tool—
statistics and numbers printed on paper hardly
look menacing, but disintegrating lungs are
practically a guarantee.

8   One of the many problems with adolescent
smoking is that the more deadly side effects
aren't felt until many years after high school,
when smoking is less of a faux-cool habit

Cavallaro 5

and more of a way of life. Asthma is highly
treatable, but lung cancer, the most lethal form
of cancer, isn't (en.wikipedia.org). I propose
banning the depiction of smoking in movies and
television geared towards young adults.
Adolescents, an extremely malleable age group,
are obviously influenced by the media and seek
to imitate it in clothing, hairstyles, music and
lifestyles. Remove the idea that smoking is an
acceptable way of life, and it will reduce the
numbers of people for whom smoking will become a
way of life. I also propose making cigarettes
more expensive; teenagers are famous for being
broke. The harder it is for that age group to
afford a deadly habit, the less likely it could
actually become a habit. America needs to be more
honest with this easily influenced age group.

9   The problem with all this is, again, the
numbers. America was founded on tobacco fields,
the trade of dried tobacco leaf between England
and the Native Americans. A cornerstone of our
economy rests on cigarettes. The biggest tobacco
companies in the world have branched out, and
now own major corporations that supply nearly
everything consumable. Richard Kluger, in his
1996 book, <u>Ashes to Ashes: America's Hundred-
Year Cigarette War, the Public Health and the
Unabashed Triumph of Philip Morris</u>, details
how Philip Morris not only dominates the
cigarette industry but has managed through its
acquisitions of other companies—from beer to
frozen vegetables—in the 1980s to insulate
itself from attack. To assault Philip Morris
would be to try to upset a major economic engine
to which many other companies on the NASDAQ are
inexorably linked.

Cavallaro 6

10   It may be quite impossible to financially overturn the tobacco companies while addicted individuals keep their cigarette plants a-humming. For example, my best friend has a pack-per-week habit which increases during midterms, finals and bad dates. One pack of cigarettes a week, at $10 a pack, amounts to $520 per year. That's a lot of money for a law school student with no job—most of a month's rent, half a year's worth of cell phone bills, and a lot of good meals at a good restaurant. I know many students who smoke a pack a day which amounts to over $3,000 a year, even if they buy cheap brands. The numbers add up, and it can be a hard choice where to apply your numbers.

11   Be selfish, America, keep your numbers to yourself.

Cavallaro 7

Works Cited

"Facts and Figures about Smoking." The Centers for Disease Control and Prevention, the Food and Drug Administration, and the American Cancer Society. 19 Jan. 2005 <http://www.thetruth.com/index.cfm?seek=facts>.

Kluger, Richard. <u>Ashes to Ashes: America's Hundred-Year Cigarette War, The Public Health and the Unabashed Triumph of Philip Morris</u>. New York: Knopf, 1996.

"Lung Cancer." <u>Wikipedia, the Free Encyclopedia</u>. 19 Jan. 2005 <http://en.wikipedia.org/wiki/Lung_cancer>.

Choosing Your Words

Whether addressing friends, foes, or the undecided, you must take care that your readers fully understand your case. In part, this is accomplished by choosing your words carefully and by accurately defining any technical, unfamiliar, foreign, or abstract terms. Here are a few specific tips to follow to inform your readers without turning them off.

Distinguishing Denotation and Connotation

Many words, even the most common, carry special suggestions or associations, **connotations,** that differ from the precise dictionary definitions, **denotations.** For example, if you looked up the word *house* in the dictionary, one of the synonyms you'd find is *shelter*. Yet if you told people you live in a shelter, they would think that you live in a facility for the homeless or some kind of animal sanctuary. That is because *shelter* implies a covering or structure that protects those within from the elements or from danger. In other words, the term is not neutral, as is the word *house*. Likewise, dictionary synonyms for *horse* include *steed* and *nag*, but the former implies an elegant and high-spirited riding animal, while the latter suggests one that is old and worn out.

The denotations of words may be the same, but their connotations will almost always differ. And the reason is that dictionary denotations are essentially neutral and emotion-free, while connotations are most often associated with attitudes or charged feelings that can influence readers' responses. Therefore, it is important to be aware of the shades of differences when choosing your words. Consider the different meanings the connotations of the bracketed choices lend these statements:

> By the time I got home I was _____ [sleepy, exhausted, weary, beat, dead].
>
> My boyfriend drives around in a red _____ [car, vehicle, buggy, clunker, jalopy].
>
> I could hear him _____ [shout, yell, bellow, scream, shriek].

Connotations can also be personal and, thus, powerful tools for shaping readers' responses to what you say. Consider the word *pig*. The dictionary definition, or denotation, would read something like this: "A domestic farm animal with a long, broad snout and a thick, fat body covered with coarse bristles." However, the connotation of *pig* is far more provocative, for it suggests someone who looks or acts like a pig; someone who is greedy or filthy; someone who is sexually immoral. (Most dictionaries list the connotations of words, although some connotations might only be found in a dictionary of slang—e.g., *The New Dictionary of American Slang,* edited by Robert L. Chapman, or *Slang!* by Paul Dickson.)

There is nothing wrong with using a word because of its connotations, but you must be aware that connotations will have an emotional impact on readers. You don't want to say something unplanned. You don't want to offend readers by using words loaded with unintentional associations. For instance, you wouldn't suggest to advertisers that they "should be more creative when hawking their products" unless you intended to insult them. Although the term *hawking* refers to selling, it is unflattering and misleading because it connotes somebody moving up and down the streets peddling goods by shouting. Linguistically, the word comes from the same root as the word *huckster,* which refers to an aggressive merchant known for haggling and questionable practices.

Connotatively loaded language can be used to create favorable as well as unfavorable reactions. If you are arguing against the use of animals in medical research, you will get a stronger response if you decry the sacrifice of "puppies and kittens" rather than the cooler, scientific, and less charged "laboratory animals."

You can understand why politicians, newspaper columnists, and anyone advocating a cause use connotative language. The loaded word is like a bullet for a writer making a strong argument. Consider the connotative impact of the italicized terms in the following excerpts taken from essays in this text:

> RCA, the corporation that took over the Victor Talking Machine Company in 1920, still uses Nipper to *hawk* its products. (Grace Conlon, "Logos, a History")

> Such hysteria is more than repugnant, it is false. In *For Your Own Good* (Free Press), a lucid and superbly researched new book on the *antitobacco jihad,* journalist Jacob Sullum pinpoints the deceit. [. . .] (Jeff Jacoby, "What the Antismoking Zealots Really Crave")

> Global consumer culture? *Supersize* it, baby. Pile on the wattage, horse-power, silicone, cholesterol and RAM until the lights *flicker,* the smoke alarms *shriek* and the cardiac paddles lurch to life. (Harry Flood, "Manufacturing Desire")

Each of the italicized words was selected not for its denotations but its negative connotations. In the first example, Grace Conlon could have chosen a more neutral word such as *sell* to convey her denotative meaning; however, she deliberately selects *hawk* to suggest irritating birdlike squawking. Similarly, Jeff Jacoby describes the organized effort against smoking as a *jihad,* which evokes the image of a holy war waged by religious extremists. And Harry Flood's description of the excesses of consumer culture features flickering lights and shrieking alarms—a jarring image of chaos and disorder.

Being Specific

To help readers better understand your argument, you need to use words that are precise enough to convey your exact meaning. If you simply say, "The weather last weekend was *terrible,*" your readers are left to come up with their own interpretations of what the weather was like. Was it hot and muggy? cold and rainy? overcast and very windy? some of each? Chances are your readers won't come up with the same weather conditions you had in mind. However, if you said, "Last weekend it rained day and night and never got above 40 degrees," readers will have a more precise idea of the weekend's weather. And you will have accomplished your purpose of saying just what you meant.

The terms *general* and *specific* are opposites just as *abstract* and *concrete* are opposites. General words do not name individual things but classes or groups of things: animals, trees, women. Specific words refer to individuals in a group: your pet canary, the oak tree outside your bedroom window, the point guard. Of course, general and specific are themselves relative terms. Depending on the context or your frame of reference, a word that is specific in one context may be general in another. For instance, there is no need to warn a vegetarian that a restaurant serves veal Oscar and beef Wellington when simply *meat* will do. In other words, there are degrees of specificity appropriate to the situation. The following list illustrates just such a sliding scale, moving downward from the more general to the more specific.

General	animal	person	book	clothing	food	machine
	feline	female	novel	footwear	seafood	vehicle
	cat	singer	American	shoes	fish	fighter jet
Specific	Daisy, my pet	Mary J. Blige	*The Great Gatsby*	her Nikes	tuna	F-17

General words are useful in ordinary conversation when the people you're addressing understand your meaning and usually don't ask for clarification. The same is true in writing when you are addressing an audience familiar with your subject. In such instances, you can get away with occasional broad statements. For example, if you are running for class president, your campaign speeches would not require a great number of specifics as much as general statements of promise and principles:

> If elected, I intend to do what I can to ensure a comfortable classroom environment for each student at this college.

But when your audience is unfamiliar with your subject or when the context requires concrete details, generalities and abstract terms fall flat, leaving people wondering just exactly what you are trying to communicate. Let's say, for instance, you write a note to your dean explaining why you'd like to change the room where your English class meets. You wouldn't get very far on this appeal:

> Room 107 Richards is too small and uncomfortable for our class.

However, if you offer some specifics evoking a sense of the room's unpleasantness, you'd make a more persuasive case for changing the room:

> Room 107 Richards has 20 fixed seats for 27 students, leaving those who come in late to sit on windowsills or the floor. Worse still is the air quality. The radiators are fixed on high and the windows don't open. By the end of the hour, it must be 90 degrees in there, leaving everybody sweaty and wilted including Prof. Hazzard.

What distinguishes this paragraph is the use of concrete details: "20 fixed seats for 27 students"; latecomers forced to "sit on windowsills or on the floor"; radiators "fixed on high"; "the windows don't open"; "90 degrees"; and everybody was left "sweaty and wilted including Prof. Hazzard." But more than simply conjuring up a vivid impression of the room's shortcomings, these specifics add substance to your argument for a room change.

Concrete language is specific language—words that have definite meaning. Concrete language names persons, places, and things: *George W. Bush, Mary Shelley, New Zealand, Venice Boulevard, book, toothpaste.* Concrete terms conjure up vivid pictures in the minds of readers because they refer to particular things or qualities that can be perceived by the five senses—that is, they can be seen, smelled, tasted, felt, and heard. Abstract words, in contrast, refer to qualities that do not have a definitive concrete meaning. They denote intangible qualities that cannot be perceived directly by the senses but are inferred from the senses—*powerful, foolish, talented, responsible, worthy.* Abstract words also denote concepts and ideas—*patriotism, beauty, victory, sorrow.* Although abstract terms can be useful depending on the context, writing that relies heavily on abstractions will fail to communicate clear meaning. Notice in the pairs below how concrete and specific details convert vague statements into vivid ones:

Abstract	He was very nicely dressed.
Concrete	He wore a dark gray Armani suit, white pinstriped shirt, and red paisley tie.
Abstract	Jim felt uncomfortable at Jean's celebration party.
Concrete	Jim's envy of Jean's promotion made him feel guilty.
Abstract	That was an incredible accident.
Concrete	A trailer truck jackknifed in the fog, causing seven cars to plow into each other, killing two, injuring eight, and leaving debris for a quarter mile along Route 17.

Abstract language is also relative. It depends on circumstances and the experience of the person using them. A *cold* December morning to someone living in Florida might mean temperatures in the forties or fifties. To residents of North Dakota, *cold* would designate air at subzero temperatures. It all depends on one's point of view. A *fair trial* might mean one thing to the prosecutor of a case, yet something completely different to the defense attorney. Likewise, what might be *offensive* language to your grandmother would probably not faze an average college student.

When employing abstract language, you need to be aware that readers may not share your point of view. Consequently, you should be careful to clarify your terms or simply select concrete alternatives. Below is an excerpt from a student paper as it appeared in the first draft. As you can see, it is lacking in details and specifics and has a rather dull impact.

> **Vague:** Last year my mother nearly died from medicine when she went to the hospital. The bad reaction sent her into a coma for weeks, requiring life-support systems around the clock. Thankfully, she came out of the coma and was released, but somebody should have at least asked what, if any, allergies she had.

Although the paragraph reads smoothly, it communicates very little of the dramatic crisis being described. Without specific details and concrete words, the reader misses both the trauma and the seriousness of the hospital staff's neglect, thus dulling the argument for stronger safeguards. What follows is the same paragraph revised with the intent of making it more concrete.

> **Revised:** Last year my mother nearly died from a codeine-based painkiller when she was rushed to the emergency room at Emerson Hospital. The severe allergic reaction sent her into a coma for six weeks, requiring daily blood transfusions, thrice weekly kidney dialysis, continuous intravenous medicines, a tracheotomy, and round-the-clock intensive care. Thankfully, she came out of the coma and was released, but the ER staff was negligent in not determining from her or her medical records that she was allergic to codeine.

Using Figurative Language

Words have their literal meaning, but they also can mean something beyond dictionary definitions, as we have seen. The sentence "Mrs. Jones is an angel" does not mean that Mrs. Jones is literally a supernatural winged creature, but a very kind and pleasant woman. What makes the literally impossible meaningful here is figurative language.

Figurative language (or a **figure of speech**) is comparative language. It is language that represents something in terms of something else—in figures, symbols, or likeness (Mrs. Jones and an angel). It functions to make the ordinary appear extraordinary and the unfamiliar appear familiar. It also adds richness and complexity to abstractions. Here, for instance, is a rather bland literal statement: "Yesterday it was 96 degrees and very humid." Here's that same sentence rendered in figurative language: "Yesterday the air was like warm glue." What this version does is equate yesterday's humid air to glue on a feature shared by each—stickiness. And the result is more interesting than the original statement.

The comparison of humid air to glue is linked by the words *like*. This example represents one of the most common figures of speech, the **simile.** Derived from the Latin *similis,* the term means similar. A simile makes an explicit comparison between dissimilar things (humid air and glue). It says that *A* is like *B* in one or more respects. The connectives used in similes are most often the words *like, as,* and *than:*

- A school of minnows shot by me like pelting rain.
- His arms are as big as hams.
- They're meaner than junkyard dogs.

When the connectives *like, as,* or *than* are omitted, then we have another common figure of speech, the **metaphor**. The term is from the Greek *meta* (over) + *pherin* ("to carry or ferry") meaning to carry over meaning from one thing to another. Instead of saying that A is like B, a metaphor equates them—A *is* B. For example, Mrs. Jones and an angel are said to be one and the same, although we all know that literally the two are separate entities.

- This calculus problem is a real pain in the neck.
- The crime in this city is a cancer out of control.
- The space shuttle was a flaming arrow in the sky.

Sometimes writers will carelessly combine metaphors that don't go with each other. Known as **mixed metaphors,** these often produce ludicrous results. For example:

- The heat of his expression froze them in their tracks.
- The experience left a bad taste in her eyes.
- The arm of the law has two strikes against it.

When a metaphor has lost its figurative value, it is called a **dead metaphor:** the *mouth* of a river, the *eye* of a needle, the *face* of a clock. Originally these expressions functioned as figures of speech, but their usage has become so common in our language that many have become **clichés** ("golden opportunity," "dirt cheap," "a clinging vine"). More will be said about clichés below, but our best advice is to avoid them. Because they have lost their freshness, they're unimaginative and they dull your writing.

Another common figure of speech is **personification,** in which human or animal characteristics or qualities are attributed to inanimate things or ideas. We hear it all the time: Trees *bow* in the wind; fear *grips* the heart; high pressure areas *sit* on the northeast. Such language is effective in making abstract concepts concrete and vivid and possibly more interesting:

- Graft and corruption walk hand in hand in this town.
- The state's new tax law threatens to gobble up our savings.
- Nature will give a sigh of relief the day they close down that factory.

As with other figures of speech, personification must be used appropriately and with restraint. If it's overdone, it ends up calling undue attention to itself while leaving readers baffled:

> Drugs have slouched their way into our schoolyards and playgrounds, laughing up their sleeves at the law and whispering vicious lies to innocent children.

For the sake of sounding literary, drugs here are personified as pushers slouching, laughing, and whispering. But such an exaggeration runs the risk of being rejected by readers as pretentious. If this happens, the vital message may well be lost. One must also be careful not to take shortcuts. Like dead metaphors, many once-imaginative personifications have become clichés: "justice is blind," "virtue triumphed," "walking death." While such may be handy catch phrases, they are trite and would probably be dismissed by critical readers as lazy writing.

Another figure of speech worth mentioning is the **euphemism,** which is a polite way of saying something blunt or offensive. Instead of toilets, restaurants have *restrooms.* Instead of a salesperson, furniture stores send us *mattress technicians.* Instead of false teeth, people in advertising wear *dentures.* The problem with euphemisms is that they conceal the true meaning of something. The result can be a kind of double-talk—language inflated for the sake of deceiving the listener. Business and government are notorious for such practices. When workers are laid off, corporations talk about *restructuring* or *downsizing*. A few years ago, the federal government announced *a revenue enhancement* when it really meant that taxes were going up; likewise, the Environmental Protection Agency referred to acid rain as *poorly buffered precipitation*; and when the CIA ordered a *nondiscernible microbinoculator,* it got a poison dart. Not only are such concoctions pretentious, they are dishonest. Fancy-sounding language camouflages hard truths.

Fancy-sounding language also has no place in good writing. When euphemisms are overdone, the result is a lot of verbiage and little meaning. Consider the example below before the euphemisms and pretentious language are reduced:

Overdone: In the event that gaming industry establishments be rendered legal, law enforcement official spokespersons have identified a potential crisis situation as the result of influence exerted by the regional career-offender cartel.

Readers may have to review this a few times before they understand what's being said. Even if they don't give up, a reader's job is not to rewrite your words. Writing with clarity and brevity shows respect for your audience. Here is the same paragraph with its pretentious wordiness and euphemisms edited down:

Revised: Should casino gambling be legalized, police fear organized crime may take over.

Of course, not all euphemisms are double-talk concoctions. Some may be necessary to avoid sounding insensitive or causing pain. To show respect in a sympathy card to bereaved survivors, it might be more appropriate to use the expression *passed away* instead of the blunt *died*. Recently, terms such as *handicapped* or *cripple* have given way to less derogatory replacements such as *a person with disabilities*. Likewise, we hear *a person with AIDS* instead of *AIDS victim,* which reduces the person to a disease or a label.

As with metaphors and personification, some euphemisms have passed into the language and become artifacts, making their usage potentially stale. People over age sixty-five are no longer "old" or "elderly," they're *senior citizens;* slums are *substandard housing;* the poor are *socially disadvantaged*. Although such euphemisms grew out of noble intentions, they tend to abstract reality. A Jules Feiffer cartoon from a few years ago captured the problem well. It showed a man talking to himself:

I used to think I was poor. Then they told me I wasn't poor, I was needy. They told me it was self-defeating to think of myself as needy, I was deprived. Then they told me underprivileged was overused. I was disadvantaged. I still don't have a dime. But I have a great vocabulary.

Although euphemisms were created to take the bite off reality, they can also take the bite out of your writing if not used appropriately. As Feiffer implies, sometimes it's better to say it like it is; depending on the context, "poor" simply might have more bite than some sanitized cliché. Similarly, some old people resent being called "seniors" not just because the term is an overused label, but because it abstracts the condition of old age. Our advice regarding euphemisms is to know when they are appropriate and to use them sparingly. Good writing simply means knowing when the right expression will get the response you want.

Avoiding Clichés

A cliché (or trite expression) is a phrase that is old and overused to the point of being unoriginal and stale. At one time, clichés were fresh and potent; overuse has left them flat. In speech, we may resort to clichés for quick meaning. However, clichés can dull your writing and make you seem lazy for choosing a phrase on tap rather than trying to think of more original and colorful wording. Consider these familiar examples:

apple of his eye

bigger than both of us

climbing the walls

dead as a doornail

head over heels

last but not least

mind over matter

ripe old age

short but sweet

white as a ghost

The problem with clichés is that they fail to communicate anything unique. To say you were "climbing the walls," for example, is an expression that could fit a wide variety of contradictory meanings. Out of context, it could mean that you were in a state of high anxiety, anger, frustration, excitement, fear, happiness, or unhappiness. Even in context, the expression is dull. Furthermore, because such clichés are ready made and instantly handy, they blot out the exact detail you intended to convey to your reader.

Clichés are the refuge of writers who don't make the effort to come up with fresh and original expressions. To avoid them, we recommend being alert for any phrases you have heard many times before and coming up with fresh substitutes. Consider the brief paragraph below, which is full of clichés marked in italics, and its revision:

Trite: *In this day and age*, a university ought to be concerned with ensuring that its women students take courses that will strengthen their understanding of their own past achievements and future *hopes and dreams*. At the same time, any school *worth its salt* should be *ready and able* to provide *hands-on experience*, activities, and courses that reflect a commitment to diversity and inclusiveness. Education must *seize the opportunity* of leading us *onward and* *upward* so that we don't slide back to the male-only curriculum emphasis of the *days of old.*

Revised: A university today ought to be concerned with ensuring that its women students take courses that will strengthen their understanding of their own past achievements and future possibilities. At the same time, any decent school should provide experience, activities, and courses that reflect a commitment to diversity and inclusiveness. Education must lead us forward so that we don't revert to the male-only curriculum emphasis of the past.

Defining Technical Terms

Special or technical vocabulary that is not clear from the context can function as an instant roadblock to freely flowing communication between you and your readers—sympathetic to your views or not. You cannot expect a novice in political science to know the meaning of *hegemony* or a nonmedical person to know exactly what you mean by *nephrological necrosis.* To avoid alienating nonexpert readers, you'll have to define such uncommon terms.

You can do so without being obtrusive or disrupting the flow of your writing with "time-outs" here and there to define terms. Notice how smoothly definitions have been slipped into the following passages:

> In fact, the phenomenon is known as recidivism—that is, a convict re-offends after having been released from confinement. (Arthur Allen, "Prayer in Prison: Religion as Rehabilitation")

> Finally, there has been no question whatever that carbon dioxide is an infrared absorber (i.e., a greenhouse gas—albeit a minor one), and its increase should theoretically contribute to warming. (Richard S. Lindzen, "Don't Believe the Hype")

> Katharine Phillips, a psychiatrist at the Brown University School of Medicine, has specialized in "body dysmorphic disorder," a psychiatric illness in which patients become obsessively preoccupied with perceived flaws in their appearances—receding hairlines, facial imperfections, small penises, inadequate musculature. (Stephen S. Hall, "The Bully in the Mirror")

Clarifying Familiar Terms

Even some familiar terms can lead to misunderstanding because they are used in so many different ways with so many different meanings: *liberal, Native American, lifestyle, decent, active.* It all depends on who is using the word. For instance, to an environmentalist the expression *big business* might connote profit-hungry and sinister industrial conglomerates that pollute the elements; to a conservative, however, the phrase might mean the commercial and industrial establishment that drives our economy. Likewise, a *liberal* does not mean the same thing to a Democrat as it does to a Republican. Even if you're writing for a sympathetic audience, be as precise as you can about familiar terms. Remember the advice of novelist George Eliot: "We have all got to remain calm, and call things by the same names other people call them by."

Stipulating Definitions

For a word that doesn't have a fixed or standard meaning, writers often offer a *stipulative* definition that explains what they mean by the term. For instance, in "The New Girl Order" (page 475), Kay S. Hymowitz argues that because of demographic and economic shifts, many countries around the world are seeing the emergence of a new breed of single young females who are unlike their grandmothers or even their mothers. This "New Girl Order," she says, is comprised of young women who have adopted the lifestyle of Carrie Bradshaw of *Sex and the City* fame. From this analogy, she stipulates a definition of the single young females "in their twenties and thirties, who spend their hours working their abs and their careers, sipping cocktails, dancing at clubs, and (yawn) talking about relationships." She goes on to refine her definition by stipulating three demographic facts: First, that they "are getting married and having kids considerably later than ever before." Second, "unlike their ancestral singles, they're looking for careers, not jobs. And that means they need lots of schooling." Third, they are moving from their "native village or town to Boston or Berlin or Seoul because that's where the jobs, boys, and bars are."

Other examples can be found in the somewhat heated dialogue, "Revisionist Feminism" (page 508), by Susan Faludi and Karen Lehrman, who take each other to task with stipulated terms. Faludi accuses Lehrman of yielding to "faux-feminism" (paragraph 6)—women's liberation as defined by the advertising industry of the 1970s, that is, "feminism as reinterpreted through television commercials for pantyhose and marketing manuals for Dress for Success bow ties." In reply, Lehrman protests Faludi's practice of "leftist" "feminist theory," which she stipulates as a refusal "to acknowledge that [. . .] equality with men has to mean sameness to men, that until all aspects of traditional femininity are abolished, women will not be free" (paragraph 7).

Stipulating your terms is like making a contract with your reader: You set down in black and white the important terms and their limits. The result is that you eliminate any misunderstanding and reduce your own vulnerability. And that can make the difference between a weak and a potent argument.

Avoiding Overdefinition

Where do you stop explaining and begin assuming your reader knows what you mean? What terms are "technical" or "specialized" or "important" enough to warrant definition? You certainly don't want to define terms unnecessarily or to oversimplify. In so doing, you run the risk of dulling the thrust of your claims while insulting the intelligence of your readers. Just how to strike a balance is a matter of good judgment about the needs and capabilities of your audience.

A good rule of thumb is to assume that your readers are almost as knowledgeable as you. This way, you minimize the risk of patronizing them. Another rule of thumb is the synonym test. If you can think of a word or short phrase that is an exact synonym for some specialized or important term in your argument, you probably don't need to define it. However, if you need a long phrase or sentence to paraphrase the term, you may want to work in a definition; it could be needed. And don't introduce your definitions with clauses like "As I'm sure you know" or "You don't need to be told that. . . ." If the audience didn't need to know it, you wouldn't be telling them, and if they do know what the terms mean, you may insult their intelligence with such condescending introductions.

Using Sarcasm and Humor Sparingly

Although we caution you against using sarcasm or humor too often, there are times when they can be very effective techniques of persuasion. Writers will often bring out their barbs for the sake of drawing blood from the opposition and snickers from the sympathetic. But artful sarcasm must be done with care. Too strong, and you run the risk of trivializing the issue or alienating your audience with a bad joke. Too vague or esoteric, and nobody will catch the joke. It's probably safest to use these touches when you are writing for a sympathetic audience; they're most likely to appreciate your wit. There is no rule of thumb here. Like any writer, you'll have to decide when to use these techniques and how to work them in artfully.

Review: To Choose Your Words Carefully . . .

- Consider both denotative and connotative meanings.
- Be as specific and concrete as your context requires.
- Use figurative language to add richness and complexity.
- Check figurative language for precision and clarity.
- Be alert for clichés and unnecessary euphemisms.
- Define technical terms that are not clear from the context.
- Define familiar terms and terms with multiple meanings.

EXERCISES

1. Let's say you were assigned to write a position paper defending the construction of a nuclear power plant in your state. What special appeals would you make were you to address your paper to the governor? to residents living next to the site where the proposed plant is to be built? to prospective construction workers and general contractors? to local environmentalists?

2. Choose one of the following claims, then list in sentence form three reasons supporting the argument. When you've finished, list in sentence form three reasons in opposition to the claim:
   a. Snowboarders are a menace to skiers.
   b. To save lives, a 55-mile-per-hour speed limit should be enforced nationwide.
   c. Condoms should be advertised on television.
   d. Students with drug convictions should be denied federally subsidized student aid.

3. Let's assume you have made up your mind on gun control. Write a brief letter to the editor of your local newspaper stating your views on the issue. In your letter, fairly and accurately represent arguments of the opposition while pointing out any logical weaknesses, flaws, impracticalities, and other problems you see. What different emphasis would your letter have were it to appear in a gun owner's newsletter? in a pro–gun control newsletter?

4. Write a letter to your parents explaining why you need an extra hundred dollars of spending money this month.

5. Each of the sentences below will take on a different meaning depending on the connotations of the words in brackets. Explain how each choice colors the writer's attitude and the reader's reaction to the statement.
   a. Sally's style of dress is really _____ [weird, exotic, unusual].
   b. If a factory is _____ [polluting, stinking up, fouling] the air over your house, you have a right to sue.
   c. Anyone who thinks that such words have no effect is _____ [unaware, ignorant, unconscious] of political history.
   d. The anti-immigration passion being stirred up in this country has become _____ [popular, trendy, common].
   e. It was clear from the way she _____ [stomped, marched, stepped] out of the room how she felt about the decision.

6. Identify the figures of speech used in the following sentences from essays in this book. In each example, note the two things being compared and explain why you think the comparisons are appropriate or not:
   a. "Carrie Bradshaw is alive and well and living in Warsaw." (Kay S. Hymowitz, "The New Girl Order")
   b. "Cops like Parks say that racial profiling is a sensible, statistically based tool." (Randall Kennedy, "You Can't Judge a Crook by His Color")
   c. "Karen, I enter into this conversation with you about feminism with some misgivings. Not because I don't want to talk to you. It is just that I suspect it will be like a phone conversation where the connection's so bad neither party can hear the other through the static." (Susan Faludi and Karen Lehrman, "Revisionist Feminism")
   d. "Of all the strange beasts that have come slouching into the 20th century, none has been more misunderstood, more criticized, and more important than materialism." (James Twitchell, "Two Cheers for Consumerism")
   e. "Magazines, newspapers, and radio and television programs round us up, rather like cattle, and producers and publishers then sell us to advertisers, usually through ads placed in advertising and industry publications." (Jean Kilbourne, "Buy This 24-Year-Old and Get All His Friends Absolutely Free")
   f. "Marketers don't feel, though, that it benefits them to encourage Americans to deal with these tensions head-on through a brew of discussion, entertainment, and argumentation aimed at broadly diverse audiences." (Joseph Turow, "Marketing a New World")

g. "Natural selection cannot push the buttons of behavior directly; it affects our behavior by endowing us with emotions that coax us toward adaptive choices." (Steven Pinker, "Why They Kill Their Newborns")

7. Rewrite the following paragraph to eliminate the clichés and trite expressions.

It is not that we don't care about what goes on up in space; it's that the vast majority of red-blooded Americans are hard put to see what these untold billions of dollars can do. While great strides have been made in space research, we ask ourselves: Is life any safer? Are material goods all the more abundant? Are we living to a ripe old age because of these vast expenditures? Beyond the shadow of a doubt, the answer is a resounding no. Those in Congress with a vested interest need to be brought back to reality, for the nation's pressing problems of crime, homelessness, and unemployment are right here on Mother Earth. Nothing is sacred including the budget for NASA, which should follow the footsteps of other programs and be slashed across the board. Yes, that will be a rude awakening to some who will have to bite the bullet, but there are just so many tax dollars to go around. And in the total scheme of things, wasting it on exploring the depths of outer space is not the way it should be.

Shaping Arguments
Thinking Like an Architect

Just as there is no best way to build a house, there is no best structure for an argument. Some essays take an inductive approach. Such an essay begins with a specific circumstance and then presents reasons and evidence in support of or in opposition to that circumstance. Other essays adopt a deductive approach. These essays begin with an idea or philosophical principle, move to a specific circumstance, then conclude with why that circumstance is right and should be maintained, or wrong and should be changed. Some essays express their conclusions in the opening paragraphs. Others build up to them in the last paragraph. Still others make use of narrative in part or as a whole—that is, a story or series of episodes or anecdotes structured on a time line. The effect is to dramatize the criteria of the author's argument rather than to argue them explicitly from point to point. As an architect designing a blueprint will tell you, the structure of a building depends on the site, the construction crew, and the prospective owners. Arguments are the same. Depending on your topic, your goals, and your readers, you'll write very different kinds of arguments.

Although no two arguments look alike, every argument has three basic structural parts: a beginning, a middle, and an end. This isn't a simplistic definition. As in architecture, each part of a structure is there for a purpose; leave out one of the parts, and the whole collapses. So let's look at those parts and the jobs they do.

Components of an Argument

What follows is an organizational pattern for argument papers—a pattern to which, with some variations, most of the essays in this book conform. We offer it to help you plan your own argument papers. Although this model provides the structure, framework, and components of most arguments, it is not a formula written in stone. You should not feel bound to follow it every time you construct an argument. In fact, you might find it more effective to move blocks of writing around or to omit material. For instance, on issues unfamiliar to your readers, it might make sense to begin with background information so the context of your discussion will be understood. With familiar issues, it might be more persuasive to open with responses to opposing views.

On especially controversial topics, you might wish to reserve your responses for the main body of the paper. Or, for dramatic effect, you might decide to save your responses until the very end, thereby emphasizing your consideration of other perspectives. As a writer, you're free to modify this model any way you like; or you may want to try different models in different drafts of your paper to see which arrangement works best in each case. As with building houses, your choices in building arguments are numerous.

The Beginning

The beginning of your argument accomplishes, in a small space, three important goals:

- It introduces you, the writer. Here your audience meets you—senses your tone, your attitude toward your subject, and the general style of the piece.
- It appeals to your readers' reason, emotions, and/or sense of ethics. This can be done in a simple value statement, an anecdote, or some high-impact statistics intended to raise your readers' interest and concern.
- It identifies the topic and indicates your stand.

Depending on the issue and the audience, the beginning of an argument can be several paragraphs in length. In most arguments, the beginning will end with a clear statement of the claim you are making—your thesis.

Although "Once upon a time . . ." is probably the most remembered introduction, it's not always the most effective; more ingenuity on your part is needed to "hook" your readers. For example, in *The Village Voice,* columnist Nat Hentoff began a column calling for eliminating duplication in the U.S. military by saying that he had telephoned the Pentagon press office for a comment on the subject. "Oh," said the officer with whom he spoke, "You want the *other* press office." As Hentoff remarked, he could have ended the column at that point; instead, he went on to develop his idea, confident that this introductory example would make his readers sympathetic to his point.

Composing good beginnings requires hard work. That's why many writers keep a journal in which they copy the strategies of writers they admire; that's how we happened to have a copy of Hentoff's introduction. As beginning arguers, you may want to develop your own repertoire of start-up strategies by copying strategies you admire into your own argument journal.

The Middle

The middle portion of your argument is where you do the argumentative work: presenting your information, responding to other views, making your case. If you think of it in terms of building construction, here's where you pour a foundation and lay the framework; put in all the walls, floors, and systems; and have the building inspector examine your work. There are a number of substages.

Provide Background Information

Before you can begin presenting your reasons, you want to be sure that your audience has the information necessary to understand the issue. Background information should answer any of the following questions depending on your topic:

- How significant is the issue? How many people are affected by it? Who are the people most affected?

- What facts, statistics, or information do your readers need to know to follow your reasons?
- What terminology or key words need to be defined so your readers will understand your meaning?
- What factors have caused the problem or situation to develop?
- What will be the consequences if the situation is not corrected?

If handled correctly, this part of your essay can be the most persuasive and convincing because it lets your readers know why you are concerned and the reasons behind that concern. Moreover, it gives your readers the opportunity to share your concern. For example, in "Buy This 24-Year-Old and Get All His Friends Absolutely Free" (page 335), Jean Kilbourne begins her essay with the claim that advertisers will spare no expense to entice us into buying their products. She includes statistics that demonstrate the millions of dollars spent to produce TV commercials and even more to air them during big-audience broadcasts such as the Super Bowl. These figures are not only informative; they create a sense of the extraordinary efforts at manipulating the consumer—at trying to separate them from their money—thereby setting the stage for the argument she will develop in her essay.

Respond to Other Points of View

As we discussed in Chapter 4, it is important to let your audience know that you have seriously deliberated other points of view before reaching your own position. By doing this, you appear informed and open-minded. In this part of your essay, you should briefly review a number of viewpoints that are different from your own. If you've engaged in debate and dialogue, as we suggested in Chapter 1, you should be aware of opposing views and common concerns. Now is your opportunity to identify them and respond. You might even acknowledge the sincerity of those holding contrary views and cite the merits of their positions. Such acknowledgments help establish your authority as a writer. They will also help you define your own position more specifically for your readers by contrasting it with others. For example, in the essay, "Revisionist Feminism," (page 508), Susan Faludi and Karen Lehrman discuss the meaning of "real feminism" in an exchange of letters. To have a productive discussion, the authors must acknowledge their differing points of view, including their different uses of the term *feminism.* Anticipating Lehrman's stand, Faludi opens her debate with "misgivings," saying that Lehrman's main complaint against feminism is that it deprives women of their femininity, "by denying them the right to display and revel in their feminine beauty and sexuality." She later says that Lehrman thinks feminism includes "women's right to express themselves through makeup, lingerie, cosmetic surgery, aerobics classes, and corsets." To Faludi's dismissive response, Lehrman offers what she sees as Faludi's warped definition of feminism: "You appear to believe that, to be allowed to use the term feminist, a woman has to adhere to a well-defined leftist political agenda, consisting of, at the very least, affirmative action, nationally subsidized day care and 'pay equity. . . .'" As the debate evolves, Lehrman addresses some of the complaints Faludi raises, explaining where Faludi oversimplifies or misses the point. In the end, Lehrman attempts to find common ground and concludes: "Instead of fighting about whether or not feminism has turned into an orthodoxy, I think it would be far more useful if this dialogue—as well as the larger feminist debate—were focused on the complexities that women must deal with today." Interestingly, out of a contentious argument comes some conciliatory, even productive discussion.

Present Reasons in Support of Your Claim

The reasons supporting your claim comprise the heart of your essay and, therefore, its largest portion. Here you explain the reasons behind your claim and present supporting evidence—facts, statistics, data, testimony of authorities, examples—to convince your readers to agree with your position or take a particular course of action. Depending on the issue, this part of your essay usually takes several paragraphs, with each reason clearly delineated for your readers. Most of the essays in this book use this approach; Laurie Essig's "Same-Sex Marriage" (page 712) is a good example.

Anticipate Possible Objections to Your Reasons

Even with a friendly audience, readers will have questions and concerns about your reasons. If you ignore these objections and leave them unanswered, you will weaken the effectiveness of your argument. Therefore, it is always wise to anticipate possible objections so you can respond to them in a constructive fashion that will strengthen and clarify your ideas. The kind of objections you anticipate, of course, will depend on your familiarity with your audience—their interests, values, beliefs, experiences, and so on. If you have carefully analyzed your audience, as we suggest in Chapter 4, you will be more aware of the objections likely to surface in response to your reasons. Raising objections and responding to them will once again demonstrate your awareness of alternative viewpoints. It will also give you an opportunity to strengthen your reasons and increase your credibility.

Review: The Structure of an Argument

The Beginning . . .
- Introduces you as a writer
- States the problem
- Establishes your position and appeal
- Presents your claim (thesis)

The Middle . . .
- Provides background information
- Responds to other points of view
- Presents arguments supporting the claim
- Anticipates possible objections

The End . . .
- Summarizes your position and implications
- Invites readers to share your conclusion and/or take action

The End

The end is usually a short paragraph or two in which you conclude your argument. Essentially, your ending summarizes your argument by reaffirming your stand on the issue. It might also make an appeal to your readers to take action. Some writers include an anecdote, a passionate summation, or even a quiet but resonant sentence. Lincoln's "Gettysburg Address," for example, ends with the quiet "government of the people, by the people, and for the people," which is one of the most memorable phrases in American political history. Looking over the essays in this book, you will find that no two end quite alike. As a writer, you have many choices; experimentation is usually the best way to decide what will work for you. Many writers copy effective conclusions into their journals so they can refresh their memories when writing their own arguments.

SAMPLE ARGUMENT FOR ANALYSIS

To illustrate this three-part argument structure, we have included two sample argument essays for you to read. The first is "Indian Bones" by Clara Spotted Elk, a consultant for Native American interests. Although it is quite brief, the essay, published in the *New York Times,* contains all the essential components of an argument essay. It is followed by an analysis of its key structural features.

Indian Bones
Clara Spotted Elk

1   Millions of American Indians lived in this country when Columbus first landed on our shores. After the western expansion, only about 250,000 Indians survived. What happened to the remains of those people who were decimated by the advance of the white man? Many are gathering dust in American museums.

2   In 1985, I and some Northern Cheyenne chiefs visited the attic of the Smithsonian's Natural History Museum in Washington to review the inventory of their Cheyenne collection. After a chance inquiry, a curator pulled out a drawer in one of the scores of cabinets that line the attic. There were the jumbled bones of an Indian. "A Kiowa," he said.

3   Subsequently, we found that 18,500 Indian remains—some consisting of a handful of bones, but mostly full skeletons—are unceremoniously stored in the Smithsonian's nooks and crannies. Other museums, individuals and Federal agencies such as the National Park Service also collect the bones of Indian warriors, women, and children. Some are on display as roadside tourist attractions. It is estimated that another 600,000 Indian remains are secreted away in locations across the country.

4   The museum community and forensic scientists vigorously defend these grisly collections. With few exceptions, they refuse to return remains to the tribes that wish to rebury them, even when grave robbing has been documented. They want to maintain adequate numbers of "specimens" for analysis and say they are dedicated to "the permanent curation of Indian skeletal remains."

5   Indian people are tired of being "specimens." The Northern Cheyenne word for ourselves is "tsistsistas"—human beings. Like people the world over, one of our greatest responsibilities is the proper care of the dead.

6   We are outraged that our religious views are not accepted by the scientific community and that the graves of our ancestors are desecrated. Many tribes are willing to accommodate some degree of study for a limited period of time—provided that it would help Indian people or mankind in general. But how many "specimens" are needed? We will not accept grave robbing and the continued hoarding of our ancestors' remains.

7   Would this nefarious collecting be tolerated if it were discovered that it affected other ethnic groups? (Incidentally, the Smithsonian also collects skeletons of blacks.) What would happen if the Smithsonian had 18,500 Holocaust victims in the attic? There would be a tremendous outcry in this country. Why is there no outcry about the Indian collection?

8   Indians are not exotic creatures for study. We are human beings who practice living religions. Our religion should be placed not only on a par with science when it comes to determining the disposition of our ancestors but on a par with every other religion practiced in this country.

9   To that end, Sen. Daniel K. Inouye will soon reintroduce the "Bones Bill" to aid Indians in retrieving the remains of their ancestors from museums. As in the past, the "Bones Bill" will most likely be staunchly resisted by the collectors of Indian skeletons—armed with slick lobbyists, lots of money and cloaked in the mystique of science.

10   Scientists have attempted to defuse this issue by characterizing their opponents as radical Indians, out of touch with the culture and with little appreciation of science. Armed only with a moral obligation to our ancestors, the Indians who support the bill have few resources and little money.

11   But, in my view, the issue should concern all Americans—for it raises very disturbing questions. American Indians want only to reclaim and rebury their dead. Is this too much to ask?

Analyzing the Structure

Now let's examine this essay according to the organizational features discussed so far.

The Beginning

Paragraph 1 clearly introduces the nature of the problem: The remains of the Indians "decimated by the advance of the white man" have wrongfully ended up "gathering dust in American museums." It isn't until paragraph 6 that Spotted Elk spells out her position: "We are outraged that our religious views are not accepted by the scientific community and that the graves of our ancestors are desecrated." (Because this essay was written for newspaper publication, the paragraphs are shorter than they might be in a formal essay; you may not want to delay your thesis until the sixth paragraph in a longer essay.) Notice, too, that in the introduction the author's persona begins to assert itself in the brief and pointed summation of the American Indians' fate. When Spotted Elk mentions the staggering decline in the population of her ancestors, we sense a note of controlled but righteous anger in her voice. Citation of the gruesome facts of history also appeals to the reader's ethical sense by prompting reflection on the Indians' demise.

The Middle

- **Background Information**   Paragraphs 2 and 3 establish the context of the author's complaint. Paragraph 2 is personal testimony to the problem—how she and other Native Americans viewed unceremonious "jumbled bones" in the museum drawer and were stunned by the representative insensitivity of their host curator, who treated the human remains as if they were a fossil. Paragraph 3 projects the problem to progressively larger contexts and magnitudes—from the single Kiowa in a drawer to the 18,500 in the Smithsonian at large; from that institution's collection to the estimated 600,000 remains in other museums, federal agencies and institutions, and "roadside tourist attractions." The broader scope of the problem is underscored here.
- **Response to Other Points of View**   In paragraph 4, Spotted Elk tersely sums up the opposing position of the "museum community and forensic scientists": ". . . they refuse to return remains to the tribes." She also states their reasoning: "They want to maintain adequate numbers of 'specimens' for analysis and say they are dedicated to the 'permanent curation of Indian skeletal remains.'"
- **Reasons in Support of the Claim**   Paragraphs 5 through 9 constitute the heart of Spotted Elk's argument. Here she most forcefully argues her objections and offers her reasons with supporting details: Indians resent being treated as specimens and want to bury their dead as do other religious people (paragraphs 5 and 6). She follows with a concession that many Indians would accommodate some degree of anthropological study for a period of time, but do not approve of the huge permanent collections that now fill museums.

   In paragraph 7, the author continues to support her claim that American Indians have been discriminated against with regard to the disposition of ancestral remains. She writes that there would be a public outcry if the remains of other ethnic groups such as Holocaust victims were hoarded. Her proposal for change appears in paragraph 8: "Our religion should be placed not only on a par with science when it comes to determining the disposition of our ancestors but on a par with every other religion practiced in this country." This is the logical consequence of the problem she has addressed to this point. That proposal logically leads into paragraph 9, where she mentions efforts by Senator Daniel Inouye to see the "Bones Bill" passed into law. Throughout, Spotted Elk uses emotional words and phrases—*grisly, unceremoniously, slick lobbyists, cloaked in mystique*—to reinforce her points.

• **Anticipation of Possible Objections**   In paragraph 10, the author addresses objections of the opposition, in this case those "[s]cientists [who] have attempted to defuse this issue by characterizing their opponents as radical Indians, out of touch with the culture and with little appreciation of science." She refutes all three charges (of being "radical," as well as out of touch with Indian culture and science) with the phrase "[a]rmed only with a moral obligation to our ancestors"—a phrase that reaffirms her strong connection with her culture. On the contrary, it is science that is out of touch with the "living religion" of Native Americans.

The End

The final paragraph brings closure to the argument. Briefly the author reaffirms her argument that Native Americans "want only to reclaim and rebury their dead." The question that makes up the final line of the essay is more than rhetorical, for it reminds us of the point introduced back in paragraph 5—that American Indians are no different than any other religious people with regard to the disposition of their ancestors. A powerful question brings the essay's conclusion into sharp focus.

As we stated in the beginning of this chapter, there is no best structure for an argument essay. As you develop your own essay, you may find it more effective to move certain structural features to locations that serve your purposes better. For instance, you may find that background information is more persuasive when you include it as support for a particular reason rather than provide it prior to your reasons. Possible objections might be raised along with each reason instead of saved for later. Ron Karpati's essay, "I Am the Enemy," provides a good example of a different approach to structuring an argument essay. Read the essay to see if you can pick out the structural elements he included and how he organized them. Following the essay, we've provided a brief analysis of its organization.

SAMPLE ARGUMENT FOR ANALYSIS

I Am the Enemy
Ron Karpati

Ron Karpati, a pediatrician and medical researcher of childhood illnesses, defends the use of animals in medical research. This article first appeared in *Newsweek*'s "My Turn" column.

1   I am the enemy! One of those vilified, inhumane physician-scientists involved in animal research. How strange, for I have never thought of myself as an evil person. I became a pediatrician because of my love for children and my desire to keep them healthy. During medical school and residency, however, I saw many children die of leukemia, prematurity and traumatic injury—circumstances against which medicine has made tremendous progress, but still has far to go. More important, I also saw children, alive and healthy, thanks to advances in medical science such as infant respirators, potent antibiotics, new surgical techniques and the entire field of

organ transplantation. My desire to tip the scales in favor of the healthy, happy children drew me to medical research.

2   My accusers claim that I inflict torture on animals for the sole purpose of career advancement. My experiments supposedly have no relevance to medicine and are easily replaced by computer simulation. Meanwhile, an apathetic public barely watches, convinced that the issue has no significance, and publicity-conscious politicians increasingly give way to the demands of the activists.

3   We in medical research have also been unconscionably apathetic. We have allowed the most extreme animal-rights protesters to seize the initiative and frame the issue as one of "animal fraud." We have been complacent in our belief that a knowledgeable public would sense the importance of animal research to the public health. Perhaps we have been mistaken in not responding to the emotional tone of the argument created by those sad posters of animals by waving equally sad posters of children dying of leukemia or cystic fibrosis.

4   Much is made of the pain inflicted on these animals in the name of medical science. The animal-rights activists contend that this is evidence of our malevolent and sadistic nature. A more reasonable argument, however, can be advanced in our defense. Life is often cruel, both to animals and human beings. Teenagers get thrown from the back of a pickup truck and suffer severe head injuries. Toddlers, barely able to walk, find themselves at the bottom of a swimming pool while a parent checks the mail. Physicians hoping to alleviate the pain and suffering these tragedies cause have but three choices: create an animal model of the injury or disease and use that model to understand the process and test new therapies; experiment on human beings—some experiments will succeed, most will fail—or finally, leave medical knowledge static, hoping that accidental discoveries will lead us to the advances.

5   Some animal-rights activists would suggest a fourth choice, claiming that computer models can simulate animal experiments, thus making the actual experiments unnecessary. Computers can simulate, reasonably well, the effects of well-understood principles on complex systems, as in the application of the laws of physics to airplane and automobile design. However, when the principles themselves are in question, as is the case with the complex biological systems under study, computer modeling alone is of little value.

6   One of the terrifying effects of the effort to restrict the use of animals in medical research is that the impact will not be felt for years and decades: drugs that might have been discovered will not be; surgical techniques that might have been developed will not be, and fundamental biological processes that might have been understood will remain mysteries. There is the danger that politically expedient solutions will be found to placate a vocal minority, while the consequences of these decisions will not be apparent until long after the decisions are made and the decision making forgotten.

7   Fortunately, most of us enjoy good health, and the trauma of watching one's child die has become a rare experience. Yet our good fortune should not make us unappreciative of the health we enjoy or the advances that make it possible. Vaccines, antibiotics, insulin and drugs to treat heart disease, hypertension and stroke are all based on animal research. Most complex surgical procedures, such as coronary-artery bypass and organ transplantation, are initially developed in animals. Presently

undergoing animal studies are techniques to insert genes in humans in order to replace the defective ones found to be the cause of so much disease. These studies will effectively end if animal research is severely restricted.

8   In America today, death has become an event isolated from our daily existence—out of the sight and thoughts of most of us. As a doctor who has watched many children die, and their parents grieve, I am particularly angered by people capable of so much compassion for a dog or a cat, but with seemingly so little for a dying human being. These people seem so insulated from the reality of human life and death and what it means.

9   Make no mistake, however: I am not advocating the needlessly cruel treatment of animals. To the extent that the animal-rights movement has made us more aware of the needs of these animals, and made us search harder for suitable alternatives, they have made a significant contribution. But if the more radical members of this movement are successful in limiting further research, their efforts will bring about a tragedy that will cost many lives. The real question is whether an apathetic majority can be aroused to protect its future against a vocal, but misdirected, minority.

Analyzing the Structure
The Beginning
In paragraph 1, Karpati introduces himself to the reader as a scientist and a pediatrician with a personal and professional interest in his topic. While his first sentence proclaims, "I am the enemy," Karpati almost immediately lets his readers know that he is only an enemy to those who oppose his work; he describes himself as a caring doctor who wishes to help children stay healthy. His second sentence informs the reader that his topic will be the use of animals as research subjects; in the next sentences, he strongly implies that the advances made in medicine are the results of research using animals. His claim, stated in paragraph 3, is that animal research is important to public health. By using the example of ill or injured children who might benefit from this work, Karpati makes a strong emotional appeal to his readers.

The Middle
Background Information
This information appears in several places in the essay. Paragraph 1 includes a list of advances in medicine that have come about, the reader assumes, through animal research. Later, in paragraph 7, Karpati lists specific drugs and surgical procedures that have resulted from using animals as research subjects. However, Karpati seems more interested in informing readers how he, a scientist who uses animals to conduct his research, is characterized negatively by animal-rights supporters.

Response to Other Points of View
Because Karpati's essay is largely a defense of his position on animal research, he focuses heavily on the views of those who oppose his position. In paragraph 2, he briefly summarizes the accusations made about him by animal-rights supporters.

In paragraph 3, he suggests that these objections are voiced by extremists in that movement. Karpati goes on to indicate that he is aware of the reasons why others wish to eliminate animal research. In paragraph 4, he acknowledges that "pain [is] inflicted on these animals in the name of medical science." He agrees with the opposition that "life is often cruel," but suggests through his examples that human suffering is more compelling to physicians than is the suffering of animals. Later, in paragraph 9, Karpati refers back to this point and cites the contribution of the animal-rights movement in making researchers more sensitive to the issue of animal suffering.

Reasons in Support of the Claim

In paragraphs 4 through 8, Karpati presents his reasons to support his claim that medical research using animals should be continued for the benefit of human health. In paragraphs 4 and 5, he explains that the alternatives to animal research—experimenting on human subjects, relying on accidental discoveries, or using computer simulation—are not satisfactory. In paragraph 6, he warns that the impact of restricting animal research will have a far-reaching and negative impact on medical science. In paragraph 7, Karpati points to the results of animal research and its significant contributions to the healthy lives that most of his readers take for granted. Finally, in paragraph 8, he reasserts the importance of human life over the well-being of animals.

Possible Objections to Reasons

Karpati has included many of the objections to his reasons along with the reasons themselves. For instance, in paragraphs 4 and 5, he anticipates that his readers might wonder why humans and computers can't be substituted for animals in research. Karpati responds that experiments on humans will largely fail and computer simulations cannot duplicate complex biological processes.

The End

In the last paragraph, Karpati summarizes his main point: The efforts of radical members of the animal-rights movement to limit the use of animals in research "will bring about a tragedy that will cost many lives." He makes a strong appeal to his readers to take action to prevent just that from happening.

Blueprints for Arguments

Our analysis of Karpati's essay gives some idea of its general organization, but it does not reflect fine subdivisions or the way the various parts of the essay are logically connected. That can be done by making an outline. Think of an outline as a blueprint of the argument you're building: It reveals structure and framework but leaves out the materials that cover the frame.

Opinions differ as to the value of making outlines before writing an essay. Some writers need to make formal outlines to organize their thoughts. Others simply scratch down a few key ideas. Still others write essays spontaneously without any preliminary writing. For the beginning writer, an outline is a valuable aid because it demonstrates at a glance how the various parts of an essay are connected, whether the organization is logical and complete, whether the evidence is sequenced properly, and whether there are any omissions or lack of proportion. Your outline need not be elaborate. You might simply jot down your key reasons in a hierarchy from strongest to weakest:

Introduction

Reason 1

Reason 2

Reason 3

Reason 4

Conclusion

This blueprint might be useful if you want to capture your readers' attention immediately with your most powerful appeal. Or you might use a reverse hierarchy, beginning with your weakest argument and proceeding to your strongest, in order to achieve a climactic effect for an audience sympathetic to your cause. The outline will help you build your case.

You might prefer, as do some writers, to construct an outline after, rather than before, writing a rough draft. This lets you create a draft without restricting the free flow of ideas and helps you rewrite by determining where you need to fill in, cut out, or reorganize. You may discover where your line of reasoning is not logical; you may also reconsider whether you should arrange your reasons from the most important to the least or vice versa in order to create a more persuasive effect. Ultimately, outlining after the first draft can prove useful in producing subsequent drafts and a polished final effort.

Outlines are also useful when evaluating somebody else's writing. Reducing the argument of the opposition to the bare bones exposes holes in the reasoning process, scanty evidence, and logical fallacies. In writing this book, we used all three processes: We developed an outline to write the first draft and sway a publisher to accept it. Then experienced teachers read the draft and suggested changes to the outline to make it more effective. Finally, one of our collaborators took all the suggestions and her own ideas and created a new outline to help us revise the text. In our case, all three strategies were equally valuable.

The Formal Outline

Some teachers like students to submit *formal outlines* with their papers to show that the students have checked their structure carefully. This kind of outlining has several rules to follow:

- Identify main ideas with capital Roman numerals.
- Identify subsections of main ideas with capital letters, indented one set of spaces from the main ideas.
- Identify support for subsections with Arabic numerals indented two sets of spaces from the main ideas.
- Identify the parts of the support with lowercase Roman numerals, indented three sets of spaces from the main ideas.

- Identify further subdivisions with lowercase letters and then italic numbers, each indented one set of spaces to the right of the previous subdivision.
- Make sure all items have at least two points; it's considered improper informal outlining to have only one point under any subdivision.

To demonstrate what a formal outline can look like, we have outlined Clara Spotted Elk's essay, "Indian Bones":

I. Hoarding of Indian remains
   A. At Smithsonian
      1. Single Kiowa at Smithsonian
      2. 18,500 others

   B. In other locations
II. Authorities' defense of collections
   A. Refusal to return grave-robbed remains
   B. Maintenance of "specimens"
III. Indians' response
   A. Outrage
      1. Desire to be seen as humans
      2. Desire to have religion accepted by science
      3. Nonacceptance of desecration of graves
      4. Resentment of lack of outcry by public

   B. Accommodation
      1. Limitation in time
      2. Service to Indians and mankind

   C. Demand equality with other religions
IV. "Bones Bill" legislation
   A. Resistance from scientific community
      1. Slick lobbyists
      2. Money
      3. Scientific mystique
      4. Characterization of Indians
         i.   Radicals
         ii. Out of touch with culture
         iii. Little appreciation of science
   B. Indian counter-resistance
      1. Few resources
      2. Little money
      3. Moral obligation to ancestors

Keep in mind that an outline should not force your writing to conform to a rigid pattern and, thus, turn your essay into something stilted and uninspired. Follow the model as a map, taking detours when necessary or inspired.

Two Basic Types of Arguments

Consider the following claims for arguments:

1. Watching television helps to eliminate some traditional family rituals.
2. Pornography poses a threat to women.
3. *Atonement* is an entertaining and beautifully filmed movie.
4. Bilingual education programs fail to help non-English-speaking children become part of mainstream society.
5. Hate crime legislation is intended to allow certain people to have more protection under the law than others.
6. Cigarette advertising should be banned from billboards everywhere.
7. Medical doctors should not advertise.
8. Americans by law should be required to vote.
9. The Ten Commandments ought to be posted in public places, schools, and government offices.
10. Pass/fail grades have to be eliminated across the board if academic standards are to be maintained.

Looking over these statements, you might notice some patterns. The verbs in the first five are all in the present tense: *helps, poses, is, fail, is intended to.* However, each of the last five statements includes "should" words: *should, should not, ought to be, have to be.* These **obligation verbs** are found in almost all claims proposing solutions to a problem.

What distinguishes the first group from the second is more than the form of the verb. The first five claims are statements of the writer's stand on a controversial issue as it currently exists. The second group are proposals for what *should* be. Of course, not every kind of argument will fit our classification scheme. However, essentially every argument in this book—and the ones you'll most likely write and read in your careers—falls into one of these two categories or a combination of each, for often a writer states his or her position on an issue, then follows it with proposals for changes. Later in this chapter, we will discuss proposals. For the moment, let's take a look at position arguments.

Position Arguments

A *position argument* scrutinizes one side of a controversial issue. In such an argument, the writer not only establishes his or her stand but also argues vigorously in defense of it. Position arguments are less likely to point to a solution to a problem. Instead, they are philosophical in nature—the kinds of arguments on which political and social principles are founded, laws are written, and business and government policies are established. Position papers also tend to address themselves to the ethical and moral aspects of a controversy. If, for instance, you were opposed to the university's policy of mandatory testing for the AIDS virus, you might write a position paper protesting your school's infringement of individual rights and invasion of privacy.

As indicated by the present tense of the verbs in the first five claims, the position argument deals with the status quo—the way things are, the current state of affairs. Such an argument reminds the audience that something *currently* is good or bad, better or worse, right or wrong. Like all arguments, they tend to be aimed at changing the audience's feelings about an issue—abortion, animal research, the death penalty, and so on. That is why many position papers tend to direct their appeals to the reader's sense of ethics rather than to reason.

By contrast, proposal arguments identify a problem and recommend a likely solution. That's why their claims contain verbs that *obligate* the readers to take some action. In this sense, they are practical rather than philosophical. For instance, if you were concerned about the spread of AIDS among college students, you might write a paper proposing that condom machines be installed in all dormitories. When you offer a proposal, you're trying to affect the future.

Features to Look for in Position Arguments
What follows are some key features of position arguments. As a checklist, they can help you evaluate someone's stand on an issue and help guide you in writing your own position papers.

The writer deals with a controversial issue. The best kind of position paper is one that focuses on a debatable issue, one in which there is clear disagreement: the war on terrorism, abortion, capital punishment, gay marriage, euthanasia, affirmative action, civil liberties, separation of church and state, censorship, sex in advertising, freedom of speech, homelessness, gun control. These are issues about which people have many different perspectives.

The writer clearly states a position. Readers should not be confused about where an author stands on an issue. Although the actual issue may be complex, the claim should be stated emphatically and straightforwardly. Don't waffle: "Using the death penalty in some situations and with some rights of appeal probably doesn't do much to lower crime anyway"; far better is an emphatic "Capital punishment is no deterrent to crime." In formulating your claim, be certain that your word choice is not ambiguous. Otherwise the argument will be muddled and, ultimately, unconvincing.

The writer recognizes other positions and potential objections. For every argument there are bound to be a number of other perspectives. Such is the nature of controversy. As a writer representing a position, you cannot assume that your readers are fully aware of or understand all the disagreement surrounding the issue you're arguing. Nor can you make a persuasive case without anticipating challenges. So in your argument you must spell out accurately and fairly the main points of the opposition and objections that might arise. We offer six reasons for doing this:

1. *You reduce your own vulnerability.* You don't want to appear ill informed or naive on an issue. Therefore, it makes sense to acknowledge opposing points of view to show how well you've investigated the topic and how sensitive you are to it. Suppose, for instance, you are writing a paper arguing that "anyone who commits suicide is insane." To avoid criticism, you would have

to be prepared to answer objections that fully rational people with terminal illnesses often choose to take their own lives so as to avoid a painful demise and curtail the suffering of loved ones. Even if you strongly disagree with your opposition, recognizing views from the other side demonstrates that you are a person of responsibility and tolerance—two qualities for which most writers of argument strive.

2. *You distinguish your own position.* By citing opposing views, you distinguish your own position from that of others. This not only helps clarify the differences but also lays out the specific points of the opposition to be refuted or discredited. Some writers do this at the outset of their arguments. Consider, for instance, how Ron Karpati sums up the views of the opposition in the opening paragraphs of his essay "I Am the Enemy."

3. *You can respond to opposing views.* A good response can challenge an opponent's ideas and examine the basis for the disagreement—whether personal, ideological, or moral. For instance, when Michael Kelley, in "Arguing for Infanticide" (page 209), responds to Steven Pinker's "Why They Kill Their Newborns" (page 200), he points out that Pinker's very logical argument for neonaticide ignores the moral and ethical values of our society regarding the relationship between mothers and their children. Kelley does not suggest that Pinker's reasons are incorrect; instead he challenges the basis for Pinker's argument.

4. *You might also challenge an opponent's logic, demonstrating where the reasoning suffers from flaws in logic.* For instance, the argument that Ms. Shazadi must be a wonderful mother because she's a great office manager does not logically follow. While some qualities of a good manager might bear on successful motherhood, not all do. In fact, it can be argued that the very qualities that make a good manager—leadership, drive, ruthlessness, determination—might damage a parent-child relationship. This logical fallacy, called a false analogy, erroneously suggests that the two situations are comparable when they are not. An example of this can be found in Jeff Jacoby's "What the Antismoking Zealots Really Crave" (page 99) when he points out that a well-known antismoking activist has compared tobacco companies to mass murderers. While the dangers of cigarette smoking are widely accepted, the comparison between profit-driven corporations and murderous criminals cannot be supported with fact and reasonable evidence.

5. *You might challenge the evidence supporting an argument.* If possible, try to point out unreliable, unrealistic, or irrelevant evidence offered by the opposition; question the truth of counterarguments; or point to distortions. The realtor who boasts oceanside property is vulnerable to challenge if the house in question is actually half a mile from the beach. Look for instances of stacking the deck. For example, a writer might argue that supporting the building of a new sports complex will benefit the community by providing new jobs. However, if she fails to mention that workers at the old sports facility will then lose their jobs, she is misleading the audience about the benefits of this change. Challenge the evidence by looking for hasty generalizations. For example, a business degree from State U. may indeed guarantee a well-paying job after graduation,

but the writer will need more than a few personal anecdotes to convince the reader that this is the case.

6. *You can gain strength through concessions.* Admitting weaknesses in your own stand shows that you are realistic, that you don't suffer from an inflated view of the virtues of your position. It also lends credibility to your argument while helping you project yourself as fair-minded. A successful example of this strategy is Ron Karpati's acknowledgment in paragraph 9 of "I Am the Enemy" (page 129) that the animal-rights movement has sensitized scientists to the needs of animals.

The writer offers a well-reasoned argument to support the position. A position paper must do more than simply state your stand on an issue. It must try to persuade readers to accept your position as credible and convince them to adjust their thinking about the issue. Toward those ends, you should make every effort to demonstrate the best reasons for your beliefs and support the positions you hold. That means presenting honest and logically sound arguments.

Persuaders use three kinds of appeal: to *reason,* to *emotions,* and to readers' sense of *ethics.* You may have heard these described as the appeals of *logos, pathos,* and *ethos.* Although it is difficult to separate the emotional and ethical components from the rational or logical structure of an argument, the persuasive powers of a position argument may mean the proper combination of these three appeals. Not all arguments will cover all three appeals. Some will target logic alone and offer as support statistics and facts. Others centering around moral, religious, or personal values will appeal to a reader's emotions as well as reason. (These arguments are most successful for a readership that need not be convinced by force of reason alone.) Arguments based on emotion aim to reinforce and inspire followers to stand by their convictions. However, relying too heavily on an emotional appeal can result in an ad misericordiam argument, one that attempts to exploit the readers' pity. The most successful arguments are those that use multiple strategies to appeal to readers' hearts and minds.

When the issue centers on right-or-wrong or good-or-bad issues, position arguments make their appeals to the audience's ethical sense. In such papers, your strategy has two intentions: one, to convince the reader that you are a person of goodwill and moral character and thus enhance your credibility and, two, to suggest that any decent and moral readers will share your position.

The writer's supporting evidence is convincing. A position paper does not end with an incontrovertible proof such as in a demonstration of a scientific law or mathematical theorem. No amount of logic can prove conclusively that your functional judgment is right or wrong; if that were the case, there would be few arguments. It is also impossible to prove that your aesthetic judgments are superior to another's or that a particular song, movie, or book is better than another. But your arguments have a greater chance of being persuasive if you can present evidence that convinces your readers that your argument is valid.

We'll say more about evidence in Chapter 6, but for now remember that a strong argument needs convincing evidence: facts, figures, personal observations, testimony of outside authorities, and specific examples. In general, the more facts supporting a position, the more reason there is for the reader to accept that position as valid. The same is true when refuting another position. An author needs to supply sound reasons and evidence to disprove or discredit an opponent's stand.

The writer projects a reasonable persona. Whenever we read an argument, we cannot help but be aware of the person behind the words. Whether it's in the choice of expressions, the tenacity of opinion, the kinds of examples, the force of the argument, the nature of the appeal, or the humor or sarcasm, we hear the author's voice and form an impression of the person. That impression, which is projected by the voice and tone of the writing, is the writer's *persona.*

Persona is communicated in a variety of ways: diction or the choice of words (formal, colloquial, slang, jargon, charged terms); the sentence style (long or short, simple or complex); and the kinds of evidence offered (from cool scientific data to inflammatory examples). As in face-to-face debates, a full range of feelings can be projected by the tone of a written argument: anger, irony, jest, sarcasm, seriousness.

Persona is the vital bond linking the writer to the reader. In fact, the success or failure of an argument might be measured by the extent to which the reader accepts the persona in an argument. If you like the voice you hear, then you have already begun to identify with the writer and are more likely to share in the writer's assumptions and opinions. If, however, that persona strikes you as harsh, distant, or arrogant, you might have difficulty subscribing to the author's argument even if it makes sense logically.

A good position argument projects a reasonable persona, one that is sincere and willing to consider opposing points of view. Steer clear of ad hominem arguments, which make personal attacks on those with whom you disagree rather than on their views. Although readers may not be convinced enough to change their stand or behavior, a writer with a reasonable persona can at least capture their respect and consideration. Remember, the success of your argument will largely depend on your audience's willingness to listen.

A word of warning. Not every persona has to be reasonable or pleasant, although for a beginner this works best. If an arrogant persona is fortified by wit and intelligence, readers may find it stimulating, even charming. A persona—whether outrageous, humorous, biting, or sarcastic—can be successful if it is executed with

---

Checklist for Writing a Position Argument

Have you:
- chosen a controversial issue?
- clearly stated a position?
- recognized other positions and possible objections?
- developed a well-reasoned argument?
- provided convincing supporting evidence?
- projected a reasonable persona?

style and assurance. Some of the best arguments in Part Two of this book have biting edges.

When you read an argument with a memorable persona, jot down in your argument journal the details of how the writer created it; that way, you can turn back to this information when you're trying to create personas for the arguments you write.

SAMPLE POSITION ARGUMENT FOR ANALYSIS

What follows is an example of a position argument whose title suggests the issue and the author's stand on it: "Is Anything Private Anymore?" In a digital world where highly personal information appears in a multitude of databases and where ubiquitous security cameras are found along highways and public streets, and in almost every conceivable public space, the author wonders if privacy still exists. Written by Sean Flynn, this essay first appeared in *Parade* Magazine in September 2007.

"Is Anything Private Anymore?"
Sean Flynn

1   Kevin Bankston was a closet smoker who hid his habit by sneaking cigarettes outside his San Francisco office. He expected anonymity on a big city street. But in 2005, an online mapping service that provided ground-level photographs captured him smoking—and made the image available to anyone on the Internet. This year, Google's Street View project caught him again.

2   Coincidence? Absolutely. Yet Bankston's twice-documented smoking highlights a wider phenomenon: Privacy is a withering commodity for all of us.

3   What you buy, where you go, whom you call, the Web sites you visit, the e-mails you send—all of that information can be monitored and logged. "When you're out in public, it's becoming a near certainty that your image will be captured," says (the newly nonsmoking) Bankston.

4   Should you care? I've interviewed numerous people on all sides of the privacy debate to find out just how wary we should be.

5   One thing is clear: In today's world, maintaining a cocoon of privacy simply isn't practical. Need a mortgage or a car loan? A legitimate lender is going to verify a wealth of private information, including your name and address, date of birth, Social Security number and credit history. We all make daily trade-offs for convenience and thrift: Electronic tollbooths mean you don't have to wait in the cash-only lane, but your travel habits will be tracked. The Piggly Wiggly discount card saves you $206 on your annual grocery bill, but it counts how many doughnuts and six-packs you buy. MySpace posts make it easy to keep in touch with friends, but your comments live on.

6   So how do you live in a digital world and still maintain a semblance of privacy? Experts say it's crucial to recognize that those bits of data are permanent—a trail of electronic crumbs that is never swept away, available to anyone with the skills and inclination to sniff it out.

7   Privacy may not feel like much of an issue for those in their teens and 20s. They've grown up chronicling their lives on popular social networking sites like MySpace or Facebook for easy retrieval by friends and strangers alike. But some young people don't realize that what was funny to college buddies might not amuse a law-firm recruiter. Employers regularly research job applicants on the Internet. Some colleges are helping students prepare: Duke University hosts seminars on how to clean up a Facebook account. "You learn why posting pictures of you riding the mechanical bull at Shooters is a bad idea," says Sarah Ball, a senior whose own page is secure and clean.

8   Amy Polumbo, 22, restricted her page on Facebook to 100 or so people who knew her password. "It was a way for me to keep in touch with friends all over the country," she says. But after she was crowned Miss New Jersey in June, someone downloaded pictures of her and threatened blackmail. She thwarted the attempt by releasing the photos herself (they're quite innocent) but suffered weeks of embarrassment.

9   "I know how easy it is for someone to take advantage of you on the Internet," says Polumbo. "The Web is a place where people can destroy your reputation if you're not careful."

10   In fact, all kinds of transgressions now are easily retrievable. An employee at a New York City bank watched his reputation shrink when his colleagues pulled up an article from a small-town newspaper about his drunk-driving arrest two years earlier. Divorce lawyers have been issuing subpoenas for electronic tollbooth records to use in custody cases. (You say you're home at 6 p.m. to have dinner with the kids, but Fast Lane says you're getting off the Massachusetts Turnpike at 7 p.m.) Abbe L. Ross, a divorce lawyer in Boston, finds a gold mine in computers: financial data, e-mails, what Web sites a soon-to-be-ex spouse looks at and for how long. "I love to look through hard drives," she says.

11   Details about you already are stashed in enormous databases. Unless you pay cash for everything, data brokers almost certainly have compiled a profile of you that will be bought and sold dozens of times to marketers and direct-mail firms. "There's almost nothing they can't find out about you," says Jack Dunning, who worked in the junk-mail business for 35 years. Right now, there are roughly 50,000 such lists for sale in a $4 billion a year industry. Now junk mail is going digital: Companies can use personal profiles and records from Internet search engines to tailor advertising—both what you see and precisely when you see it—to individual consumers.

12   And new databases are being created all the time. Most of the major proposals for health-care reform, for example, include compiling medical records into easily and widely accessible digital files. In July, the FBI requested $5 million to pay the major phone companies to maintain logs of your calls—information the Feds can't legally stockpile themselves but might find useful later.

13   Surveillance cameras are increasingly ubiquitous in our post-9/11 world. Indeed, New York City plans to ring the financial district with them, as central London did several years ago.

14   Of course, there are upsides. London's network of cameras helped capture failed car bombers in June. And streamlined electronic medical records would make health care safer and more efficient.

15   Still, most experts say we need to be vigilant about the increasing encroachments on our privacy.

16   The ability to collect information and images has outpaced the security available to protect them. Since January 2005, nearly 160 million personal records have been stolen or inadvertently posted online.

17   And even if information stays secure, the big question remains: Who should be allowed to access these databases? The FBI might find evidence against a few bad guys in millions of phone records, but the government could track all of your calls too. (President Bush has acknowledged that the National Security Agency tapped phone calls, though whose and how many is unknown.)

18   Even more disturbing: All of those data files can be linked and cross-referenced. At the 2001 Super Bowl in Tampa, fans were scanned with cameras linked to facial-recognition software in a hunt for suspected terrorists. Some privacy advocates worry that police could videotape anti-war marches and create a library of digital faces or start mining Web pages for personal information.

19   Kevin Bankston was only caught smoking, but he's worried about larger implications: "The issue isn't whether you have anything to hide," he says. "The issue is whether the lack of privacy would give the government an inordinate amount of power over the populace. This is about maintaining the privacy necessary for us to flourish as a free society."

Analysis of Sample Position Argument

The writer deals with a controversial issue. Most people assume that personal privacy is a given, an inherent right. But is the right to privacy a realistic expectation in today's world? Few people realize that almost every electronic transaction, whether a bank transaction or a store purchase, leaves a permanent digital record. Nor do they realize that every phone call, e-mail, grocery store purchase, or Facebook entry becomes part of huge data systems accessible to others. Controversy arises from the fact that such personal information can be used by businesses to track spending habits and, thus, target customers. Also controversial is how the government can keep tabs on its citizenry. That issue is even more controversial since some forms of surveillance—for example, at airports, on highways, and in commercial and financial areas—are considered essential in the fight against terrorism. Of course, to many people, such surveillance constitutes an infringement on individual privacy and, thus, a diminishing of civil liberties. In his essay, Flynn clearly addresses the controversy that in our digital world it may be impossible to protect personal information.

The writer clearly states a position. The title of Flynn's essay implies the author's stand: that personal privacy no longer exists. He begins the essay with an anecdote, illustrating the erosion of privacy. He recounts the story of a young man who was a closet smoker but concealed this by taking cigarette breaks outside his office on a street where he expected anonymity. But, as the writer points out, an "online mapping service that provided ground-level photographs captured him smoking—and made the image available to anyone on the Internet" (paragraph 1). He concludes this anecdote with a blunt generalization, "Privacy is a withering commodity for all of us" (paragraph 2). This is a clear statement of his position. Several times in the essay after citing examples of the violation of privacy he reiterates his position. For instance, after discussing the ready availability of telephone and health records Flynn states, "Still, most experts say we need to be vigilant about the increasing encroachments on our privacy" (paragraph 15). Following that, he points out that "The ability to collect information and images has outpaced the security available to protect them" (paragraph 16). Clearly, he has surveyed the many ways privacy is compromised and has concluded that our privacy is rapidly eroding.

The writer recognizes other positions and possible objections. Flynn tries to take a balanced view by citing other points of view. At the end of paragraph 5, for example, he cites the consumer perks built into some everyday consumer transactions: "We all make daily trade-offs for convenience and thrift: Electronic tollbooths mean you don't have to wait in the cash-only lane, but your travel habits will be tracked. The Piggly Wiggly discount card saved you $206 on your annual grocery bill, but it counts how many doughnuts and six-packs you buy. MySpace posts make it easy to keep in touch with friends, but your comments live on." Later in the piece when the author tackles the invasion of privacy in the fight against terrorism, he acknowledges the other side: "Of course there up upsides. London's network of cameras helped capture failed car bombers in June" (paragraph 14). And referring to the prospect of health care digital files that would be "easily and widely accessible," the author acknowledges that these "streamlined electronic medical records would make health care safer and more efficient" (paragraph 14).

As the author explores the scope and consequences of the invasion of privacy, his tone remains matter-of-fact and objective. His most emotionally potent comment comes at the conclusion of the piece when he refers back to the young man in paragraph 1. It is only here that his tone approaches that of a warning when he cites the ominous consequences of surveillance in public places: "Kevin Bankston was only caught smoking. . . . 'This is about maintaining the privacy necessary for us to flourish as a free society'" (paragraph 19).

The writer offers well-developed reasons to support the position. Flynn offers concrete, concise, and convincing evidence to support his position that personal privacy is greatly compromised today. He describes virulent threats to privacy and documents these threats with examples to which his audience, the general public, can relate. One of his claims is that in today's world of commerce, it is almost impossible to maintain personal privacy—that nearly every transaction is recorded electronically and leaves a trail that is permanent and that can be available to anyone skilled "to sniff it out" (paragraph 6). And he gets specific: "Need a mortgage or a car loan? A legitimate lender is going to verify a wealth of private information, including your name and address, date of birth, Social Security number and credit history" (paragraph 5). Later, he argues that because of the enormous databases, "Companies can use personal profiles and records from Internet search engines to tailor advertising—both what you see and precisely when you see it—to individual consumers" (paragraph 11). For support, Flynn quotes an authority in the field of direct-mail and marketing: "'There's almost nothing they can't find out about you,' says Jack Dunning, who worked in the junk-mail business for 35 years" (paragraph 11).

Another threat Flynn names are the social networking sites that make personal information available to everyone, including potential employers as well as thieves and sexual predators. He supports his position with reference to students who naively chronicle their lives on MySpace or Facebook. Young people may not know that "employers regularly research job applicants on the Internet," Flynn writes. What may amuse college pals "might not amuse a law-firm recruiter" (paragraph 7). He further supports his position with another piece of anecdotal evidence: reference to the newly crowned Miss New Jersey, whose Facebook page contained photographs that were used as blackmail. Flynn even quotes her directly: "'The Web is a place where people can destroy your reputation if you're not careful'" (paragraph 9).

Another argument Flynn makes to support his claim of a diminishing privacy is the ubiquitous use of surveillance cameras in public places. In paragraph 18, he offers the powerful example of the 2001 Super Bowl in Tampa, Florida, where "fans were scanned with cameras linked to facial-recognition software in a hunt for suspected terrorists." Flynn's logical concern is that "police could videotape anti-war marches and create a library of digital faces or start mining Web pages for personal information." Building on all his specific concerns, Flynn concludes with larger implications: that the increased lack of privacy could "'give the government an inordinate amount of power over the populace'" (paragraph 19).

The writer's supporting evidence is convincing. Flynn's evidence is very convincing. He supports his position in a variety of ways. He uses anecdotes that the average person can identify with, whether it be references to the smoker Kevin Bankston or the experience of young people using Facebook. He makes use of expert opinion, quoting, for instance, Jack Dunning, who worked for 35 years in the direct-mail business. Throughout the piece, he also cites numerous examples of our compromised privacy.

The writer projects a reasonable persona. The tone of this essay is reasonable and balanced. Flynn's purpose is to alert the general public to the many ways personal data is, in fact, part of public or available records. His tone is friendly as his intention is not to alarm but to inform—to enhance awareness so that people can take sensible precautions. Thus, he gives numerous examples but does not inflate them or create a sense of panic.

Proposal Arguments

Position arguments examine existing conditions. *Proposal arguments,* however, look to the future. They make recommendations for changes in the status quo—namely, changes in a policy, practice, or attitude. Essentially, what every proposal writer says is this: "Here is the problem, and this is what I think should be done about it." The hoped-for result is a new course of action or way of thinking.

Proposals are the most common kind of argument. We hear them all the time: "There ought to be a law against that"; "The government should do something about these conditions." We're always making proposals of some kind: "Van should work out more"; "You ought to see that movie"; "We should recycle more of our trash." As pointed out earlier in this chapter, because proposals are aimed at correcting problems, they almost always make their claims in obligation verbs such as *ought to, needs to be,* and *must.*

Sometimes proposal arguments take up local problems and make practical recommendations for immediate solutions. For instance, to reduce the long lines at the photocopy machines in your campus library, you might propose that the school invest in more copiers and station them throughout the building. Proposal arguments also seek to correct or improve conditions with more far-reaching consequences. If, for example, too many of your classmates smoke, you might write a proposal to your school's administration to remove all cigarette machines from campus buildings or to limit smoking areas on campus.

Still other proposals address perennial social issues in an effort to change public behavior and government policy. A group of physicians might recommend that marijuana be legalized for medical use. An organization of concerned parents might ask the federal government to ban toys that contain toxic or flammable materials. Everyone has ideas about things that should be changed; proposals are the means we use to make those changes happen.

Features to Look for in Proposal Arguments

Proposals have two basic functions: (1) They inform readers that there is a problem; (2) they make recommendations about how to correct those problems. To help you sharpen your own critical ability to build and analyze proposal arguments, we offer some guidelines.

The writer states the problem clearly. Because a proposal argument seeks to change the reader's mind and/or behavior, you first must demonstrate that a problem exists. You do this for several reasons. Your audience may not be aware that the problem exists or they may have forgotten it or think that it has already been solved. Sympathetic audiences may need to be reinspired to take action. It is crucial, therefore, that proposals clearly define the problem and the undesirable or dangerous consequences if matters are not corrected.

For both uninformed and sympathetic audiences, writers often try to demonstrate how the problem personally affects the reader. An argument for greater measures against shoplifting can be more convincing when you illustrate how petty thefts inevitably lead to higher prices. A paper proposing the elimination of pesticides might interest the everyday gardener by demonstrating how much carcinogenic chemicals can contaminate local drinking water. To make the problem even more convincing, the claim should be supported by solid evidence—statistics, historical data, examples, testimony of witnesses and experts, maybe even personal experience.

The writer clearly proposes how to solve the problem. After defining the problem clearly, you need to tell your readers how to solve it. This is the heart of the proposal, the writer's plan of action. Besides a detailed explanation of what should be done and how, the proposal should supply reliable supporting evidence for the plan: testimony of others, ideas from authorities, statistics from studies.

The writer argues convincingly that this proposal will solve the problem. Perhaps the first question readers ask is "How will this solution solve the problem?" Writers usually address this question by identifying the forces behind the problem and demonstrating how their plan will counter those forces. Suppose, for instance, you propose putting condom machines in all college dorms as a means of combating the spread of AIDS. To build a convincing case, you would have to summon evidence documenting how condoms significantly reduce the spread of AIDS. To make the connection between the problem and your solution even stronger, you might go on to explain how readily available machines leave students little excuse for unsafe sex. Students cannot complain that they jeopardized their health because they couldn't make it to a drugstore.

The writer convincingly explains how the solution will work. Generally readers next ask how the plan will be put into action. Writers usually answer by detailing how their plan will work. They emphasize their plan's advantages and how efficiently (or cheaply, safely, conveniently) it can be carried out. For the condom machine proposal, that might mean explaining how and where the machines will be installed and how students can be encouraged to use them. You might cite advantages of your proposal, such as the easy installation of the machines and the low price of the contents.

The writer anticipates objections to the proposed solution. Writers expect disagreement and objections to proposal arguments: Proposals are aimed at changing the status quo, and many people are opposed to or are fearful of change. If you want to persuade readers, especially hostile ones, you must show that you respect their sides of the argument too. Most proposal writers anticipate audience response to fortify their case and establish credibility. (See Chapter 4 for more discussion of audience response.)

The writer explains why this solution is better than the alternatives. Although you may believe that your solution to the problem is best, you cannot expect readers automatically to share that sentiment. Nor can you expect readers not to wonder about other solutions. Good proposal writers investigate other solutions that have been tried to solve this problem so they can weigh alternative possibilities and attempt to demonstrate the superiority of their plan and the disadvantages of others. If you are knowledgeable about ways the problem has been dealt with in the past, you might be able to show how your plan combines the best features of other, less

---

Checklist for Writing a Proposal Argument

Have you:
- stated the problem clearly?
- proposed a solution clearly?
- explained why the solution will work?
- demonstrated how the solution will work?
- addressed possible objections?
- shown why the solution is better than alternatives?
- projected a reasonable persona?

successful solutions. For instance, in the condom machine proposal you might explain to your readers that universities have attempted to make students more aware that unsafe sex promotes the spread of AIDS; however, without the easy availability of condom machines, students are more likely to continue to engage in unsafe sex. The promotion of AIDS awareness and the presence of condom machines might significantly reduce that problem.

The writer projects a reasonable persona. As in position arguments, your persona is an important factor in proposals, for it conveys your attitude toward the subject and the audience. Because a proposal is intended to win readers to your side, the best strategy is to project a persona that is fair-minded. Even if you dislike or are angry about somebody else's views on an issue, projecting a reasonable and knowledgeable tone will have a more persuasive effect than a tone of belligerence.

If you are arguing for condom machines in dormitories, you would be wise to recognize that some people might object to the proposal because availability might be interpreted as encouragement of sexual behavior. So as not to offend or antagonize such readers, adopting a serious, straightforward tone might be the best mode of presenting the case.

SAMPLE PROPOSAL ARGUMENT FOR ANALYSIS

The following argument was written by Amanda Collins, a first-year English composition student, whose assignment was to write a proposal argument. In her paper, she argues for the implementation of foreign language teaching in American elementary schools, focusing in particular on her own home town of East Bridgewater, Massachusetts. Read her essay and respond to the questions that follow. Note that she used research to support her ideas and documentation to acknowledge her sources. The style of documentation used in this paper is MLA, which we discuss in detail in the Documentation Guide.

```
                                        Collins 1

     Amanda Collins
     Professor Ingram
     ENG 1350
     July 29, 2007
               Bring East Bridgewater Elementary
                      into the World
     Introduction
            According to a survey of ten European
     countries and Russia, the average age of
     students beginning foreign language instruction
```

Collins 2

is eight (Bergentoft 13). In Sweden, ninety-nine percent of the students in primary school study English. One hundred percent of the students study English in secondary schools (Bergentoft 19). However, "across the United States, only about one in three elementary schools offers its students the opportunity to gain some measure of skill in another language" (Met 37). The United States falls drastically short of the standards being set by the rest of the world.

2   The Commonwealth of Massachusetts is no exception. According to a report from the Center for Applied Linguistics (CAL), only forty-four schools across the state offer foreign language programs in primary school ("National Directory"). Schools not offering foreign language study leave their students at a disadvantage. Foreign language needs to be considered as vital to a child's education as are math, science and reading. Parents would not be happy if their children began math or English studies in high school. So why shouldn't parents be outraged that second languages do not hold much significance in the Massachusetts curriculum (Brown 166)? East Bridgewater must take steps to change this and open Central Elementary School to foreign language learning.

3   The world is changing as are the skills one needs to succeed. Globalization brings us together. People around the world are connected to each other more than ever before, whether through international communication, travel, or commerce. In a world today that is constantly crossing borders "there is a need for linguistically and culturally competent Americans" (Brown 165). And learning languages

is one way to reach such competency. America's
students need to be prepared for entrance into
this ever-merging world where they will compete
with their international peers who are fluent in
two or three languages. It is time to adopt a
plan like those proven successful elsewhere in
America and abroad. It's time to give East
Bridgewater's students an advantage. In order to
do this, East Bridgewater must live up to the
school system's motto, "There is no better place
to learn," and mandate foreign language education
in the elementary curriculum for every child.

4   Although the Massachusetts Department of
Education adopted a curriculum framework in
August of 1999 that includes foreign language in
the requirements for elementary schools, it is
still a recommendation, not yet a requirement
(MA Department of Education). Massachusetts's
new Curriculum Framework for World Languages
states that "students should graduate from high
school able to read, write, and converse in a
world language in order to participate in the
multilingual, interdependent communities of the
twenty-first century . . . to develop proficiency,
this framework recommends a sequence of language
learning that starts in kindergarten and
continues through grade twelve and beyond . . .
the World Languages discipline is about making
connections" (MA Department of Education). The
framework places the same value on learning a
foreign language as is placed on mathematics,
reading and science. Despite the framework's
passing, foreign language is not mandated in
the elementary curriculum. There is a real need
not only to finalize the benefits that students
gain by learning languages at an early age, but

Collins 4

also to work toward advancing our schools'
curricula to include Foreign Language in
Elementary School (FLES).

Why Should Children Learn Foreign Language?

Language is an important aspect of the
education of students of all ages. It is becoming
more important for citizens to be well versed in
a language other than their own. The United
States was basically a self-sufficient and self-
contained country before the World Wars. "Rapid
and widespread political, economic, and military
changes after World War II gave rise to issues
that were global in scope, and many people became
aware of the impact that events outside U.S.
borders had on domestic affairs" (Smith 38). The
United States was learning just how fundamental
foreign languages are.

One reason is that transcontinental
communications have become essential to everyday
life in the world. With so much cross-cultural
interaction, we must prepare American children
to grow into adults capable of interacting with
other cultures. The future of the United States
depends on continued and constant communication
with foreign countries that speak languages
other than our own. There are only about 45
other countries outside of the United States
where English is spoken. So, in order to
maintain the status that this country now
enjoys, we must train American children to
comprehend changes in the global community.
Students must learn foreign languages.

In 1999 a study entitled Exploring the
Economics of Language found that "multilingual
societies have a competitive advantage over
monolingual societies in international trade"

(Met 36). The study went on to point out that businesses that had people with the proper language skills to negotiate and carry out commerce with foreign enterprises were at a distinct advantage over those that lacked such talent. So it stands to reason that giving America's students the opportunity to learn a foreign language increases their chances of succeeding in the business world. Likewise, the country benefits since successful businesses on the world level only help the American economy. As Andrew Smith asserts, there is a need to "prepare our students to meet the challenges of our increasingly, sometimes dangerously, interconnected world. It is not likely that the United States will exert global leadership for long with a citizenry that is globally deaf, dumb, and blind" (41).

Besides the business industry, other jobs require expertise in a second language. The State Department, the Central Intelligence Agency, and the National Security Agency are among more than 70 government agencies that require proficiency in foreign languages (Met 36). The non-profit service industries need employees to interact with other cultures and speak other languages. The Red Cross, for example, not only aids victims in the United States but throughout the world. Additionally, the Internet and other electronic communications, though originally English-based, are becoming more linguistically diverse, making proficiency in other languages indispensable. Again, we must not deprive students the opportunity to advance in such career paths; we must provide them language training to make possible such career success.

Collins 6

Other Benefits to Learning a Language Early

9   While most people have the ability to learn a foreign language at any age, there are benefits to starting that process when students are young (Lipton 1115). In 1959 neurologist Wilder Penfield claimed that the brain was best able to comprehend language before the age of ten. Later, research by scientists Chugani and Phelps resulted in the same conclusion: that the ideal time to begin studying a foreign language is before puberty (Lipton 1114). Thompson, Giedd et al. discovered in the year 2000 that the area of the brain associated with language learning grew the most rapidly from age six to thirteen and then slowed. Another researcher suggested that children learning a language before the age of twelve will develop a more authentic accent (Lipton 1114). So, this scientific evidence makes a strong case that foreign language learning must begin at a young age. But there are other studies that make the case even stronger.

10   In 1987, a Connecticut test of twenty-six thousand students revealed that children who began foreign language education before grade four did significantly better on speaking, listening, reading, writing and cultural understanding tests than students who started language learning in seventh grade or after (Brown 165). This and other similar studies initiated further investigation into the academic benefits of early foreign language learning.

11   Numerous studies have been conducted to evaluate the ways in which learning a language will enhance the simultaneous learning of other

subjects. "Learning [foreign] languages . . . provides a unique conduit to higher-order thinking skills. From the early stages of learning, students move from a representational knowledge base to comparison, synthesis, and hypothesis, all elements of higher-order thinking skills" (Brown 167). A student can gain better understanding of the grammar of their native language when they study the grammar of a foreign tongue, and students who can speak another language can develop stronger reading skills (Met 38). On the national level, there is a call for improved literacy, which is why it is important for parents and educators to recognize how FLES helps students learn to read and write (Bruce 608). FLES students scored higher on the 1985 Basic Skills Language Arts Test than non-FLES students. Foreign language study has helped improve standardized test scores in mathematics and reading for students from a variety of backgrounds. Bilingualism also improves "cognitive functioning, such as metalinguistic skills and divergent thinking" (Met 38). It has even been suggested that students gain more creativity. Foreign language study helps students become more academically successful overall.

12   Additionally, since the world is full of many cultures, studying a foreign language helps prepare students for the cultural understanding that is necessary for the acceptance of such diversity. Brown states, "no other subject matter in the elementary school prepares students for the realization that there are other languages and cultures beyond their own" (167). This in turn aids in teaching students geography, history, and social studies because

Collins 8

they will have something to build off of knowing
that the United States is not the only country
of consequence. Researchers Carpenter and Torney
found that younger students studying languages
are more open to other cultures and develop more
positive attitudes toward foreign cultures and
languages (Lipton 1114). From brain functions,
to academics, to character development, learning
foreign languages in elementary school is proven
to be profitable.

Optimal Solution for East Bridgewater

13   There is no doubt that East Bridgewater
must adopt some version of a FLES program. Based
on the current circumstances at the Central
Elementary School, I recommend that the East
Bridgewater School Committee adopt a Sequential
FLES program in which students study a language
no more than thirty minutes per session up to
five times a week.

14   As for the specific language, that decision
can be left up to the School Committee. However,
it is suggested that only one language be taught
for the first year, or at least until the
program is underway and running smoothly. And it
makes sense to recommend Spanish since that
language is used more often than other foreign
languages in the United States.

15   Language instruction should take place at
least three times a week for thirty minutes.
Each school day is six hours long, minus time
for lunch and recess. In order to arrange for
the addition of a language program, the length
of other lessons per day would have to be
shortened slightly, but never by more than ten
minutes each. This should not be a problem.
Foreign languages are as equally important to a

Collins 9

child's education as math, reading or science, and, therefore, would advance students' education in the long run. Since it has been proven that the study of a second language enhances students' performances in other subjects, the amount of time shaved from each subject's session would be more than made up for in the students' overall success.

To fund this undertaking, East Bridgewater should apply to the Federal Language Assistance Program (FLAP). As of the year 2000, Springfield and Medford were the only two towns to receive FLAP grants. Funds are also available through Goals 2000: Educate America Act of 1994. Under the Improving America's Schools Act of 1994, Title VII grants are given out for foreign language assistance. In the year 2001, the Massachusetts Board of Education received two, and Newton, Malden, Medford, Salem, and Springfield Public Schools each received a grant. East Bridgewater has the opportunity to apply for all of these grants.

Meetings should be scheduled with parents to discuss the importance of foreign language education. Brochures outlining fundraising activities should be distributed. The costs of the meetings and printed materials would be minimal, and they would be more than paid off with the benefits of the program. When parents and communities join together, fundraisers can bring in large revenues. East Bridgewater can hold benefits similar to the concert and art auction held by parents in Athens, Georgia. These grants and locally raised money can also help defray the cost of adding teachers to the staff and carrying out the proper training.

Collins 10

Books and other teaching materials can be
purchased from grant funds as well. There really
is no shortage of money available. Once a town
or district realizes the advantages of foreign
language and expresses desire to include it in
their elementary school, the government and
private agencies could offer funds to help get
those programs underway.

Teaching foreign language to students is a
necessity. Linguistic and national borders are
becoming a thing of the past as the result of
globalization. It is a school's responsibility
and a student's right to have every opportunity
afforded them to become globally aware and
literate citizens. East Bridgewater's School
Committee shares that responsibility as
educators of this country's future leaders. Now
is the time to act and close the gap on the
foreign language deficiency that exists in East
Bridgewater's Central Elementary School.

18

Collins 11

Works Cited

Bergentoft, Rune. "Foreign Language Instruction:
A Comparative Perspective." <u>The Annals of
the American Academy of Political and
Social Science</u> 532 (1994): 8–34.
Brown, Christine L. "Elementary School Foreign
Language Programs in the United States." <u>The
Annals of the American Academy of Political
and Social Science</u> 532 (1994): 164–76.

Collins 12

Bruce, Anita. "Encouraging the Growth of Foreign
     Language Study." The Modern Language
     Journal 86 (2002): 605–09.

Caccavale, Therese. "Holliston Public Schools
     Foreign Language." (12 Nov. 2004) <http://
     teacherweb.com/MA/HollistonHighSchool/
     HollistonPublicSchoolsForeignLanguage/>.

Lambert, Richard D. "Problems and Processes in
     U.S. Foreign Language Planning." The Annals
     of the American Academy of Political and
     Social Science 532 (1994): 47–58.

Lipton, Gladys C. "The FLES Advantage: FLES
     Programs in the Third Millennium." The
     French Review 74 (2001): 1113–24.

Massachusetts Department of Education. "World
     Languages Curriculum Framework," Jan. 1996
     <http://www.doe.mass.edu/frameworks/foreign/
     1996/default.html>.

Met, Myriam. "Why Language Learning Matters."
     Educational Leadership 59 (2001): 36–40.

"National Directory of Early Foreign Language
     Programs." ERIC/CLL Online Digest
     <http://www.maltsite.org/worksh01/MetNet/
     National%20Directory%20of%20E%23EB7.htm>.

Smith, Andrew F. "How Global Is the Curriculum?"
     Educational Leadership 60 (2002): 38–41.

QUESTIONS FOR ANALYSIS AND DISCUSSION ———

Briefly summarize the main points of Amanda Collins's essay. Then answer the following questions about the essay to see how it fulfills our guidelines for a proposal argument:

1. Where does Collins identify the problem? Explain how she demonstrates that the problem is significant. Does she explain how the problem might affect today's young students? Where does she do this?

2. What does Collins propose to solve the problem? In what paragraph do you find the solution stated?

3. According to Collins's essay, how will her solution help to solve the problem? Where does she demonstrate this?

4. Does Collins explain how her solution will work? Where does she do this? Does she provide enough detail for you to understand how it will work?

5. Has Collins anticipated objections to her solution? in which paragraphs? Find an example of this. How does she respond to the objection? How does she acknowledge her audience's concerns?

6. Does Collins seem aware of other programs that have been tried to solve the problem? Where does she refer to them in her essay?

7. What attitude about her subject does Collins convey to her readers? Does she seem reasonable and balanced? If so, find some examples of how she conveys this.

Analyzing the Structure
The Beginning

Amanda Collins has already segmented her paper according to four parts: "Introduction," "Why Should Children Learn Foreign Language?" "Other Benefits to Learning a Language Early," and "Optimal Solution for East Bridgewater." Her "Introduction" constitutes the beginning of the essay. The middle includes those paragraphs grouped under her next two parts ("Why Should Children Learn Foreign Language?" and "Other Benefits to Learning a Language Early"). The end corresponds to those paragraphs under "Optimal Solution for East Bridgewater."

In paragraph 1, Amanda introduces the problem: that compared with several foreign countries only about a third of the elementary schools in America offers foreign language teaching. And this creates a disadvantage not only for children who are preparing for a global world but also for America. Then in paragraph 2, she tightens her focus to the state of Massachusetts, which, characteristic of the rest of the country, offers a paltry response—in this case, only 44 schools statewide with foreign language programs at the primary school level. She concludes that paragraph with a point-blank proposal that "East Bridgewater must take steps to change this and open Central Elementary School to foreign language learning."

As her audience, we get a sense of Amanda from these introductory paragraphs. We hear both concern and sincerity in Amanda's tone. We also are clear on her positions. Equating foreign language learning with math and writing, she projects a sense of urgency if American young people are to grow up to function successfully in a world that is linguistically and culturally interconnected and competitive. She appeals to both reason and emotion when she states: "It is time to adopt a plan like those proven successful elsewhere in America and abroad. It's time to give East Bridgewater's students an advantage." She also appeals to a sense of ethics, reminding authorities of their responsibility and duty to live up to the school system's motto, "There is no better place to learn." And she concludes this part of the argument with an insistence that East Bridgewater mandate that foreign language be taught at Central Elementary so students can begin to share in the benefits to come.

The Middle

The next eight paragraphs Amanda has divided into two sections: "Why Should Children Learn Foreign Language?" and "Other Benefits to Learning a Language Early." These represent the middle of Amanda's essays, for this is where she makes her case, where she does the real arguing for her proposal.

Background Information Paragraphs 1, 2, and 4 set the context for Amanda Collins's complaint and the basis for her proposal. In paragraph 1, she says how America "falls drastically short of the standards being set by the rest of the world." She then goes on in the next paragraph to say that the Commonwealth of Massachusetts is characteristic of the larger problem with only 44 schools statewide—a small percentage—offering foreign language programs in primary schools. Paragraph 4 focuses on how despite an adopted curriculum that includes a foreign language requirement in Massachusetts schools, it has still not been mandated, and that means East Bridgewater students are still being deprived.

Reasons in Support of the Claim Paragraphs 5 through 12 make up the heart of Amanda's essay. This is where she supports her claim that it's important for children to learn foreign languages. And she offers several reasons. One key point is the competition in international business that American students will eventually face in the multilingual world of commerce. As evidence, she cites a source (paragraph 6) that claims how only 45 countries besides the United States speak English, implying that most of the rest of the 160 or so countries do not. So in a majority of the world's nations, commerce is conducted in foreign tongues.

She also refers to a study that supports her claim that "monolingual societies" are at a distinct disadvantage over those where other languages are spoken. She summons the support of Andrew Smith (paragraph 7) who also sees a need to prepare our children for an increasing global economy and culture. In the next paragraph, she points out that besides business, other careers require expertise in a second language. She cites the nonprofit organizations as well as some 70 government agencies, including the CIA, that require proficiency in foreign languages. She concludes with an appeal that with the Internet and other electronic communications, once English-based, the world is becoming more linguistically diverse, making proficiency in other languages indispensable. Again, she argues, we must not deprive students the opportunity to advance in such career paths; we must provide them language training to make possible such career success.

In paragraphs 9 through 12, Amanda offers other benefits to early language learning besides career success, thus bolstering her claim. Predicated on the evidence that children best learn foreign languages at a young age, she argues first that kids who learn foreign languages develop more authentic accents. Second, foreign language learning also helps children perform better in speaking, writing, and even mathematics. As evidence, she cites numerous studies supporting her reasons and allowing her to conclude that "younger students studying languages are more open to other cultures and develop more positive attitudes toward foreign cultures. . . . From brain functions, to academics, to character development, learning foreign languages in elementary school is proven to be profitable."

Response to Other Points of View Although Amanda cites no specific opposing points of view, she implies that America may be slow to develop language programs at the primary level because of a general apathy and/or the belief that speaking English is good enough. She hints at this when she mentions America's pre–World Wars sense of self-sufficiency and self-containment. And even though Americans had learned "how fundamental foreign languages" were following World War II, vigorous response to implement foreign language study, especially on the primary school level, has been lacking.

Anticipates Possible Objections to Reasons Amanda indirectly anticipates opposition to early language training. With considerable supporting evidence, she argues that the earlier children learn foreign languages the better. What she possibly has in mind here is the counterclaim that if people need to learn a foreign language for their careers they can take courses as adults. To counter that, she cites scientific studies that confirm how young children absorb foreign languages faster and more efficiently than adolescents or adults.

The End

The final five paragraphs constitute the end of Amanda's argument. And here she returns to the problem in East Bridgewater and offers specific proposals on implementing foreign language training in Central Elementary School. She recommends a program of half-hour sessions three to five times a week; she suggests Spanish since it is the second most-spoken language in America; she suggests various means of funding the program; and she concludes with recommendations of getting parents involved. She concludes with reaffirmations of her argument that it is important for young students to learn foreign languages and that it is a school's responsibility to provide students that opportunity. Her final sentence rounds out her argument and nicely returns to the home front: "Now is the time to act and close the gap on the foreign language deficiency that exists in East Bridgewater's Central Elementary School."

Narrative Arguments

Sometimes position and proposal arguments do not take on the familiar shapes as just discussed. Sometimes the author's position on an issue is implied rather than straightforwardly stated. Sometimes instead of a well-reasoned argument bound by a hierarchy of supporting details, the evidence is incorporated in a dramatic illustration of the issue. So is the author's stand. What we're talking about is argument in the form of a *narrative.*

Instead of spelling out the claims and making explicit points, the narrative argument relies on a scene, a series of episodes, or a story to advocate a change of behavior or way of thinking. Whether true or hypothetical, a narrative may serve as the body of an argument or it may be used at the beginning as a springboard to the central claim and discussion. Either way, a narrative can be a powerful strategy for winning the sympathy of an audience by describing experiences that evoke emotional responses. Below is an argument aimed at getting people to protest a governmental proposal to remove grizzly bears from list of animals protected by the Endangered Species Act. It begins with a student's personal narrative, an account that is emotionally appealing and that leads into an explicit appeal.

> We'd been hiking for three hours east of Yellowstone's Slough Creek when our guide motioned us to stop. "Bears," he whispered. We heard a piercing sound— more like a wailing cry than a roar. We cut through some sage and over a rise when we saw a grizzly bear mother and two yearling cubs. From about a hundred yards we watched in hushed fascination as the adorable cubs romped and wrestled in the grass while the mother watched from a short distance. They were seemingly unaware of our presence and continued to cavort, one cub trying to engage the mother in play by nudging her with his nose. This went on for several minutes until the mother made a sound and stood erect, sniffing the air. She must have sensed danger because she bellowed for the cubs to follow. In a moment they tumbled down a ravine and out of sight.
>
> To see that mother grizzly and her young at such close range was not just a rare experience but an eye-opener. It was a reminder that these magnificent, elusive creatures are in a constant struggle to survive. They reproduce only every three years and spend at least that time rearing their cubs. They are vulnerable to hunters, traffic, and male grizzlies which will kill their own cubs in order to render nursing mothers fertile again. While their numbers have increased over the past decades, these bears are threatened once again.
>
> The current administration has recently proposed taking grizzlies off the Endangered Species list, thus stripping them of the kind of protection from hunters that could push them to the edge of extinction once again. We must do everything in our power to make people aware of the continuing struggle to save these iconic vestiges of frontier America.

The appeal here makes a case for protecting the grizzlies by re-creating an encounter with a mother bear and her cubs, thus invoking in the reader identification with the author's sympathy for the creatures. Even if the reader has never encountered grizzly bears in the wild, the narrative evokes in readers at least yearnings for such. To anyone who has ever visited a zoo or seen wildlife movies, the description of the cubs at play has a strong emotional appeal.

While this strategy—the use of a story—differs from the standard position and proposal argument, the narrative argument still has three basic parts—in this sample, a paragraph for each. The first is the actual narrative, the "story" in which the author invites the reader to partake in the experience. Because the encounter is told on a time line, it has its own three-part structure—a beginning, middle, and end. The first paragraph is devoted to the author's observations of the animals "cavorting"; the final sentence concludes with the animals' sensing danger and eventually departing. In essence, this opening paragraph is the author's invitation to share in the emotional experience of the encounter. The second paragraph shifts to an appreciation of that experience and an evaluation of the vulnerability of the animals. Here the author reminds us that these "magnificent" creatures are threatened by a variety of forces, and the author names specifics—hunters, vehicular traffic, and other grizzlies. In the third paragraph, the author states the specific problem that could further endanger the animals—the current administration's proposal to remove them from the Endangered Species list. And it concludes with a proposal for people who care to "do everything in . . .[their] power to make people aware of the continuing struggle to save" the grizzlies.

A narrative can also constitute other peoples' experiences as in the third-person account below of a teenager's death by drug overdose. Like the above first-person narrative, the Web log entry that follows is constructed on a time line, moving from the deeper to the more recent past.

> Megan B. started smoking marijuana and drinking alcohol at the age of thirteen. But when those didn't work for her she decided she needed to step it up a level. So by fourteen she began using cocaine as well as taking prescription drugs including Ritalin, Xanax, and Percocet. There was no need to go to a doctor for prescriptions. Friends got them from their parents' medicine cabinets. Like so many kids, she regarded prescription drugs as "safer" than other drugs. She figured that since people took them legally all the time, she'd be fine with them. By the time she was sixteen, she had graduated to heroin, sniffing it with friends to calm herself and get sleep. The stuff was easy to get and only a few dollars a bag. But then her heroin use started spiraling out of control. She missed curfews. She missed school; she didn't come home nights, saying she was staying at friends' homes. When her parents asked if she was taking drugs, she, of course, lied. For some time they believed her. Then two months before her seventeenth birthday, she died from an overdose. Her parents had missed the warning signs—the erratic behavior, her bouts of depression, restlessness, angry denials—discounting them as teenage rebelliousness. By the time they tried to intervene, to get professional help, Megan was dead.

What makes this narrative so effective is its objective tone, its matter-of-fact chronicling of Megan B.'s sad demise. Nowhere in the passage does the author take on an admonishing or threatening tone; nor does she cite a lot of dry statistics about drugs and young people's deaths. Instead, the author creates a growing sense of inevitability that climaxes in the stark final announcement, "By the time they tried to intervene, to get professional help, Megan was dead." The Internet has hundreds of websites with narratives of the accidental deaths of drug victims. Likewise, there are dedicated sites with stories of deaths due to drunk driving, guns, house poisons, suicide, and other tragedies.

Features to Look for in Narrative Arguments

For a narrative argument to be successful, it should tell a story that clearly dramatizes a controversial issue. It should also meet some of the following basic criteria, which we offer as a checklist to evaluate your own or other writers' narratives.

The writer's narrative illustrates a controversial issue. Like either a position or proposal argument, the narrative should tell a story that dramatizes an experience or series of experiences relevant to a controversial issue.

The narrative is a scene, a series of episodes, or a story that advocates a change of behavior or way of thinking. A narrative is more than just the citation of personal evidence—yours or someone else's—in support of your stand on an issue. Instead, a narrative is a story or running account of a series of events, usually arranged in chronological order, that illustrate someone's experience with some aspects of the issue being debated. Even if your audience is aware of the problem and may even be sympathetic, framing your argument as a narrative has the potential to invite the reader to identify personally with the character or characters in the discourse and, as a result, move them to action. A paper proposing stricter laws against drunk drivers, for instance, might be especially persuasive if it is cast as a real-life account of someone who experienced injury in an automobile accident that a drunk driver caused.

The narrative should be credible. Whether your narrative is based on your own personal experience or someone else's, it should have credibility if it is going to win the sympathy of an audience. If because of inaccuracies, contradictions, or unbelievable exaggeration the story strains for validity, your narrative will lose its power to persuade.

The narrative should be representative. No matter how credible, your narrative should be *representative* of the issue. Say, for instance, you were stopped for exceeding the speed limit by 30 miles per hour in a town you passed through infrequently. In your narrative, you describe how the police officer not only reprimanded you but also put you under arrest, escorting you to the police station where you were put in a jail cell overnight. No matter how harrowing that narrative may be, no matter how unpleasant the police reaction was, your case would be weak if you argued that the town's police force was out of control and should be investigated by the district attorney's office. Unless you had other evidence that police overreaction or excessive punishment was standard in that town, your narrative would not be symptomatic of a real problem. In contrast, the tragic story of Megan B. whose drug abuse was not dealt with in time is representative of hundreds of young people who annually fall victim to drug overdoses.

The narrative must avoid sentimentality. Opening an argument with a strong narrative has the potential of snagging the readers' attention and sympathy from the start. But you should be careful not to let your appeal become too emotional or sink into melodrama, otherwise your argument will lose sympathy. Choose your words and present facts and details carefully. Avoid words and expressions that are emotionally too loaded, too forceful.

SAMPLE NARRATIVE ARGUMENT

Narratives can have a greater impact on the reader than other kinds of arguments because narratives appeal to values and emotions common to most people and, thus, have more impact than cool logic and dry statistical data. What follows is an appeal for people to be open-minded about physician-assisted suicide. It's an argument that is fashioned on a narrative that takes up most of the essay. Like other narratives, it is structured on a time line—and one that is particularly poignant since much of it chronicles the author's grappling with his own terminal medical condition.

Jerry Fensterman is the former director of development for Fenway Community Health in Boston, Massachusetts. This article appeared as a guest editorial in the *Boston Globe* on January 31, 2006.

I See Why Others Choose to Die
Jerry Fensterman

1   The US Supreme Court's recent decision to let stand Oregon's law permitting physician-assisted suicide is sure to fuel an ongoing national debate. Issues of life and death are deeply felt and inspire great passions. It would be wonderful, and unusual, if all those joining the fray would do so with the humility and gravity the matter deserves.

2   I am approaching 50, recently remarried, and the father of a terrific 13-year-old young man. By every measure I enjoy a wonderful life. Or at least I did until April 2004, when I was diagnosed with kidney cancer. Surgery was my only hope to prevent its spread and save my life. The discovery of a new lump in December 2004 after two surgeries signaled that metastasis was underway. My death sentence had been pronounced.

3   Life may be the most intense addiction on earth. From the moment I first heard the words "you have cancer" and again when I was told that it was spreading out of control, I recognized my addiction to life almost at the cellular level. I have tried since then, as I did before, to live life to the fullest. I also committed myself to doing everything within my power to extend my life.

4   Toward that end I am participating in my third clinical trial in a year. I have gained some small benefit from it. I am, however, one of the first people with my cancer to try this drug. Its median benefit seems to be only on the order of three months. So my expectations are modest. The side effects of these drugs are significant, as are the symptoms of the cancer's gallop through my body. All things considered, I believe I have earned my merit badge for "doing all one can in the face of death to stay alive."

5   That the experience has changed me is obvious. I have a few scars, have lost 50 pounds, and my hair is thinner. I rely on oxygen nearly all the time, can no longer perform the job I loved, and have difficulty eating. More profoundly, my universe has contracted. Simply leaving home has become an enormous task, and travel is essentially out of the question. I can no longer run, swim, golf, ski, and play with my son. I haven't yet learned how to set goals or make plans for a future that probably consists of weeks or months, not years. I am also nearing a point where I will not be able to take care of my most basic needs.

6   Mine has been a long, difficult, and certain march to death. Thus, I have had ample time to reflect on my life, get my affairs in order, say everything I want to the people I love, and seek rapprochement with friends I have hurt or lost touch with. The bad news is that my pain and suffering have been drawn out, the rewarding aspects of life have inexorably shrunk, and I have watched my condition place an increasingly

great physical and emotional burden on the people closest to me. While they have cared for me with great love and selflessness, I cannot abide how my illness has caused them hardship, in some cases dominating their lives and delaying their healing.

7   Perhaps the biggest and most profound change I have undergone is that my addiction to life has been "cured." I've kicked the habit! I now know how a feeling, loving, rational person could choose death over life, could choose to relieve his suffering as well as that of his loved ones a few months earlier than would happen naturally.

8   I am not a religious person, but I consider myself and believe I have proved throughout my life to be a deeply moral person. Personally I would not now choose physician-assisted suicide if it were available. I do not know if I ever would. Yet now, I understand in a manner that I never could have before why an enlightened society should, with thoughtful safeguards, allow the incurably ill to choose a merciful death.

9   The Supreme Court's ruling will inflame the debate over physician-assisted suicide. Besides adding my voice to this debate, I ask you to carefully search your soul before locking into any position. If you oppose physician-assisted suicide, first try to walk a mile in the shoes of those to whom you would deny this choice. For as surely as I'm now wearing them, they could one day just as easily be on your feet or those of someone you care deeply about.

Analysis of Sample Narrative Argument

Unlike the Megan B. and grizzly bear examples, Fensterman does not begin with a story and conclude with his claim. Instead, he opens with an acknowledgment of the U.S. Supreme Court's ruling to let stand the law permitting physician-assisted suicide. He then follows with seven paragraphs that personalize his coming to terms with his "death sentence." These paragraphs constitute the body of the piece and, like most narratives, the contents are structured on a time line. In this case, the narrative begins in April 2004 when the author was diagnosed with kidney cancer and then relates events occurring in the next year and a half. In his final two paragraphs, he refers back to the controversy, saying that he would not choose physician-assisted suicide at this time and does not know if he ever would. But he has learned through his own experience of terminal illness why the option should be available.

Analyzing the Structure
The Beginning

Paragraph 1 constitutes the beginning of Fensterman's narrative argument. In it, he names the controversy, which his following narrative dramatizes. Here he specifically cites the U.S. Supreme Court's recent ruling "to let stand Oregon's law permitting physician-assisted suicide." Acknowledging how this will only fuel the ongoing national debate, he asks, because the issue is a matter of life and death, that people enter it "with the humility and gravity the matter deserves," thus anticipating his own personal story.

The Middle

Paragraphs 2 through 7 constitute Fensterman's personal narrative of his "death sentence." He immediately identifies himself as a 50-year-old recently remarried man and a father who "enjoys a wonderful life" and who clearly has a lot to live for. But in April 2004, he was diagnosed with cancer of the kidney. Over the next five paragraphs (3–7), he chronicles the events of the next two years. In December 2004, a new lump was discovered following two surgeries, signaling the cancer had spread. That "death sentence" announcement made Fensterman recognize his "addiction to life almost at the cellular level" (paragraph 3). As he says, since then he has dedicated himself to prolonging his life including participating in another clinical trial. But the benefits were short-lived and the side effects were significant—scars, weight loss, thinning of his hair. Worse, his universe "was contracted." He could no longer work, travel, "run, swim, golf, ski, and play" with his son. In paragraphs 6 and 7, as he approaches death, he says that he is reflecting on his life, getting his affairs in order, and contacting family members and friends. But what pains him the most is how his condition has become "an increasingly great physical and emotional burden on the people" to whom he is closest. And this hardship is what he "cannot abide" (paragraph 6). He concludes in his personal narrative that he has become "cured" of his "addiction to life." As a result, he says he now understands "how a feeling, loving, rational person could choose death over life, could choose to relieve his suffering as well as that of his loved ones a few months earlier than would happen naturally" (paragraph 7).

The End

The final two paragraphs (8 and 9) make up the end of Fensterman's piece. Here he returns to the present tense and to his request for open-mindedness. Even after all the anguish he has undergone and the hardship no doubt assumed by his loved ones, Fensterman surprisingly announces that he "would not now choose physician-assisted suicide if it were available." That statement makes even stronger his appeal that "an enlightened society . . . allow the incurably ill to choose a merciful death." At the end of paragraph 9, he shifts to a powerful personal appeal, asking those who might be opposed to physician-assisted suicide to "walk a mile in the shoes of those to whom you would deny this choice." And he concludes with a reminder that he is wearing shoes that could one day "be on your feet or those of someone you care deeply about."

Analyzing the Narrative Features

The writer's narrative dramatizes a controversial issue. In the opening paragraph of Fensterman's piece, he cites the topic he will ultimately be addressing through his narrative argument, namely, the recent U.S. Supreme Court's decision to let stand Oregon's law permitting physician-assisted suicide. But his focus is a plea for open-minded debate, informed by an appreciation of the experience of a person suffering with a terminal illness. He recognizes that the passage of this law will provoke debate about the rightness or wrongness of physician-assisted suicide. But he wants to argue that one should be acutely aware of the feelings and circumstances of patients suffering a terminal illness before denying them the right to end their lives through physician-assisted suicide.

The writer's narration is credible. Fensterman's narrative is highly credible. He establishes credibility in paragraph 2 by forthrightly identifying himself and his plight: "I am approaching 50, recently remarried, and the father of a terrific 13-year-old young man. By every measure I enjoy a wonderful life. Or at least I did until April 2004, when I was diagnosed with kidney cancer." He is an ordinary man, leading an ordinary life, and grateful for ordinary things. However, like everyone else's, his life is fragile, and it nearly crashed down around him when he was diagnosed with cancer. This is a situation everyone can identify with and one everyone secretly fears. At the same time, anyone who knows of the ravages of cancer or knows someone who has suffered from it can identify personally and intensely with the piece. Thus, Fensterman's material is quite credible.

The writer's narrative is representative of the issue. Fensterman's narrative could not be more representative of the issue. His reflection on the various stages of cancer diagnosis and treatment represent what so many people go through. In paragraph 3, he says that he recognizes that "Life may be the most intense addiction on earth. From the moment I first heard the words 'you have cancer' and again when I was told that it was spreading out of control, I recognized my addiction to life almost at the cellular level." He acknowledges the physical toll the disease takes: "I have a few scars, have lost 50 pounds, and my hair is thinner. I rely on oxygen nearly all the time, can no longer perform the tasks I love. . . . Simply leaving home has become an enormous task" (paragraph 5). His description of the emotional and physical toll of the disease reflects what many cancer victims feel. He also acknowledges the burden of his illness on those he loves: "While they have cared for me with great love and selflessness, I cannot abide how my illness has caused them hardship, in some cases dominating their lives and delaying their healing" (paragraph 6). Such a painful sentiment can be widely shared.

The writer's narrative avoids sentimentality. A subject such as imminent death is difficult to discuss without being emotional. Yet Fensterman manages to do just that while avoiding sentimentality. He is straightforward in his description of his own physical and emotional suffering. And in the proclamation that concludes the various stages he has gone through he dispassionately states, "Perhaps the biggest and most profound change I have undergone is that my addiction to life has been 'cured.' I've kicked the habit" (paragraph 7).

The writer's narrative advocates a change of behavior or a way of thinking. Clearly, Fensterman has used the story of his personal struggle with cancer to influence the debate over the appropriateness of physician-assisted suicide. Every aspect of his narrative does that—from the diagnosis of the disease (paragraph 2), to his awareness of the toll cancer treatment is taking on his body and on the family and friends he loves (paragraphs 4, 5, and 6), to his realization that "I now know how a feeling, loving, rational person could choose death over life, could choose to relieve his suffering as well as that of his loved ones a few months earlier than would happen naturally." Although he admits that he personally would not choose physician-assisted suicide, the entire point of his narrative is to use his experience to illustrate that in the face of terminal suffering a person should have a choice. As he so powerfully concludes, "If you oppose physician-assisted suicide, first try to walk a mile in the shoes of those whom you would deny this choice. For as surely as I'm now wearing them, they could one day just as easily be on your feet or those of someone you care about deeply" (paragraph 9).

Checklist for Writing a Narrative Argument
• Does your narrative dramatize a controversial issue? • Is your narrative credible? • Is your narrative representative of the issue? • Does your narrative avoid sentimentality? • Does your narrative advocate a change of behavior or a way of thinking?

EXERCISES

1. Look in several current issues of a local or national newspaper to find examples of essays written by columnists about controversial issues. You might find these in your college library or online. Make a list in your journal of the strategies different writers use to begin their essays. Bring your examples to class and work in a group to share your findings. You may want to photocopy your examples so that each member has a "catalogue" of good introductions to consider.

2. Repeat exercise 1, but this time collect examples of conclusions from argument essays. Your goal here is to compile a catalogue of endings to consult for examples.

3. Construct a formal outline for one of the essays other than "Indian Bones" in this chapter. Compare it with another student's. If there are places where your outlines differ, analyze how your readings are different.

4. Go back to the examples you found for exercise 1. Divide the essays you and the members of your group found into position and proposal arguments.

5. In your journal, respond to the ideas in Amanda Collins's, Sean Flynn's, or Jerry Fensterman's essay. With which of their reasons do you agree? How would you refute any of their reasons? Make a pro/con checklist that lists their reasons and points you might use to debate them.

6. Through the Internet or your library resources, do some reading on either Karpati's or Fensterman's subject to find out how others view the issue. Create a dialogue among the various positions on the issue and explore their points of view to find common or shared concerns or values. With this knowledge, deliberate about how you stand on the issue.

7. If you were to write an argument essay of your own on either subject, how would you begin your essay? Experiment with a few introductions.

8. Write a first draft of your own essay on either topic.

9. Write a narrative argument on some debatable issue with which you have had personal experience.

CHAPTER 6

Using Evidence

Thinking Like an Advocate

Because this is a democracy, there's a widespread conviction in our society that having opinions is our responsibility as citizens—a conviction supported by our fast-forward multimedia culture. You see it on the nightly news every time a reporter sticks a microphone in the face of somebody on the street, or whenever Oprah Winfrey moves into the studio audience. It's the heart of talk radio and television programs. In newspapers and magazines, it comes in the form of "opinion polls" that tally up our positions on all sorts of weighty issues:

"Should the use of marijuana for medical purposes be legalized?"

"Is the economy this year in better shape than it was last year at this time?"

"Do you think that the American judicial system treats people equally whether they are rich or poor?"

"Is the U.S. government doing enough to prevent acts of domestic terrorism?"

"Do men and women have the same opportunities for promotions and raises in the workplace?"

"Should schoolchildren be required to recite the Pledge of Allegiance in school?"

All this on-the-spot opinion-making encourages people to take an immediate stand on an issue, whether or not they have sufficient understanding and information about it. However, holding an opinion on a matter does not necessarily mean that you have investigated the issue or that you've carefully considered the views of others or that you've gathered enough information to support your position. If you want to make successful arguments, you need more than a gut reaction or simple reliance on yourself for the "truth."

This means thinking of yourself as an *advocate*—a prosecutor or defense attorney, if you like. You need a case to present to the jury of your readers, one that convinces them that your interpretation is plausible. Like an advocate, when you're constructing an argument you look for support to put before your readers: facts, statistics, people's experiences—in a word, *evidence.* The jury judges your argument both on the evidence

169

you bring forth and on the interpretation of that evidence. So, like an advocate, to write successful arguments you need to understand and weigh the value of the *supporting evidence* for your case.

How Much Evidence Is Enough?

Like any advocate, you need to decide *how much* evidence to present to your readers. Your decision will vary from case to case, although with more practice you'll find it easier to judge. Common sense is a good predictor: If the evidence is enough to persuade you, it's probably enough to persuade like-minded readers. Unsympathetic readers may need more proof. The more unexpected or unorthodox your claim, the more evidence you need to convince skeptical readers. It's often as much a case of the *right* evidence as it is the *right amount* of evidence. One fact or statistic, if it touches on your readers' most valued standards and principles, may be enough to swing an argument for a particular group. Here's where outlining (Chapter 5) can help; an outline helps you make sure you present evidence for every assertion you make.

It's easier to gather too much evidence and winnow out the least effective than to have too little and try to expand it. One of our instructors used to call this the "Cecil B. DeMille strategy," after the great Hollywood producer. DeMille's theory was that if audiences were impressed by five dancers, they'd really be overwhelmed by five hundred—but just to be sure, he'd hire a thousand. That's a good strategy to have when writing arguments; you can always use a sentence such as "Of the 116 explosions in GMC trucks with side-mounted fuel tanks, four cases are most frequently cited" and then go on to discuss those four. You've let your readers know that another 112 are on record so they can weigh this fact when considering the four you examine in particular. You may never need a thousand pieces of evidence—or dancers—in an argument, but there's no harm in thinking big!

Why Arguments Need Supporting Evidence

Evidence is composed of facts and their interpretations. As we said in Chapter 1, facts are pieces of information that can be verified—that is, statistics, examples, testimony, historical details. For instance, it is a fact that SAT verbal scores across the nation have gone up for the last ten years. One interpretation might be that students today are spending more time reading and less time watching television than students in the last decade. Another interpretation might be that secondary schools are putting more emphasis on language skills. A third might be that changes in the test or the prevalence of test-preparation courses has contributed to the higher scores.

In everyday conversation, we make claims without offering supporting evidence: "Poverty is the reason why there is so much crime"; "The president is doing a poor job handling the economy"; "Foreign cars are better than American cars." Although we may have good reasons to back up such statements, we're not often called upon to do so, at least not in casual conversation. In written arguments, however, presenting evidence is critical, and a failure to do so is glaring. Without supporting data and examples, an argument is hollow. It will bore the reader, fail to convince, and collapse under criticism. Moreover, you'll be in danger of making a hasty generalization by drawing a conclusion with too little evidence. Consider the following paragraph:

> Video games are a danger to the mental well-being of children. Some children play video games for hours on end, and the result is that their behavior and concentration are greatly affected. Many of them display bad behavior. Others have difficulty doing other, more important things. Parents with young children should be stricter about what video games their children play and how long they play them.

Chances are this paragraph has not convinced you that video games are a threat to children. The sample lacks the details that might persuade you. For instance, exactly what kind of bad behavior do children display? And what specific video games out of the hundreds on the market are the real culprits? How is concentration actually affected? What "more important things" does the author mean? And how many hours of video consumption need occur before signs of dangerous behavior begin to manifest themselves?

Consider how much sharper and more persuasive the following rewrite is with the addition of specific details, facts, and examples:

> Video games may be fun for children, but they can have detrimental effects on their behavior. They encourage violent behavior. A steady dose of some of the more violent games clearly results in more aggressive behavior. One study by the Department of Psychology at State University has shown that after two hours of "Urban Guerrilla," 60 percent of the 12 boys and 20 percent of the 12 girls tested began to mimic the street-fighting gestures—punching, kicking, karate-chopping each other. The study has also shown that such games negatively affect concentration. Even half an hour after their game playing had lapsed, the boys had difficulty settling down to read or draw. Since my parents restricted my little brother's game playing to weekends, he concentrates when completing his homework and has fewer fights with his best friend.

The statistics from the academic study, as well as the concrete case of the writer's own brother, give readers something substantial to consider. Presenting supporting evidence puts meat on the bones of your argument. (In Chapter 9, we will go into greater depth about how to gather research evidence, particularly from the library and the Internet.)

Forms of Evidence

We hope that when you begin to develop an argument, you utilize debate, dialogue, and deliberation, as we suggested in Chapter 1. As you do this, you need to expand and deepen your understanding of the issue by collecting useful evidence from both sides of the issue. Don't neglect this critical step: Remember, the bulk of your argument is composed of material supporting your claim.

Writers enlist four basic kinds of evidence to support their arguments: personal experience (theirs and others'), outside authorities, factual references and examples, and statistics. We'll examine each separately, but you'll probably want to use combinations of these kinds of evidence when building your arguments in order to convince a wide range of readers.

Personal Experience—Yours and Others'

The power of personal testimony cannot be underestimated. Think of the number of movies that have failed at the box office in spite of huge and expensive ad campaigns. Think of the number of times you've read a book on the recommendation of friends—or taken a certain course or shopped at a particular store. You might have chosen the college you're attending based on the recommendation of someone you know. Many people find the word-of-mouth judgments that make up personal testimony the most persuasive kind of evidence.

In written arguments, the personal testimony of other people is used to affirm facts and support your claim. Essentially, their experiences provide you with eyewitness accounts of events that are not available to you. Such accounts may prove crucial in winning over an audience. Suppose you are writing about the rising abuse of alcohol among college students. In addition to statistics and hard facts, your argument can gain strength from quoting the experience of a first-year student who nearly died one night from alcohol poisoning. Or, in an essay decrying discrimination against minorities in hiring, consider the authenticity provided by an interview of neighborhood residents who felt they were passed over for a job because of race or ethnic identity.

Your own eyewitness testimony can be a powerful tool of persuasion. Suppose, for example, that you are writing a paper in which you argue that the big teaching hospital in the city provides far better care and has a lower death rate than the small rural hospital in your town. The hard facts and statistics on the quality of care and comparative mortality rates you provide will certainly have a stark persuasiveness. But consider the dramatic impact on those figures were you to recount how your own trip to the rural emergency room nearly cost you your life because of understaffing or the lack of critical but expensive diagnostic equipment.

Personal observation is useful and valuable in arguments. However, you should be careful not to draw hasty generalizations from such testimony. The fact that you and three of your friends are staunchly in favor of replacing letter grades with a pass/fail system does not support the claim that the entire student body at your school is in favor of the conversion. You need a much greater sample. Likewise, the dislike most people in your class feel for a certain professor does not justify the claim that the university tenure system should be abolished. On such complex issues, you need more than personal testimony to make a case.

You also have to remember the "multiple-perspective" rule. As any police officer can tell you, there are as many versions of the "truth" of an incident as there are people who saw it. The people involved in a car accident see it one way (or more), yet witnesses in a car heading in the other direction may interpret events differently, as will people in an apartment six stories above the street on which the accident took place. Your job is to sort out the different testimonies and make sense of them. Personal experience—yours and that of people you know—is valuable. However, on bigger issues you need statistics and data, as well as the evidence provided by outside authorities.

Outside Authorities

Think of the number of times you've heard statements such as these:

"Scientists have found that . . ."

"Scholars inform us that . . ."

"According to his biographer, President Lincoln decided that . . ."

What these statements have in common is the appeal to outside authorities— people recognized as experts in a given field, people who can speak knowledgeably about a subject. Because authoritative opinions are such powerful tools of persuasion, you hear them all the time in advertisements. Automobile manufacturers quote the opinions of professional race car drivers; the makers of toothpaste cite dentists' claims; famous basketball players push brand-name sneakers all the time. Similarly, a good trial lawyer will almost always rely on forensic experts or other such authorities to help sway a jury.

Outside authorities can provide convincing evidence to support your ideas. However, there are times when expert opinion can be used inappropriately. This faulty use of authority can undermine the effectiveness of your argument. For the most part, experts usually try to be objective and fair-minded when asked for opinions. But, an expert with a vested interest in an issue might slant the testimony in his or her favor. The dentist who has just purchased a huge number of shares in a new toothpaste company would not be an unbiased expert. You wouldn't turn for an unbiased opinion on lung cancer to scientists working for tobacco companies, or ask an employee facing the loss of his or her job to comment on the advisability of layoffs. When you cite authorities, you should be careful to note any possibility of bias so your readers can fairly weigh the contributions. (This is often done through *attribution*; see Chapter 9.) Knowing that Professor Brown's research will benefit from construction of the supercollider doesn't make her enthusiasm for its other potential benefits less credible, but it does help your readers see her contributions to your argument in their proper context.

You should also check the credentials of those experts you are citing as evidence. Certainly claims supported by the research of reliable authorities in the field can add to the validity of your argument. But research is often debated, and evidence often disputed. So you should evaluate the credentials of the expert or experts who conducted the studies—what organizations, institutions, and universities they are affiliated with; their educational background; the books and/or journals where they may have published their results. It would also be wise to familiarize yourself with the actual research to be certain that it looks like valid and convincing support for your argument.

Another faulty use of authority is the use of an expert to provide evidence in a subject area in which he or she possesses no expertise. If you are going to cite authorities, you must make sure that they are competent; they should have expertise in their fields. You wouldn't turn to a professional beekeeper for opinions on laser surgery any more than you would quote a civil engineer on macroeconomic theory. And yet, just that is done all the time in advertising. Although it makes better sense to ask a veterinarian for a professional opinion about what to feed your pet, advertisers hire known actors to push dog food (as well as yogurt and skin cream). Of course, in advertising, celebrity sells. But that's not the case in most written arguments. It would not impress a critical reader to cite Tom Cruise's views on the use of fetal tissue or the greenhouse effect. Again, think about the profile of your audience. Whose expertise would they respect on your topic? Those are the experts to cite.

Factual References and Examples

Facts do as much to inform as they do to persuade, as we mentioned in Chapter 1. If somebody wants to sell you something, they'll pour on the details. For instance, ask the used car salesperson about that red 2003 Ford Explorer in the lot and he or she will hold forth about what a "creampuff" it is: only 18,400 original miles, mint condition, five-speed transmission with overdrive, all-black leather interior, and loaded—AC, power brakes, cruise control, CD player, premium sound system, captain's chair, and so on. Or listen to how the cereal manufacturers inform you that their toasted Os now contain "all-natural oat bran, which has been found to prevent cancer." Information is not always neutral. The very selection process implies intent. By offering specific facts or examples about your claim, you can make a persuasive argument.

The strategy in using facts and examples is to get readers so absorbed in the information that they nearly forget they are being persuaded to buy or do something. So common is this strategy in television ads that some have been given the name "infomercials"—ads that give the impression of being a documentary on the benefits of a product. For instance, you might be familiar with the margarine commercial narrated by a man who announces that at 33 years of age he had a heart attack. He then recounts the advice of his doctor for avoiding coronary disease, beginning with the need for exercise and climaxing with the warning about cutting down on cholesterol. Not until the very end of the ad does the narrator inform us that, taking advantage of his second chance, the speaker has switched to a particular brand of margarine, which, of course, is cholesterol free.

In less blatant form, this "informational" strategy can be found in newspaper columns and editorials, where authors give the impression that they are simply presenting the facts surrounding particular issues when in reality they may be attempting to persuade readers to see things their way. For instance, suppose in an apparently objective commentary a writer discusses how history is replete with people wrongfully executed for first-degree murder. Throughout the piece, the author cites several specific cases in which it was learned too late that the defendant had been framed or that the real killer had confessed. On the surface, the piece may appear to be simply presenting historical facts, but the more subtle intention may be to convince people that capital punishment is morally wrong. The old tagline from *Dragnet,* "Just the facts, ma'am," isn't quite the whole picture. How those facts are used is also part of their persuasive impact.

Often facts and examples are used to establish cause-and-effect relationships. It's very important, when both writing and reading arguments, to test the links the facts forge. While one event may indeed follow another, you can't automatically assume a causal relationship. This can result in a logical fallacy, in this case post hoc, ergo propter hoc. For instance, it may rain the day after every launch of the space shuttle, but does that prove that shuttle launches affect the weather in Florida? Similarly, we are all familiar with politicians who claim credit for improvements in the economy that have little to do with the legislation they have proposed. They hope to gain votes by having the public believe that there is a direct causal relationship between their actions and the economic improvement. Often this strategy backfires when opponents point out the lack of any actual connection.

Sometimes even experts disagree; one might see the rise in prostate cancer rates for vasectomy patients as reason to abolish the surgery; another might point to other contributing causes (diet, lack of exercise, hormonal imbalance). If you don't have the expertise to determine which of the conflicting experts is correct, you'll probably decide based on the *weight of the evidence*—whichever side has the most people or the most plausible reasons supporting it. This, in fact, is how most juries decide cases.

Statistics

People are impressed by numbers. Saying that 77 percent of the student body at your school supports a woman's right to choose is far more persuasive than saying that a lot of people on campus are pro-choice. **Statistics** have a special no-nonsense authority. Batting averages, medical statistics, polling results (election and otherwise), economic indicators, the stock market index, unemployment figures, scientific ratings, FBI statistics, percentages, demographic data—they all are reported in numbers. If they're accurate, statistics are difficult to argue against, though a skillful manipulator can use them to mislead.

The demand for statistics has made market research a huge business in America. During an election year, weekly and daily results on voters' opinions of candidates are released from various news organizations and TV networks, as well as independent polling companies such as the Harris and Gallup organizations. Most of the brand-name products you buy, the TV shows and movies you watch, or the CDs you listen to were made available after somebody did test studies on sample populations to determine the potential success of these items. Those same statistics are then used in promotional ads. Think of the number of times you've heard claims such as these:

"Nine out of ten doctors recommend Zappo aspirin."

"Our new Speed King copier turns out 24 percent more copies per minute."

"Sixty-eight percent of those polled approve of women in military combat roles."

Of course, these claims bear further examination. If you polled only ten doctors, nine of whom recommended Zappo, that's not a big enough sample to imply that 90 percent of *all* doctors do. To avoid drawing a hasty generalization from too small a sample, avoid using sweeping words such as *all, always, never,* or *none.* Either be straightforward about the statistics supporting your claim or limit your claim with qualifiers such as *some, many, often,* or *few.* As Mark Twain once observed, "There are lies, damned lies, and statistics."

Numbers don't lie, but they can be manipulated. Sometimes, to sway an audience, claim makers will cite figures that are inaccurate or dated, or they will intentionally misuse accurate figures to make a case. If, for instance, somebody claims that 139 students and professors protested the invitation of a certain controversial guest to your campus, it would be a distortion of the truth not to mention that another 1,500 attended the talk and gave the speaker a standing ovation. Providing only those numbers or statistics that support the writer's claim and ignoring or concealing figures that might indicate otherwise is one way of stacking the deck. While this practice might deceive—at least temporarily—an uninformed audience, the writer risks damaging his or her credibility once the true figures are revealed.

Be on guard for the misleading use of statistics, a technique used all too frequently in advertising. The manufacturer that claims its flaked corn cereal is 100 percent cholesterol free misleads the public because no breakfast cereal of any brand contains cholesterol (which is found only in animal fats). French fries prepared in pure vegetable oil are also cholesterol free, but that doesn't mean that they're the best food for your health. Manufacturers that use terms like *cholesterol free, light,* and *low fat* are trying to get you to buy their products without really examining the basis for their nutritional claims. Although it's tempting to use such crowd-pleasing statistics, it's a good idea to avoid them in your own arguments because they are deceptive. If your readers discover your deception, your chances of persuading them to accept your position or proposal become unlikely.

Different Interpretations of Evidence

As we already said, evidence consists of solid facts, scientific studies and data, historical analysis, statistics, quotations from accepted authorities, and pertinent examples, as well as personal narratives that your audience will find relevant and compelling.

But not all evidence is of equal worth or value; not all evidence makes an argument valid. And not all scientific facts have a single interpretation. This is why different people can look at the same scientific data and have completely different interpretations. Although they may not argue over facts or the data, they will strenuously debate the interpretations of facts. In fact, some of the most hotly contested issues in society and politics revolve around the interpretation of the evidence. And the reason that people disagree about interpretation is that people hold fundamental differences in underlying beliefs, values, and assumptions.

Different Definitions

People will disagree based on different definitions of terms and concepts. If your parents say to be home at a "reasonable" hour, does that mean 11 p.m. or 2 a.m.? What might be deemed "reasonable" to your parents may not be the same to you, especially if you showed up at 3 a.m. But if they specified to be home no later than 1 a.m., then you have precision, which means a 3 a.m. arrival would not be "reasonable."

The point is that arguments over the definition of a subjective term such as "reasonable" will never resolve the argument. The same is true when critics declare that this book or movie is the "best of the year." There will always be dissenters, even people who may think the selection or award winner was far worse than its competition. Criteria differ from person to person. For instance, what is "violent" to a 16-year-old video game fan is not the same as what is violent to an acknowledged pacifist. What is pornography to some is erotic art to others. In fact, for decades the U.S. Supreme Court could not come up with a clear definition of *pornography* in order to determine laws and regulations and eventually gave up, deciding that any regulation of such— with the exception of child pornography, which is prohibited under law—was an infringement on rights of free speech. Such avoidance by the courts essentially freed itself from the decades-long trap of word play.

The point is that language is relative; it is difficult for people to agree completely on the definition of any complex word. And adding to their complexity are the different connotations of words—connotations that signal different emotional reactions in an audience. Consider such charged words as "evil," "racist," "liberal," "Nazi," "religious extremist," even "terrorist." Often arguments are made in which such terms are employed beyond their dictionary definitions for the purpose of arousing strong reactions. With the proper audience, the effect can be powerful.

Different Interpretations of Tradition and Past Authority

It can be said that evidence sometimes lies in the eyes of the beholder. That is, what is evidence to some people may not be evidence to others. The reason is that writers often appeal to authority and traditions that for them have special weight. This is especially evident in arguments based on moral values and beliefs, such as those regarding the death penalty, euthanasia, abortion, and same-sex marriages. Such appeals may be persuasive to those who believe in the authority or tradition, but not persuasive to others who don't share in those beliefs.

Sometimes people will claim that something is right because it has always been practiced. Consider, for instance, the following statements:

"When we were kids, we walked to school. So, you're not taking the car."

"Women have always taken their husband's last name in marriage, so why should we change now?"

"The ancient Greeks and Romans practiced euthanasia in order to end a patient's unnecessary suffering, so why shouldn't we?"

Each of these claims is a familiar appeal to tradition. Of course, such appeals raise the question that because something is an old practice does not necessarily mean it should be continued today. The logical fallacy is that behavior is never necessarily right simply because it has always been done.

Yet, when the appeal is to a higher authority, then a different set of beliefs and assumptions may prevail. For instance, the dominant argument against gun control is the Second Amendment of the U.S. Constitution guarantee: "A well regulated militia, being necessary to the security of a free state, the right of the people to keep and bear arms, shall not be infringed." For the National Rifle Association and others, those words represent the highest legal authority in preserving and protecting the rights of law-abiding citizens to have guns in our American democracy. But the endless debates on gun control do not center on whether or not people have the right to own guns but on the interpretation of that amendment regarding the regulation of guns. While many people would agree that hunters, sportspeople, and collectors have the right to own guns, nearly everybody would argue that the Second Amendment does not give individuals the unlimited right to own any weapons they like. And that is where the debates become heated—on the question of just how much governmental restriction is too much.

Likewise, the First Amendment is often enlisted as the highest authority on an individual's right to free speech in America. But like gun control, that right is limited by the court's interpretation. You cannot in the eyes of the law intentionally publish lies about a public figure, claiming, for instance, that a local politician sells illegal drugs on the side. Such a claim is libelous and an abridgment of your free-speech rights—and, of course, grounds for a lawsuit. Nor, in the eyes of the law, can you get away with crying "Fire!" in a crowded theater if there is no fire, because the ensuing panic could lead to injury.

While there are some restraints on the rights to free speech, the powerful First Amendment has been invoked to protect flag burning, nude dancing, Internet pornography, Nazi party parades, and Ku Klux Klan rants, to varying degrees of success. And although such claims may seem to undermine the guarantee by protecting dubious and malicious intentions, restriction of the principle could give way to even greater dangers—the tyrannical abuse by government. In several other free and democratic societies, censorship laws empower governments legally to prohibit certain kinds of speech that are protected by the U.S. Constitution.

Religious tradition is another powerful authority that is invoked in arguments on major social issues. References to Biblical or Koranic prohibitions are often presented as evidence against arguments in favor of certain public practices. For instance, consider same-sex marriages. Because of scriptural laws against homosexuality, many people argue that gay and lesbian couples should not be allowed to wed under the eyes of the law. The same is true regarding capital punishment. The Sixth Commandment from the Old Testament of the Bible says, "Thou shall not kill." For years, people opposed to legalized abortion have employed such "evidence." The same Commandment has also been referenced by others in opposition to capital punishment and euthanasia. But the problem with strict appeal to such authority for evidence is that, like tradition, interpretation of religious taboos can be ambiguous and contradictory. For instance, the Old Testament of the Bible also argues, "An eye for an eye, and a tooth for a tooth"—thus, "evidence" that can be enlisted in an argument in favor of the death penalty. Once again, familiarity with your audience should help you determine just the kind of authority and tradition you enlist as evidence. If, for instance, you knew you were addressing religiously conservative readers, summoning the moral import of the scriptures could be very persuasive on some of these public issues.

Different Interpretations of Scientific Data

As we said earlier, scientific data is a persuasive form of evidence. In fact, in most arguments scientific evidence is universally perceived as valid and acceptable. But not everybody interprets scientific evidence in the same way, nor do they draw the same conclusions. For example, one of the most talked about issues of our times is global warming. Over the last several decades, scientific data point to rising average temperatures of the earth's atmosphere and oceans. They also cite the rise in carbon dioxide in the atmosphere, one of the components of the so-called "greenhouse gas." These are the hard facts. Many scientists have looked at the data and determined that there is a direct relationship—namely, that the rise in CO_2 has caused the rise in oceanic and atmospheric temperatures; they blame the effect on human consumption of fossil fuels. These scientists warn that unless something drastic is done, the world's weather will change for the worse for many populated areas, while polar caps will continue to melt and raise sea levels to catastrophic proportions, leading to global coastal flooding.

However, not everybody draws the same conclusion from the data. Not everybody blames the global warming phenomenon on human activity. Nor do they warn of catastrophic climate changes and serious effects on life. Nor do they offer the same political responses. In the following article, scientist Siegfried Frederick Singer responds to the alarms of many, including former vice president Al Gore, narrator of the Academy Award-winning movie, *An Inconvenient Truth*, and author of the book of the same title, and winner of the 2008 Nobel Peace Prize for his work on behalf of the environment.

The Great Global Warming Swindle

S. Fred Singer

Singer, an atmospheric physicist, is a research fellow at the Independent Institute, is Professor Emeritus of Environmental Sciences at the University of Virginia, and is a former founding director of the U.S. Weather Satellite Service. He is author of *Hot Talk, Cold Science: Global Warming's Unfinished Debate* (The Independent Institute, 1997). This article appeared on May 22, 2007, in the *San Francisco Examiner.*

1   Al Gore's *An Inconvenient Truth* has met its match: a devastating documentary recently shown on British television, which has now been viewed by millions of people on the Internet. Despite its flamboyant title, *The Great Global Warming Swindle* is based on sound science and interviews with real climate scientists, including me. *An Inconvenient Truth*, on the other hand, is mostly an emotional presentation from a single politician.

2   The scientific arguments presented in *The Great Global Warming Swindle* can be stated quite briefly:

3   1. There is *no* proof that the current warming is caused by the rise of greenhouse gases from human activity. Ice core records from the past 650,000 years show that temperature increases have *preceded—not resulted from—*increases in CO_2 by hundreds of years, suggesting that the warming of the oceans is an important *source* of the rise in atmospheric CO_2. As the dominant greenhouse gas, water vapor is far, far more important than CO_2. Dire predictions of future warming are based almost entirely on computer climate models, yet these models do not accurately understand the role of water vapor—and, in any case, water vapor is not within our control. Plus, computer models cannot account for the observed cooling of much of the past century (1940–75), nor for the observed *patterns* of warming—what we call the "fingerprints." For example, the Antarctic is cooling while models predict warming. And where the models call for the middle atmosphere to warm faster than the surface, the observations show the exact opposite.

4   The best evidence supporting natural causes of temperature fluctuations are the changes in cloudiness, which correspond strongly with regular variations in solar activity. The current warming is likely part of a natural cycle of climate warming and cooling that's been traced back almost a million years. It accounts for the Medieval Warm Period around 1100 A.D., when the Vikings settled Greenland and grew crops, and the Little Ice Age, from about 1400 to 1850 A.D., which brought severe winters and cold summers to Europe, with failed harvests, starvation, disease, and general misery. Attempts have been made to claim that the current warming is "unusual" using spurious analysis of tree rings and other proxy data. Advocates have tried to deny the existence of these historic climate swings and claim that the current warming is "unusual" by using spurious analysis of tree rings and other proxy data, resulting in the famous "hockey–stick" temperature graph. The hockey-stick graph has now been thoroughly discredited.

5   2. If the cause of warming is mostly natural, then there is little we can do about it. We cannot control the inconstant sun, the likely origin of most climate variability. None of the schemes for greenhouse gas reduction currently bandied about will do any good; they are all irrelevant, useless, and wildly expensive:
      • Control of CO_2 emissions, whether by rationing or elaborate cap-and-trade schemes
      • Uneconomic "alternative" energy, such as ethanol and the impractical "hydrogen economy"
      • Massive installations of wind turbines and solar collectors
      • Proposed projects for the sequestration of CO_2 from smokestacks or even from the atmosphere

6   Ironically, *even if* CO_2 were responsible for the observed warming trend, all these schemes would be ineffective—unless we could persuade every nation, including China, to cut fuel use by 80 percent!

7   3. Finally, no one can show that a warmer climate would produce negative impacts overall. The much-feared rise in sea levels does not seem to depend on short-term temperature changes, as the rate of sea-level increases has been steady

since the last ice age, 10,000 years ago. In fact, many economists argue that the opposite is more likely—that warming produces a net benefit, that it increases incomes and standards of living. Why do we assume that the present climate is the optimum? Surely, the chance of this must be vanishingly small, and the economic history of past climate warmings bear this out.

8   But the main message of *The Great Global Warming Swindle* is much broader. Why should we devote our scarce resources to what is essentially a non-problem, and ignore the real problems the world faces: hunger, disease, denial of human rights—not to mention the threats of terrorism and nuclear wars? And are we really prepared to deal with natural disasters; pandemics that can wipe out most of the human race, or even the impact of an asteroid, such as the one that wiped out the dinosaurs? Yet politicians and the elites throughout much of the world prefer to squander our limited resources to fashionable issues, rather than concentrate on real problems. Just consider the scary predictions emanating from supposedly responsible world figures: the chief scientist of Great Britain tells us that unless we insulate our houses and use more efficient light bulbs, the Antarctic will be the only habitable continent by 2100, with a few surviving breeding couples propagating the human race. Seriously!

9   I imagine that in the not-too-distant future all the hype will have died down, particularly if the climate should decide to cool—as it did during much of the past century; we should take note here that it has not warmed since 1998. Future generations will look back on the current madness and wonder what it was all about. They will have movies like *An Inconvenient Truth* and documentaries like *The Great Global Warming Swindle* to remind them.

The effectiveness of *The Great Global Warming Swindle* rests entirely on a challenge to the validity of the evidence used by those who claim that global warming is caused by greenhouse gases, or emissions due to the burning of fossil fuels. First, Singer discredits these arguments in a general sense, pointing out that they are based on emotion and fear, not on sound science. He then breaks his argument into three parts. In the first, Singer points out that 650,000 years of evidence point to the fact that temperature increases have preceded—not resulted from—increases in CO_2 by hundreds of years. He says scientific evidence shows that the warming of oceans accounts for the rise in atmospheric CO_2. Singer also questions the validity of computer models, the cornerstone of the evidence offered by the global-warming contingent. He points out that computer models do not take into account the role of warming oceans and their impact on water vapor. He notes the role of solar activity and explains how it accounts for the "Medieval Warm Period" around 1100 AD as well as the "Little Ice Age" beginning three hundred years later.

In his second argument, he points out that since global warming is natural little can be done about it. Arguments to develop alternative fuels are expensive and a large drain on the economy. Finally, he says that the fight against global warming diverts resources that should be used to fight bigger issues such as terrorism, nuclear threats, disease, hunger, and human rights.

Some Tips About Supporting Evidence

Because, as argument writers, you'll be using evidence on a routine basis, it will help you to develop a systematic approach to testing the evidence you want to use. Here are some questions to ask yourself about the evidence you enlist in an argument.

Do You Have a Sufficient Number of Examples to Support Your Claim?

You don't want to jump to conclusions based on too little evidence. Suppose you want to make the case that electric cars would be better for the environment than motor vehicles. If all you offer as evidence is the fact that electric vehicles don't pollute the air, your argument would be somewhat thin. Your argument would be much more convincing if you offered the following evidence: that in addition to zero emission at the tailpipe—which is good for the atmosphere—electric cars do not use engine fluids or internal combustion parts, all of which constitute wastes that contaminate our landfills and water supplies. Furthermore, because electric vehicles don't use gasoline or oil, the hazards associated with storage of such fluids are eliminated.

Preview: To Evaluate Supporting Evidence, Ask . . .

- Is the evidence sufficient?
- Is the evidence detailed enough?
- Is the evidence relevant?
- Does the evidence fit the claim?
- Is the evidence up-to-date and verifiable?
- Is the evidence appropriate for the audience?
- Is the evidence biased?
- Is the evidence balanced and fairly presented?

Likewise, you should avoid making hasty generalizations based on your own experience as evidence. For instance, if your Acme Airlines flight to Chattanooga was delayed last week, you shouldn't conclude that Acme Airlines always leaves late. However, you would have a persuasive case were you to demonstrate that over the last six months 47 percent of the frequent flyers you interviewed complained that Acme flights left late.

Is Your Evidence Detailed Enough?

The more specific the details, the more persuasive your argument. Instead of generalizations, cite figures, dates, and facts; instead of paraphrases, offer quotations from experts. Remember that your readers are subconsciously saying, "Show me! Prove it!" If you want to tell people how to bake bread, you wouldn't write, "Mix some flour with some yeast and water"; you'd say, "Dissolve one packet of yeast in 1 cup of warm water and let it sit for ten minutes. Then slowly mix in 3 cups of sifted whole wheat flour." Or, as in our electric car example above, instead of simply asserting that there would be none of the fluid or solid wastes associated with internal combustion vehicles, specify that in electric vehicles there would be no motor oil, engine coolants, transmission fluid or filters, spark plugs, ignition wires, and gaskets to end up in landfills. What your readers want are specifics—and that's what you should give them.

Is Your Evidence Relevant to the Claim You Make or Conclusion You Reach?

Select evidence based on how well it supports the point you are arguing, not on how interesting, novel, or humorous it is or how hard you had to work to find it. Recall that using evidence that is unrelated or irrelevant is a logical fallacy called a non sequitur. For instance, if you are arguing about whether John Lennon was the most influential songwriter in rock-and-roll history, you wouldn't mention that he had two sons or that he owned dairy cattle; those are facts, but they have nothing to do with the influence of his lyrics. Historian Barbara Tuchman relates that in writing *The Guns of August,* she discovered that the Kaiser bought his wife the same birthday present every year: 12 hats of his choosing, which he required her to wear. Tuchman tried to use this detail in Chapter 1, then in Chapter 2, and so on, but was finally obligated to relegate the detail to a stack of notecards marked "Unused." It just didn't fit, even though for her it summarized his stubborn selfishness. (She did work it into a later essay, which is why we know about it.) Learn her lesson: Irrelevant evidence distracts an audience and weakens an argument's persuasive power.

Does Your Conclusion (or Claim) Exceed the Evidence?

Don't make generalizations about entire groups when your evidence points to select members. Baseball may be the national pastime, but it would be unwise to claim that *all* Americans love baseball. Experience tells you that some Americans prefer football or basketball, while others don't like any sports. Claims that are out of proportion to the evidence can result in a fallacy called the **bandwagon appeal.** The bandwagon appeal suggests to the audience that they should agree with the writer because everyone else does, rather than because the writer has supplied compelling evidence to support the reasons and claim. This is a favorite strategy of advertisers, who work to convince us that we should buy a certain product because everyone else is doing so. While this strategy is in itself fallacious, these salespeople are often unable to produce adequate evidence to support their sweeping claims of nationwide popularity for their product.

Is Your Evidence Up-to-Date and Verifiable?

You want to be sure that the evidence you enlist isn't so dated or vague that it fails to support your claim. For instance, figures demonstrating an increase in the rate of teen pregnancy will not persuade your audience if the numbers are ten years old. Similarly, it wouldn't be accurate to say that Candidate Oshawa fails to support the

American worker because 15 years ago he purchased a foreign car. His recent and current actions are far more relevant.

When you're citing evidence, your readers will expect you to be specific enough for them to verify what you say. A writer supporting animal rights may cite the example of rabbits whose eyes were burned by pharmacological testing, but such tests have been outlawed in the United States for many years. Another writer may point to medical research that appears to abuse its human subjects, but not name the researchers, the place where the testing took place, or the year in which it occurred. The readers have no way of verifying the claim and may become suspicious of the entire argument because the factual claims are so difficult to confirm.

Is Your Evidence Appropriate for Your Audience?

As discussed in Chapter 3, before you write, it is important to spend some time identifying the audience you will address in your argument. Knowing your audience helps you determine the slant of your argument as well as your language and voice. Likewise, it will influence the evidence you choose to present, the sources of information you use, and the kind of authorities or experts in the field you cite to support your point of view. And that evidence could help make the difference between a convincing argument and one that fails.

Imagine that you are writing an argument against the use of steroids by college students. If you are writing a paper for your biology professor and are discussing the damaging effect of steroids on the body, you would use highly technical evidence—evidence most likely from medical journals aimed at scientists and medical professionals or from your biology textbook. If, however, you are writing an article for your college newspaper, your audience would be your peers, young adults both male and female who may be experimenting or tempted to experiment with steroids. Your focus might be on issues of peer pressure to look good or to succeed in athletics. Therefore the evidence you select might include quotations from known health professionals published in psychology journals or specialized websites, or from newspaper articles addressing the impact of steroids on one's mental and emotional health. Such evidence would not be highly technical.

Let's take another example. Assume that you decided to write a paper arguing that healthier food should be served in your student cafeteria. If you were addressing your peers, the evidence you cite might come from general publications devoted to nutrition or you might quote one of the many health and diet gurus published widely today. Your evidence would be geared to convince your peers that a healthier diet would lead to healthier and trimmer bodies and possibly better frames of mind. In contrast, if your goal was to convince the university's trustees, your argument would focus on the obligation of the university to provide a healthy diet. You might argue that doing so not only enhances the well-being of the student body but also the reputation of the university. And this enhancement translates into more student applications for admission. To support these arguments you would use evidence based on your own personal experience as well as experiences of your peers. Additionally, evidence taken from publications geared to university administrators would be convincing.

Keep in mind that whether your audience is a peer group, a professor, or a college administrator, you must document your evidence—you must let your reader know where you got your support material. You must document the source of any idea you *summarize* or *paraphrase or quote* directly from. The most widely used forms of documentation used in colleges and universities are the Modern Language Association (MLA) style, used widely in the humanities, and the American Psychological Association (APA) style, used widely in the social sciences. These are explained in greater detail in Chapter 9, Researching Arguments.

Is Your Evidence Slanted?

Sometimes writers select evidence that supports their case while ignoring evidence that does not. Often referred to as stacking the deck, this practice makes for an unfair argument, and one that could be disastrous for the arguer. Even though some of your evidence has merit, your argument will be dismissed if your audience discovers that you slanted or suppressed evidence.

For example, suppose you heard a friend make the following statements: "If I were you, I'd avoid taking a course with Professor Gorman at all costs. He gives surprise quizzes, he assigns 50 pages a night, and he refuses to grade on a curve." Even if these reasons are true, that may not be the whole truth. Suppose you learned that Professor Gorman is, in fact, a very dynamic and talented teacher whose classes successfully stimulate the learning process. By holding back that information, your friend's argument is suspect.

Sometimes writers will take advantage of their readers' lack of information on a topic and offer evidence that really doesn't support their claims. Recently several newspapers reported that a study written up in the *Archives of Internal Medicine* proved that eating nuts prevents heart attacks. According to the study, some thirty thousand Seventh-Day Adventists were asked to rate the frequency with which they ate certain foods. Those claiming to eat nuts five or more times a week reported fewer heart attacks. What the newspapers failed to report was that most Seventh-Day Adventists are vegetarians, and that those who ate more nuts also ate fewer dairy products (which are high in cholesterol and saturated fat, both of which contribute to heart disease) and eggs (also high in cholesterol) than others in the study. Newspapers have failed to report that all the subsequent pro-nut publicity was distributed by a nut growers' association.[1]

It is to your benefit to present all relevant evidence so that you clearly weigh both sides of an issue. As we discussed in Chapter 4, you want to demonstrate to your readers that you have made an effort to consider other perspectives and that your conclusions are fair and balanced. Otherwise your argument might not be taken seriously. Let's return to the argument that electric cars are more beneficial to the environment than cars with internal combustion engines. Your key evidence is the fact that electric cars do not use petroleum products and various motor parts that contribute to the pollution of air, land, and waterways. If you left your argument at that,

---

[1]Mirkin, Gabe, and Diana Rich. *Fat Free Flavor Full*. Boston: Little, Brown, 1995, 51.

you would be guilty of suppressing an important concern regarding electric vehicles: the disposal of the great amounts of lead in the huge electric vehicles' batteries. Failure to acknowledge that opposing point reduces your credibility as a writer. Readers would wonder either about your attempt at deception or about your ignorance. Either way, they would dismiss your argument.

To Test Your Evidence for Logical Fallacies, Ask These Questions

Stacking the deck	Did I present evidence that only supports my point of view? Have I withheld evidence that might contradict it?
Non sequitur	Is my evidence related and relevant to the reasons or claim it is supporting?
Hasty generalization	Have I provided sufficient evidence to support my conclusions?
Dicto simpliciter	Does my evidence cover exceptions to any generalizations that I've made?
Red herring	Does all of my evidence pertain to the true issue? Have I tried to distract my audience's attention with irrelevant concerns?
Bandwagon appeal	Can my evidence stand on its own? Have I argued that my audience should support my ideas because they reflect a popular viewpoint?
Faulty use of authority	Are the authorities I cite actually experts in my subject area? Could my authorities be biased because of their background or their professional or political associations?

A much better strategy would be to confront this concern and then try to overcome it. While acknowledging that lead is a dangerous pollutant, you could point out that more than 95 percent of battery lead is recycled. You could also point out that progress is being made to improve battery technology and create alternatives such as the kinds of fuel cells used in spacecraft.[2] The result is a balanced presentation that makes your own case stronger.

---

[2]May, Thomas, J. "Electric Cars Will Benefit the Environment and the Economy." *Boston Globe* 10 Aug. 1994: 15.

In summary, using evidence means putting yourself in an advocate's place. You'll probably do this while building your argument, and certainly when you revise; then you should see yourself as an advocate for the other side and scrutinize your evidence as if you were going to challenge it in court. As a reader, you need to keep that Missouri "show me!" attitude in mind at all times. A little healthy skepticism will help you test the information you're asked to believe. The next chapter will help you do so.

SAMPLE ARGUMENT FOR ANALYSIS

The following is a paper written by a student, Arthur Allen. In it, Allen considers the high rate of recidivism in America—that is, convicts committing more crimes after they've been released from prison. In his paper, he argues that religion might be a better form of rehabilitation than just more harsh punishment. Read the essay carefully and take notes about it in your argument journal. Then, either individually or in your peer group, answer the questions that follow. Notice the style is MLA, which is discussed in the documentation guide.

Allen 1

Arthur Allen
Professor Capobianco
English 097
February 22, 2005

Prayer in Prison: Religion as Rehabilitation

1   Prisons don't work if the prisoners are released only to commit more crimes. Unfortunately, that happens all too frequently. In fact, the phenomenon is known as recidivism—that is, a convict re-offends after having been released from confinement. The challenge faced within prisons across America is how best to minimize recidivism in order to ensure that the convicts do not commit more crimes. There are two main schools of thought regarding the prevention of recidivism: increasing the harshness of the punishment (most often by increasing time in prison) or offering convicts rehabilitation programs.

---

2   The Canadian crime-reduction research
group, Canada Safety Council, found that
"[T]here is little evidence that harsh penalties
are the best way to prevent further offences."
The council cites studies in Australia, Canada,
and America, all pointing to this conclusion. In
fact, the group finds that "long prison
sentences without other remedial programs may
actually increase the chances of re-offending
after release" (CSC). However, a seemingly more
effective method of reducing recidivism, while
largely controversial, is rehabilitation, more
often than not using a religious basis.

3   The obvious concern with religion-based
rehabilitation is the perceived clash with the
Constitution, which prohibits the government from
making any "law respecting an establishment of
religion or forbidding free exercise thereof"
(O'Connor 531). There are no questions, however,
about its effectiveness: In Texas, about 40% of
parolees who do not participate in any form of
rehabilitation program return to prison within
three years; in the same amount of time, less than
5% of those who participated in a rehabilitation
program were rearrested (Bradley). Other
implementations of these types of programs have
been comparably successful in Louisiana (van Wel)
as well as in Iowa, Kansas and Minnesota (Alter).

4   One of the major rehabilitation programs
nationally is the Interchange Freedom Initiative
(IFI) Program, a third-party rehabilitation
program based on offering religion to inmates.
Sam Dye, director of the Interchange program in
Iowa says,

          The only true lasting change that
          is worth anything is change that
          comes from the inside out, change

                                                  Allen 3

           from the heart. You can coerce a
           person, from the outside, to do
           what you want them to do, but once
           that external pressure is gone,
           typically people go back to act
           the way they did before. So if you
           really want to change a person,
           you have to get a hold of their
           heart. (Bradley)

This seems to make sense: The prisoner must be
changed from the inside out in order to keep that
prisoner from committing a future crime. That is
to say, prisoners will not change simply because
they have been told they were wrong or because
they were punished severely. Recidivism occurs
when there is no change in the status quo of the
life of the criminal. If a person is pushed to
the point where he or she needs to sell drugs and
rob stores in order to pay the bills, a harsh
prison life will not change that situation.

5   However, the question surrounding
rehabilitation programs is not about their
effectiveness but about their constitutionality.
Les Nester, a lawyer and critic of the IFI
program, says, "the concerns would be that the
state is actually promoting and advancing
Christianity. If you look at the programming,
it is very sectarian, very evangelical
programming. . . . I think the IFI program is a
brainwash tactic." He argues that since the
state government is promoting the use of
rehabilitation programs that use Christianity
as a way to rehabilitate criminals, the state
is declaring affiliation with a specific
religion. However, the IFI is not purely a
Christian program. It incorporates many faiths,
including Judaism and Islam, in its treatment

Allen 4

of prisoners. One graduate of the program
states, "I think Islam has everything to do
with my growth and development and my
transformation that I have accomplished, in the
sense that Islam taught me for the first time
what it is to take responsibility for my
actions" (Neary).

6   The argument for inclusion of any religion
rather then exclusion of all religions is summed
up succinctly in an article written by William
Bennett featured in the book Opposing Viewpoints.
In his article he stated, "The First Amendment
does not require the government to be neutral on
the subject of religion. It requires it to be
neutral only on any one particular form of
religion" (Dudley 54). In other words, while the
government should not show favoritism toward one
particular religion, it also does not have the
obligation of pretending religion does not
exist. Thus, this distinction allows the
government to sponsor religious programs in the
context of furthering the social good (reduction
of crime) as long as it does not promote one
religious program over another.

7   In another article in the same book Opposing
Viewpoints, John Swomley argues that the
government could not give funding to one religious
group without giving funding to all religious
groups; this argument then implies that the
government could not provide any funding to
religious rehabilitation programs in prisons if it
did not give funding to all 300-plus religious
groups (Dudley 62). This argument is backwards:
The government is free to give money to any
religious group it sees fit. It is prohibited,
however, from denying one group funding in the

same situation where it would grant another group that same funding. To say that the government is responsible for giving "all or none" to religious groups would be like saying the government is required to either employ all races in government positions or employ none of them. If a religion-based rehabilitation program wants to operate, it should not be denied funds, but should be funded equally as all other religion-based rehabilitation programs representing different faiths.

8   Furthermore, civil liberties groups have actually held back from suing the IFI program because it provides a number of unique services including a support community both for convicts in prison and for those who have been released. As one graduate of the IFI program puts it, "Now I have someone I can call, even in the middle of the night. And when I start feeling bad ... who you gonna call? You call your brother, he uses drugs. You call your sister, she's using drugs. Mom's upset with you. Dad's gone. Whereas, with IFI, I was given a family." In other words, because it is a third-party non-profit program the IFI is not only able to reach prisoners in a way government officials can't by offering spiritual growth and continuity, but also it provides follow-through support after prison by offering a new family to which the convicts feel a sense of loyalty and responsibility (Bradley).

9   As an alternative to harsher punishments, rehabilitation is clearly superior. When prison is the necessary evil in a person's life, the harshness of it will make little difference. The change must truly come from the inside out. And faith-based rehabilitation programs have proven successful.

Allen 6

Works Cited

Alter, Alexandra. "Study Touts Faith-Based
    Prison Rehabilitation Program." The Pew
    Forum on Religion and Public Life. 19 June
    2003 <http://pewforum.org/news/
    display.php?NewsID=2333>.

Bradley, Barbra. God Pods, NPR News. Iowa, 2001.

Canada Safety Council. Crime, Punishment Safety.
    2004. <http://www.safety-council.org/info/
    community/crime.html>.

Dudley, William, et al. Religion in America:
    Opposing Viewpoints. San Diego: Greenhaven
    Press, 2001.

Neary, Lynn. Sing Sing Studies. NPR News,
    Washington DC. 1998.

O'Connor, Karen, and Larry J. Sabato. American
    Government: Continuity and Change, 2004
    Edition. New York: Pearson Education, 2004.

Van Wel, Alex. "US Prison Rehabilitation Through
    Faith." BBC News. 2 Oct. 2002 <http://
    news.bbc.co.uk/1/hi/americas/2284591.stm>.

QUESTIONS FOR ANALYSIS AND DISCUSSION ─────

1. What claim (Chapter 1) is Allen arguing? What are the reasons for his claim? What do you think the pros and cons he listed in developing this argument might have been?

2. Who is Allen's target audience? What clues does he give you? What values and prejudices might the readership hold?

3. What different forms of evidence (personal, outside authorities, factual references, statistics) does Allen provide? Which form(s) of evidence does he rely on most?

4. Evaluate the supporting evidence that Allen provides. Is it relevant? Is it detailed enough? Does it seem dated and verifiable? Does his claim exceed his evidence? Does his evidence strike you as slanted? If you were his reader, would you be persuaded by his reasons? What

changes (if any) in evidence would you recommend to help him make his argument more persuasive?

5. Use debate, dialogue, and deliberation to respond to Allen's essay in your journal. See Chapter 1 to review this process.

   a. Create a dialogue to help you understand and respond productively to Allen's ideas.

   b. Given what you've learned through debate and dialogue, write at least a page in which you deliberate about the conflicting issues that Allen raises in his essay. How does your understanding of Allen's position change or modify your own viewpoint? Is there a way to reconcile conflicting concerns about this subject?

CHAPTER 7

Establishing Claims
Thinking Like a Skeptic

You have decided the issue you're going to argue. With the aid of debate and dialogue, you've sharpened your ideas and considered alternative perspectives and common concerns. You've thought about your audience and determined what you have in common, where you might agree, and where you might disagree. After deliberating, you have formulated a working claim, and you have gathered solid evidence to support it. Now it's time to establish the logical structure of your argument and decide how best to arrange this material to persuade your readers.

If you've ever tried handing in a paper made up of slapped-together evidence and first-draft organization, you've probably discovered a blueprint for disaster. Perhaps you didn't test your work, didn't revise it, or didn't think about how it would appeal to a reader. You assumed that because *you* understood how the parts fit together, your readers would as well. To help you detect and correct these problems, this chapter focuses on thinking like a *skeptic*—a skeptical building inspector, to be exact—because a skeptical attitude works best.

To construct a persuasive argument, one that has a chance of convincing your readers, you have to pay careful attention to the logical structure you are building. You can't take anything for granted; you have to question every step you take, every joist and joint. You have to ask yourself if you're using the right material for the right purpose, the right tool at the right time. In other words, you have to think like a building inspector examining a half-built two-story house—one whose builder is notoriously crafty at compromising quality. A healthy skepticism—and a logical system—help uncover flaws before they create a disaster.

The Toulmin Model

Stephen Toulmin, a British philosopher and logician, analyzed hundreds of arguments from various fields of politics and law.[1] He concluded that nearly every argument has certain patterns and parts. The best arguments, Toulmin found, are those addressed to

---

[1]Toulmin, Stephen. *The Uses of Argument.* Cambridge: Cambridge UP, 1958.

a skeptical audience, one eager to question the reasoning where it seems faulty, to demand support for wobbly assumptions, and to raise opposing reasons.

The slightly retooled version of the Toulmin model we describe below encourages you to become a skeptical audience. It provides useful everyday terms to help you unearth, weigh, and, if necessary, fix an argument's logical structures. It lets you verify that the major premises in your argument or those of your opposition are clear and accurate, helps you determine whether repairs to your claims are needed and whether counterarguments are addressed. It shows you where supporting evidence may be needed and helps you avoid logical fallacies. And, since Toulmin's terms are designed to be broadly practical, they allow you to present your case to a wide variety of readers.

Toulmin's Terms

According to Toulmin, a fully developed argument has six parts. They are the *claim,* the *grounds,* the *warrant,* the *backing,* the *qualifiers,* and the *rebuttals.*

The Claim

The **claim** is the assertion you are trying to prove—the same term as discussed in Chapter 1. It is the position you take in your argument, often as a proposal with which you are asking your reader to agree. In a well-constructed argument, each part makes its ultimate claim, its conclusion, seem inevitable.

The Grounds

Just as every argument contains a claim, every claim needs supporting evidence. The **grounds** are the hard data—statistics, research studies, facts, and examples that bolster your claim and that your audience accepts without requiring further proof.

The Warrant

The claim is usually stated explicitly. However, underlying the claim are a number of assumptions and principles that are also critical to the success of your argument. These are the **warrants** that implicitly support your argument by connecting your claim to the grounds. They enable your audience to follow the reasoning in your argument. They explain why the hard evidence supports your claim. So the success of your argument depends on whether the audience accepts these often half-buried assumptions, commonly held values, legal or moral principles, laws of nature, commonsense knowledge, or shared beliefs.

Let's look at a few examples. We are all familiar with the advertiser that promises that its shampoo will eliminate dandruff. The basic **claim** here is that you should shampoo your hair with this manufacturer's product. And as **grounds** the manufacturer says that studies have shown that 60 percent of those people who use their shampoo no longer have dandruff. One underlying **warrant** here is that people don't want dandruff—a commonly held assumption that you share with your audience. Another is that we assume 60 percent to be a sufficient proportion to accept the claim. Because warrants are based on commonly held values or patterns of reasoning, they are not easily detected. Here's another example:

> **Claim:** Cigarette smoking is harmful to your health.
>
> **Grounds:** The U.S. Surgeon General has warned that cigarettes cause a number of diseases including cancer, heart trouble, and injury to fetuses in pregnant women.
>
> **Warrant:** The Surgeon General is a medical authority we can trust.

At times, warrants can be a challenge to determine since they are often based on unstated but commonly held assumptions. And that is why it is important to find them. More on that below.

The Backing

Because your warrant is an assumption, you cannot be certain that it will always be accepted by your readers. So you must provide reasons to back it up. These reasons, called **backing,** indicate that the warrant is reliable in a particular argument, though it doesn't have to be true in all cases at all times.

The Qualifiers

Qualifiers provide a way to indicate when, why, and how your claim and warrant are reliable. They're words or phrases such as *often, probably, possibly, almost always;* verbs like *may* and *might, can* and *could;* or adjectives and adverbs that yoke your claim to some condition. The subtlest kind of qualifier is an adjective that acknowledges that your claim is true to a degree: "Coming from a dysfunctional family *often* makes it *harder* to resist the angry lure of crime." The qualifiers *often* and *harder* imply that the statement is conditional and not absolute. They allow for exceptions.

You need to consider a few guidelines about using qualifiers; like antibiotics, they're too powerful to use unwisely. Using too few qualifiers can indicate that you're exaggerating your argument's validity. As we've mentioned in previous chapters, common fallacies, such as *hasty generalizations,* are often potentially valid arguments that go astray by not qualifying their claims enough, if at all. Using *no* qualifiers can result in a claim that is too general and sweeping. Although many students think a qualified claim is a weak claim, in fact, the qualified claim is often the most persuasive. Few truths are *completely* true; few claims are *always* right. A well-qualified claim, then, shows that the writer respects both the difficulty of the issue and the intelligence of the reader.

Nevertheless, qualifiers alone cannot substitute for reasoning your way to the tough, subtle distinctions on which the most persuasive arguments depend. For example, look at the claim that "Innocent people have an inviolable right to life." It's wisely qualified with the word "innocent" since just saying "People have an inviolable right to life" wouldn't hold up. Hitler, after all, was human. Did he too have "an inviolable right to life"? But even *innocent* is not qualification enough. It raises too many tough, troubling questions. "Innocent" of what? "Innocent" by whose judgment, and why? What if killing a few innocent people were the only way to end a war that is killing *many* innocent people?

Using a lot of qualifiers, therefore, is no guarantee that your argument is carefully reasoned. In fact, strongly qualifying your argument's claim may be a sign that you doubt your argument's validity. But such doubt can itself be encouraging. Misusing or overusing qualifiers can indicate that your instinct of anxiety is right—that you've discovered better reasons to doubt your initial argument than to defend it. In fact, acknowledging the appeal of a flawed claim—and describing how you only discovered its flaws once you tried trumpeting its strengths—is an effective way of earning the reader's respect. It shows you to be an honest arguer capable of learning from errors—and thus worth learning *from*.

Deciding what to state and what to imply is a large part of writing any good argument. Just as a building's cross-beams don't have to be visible to be working, not everything important in an argument has to be stated. For example, if someone were to claim that winters in Minnesota are "mostly long and cold," we probably wouldn't stop the flow of argument to ask him to define the qualifier *mostly*. We'd instead keep the qualifier in mind, and let the Minnesotan's definition of "mostly" emerge, implied, from the rest of the story. Similarly, it's sometimes wise to leave your argument's qualifiers implied.

Still, it's often better to risk belaboring the obvious. To minimize the chances that your reader will misunderstand (or altogether miss) your meaning, qualify your claims as clearly and explicitly as possible. "Reading" the argument you're writing like a skeptical reader will help you decide which qualifiers are needed, where they are needed, and how explicitly they need to be stated.

The Rebuttals

Reading your argument skeptically also allows you to participate, answer, and even preempt rebuttals. **Rebuttals** represent the exceptions to the claim. There are many different kinds of rebuttals, and any persuasive argument ought to acknowledge and incorporate the most important ones. Rebuttals are like large-scale qualifiers. They acknowledge and explain the conditions or situations in which your claim would not be true—while still proving how your claim *is* true under other conditions. It's wise, then, to anticipate such rebuttals by regularly acknowledging all your argument's limits. This acknowledgment will prompt you to craft your claims more carefully.

Let's say, for example, that a sportswriter argues that allowing big-market baseball teams to monopolize talent ruins competition by perpetuating dynasties. Your rebuttal might be to cite the overlooked grounds of ignored evidence—grounds that complicate, if not contradict, the writer's claim: "Then why have small-market teams won four of the last ten World Series?" Had the sportswriter anticipated and integrated this rebuttal, she could have improved the argument—from her warrant on up. Her argument could have taken into account this rebuttal in the form of more careful qualifications. "While the rule of money doesn't guarantee that the richer teams will always win the World Series, it does make it more difficult for hard-pressed teams to compete for available talent." This is now, of course, a less sweeping claim—and, therefore, more precise and persuasive.

Of course, no writer can anticipate their readers' every rebuttal, nor should the writer even try. But you should test your argument by trying to rebut it yourself or working with classmates in small groups. Then revise your arguments with those rebuttals in mind.

	Review: Six Parts of an Argument	
	Claim	The assertion you are trying to prove
	Grounds	The supporting evidence for the claim
	Warrant	A generalization that explains why the evidence supports the claim
	Backing	The reasons that show the warrant is reliable
	Qualifiers	The words that show when, how, and why your claim is reliable
	Rebuttal	The exceptions to the claim

Finding Warrants

Finding your warrants in order to explicate your argument can help you in several ways: You persuade your reader more effectively, detect flaws in your own argument, and identify the cause of otherwise confusing debates more quickly.

For example, let's say you want to argue the claim that all students in American schools should be taught in English rather than in the students' native or family languages. The grounds supporting this claim are results of research showing a high correlation between English fluency and socioeconomic success.

For your audience to accept the connection between your claim and your grounds, you and they must agree on several warrants that underlie it. (Remember that warrants are underlying assumptions or common knowledge.) The first might be the assumption that schools prepare students for socioeconomic success in U.S. society. Since one of the purposes of an education is to develop skills such as reading, writing, and thinking critically, skills that are considered basic requirements for success, most of your audience would likely accept this assumption. Therefore, it can be left implied and unstated.

The second warrant implied by your claim may not be as readily acceptable to your audience as the one above and will need to be explicitly supported in your essay: that our English language skills affect whether we are successful. The third warrant, implied by the second, is that individuals who are not fluent in English will not be successful members of society. These warrants will need considerable backing to show that they are reliable. How do English language skills enable individuals to attain socioeconomic success? How are individuals who lack fluency in English adversely affected? You will want to provide additional backing in the form of evidence, examples, and statistics to demonstrate that English language skills have a significant impact on an individual's chances for social and economic success.

Your fourth and final warrant is particularly important because it establishes a critical link between your claim that all students should be taught in English and the need for fluency to succeed. This warrant assumes nonnative speaking students will achieve greater fluency in English in the English-only classroom. You will need additional backing to prove this warrant, especially when you take into account possible rebuttals. For instance, what about students who enter U.S. schools with no English skills at all? How can they learn the required curriculum with no fluency in English? Will English-only classrooms fail to teach them language skills as well as subject matter? Will this approach alienate them from the American educational system and, thus, from success in our society? Making your responses to these rebuttals explicit will strengthen your argument.

Using Toulmin's approach to analyze your argument allows you to dig beneath the surface of your claim to find the underlying assumptions that form its foundation. It also allows your audience to see that even if they disagree with your claim, they may agree with many of the principles and assumptions that support it. Revealing this common ground, however hidden it lies, can provide opportunities to begin a dialogue that emerges from the recognition of shared values and beliefs. For instance, take the notoriously divisive issue of capital punishment. Those who support capital punishment say, in essence, "A human life is so precious that anyone who is guilty of depriving another of it should forfeit his or her own life." The opposing side says, in effect, "Human life is so precious that we have no right to deprive another of it no matter what the cause." By digging down to the warrants that underlie these positions, we may be surprised to find that the two sides have much in common: a respect for and appreciation of the value of human life. This discovery, of course, is no guarantee that we can reconcile dramatically opposing views on a particular issue. But the recognition of commonality might provide a first step toward increasing understanding—if not consensus—between opposing sides.

Digging deeply to excavate your warrants can also help you avoid two common logical fallacies: post hoc, ergo propter hoc and slippery slope arguments. A post hoc, ergo propter hoc fallacy occurs when the writer mistakenly draws a causal relationship between two or more events or situations that are unrelated or simply coincidental. Similarly, a slippery slope argument is based on an assumption that a particular outcome is inevitable if certain events happen or if a situation is allowed to continue. In both cases, the writer fails to identify and support the underlying warrants that would create a convincing logical link.

To Avoid Errors in Logic, Check for These Logical Fallacies

Post hoc, ergo propter hoc	Be certain to demonstrate a cause-effect relationship between events by uncovering all warrants that underlie your claim.
Slippery slope argument	Make explicit the chain of events that link a situation to its possible outcome. Provide proof that this progression will inevitably occur.

Warrants	
Notice the many layers of warrants that can underlie a single claim:	
Claim	All students in American public schools should be taught in English-only classrooms.
Grounds	Research shows high correlation between English fluency and socioeconomic success in America.
Warrant	Schools prepare students for success in our society.
Warrant	Success in American society can be determined by our English language skills.
Warrant	Individuals who are not fluent in English will not succeed in our society.
Warrant	Teaching classes only in the English language will ensure that students will be fluent in English.

SAMPLE ARGUMENTS FOR ANALYSIS

Now let's turn to two sample arguments to see how our version of the Toulmin model can help you test your own arguments more effectively. The first piece, originally published in the *New York Times Magazine,* provides a very logical but highly provocative argument about a crime that has received considerable media attention: infanticide. The author, Steven Pinker, who wrote this piece while director of the Center for Cognitive Neuroscience at Massachusetts Institute of Technology, is currently the Johnstone Family Professor of Psychology in the Department of Psychology at Harvard University. He is the author of *How the Mind Works* (1997) and most recently *The Stuff of Thought* (2007). Following Pinker's essay is a point-by-point counterargument (page 209) by Michael Kelley published a few days later in the *New York Times.*

Why They Kill Their Newborns

Steven Pinker

1   Killing your baby. What could be more depraved? For a woman to destroy the fruit of her womb would seem like an ultimate violation of the natural order. But every year, hundreds of women commit neonaticide: They kill their newborns or let them die. Most neonaticides remain undiscovered, but every once in a while a janitor follows a trail of blood to a tiny body in a trash bin, or a woman faints and doctors find the remains of a placenta inside her.

2   Two cases have recently riveted the American public. Last November, Amy Grossberg and Brian Peterson, 18-year-old college sweethearts, delivered their baby in a motel room and, according to prosecutors, killed him and left his body in a dumpster. They will go on trial for murder next year and, if convicted, could be sentenced to death. In June, another 18-year-old, Melissa Drexler, arrived at her high-school prom, locked herself in a bathroom stall, gave birth to a boy and left him dead in a garbage can. Everyone knows what happened next: she touched herself up and returned to the dance floor. In September, a grand jury indicted her for murder.

3   How could they do it? Nothing melts the heart like a helpless baby. Even a biologist's cold calculations tell us that nurturing an offspring that carries our genes is the whole point of our existence. Neonaticide, many think, could be only a product of pathology. The psychiatrists uncover childhood trauma. The defense lawyers argue temporary psychosis. The pundits blame a throwaway society, permissive sex education and, of course, rock lyrics.

4   But it's hard to maintain that neonaticide is an illness when we learn that it has been practiced and accepted in most cultures throughout history. And that neonaticidal women do not commonly show signs of psychopathology. In a classic 1970 study of statistics of child killing, a psychiatrist, Phillip Resnick, found that mothers who kill their *older* children are frequently psychotic, depressed or suicidal, but mothers who kill their newborns are usually not. (It was this difference that led Resnick to argue that the category infanticide be split into neonaticide, the killing of a baby on the day of its birth, and filicide, the killing of a child older than one day.)

5   Killing a baby is an immoral act, and we often express our outrage at the immoral by calling it a sickness. But normal human motives are not always moral, and neonaticide does not have to be a product of malfunctioning neural circuitry or a dysfunctional upbringing. We can try to understand what would lead a mother to kill her newborn, remembering that to understand is not necessarily to forgive.

6   Martin Daly and Margo Wilson, both psychologists, argue that a capacity for neonaticide is built into the biological design of our parental emotions. Mammals are extreme among animals in the amount of time, energy and food they invest in their young, and humans are extreme among mammals. Parental investment is a limited resource, and mammalian mothers must "decide" whether to allot it to their newborn or to their current and future offspring. If a newborn is sickly, or if its survival is not promising, they may cut their losses and favor the healthiest in the litter or try again later on.

7   In most cultures, neonaticide is a form of this triage. Until very recently in human evolutionary history, mothers nursed their children for two to four years before becoming fertile again. Many children died, especially in the perilous first year. Most women saw no more than two or three of their children survive to adulthood, and many did not see any survive. To become a grandmother, a woman had to make hard choices. In most societies documented by anthropologists, including those of hunter-gatherers (our best glimpse into our ancestors' way of life), a woman lets a newborn die when its prospects for survival to adulthood are poor. The forecast might be based on abnormal signs in the infant, or on bad circumstances for successful motherhood at the time—she might be burdened with older children, beset by

war or famine or without a husband or social support. Moreover, she might be young enough to try again.

8   We are all descendants of women who made the difficult decisions that allowed them to become grandmothers in that unforgiving world, and we inherited that brain circuitry that led to those decisions. Daly and Wilson have shown that the statistics on neonaticide in contemporary North America parallel those in the anthropological literature. The women who sacrifice their offspring tend to be young, poor, unmarried and socially isolated.

9   Natural selection cannot push the buttons of behavior directly; it affects our behavior by endowing us with emotions that coax us toward adaptive choices. New mothers have always faced a choice between a definite tragedy now and the possibility of an even greater tragedy months or years later, and that choice is not to be taken lightly. Even today, the typical rumination of a depressed new mother—how will I cope with this burden?—is a legitimate concern. The emotional response called bonding is also far more complex than the popular view, in which a woman is imprinted with a lifelong attachment to her baby if they interact in a critical period immediately following the baby's birth. A new mother will first coolly assess the infant and her current situation and only in the next few days begin to see it as a unique and wonderful individual. Her love will gradually deepen in ensuing years, in a trajectory that tracks the increasing biological value of a child (the chance that it will live to produce grandchildren) as the child proceeds through the mine field of early development.

10   Even when a mother in a hunter-gatherer society hardens her heart to sacrifice a newborn, her heart has not turned to stone. Anthropologists who interview these women (or their relatives, since the event is often too painful for the woman to discuss) discover that the women see the death as an unavoidable tragedy, grieve at the time and remember the child with pain all their lives. Even the supposedly callous Melissa Drexler agonized over a name for her dead son and wept at his funeral. (Initial reports that, after giving birth, she requested a Metallica song from the deejay and danced with her boyfriend turned out to be false.)

11   Many cultural practices are designed to distance people's emotions from a newborn until its survival seems probable. Full personhood is often not automatically granted at birth, as we see in our rituals of christening and the Jewish bris. And yet the recent neonaticides will seem puzzling. These are middle-class girls whose babies would have been kept far from starvation by the girl's parents or by any of thousands of eager adoptive couples. But our emotions, fashioned by the slow hand of natural selection, respond to the signals of the long-vanished tribal environment in which we spent 99 percent of our evolutionary history. Being young and single are two bad omens for successful motherhood, and the girl who conceals her pregnancy and procrastinates over its consequences will soon be disquieted by a third omen. She will give birth in circumstances that are particularly unpromising for a human mother: alone.

12   In hunter-gatherer societies, births are virtually always assisted because human anatomy makes birth (especially the first one) long, difficult and risky. Older women act as midwives, emotional supports and experienced appraisers who help decide whether the infant should live. Wenda Trevathan, an anthropologist and trained midwife, has studied pelvises of human fossils and concluded that childbirth has been

physically torturous, and therefore probably assisted, for millions of years. Maternal feelings may be adapted to a world in which a promising newborn is heralded with waves of cooing and clucking and congratulating. Those reassuring signals are absent from a secret birth in a motel room or a bathroom stall.

13 So what is the mental state of a teen-age mother who has kept her pregnancy secret? She is immature enough to have hoped that her pregnancy would go away by itself, her maternal feelings have been set at zero and she suddenly realizes she is in big trouble.

14 Sometimes she continues to procrastinate. In September, 17-year-old Shanta Clark gave birth to a premature boy and kept him hidden in her bedroom closet, as if he were E.T., for 17 days. She fed him before and after she went to school until her mother discovered him. The weak cry of the preemie kept him from being discovered earlier. (In other cases, girls have panicked over the crying and, in stifling the cry, killed the baby.)

15 Most observers sense the desperation that drives a woman to neonaticide. Prosecutors sometimes don't prosecute; juries rarely convict; those found guilty almost never go to jail. Barbara Kirwin, a forensic psychologist, reports that in nearly 300 cases of women charged with neonaticide in the United States and Britain, no woman spent more than a night in jail. In Europe, the laws of several countries prescribed less-severe penalties for neonaticide than for adult homicides. The fascination with the Grossberg-Peterson case comes from the unusual threat of the death penalty. Even those in favor of capital punishment might shudder at the thought of two reportedly nice kids being strapped to gurneys and put to death.

16 But our compassion hinges on the child, not just on the mother. Killers of older children, no matter how desperate, evoke little mercy. Susan Smith, the South Carolina woman who sent her two sons, 14 months and 3 years old, to watery deaths, is in jail, unmourned, serving a life sentence. The leniency shown to neonaticidal mothers forces us to think the unthinkable and ask if we, like many societies and like the mothers themselves, are not completely sure whether a neonate is a full person.

17 It seems obvious that we need a clear boundary to confer personhood on a human being and grant it a right to life. Otherwise, we approach a slippery slope that ends in the disposal of inconvenient people or in grotesque deliberations on the value of individual lives. But the endless abortion debate shows how hard it is to locate the boundary. Anti-abortionists draw the line at conception, but that implies we should shed tears every time an invisible conceptus fails to implant in the uterus—and, to carry the argument to its logical conclusion, that we should prosecute for murder anyone who uses an IUD. Those in favor of abortion draw the line at viability, but viability is a fuzzy gradient that depends on how great a risk of an impaired child the parents are willing to tolerate. The only thing both sides agree on is that the line must be drawn at some point before birth.

18 Neonaticide forces us to examine even that boundary. To a biologist, birth is as arbitrary a milestone as any other. Many mammals bear offspring that see and walk as soon as they hit the ground. But the incomplete 9-month-old human fetus must be evicted from the womb before its oversized head gets too big to fit through its mother's pelvis. The usual primate assembly process spills into the first years in the world. And that complicates our definition of personhood.

19   What makes a living being a person with a right not to be killed? Animal-rights extremists would seem to have the easiest argument to make: that all sentient beings have a right to life. But champions of that argument must conclude that delousing a child is akin to mass murder; the rest of us must look for an argument that draws a small circle. Perhaps only the members of our own species, Homo sapiens, have a right to life? But that is simply chauvinism; a person of one race could just as easily say that people of another race have no right to life.

20   No, the right to life must come, the moral philosophers say, from morally significant traits that we humans happen to possess. One such trait is having a unique sequence of experiences that defines us as individuals and connects us to other people. Other traits include an ability to reflect upon ourselves as a continuous locus of consciousness, to form and savor plans for the future, to dread death and to express the choice not to die. And there's the rub: our immature neonates don't possess these traits any more than mice do.

21   Several moral philosophers have concluded that neonates are not persons, and thus neonaticide should not be classified as murder. Michael Tooley has gone so far as to say that neonaticide ought to be permitted during an interval after birth. Most philosophers (to say nothing of nonphilosophers) recoil from that last step, but the very fact that there can be a debate about the personhood of neonates, but no debate about the personhood of older children, makes it clearer why we feel more sympathy for an Amy Grossberg than for a Susan Smith.

22   So how do you provide grounds for outlawing neonaticide? The facts don't make it easy. Some philosophers suggest that people intuitively see neonates as so similar to older babies that you couldn't allow neonaticide without coarsening the way people treat children and other people in general. Again, the facts say otherwise. Studies in both modern and hunter-gatherer societies have found that neonaticidal women don't kill anyone but their newborns, and when they give birth later under better conditions, they can be devoted, loving mothers.

23   The laws of biology were not kind to Amy Grossberg and Melissa Drexler, and they are not kind to us as we struggle to make moral sense of the teen-agers' actions. One predicament is that our moral system needs a crisp inauguration of personhood, but the assembly process for Homo sapiens is gradual, piecemeal and uncertain. Another problem is that the emotional circuitry of mothers has evolved to cope with this uncertain process, so the baby killers turn out to be not moral monsters but nice, normal (and sometimes religious) young women. These are dilemmas we will probably never resolve, and any policy will leave us with uncomfortable cases. We will most likely muddle through, keeping birth as a conspicuous legal boundary but showing mercy to the anguished girls who feel they had no choice but to run afoul of it.

An Analysis Based on the Toulmin Model

Clearly Steven Pinker has taken a controversial stance on a disturbing social issue. In fact, in light of civilized society's attitudes toward the sacredness of the mother-infant bond, his position is one that many people might find shocking and repugnant. How could he propose that neonaticide, the murder of one's newborn infant, be viewed as an acceptable form of behavior, one that we have inherited from our evolutionary ancestors? As Pinker readily admits in the first three paragraphs of his essay, neonaticide seems alien to most of the values we as civilized people cherish. Nevertheless, Pinker argues that while it may be regarded as immoral, neonaticide is not necessarily the act of a mentally deranged woman, but rather a difficult decision guided by an instinct for survival handed down to a mother by generations of women before her. While he does not condone or endorse this practice, Pinker urges his readers to try to understand a context that might drive women to commit such an act.

No matter how repugnant an idea may be, it cannot be repudiated unless it is understood. Therefore it is important to be detached and put aside emotion when confronted with ideas that are unacceptable. Genocide, child slavery, and child prostitution, for example, are topics most people would rather avoid. But to understand the forces underlying these practices, and to eradicate them, one must be knowledgeable about them. This might require digesting material that is disturbing and contrary to all the values held by a civilized society.

So while your first reaction to Pinker's ideas may be to dismiss them as outrageous and unworthy of serious consideration, a close analysis of his argument using the Toulmin method may demonstrate how carefully Pinker has crafted his argument to challenge many of our assumptions about human behavior and, in particular, motherhood.

Claims and Grounds

Pinker presents the first part of his claim in paragraph 4 of his essay: Neonaticide is not an abnormal behavior but one that has been practiced "in most cultures throughout history." This statement seems to contradict the popular notion of neonaticide. Because our society regards neonaticide as an immoral act, many people likely assume that it is a rare occurrence. However, Pinker anticipates this assumption in paragraph 1 by reminding us that neonaticide *does* occur in our own society. It is, he claims, more common than we realize, since most murders of newborn babies go undetected. Only "every once in a while" do we discover that this act has taken place because some physical evidence is found. While Pinker offers no grounds for his assertion that "every year, hundreds of women commit neonaticide," his audience's familiarity with newspaper accounts of newborns abandoned in dumpsters and public restrooms lends credibility to his statement. This point is important because it establishes a link between contemporary women's behavior and the practices of our "long-vanished tribal environment."

Pinker develops this idea further in paragraphs 6 through 8 by suggesting that this behavior has been programmed into our "biological design" through human evolutionary development. He provides the grounds to support this part of his claim by citing two scholarly sources: Philip Resnick's study of child-killing statistics, which indicates that women who kill their newborn babies are typically not mentally ill, and research by Martin Daly and Margo Wilson that suggests neonaticide may be an intrinsic part of our "biological design," a necessity for human beings with limited resources to invest in their offspring. Relying on these grounds, Pinker goes on to argue in paragraph 9 that neonaticide is an "adaptive choice," one that is preferable to nurturing an infant whose continued survival is in doubt because of either the physical condition of the child or environmental difficulties for the mother.

So far, then, we have found two of the essential parts of the Toulmin model in Pinker's essay:

Claim	Neonaticide is not a pathologic behavior but can be, rather, the result of evolutionary development.
Grounds	Various anthropological studies indicate that neonaticide is a common and accepted practice in many contemporary societies; studies by psychologists argue that neonaticide is a normal part of our parenting emotions; research by psychologists demonstrates that women who commit neonaticide are not mentally ill.

Warrants, Backing, and Rebuttals

Now let's move on to Pinker's warrants, which work to support his claim. Pinker never directly states, yet he strongly implies as a *warrant,* that "biology is destiny." It is clear from his claim and the grounds used to support it that Pinker believes the biological impulses of a new mother who commits neonaticide may overwhelm her civilized sense of what is morally or even emotionally right. Human beings, according to Pinker, are at the mercy of their neurological programming. Pinker offers *backing* for this *warrant* in paragraph 10 when he relates interviews by anthropologists with women who have killed their newborn babies and who appear to grieve sincerely for their children, regarding their actions as "an unavoidable tragedy." These women, according to Pinker, were compelled to make a difficult choice, which each did in spite of her maternal feelings toward the newborn. Pinker reinforces this point later in the essay when he states in paragraph 23 that "the laws of biology were not kind to Amy Grossberg and Melissa Drexler," two young women who killed their infants just after birth. Pinker strongly implies that biological forces were at work when these women made their decisions.

Pinker's warrant provides plenty of opportunity for *rebuttal* because even if the reader accepts the idea that human beings, despite the teachings of civilized society, are still subject to the dictates of more primitive and instinctive urges, Pinker asserts that the urge to kill one's baby is stronger than, say, the maternal instinct to nurture that infant. We have all heard of situations in which a mother has risked or sacrificed her own life to save that of her child. Why, we might ask, wouldn't this emotion dominate the behavior of a new mother? Pinker acknowledges this rebuttal in paragraph 11 when he points out that the neonaticides we read about in newspapers are often committed by middle-class girls who have the resources to support a child or the option to give the baby up for adoption.

Pinker responds to this rebuttal in two ways: First, he reiterates his claim that the internal forces of our evolutionary background are stronger than the individual's own sense of right and wrong. These young women are responding to the "signals of the long-vanished tribal environment in which we spent 99 percent of our evolutionary history." Moreover, Pinker goes on to suggest, neonaticide is triggered by environmental and social factors, specifically the age, marital status, and isolation of the new mother, that work to suppress more positive maternal responses. As he explains in paragraph 12, maternal feelings are more likely to emerge in an atmosphere of "cooing and clucking and congratulating" than in a "motel room or bathroom stall."

Pinker goes on to support his argument with several additional layers of warrants: If human behavior is controlled by deeply ingrained biological forces, then we can't be held legally responsible for these actions. In other words, while we may deeply deplore the act of neonaticide, we cannot fault these women for acting on an impulse they may not completely understand or feel able to control. In paragraph 15, Pinker provides backing for this claim by observing that few women in the United States are actually incarcerated for this crime and several European countries treat neonaticide less severely than other forms of homicide. Thus, although the killing of one's baby generates strong moral outrage in our society, we treat it less severely than most other offenses in the same category.

Logically, then, the next question must be "Why is this the case?" When older children are murdered by their mothers, as in Pinker's example of Susan Smith in paragraph 16, we waste little sympathy on the plight of the mother. We can agree with Pinker that "our compassion hinges on the child." Why do we react, according to Pinker, in a very different way to the death of a newborn? Pinker has very carefully brought us to his next warrant, which even he admits is the "unthinkable": Our reaction to the killing of a newborn and the killing of an older child is different because a newborn is not yet a "full person."

Pinker provides backing for his warrant in paragraphs 18 through 20. In paragraph 18, he points out a fact most readers would agree with: Unlike other mammals, human babies are helpless at birth. They are "incomplete." It will take an infant several years to achieve the level of physical development that some mammals enjoy at birth. Thus, a newborn baby cannot claim its rights as a person based on its physical completeness. Then, Pinker asks, on what basis can a newborn be seen as possessing "a right not to be killed"? By what traits do we define a person with a right to life? In paragraph 20, Pinker calls on the *backing* of "moral philosophers" who describe the traits human beings must possess to be considered fully human. Pinker concludes that newborn babies "don't possess these traits any more than mice do."

Anticipating that most readers will have a strong negative response to these ideas, Pinker acknowledges several rebuttals to this warrant. In paragraph 17, he recognizes that neither side of the abortion debate would agree with his assertion that birth should not be a marker to determine when a human being is given a right to life. To antiabortionists, who maintain that "personhood" begins at conception, Pinker responds that if we adopt this viewpoint, the destruction of any fertilized human egg would be considered murder. To those in favor of abortion rights, who consider personhood to begin when the baby is capable of living outside the protection of the mother's body, Pinker counters that this depends on the condition of the infant and the willingness of the parents to accept the risks inherent in a premature birth. In paragraph 19, Pinker also rejects the position that all life deserves to be preserved. If this were practiced, Pinker reasons, then "delousing a child is akin to mass murder." Pinker's stance forces us to reexamine how we define a "person" and how we can determine at what point the right to live unharmed begins.

We can briefly summarize Pinker's warrants and backing as follows:

Warrant 1	Biology is destiny. We are at the mercy of our neurological programming, which has been handed down from our evolutionary ancestors.
Backing	Examples of women who grieve for the newborns they killed; references to Melissa Drexler and Amy Grossberg, who killed their newborn infants.
Warrant 2	If human behavior is controlled by deeply ingrained biological forces, then women can't be held legally responsible for following their natural impulses.
Backing	Examples of lenient criminal treatment of women who commit neonaticide; examples of less severe penalties for women who kill newborns, as opposed to those given for the murder of older children or adults.
Warrant 3	A newborn infant is not a full person. Neonates do not yet possess those human qualities that bestow on them the right to life.
Backing	A description of a newborn infant's physical helplessness; a definition of a "full person" according to some moral philosophers; a comparison of the intellectual and moral awareness of a newborn infant with that of a mouse.

Qualifiers

Throughout his essay, Pinker is careful to use *qualifiers* that limit and clarify his claim. There are many examples of these; we will point out a few that appear early in the essay along with our emphasis and comments:

Paragraph 4	"But it's *hard* [difficult but not impossible] to maintain that neonaticide is an illness when we learn that it has been practiced and accepted in *most* [but not all] cultures throughout history. And that neonaticidal women do not *commonly* [typical but not in all cases] show signs of psychopathology."
Paragraph 5	"But normal human motives are *not always* [happens some of the time] moral, and neonaticide *does not have to be* [but it could be] a product of malfunctioning neural circuitry or a dysfunctional upbringing."

By using qualifiers, Pinker demonstrates his awareness that his claim may not always be true under all circumstances and accounts for the differing experiences of his audience.

As we stated at the beginning of this chapter, to construct a persuasive argument, you must pay careful attention to the logical structure you are building. As the Toulmin method illustrates, unless your claim is supported by a firm foundation (your warrants) and well buttressed by convincing grounds and backing, your structure will not withstand the rebuttals that will test its strength.

Pinker's view on neonaticide is disturbing, to say the least. For his essay to be persuasive, the reader must be willing to accept each of his warrants and the backing he uses to support them. Four days after Pinker's essay appeared in the *New York Times,* the following article was published in the *Washington Post.* As you read the article, notice how author Michael Kelley, a senior writer at the *National Journal,* attacks Pinker's claim by questioning each of his warrants and their backing. Calling Pinker's premise one of the "most thoroughly dishonest constructs anyone has ever attempted to pass off as science," Kelley also levels severe criticism at one of Pinker's sources, Michael Tooley. Kelley comments that Pinker's citation of Tooley's radical views, even though he may not directly agree with them, makes him "guilty by association." Kelley's accusation demonstrates why you should choose your sources carefully. Your audience will associate your views with the company they keep.

Arguing for Infanticide
Michael Kelley

1   Of all the arguments advanced against the legalization of abortion, the one that always struck me as the most questionable is the most consequential: that the widespread acceptance of abortion would lead to a profound moral shift in our culture, a great devaluing of human life. This seemed to me dubious on general principle: Projections of this sort almost always turn out to be wrong because they fail to grasp that, in matters of human behavior, there is not really any such thing as a trendline. People change to meet new realities and thereby change reality.

2   Thus, for the environmental hysterics of the 1970s, the nuclear freezers of the 1980s and the Perovian budget doomsayers of the 1990s, the end that was nigh never came. So, with abortions, why should a tolerance for ending human life under one, very limited, set of conditions necessarily lead to an acceptance of ending human life under other, broader terms?

3   This time, it seems, the pessimists were right. On Sunday, Nov. 2, an article in the *New York Times,* the closest thing we have to the voice of the intellectual establishment, came out for killing babies. I am afraid that I am sensationalizing only slightly. The article by Steven Pinker in the *Times Magazine* did not go quite so far as to openly recommend the murder of infants, and printing the article did not constitute the *Times'* endorsement of the idea. But close enough, close enough.

4   What Pinker, a professor of psychology at the Massachusetts Institute of Technology, wrote and what the *Times* treated as a legitimate argument, was a

thoroughly sympathetic treatment of this modest proposal: Mothers who kill their newborn infants should not be judged as harshly as people who take human life in its later stages because newborn infants are not persons in the full sense of the word, and therefore do not enjoy a right to life. Who says that life begins at birth?

5   "To a biologist, birth is as arbitrary a milestone as any other," Pinker breezily writes. "No, the right to life must come, the moral philosophers say, from morally significant traits that we humans happen to possess. One such trait is having a unique sequence of experiences that defines us as individuals and connects us to other people. Other traits include an ability to reflect upon ourselves as a continuous locus of consciousness, to form and savor plans for the future, to dread death and to express the choice not to die. And there's the rub: our immature neonates don't possess these traits any more than mice do."

6   Pinker notes that "several moral philosophers have concluded that neonates are not persons, and thus neonaticide should not be classified as murder," and he suggests his acceptance of this view, arguing that "the facts don't make it easy" to legitimately outlaw the killing of infants.

7   Pinker's casually authoritative mention of "the facts" is important, because Pinker is no mere ranter from the crackpot fringe but a scientist. He is, in fact, a respected explicator of the entirely mainstream and currently hot theory of evolutionary psychology, and the author of *How the Mind Works,* a widely read and widely celebrated book on the subject.

8   How the mind works, says Pinker, is that people are more or less hard-wired to behave as they do by the cumulative effects of the human experience. First cousins to the old Marxist economic determinists, the evolutionary psychologists are behavioral determinists. They believe in a sort of Popeye's theory of human behavior: I do what I do because I yam what I yam because I wuz what I wuz.

9   This view is radical; it seeks to supplant both traditional Judeo-Christian morality and liberal humanism with a new "scientific" philosophy that denies the idea that all humans are possessed of a quality that sets them apart from the lower species, and that this quality gives humans the capacity and responsibility to choose freely between right and wrong. And it is monstrous. And, judging from the writings of Pinker and his fellow determinists on the subject of infanticide, it may be the most thoroughly dishonest construct anyone has ever attempted to pass off as science.

10   Pinker's argument was a euphemized one. The more blunt argument is made by Michael Tooley, a philosophy professor at the University of Colorado, whom Pinker quotes. In this 1972 essay "Abortion and Infanticide," Tooley makes what he calls "an extremely plausible answer" to the question: "What makes it morally permissible to destroy a baby, but wrong to kill an adult?" Simple enough: Personhood does not begin at birth. Rather, "an organism possesses a serious right to life only if it possesses the concept of a self as a continuing subject of experiences and other mental states, and believes that it is itself such a continuing entity."

11   Some would permit the killing of infants "up to the time an organism learned how to use certain expressions," but Tooley finds this cumbersome and would simply

establish "some period of time, such as a week after birth, as the interval during which infanticide will be permitted."

12   And Tooley does not bother with Pinker's pretense that what is under discussion here is only a rare act of desperation, the killing of an unwanted child by a frightened, troubled mother. No, no, no. If it is moral to kill a baby for one, it is moral for all. Indeed, the systematic, professionalized use of infanticide would be a great benefit to humanity. "Most people would prefer to raise children who do not suffer from gross deformities or from severe physical, emotional, or intellectual handicaps," writes eugenicist Tooley. "If it could be shown that there is no moral objection to infanticide the happiness of society could be significantly and justifiably increased."

13   To defend such an unnatural idea, the determinists argue that infanticide is in fact natural: In Pinker's words, "it has been practiced and accepted in most cultures throughout history." This surprising claim is critical to the argument that the act of a mother killing a child is a programmed response to signals that the child might not fare well in life (because of poverty, illegitimacy or other factors). And it is a lie.

14   In fact, although millions of mothers give birth every year under the sort of adverse conditions that Pinker says trigger the "natural" urge to kill the baby, infanticide is extremely rare in all modern societies, and is universally treated as a greatly aberrant act, the very definition of a moral horror. The only cultures that Pinker can point to in which infanticide is widely "practiced and accepted" are those that are outside the mores of Western civilization: ancient cultures and the remnants of ancient cultures today, tribal hunter-gatherer societies.

15   And so goes the entire argument, a great chain of dishonesty, palpable untruth piled upon palpable untruth. "A new mother," asserts Pinker, "will first coolly assess the infant and her situation and only in the next few days begin to see it as a unique and wonderful individual." Yes, that was my wife all over: cool as a cucumber as she assessed whether to keep her first-born child or toss him out the window. As George Orwell said once of another vast lie, "You have to be an intellectual to believe such nonsense. No ordinary man could be such a fool."

QUESTIONS FOR ANALYSIS AND DISCUSSION ────────

1. Briefly outline the basic Toulmin components of Kelley's argument: What is his claim? What grounds does he use to support it? Then find and identify Kelley's warrants and the backing he provides to demonstrate their reliability.

2. To what aspects of Pinker's claim and warrants does Kelley object? On what grounds does he object?

3. Pinker limits his discussion of neonaticide to the behavior of "depressed new mothers" (paragraph 9). Does Kelley ignore this distinction in his response to Pinker? How does Kelley shift the discussion from Pinker's "anguished girls" (paragraph 23) to "millions

of mothers" (paragraph 14 in Kelley)? Do you think this is a fair interpretation of Pinker's intent?

4. Kelley begins his essay with a reference to the legalization of abortion. On what basis does he suggest a link between the "widespread
acceptance of abortion" and Pinker's theories about neonaticide?

5. In paragraph 3 of his essay, Kelley states that Pinker "did not go quite
so far as to openly recommend the murder of infants." Discuss the implications of Kelley's use of the qualifiers *quite* and *openly*. What do
you think he intends to imply about Pinker's objectives?

6. In paragraph 10, what does Kelley mean by describing Pinker's
argument as "euphemized"? What connection does Kelley make between Pinker's views and the theories expressed by Michael Tooley
in his 1972 essay? Does your analysis of Pinker's claim and warrants lead you to believe that Pinker endorses Tooley's theories, as
Kelley asserts?

7. In your journal, discuss your own response to Kelley's essay. Which
reasons do you find particularly persuasive? With which reasons do
you disagree, and why?

8. In paragraph 9, Kelley criticizes Pinker's attempt to take a "scientific" approach to a serious moral issue by suggesting that humans
lack "the capacity and responsibility to choose freely between right
and wrong." In your journal, consider how Pinker might respond to
that statement. Would he agree with Kelley's interpretation of his
ideas? How would Pinker suggest that society should deal with the
problem of neonaticide?

SAMPLE STUDENT ARGUMENT FOR ANALYSIS

The previous two essays focused on parental love becoming grossly dysfunctional as the possible result of tragic neurological wiring. What follows is a paper
about the effects of parental love on children of divorce. Given the fact that half
of all children will see their parents' marriage terminate by the time they turn 18,
divorce has become an American way of life. While society may shake its collective head at such a statistic, lamenting the loss of the traditional family, not
all children of divorce see it as a problem. In the following essay, Lowell Putnam
explores the effect of his parents' divorce on his development, arguing that divorce should not be a taboo topic, and that children of broken homes are not
always damaged.

Putnam wrote this essay when he was a college freshman. When he is not living
on campus, he splits his time between his mother's home in New York and his father's home in Massachusetts.

Read through Putnam's essay and make notes in your journal. Notice whether
and how its parts work together—and, if possible, where some of the parts may need
to be reworked. Then respond to the questions that follow.

Lowell Putnam

Professor Ramos

English 201

March 6, 2008

Did I Miss Something?

1	The subject of divorce turns heads in our society. It is responsible for bitten tongues, lowered voices, and an almost pious reverence saved only for life-threatening illness or uncontrolled catastrophe. Having grown up in a "broken home," I am always shocked to be treated as a victim of some social disease. When a class assignment required that I write an essay concerning my feelings about or my personal experiences with divorce, my first reaction was complete surprise. An essay on aspects of my life affected by divorce seems completely superfluous, because I cannot differentiate between the "normal" part of my youth and the supposed angst and confusion that apparently come with all divorces. The separation of my parents over sixteen years ago (when I was three years old) has either saturated every last pore of my developmental epidermis to a point where I cannot sense it or has not affected me at all. Eugene Ehrlich's Highly Selective Dictionary for the Extraordinarily Literate (1997) defines divorce as a "breach"; however, I cannot sense any schism in my life resulting from the event to which other people seem to attribute so much importance. My parents' divorce is a ubiquitous part of who I am, and the only "breach" that could arrive from my present familial arrangement would be to tear me away from what I consider my normal living conditions.

2   Though there is no doubt in my mind that many unfortunate people have had their lives torn apart by the divorce of their parents, I do not feel any real sense of regret for my situation. In my opinion, the paramount role of a parent is to love his or her child. Providing food, shelter, education, and video games are of course other necessary elements of successful child rearing, but these secondary concerns stem from the most fundamental ideal of parenting, which is love. A loving parent will be a successful one even if he or she cannot afford to furnish his or her child with the best clothes or the most sophisticated gourmet delicacies. With love as the driving force in a parent's mind, he or she will almost invariably make the correct decisions. When my mother and father found that they were no longer in love with each other after nine years of marriage, their love for me forced them to take the precipitous step to separate. The safest environment for me was to be with one happy parent at a time, instead of two miserable ones all the time. The sacrifice that they both made to relinquish control over me for half the year was at least as painful for them as it was for me (probably even more so), but in the end I was not deprived of a parent's love, but merely of one parent's presence for a few weeks at a time. My father and mother's love for me has not dwindled even slightly over the past fifteen years, and I can hardly imagine a more well-adjusted and contented family.

3   As I reread the first section of this essay, I realize that it is perhaps too optimistic and cheerful regarding my life as a

child of divorced parents. In all truthfulness,
there have been some decidedly negative
ramifications stemming from our family
separation. My first memory is actually of a
fight between my mother and father. I vaguely
remember standing in the end of the upstairs
hallway of our Philadelphia house when I was
about three years old, and seeing shadows
moving back and forth in the light coming
from under the door of my father's study,
accompanied by raised voices. It would be naïve
of me to say that I have not been at all
affected by divorce, since it has permeated my
most primal and basic memories; however, I am
grateful that I can only recall one such
incident, instead of having parental conflicts
become so quotidian that they leave no mark
whatsoever on my mind. Also, I find that having
to divide my time equally between both parents
leads to alienation from either side of my
family. Invariably, at every holiday occasion,
there is one half of my family (either my
mother's side or my father's) that has to
explain that "Lowell is with his
[mother/father] this year," while aunts,
cousins, and grandparents collectively arch
eyebrows or avert eyes. Again, though, I should
not be hasty to lament my distance from loved
ones, since there are many families with
"normal" marriages where the children never
even meet their cousins, let alone get to spend
every other Thanksgiving with them. Though
divorce has certainly thrown some proverbial
monkey wrenches into some proverbial gears, in
general my otherwise strong familial ties have
overshadowed any minor blemishes.

4   Perhaps one of the most important reasons
for my absence of "trauma" (for lack of a better
word) stemming from my parents' divorce is that
I am by no means alone in my trials and
tribulations. The foreboding statistic that
sixty percent of marriages end in divorce is no
myth to me, indeed many of my friends come from
similar situations. The argument could be made
that "birds of a feather flock together" and
that my friends and I form a tight support
network for each other, but I strongly doubt
that any of us need or look for that kind of
buttress. The fact of the matter is that divorce
happens a lot in today's society, and as a
result our culture has evolved to accommodate
these new family arrangements, making the
overall conditions more hospitable for me and my
broken brothers and shattered sisters.

5   I am well aware that divorce can often lead
to issues of abandonment and familial proximity
among children of separated parents, but in my
case I see very little evidence to support the
claim that my parents should have stayed married
"for the sake of the child." In many ways, my
life is enriched by the division of my time with
my father and my time with my mother. I get to
live in New York City for half of the year, and
in a small suburb of Boston for the other half.
I have friends who envy me, since I get "the
best of both worlds." I never get double-teamed
by parents during arguments, and I cherish my
time with each one more since it only lasts half
the year.

6   In my opinion, there is no such thing as a
perfect life or a "normal" life, and any small
blips on our karmic radar screen have to be

Putnam 5

dealt with appropriately but without any
trepidation or self-pity. Do I miss my father
when I live with my mother (and vice versa)? Of
course I do. However, I know young boys and
girls who have lost parents to illness or
accidental injury, so my pitiable position is
relative. As I look back on the last nineteen
years from the relative independence of college,
I can safely say that my childhood has not been
at all marred by having two different houses to
call home.

QUESTIONS FOR ANALYSIS AND DISCUSSION

1. Identify Putnam's claim. Where does he state it in his essay? From
   your experience, do you agree with him? Do you agree that people
   discuss divorce "in an almost pious reverence saved only for life-
   threatening illness"?
2. On what grounds does Putnam base his claim? Find specific evidence
   he presents to support his claim. Do you find it convincing and
   supportive?
3. Do you agree with Putnam's definition of what makes a good parent?
4. Putnam has several warrants, some of them stated explicitly and some
   implied. In paragraph 2, he states: "A loving parent will be a successful one even if he or she cannot afford to furnish his or her child with
   the best clothes or the most sophisticated gourmet delicacies." Do you
   agree with his warrant? On what commonly shared values or beliefs
   does he base this warrant? Are there any aspects of his warrant with
   which you disagree? What backing does Putnam provide to support
   his warrant? Is it sufficient?
5. What other warrants underlie Putnam's claim? In a small peer group,
   identify several layers of warrants and discuss whether these need additional backing to be convincing.
6. Notice the qualifier Putnam uses in paragraph 3 when he says, "In
   all truthfulness, there have been *some* decidedly negative ramifications stemming from our family separation" (emphasis added). What
   limitations does this qualifying statement put on his argument? Does
   this limitation weaken his argument at all?

7. Does Putnam acknowledge and address anticipated rebuttals to his argument? Can you locate any in his essay? What rebuttals can you make in response to his argument?

8. If you are a child of divorced parents, write about the experience as it affected your emotional and psychological outlook. How did it impact your life growing up, and how did it affect your adult view of marriage? Answer the same questions if your parents remained married, considering in your response how your life may have been different if your parents had divorced while you were young.

9. In your peer group, discuss the effects of divorce on children. Further develop Putnam's idea that it is just another way of life. Compare notes with classmates to assemble a complete list. Based on this list, develop your own argument about the effects of divorce on children.

CHAPTER 8

Using Visual Arguments

Thinking Like an Illustrator

Ours is a visual world. From the first cave paintings of prehistoric France to the complicated photomosaic posters that adorn dormitory walls today, we are inspired, compelled, and persuaded by visual stimuli. Everywhere we look there are images vying for our attention—magazine ads, T-shirt logos, movie billboards, artwork, traffic signs, political cartoons, statues, and storefront windows. Glanced at only briefly, visuals communicate information and ideas. They may project commonly held values, ideals, and fantasies. They can relay opinion, inspire reaction, and influence emotion. And because the competition for our attention today is so great, and the time available for communication is so scarce, images must compete to make an impression or risk being lost in a blur of visual information.

Because the goal of a calculated visual is to persuade, coax, intimidate, or otherwise subliminally influence its viewer, it is important that its audience can discern the strategies or technique it employs. In other words, to be a literate reader of visuals, one must be a literate reader of arguments.

Consider the instant messages projected by brand names, company logos, or even the American flag. Such images may influence us consciously and unconsciously. Some visual images, such as advertisements, may target our emotions, while others, such as graphics, may appeal to our intellect. Just as we approach writing with the tools of critical analysis, we should carefully consider the many ways visuals influence us.

Common Forms of Visual Arguments

Visual arguments come in many different forms and use many different media. Artists, photographers, advertisers, cartoonists, and designers approach their work with the same intentions that authors of written material do—they want to share a point of view, present an idea, inspire, or evoke a reaction. For example, think back to when you had your high school yearbook photo taken. The photographer didn't simply sit you down and start snapping pictures. More likely, the photographer told you how to sit, tilt your head, and where to gaze. You selected your clothing for the picture carefully and probably spent more time on your hair that day. Lighting, shadow, and setting were also thoughtfully considered. You and your photographer crafted an image of how you wanted the world to see you—an image of importance because it would be forever recorded in your yearbook, as well as distributed to family and friends as the remembrance of a milestone in your life. In effect, you were creating a visual argument.

While there are many different kinds of visual arguments, the most common ones take the form of artwork, advertisements, editorial cartoons, and news photos. These visuals often do not rely on an image alone to tell their story, although it is certainly possible for a thoughtfully designed visual to do so. More often, however, advertisements are accompanied by ad copy, editorial cartoons feature comments or statements, and news photos are placed near the stories they enhance.

Ancillary visuals—that is, graphs, charts, and tables—have great potential for enhancing written arguments and influencing the audience. They provide snapshots of information and are usually used to provide factual support to written information. We will discuss these types of visuals, and how you can use them to enhance your own written arguments, later in this chapter. But first, let us examine some powerful visual images and the ways they capture our attention, impact our sensibilities, and evoke our responses.

Analyzing Visual Arguments

As critical readers of written arguments, we do not take the author simply at face value. We consider the author's purpose and intent, audience, style, tone, and supporting evidence. We must apply these same analytical tools to "read" visual arguments effectively. As with written language, understanding the persuasive power of "visual language" requires a close examination and interpretation of the premise, claims, details, supporting evidence, and stylistic touches embedded in any visual piece. We should ask ourselves the following four questions when examining visual arguments:

- Who is the target *audience?*
- What are the *claims* made in the images?
- What shared history or cultural *assumptions*—or warrants—does the image make?
- What is the supporting *evidence?*

Like works of art, visuals often employ color, shape, line, texture, depth, and point of view to create their effect. Therefore, to understand how visuals work and to analyze the way visuals persuade, we must also ask questions about specific aspects of form and design. For example, some questions to ask about print images such as those in newspaper and magazine ads include:

- What in the frame catches your attention immediately?
- What is the central image? What is the background image? foreground images? What are the surrounding images? What is significant in the placement of these images? their relationship to one another?

- What verbal information is included? How is it made prominent? How does it relate to the other graphics or images?
- What specific details (people, objects, locale) are emphasized? Which are exaggerated or idealized?
- What is the effect of color and lighting?
- What emotional effect is created by the images—pleasure? longing? anxiety? nostalgia?
- Do the graphics and images make you want to know more about the subject or product?
- What special significance might objects in the image have?
- Is there any symbolism embedded in the images?

Considering these questions helps us to survey a visual argument critically and enables us to formulate reasoned assessments of its message and intent. In the next pages of this chapter, we will analyze in greater detail some visual arguments presented in art, advertising, editorial cartoons, and photographs. Part Two of this book continues the investigation of visual arguments as they connect to the topics of each chapter.

Art

The French artist Georges Braque (1882–1963) once said, "In art, there can be no effect without twisting the truth." While not all artists would agree with him, Braque, who with Pablo Picasso originated the cubist style, "saw" things from a different perspective than the rest of us, and he expressed his vision in his paintings. All art is an interpretation of what the artist sees. It is filtered through the eyes of the artist and influenced by his or her own perceptions.

Throughout history, artists have applied their craft to advance religious, social, and political visual arguments. Portraits of kings and queens present how the monarchs wanted their people to see them, with symbolic tools of power such as scepters, crowns, and rich vestments. Art in churches and cathedrals was used as a means of visual instruction for people who could not read. Much of modern art reveals impressions, feelings, and emotions without remaining faithful to the actual thing depicted. While entire books are written about the meaning and function of art, let's examine how one particular artist, Pablo Picasso (1881–1973), created a visual argument.

Pablo Picasso's *Guernica*

Pablo Picasso, with fellow artist Georges Braque, invented a style of painting known as **cubism.** Cubism is based on the idea that the eye observes things from continually changing viewpoints, as fragments of a whole. Cubism aims to represent the essential reality of forms from multiple perspectives and angles. Thus, cubist paintings don't show reality as we see it. Rather, they depict pieces of people, places, and things in an unstable field of vision.

Figure 8.1   Pablo Picasso, Guernica, 1937

Picasso's painting *Guernica* (Figure 8.1, page 222) represents the essence of cubism. During the Spanish Civil War, the German air force bombed the town of Guernica, the cultural center of the Basque region in northern Spain and a Loyalist stronghold. In only a few minutes on April 26, 1937, hundreds of men, women, and children were massacred in the deadly air strike. Two months later, Picasso expressed his outrage at the attack in a mural he titled simply, *Guernica*.

The mural is Picasso's statement about the horror and devastation of war. The painting is dynamic and full of action, yet its figures seem flat and static. It is balanced while still presenting distorted images and impressions. It is ordered while still evoking a sense of chaos and panic. To better understand Picasso's "statement," let's apply some of the questions about visual arguments described earlier in the chapter to this painting.

Who Is Picasso's Target Audience?

Knowing the history of the painting can help us understand whom Picasso was trying to reach. In January 1937, Picasso was commissioned to paint a mural for the 1937 *Exposition Internationale des Arts et Techniques dans la Vie Moderne,* an art exhibition to open in France in May of that same year. Although he had never been a political person, the atrocity of Guernica in April compelled him to express his anger and appeal to the world.

Before the mural went on display, some politicians tried to replace it with a less "offensive" piece of art. When the picture was unveiled at the opening of the expo, it was received poorly. One critic described it as "the work of a madman." Picasso had hoped that his work would shock people. He wanted the outside world to care about what happened at Guernica. However, Picasso may have misjudged his first audience. In 1937, Europe was on the brink of world war. Many people were in denial that the war could touch them and preferred to ignore the possibility that it was imminent. It was this audience who first viewed *Guernica*—an audience that didn't want to see a mural about war, an audience that was trying to avoid the inevitable. Years later, the mural would become one of the most critically acclaimed works of art of the twentieth century.

What Claims Is Picasso Making in the Images?

Picasso's painting comprises many images that make up an entire scene. It depicts simultaneously events that happened over a period of time. The overall claim is that war itself is horrible. The smaller claims address the injustice of Guernica more directly. A mother wails in grief over her dead infant, a reminder that the bombing of Guernica was a massacre of innocents. Picasso also chose to paint his mural in black and white, giving it the aura of a newspaper, especially in the body of the horse. He could be saying, "This is news" or "This is a current event that you should think about."

It should be mentioned that Picasso created many versions of the images in the mural, carefully considering their position, placement, and expression, sometimes drawing eight or nine versions of a single subject. He thoughtfully considered how the images would convey his message before he painted them in the mural.

What Shared History or Cultural Assumptions Does Picasso Make?

The assumptions in any argument are the principles or beliefs that the audience takes for granted. These assumptions implicitly connect the claim to the evidence. By naming his mural *Guernica*, Picasso knew that people would make an immediate connection between the chaos on the wall and the events of April 26, 1937. He also assumed that the people viewing the painting would be upset by it. In addition, there are symbols in the painting that would have been recognized by people at the time—such as the figure of the bull in the upper-left-hand corner of the mural, a long-time symbol for Spain.

What Is Picasso's Supporting Evidence?

Although Picasso was illustrating a real event, cubism allowed him to paint "truth" rather than "reality." If Picasso was trying to depict the horror of Guernica, and by extension, the terror and chaos of war, all the components of his mural serve as supporting evidence. The wailing figures, panicked faces, the darkness contrasted by jumbled images of light all project the horror of war. Even the horse looks terrified. Overall, *Guernica* captures the emotional cacophony of war. Picasso wasn't just trying to say, "War is hell." He was also trying to impress upon his audience that such atrocities should never happen again. In essence, Picasso was making an appeal for peace by showing its opposite, the carnage of war.

QUESTIONS FOR ANALYSIS AND DISCUSSION

Referring to the more specific questions regarding visual arguments discussed earlier in the chapter, apply them to Picasso's painting.

1. What images in the painting catch your attention, and why?
2. What is the central image? Is there a central image? What appears in the foreground? What is significant about the placement of the images? How do they relate to one another?
3. What verbal information, if any, is included, and why? (Remember that Picasso did title his painting *Guernica*. What might have happened if he had named it something more abstract?)
4. What specific details are emphasized? What is exaggerated or idealized?
5. What is the effect of color and light?
6. Does the image make you want to know more?
7. What symbolism is embedded in the image?

Norman Rockwell's *Freedom of Speech*

Picasso's mural was designed to be displayed in a large hall at the World Exposition and later, presumably, in a museum. Other artists had less grand aspirations for their work. Norman Rockwell (1894–1978) was an artist who featured most of his work

Figure 8.2   Norman Rockwell, Freedom of Speech, *1943*

on the covers of magazines, most notably *The Saturday Evening Post,* a publication he considered "the greatest show window in America." In 47 years, Rockwell contributed 321 paintings to the magazine and became an American icon.

On January 6, 1941, President Franklin Delano Roosevelt addressed Congress, delivering his famous "Four Freedoms" speech. Against the background of the Nazi domination of Europe and the Japanese oppression of China, Roosevelt described the four essential human freedoms—freedom of speech, freedom of worship, freedom from want, and freedom from fear. Viewing these freedoms as the fundamental basis on which our society was formed, Roosevelt called upon Americans to uphold these liberties at all costs. Two years later, Rockwell, inspired by Roosevelt's speech, created his famous series of paintings on these "Four Freedoms," reproduced in four consecutive issues of *The Saturday Evening Post.* So popular were the images that they were used by the U.S. government to sell war bonds, to inspire public support for the war effort, and to remind people of the ideals for which they were fighting. The paintings serve as an example of how art can sometimes extend into advertising.

Let's take a closer look at one of the four paintings, *Freedom of Speech* (Figure 8.2 on page 225). When the war department adopted the painting for the war bond effort, it added two slogans to the image. The command "Save Freedom of Speech" was printed at the top of the painting in large, capital letters and, in even larger typeface, "Buy War Bonds" was printed at the bottom. As we analyze this painting, we will also make references to its later use as part of the effort to sell war bonds.

Before he took a brush to his canvas, Rockwell consciously or unconsciously asked himself some of the same questions writers do when they stare at a blank piece of paper while preparing to create a written argument. After determining that he would use the American small-town vehicle of democracy, the town meeting, as the means to express the theme of freedom of speech, he then painted his "argument."

Who Is Rockwell's Audience?

The Saturday Evening Post was widely read in America in the 1930s and 1940s. Rockwell would have wanted his work to appeal to a wide audience, readers of the magazine. If we examine the people in the painting—presumably based on Rockwell's Arlington, Vermont, friends and neighbors—we can deduce the kind of audience the artist was hoping to touch: small-town citizens from a middle-income, working-class environment. Like the language of an argument written for a "general audience," the figures represent what Rockwell considered all-American townsfolk.

The venue is a meetinghouse or town hall because people are sitting on benches. The figures represent a generational cross-section of men and women, from the elderly white-haired man to the left of the central standing figure to the young woman behind him. Style of dress reinforces the notion of class diversity, from the standing man in work clothes to the two men dressed in white shirts, ties, and suit jackets. The formality of the seated figures also opens audience identity to life beyond a small, rural community. That is, some of the men's formal attire and the woman in a stylish hat broaden the depiction to include white-collar urban America. While diversity in age and class is suggested, diversity of race is not. There are no Asians, African Americans, or other nonwhites in the scene. This exclusion might be a reflection of the times and, perhaps, the popular notion of what constituted small-town America 65 years ago. While such exclusion would be unacceptable today, it should be noted that in the years following this painting's completion, Rockwell used his considerable talent and fame to champion the civil rights struggle.

What Is Rockwell's Claim?

When the government adopted Rockwell's painting for their World War II effort campaign to sell war bonds, they added the caption: "Save Freedom of Speech. Buy

War Bonds." When we consider the poster as an advertising piece, this essentially becomes the poster's claim. And we know the artist's intention, to illustrate the theme of freedom of speech. Rockwell's challenge was in how he makes his claim—how he dramatizes it on canvas. Just as a writer uses words to persuade, the artist makes his claim in symbolic details of the brush.

It has been said that Norman Rockwell's paintings appeal to a dreamy-eyed American nostalgia and at the same time project a world where the simple acts of common folk express high American ideals. In this painting, we have one of the sacred liberties dramatized by a working-class man raised to the figure of a political spokesperson in the assembly of others. Clearly expressing his opinion as freely as anybody else, he becomes both the illustration and defender of the democratic principles of freedom and equality.

What Are Rockwell's Assumptions?

As with written arguments, the success of a visual argument depends on whether the audience accepts the assumptions (the values, legal or moral principles, commonsense knowledge, or shared beliefs) projected in the image. One assumption underlying Rockwell's illustration is that freedom of speech is desirable for Americans regardless of gender, class, or position in society. We know this instantly from the facial expressions and body language of the figures in the canvas. For instance, the face of the man standing seems more prominent because it is painted against a dark blank background and is brighter than any others, immediately capturing our attention. His face tilts upward with a look of pride, lit as if by the inspiration of the ideals he represents—freedom of expression. One might even see suggestions of divine inspiration on his face as it rises in the light and against the night-blackened window in the background. The lighting and man's posture are reminiscent of religious paintings of past centuries. Additionally, the man's body is angular and rough, while his facial characteristics strongly resemble those of a young Abraham Lincoln—which suggests a subtle fusion of the patriotic with the divine. The implied message is that freedom of speech is a divine right.

As for the surrounding audience, we take special note of the two men looking up at the speaker. The older man appears impressed and looks on with a warm smile of approval, while the other man on the right gazes up expectantly. In fact, the entire audience supports the standing man with reasonable, friendly, and respectful gazes. The speaker is "Everyman." And he has the support and respect of his community. Rockwell's audience, subscribers of *The Saturday Evening Post,* saw themselves in this image—an image that mirrored the values of honest, decent, middle America.

What Is Rockwell's Supporting Evidence?

The key supporting image in Rockwell's painting is the sharp contrast between the standing man and those sitting around him. Not only is he the only one standing in the room but he is also the only working-class person clearly depicted. He stands out from the other people in the room. It is significant that those around him look up to him—a dramatic illustration of what it means to give the common man his say. Were the scene reversed—with the central figure formally dressed and those looking up approvingly attired in work clothes—we would have a completely different message: That is, a representative of the upper class perhaps "explaining" higher concepts to a less-educated class of people. The message would be all wrong. In the painting, class barriers are transcended as the "common man" has risen to speak his mind with a face full of conviction, while upper-class people look on in support. That's the American ideal in action.

Because this is a painting instead of a newspaper photograph, every detail is selected purposely and, thus, is open to interpretation. One such detail is the fold of papers sticking out of the man's jacket pocket. What might those papers represent? And what's the point of such a detail? What associations might we make with it? There are words printed on the paper, but we cannot read them, so we're left to speculate. The only other paper in the painting is in the hand of the man on the right. The words "report" and "town" are visible. So, we might conclude that the speaker's pocket contains the same pamphlet, perhaps a summary report of the evening's agenda or possibly a resolution to be voted on. Whatever the documentation is, it is clear that the man doesn't need it, that his remarks transcend whatever is written on that paper. And here lies more evidence of Rockwell's claim and celebration of the unaided articulation of one man's views out of many—the essence of freedom of speech.

QUESTIONS FOR ANALYSIS AND DISCUSSION

Referring to the more specific questions regarding visual arguments discussed earlier in the chapter, apply them to Rockwell's painting.

1. What images in the painting catch your attention, and why?
2. What is the central image? Is there a central image? What appears in the foreground? What is significant about the placement of the images? How do they relate to one another?
3. What verbal information, if any, is included, and why?
4. What specific details are emphasized? What is exaggerated or idealized?
5. What is the effect of color and light?
6. Does the image make you want to know more?
7. What symbolism is embedded in the image?

Advertisements

Norman Rockwell sought to embody a concept through his art, and as a result, his painting tries to prompt reflection and self-awareness. In other words, his visuals serve to open the mind to a new discovery or idea. Advertising also selects and crafts visual images. However, advertising has a different objective. Its goal is not to stimulate expansive and enlightened thought but to direct the viewer to a single basic response: Buy this product!

Images have clout, and none are so obvious or so craftily designed as those that come from the world of advertising. Advertising images are everywhere—television, newspapers, the Internet, magazines, the sides of buses, and on highway billboards. Each year, companies collectively spend more than $150 billion on print ads and television commercials (more than the gross national product of many countries). Advertisements comprise at least a quarter of each television hour and form the bulk of most newspapers and magazines. Tapping into our most basic emotions, their appeal goes right to the quick of our fantasies: happiness, material wealth, eternal youth, social acceptance, sexual fulfillment, and power.

Yet, most of us are so accustomed to the onslaught of such images that we see them without looking and hear them without listening. But if we stopped to examine how the images work, we might be amazed at their powerful and complex psychological force. And we might be surprised at how much effort goes into the crafting of such images—an effort solely intended to make us spend our money.

Like a written argument, every print ad or commercial has an *audience, claims, assumptions,* and *evidence.* Sometimes these elements are obvious; sometimes they are understated; sometimes they are implied. They may boast testimonials by average folk or celebrities, or cite hard scientific evidence. And sometimes they simply manipulate our desire to be happy or socially accepted. But common to every ad and commercial, no matter what the medium, is the *claim* that you should buy this product.

Print ads are potentially complex mixtures of images, graphics, and text. So in analyzing an ad, you should be aware of the use of photography, the placement of those images, and the use of text, company logos, and other graphics such as illustrations, drawings, sidebar boxes, additional logos, and so on. You should also keep in mind that every aspect of the image has been thought about and carefully designed. Let's take a look at how a recent magazine ad for Toyota uses some of these elements, including emotional appeal, the use of color and light, and text placement, to convince us that Toyota Tacoma trucks are better than other brands.

Toyota Tacoma Truck Ad

When analyzing a print ad, we should try to determine what first captures our attention. In the Toyota Tacoma truck ad (Figure 8.3 on page 230), the image of a dog immediately catches our eye. Completely saturated by some recent, possibly mischievous activity, he shakes himself off in the back seat of his owner's truck. The viewer can't help but be amused at the dog's innocent exuberance. Second, we are drawn to the bold, horizontal line of text rendered in white and cutting through the middle of the ad reading, "A ROOMY CAB. BECAUSE REAL DOGS DON'T FIT IN HANDBAGS." Third, our eye takes in the roomy and plush interior of the truck, pristine but now soaked by a wet puppy. Fourth, in the

Figure 8.3

background, we see the owner of the truck and most likely owner of the dog, a young man whose facial expression seems to be dismay rather than rage. Finally, in the lower right-hand corner we notice the text highlighting the features of the

OGS DON'T FIT IN HANDBAGS.

TACOMA THE ALL-NEW ROOMIER TOYOTA TACOMA. With 60/40 split rear seats, an available 270-watt JBL sound system and room for five, Tacoma's totally redesigned interior has everything you need to keep it real. Not to mention comfortable too. toyota.com

Double Cab model shown with available TRD Off-Road Package. ©2004 Toyota Motor Sales, U.S.A., Inc.

"ALL-NEW ROOMIER TOYOTA TACOMA," pointing out that the Toyota Tacoma "has everything you need to keep it real. Not to mention comfortable too."

This ad plays on two important American images: (1) a boy and his dog; (2) a young man and his car. Subtly, the iconic image of a boy and his dog evokes feelings of youthful optimism, innocent mischief, and emotional warmth. At the same time, this ad fuses that all-American icon with the equally powerful iconic image of a young man and his car and with it all the associations of independence, ruggedness, and adventure.

Who Is the Audience for the Ad?

The target audience for this ad is males from age 16 to 30 who aspire to own a truck and who might connect to the idea of owning a dog. The composition of the ad is such that the left half emphasizes the qualities of a vehicle that typical young men value—a spacious interior, plush upholstery, a rugged steering wheel, a space-age console, and a high-tech sound system. The right half, showing the wet animal, appeals to the affection most young men would share for a vigorous and mischievous dog.

What Is the Claim?

Because advertisers are vying for our attention, they must project their claim as efficiently as possible in order to discourage us from turning the page. The stated or implied claim of all advertising is that the product will make life better for us. Of course, most ads aren't so bald in their claims. But the promise is there by inference. The claim of *this* ad is that if a young man owns a Toyota Tacoma truck he will experience the essence of young American manhood. Examine the statement that runs through the center of the ad: "A ROOMY CAB. BECAUSE REAL DOGS DON'T FIT IN HANDBAGS." What does this statement really mean? In other words, what is suggested but not directly said? First consider "A ROOMY CAB." This three-word (verbless) sentence grabs our attention and directs it to the interior of the truck. It announces "spaciousness" while drawing us to the other interior features (the upholstery, color-coordination, styling, console, sound system, etc.). The second part of the text, "BECAUSE REAL DOGS DON'T FIT IN HANDBAGS," invites us to share a joke. Anyone aware of our culture knows that celebrities such as Britney Spears and Paris Hilton carry miniature dogs in handbags—a fad that the average American male might find ludicrous. Thus, the young male audience is automatically distinguished from the frivolous dog-toting fad and identifies with the image of the rugged guy and his dog. In other words: *Real* men don't carry *real* dogs in a handbag. Instead, they'd drive around with a dog in their Tacoma.

Ultimately, the goal of the ad is to make its target audience identify with the young man in the ad. They love dogs, they identify with the energy and free spirit of the animal, they might be slightly annoyed with the mess but will easily forgive the pup, and they like the simple but manly features of the Toyota Tacoma—the roominess, the high-tech console, the rugged steering wheel. Thus, the ad's claim: If you buy the Toyota Tacoma truck, you will experience the exhilaration, power, and adventure of young manhood.

What Is the Evidence?

The evidence for the desirability of the Toyota Tacoma is in the visuals as discussed above. Additionally, the text at the bottom right spells out some of other benefits of the vehicle: "THE ALL-NEW ROOMIER TOYOTA TACOMA. With 60/40 split rear seats, an available 270-watt JBL sound system and room for five, Tacoma's totally redesigned interior has everything you need to keep it real. Not to mention comfortable too. **toyota.com.**" The text is a synopsis of some outstanding features of the truck.

What Are the Assumptions?

The creators of this ad made several assumptions about us, the audience: (1) that we are familiar with the trend of carrying small dogs in handbags; (2) that we share an affection for pets; (3) that we share the idea that real men are rugged, need roomy cars, and need freedom; and (4) that rugged, sporty vehicles appeal to young men.

Sample Ads for Analysis

Apply the principles of critical analysis described in the above section on advertising, as well as the elements of form and design discussed earlier in the chapter, to the ads that appear in the following pages.

Figure 8.4

Granola Bites

1. What first caught your eye in this ad? In what order do you look at other elements in the ad? Do you think the advertiser intends you to look at each component of the ad in a particular order? Why?

2. Do you find this ad visually pleasing? Why or why not? Consider the placement of the copy and graphics in your response. Why do you suppose the swing and other playground apparatus are simple black-and-white sketches instead of an imposed photo of a real swing and playground? (The original ad is in color.)

3. Who might be the target audience for this ad? Consider gender, age group, socioeconomic level, lifestyle, and self-image. Defend your answers using specifics in the ad as support.

4. There is a minimal amount of text in this ad. How does the wording relate to the visuals? With reference to the copy, what is the implied argument in the copy? What is the claim? What are the warrants? What comprises the evidence?

5. The iconic Quaker image appears on the box in the ad. What does the image convey? In other words, what associations do you make with the image? Does this image appeal to the parent, the child, or both?

Figure 8.5

Victoria's Dirty Secret

1. In what ways does the model look like the typical Victoria's Secret model? Be specific. In what ways does this model differ? Consider her attire, the wings, hair styling, expression, body posture, shoes, and so on. If you see any differences, how would you explain them? How do the similarities and/or differences contribute to the ad's criticism of the catalogue production of Victoria's Secret?

2. Consider the chain saw. What is the effect of having the model holding a sketched chain saw instead of a real one? And what do you make of the style of the drawing? Why not have a more realistic drawing than this roughly drawn one?

3. After reading the text of the ad, consider some of the characteristics of its argument. What is the basic claim? Locate specific evidence. Are opposing points of view presented? Where specifically?

4. Is this ad a proposal or a position argument? Explain your answer.

5. Visual arguments should inspire or provoke a reaction. On a scale of one to ten, how persuasive is this ad? Are you inspired to take action—specifically to contact Leslie H. Wexner, CEO of Victoria's Secret's parent company? Does it inspire you to get involved with ForestEthics' campaign?

6. Consider the small photograph insert. What is depicted, and how well does it illustrate the argument being made in the ad? How does it relate to the image of the model? Explain in detail.

Editorial or Political Cartoons

Editorial cartoons have been a part of American life for over a century. They are a mainstay feature on the editorial pages in most newspapers—those pages reserved for columnists, contributing editors, and illustrators to present their views in words and pen and ink. As in the nineteenth century when they first started to appear, such editorial cartoons are political in nature, holding up political and social issues for public scrutiny and sometimes ridicule.

A stand-alone editorial cartoon—as opposed to a strip of multiple frames—is a powerful and terse form of communication that combines pen-and-ink drawings with dialogue balloons and captions. They're not just visual jokes, but visual humor that comments on social/political issues while drawing on viewers' experience and knowledge.

The editorial cartoon is the story of a moment in the flow of familiar current events. And the key words here are *moment* and *familiar.* Although a cartoon captures a split instant in time, it also infers what came before and, perhaps, what may happen next—either in the next moment or in some indefinite future. And usually the cartoon depicts a specific moment in time. One of the most famous cartoons of the last 50 years is the late Bill Mauldin's Pulitzer Prize–winning drawing of the figure of Abraham Lincoln with his head in his hands. It appeared the morning after the assassination of President John Kennedy in 1963. There was no caption nor was there a need for one. The image represented the profound grief of a nation that had lost its leader to an assassin's bullet. But to capture the enormity of the event, Mauldin brilliantly chose to represent a woeful America by using the figure of Abraham Lincoln as depicted in the sculpture of the Lincoln Memorial in Washington, D.C. In so doing, the message implied that so profound was the loss that it even reduced to tears the marble figure of a man considered to be our greatest president, himself assassinated a century before.

For a cartoon to be effective, it must make the issue clear at a glance and it must establish where it stands on the argument. In the Mauldin illustration, we instantly recognize Lincoln and identify with the emotions. We need not be told the circumstances, since by the time the cartoon appeared the next day, all the world knew the horrible news that the president had been assassinated. To convey less obvious issues and figures at a glance, cartoonists resort to images that are instantly recognizable, that we don't have to work hard to grasp. Locales are determined by giveaway props: An airplane out the window suggests an airport; a cactus and cattle skull, a desert; an overstuffed armchair and TV, the standard living room. Likewise, human emotions are instantly conveyed: Pleasure is a huge toothy grin, fury is steam blowing out of a figure's ears, love is two figures making goo-goo eyes with floating hearts overhead. People themselves may have exaggerated features to emphasize a point or emotion.

In his essay "What Is a Cartoon?" Mort Gerberg says that editorial cartoons rely on such visual clichés to convey their messages instantly. That is, they employ stock figures for their representation—images instantly recognizable from cultural stereotypes like the fat-cat tycoon, the mobster thug, and the sexy female movie star. And these come to us in familiar outfits and props that give away their identities and profession.

The cartoon judge has a black robe and gavel; the prisoner wears striped overalls and a ball and chain; the physician dons a smock and holds a stethoscope; the doomsayer is a scrawny long-haired guy carrying a sign saying, "The end is near." These are visual clichés known by the culture at large, and we instantly recognize them.

The visual cliché may be what catches our eye in the editorial cartoon, but the message lies in what the cartoonist does with it. As Gerberg observes, "The message is in twisting it, in turning the cliché around."

Jack Ohman's "Cloned Embryo Department" Cartoon

Consider Jack Ohman's cartoon (from *The Oregonian*) in Figure 8.6 that addresses the issue of human cloning. The visual cliché is a woman shopping in a supermarket. We know that from the familiar props: the shopping cart, the meat display unit, the department banner, and hint of shelving in the background. Even the shopper is a familiar figure, an elderly woman in an overcoat pushing her cart. The twist, of course, is that instead of a refrigeration unit displaying lamb, beef, and poultry, we see trays of neatly arranged embryonic clones with their genetic specialties indicated by pop-up signs.

The issue, of course, is the debate on human cloning. The cartoon was published on December 10, 2001, shortly after the announcement by the genetics firm Advanced Cell Technology in Worcester, Massachusetts, that they had cloned the first human embryo. (The embryos only survived a few cell divisions before they

Figure 8.6   Cartoon by Jack Ohman

perished.) Although the lab claimed that the intention of cloning was not to create human beings but to treat particular human ailments such as Parkinson's disease, cancer, and strokes, the publicity fanned the flames of debate over the ethics and morality of cloning. Some people view such breakthroughs as medically promising; others fear we are crossing the line and playing God. In the United States, there is a ban on using federal money for cloning research or projects, but no ban on private funding. Early in 2005, the British scientific team that had cloned the famous sheep Dolly was granted a license to clone human embryos for medical research.

The cartoon's joke is in the twist—the gap between the familiar and the unexpected. The familiar is the supermarket cliché; the unexpected is the casual display of embryos flagged for desirable traits in a supermarket's "Cloned Embryo Department." Of course, the scene depicts some indefinite future time when cloning is permitted by law and widely practiced.

What Is the Cartoon's Claim?

The claim in this cartoon is that natural birth is better than genetic engineering. That is implicit in the satirical image of the human talents and traits quantified and commercialized in the meat section of the supermarket. And it is explicit in the woman's thoughts, "I miss the stork. . . ."

What Are the Cartoon's Assumptions?

This cartoon makes the assumptions that people see human beings as more complex and elusive than particular traits and talents, and that purchasing babies according to desired traits is perverse and unnatural. It also presumes that readers are familiar with the recent developments in cloning. Although the cartoon appeared shortly after the statement by Advanced Cell Technology, its success is not necessarily dependent on the audience's knowledge of that announcement.

What Is the Cartoon's Evidence?

The cartoon presents the darkly satirical notion that instead of relying on natural procreation, we would someday shop for scientifically perfected babies in a supermarket. Next to more "serious" preferences such as embryos cloned from donors with "1600 SAT" scores and "20/20 vision" are the embryos cloned from people good at juggling and ear wiggling. It is in these juxtapositions that the cartoonist reveals where he stands on the issue. He is mocking our society by reducing the aspirations of would-be parents to having kids with narrowly specific talents.

Ohman's stand is then clearly and more powerfully conveyed by the older woman's private thought—"I miss the stork. . . ." The message is that in the imagined new world where we can shop for our ideal babies, there will be those who yearn for the good old days. Of course, "the stork" is a polite metaphorical reference to sexual reproduction—a term appropriate for the shopper in the drawing, an elderly woman conservatively dressed. However, the term is another cliché, and in a curious twist it plays off the standard supermarket meat department display—as if *stork* were another kind of meat or poultry option.

"BACK IN AUGHT-FIVE WE HAD TO CHOOSE BETWEEN HIGHWAYS AND EDUCATION..."

Figure 8.7   Cartoon by Pat Bagley

QUESTIONS FOR ANALYSIS AND DISCUSSION

Apply the principles of critical analysis described in the above section on editorial cartoons, as well as the elements of form and design discussed earlier in the chapter, to the cartoons. First take a look at Figure 8.7.

1. What is the claim or claims embodied in the visual elements of this political cartoon? What constitutes the evidence of the claim or claims? Cite the specific pieces of evidence.
2. Consider the audience for this cartoon. What groups of citizens would be most likely to have a strong reaction? Does the cartoon suggest a solution to the problems depicted? Are the problems interrelated?
3. What is the tone of the cartoon? Would you describe it as comical? satirical? facetious? overstated? amusing? disturbing?
4. This cartoon originally appeared on the editorial page in *The Salt Lake City Tribune*. Is the cartoon particular to the Salt Lake City area? Why or why not? What could you change in the piece so that it applied to a different city or area?
5. What is the grill-like tray on the top of the cars? And what is the bumper extension jutting off each car? How do they fit into the ad? What is the significance of the insignia on the vehicle on the lower right corner that says "SUV2020"?

6. What might "back in aught-five we had to choose" most likely refer to?
7. Based on the cartoonist's "argument," what do you think he is advocating? Is he for or against highway improvement? for or against education? Can you tell? Does it matter?

QUESTIONS FOR ANALYSIS AND DISCUSSION

Refer to the cartoon in Figure 8.8.

1. What is happening in this cartoon? Whom does the first kid "hate"? Does the cartoon make more sense when we know that it appeared shortly after September 11, 2001? Why or why not?
2. Consider the comment made by the middle kid in the cartoon, who agrees at first, but then asks a clarifying question. Is this significant? Why doesn't the first kid ask the same thing?

Figure 8.8   Cartoon by Daryl Cagle

3. What is the cartoonist's claim in this cartoon? What evidence does he provide? Explain.
4. Although this cartoon was drawn in the context of the events following September 11, 2001, would it have been equally effective ten years ago? ten years into the future? Would the previous cartoon be as timeless? Explain.

News Photographs

Although editorial cartoons can stand on their own, they are frequently featured on editorial pages in newspapers that include commentary on the topic they depict. Photographs are another vehicle used to augment commentary in newspapers, journals, and magazines. Indeed, sometimes the photograph *tells* the story better than words ever could, because it has the ability to touch our deepest emotions instantly.

At first glance, you may think that photos are simply snapshots of an event or moment. But most photographs presented in leading newspapers and journals are the result of effort and planning. Photojournalists are constantly making editorial decisions when they take a picture. They think about where to take the photo, the right moment, whom to include, the angle, the lighting, depth, and speed of film. They consider the subject matter and how it might affect an audience. In some cases, they think about why they are taking the picture and what argument they want to present on film. Some of the most compelling photographs in history come from photojournalists capturing one moment. These photos are not posed, but they still tell a story. Some famous photos include the shot of a sailor kissing a nurse in New York City's Times Square when victory was declared at the end of World War II. Or, who can forget the Pulitzer Prize–winning photo of firefighter Chris Fields carrying the lifeless body of 1-year-old Baylee Almon from the wreckage of the federal office building after the Oklahoma City bombing? While we might not recall the names of the people involved, the image itself remains stamped on our memory.

As a unit, the news story and the photo work together to tell a story. The best photos often tell a story without using any words. But knowing the context in which the photo was taken is important as well. At the very least, the date and location establish the circumstances. Consider Figure 8.9, a photograph of the coffins of American troops in a cargo plane at Kuwait International Airport about to be transported home. This photograph, taken by Tami Silicio, who was working on contract in the military area of the Kuwait Airport, was published in *The Seattle Times* on April 7, 2004. Editors of the newspaper decided to publish the photograph despite a ban by the Pentagon since 1991 of news coverage and photographs of dead soldiers' homecomings. The photograph generated much controversy. Those favoring the ban argue that restricting coverage of the arrival of coffins bearing U.S. dead from Iraq and Afghanistan affords grieving families privacy and sensitivity in their deepest moment of grief. Others who favor the dissemination of images of flag-draped coffins point out that the coffins are treated with the greatest esteem

Figure 8.9

and most formal of protocol. They believe showing the flag-draped coffins is a solemn tribute that honors the supreme sacrifice made by these men and women. Some fear that such pictures would demoralize soldiers and jeopardize support for the war. The fact that a single photograph can generate so many different reactions attests to the power of the visual image.

Who Is the Target Audience?

Because this photograph was published on the front page of *The Seattle Times,* the editors were very aware that the photograph was newsworthy and powerful. They knew that every reader would bring his or her own response to the photograph. Likewise, the editors realized that the image would generate many different responses, some negative, some positive.

What Is the Purpose of the Image?

The image captures a moment in time, a moment the photographer felt was important to save. Tami Silicio, the photographer, said she felt that the photograph would help the families of fallen soldiers understand the incredible care and ceremony with which the remains of fallen soldiers are treated. The photograph shows coffins draped with flags, lined up in ordered and precise rows, tended to by soldiers in uniform in preparation for their return flight to the United States.

What Are the Claims Made in the Image?

One could argue that the picture is a neutral photograph, simply showing flag-draped coffins being prepared for flight to the United States. No elements of the photograph seem to stress a particular point of view or to argue for an opinion. But given the context of war, the viewer of the image can bring many different interpretations to the photograph. Thus, the viewer imposes the claim on the picture. One viewer might be moved by the details suggesting the careful and precise treatment of the coffins. For them, the claim is that military dead are honored and revered for their supreme sacrifice. Another viewer might see a picture of human suffering. The claim for that viewer is that war is about the loss of human life. Another viewer might see the photograph as a violation of privacy. For that viewer, the claim is a lack of respect for grieving families.

What Assumptions Does the Image Make?

The photographer assumes that most people will find this photo arresting and will take a long look at it. Given the context, namely a time of war in Iraq and Afghanistan, it is assumed the photograph is emotionally charged.

QUESTIONS FOR ANALYSIS AND DISCUSSION

Consider the photograph in Figure 8.10 taken by *Boston Globe* photojournalist Suzanne Kreiter. It shows two panhandlers on a Boston street. The photograph accompanied an article, "A Street to Call Home," which reports on how some homeless people panhandle on the very spot where they live.

1. This photograph accompanied an article about homelessness in an urban area of the Northeast. What assumptions about the audience does the photographer make?
2. What details in the photograph convey homelessness to the viewer? Consider objects, location, and background.
3. A close examination of the two main figures in this photograph makes a strong statement about their character. Consider their position, posture, relationship to one another, the direction of their gazes, the facial expressions, and their clothing, and describe the character of these individuals.
4. Would you describe these people as heroic? downtrodden? defiant? helpless victims? noble survivors? Explain why.
5. What argument about homelessness is embedded in this photograph? In other words, what is the claim?
6. Does the background of the photograph detract from or add to the meaning of the photograph?
7. How do you expect to see the homeless depicted? Is this expectation based on stereotype? Does this image of the homeless reinforce or contradict the stereotypical view of the homeless? Explain your

Figure 8.10

answer. Does this photograph change your idea of urban poverty? Why or why not?

8. Do you see any similarities in style or content between this photo- graph and Norman Rockwell's "Freedom of Speech"?

Ancillary Graphics: Tables, Charts, and Graphs

Art, advertisements, editorial cartoons, and news photos all present interesting visual ways to persuade, and knowing how they do this improves your critical thinking and analytical skills. Ancillary graphics, however, such as tables, charts, and graphs, are some visual tools you can use in your own persuasive essays. In Chapter 6, we discussed how numerical data and statistics are very persuasive in bolstering an argument. But a simple table, chart, or graph can convey information at a glance while conveying trends that support your argument. In fact, such visuals are preferable to long, complicated paragraphs that confuse the reader and may detract from your argument.

Ancillary graphics usually take the form of tables, charts, graphs (including line, bar, and pie graphs), and illustrations such as maps and line drawings (of a piece of equipment, for example).

Numerical Tables

There are many ways of representing statistical data. As you know from courses you've taken in math or chemistry, the simplest presentation of numerical data is the table. Tables are useful in demonstrating relationships among data. They present numerical information in tabular fashion arranged in rows or columns so that data elements may be referenced and compared. Tables also facilitate the interpretation of data without the expense of several paragraphs of description.

Suppose you are writing a paper in which you argue that part-time faculty at your institution teach more hours, but are underpaid and undersupported when it comes to benefits. Your research reveals that most part-time faculty receive less than $4,000 per course, and nearly one-third earn $3,000 or less per course—which is little more than the minimum wage. You also discover that the treatment of part-timers at your own school reflects a national trend—faced with rising enrollments and skyrocketing costs, colleges and universities have come to rely more on part-time instructors. Moreover, while they may carry heavier teaching loads, these part-time faculty do not receive the same benefits as full professors. Your claim is that such lack of support is not only unfair to the instructors but also that it compromises the nature of higher education since low compensation drives instructors to take on other jobs to meet the cost of living.

Presenting this information in a table will allow you to demonstrate your point while saving space for your discussion. The tables below provide the results of a survey conducted by the Coalition on the Academic Work Force (CAW), describing how history faculty are facing this situation.

As the title indicates, the table reproduced in Figure 8.11 shows the percentage of history courses taught by full- and part-time faculty. The table intends to help readers understand how much institutions have come to depend on part-time instructors, especially graduate teaching assistants and part-time nontenure-track teachers—people who are paid the least and often denied the benefits enjoyed by full-time faculty. The horizontal rows break down faculty types into five discrete categories—from "Full-Time Tenure Track" at the top to "Graduate Teaching Assistants" at the bottom. The three vertical columns tabulate the percentages according to categories: "Intro Courses," "Other Courses," and "All Courses," which is the median—the calculated halfway point between the other two categories.

Percentage of History Courses Taught, by Faculty Type

	Intro Courses	Other Courses	All Courses
Full-Time Tenure Track	49%	72%	59%
Full-Time Nontenure Track	9%	5%	7%
Part-Time Tenure Track	1%	1%	1%
Part-Time Nontenure Track	23%	15%	19%
Graduate Teaching Assistants	17%	8%	13%
Percentage of All Courses Taught	55%	45%	
Number of Courses Taught	5,825	4,759	10,584

Source: AHA Surveys.

Figure 8.11

Reading from left to right along the first row, we see that 49 percent of the introductory history courses and 72 percent of the "other courses" were taught by full-time tenure-track faculty. This compares with 41 percent of the introductory courses taught by part-timers (part-time tenure track [1%] + part-time nontenure-track faculty [23%] + graduate teaching assistants [17%]). The last column, which represents the median percentage of intro and other courses, tells us that part-timers taught 33 percent or a third of all history courses. That is a compelling figure when tabulated for comparison to full-time faculty.

The second table (Figure 8.12) presents the reported benefits for nontenure-track and part-time faculty. Here nine categories of benefits are tabulated according to three categories of faculty. (Presumably nearly 100 percent of history departments provide full-time tenure-track faculty the kinds of support and benefits listed.) The first line shows the comparative institutional support for travel to professional meetings for the three categories of instructors: 76.9 percent for full-time nontenure track, 46.4 for part-time faculty paid a fraction of full-time salary, and 15.2 for part-time faculty paid by the course.

The fifth line down tabulates the copaid health plan for the three categories of faculty. As we can see at a glance, 72 percent of the institutions with full-time non-tenure-track faculty and 63 percent of the departments with part-time faculty paid a fraction of full-time salaries provide some kind of health plan copaid by the school and faculty member. This compares with just 13 percent of institutions providing such a benefit to part-time faculty paid on a per-course basis. Similarly, 32 percent of the institutions with full-time nontenure-track faculty provided a health plan paid for by the school, as compared to 2.26 percent of those with faculty paid by the course. Reading across the other benefits categories reveals how much more generous institutions were to full-time nontenure-track faculty than to part-timers—including retirement plans and insurance.

History Departments, Benefits

	% for Full-Time Nontenure-Track Faculty	% for Part-Time Faculty (Paid by semester)	% for Part-Time Faculty (Paid by course)
Support Travel to Prof. Mtgs.	76.9	46.4	15.2
Support Attendance at Prof. Mtgs.	41.0	28.6	22.9
Provide Regular Salary Increases	68.4	53.6	28.1
Access to Research Grants	52.1	39.3	13.3
Health Plan Paid by Both	72.17	62.96	12.99
Health Plan Paid by School	32.17	22.22	2.26
Health Plan Paid by Employee	1.74	7.41	3.95
Retirement Plan	73.91	55.56	10.17
Life Insurance	76.52	44.44	5.65

Source: AHA Surveys.

Figure 8.12

As the above paragraphs demonstrate, explaining all this information in the body of your text can be complicated and confusing. And when you are trying to prepare a compelling argument, simplicity of style and clarity of text are essential. Using tables helps you clearly depict data while you move forward with your discussion.

Line Graphs

Line graphs show the relationship between two or more sets of numerical data by plotting points in relation to two axes. The vertical axis is usually used to represent amounts, and the horizontal axis normally represents increments of time, although this is not always the case. Line graphs are probably easier for most people to read than tables, and they are especially useful when depicting trends or changes over time. Consider the graph in Figure 8.13 on page 250.

This graph plots the comparative increase and decrease of full- and part-time faculty over a 25-year period (based on data from American Historical Association

[AHA] surveys). The vertical or *y*-axis represents the percentage of part-time faculty, and the horizontal or *x*-axis represents the time starting from 1980. There are two lines on the graph: The upper line represents the decreasing percentage of full-time history faculty of the colleges and universities surveyed, while the lower line represents the increase in part-time history faculty over the same 25-year pe-riod. The declining slope of the upper line instantly captures the decreasing depen-dence on full-time faculty, whereas the rising slope of the lower line illustrates the increasing dependence on part-time hires. Because the data are plotted on the same graph, we understand how the two are interrelated.

We also notice that neither line is straight but slightly curving. The upper line (full-time faculty) curves downward, while the lower line (part-time faculty) curves upward. Around the year 2005, these lines cross just below the 50th percentile level on the *y*-axis—that is, more than half the college history courses surveyed are currently being taught by part-timers. Also, if we extrapolate both lines toward the right along the curves they are defining, we will eventually arrive at some hypothetical future date when 100 percent of all history courses are taught by part-time faculty and none by full-timers. While we presume that most colleges and universities would not allow this to happen, the trend suggests just how the increased dependence on part-timers is changing the nature of higher education, as fewer courses are taught by full-time faculty. The graphs indeed make a persuasive argument.

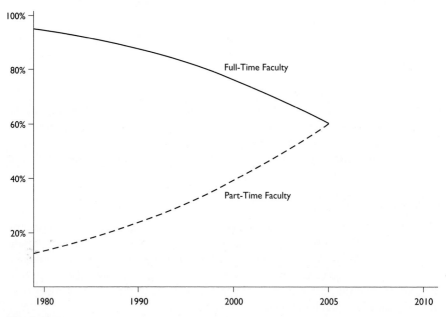

Figure 8.13

Bar Graphs

Bar graphs are often used to compare parts and enable readers to grasp complex data and the relationships among variables at a glance. A bar graph uses horizontal or vertical bars and is commonly used to show either quantities of the same item at different times, quantities of different items at the same time, or quantities of the different parts of an item that make up the whole. They are usually differentiated by contrasting colors, shades, or textures, with a legend explaining what these colors, shades, or textures mean.

The bar graph in Figure 8.14 shows the increase of part-time and adjunct faculty in history departments over a 25-year period as broken down by type of employment and gender (based on data from the AHA survey of the historical profession and unpublished data from AHA departmental surveys). As indicated, the graph demonstrates a dramatic increase in that time period. In 1980, only 4.3 percent of male and 2.0 percent of female history faculty were part-time—a total of 6.3 percent. Two and a half decades later, part-time male and female faculty increased to over 24 percent. This number could be even larger if graduate teaching assistants were included. As this graph shows, the appeal of bar graphs is that they take comparative amounts of data and transform them into instant no-nonsense images.

Pie Charts

Pie charts present data as wedge-shaped sections of a circle or "pie." The total amount of all the pieces of the pie must equal 100 percent. They are an efficient way of demonstrating the relative proportion of the whole something occupies—an instant

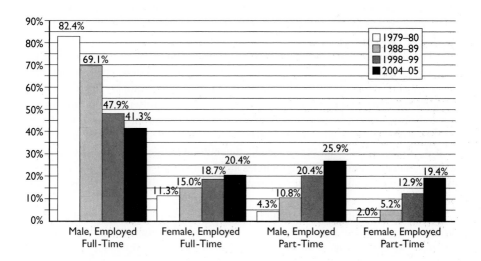

Figure 8.14

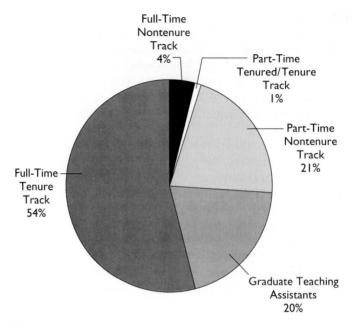

Full-Time
Nontenure
Track
4%

Part-Time
Tenured/Tenure
Track
1%

Part-Time
Nontenure
Track
21%

Full-Time
Tenure
Track
54%

Graduate Teaching
Assistants
20%

Figure 8.15

way to visualize "percentages" without thinking in numbers. But when using pie charts, it is best to include six or fewer slices. If more pieces than that are used, the chart becomes messy and its impact is muted. Figure 8.15 dramatically demonstrates the portion of all history courses in the CAW survey that were taught by part-time faculty, including graduate students.

This pie chart clearly reveals that the combined wedges of graduate teaching assistants and part-time instructors form a substantial portion of the pie. In fact, they comprise almost half of the teaching population. This image quickly and powerfully demonstrates the point of your argument that part-time faculty make up a disproportionately large part of history faculty while receiving a disproportionately small percentage of the benefits. The chart allows readers to visualize the information as they read it. (In the student sample in the Documentation Guide that follows Chapter 9, writing student Shannon O'Neill includes a pie chart along with an editorial cartoon to bolster her written argument, "Literature Hacked and Torn Apart: Censorship in Public Schools." See page 304.)

Used together, these visuals can play an invaluable role in bolstering a written argument on behalf of part-time faculty. Instead of blinding readers with reams of raw data, these pictorials organize numbers and bring their significance to life. Comparative benefits and changing dependencies are transformed into easy-to-understand tables, graphs, and charts. At a glance, complex ideas and confusing numbers are organized into memorable images.

Tips for Using Ancillary Graphics

While understanding the types of ancillary graphics at your disposal is important, it is also important to know how to use them properly. Here are a few guidelines to consider when using graphics in your persuasive essays:

- Include only the data you need to demonstrate your point.
- Make a reference to the chart or graphic in the body of your text.
- Try to keep the graphic on the same page as your discussion.
- Present only one type of information in each graph or chart.
- Label everything in your graph and provide legends where appropriate.
- Assign a figure number to each graphic for easy reference.
- Don't crowd your text too closely around the graphic.
- Remember to document the sources used to create the graphics.

As you begin to incorporate visuals into your own papers, consider the discussion provided earlier in this chapter regarding visual arguments. Consider why you wish to use the graphic and what you want it to do. Think about your audience's needs.

SAMPLE STUDENT ARGUMENT FOR ANALYSIS

Lee Innes, a first-year business major, was interested in the subject of women in sports. He realized what an enormous topic it was and that he needed to narrow it down. He began by asking questions about women in today's world of sports. Why do male athletes dominate the world of sports? What is the impact of sex-role stereotyping on women's athletics? What is Title IX and what is its impact on college athletics? Is scholarship money unfairly distributed to male athletes? In what major sports do women excel? In what major sports do women receive the most attention or the highest salaries or the most product endorsement fees? Why is it that tennis, volleyball, and soccer are among the sports in which women receive the most attention? Why does a sport like women's beach volleyball attract a large and enthusiastic audience?

As Lee thought about the answers, he realized that although each question presented an interesting issue to explore, he had to narrow the focus of his wide-ranging topic to one that he could cover in a paper of reasonable length. While anticipating the 2008 Summer Olympics in Beijing, he thought back on the 2004 summer games in Greece, an event he had followed closely. He recalled feeling conflicted as he watched the women's beach volleyball. The athletic skill and strength of the women was dazzling. But their athletic feats attracted less attention than their scant bikinis. Reflecting on this, Lee realized he had a narrowly defined and specific topic. He decided he would focus only on the issue of women's volleyball and uniform selection process. His essay would consider the controversial issue of women as sexual spectacles in the Olympics. In particular, he was interested in the question of who was responsible for the selection of the uniform and how the women athletes felt about it. He wondered if this was a case of sexism in sport. He arrived at a *working* claim that both limited the range of his topic and very clearly expressed his point of view about it:

> Women in all sports, including Olympic beach volleyball, should be judged and promoted on their skill as athletes not on how they look in bikinis.

His working claim helped him concentrate his research on those areas that pertained most directly to his ideas. In addition to referencing expert views as they appeared in various magazines, newspapers, and on websites, Lee also bolstered his claim—and argument—by including an illustration of men's versus women's Olympic uniforms. The visuals clearly enhanced his written argument.

Innes 1

Lee Innes

Professor Khoury

Writing 122

February 19, 2008

A Double Standard of Olympic Proportions

1   As the Beijing Olympics of 2008 approach, I find myself considering the pressing issues facing this international event. Will America prove to be an athletic force? Will banned, performance enhancing substances taint the games again? And will the women's volleyball team still sport skimpy bikini uniforms?

2   Admittedly, the last question may carry less weight than the others, but as a stereotypical red-blooded heterosexual male, I certainly appreciated the sexy aesthetics of the volleyball competition in 2004 in Athens, Greece. However, the display—and it indeed seemed to be just that—troubled me on a more visceral level. If I had been reading a popular magazine targeting young males, *Maxim* or *FHM* for example, ogling young women in bikinis would have felt fine. But this was the Olympics, and

these women were representing my country—the United States—in an athletic competition.

So to be honest, as both an athlete and an American, I cringed each time one of the women paused to adjust her "uniform." How could these women concentrate on winning Olympic gold with the constant threat of a wedgie on international television? Just what were these women thinking when they picked this uniform, I wondered? How could I take their sporting event seriously when it was so obvious that they didn't take *themselves* seriously? And how could they objectify themselves in this way as they represented not only U.S. athletes, but in many ways, female athletes in particular.

When I shared this observation with a friend who played college volleyball herself, I was surprised to learn that not only did the women of the U.S. Volleyball Team *not* pick those uniforms; they were *forced* to wear it by the Olympic committee. At the time, I was shocked—both by the idea that an official sports organization would require such a uniform, and by the fact that women had not reacted with more outrage.

In 1998, the International Volleyball Federation (FIVB), based in Switzerland, decided volleyball uniforms should be standardized. It was this organization who chose the bikini uniform worn by the Olympic athletes. Interestingly, there was only one woman on the committee when they designed and implemented the uniform. Kristine Drakich, in a 1997 interview with the Canadian Association for the Advancement of Women and Sport and Physical Activity, commented that she was the only female athlete representative for the International Volleyball Federation's Beach

Innes 3

Volleyball World Council at that time. The
council, she observed, was "an intimidating
place for anybody . . . this is a place with
about 50 members, all men, except for my
position" (Robertson). One can surmise that a
predominantly male committee was responsible
for voting in favor of adopting the bikini
uniform for women for beach volleyball
competition. (It makes one wonder if Hugh
Heffner sat in on the meetings.)

6   Perhaps more at issue and culturally
significant is that the men's beach volleyball
uniform was nowhere near as revealing. The men's
uniform featured a tank top and loose-fitting
shorts. The women's uniform, in addition to the
bikini top, sports a brief with a waistline that
falls below the belly button. And the women's
uniform bottoms must be two and a half inches
wide on the sides, providing very little
coverage, even for the toned glutes of these
women. That's only *five* inches wide.

7   Surprisingly, the women's uniform provoked
little public outcry, and not for lack of
publicity. Jeanne Moos reported on the decision
in a *CNN Online* article, "Women's volleyball
uniforms will be standardized in order to banish
t-shirts and shorts." Moos expressed her own
viewpoint bluntly, "Beach volleyball has now
joined go-go girl dancing as perhaps the only
two professions where a bikini is the required
uniform." Yet, the announcement of the FIVB's
decision created little more than a ripple of
controversy. (See FIVB diagrams comparing men's
uniforms to women's.)

8   Opponents of the uniform seemed to become
more vocal as the extensive television coverage
of the Olympic beach volleyball matches brought

Innes 4

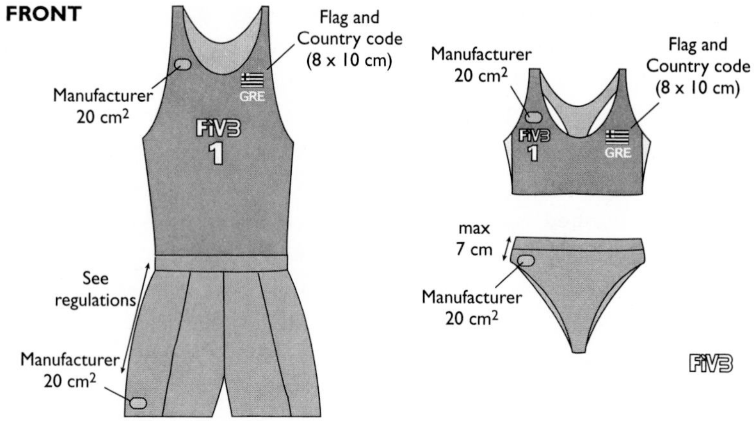

Fig. 1. Men's volleyball uniforms are shown on the left and women's volleyball uniforms are on the right.

the issue to the public eye. Jeneé Osterheldt reported in the August 20, 2004 *Kansas City Star* that the required uniform was upsetting some sports officials and players. "[Female] players can't cover up, even if they want to. . . . Donna Lopiano, executive director of the Women's Sports Foundation, [says] 'It's like telling a swimmer she has to wear a bikini instead of a high-performance suit, when the material has been shown to increase speed. Elasticized attire on leg muscles, especially larger muscles like the thigh, has been proven to reduce fatigue. If you are looking for performance enhancement, you wouldn't choose bikini bottoms" (Osterheldt Al).

But Lopiano's statement addressed what seems to be an irrelevant detail to the IFVB board. Official commentary on the "performance enhancement" of the uniforms is absent from the literature. It would appear that performance has little, if anything, to do with the decision at

all. The uniforms, it seems, were not designed
for functionality, but for marketing purposes. In
a *Business Week* article addressing the "comeback"
of beach volleyball as a legitimate sport,
Leonard Armato, the marketing man responsible for
getting volleyball on NBC as an athletic event,
was quoted admitting, "[Beach volleyball is] an
incredibly sexy sport. We're not embarrassed that
the women [wear] bikinis." Based on ticket sales
for beach volleyball in Athens, it seems like the
IFVB had the right idea.

10   The larger issue is whether athletes
themselves mind the uniforms. Patrick Hruby, a
reporter for *The Washington Times,* noted that
athletes' complaints about bikinis were few, and
even then it wasn't about their own outfits,
most objections were made over the decision to
have a group of bikini-clad dancing girls
entertain between sets during the 2004 beach
competition. Hruby reported, "A handful of
female players, most notably from Australia,
have carped that the dance team is offensive, a
sexist distraction in an otherwise serious
tournament. No objections from Team Netherlands,
however, whose playing uniforms are skimpier—and
more orange—than the dancer's outfits."

11   Even when the IFVB rendered its initial
decision in 1999, few players complained, and
even those who did seemed to lack spirit. "I'm
kind of bummed—I like my tights," said the
sport's perhaps most famous player, Gabrielle
Reece, to a CNN reporter at the time. Reece, who
was known for wearing black Lycra tights rather
than a bikini suit while playing, added "You
take one step, that bathing suit goes straight
up. You're always yanking and fiddling" (Moos).

Innes 6

12   "Bummed" doesn't exactly express the
feminist fury one might expect. If the Williams
sisters of tennis fame have taught us anything,
women like to choose what to wear, and will
often select uniforms that are both performance
enhancing and flattering. If they choose to be
sexy, that's one thing. But to be ordered to
wear a sexy uniform with no alternatives, one
would expect more protests than were reported in
media outlets.

13   All of which then leads me to my next
question: If the women aren't complaining, is
there anything wrong here? As we approach this
next summer Olympiad, is it permissible for me
to enjoy both the view, so to speak, as well as
the competition? It would appear be the case.
Michael Noble commented in his article "Can't
Wait for the Next Olympixxx" printed in the
Canadian newspaper *The Townie*,

>   Of course there is a sexual
>   element to all sports, male and
>   female, and there always has been.
>   Tight pants, skirts, shorts and
>   bathing suits can be found
>   throughout the Olympic lineup. In
>   proper and respectful sports
>   though, admiring the bodies within
>   these suits is kept on a "wink-
>   wink, nudge-nudge" level. They
>   know what you're looking at, but
>   they don't make new rules to
>   accentuate it.
>   Volleyball has taken a
>   different route. Instead of a
>   nudge and a wink, it's a point and
>   a yell—"Hey everyone, take a look

at this ass!" Clearly women's
sports are changing. At one time,
female athletes were all portrayed
as manly "butches." Today they're
shown as suped-up sex machines.
You've come a long way, baby.

14   Indeed, the 2004 beach volleyball events
seemed more party than competition. Between the
scanty uniforms, the dancing-girls, and the
larger than life announcer, Stefano Cesare, it
was easy to forget that the athletes were
competing for Olympic gold. In fact, the beach
volleyball cheerleaders, a troupe from the
Canary Islands called "Personal Plus," gyrating
to the latest techno-pop, often made viewers
forget to look at the *athletes* at all. One is
hard pressed to recall cheerleaders at other
sporting events. Where was Personal Plus during
the track and field competitions?

15   However, one could also argue that
such media attention and the addition of
gyrating cheerleaders helped out both the
sport and the athletes. Since their victory
in Athens, teammates Kerri Walsh and Misty
May have enjoyed tremendous popularity. One
could argue that their cute bikinis certainly
didn't hurt their careers. Donning bikinis
long before their foray into Olympic glory,
the pair was in a Visa ad during the 2004
Super Bowl, playing beach volleyball in the
snow and ice. Their likenesses have been
displayed on McDonald's wrappers and boxes.
And after their Olympic win, they were
featured on the front page of practically
every sports section of every newspaper in
the country. Even the *Wall Street Journal*
ran a photo.

16   Reflection on the issue at hand—is it fair that a group of men have mandated what most female athletes seem to agree is a less than ideal uniform—seems to have no satisfactory answer. A look at the uniforms in the *2007 Beach Volleyball Handbook* leads one to presume that little will change in Beijing. Despite the lack of vocal protest, I am still left with the gnawing feeling that something is amiss. Perhaps Andrea Lewis, a writer for the Progressive Media Project, summarizes it best. "The [2004] games in Athens were a great showcase for athletic talents of both genders, but it's still an Olympian task for women to be treated equally."

Innes 9

Works Cited

"Beach Volleyball Uniforms." Drawing.
<http://www.fivb.ch/en/volleyball/Rules/
RulesCASEBOOK_2001-2004.pdf>.

Hruby, Patrick. "A Day at the Beach." The
Washington Times 20 August 2004, online
edition.

Khermouch, Gerry. "Son of a Beach Volleyball."
Business Week 20 Apr. 2002.

Lewis, Andrea. "Women Athletes Shined at Olympic
Games." Progressive Media Project 30 August
2004 <http://www.progressive.org/
mediaproj04/mpla3004.html>.

Moore, David Leon. "Beach Volleyball's Dynamic
Duo." USA Today 13 August 2004. <http://
www.usatoday.com/sports/olympics/athens/
volleyball/ 2004-08-12-beach-volleyball-
portrait_x.htm>.

Moos, Jeanne. "Bikini Blues—Beach Volleyball
Makes the Swimsuit Standard." CNN Online 13
January 1999. <http://www.cnn.com/STYLE/
9901/13/vollyball.bikini/>.

Osterheldt, Jeneé. "Olympic Athletes Prance Chic
to Cheek." Kansas City Star 20 Aug. 2004,
late ed.: Al.

Robertson, Sheila. "Insight Into An Activist."
ACTION (Canadian Association for the
Advancement of Women and Sport and
Physical Activity) Springs 1998. <http://
www.caaws.ca/Leadership/Activist.htm>.

QUESTIONS FOR ANALYSIS AND DISCUSSION

1. Do you agree with Lee Innes's working claim here? What are your thoughts about the role of male and female athletic attire? about the use of attire to promote or popularize a sporting event? In your journal, respond to Innes's ideas by exploring your own views on the media's promotion of women athletes and whether or not the promotion is based on talent or appearance.

2. Consider the effectiveness of the author's use of the visuals comparing beach volleyball uniforms for men and women. Do the illustrations bolster Innes's argument? Were you impressed with their comparisons? Did the visuals convince you that there's an inequity if not sexual exploitation in uniform guidelines? Explain your answers.

3. Even if you didn't watch the women's beach volleyball competition in the 2004 or 2008 Olympics or don't follow the sport, do you think that most fans are concerned with what Innes and others see as sexual exploitation? Do you think that the media will ever respond to Innes's concern? Why or why not?

4. What do you make of the fact that few female athletes complained that they had to wear bikinis? Does that weaken Innes's argument? Or do you see that lack of concern as legitimate disinterest? Or as suggested by the article, do you think that the lack of complaints suggests more deeply rooted gender issues in our culture?

5. In Innes's last paragraph, he wonders if there's really a problem in what female athletes wear. What specific counterarguments to his position does he cite? In spite of these, why is he still left with a "gnawing sense that something isn't right here"? Do you agree? Are you also convinced as Andrea Lewis claims that rendering equal treatment for woman athletes is "an Olympian task"?

6. In your journal, write an entry as if done by a member of the Women's Olympic Volleyball Team after the first day of competition. In it, explore how she felt about her uniform.

CHAPTER 9

Researching Arguments

Thinking Like an Investigator

Most arguments derive their success from the evidence they contain, so good argumentative writers learn to find evidence in many sources and present the best evidence to support their claims. In the academic world, much of that evidence is gathered through *research,* either conducted in a lab or field or through examination of the previously published work of other investigators and scholars. The research paper you may be asked to write challenges you to learn how more experienced writers find and present evidence that meets the standards of the academic community.

When you walk through the library, you are surrounded with researched arguments. The book claiming that the Kennedy assassination was part of a CIA conspiracy is a researched argument. So are the journal articles asserting that Shakespeare's plays were written by Sir Francis Bacon and the research report that claims AZT is an effective treatment for some AIDS patients. The article in *Fortune* on the need for changes in the capital gains tax is one, too, as is the review claiming that Nirvana was the most important band of the 1990s. All these arguments have something in common: To back up their claims, their authors have brought in supporting evidence that they gathered through a focused research effort. That evidence gives you and readers like you grounds by which to decide whether you will agree with the authors' claims. Libraries, then, aren't just storehouses for history; they provide good writers with valuable information to support their ideas.

In the previous chapters, we've stressed the importance of finding evidence that will impress readers of your argument's merits. To review, researched evidence plays an important role in convincing readers of the following:

- Expert, unbiased authorities agree with your position in whole or in part, adding to your credibility.
- Your position or proposal is based on facts, statistics, and real-life examples, not mere personal opinion.
- You understand different viewpoints about your subject as well as your own.
- Your sources of information are verifiable, since researched evidence is always accompanied by documentation.

A good analogy to use, once again, is that of the lawyer presenting a case to a jury. When you write a researched argument, you're making a case to a group of people who will make a decision about a subject. Not only do you present your arguments in the case but also you call on witnesses to offer evidence and expert opinion, which you then interpret and clarify for the jury. In a researched argument, your sources are your witnesses.

Writing an argumentative research paper isn't different from writing any other kind of argument, except in scale. You will need more time to write the paper in order to conduct and assimilate your research, the paper is usually longer than nonresearched papers, and the formal presentation (including documentation) must be addressed in more detail. The argumentative research paper is an extension and refinement of the essays you've been writing. It's not a different species of argument.

Sources of Information

There are two basic kinds of research sources, and depending partly on the type of issue you've picked to research, one may prove more helpful than the other. The first kind is *primary sources,* which include firsthand accounts of events (interviews, diaries, court records, letters, manuscripts). The second is *secondary sources,* which interpret, comment on, critique, explain, or evaluate events or primary sources. Secondary sources include most reference works and any books or articles that expand on primary sources. Depending on whether you choose a local or a more global issue to write about, you may decide to focus more on primary or more on secondary source, but in most research, you'll want to consider both.

Primary Sources

If you choose a topic of local concern to write about, your chief challenge will be finding enough research material; very current controversies or issues won't yet have books written about them, so you may have to rely more heavily on electronic databases, which you can access through a computer, or interviews and other primary research methods to find information. If you choose a local issue to argue, consider the following questions.

- Which experts on campus or in the community might you interview to find out the pros and cons of the debated issue? an administrator at your college? a professor? the town manager? Think of at least two local experts who could provide an overview of the issue from different angles or perspectives.
- What local resources—such as a local newspaper, radio station, TV station, or political group—are available for gathering printed or broadcast information? If one of your topics is a campus issue, for example, the student newspaper, student committees or groups, university online discussion groups, or the student government body might be places to search for information.

Once you determine that you have several possible sources of information available locally, your next step is to set up interviews or make arrangements to read or view related materials. Most students find that experts are eager to talk about local issues and have little problem setting up interviews. However, you'll need to allow plenty of time in your research schedule to gather background information, phone for interviews, prepare your questions, and write up your notes afterward. If you're depending on primary research for the bulk of your information, get started as soon as the paper is assigned.

Preparing for Interviews

A few common courtesies apply when preparing for interviews. First, be ready to discuss the purpose of your interview when setting up an appointment. Second, go into the interview with a list of questions that shows you have already thought about the issue. Be on time and have a notebook and pen to record important points. If you think you may want to quote people directly, ask their permission to do so and read the quotation back to them to check it for accuracy.

Conducting Interviews

Be prepared to jot down only key words or ideas during the interview, reserving time afterward to take more detailed notes. Keep the interview on track by asking focused questions if the interviewee wanders while responding to your question. When you are leaving, ask if it would be okay to call if you find you have additional questions later.

Writing Up Interviews

As soon as possible after the interview, review the notes you jotted down and flesh out the details of the conversation. Think about what you learned. How does the information you gathered relate to your main topic or question? Did you gather any information that surprised or intrigued you? What questions remain? Record the date of your interview in your notes as you may need this information to document your source when you write the paper.

Preparing Interview Questions

Consider the following guidelines as you prepare questions for an interview:

- Find out as much information as you can about the issue and about the expert's stand on the issue before the interview. Then you won't waste interview time on general details you could have found in the newspaper or on the local TV news.
- Ask open-ended questions that allow the authority to respond freely, rather than questions requiring only "yes" or "no" answers.
- Prepare more questions than you think you need and rank them in order of priority according to your purpose. Using the most important points as a guide, sequence the list in a logical progression.

Secondary Sources

Although many primary sources—published interviews, public documents, results of experiments, and first-person accounts of historical events, for example—are available in the college library, the library is also a vast repository of secondary source material. If your topic is regional, national, or international in scope, you'll want to consider both of these kinds of sources. For example, if your topic is proposed changes to the Social Security system, you might find information in the *Congressional Record* on committee deliberations, a primary source, and also read editorials on the op-ed page of the *New York Times* for interpretive commentary, a secondary source.

A Search Strategy

Because the sheer amount of information in the library can be daunting, plan how you will find information before you start your search. Always consult a reference librarian if you get stuck in planning your search or if you can't find the information you need.

Preview: A Search Strategy

- Choose your topic.
- Get an overview of your topic.
- Compile a working bibliography.
- Locate sources.
- Evaluate sources.
- Take notes.

Choosing Your Topic

Your argument journal may remind you of potential topics, and Chapter 3 covered how to develop a topic. But what if you still can't think of a topic? You might try browsing through two print sources that contain information on current issues:

Facts on File (1940 to the present). A weekly digest of current news.

Editorials on File (1970 to the present). Selected editorials from U.S. and Canadian newspapers reprinted in their entirety.

If you have access to the Internet, the *Political Junkie* website will provide you with ideas from the latest news stories in national and regional newspapers and magazines, columnists' viewpoints on current issues, up-to-the-minute reports on public figures, and links to the websites of numerous political and social organizations. You can access this site at <http://www.politicaljunkie.com>. Also, think about which subjects you find interesting from the essays in Part Two of this book. These four sources should give you a wealth of ideas to draw on.

Getting an Overview of Your Topic

If you know little about your topic, encyclopedias can give you general background information. Just as important, encyclopedia articles often end with bibliographies on their subjects—bibliographies prepared by experts in the field. Using such bibliographies can save you hours in the library.

If your library houses specialized encyclopedias related to your topic either in print or through computer, check them first. If not, go to the general encyclopedias. Following is a list of general and specialized encyclopedias you may find helpful.

General Encyclopedias

Academic American Encyclopedia. Written for high school and college students.

New Encyclopedia Britannica and *Britannica Online. Micropaedia* is a ten-volume index of the *New Encyclopedia Britannica.*

Encyclopedia Americana. Extensive coverage of science and technology and excellent on American history.

Specialized Encyclopedias

Encyclopedia of American Economic History (1980). Overview of U.S. economic history and aspects of American social history related to economics.

Encyclopedia of Bioethics (1995). Covers life sciences and health care.

Encyclopedia of Philosophy (1972). Scholarly articles on philosophy and philosophers.

Encyclopedia of Psychology (1994). Covers topics in the field of psychology.

Encyclopedia of Religion (1993). Covers theoretical, practical, and sociological aspects of religion worldwide.

Encyclopedia of Social Work (1995). Covers social work issues including minorities and women.

Encyclopedia of World Art (1959–1983). Covers artists and artworks and contains many reproductions of artworks.

McGraw-Hill Encyclopedia of Science and Technology (1997). Covers physical, natural, and applied sciences.

This is just a brief listing of the many encyclopedias available in areas that range from marriage and the family to folklore and social history. Your librarian can assist you in finding the encyclopedia you need. Be sure to check the dates of encyclopedias so you locate the most current information available.

Compiling a Working Bibliography

Because you don't know at the beginning of your search which sources will prove most relevant to your narrowed topic, keep track of every source you consult. Record complete publication information about each source in your notebook, on 3" × 5" index cards, or on printouts of online sources. The list that follows describes the information you'll need for particular kinds of sources.

For a Book

- Authors' and/or editors' names
- Full title, including subtitle
- Place of publication (city, state, country)
- Date of publication (from the copyright page)
- Name of publisher
- Volume or edition numbers
- Library call number

For an Article

- Authors' names
- Title and subtitle of article
- Title of periodical (magazine, journal, newspaper)
- Volume number and issue number, if any
- Date of the issue
- All page numbers on which the article appears
- Library location

For an Electronic Source

- Authors' names, if given
- Title of material accessed
- Name of periodical (if applicable)
- Volume and issue numbers (if applicable)
- Date of material, if given
- Page numbers or numbers of paragraphs (if indicated)
- Title of the database
- Publication medium (e.g., CD-ROM, diskette, microfiche, online)
- Name of the vendor, if relevant
- Electronic publication date
- Date of access to the material, if relevant
- Path specification for online media (e.g., FTP information; directory; file name)

Note that for electronic sources, which come in many different formats, you should record all the information that would allow another researcher to retrieve the documents you used. This will vary from source to source, but the important point is to give as much information as you can.

Your instructor may ask you to prepare an *annotated bibliography,* in which you briefly summarize the main ideas in each source and note its potential usefulness. You will also want to evaluate each source for accuracy, currency, or bias.

Sample Entries for an Annotated Bibliography

Shannon O'Neill, a second-year journalism major, decided to write her argument essay on book banning in the public schools. Here are some sample entries from her annotated bibliography. (Shannon O'Neill's paper can be found on pages 304–315 in the Documentation Guide.)

Barnhisel, Greg, ed. *Media and Messages: Strategies and Readings in Public Rhetoric.* **New York: Pearson Education, 2005.** This book contains many useful essays, editorials, and articles examining contemporary issues in the media and presents a balanced view of a large variety of topics. Barnhisel draws summaries and conclusions based on information in each chapter, which is useful. The book is unbiased because it presents criticisms from all angles. I used an article and an editorial from this text in my paper because they give interesting perspectives on censorship of the written word; one focused on the censorship of student newspapers, and the other criticized the idea of what's "politically correct" and how that relates to censorship. Both pieces advocate against censorship, though, and while the text as a whole is balanced, there aren't any helpful pieces advocating for censorship of the written word; rather, they focused on censorship of the visual media or of the Internet.

"Keeping the Faith in Public Schools." *Gateways to a Better Education.* **2004. 5 Feb. 2005** <http://www.gtbe.org>. This website is for a national organization that promotes the spread of Christian values. While it does not advocate for the censorship or removal of specific works, it encourages parents to challenge their children's curriculum and take an active part in deciding what should or should not be taught in public schools—all with a Christian agenda. This site is clearly biased, but it is an important and useful source for the presentation of the religious argument for book censorship.

"Challenged and Banned Books." American Library Association. 2005. 5 Feb. 2005 <http://www.ala.org/ala/oif/bannedbooksweek/challengedbanned/challengedbanned.htm#web>. This organization's website is an extremely useful source because it gives background information on the banning and censoring of books and gives recent lists of frequently banned books and authors. It also gives statistics on reasons for challenges, which I used for a pie chart. The site could be considered biased, though, because it encourages the idea of free speech and discourages censorship based on the premise of the First Amendment. It also encourages people to read banned books and coined Banned Book Week, which celebrates books that have been banned or challenged.

A working bibliography (as opposed to an annotated bibliography) would include the complete publication information for each source, but not the evaluation of its usefulness to the paper.

Locating Sources

Your college library offers a range of methods and materials for finding the precise information you need. Here is a brief guide to locating periodicals, books, and electronic sources.

Finding Periodicals

Instead of going to the periodicals room and leafing page by page through magazines, journals, and newspapers to find information pertinent to your topic, use periodical indexes to locate the articles you need. Your college library will have these indexes available in print, CD-ROM, or online databases. The form you choose will depend on what is available and how current your information must be. When deciding whether to use the printed or electronic versions, carefully note the dates of the material the indexes reference. For example, you cannot use the CD-ROM version of *The Readers' Guide to Periodical Literature* to find a source from 1979. However, for a more current source (from 1983 to present), use the CD-ROM version since it provides abstracts of articles. These will allow you to decide whether locating the full article is worth your time and effort. Here is a list of some of the periodical indexes often available in college libraries. If your library does not have these indexes, ask the reference librarian the best way to find periodical articles in your library.

Periodical Indexes

General

Readers' Guide to Periodical Literature. 1915 to present. Print. Indexes popular journals and magazines and some reviews of movies, plays, books, and television.

Readers' Guide Abstracts. 1983 to present. Same content as *Readers' Guide* but with abstracts.

Newspaper Abstracts. 1985 to present. Abstracts of articles in national and regional newspapers.

New York Times. 1851 to present. Extensive coverage is national and international.

Periodical Abstracts. 1986 to present. Abstracts and full-text articles from more than 950 general periodicals.

ABI/Inform. August 1971 to present. About eight hundred thousand citations to articles in 1,400 periodicals. Good source for business-related topics. Complete text of articles from five hundred publications since 1991.

LexisNexis Universe. Full-text access to newspapers, magazines, directories, legal and financial publications, and medical journals.

Specialized

Applied Science and Technology Index/Applied Science and Technology Abstracts. 1913 to present. Covers all areas of science and technology.

Art Index/Art Abstracts. 1929 to present. Wide coverage of art and allied fields.

Business Periodicals Index. 1958 to present. Covers all areas of business.

Education Index/Education Abstracts. 1929 to present. June 1983 to present. Covers elementary, secondary, and higher education.

PAIS International in Print/PAIS Database (formerly *Public Affairs Information Service Bulletin*). 1915 to present. Excellent index to journals, books, and reports in economics, social conditions, government, and law.

Ethnic Newswatch. 1990 to present. Indexes news publications by various ethnic groups. Includes full texts of most articles.

Social Sciences Index (*International Index* 1907–1965; *Social Sciences and Humanities* 1965–1974; *Social Sciences Index* 1974 to present). 1907 to present.

Indexes scholarly journals in political science, sociology, psychology, and related fields.

Humanities Index. (See *Social Sciences Index* entry for name changes.) 1907 to present. Covers scholarly journals in literature, history, philosophy, folklore, and other fields in the humanities.

America: History and Life. 1964 to present. Index and abstracts to articles in more than 2,000 journals. Covers the histories and cultures of the United States and Canada from prehistory to the present.

SPORT Discus. 1975 to present. Covers sports, physical education, physical fitness, and sports medicine.

Social Issues Researcher (SIRS). Full-text articles from newspapers, journals, and government publications related to the social sciences.

Congressional Universe. Offers a legislative perspective on congressional bills, hearings, public laws, and information on members of Congress.

Sociofile. 1974 to present. Coverage includes family and socialization, culture, social differentiation, social problems, and social psychology.

Essay and General Literature Index. 1900 to present. Indexes essays and chapters in collected works. Emphasis is on social sciences and humanities.

Finding Books

Your library catalogue, whether available in printed (card), electronic, or microform format, indexes the books your library holds. (You may be able to access other kinds of sources using the catalogue as well, for example, government documents or maps.) Every catalogue provides access to books in three basic ways: by author, title, and general subject. If the catalogue is electronic, you can also use keyword searching to locate books. In a keyword search on a computer terminal, you type in a word related to your topic, and the catalogue lists all the sources that include that word.

To make keyword searching more efficient, you can often combine two or more search terms. For example, if you know that you want information on "violence" and can narrow that to "violence and music not rap music," the catalogue will give you a much shorter list of sources than if you had typed only "violence," which is a very broad topic. This is called Boolean searching, and the typical ways you can combine terms are to use "and" to combine search terms; "or" to substitute search terms (e.g., "violent crime" or "assault"); and "not" to exclude terms. For example, suppose you are looking for information on cigarette smoking by teenagers. In a Boolean search, you could use the search phrase: "teenager or youth and smoking not marijuana."

If you are searching by subject rather than author or title, it's useful to know that libraries organize subject headings according to the *Library of Congress Subject Headings (LCSH).* These are large red books, usually located near the library's catalogue. You will save time and be more successful if you look up your subject in the *LCSH.* For example, if you search the catalogue using the term "movies," you won't find a single source. If you look up "movies" in the *LCSH,* it will tell you that the subject heading is "motion pictures." Type in "motion pictures," and you'll find the sources you need.

Listed below are other useful sources of information.

Biographies

There are so many different biographical sources it is difficult to know which one has the information you need. The following titles will save you a lot of time:

Biography and Genealogy Master Index. (Spans from B.C. to the present.) Index to more than one million biographical sources.

Biographical Index. 1947 to present. International and all occupations. Guide to sources in books, periodicals, letters, diaries, etc.

Contemporary Authors. 1962 to present. Contains biographical information about authors and lists of their works.

Almanacs

World Almanac and Book of Facts. 1968 to present. Facts about government, business, society, etc. International in scope.

Statistical Abstract of the United States. 1879 to present. Published by the U.S. Bureau of the Census. Good source for statistics about all aspects of the United States including economics, education, society, and politics.

Statistical Masterfile. 1984 to present. State and national government statistics and private and international.

Reviews, Editorials

Book Review Digest. 1905 to present. Index to book reviews with excerpts from the reviews.

Book Review Index. 1965 to present. Indexes to more books than the above but doesn't have excerpts from reviews.

Bibliographies

Look for these in journal articles, books, encyclopedia articles, biographical sources, etc.

Finding Internet Sources

The Internet offers countless possibilities for research using government documents, newspapers and electronic journals, websites, business publications, and much more. You may have access to the Internet through either campus computer labs or your own computer. The easiest way to access the Net is by using the World Wide Web (WWW), a point-and-click system in which related documents are linked.

To make your search easier and more efficient, you can rely on several of the powerful search engines available for exploring the World Wide Web. Each of the search engines we've listed below uses keyword searches to find material on your topic. These words can specify your topic, supply the title of a book or article about your topic, name a person associated with your topic, and so on. It's important to try out a number of keyword combinations when you are searching for resources. For instance, if your topic is assisted suicide, you might also search under *euthanasia* and *physician-assisted suicide.* By adding additional terms such as *terminal illness, legalization,* and *patient's rights,* you may be able to both narrow your search and find material filed under different topic headings that are related to your subject.

Here is a list of the more popular search engines. You'll find them useful for locating information on the Internet:

Google *<http://www.google.com>*
This search engine is the first line for searching and the most popular. It will give you a lot of options. Keywords can be used for subject searches or to find a phrase that appears in the sources. You may also supply the name of a person or a title to prompt your search. It will search for each of your keywords separately or as a unit. You can also limit or expand the time parameters of your search from the current date to up to two years. A word of caution: Information found on Google may not always be appropriate or credible. (See section below on evaluating sources.)

Yahoo! *<http://www.yahoo.com>*
Yahoo! works just like *Google*. It will also expand your search by linking you to two other search engines if you request them.

About.com *<http://www.about.com>*
Although not as useful for academic research as are *Google, Dogpile*, and *Yahoo!* this search engine connects users to a network of experts or "guides" who offer practical solutions to common problems spanning a wide field of topics.

In addition to the traditional search engines, there are others that conduct "meta searches"; that is, they allow you to leverage the power of many popular search engines at the same time. Combined, these engines cover more of the Internet than a single search engine can cover. Here is a list of some of the most popular and powerful meta-search engines:

Dogpile *<http://www.dogpile.com>*
This is a popular meta-search engine that combines the power of several other major search engines including *Google, Yahoo! Search, Live Search, Ask.com*, and *LookSmart*. It displays results from each different search engine.

ixquick.com *<http://ixquick.com>*
This meta-search engine ranks results based on the number of "top 10" rankings a site receives from the various search engines.

Zworks.com *<http://zworks.com>*
Like *Ixquick*, when you use *Zworks* you are searching many popular search engines at the same time. Combined, these engines cover more databases on the Internet than any one search engine covers.

Wikipedia *<http://wikipedia.org>*
Websites that are managed by their readers are called wikis. Users can log in and add or edit pages, updating and correcting information. The interaction creates an online collaboration of information. Perhaps the best-known and most popular is *Wikipedia,* an online multilingual encyclopedia. Wikipedia covers a vast range of topics with articles that are useful and current and that offer links to related pages and additional information. But users should be warned that

unlike written articles, Wikipedia entries may be lacking in substance and balance. Also, because the entries are created by "regular" readers and are constantly being revised, material is subject to error and misinformation.

When you are using any search engine, be sure to check the instructions so you can use it as effectively as possible. Also, don't rely on only one search engine. Use several to give yourself access to the broadest range of materials.

Three additional websites that may help you if you are searching for information related to government, politics, legislation, or statistics are the following:

Library of Congress <*http://www.loc.gov*>
This website provides information about the U.S. Congress and the legislative process. It will search for past legislative bills by topic, bill number, or title; allow you to read the *Congressional Record* from the current and past years' Congresses; find committee reports by topic or committee name; and provide full-text access to current bills under consideration in the House of Representatives and the Senate.

U.S. Census Bureau <*http://www.census.gov*>
You can find facts, figures, and statistics derived from the last census at this site. There is also some information about world population.

White House <*http://www.whitehouse.gov*>
At this site, you can find current and past White House press briefings and news releases, as well as a full range of statistics and information produced by federal agencies for public use.

Remember that the Internet is constantly changing, so no book will be completely up to date on how to access its information. Check to see if your college has workshops or courses on using the Internet—it's an important research tool, and it's worth your time to learn how to navigate in cyberspace.

Evaluating Sources

The first examination of your sources isn't intended to find the precise information you'll use in your final paper; rather, it is a preliminary assessment to help you decide whether the material is *relevant* and *reliable* for your purposes.

Print Sources

You can often sense a print source's relevance by skimming its preface, introduction, table of contents, conclusion, and index (for books) or abstract and headings (for articles) to see whether your topic appears and how often. Many students mark their bibliography cards with numbers (1 = most relevant, 2 = somewhat relevant, 3 = not very relevant) to help them remember which sources they most want to examine. If a source contains no relevant material, mark the bibliography card "unusable" but don't discard it; if you refine your topic or claim later, you may want to go back to that source.

The reliability of a printed source is judged in a number of ways:

- Check the date: Is it recent or timely for your topic?
- Look at the citations: Is the author's evidence recent or timely?
- Is the author an expert in the field? To find out, use the biographical sources listed earlier in this chapter or find book reviews in the reference section.
- Where does the author work? A source's credentials may influence your readers. You may also find out what biases the author may have; for example, if the author is the founder of Scientists Against Animal Research, you'll have a good idea about his or her personal beliefs on that subject.

Electronic Sources

Using material that you find on the Internet will present special challenges in determining the value of a source. Unlike most printed journal and newspaper articles and books, Internet materials are not necessarily reviewed by editors or professional colleagues to determine whether the facts are correct and the conclusions reliable. Anyone who has (or knows someone who has) the technical skills can develop a website and post opinions for the world to read. Sometimes it's difficult to determine whether the information you find on the Web is worth using. While there are no hard-and-fast rules to indicate whether an Internet source is reliable, here are a few suggestions that will help you evaluate whether you have found a credible source:

- **Domain address**   Each Internet host computer is assigned a domain indicating the type of organization that created the site. This domain indicator appears at the end of the address. Most sites will be labeled one of the following:

  edu for an educational site

  gov for a government site

  com for a commercial site

  org for an organizational site

  While we can't vouch for the quality of all the material at these different domains, it is more likely that sites affiliated with an educational institution or a government office will provide information that has been carefully researched and prepared. Although commercial sites and sites sponsored by organizations may also provide valid information, it is important to check carefully for bias or misinformation that might be made available to further the interests of the business or organization.
- **Author of the site**   Try to identity the author or authors of the material published at the site. Is the author a professional or an authority in a field relevant to the topic? The director of a public health clinic may have opinions worth considering on the medical use of marijuana; he may or may not have the same level of credibility in a discussion about punishment for juvenile criminals.
- **Identity of the organization**   If the site is maintained by an organization, find out what interests, if any, the organization represents. Who created the organization? A government-appointed committee investigating public support

of family planning will have a very different agenda from a committee organized by private interest groups. While both groups may be scrupulously honest in their presentation of the facts, each may interpret those facts with a particular bias. Your awareness of their "slant" will help you decide how to use the information. The reference section of most libraries can provide directories of associations and organizations.

- **Date of posting**   Check the date when the site was posted. Has the site been updated recently? If not, is the material still current and relevant?

- **Quality of references**   Are sources provided to support the information posted on the site? Most credible sites will document their facts, research studies, and statistics. Many articles and essays will be followed by a bibliography. It's always a good idea to double-check these references to determine whether the information is accurate. The absence of any references to support statements of fact and statistics may indicate that the site is unreliable.

- **Quality of material**   Look for indications that the material has been written or assembled by an educated, well-informed individual who offers a balanced and thoughtful perspective on the issue. Is the written text free of obvious grammatical mistakes, spelling errors, problems with sentence structure, and so on? Does the author indicate awareness and respect for other views even while disagreeing with them? Is the coverage of material thorough and well supported? Although poorly written and executed websites can be obvious indications of low reliability, don't be fooled by slick, attractive presentations either. You need to investigate beneath the surface to determine whether the content of the site meets academic standards of fairness and thoroughness.

- **Intended use**   Consider how you will use the material at the site. If you are looking for reliable statistics and factual information, then checking the author's credentials and the status of the organization or company will be important to maintaining your own credibility. However, there are times when personal examples and experiences of individuals who are not professionally qualified may still be of value. For example, a student writing a paper on Alzheimer's disease came across a site in which an Alzheimer's victim kept a diary of the progression of her illness. Even though she was not qualified to give expert medical opinion on the disease itself, her diary provided a unique insight into the feelings and perceptions of someone experiencing the loss of her intellectual capabilities. In her paper, the student writer was able to incorporate some of this compelling personal testimony.

Let's see how this advice works in practice. Shannon decided to do an Internet search to find background information for her argument essay on book banning in the public schools. (Sample entries from her annotated bibliography appear earlier in this chapter.) Using several search engines and a keyword search, Shannon had no trouble finding a large number of sites concerned with this subject. However, before relying on the information she found at the sites, Shannon had to determine which sites were reliable. To do this, she examined several features of each site, as recommended above.

The first site Shannon found was called *The Online Books Page: Banned Books Online* <http://onlinebooks.library.upenn.edu/banned-books.html>. Using the criteria from the list we've provided, Shannon made the following evaluation of the site (see Figure 9.1):

- **Domain address** As Shannon noted, the domain address identified the website as being based at the University of Pennsylvania, a well-known and reputable school.
- **Author of the site** At the end of the site, the author identified himself by name. Using the home page link "About Us" under "The Inside Story" (see Figure 9.1), Shannon found information about the author who identified himself as a computer scientist who works in a library at the University of Pennsylvania and who received a PhD in computer science at Carnegie Mellon University. But since this description didn't indicate any special expertise on the subject of banned books, Shannon returned to the home page and clicked on the link "Banned Books."
- **Identity of the organization** That link provided on the home page allowed Shannon to gather more information about *The Online Books Page* and its

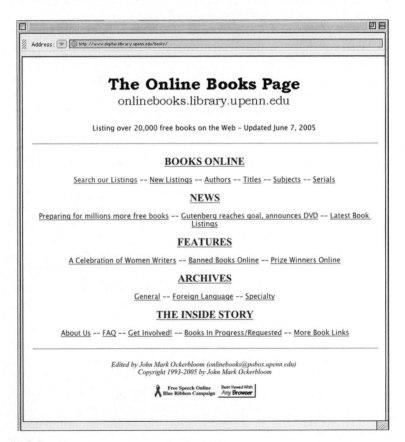

Figure 9.1

author. Shannon found a number of links that provided her with considerable information on banned books including classics by Geoffrey Chaucer and John Milton. Another link specified the criteria used to determine which books were placed on the banned book list. Still other links provided further background information about the goals of the site and its association with the Library of Congress. This information and the support of well-known and credible organizations and projects made Shannon feel confident about the value of this site.

- **Date of posting** Shannon noted that the material on the website was current, having last been updated in the very month in which she was doing her research. The site itself contained information about both recent attempts to limit public library Internet access and historical accounts of book banning.

- **Quality of references** The author provided frequent references to other websites on banned books, as well as to printed books on censorship. Checking through the Internet and the college library, Shannon confirmed that these references were used reliably and even decided to incorporate some of them into her research.

- **Quality of material** Shannon found the text well written and the entire site organized and thorough. To evaluate whether the author's perspective was well balanced, Shannon checked to see if books from all ends of the political spectrum were included in the list. She discovered that the list included a group of diverse books, from the Bible to the Qur'an to works of nineteenth-century poetry to contemporary books that had been criminalized under "hate speech" laws in other countries. Although it was clear to Shannon that the author of the site did not approve of book banning, this bias did not seem to distort the information he provided.

- **Intended use** Shannon was interested in finding out the titles of books that were banned, those responsible for the banning, and the reasons behind the decisions. She found *The Online Books Page* very useful. Shannon was particularly impressed by its range of titles. The site's list covered classic and historical works, as well as more modern ones. The explanations that accompanied each listing briefly explained the circumstances surrounding the book's censorship and provided specific dates and information about it.

After carefully evaluating *The Online Books Page: Banned Books Online,* Shannon concluded that it was a reliable source that might supply her with valuable information for her argument essay.

Shannon found three other websites that were also concerned with the issue of banned books. However, after using the criteria outlined above to evaluate the three, Shannon decided not to use them. Here are some of the reasons why:

- **Domain address** Two of the sites had addresses that indicated that they had no association with any educational institution, government, business, or organization; the websites were developed by individuals for their own personal use. Shannon decided that the materials on these sites were more likely to reflect personal opinion than careful research. The third site was maintained by an organization that Shannon decided to investigate further.

- **Author of the site**   By using the links provided in each site, Shannon discovered that one author was a student writing a paper for an Internet course; another was an individual who supplied some personal information about his life (as well as family photographs), but nothing that indicated expertise on book banning; and the third was identified as a news editor for a newspaper published in California. Shannon needed more information before she could conclude that any of these authors was a reliable source.
- **Identity of the organization**   Only the site authored by the newspaper editor indicated an association with an organization. Using links in the site, Shannon found that he was affiliated with a religious group that strongly advocated the elimination of different races and religions in American life. After reading several articles on the group's website, Shannon concluded that the material contained strong political and racial bias that made her question the reliability of the newspaper editor.
- **Date of posting**   None of the sites had been updated within the past year. Although Shannon was interested in both historical and current information on book banning, she was concerned that the authors had made no attempts to keep the information in the sites current and timely.
- **Quality of references**   Only one site contained a list of related readings, and none of the sites used references to support statements of fact or opinion.
- **Quality of material**   Shannon immediately noticed the poor writing quality of the student paper. It was filled with misspellings and grammatical errors and was poorly organized. The second site demonstrated better quality writing, but the author did not develop or support his ideas sufficiently. For instance, he based much of his claim on an "informal survey" without specifying the details of how the survey was conducted. The site authored by the newspaper editor did not reflect respect for other viewpoints or any attempt to present a balanced perspective on the issue of book banning.
- **Intended use**   Shannon wanted to be sure that the information she used in her argument essay was accurate. The absence of information about two of the authors and the political affiliations of the third caused her to doubt that any of these sites could be relied on for accuracy.

As Shannon discovered, the Internet can offer a wide array of source material to research, but it does take additional effort to determine which sources will meet the academic standards required for research. If you remember to think like an investigator and examine your findings carefully, you'll discover reliable and valuable information and ideas for your argument essays.

Taking Notes

There are as many different styles of note taking as there are writers. Some people like to use 4" × 6" cards, recording one idea on each card. This is useful because you can easily shift cards around as you change your outline; you don't have to recopy material as often. Other students take their notes in their argument journals or on sheets of wide computer paper so they can make notes or copy bibliographic references in the margins. If you decide to use note cards, we offer two words of advice: First, mark every note card in some way to identify the source. You might want to use the author's name, a short abbreviation of the title, or some kind of numbering system tying your note cards and bibliography together. Don't neglect this or you'll find yourself desperately searching for a reference at 2 a.m. on the day your paper is due, with no way to track it down. Second, on each note card indicate whether it's a summary, paraphrase, or direct quote; some people use different-colored cards, pens, or highlighters to distinguish the three kinds of notes. Other people use the initials *S, P,* and *Q* to make the cards. This designation proves useful when deciding how and when to *document* your sources (see the Documentation Guide).

Most research notes fall into three categories: summary, paraphrase, and quotation.

You may also make use of online note-taking. The Internet offers several sites that help students to take, manage, and store their notes and documents—including images and audio data—securely online. Most of these services offer easy systems for organizing notes according to categories just as you would with 3" × 5" cards or manila file folders as well as search engines for finding old notes. You can also create as many folders as you like, while assigning as many notes as desired to each folder. Because these services are Web applications rather than desktop programs, you can access material from any computer.

Some of these services require a fee such as NoodleTools <http://www.noodletools .com> which offers students innovative software that searches, accesses, records, and organizes information using online note cards. It also formats your bibliography in MLA or APA style. (NoodleTools is included in Pearson Longman's MyCompLab. If this book was packaged with an access code to MyCompLab, you will have free access to NoodleTools.) In spite of the fee, NoodleTools is an excellent resource that might be worth the money for all the conveniences offered. Other online services are free, such as mynoteit.com, *Google Docs*, WordPress.com, and Yahoo! Notepad, which is accessible upon opening a free e-mail account with Yahoo!

A word of caution. You can lose track of sources if the particular research link goes down. To avoid such pitfalls, you should always make copies of your information on CDs, discs, and/or data sticks. You should also make hard copies and print notes with particularly important information.

Summary

Summary is most useful when you want to record the author's main idea without the background or supporting evidence. To summarize accurately, you condense an extended idea into a sentence or more in your own words. Your goal is to record the *essence* of the idea as accurately as possible in your own words.

Here's Shannon's summary of a passage from one of her sources:

Original
In Mark Twain's lifetime, his books *Tom Sawyer* and *Huckleberry Finn* were excluded from the juvenile sections of the Brooklyn Public Library (among

other libraries), and banned from the library in Concord, MA, home of Henry Thoreau. In recent years, some high schools have dropped *Huckleberry Finn* from their reading lists, or have been sued by parents who want the book dropped. In Tempe, Arizona, a parent's lawsuit that attempted to get the local high school to remove the book from a required reading list *went as far as a federal appeals court* in 1998. (The court's *decision in the case*, which affirmed Tempe High's right to teach the book, has some interesting comments about education and racial tensions.) The Tempe suit, and other recent incidents, have often been concerned with the use of the word "nigger," a word that also got *Uncle Tom's Cabin* challenged in Waukegan, Illinois. (From Ockerbloom, John Mark. *The Online Books Page: Banned Books Online.* <http://digital.library.upenn.edu/books/banned-books.html>.)

Shannon's Summary
Mark Twain's *Huckleberry Finn* is one of the most infamously banned books, as some say it promotes racism by using the "n" word. In 1998, parents in Arizona filed a lawsuit attempting to remove the book from a high school reading list, and the suit went all the way to the federal appeals court. The court's decision returned the book to the reading list.

For more on writing summaries, see Chapter 2.

Paraphrase

Paraphrasing is useful when you want to preserve an author's line of reasoning or specific ideas but don't want or need to use the original words. When you paraphrase, you restate the original in your own words and sentence structure as accurately as possible.

Here is an excerpt from another source that Shannon used in her paper:

Original
Textbook publishers are sensitive, as well, to the often right-wing committees and boards of education that purchase books for large states like Texas and California, and so will also delete references to evolution or the scientifically hypothesized age of the Earth. (From Barnhisel, Greg, ed. *Media and Messages: Strategies and Readings in Public Rhetoric*, p. 422.)

Shannon's Paraphrase
When they prepare their book lists, publishers put their business at risk if they forget that states with large, expensive, book-consuming school systems— Texas, for example—often have very particular and unyielding opinions about any number of sensitive topics. Evolution, for example, is not discussed in some of the science textbooks students use in school—an inappropriate move that denies students exposure to an important scientific theory.

Quotation

Direct quotation should be used only when the author's words are particularly memorable or succinct, or when the author presents factual or numerical evidence that can't be easily paraphrased. You must copy the author's *exact* wording, spelling, capitalization, and punctuation, *as you find it* (even if it contains an obvious mistake). Proofread every direct quotation at least twice; it's easier than you think to leave something out, change a verb tense, or add a word or two. If you want to add words for grammatical completeness or clarity, put them in square brackets such as these [ ]. If you want to eliminate words, mark the omission with three spaced periods, called *ellipsis points* (if the omission comes at the end of a sentence, the ellipsis is typed with four spaced periods), and put them within square brackets. If you find a source you are certain to quote from, it might be worthwhile to photocopy it to avoid errors when rewriting the words.

Here is an example of the effective use of quotation, based on another of Shannon's sources:

Original
Congress shall make no law respecting an establishment of religion, or prohibiting the free exercise thereof; or abridging the freedom of speech, or of the press; or the right of the people peaceably to assemble, and to petition the Government for a redress of grievances. ("About the First Amendment." *First Amendment Center.* <http://www.firstamendmentcenter.org/about.aspx?item=about_firstamd>.)

Shannon's Effective Use of Quotation
According to the First Amendment, citizens of the United States are guaranteed the right to freedom of speech, which also includes the freedoms of thought and expression: "Congress shall make no law respecting an establishment of religion, or prohibiting the free exercise thereof; or abridging the freedom of speech, or of the press [. . .]."

Drafting Your Paper

Sometimes the sheer size of a researched argument paper can be intimidating. As a result, some writers suffer from "writer's block" when they start composing the paper. Here are several strategies for starting your draft.

1. **Write a five-minute summary.** The five-minute summary asks you to write a quick, one- or two-paragraph description of what your final paper will say. Basically you're creating a thumbnail sketch of the paper to clarify in your own mind how the paper will come together. The summary doesn't have to be formal; some people don't even use complete sentences. Almost always, these summaries dispel writer's block and get your creativity flowing.
2. **Divide the paper into sections.** Dividing the paper into sections makes the task of writing a long paper more manageable. Most writers divide a paper, as we did in Chapter 5, into beginning, middle, and end, and further subdivide the middle.
3. **First, draft the sections you're confident about.** Drafting the sections you feel most confident about first builds momentum for drafting other parts of the paper. As reported by many students, this strategy might also lead you to alter the slant or emphasis of the final paper, thereby resulting in a better outcome.

4. **Use a simple code to indicate sources.** Using a simple code to indicate sources will save you a great deal of time in revising your paper. As you write your draft, you may not want to interrupt the flow of your ideas to copy quotations or summaries from note cards; instead, you can insert into your draft the author's or source's name and a quick reference to the content so that you'll know on a later draft what you intended to include. Here's an example of how Shannon used coded references in her first draft:

> Attempts to ban books in public schools is on the rise. [People, Attacks 6] John Steinbeck's *Of Mice and Men* is a frequent target of protest for parents. [Mitchell, NYT B17]

Here you can see Shannon's code at work as she refers to notes from a report published by People for the American Way and an article from page B17 of the *New York Times*. Later, she will have to incorporate these sources into her first draft and provide parenthetical citations; for the time being, she simply lists in shorthand the evidence to support her general statements.

Incorporating Your Research

Because the effort in finding sources and taking notes is so time-consuming, some writers think that their work will be "wasted" if they don't somehow cram all the notes they've taken into their final papers. Unfortunately, the results of such cramming often look less like a paper and more like note cards stapled together in a long string with an occasional sentence wedged between to provide transitions. Every successful writer ends up gathering more research data than is needed for a paper. But isn't it better to have plenty of material to pick and choose from than not have enough to make a persuasive case? The five tests we explained at the end of Chapter 6 (sufficiency, detail, relevance, avoidance of excess, and appropriateness) should determine which notes to incorporate into the final draft. Here, too, the flexibility of having one note per card may help you because you can shuffle and change the sequence of sources to see which order of presentation will have the most impact on your readers. If you're working with a computer, you may find yourself marking and moving blocks of text around as you judge the arrangement of your evidence. The first arrangement you come up with may not always be the best. Allow yourself some flexibility!

When incorporating sources into your paper, you don't want the "seams" to show between your own writing and the summaries, paraphrases, and quotations from your sources. So it's worth the effort to spend some time writing sentences and phrases that smoothly introduce sources into the text. Consider these two examples:

Awkward	The Anaheim school board decided to ban *Beloved,* and this was "not an example of censorship, but an isolated incident."
Revised	The school board in the Anaheim, California, school system stated that their decision to ban *Beloved* was "not an example of censorship, but an isolated incident."

Remember that while *you,* the writer, may understand how a particular source supports your points, your *readers* may miss the connections unless you provide them. "But I know what I meant!" isn't much of a defense when your readers can't follow your chain of thought. Again we fall back on the analogy of making a case to a jury: A good attorney not only presents a witness's testimony but also helps the jury understand what that testimony means.

Attribution

Many students fail to understand the importance of introducing their sources when they incorporate them into a paper. This introduction is called **attribution,** and it is an important part of the process of documentation. Attribution shows your readers that your evidence comes from identifiable, reliable sources. When the attribution contains the name of a book or the author's professional affiliation or other credentials, it also suggests to your readers how reliable the source may be. For instance, if you present a statistic on divorce and attribute it to the book *How to Pick Up Women,* your readers are less likely to respect that statistic than if it came from the U.S. Census Bureau. Likewise, if you cite evidence that eating rutabagas prevents colon cancer, your readers will treat the evidence differently if it comes from an unbiased researcher at the Mayo Clinic rather than from one at the American Rutabaga Institute. In neither case is the evidence less likely to be true, but the attribution in both cases makes the difference in plausibility.

Many students have only one phrase in their repertoires for attribution: "According to...." This works, but it is not very informative. By choosing a more connotative argumentative verb, as you do when you state a position or proposal, you can signal to your readers the source's attitude toward the statement. For instance, consider this sentence:

Senator Smith _____ that the change is needed.

Using the list of attribution verbs on page 286, look at how changing the verb can change the way your audience regards Smith's position (not all these verbs will work in this sentence structure).

If you're not sure of the connotations of any of these verbs, or you're not sure that the sentence you created works with a particular choice, consult an unabridged dictionary or your instructor. Clumsy attribution can distract readers in the same way typos and grammatical errors can, so you want to make your attributions as smooth as possible. (For placement of a bibliographic reference after attributed material, see the next section on documentation.)

Revising and Editing Your Paper

After you have worked your source material into a draft, it's time to look at your writing skeptically, as your readers will. Start by testing all the parts of your argument. This may not be easy to do because you've been living with this topic for several weeks and may have lost your objectivity and ability to see the gaps. (If

Attribution Verbs

Source Is Neutral

comments	observes	says
describes	points out	sees
explains	records	thinks
illustrates	reports	writes
notes		

Source Implies or Suggests, but Doesn't Actually Say So

analyzes	asks	assesses
concludes	considers	finds
predicts	proposes	reveals
shows	speculates	suggests
supposes	infers	implies

Source Argues

alleges	claims	contends
defends	disagrees	holds
insists	maintains	argues

Source Agrees with Someone/Something Else

admits	agrees	concedes
concurs	grants	allows

Source Is Uneasy or Disagrees

belittles	bemoans	complains
condemns	deplores	deprecates
derides	laments	warns

you're working in writing groups, ask another member to read your paper and offer you some feedback on it.) Then change, delete, add, or reorganize material to make your case more effectively.

To help you revise your argument, we recommend making an outline of the draft *as you've written it*—not as you intended to write it. This will serve as an X-ray of the paper, helping you detect any holes or imbalances. Moreover, it will show you the actual order in which points are presented so that you can consider reorganizing or changing your argumentative strategy. The strategies explained in Chapters 6 and 7 for assessing evidence and considering claims ought to help you at this stage; apply them as stringently to your own writing as you would to an essay you're reading.

If you made notes in your argument journal at an earlier date about connections you wanted to make in your final paper, now is the time to include those connections if, in fact, they fit into the paper's final shape. You might also consider other kinds of evidence to include. Can you think of personal experiences or those of other people to support the evidence of your outside authorities? Have you found facts and statistics to buttress the opinions you present? What are your readers' criteria for judging an issue? Have you presented claims that meet those criteria and phrased them in that manner? It's also time to make sure that all transitions between points are included and are accurate. For instance, if you switch points around, make sure that the point you call "second" is actually the second, not the third or fourth. Also, check to be sure you've included documentation for all your sources and that you have bibliographic note cards or other records of documentation information to prepare the notes in your final copy. Then polish your prose so that your sentences are smooth, your paragraphs are complete, and your grammar and punctuation are precise. Many students "let down" their efforts when they sense their papers are nearing completion; as a result, their final grades suffer. The revising and editing stage requires sharp attention. Don't undercut all your hard research efforts by presenting your argument in anything but its best form.

Preparing and Proofreading Your Final Manuscript

Once you have polished the draft to your satisfaction, it is time to attend to the presentation of your paper. Flawless presentation is important in research, not only because of the appreciation it will win from your instructor and readers, but also because it will reinforce your credibility with your readers. A sloppy paper with typographical or grammatical errors, missing documentation, or illegible print makes your readers think that your argument might be sloppy as well. A well-prepared paper suggests to your readers that you have taken extra care to ensure that everything is correct—not only the presentation, but the content as well. This good impression may make readers more inclined to accept your arguments.

Most instructors expect research papers to be neatly and legibly typed with clear titles, double spacing, standard margins (1-inch) and type sizes (10- or 12-point), and minimal handwritten corrections. Your last name and the page number should appear in the upper-right-hand corner of every page after the title page. For English courses, the standard guide to manuscript format is the *MLA Handbook for Writers of Research Papers,* 6th edition. MLA requirements are spelled out in most college composition handbooks and illustrated in Shannon's final paper (see the Documentation Guide). Before you submit your paper, proofread it carefully for typographical errors, misspellings, omitted words, and other minor errors. If possible, let several hours elapse before your final proofreading so you can see what you've actually typed instead of what you *think* you typed. Never let the pressure of a deadline keep you from proofreading your paper. Readers get annoyed by minor errors, and annoyed readers are less likely to be persuaded by the content of your argument.

Plagiarism

Plagiarism is a crime in the academic community. The scholarly world operates by exchanging information and acknowledging the sources of this information. If you fail to acknowledge your sources or make it appear that someone else's work is actually your own, you are sabotaging the exchange of scholarly information. You're blocking the channels. Perhaps it doesn't seem important to you now, but you should know that plagiarism has very serious consequences. It can earn you a failing grade on an assignment or for a course, a suspension or even expulsion from school, and/or a permanent notation on the transcripts that future employers and graduate schools will see. Even if you are never caught, you've still stolen ideas and words from someone.

Plagiarism falls into two categories: intentional and accidental. Intentional plagiarism includes copying a phrase, a sentence, or a longer passage from a source and passing it off as your own; summarizing or paraphrasing someone else's ideas without acknowledgment; and buying or borrowing a paper written by someone else and submitting it as your own. Accidental plagiarism includes forgetting to place quotation marks around someone else's words and not acknowledging a source because you were ignorant of the need to document it. Carelessness and ignorance are not defenses against plagiarism.

Many questions about plagiarism involve the tricky subject of *common knowledge*—that is, standard information in a field of study, as well as commonsense observations and proverbial wisdom. Standard information includes the major facts in a discipline—for example, the chemical formula for water is H_2O or the Seneca Falls Convention for Women's Rights took place in 1848. If most of your sources accept such a fact without acknowledgment, you can assume it is common knowledge to readers in that field. However, if you're dealing with lesser-known facts (the numbers of soldiers at the Battle of Hastings), interpretations of those facts (assessments of the importance of the Seneca Falls meeting), or a specialist's observation (a scholar's analysis of Susan B. Anthony's rhetoric), you'll need to provide documentation.

Commonsense information, such as the notions that politicians are concerned with getting votes or that icy roads make driving dangerous, need not be documented. Proverbs and clichés don't need documentation either, although proverbs taken from recognized poems or literary works do. (Thus, "A stitch in time" needs no documentation, but "To be or not to be" should carry a reference to *Hamlet.*)

Here are four simple rules to help you avoid plagiarism:

1. *Take your research notes carefully.* Write down (or print out) a full bibliographical reference for each source (the forms for these appear in the Documentation Guide). Also, note whether you are quoting, paraphrasing, or summarizing what you find in your source (see earlier discussion in this chapter). If your notes are clear and thorough, you'll never have to worry about which words and ideas are yours and which come from your sources.
2. *Always introduce your source carefully so that your audience knows to whom they're listening.* Proper attribution is a signal to your readers that you're switching from your own work to someone else's. It also is a signal to you to check that a source is represented accurately (with no exaggeration) and that a bibliographic citation appears in your list of Works Cited or References.
3. *When in doubt, document.* While it is possible to overdocument, it is not an intellectual crime to do so. Rather, it reveals a lack of self-confidence in your own

argument or your determination to prove to your instructor and readers that you've seen every source ever published on your subject. However, overdocumenting is a less serious academic sin than plagiarizing!

4. *Enter the documentation right after the use of the source; it doesn't "carry over" between paragraphs or pages.* It is tempting, especially when using one source for an extended period, to leave all the documentation until the end of a large passage of text (which might be several paragraphs or several pages in length). But even if you weave attribution skillfully throughout the whole passage, the convention in academics is that you document a source in each paragraph in which you use it. If another source intervenes, it is twice as important that the main source be documented in every paragraph of use. So if you use the same article in four successive paragraphs, each of those paragraphs must have some parenthetical source reference. With skillful attribution, the parenthetical reference can be reduced to a simple page number, which won't interrupt the "flow" of your text.

To understand how plagiarism works, let's look at some of the ways writers might handle, or mishandle, this passage from Dennis Baron's article "English in a Multicultural Society," which appeared in the Spring 1991 issue of *Social Policy.* Here's the original passage from page 8:

> The notion of a national language sometimes wears the disguise of inclusion: we must all speak English to participate meaningfully in the democratic process. Sometimes it argues unity: we must speak one language to understand one another and share both culture and country. Those who insist on English often equate bilingualism with lack of patriotism. Their intention to legislate official English often masks racism and certainly fails to appreciate cultural difference; it is a thinly veiled measure to disenfranchise anyone not like "us."

Plagiarized Use
Supporters of U.S. English argue we must all speak one language to understand one another and share both culture and country. But Dennis Baron argues that "[t]heir intention to legislate official English often masks racism and certainly fails to appreciate cultural difference" (8). English-only legislation really intends to exclude anyone who is not like "us."

This is plagiarism because the writer has copied Baron's words in the first sentence and paraphrased them in the last, but made it appear as though only the middle sentence were actually taken from Baron's article.

Plagiarized Use
Calls for a national language sometimes wear the disguise of inclusion, according to linguist Dennis Baron. When U.S. English argues that we must all speak English to participate meaningfully in the democratic process, or that we must speak one language to understand one another and share both culture and country, Baron says they are masking racism and failing to appreciate cultural difference (8).

Here the plagiarism comes in presenting Baron's actual words without quotation marks, so it looks as if the writer is paraphrasing rather than quoting. Even with the attribution and the citation of the source, this paragraph is still an example of plagiarism because the direct quotations are disguised as the writer's paraphrase.

Acceptable Use

Linguist Dennis Baron argues that supporters of official English legislation use the reasons of inclusions, unity, and patriotism to justify these laws, but that their efforts may hide racist and culturally intolerant positions. Baron says that sometimes English-only laws are "thinly veiled measure[s] to disenfranchise anyone not like 'us'" (8).

Here the source is properly handled. The writer paraphrases most of the original text in the first sentence, then skillfully incorporates a direct quotation in the second (note the use of square brackets to make the noun agree in number with the verb, and the conversion of double quotation marks from the original into single quotation marks in the quote). The attribution clearly says that both points are taken from Baron, but the quotation marks show where Baron's actual words, rather than the writer's, are used.

Documentation Guide
MLA and APA Styles

A lmost every academic discipline has developed its own system of *documenta-tion,* a method of indicating where the writer's evidence may be found. A good way to think of the rules of documentation is by analogy to a sport, for example, basketball: Academic readers expect you to play by the established rules (what to document, how to avoid plagiarism, how to attribute sources). If you want to play the game, you have to observe the rules. At the same time—as you probably know—there are accepted variations to the rules (e.g., 30- or 45-second shot clocks, the dimensions of the 3-point line) in certain basketball leagues. The various styles of documentation used in the humanities, social sciences, and natural sciences are rather like these acceptable variations in basketball.

You must document any ideas or words you *summarize, paraphrase,* or *quote di-rectly* from a source. The two most common systems of documentation used in colleges and universities are the Modern Language Association (MLA) style, used widely in the humanities, and the American Psychological Association (APA) style, used widely in the social sciences. We will explain them in detail later in this chapter. (Some of your courses may also require you to use the Council of Biology Editors, or CBE, style; *The Chicago Manual of Style,* which you might know as Turabian style; or a journalistic style guide such as *The Associated Press Style Book.*) Think of these systems not as annoyances for you as a writer but as rule books for playing the game of researched writing on different courts. Your instructor will tell you which rules to follow.

Where Does the Documentation Go?

Fortunately, both MLA and APA styles have abandoned footnotes in favor of paren-thetical citations within the paper and a source list at the end of the paper. This setup is much neater than the footnote approach. In both styles, you use a brief reference or attribution to your source in parentheses within the body of the paper and a full bibliographical citation in a list of Works Cited (MLA) or References (APA). (These are the equivalents of what you probably called a "Bibliography" in high school.) Documenting your sources, if performed properly, will help you avoid plagiarism. The shape that citations take in the two systems, however, is a little different, so make sure you observe the forms carefully.

291

Documentation Style

Let's look at how both systems handle documentation for some of the most commonly used information sources. Suppose you want to quote from Matt Bai's article "The New Boss," which appeared in the January 30, 2005, issue of the *New York Times Magazine.* Here's how it would appear in your list of sources or bibliography:

MLA   Bai, Matt. "The New Boss." <u>New York Times Magazine</u>
          30 Jan. 2005: 38+.

APA   Bai, M. (2005, January 30). The new boss. *New York
          Times Magazine*, pp. 38-45, 62, 68, 71.

As you can see, each style orders information differently.

Likewise, both styles use a parenthetical reference in the paper to show where the evidence comes from, but again they do it differently.

MLA   One author talks about giving "added value" to
          employers, some of whom have come to view him,
          warily, as a partner (Bai, 42).

If the author's name appears in your attribution, only the page number needs to go in the parentheses:

MLA   Matt Bai talks about giving "added value" to
          employers, some of whom have come to view him,
          warily, as a partner (42).

Both references tell your readers that they can find this source in your Works Cited list, alphabetized by the last name *Bai.* If you had more than one reference to Bai in your Works Cited list, then you would add a shortened form of the title in the parentheses so readers would know to which Bai article you were referring (Bai, *Boss*, 42).

The APA style references for the same situations would be

APA   One author talks about giving "added value" to
          employers, some of whom have come to view him,
          warily, as a partner (Bai, 2005, p. 42).

or

APA   Bai (2005) talks about giving "added value" to
          employers, some of whom have come to view him,
          warily, as a partner (p. 42).

When you use more than one work by an author in your paper, APA style distinguishes them by date of publication. For example, if you cited two Bai articles from 2005, the earlier one would be designated 2005a, and the second as 2005b.

Using parenthetical citations for electronic sources can be much trickier because such sources typically have no page numbers. If your source uses paragraph numbers, provide the paragraph number preceded by *par.* or *para.* If you need to include the author's name or a brief title, place a comma after the name or title. If another type of designation is used in the source to delineate its parts (such as *screens* or *Part II*), write out the word used for that part:

MLA   Between 2000 and 2004, the message delivered by political advertisements changed dramatically (Edwards, par. 15).

APA   Between 2000 and 2004, the message delivered by political advertisements changed dramatically (Edwards, 2005, para. 15).

If your source has no numbering, no page or paragraph numbers should appear in your parenthetical reference unless your instructor indicates that you should do otherwise. Some instructors ask students to number the paragraphs of electronic sources to make references easier to locate.

A Brief Guide to MLA and APA Styles

The handbooks for MLA and APA documentation are available in most college libraries. If you don't find the information you need in the following brief guide, look for these books or websites:

MLA   Gibaldi, Joseph. <u>MLA Handbook for Writers of Research Papers</u>. 6th edition. New York: MLA, 2003.

The website of the Modern Language Association is <http://www.mla.org>.

APA   *Publication Manual of the American Psychological Association* (5th ed.). (2001). Washington, DC: American Psychological Association.

The American Psychological Association does not provide a guide to documentation on its website; however, the Purdue University Online Writing Lab provides a useful guide to APA documentation: <http://owl.english.purdue.edu/handouts/research/r_apa.html>.

Books

MLA   Author. <u>Title</u>. Edition. City of Publication: Publisher, Year.

APA   Author. (Year of Publication). *Title*. City of Publication, State: Publisher.

One Author

MLA   Riffenburgh, Beau. <u>Shackleton's Forgotten Expedition: The Voyage of the Nimrod</u>. New York and London: Bloomsbury, 2004.

APA   Riffenburgh, B. (2004). *Shackleton's forgotten expedition: The voyage of the Nimrod*. New York and London: Bloomsbury.

MLA uses the author's full first name plus middle initial, whereas APA uses the initial of the first name (unless more initials are needed to distinguish among people with the same initials). APA capitalizes only first words and proper nouns in titles and subtitles; MLA capitalizes all words except prepositions, conjunctions, and articles. MLA lists only the city; APA lists the city but also includes the state if the city is not well known or could be confused with another. Finally, MLA permits the shortening of certain publishers' names, whereas APA just drops unnecessary words such as *Co., Inc.*, and *Publishers*.

Two or More Authors

MLA   Schweikart, Larry, and Michael Allen. A Patriot's History of the United States. New York: Sentinal, 2004.

APA   Schweikart, L., & Allen, M. (2004). *A patriot's history of the United States*. New York: Sentinel.

In MLA style, only the first author's name is given in inverted form. In APA style, the ampersand (&) is used to join authors' names. The ampersand is also used in parenthetical references in text, for example "(Schweikart & Allen, 2004, p. 63)," but not in attributions, for example, "According to Pyles and Algeo". In MLA style, for works with more than three authors you may replace all but the first author's name by the abbreviation *et al.* In APA style, list the names of up to six authors, and use the abbreviation *et al.* to indicate the remaining authors.

More Than One Book by an Author

MLA   Ambrose, Stephen E. Citizen Soldier. New York: Simon & Schuster, 1997.

---. Nothing Like It in the World. New York: Simon & Schuster, 2000.

In MLA style, if you cite more than one work by a particular author, the individual works are listed in alphabetical order. For the second and any additional entries, type three hyphens and a period instead of the author's name; then skip a space and type the title, underlined or italic.

In APA style, when you cite more than one work by an author, the author's name is repeated for each work. The order of the entries is based on the publication dates of the titles, with the earliest-published given first, instead of alphabetical order. If two works by one author are published in the same year, alphabetization is done by title and the letters *a, b*, etc., are placed immediately after the year.

Book with an Editor

MLA   Todd, Janet, ed. <u>The Collected Letters of Mary Wollstonecraft</u>. New York: Columbia UP, 2004.

APA   Todd, J. (Ed.). (2004). *The collected letters of Mary Wollstonecraft*. New York: Columbia University Press.

Essay in a Collection or Anthology

MLA   Fisher, M. F. K. "Gare de Lyon." <u>Americans in Paris: A Literary Anthology</u>. Ed. Adam Gopnik. New York: Library of America, 2004. 581–91.

APA   Fisher, M. F. K. (2004). Gare de Lyon. In A. Gopnik (Ed.), *Americans in Paris: A literary anthology* (pp. 581–591). New York: Library of America.

Book in a Later Edition

MLA   Randel, Don Michael, ed. <u>The Harvard Dictionary of Music</u>, 4th ed. Cambridge: Harvard UP, 2003.

APA   Randal, D. M. (Ed.). (2003). *The Harvard dictionary of music* (4th ed.). Cambridge, MA: Harvard University Press.

Multivolume Work

MLA   Doyle, Arthur Conan. <u>The New Annotated Sherlock Holmes</u>, Ed. Leslie S. Klinger. 2 vols. New York: Norton, 2004.

APA   Doyle, A. C. (2004). *The new annotated Sherlock Holmes* (L. S. Klinger, Ed.). (Vols. 1–2). New York: Norton.

Book with a Group or Corporate Author

MLA   American Medical Association. <u>Family Medical Guide</u>, 4th ed. Hoboken: Wiley, 2004.

APA   American Medical Association. (2004). *Family medical guide* (4th ed.). Hoboken, NJ: Wiley.

Begin the entry with the corporate or group name alphabetized by the first letter of the main word (not including *a, an,* or *the*).

Article from Reference Work

MLA Bragg, Michael B. "Aircraft Deicing." The McGraw-
Hill Encyclopedia of Science and Technology.
9th ed. 2002.

APA Bragg, M. (2002). Aircraft deicing. In *The McGraw-
Hill encyclopedia of science and technology*
(Vol. 1, pp. 339-342). New York: McGraw-Hill.

If the reference book is widely available (such as a major encyclopedia or bibliography), a short bibliographic form as shown here is acceptable in MLA; APA recommends including more information rather than less. For a less widely known reference book, MLA recommends using the form for a book, multiple-authored book, or series, depending on what the book is.

Editor's Preparation of a Previous Work

MLA Lovecraft, H. P. Tales. Ed. Peter Straub, New York:
Library of America, 2005.

APA Lovecraft, H. P. (2005). *Tales* (P. Straub, Ed.).
New York: Library of America. (Original work
published c. 1801)

Translated Work

MLA Mankell, Henning. One Step Behind. Trans. Ebba
Segerberg. New York: New Press, 2002.

APA Mankell, H. (2002). *One step behind* (E. Segerberg,
Trans.). New York: New Press. (Original work
published 1997)

In APA style, the date of the translation is placed after the author's name. The date of the original publication of the work appears in parentheses at the end of the citation. This text would be cited in a paper as (Mankell, 1997/2002).

Anonymous Work

MLA The Chicago Manual of Style: The Essential Guide
for Writers, Editors, and Publishers. 15th ed.
Chicago and London: U of Chicago P, 2003.

APA *The Chicago manual of style: The essential guide
for writers, editors, and publishers* (15th
ed.). (2003). Chicago and London: University
of Chicago Press.

Articles

MLA format and APA format for articles in journals, periodicals, magazines, newspapers, and so on, are similar to the formats for books. One of the few differences concerns the volume number of each issue. Volume numbers for magazines or journals found in a library or acquired by subscription (these usually appear six times a year or less frequently) should be included in your entry. If a journal appears monthly or more frequently, or can be acquired on newsstands, you can usually omit the volume number. If the journal has continuous pagination (i.e., if the January volume ends on page 88 and the February volume begins on page 89), you don't need to include the month or season of the issue in your citation. If the journal starts over with page 1 in each issue, then you must include the month or season in your citation.

Magazines and newspapers (unlike scholarly journals) often carry articles on to continuation pages (e.g., pages 35–37 and then continued on 114–115). MLA permits the use of the form "35+" instead of giving all the pages on which such articles appear. With APA style, all page numbers must be noted.

MLA	Author. "Article Title." Journal or Magazine Title volume number (Date): inclusive pages.

APA	Author. (Date). Article title. *Journal or Magazine Title, volume number,* inclusive pages.

Scholarly Journal with Continuous Pagination

MLA	Atkinson, A. B. "Social Europe and Social Science." Social Policy and Society 2 (2003), 261–72.

APA	Atkinson, A. B. (2003). Social Europe and social science. *Social Policy and Society, 2,* 261–272.

Scholarly Journal with Each Issue Paged Separately

MLA	Baron, Dennis. "English in a Multicultural America." Social Policy 31 (Spring 1991): 5–14.

If this journal used issue numbers instead of seasons, the form would be *Social Policy* 31.1 (1991): 5–14.

APA	Baron, D. (1991). English in a multicultural America. *Social Policy,* 31, 5–14.

Magazine Article

MLA	Wong, Kate. "The Littlest Human." Scientific American Feb. 2005: 56–65.

APA	Wong, K. (2005, February). The littlest human. *Scientific American,* 56–65.

This is the form for a magazine that appears monthly. For a magazine that appears bimonthly or weekly, see the examples under "Anonymous Article."

Anonymous Article

MLA "Lessons from the U.S. Army." Fortune 22 Mar.
        1993: 68+.

APA Lessons from the U.S. Army. (1993, March 22).
        Fortune, 68-71.

Review

MLA Vaill, Amanda. "Brooklyn Bohemians." Rev. of
        February House, by Sherill Tippins. New York
        Times Book Review 6 Feb. 2005: 8.

APA Vaill, A. (2005, February 6). Brooklyn Bohemians
        [Review of the book *February house*]. *The New
        York Times Book Review,* p. 8.

When newspapers designate sections with identifying letters (e.g., *A, B*), that information is included in the reference. With MLA style, a "4+" indicates that the review begins on page 4 and continues on other nonadjacent pages in the newspaper. APA includes initial articles such as "The" in a newspaper title; MLA omits them. If the reviewer's name does not appear, begin with "Rev. of *Title*" in the MLA system or [Review of the book *Title*]" in the APA system. If the reviewer's name does not appear, but the review has a title, begin with the title of the review in both systems.

Newspaper Article

MLA Begley, Sharon. "Reversing Partial Blindness." Wall
        Street Journal 1 Feb. 2005: D1.

APA Begley, S. (2005, February 1). Reversing partial
        blindness. *The Wall Street Journal,* p. D1.

Newspaper Editorial

MLA Judge, Michael. "Epitaph on a Tyrant." Editorial.
        Wall Street Journal 7 Feb. 2005: A19.

APA Judge, M. (2005, February 7). Epitaph on a tyrant
        [Editorial]. *The Wall Street Journal,* p. A19.

Letter to the Editor of a Magazine or Newspaper

MLA Rafferty, Heather A. Letter. "The Other 'CIA.'"
        Weekly Standard 7 Feb. 2005: 5.

APA   Rafferty, H. (2005, February 7). The other "CIA"
        [Letter to the editor]. *The Weekly Standard*,
        p. 5.

If the newspaper or magazine doesn't give a title to the letter, for MLA style use the word *Letter* followed by a period after the author's name. Do not underline the word or enclose it in quotation marks. For APA style, skip that information and use the rest of the citation form.

Electronic Sources
Editorial or Letter to the Editor

MLA   Baker, Stewart. "The Net Escape Censorship? Ha!"
        Editorial. <u>Wired</u> 3.09. 1 Apr. 1998. 19 Jan.
        2005 <http://www.wired.com/wired/3.09/
        departments/baker.if.html>.

If this were a letter to the editor, *Editorial* would be replaced by *Letter.*

APA   Baker, S. (1998, April 1). The net escape censorship?
        Ha! [25 paragraphs]. *Wired* [Online serial],
        3.09. Retrieved January 19, 2005 from http://
        www.wired.com/wired/3.09/departments/
        baker.if.html

E-Mail

MLA   Mendez, Michael R. "Re: Solar power." E-mail to
        Edgar V. Atamian. 11 Sept. 2003.

In APA, electronic correspondence via e-mail, listservs, and newsgroups typically does not appear in the reference list. It is cited only in an in-text reference: (M. Mendez, personal communication, September 11, 2003).

Listserv

MLA   Kosten, Arthur. "Major Update of the WWWVL Migration
        and Ethnic Relations." Online posting. 7 Apr.
        1998. <u>ERCOMER News</u>. 7 May 1998 <http://
        www.ercomer.org/archive/ercomernews/0002.html>.

APA   Kosten, R. (1998, April 7). Major update of the
        WWWVL migration and ethnic relations. [*ERCOMER
        News* 1998, May 7]. Message posted to http://
        www.ercomer.org/archive/ercomernews/0002.html

Online Magazine Article

MLA Stevens, Sue. "New Rules Could Trick or Treat Your
Portfolio." <u>Forbes</u> 28 Oct. 2004. 3 Nov. 2004
<http://www.forbes.com/feeds/mstar/2004/10/29/
mstart_11_18655_132.html>.

APA Stevens, S. (2004, October 28). New rules could
trick or treat your portfolio. *Forbes*.
Retrieved November 3, 2004, from
http://www.forbes.com/feeds/mstar/2004/10/29/
mstart_11_18655_132.html

Both MLA and APA give date of access for electronic sources. MLA places the
date of access right before the URL address. APA uses the word "Retrieved"
followed by the date of access and then the word "from" followed by the URL. Note
that MLA uses angle brackets to enclose the URL address; APA does not.

Article in Electronic Journal

MLA Ward, Barbara. "The Best of Both Worlds: A Hybrid
Statistics Course." <u>Journal of Statistics
Education</u> 12.3. Nov. 2004. 1 Dec. 2004
<http://www.amstat.org/publications/jse/v12n3/
ward.html>.

APA Ward, B. (2004). The best of both worlds: A hybrid
statistics course. *Journal of Statistics
Education*, *12*(3). Retrieved December 1, 2004,
from http://www.amstat.org/publications/jse/
v12n3/ward/html

CD-ROM

MLA "Electrometer." <u>The McGraw-Hill Encyclopedia of
Science and Technology</u>. 9th ed. CD-ROM. New
York: McGraw-Hill. 2002.

APA Electrometer. (2002). In *The Encyclopedia of Science
and Technology*. [CD-ROM]. New York: McGraw-Hill.

Online Book

MLA Clark, Rufus W. <u>The African Slave Trade</u>. Boston:
American Tract Society: 1860. 19 June 1998
<http://moa.umdl.umich.edu/cgi/bin/moa/
idx?notisid=AHL6707>.

APA   Clark, R. W. (1860). *The African slave trade*
          [Electronic version]. Retrieved June 19, 1998,
          from http://moa.umdl.umich.edu/cgi-bin/moa/
          idx?notisid=AHL6707

Web Page

MLA   Using Modern Language Association (MLA) Format.
          Purdue University Online Writing Lab. 2 Feb.
          2005 <http://owl.english.purdue.edu/handouts/
          research/r_mla.html>.

APA   Purdue University Online Writing Lab (n.d.) *Using*
          Modern Language Association (MLA) format.
          Retrieved February 2, 2005, from http://
          owl.english.purdue.edu/handouts/research/
          r_mla.html

For MLA, begin the entry with the title of the site (underlined or italic). Follow with the name of the individual who created the website (first name first), if available, and then a period. Then write the name of the organization associated with the site, if available; the date of access; and the electronic address.

For APA, begin with the last name of the author followed by initials and period. Follow with the date of publication or latest update. Use "(n.d.)" if no date is available. If there is no author, begin with the title of the site, and then the date of publication or update. Follow with the name of the organization associated with the site, if available; the medium; the electronic address; and the date of access.

Article Retrieved from a Database

MLA   Schoem, David. "Transforming Undergraduate
          Education: Moving beyond Distinct
          Undergraduate Initiatives." Change
          Nov.-Dec. 2002. EBSCO Bergen County
          Cooperative Lib. System, NJ. 15 Feb. 2005
          <http://web31.epnet.com>.

APA   Schoem, D. (2002 November-December). Transforming
          education: Moving beyond distinct undergraduate
          initiatives. *Change, 34*(6), 50-55. Retrieved
          February 15, 2005, from http://web31.epnet.com

To document material from a database in MLA, underline or italicize the database service, give the name of the library or library service, the date of access, and the URL if known. APA gives the data of access and names the database.

Miscellaneous Sources
Film, Filmstrip, Slide Program, Videotape, DVD

MLA   Forster, Marc, dir. <u>Finding Neverland</u>. Perf. Johnny
Depp, Kate Winslet, Julie Christie, and Dustin
Hoffman. Miramax, 2004.

APA   Forster, M. (Director). (2004). *Finding neverland*
[Motion picture]. United States: Miramax.

To cite a filmstrip, slide program, videotape, or DVD in MLA style, include the name of the medium after the title without underlining (italicizing) or using quotation marks. If you are citing the work as a whole, rather than the work of one of the creative artists involved in the project, start with the title instead. For instance,

MLA   <u>Harry Potter and the Sorcerer's Stone</u>. Dir. Chris
Columbus. DVD. Warner Bros. 2001.

In APA style, substitute "[Motion Picture]" for the name of the medium, for example, "DVD."

Television or Radio Program

MLA   <u>Island at War</u>. Dirs. Thaddeus O'Sullivan and Peter
Lydon. Masterpiece Theatre. PBS. WGBH, Boston.
23 Jan. through 20 Feb. 2005.

APA   Rushton, J. (Producer). (2005). *Island at war*
[Television series]. Boston: WGBH.

Interview

MLA   Pennington, Linda Beth. Personal interview. 20 April
2003.

In APA, personal communications including interviews do not appear in the reference list. They are cited only in an in-text reference: (L. Pennington, personal interview, April 20, 2003).

The APA doesn't offer formal forms for "unrecoverable" materials such as personal letters or e-mail messages, lectures, and speeches, and in professional practice these are not included in reference listings. However, in collegiate writing assignments, most instructors will ask you to include them. You may, therefore, have to design a hybrid citation form based on these more standard forms. Remember that the APA encourages you to provide more, rather than less, information in your citations. The MLA has forms for almost any kind of communication, even nonrecoverable ones. Consult the *MLA Handbook for Writers of Research Papers,* 6th edition, to find additional forms.

SAMPLE RESEARCH PAPERS

Following are two sample student research papers, the first in MLA format and the second in APA format. As you read them, notice the margins and other format requirements of the two different styles, such as the use of running heads, the placement of titles, and the different citation forms. We have added marginal annotations to highlight these special features and to demonstrate the structural elements of the arguments.

As these research papers demonstrate, the researched argument is different from the other arguments you've written only in quantity and format, not in quality. You still must make a claim and find evidence to support it, tailor your presentation to your readers, and use a logical structure that considers the various sides of an issue. As you progress in your academic life and, later, in your professional life, you will find that variations on the researched argument can become successful senior projects, theses, sales proposals, journal articles, grant proposals—even books—so mastering the skills of argumentative writing will serve you well.

O'Neill 1

1/2"

1"

Shannon O'Neill

Professor Martinez

English 111

February 7, 2007

Literature Hacked and Torn Apart:

Censorship in Public Schools

Ever since Janet Jackson's "wardrobe malfunction" at the 2004 Super Bowl, the concept of censorship has been both embraced and attacked. But beyond the highly publicized debates over restrictions in the mainstream media, an industry of censorship is lurking in the fine print: the banning of books in public schools.

According to the First Amendment, citizens of the United States are guaranteed the right to freedom of speech, which also includes the freedoms of thought and expression: "Congress shall make no law respecting an establishment of religion or prohibiting the free exercise thereof; or abridging the freedom of speech, or of the press [...]" ("About the First Amendment"). Although rooted in the Constitution, these rights are considered inconvenient by some people who censor the voices of others in order to promote a private agenda.

Greg Barnhisel of Duquesne University observes that book banning is nothing new and that since the advent of the printing press "society has bemoaned how information or entertainment corrupts the youth and coarsens the intellectual atmosphere." He says that in the early 1800s, "parents fretted about the craze for rebellious Romantic writers like Byron and Goethe that resulted in a rash of faddish suicides of young men imitating the melancholy heroes of literature" (465).

1"

1" margin on each side and at bottom

Heading appears on first page

Double-space between title and first line and throughout

Introduces general topic and position

Bracketed ellipsis indicates words omitted from quotation

Use of authority

Narrows topic to book banning

Gives sense of history

1/2"

1"

O'Neill 2

Last name and page number at right-hand corner of each page

As it turns out, parents of schoolchildren are still the loudest advocates for book censorship. Taking the authority of school systems into their own hands, they arrogantly assert that what they think is best for <u>their</u> children to read is what is best for <u>all</u> children. According to the American Library Association's Web site, 6,364 challenges to books were reported between 1990 and 2000. Seventy-one percent of those challenges were to literature in schools or school libraries, and parents initiated 60 percent of them. Reasons for challenges ranged from "promoting homosexuality" to "promoting a religious viewpoint" (see Fig. 1).

Identifies opposition and cites statistics

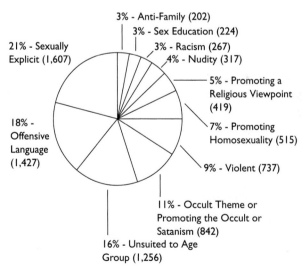

Reasons for Challenges Between 1990 and 2000

3% - Anti-Family (202)
3% - Sex Education (224)
3% - Racism (267)
4% - Nudity (317)
5% - Promoting a Religious Viewpoint (419)
7% - Promoting Homosexuality (515)
9% - Violent (737)
11% - Occult Theme or Promoting the Occult or Satanism (842)
16% - Unsuited to Age Group (1,256)
18% - Offensive Language (1,427)
21% - Sexually Explicit (1,607)

Supports evidence with pie chart

Fig. 1.

O'Neill 3

Cites specific
opposition
group and its
position

Direct
quotation

Online website
source in
parentheses

Claim

Quotes
opposition
stand

One group of parents is particularly outspoken on this issue. Gateways to a Better Education, a national organization devoted to the promotion of Christian values in public schools, "envisions schools enriched by the academically legitimate and legally appropriate inclusion of Christian expression, thought, and values." Their Web site continues, "We are making the case that implementing our vision is culturally appropriate, academically legitimate, legally permitted and morally imperative" (Gateways to a Better Education). Their case, however braced with adjectives, is "imperative" only if you share their vision of the importance of using the classroom to advocate Christian beliefs. If unchecked, such efforts can blur the separation of church and state, imposing religious ideals on students (and parents) who may not share those beliefs.

In an article on the group's Web site, Gateways Spokesperson Eric Buehrer asserts that parents—and teachers—have the moral obligation to censor the material presented to students: "There are many educators who believe that when parents question something being taught in the classroom, it's meddling. When parents ask to have something removed...it's censorship! But is it? To hear certain groups tell it, you'd conclude that Hitler is alive and well and lurking in the wings of Hooterville High School." While Beuhrer does not advocate the banning of a specific book in his article, he supports and encourages parents who wish to challenge books on a local level ("Challenging a Book in Your School").

O'Neill 4

Denying students access to literature that does not support a particular individual's religious or personal moral beliefs is detrimental to the learning process. By questioning the authority of the schools, parents are questioning the art of learning itself. Books should be selected based on established academic principles and not on the fulfillment of religious or moral goals or agendas.

Censors of high school literature have criticized many classic, exemplary literary works. The Online Books Page Web site reports that in 1996 a New Hampshire school district removed Shakespeare's Twelfth Night from the curriculum because the school board felt it encouraged alternative lifestyles. One of the play's characters is a young woman disguised as a young man (Ockerbloom).

Mark Twain's Huckleberry Finn is one of the most infamously banned books, as some say it promotes racism by using the "n" word. In 1998, parents in Arizona filed a lawsuit attempting to remove the book from a high school reading list, and the suit went all the way to the federal appeals court. The court's decision returned the book to the reading list (Ockerbloom).

Sometimes, in their zeal to protect young readers from offense, even well-intended people miss the point. Literature is created in a context, reflecting the fears and prejudices of contemporary society. Twain did not intend to ridicule African Americans, then or now. Quite to the contrary, his work reflected the dialect and prejudice of the book's period. Reading the book, we join Huck Finn on a moral journey that

Reasons
support
author's
claim

Specific
evidence

Specific
evidence

Acknowledges
possible
objections

Responds to
objections

O'Neill 5

leads him to question and finally reject the
accepted social institutions of his time—many of
which hypocritically promoted moral values while
embracing the oppression of African Americans
(Twain). Today, we consider the "n" word brutal
and insulting, but without it, the book would be
less effective in helping us understand our sad
history of racism and tolerance for slavery.
Excising the word to avoid offense is an odd
sort of denial, a way to pretend that people of
the time spoke respectfully to those whose lives
they brutalized. When we remove it from text, we
are reaching back in time and altering the
record of what people said.

Robert Lipsyte's novel, <u>One Fat Summer</u>,
the story of an overweight boy who gains self-
confidence, was removed from a seventh-grade
class in Levittown, New York because one parent
complained about its mention of adolescent
sexuality. The teachers in the district,
however, praised the book for addressing the
difficulties of growing up, and claimed that the
students enjoyed reading it (Vinciguerra). In
fighting to have the book removed, the critic
confronted reality and ignored it, asserting in
effect that adolescent students are unaware of
sex—a notion that even the most conservative
students and parents alike would regard as
preposterous. Moreover, did the parent stop to
consider that the book might help an overweight
adolescent gain self-confidence? Apparently not.
Where students understood and benefited from the
book's lessons, others peeked beneath the covers
and saw something dangerous.

Also under attack is a book that has
encouraged kids to read rather than sit in front

Specific evidence

Reason supporting claim

Acknowledges possible objection

Responds to objection

Reason supporting claim

O'Neill 6

of the TV—J.K. Rowling's <u>Harry Potter</u> series.
Number two on the American Library Association's
list of the most frequently challenged books of
2003, the series has also climbed the ladder of
success. The fifth in the series, <u>Harry Potter
and the Order of the Phoenix</u>, had the largest
first printing of any work of fiction—8.5
million copies. The series' fourth book, <u>Harry
Potter and the Goblet of Fire</u>, sold its entire
first printing—3.8 million copies—within the
first two days (Rutten). The American Library
Association states that the reason for the
challenges against the series is that it
contains wizardry and magic, and thereby, some
say, embraces the occult.

Specific evidence

Cites statistics

  An article on the Christian Web site <u>Surf-
In-The-Spirit</u>, cites Biblical passages and
claims that the <u>Harry Potter</u> series persuades
children to enjoy the "ungodly practice" of
magic. The author asserts that reading the books
promotes Satan's goals of destruction:

Acknowledges opposition with direct quotation

    Our children are the next
    generation, and Satan's goals are
    to destroy their lives and condemn
    their souls. He will surely
    succeed if parents fall into the
    trap of believing that these books
    "are only a story" and are just
    innocent evil. There is no such
    thing as innocent evil! This is
    the worst kind of evil, because it
    has deceived so many Christians
    and non-believers into accepting
    it. (Smith)

Long quotation (more than four lines); left margin indented one inch (10 spaces) double-spaced

Christians and others have the right to believe
that witchcraft and wizardry are Satan's work.

Parenthetical reference appears after final punctuation

The Harry Potter books, though popular, may be less than enlightening as literature. But banning the books from circulation is yet another way of imposing personal beliefs on others who may have a different opinion about spells and magic.

Response to opposition

Conservatives are certainly not alone in promoting censorship: liberals share the affliction. The art of deciding what is politically correct has become an industry in itself. The English language has been hacked and torn apart in the effort to promote equality, but the result is often a disconnection from reality. It seems like nothing is acceptable enough for literature, since both political spectrums endure a conflicting battle (see Mike Cramer cartoon below).

Acknowledges other sources of censorship — liberals

In her essay, "Cut on the Bias" educational scholar Diane Ravitch says that the educational publishing industry embraces specific guidelines that prevent the exposure of controversial words

Supports claim with editorial cartoon

Fig. 2. "This is acceptable!" cartoon.

Cartoon courtesy of Mike Cramer.

or topics, notably those involving gender, race, religion, or the most disturbing three-letter word of all, sex. Ravitch collected a list of over 500 words that are banned by one or more publishers, including "landlord," "senior citizen," "yacht," and "actress" (428). "Founding Fathers" is avoided because it is supposedly sexist, and a story about animals living in a rotted tree trunk was criticized because it could be offensive to people who live in low-income apartments (Barnhisel 422). It cannot be denied that the country's Founding Fathers were indeed men. That is not to say that women were not capable of running a revolution to a successful conclusion. The sad fact is, during the establishment of the United States, women were not <u>considered</u> capable—and the women's rights movement was many long years in the future.

When they prepare their book lists, publishers put their business at risk if they forget that states with large, expensive, book-consuming school systems—Texas for example— often have very particular and unyielding opinions about any number of sensitive topics. Evolution, for example, is not discussed in some of the science textbooks students use in school—an inappropriate move that denies students exposure to an important scientific theory (Barnhisel 422). Ravitch correctly asserts that the enforcement of politically correct—but historically inaccurate—language is promoting denial and ignorance: "[B]owdlerization is not only dishonest, it leads to the dumbing down of language and ideas. And of one thing I'm convinced: The widespread censorship of

Use of authority

Specific evidence

Claim with evidence

Cites authority

Quotation of authority

language and ideas in education caused by the demands of advocacy groups will not end unless it is regularly exposed to public review and ridicule" (429).

Turning the First Amendment on its head through censorship of books is not enough for some people. Children's writing is subject to censorship as well. As Jill Rosen explains in her article, "High School Confidential," "Yanked newspaper stories, disappointed student journalists and resolute administrators are an unfortunately common part of the high-school experience. Censorship occurs so consistently, so ubiquitously that it's almost clichéd, no more eyebrow-raising than the cafeteria serving mystery meat or a nerd getting books smacked out of his arms in the hallway." In 2000, 518 calls for help with censorship were registered by the Student Press Law Center—up 41 percent from 1999. Rosen claims that school administrators are allowed to do this because of the Supreme Court's 1988 decision in <u>Hazelwood School District v. Kuhlmeier</u>. Before the case, "papers operated under the premise that a student's right to free speech should only be limited in cases where it could disrupt school or invade the rights of others" (498).

Barnhisel states that public control over morality is especially difficult in a country as diverse as the United States: "For every George W. Bush fighting for 'family values,' [...] there is a Madonna or Johnny Knoxville seeking to expand the bounds of what's permissible." He says that standards are "handled by thousands of different people and groups with thousands of different agendas and values and hundreds of

Cites authority with quotation

Cites statistics

Cites authority to support claim

O'Neill 10

ways of enforcing their desires" (471). The
plethora of ideals and desires makes censorship
a complicated issue.

　　If we ban everything that might offend
anyone, what is left to write? Books that
promote diversity, alternative lifestyles,
and the struggles of minorities, expose
children to the truth about life. Senseless
and gratuitous violence is woven into the
plots of television shows and movies to enhance
their popularity, but Maya Angelou's true and
heartbreaking accounts of rape and prejudice
in her memoir, I Know Why the Caged Bird Sings,
are not thought of as suitable for reading by
some, such as the organization Parents Against
Bad Books In Schools.

Cites
evidence to
support claim

　　Censorship denies reality and creates false
worlds in which certain words or actions do not
exist. U.S. Supreme Court Justice Louis D.
Brandeis put it perfectly when he said, "Fear of
serious injury alone cannot justify oppression
of free speech and assembly. Men feared witches
and burnt women. It is the function of speech to
free men from the bondage of irrational fears"
("Public Education").

　　Should parents be concerned about what
their children are reading? Of course they
should. The issue is not about parental
control and supervision. It is about efforts
to censor reading material for everyone in
order to advance a narrow and not necessarily
shared agenda.

Works Cited

"About the First Amendment." <u>First Amendment Center</u>. 12 Feb. 2005. 12 Feb. 2005 <http://firstamendmentcenter.org/ about.aspx?item-about_firstamd>.

Barnhisel, Greg, ed. <u>Media and Messages: Strategies and Readings in Public Rhetoric</u>. New York: Pearson Education, 2005.

Buehrer, Eric. "Challenging a Book in Your School." <u>Gateways to a Better Education</u>. 1998. 5 Feb. 2005 <http://www.gtbe.org/ news/index.php/1/14/35.html>.

Challenged and Banned Books. <u>American Library Association</u>. 2005. 5 Feb. 2005. <http://www.ala.org/ala/oif/ bannedbooksweek/challengedbanned/ challengedbanned.html# web>.

Cramer, Mike. Cartoon. 26 July 1993. <u>Illinois Issues</u>. 6 Feb. 2005 <http:// www.lib.nlu.edu/ipo/ii930724.html.

Ockerbloom, John Mark. <u>The Online Books Page: Banned Books Online</u>. 2004. 17 Jan. 2005 <http://digital.library.upenn.edu/books/ banned-books. html>.

PABBIS (Parents Against Bad Books In Schools). "Book Titles H-L." n.d. <http:// www.sibbap.org/bookshl.htm>.

"Public Education: Schools and Censorship: Banned Books." <u>People for the American Way</u>. n.d. <http://www.pfaw.org/pfaw/general/ default.aspx?oid=10038>.

Ravitch, Diane. "Cut on the Bias." Barnhisel 428–429.

Rosen, Jill. "High School Confidential." Barnhisel 496–502.

(margin notes)

List is alphabetical by author's last name. Use title if no author. Double-space throughout

Title of books, journals, and newspapers are underlined

Websites are constantly updated. Include date of access

Website with individual author

O'Neill 12

Rutten, Tim. "It's All Hillary and Harry." <u>Los
Angeles Times</u>. 18 June 2003. 6 Feb. 2005
<http://www.chicagotribune.com/features/
chi030618harrybooks.1,4261048.
story?ctrack=1&cset=true>.

Smith, Kathy A. "Harry Potter: Seduction into
the Dark World of the Occult—Part One."
<u>Surf-in-the-Spirit</u>. 2000. Fill the Void
Ministries. 6 Feb. 2005 <http://
www. surfinthespirit.com/entertainment/
harry-potter-1. shtml>.

Twain, Mark. <u>Adventures of Huckleberry Finn</u>.
Ed. Susan K. Harris. Boston: Houghton
Mifflin, 2000.

Vinciguerra, Thomas. "A 1977 Novel Comes
Under Scrutiny." <u>New York Times</u> 8 June
1997, LI ed., sec. 13:8.

↑ 1/2"

Abbreviated title and number appear on each page, including the title page

Running head: PUBLIC POLICY PROPOSAL

Public Policy Proposal:
Legalization of Marijuana for Medical Purposes
Robin Fleishman
Vanderbilt University

If your instructor requires an abstract of your paper, locate it on the second page of your paper

Public Policy Proposal: Legalization of
Marijuana for Medical Purposes

Currently marijuana is an illegal substance
in the United States. Even those who need the
drug for medical purposes may not obtain it
legally. Significant amounts of research have
found that the health risks associated with
marijuana are minimal, especially compared to
those of current legal drugs, such as alcohol
and tobacco. Considerable debate has raged over
the issue of legalizing marijuana for medicinal
use, pitting the great benefits marijuana has
afforded those in medical need against the
negative social perceptions of the drug. In
this paper, I will argue that in spite of all
the legal resistance against marijuana, the
substance should be legalized for medical use
since it has proven beneficial in treating
people with serious pathologies.

Medicinal marijuana has been found to
help patients who are suffering from a variety
of diseases including Alzheimer's disease,
glaucoma, cancer, AIDS, and multiple sclerosis.
A number of studies of the medicinal effects
of marijuana found that with many patients "who
suffer simultaneously from severe pain, nausea,
and appetite loss, cannabinoid drugs might
offer broad-spectrum relief not found in any
other single medication" (Joy et al., 1999).
Making marijuana an illegal substance denies
this treatment to millions of Americans who
may greatly benefit from the drug.

Glaucoma is a common disease that can be
relieved with marijuana use. Glaucoma is caused
by high intraocular pressure (IOP) of the eye
which can lead to blindness. Marijuana has "been

Double-space
between title
and first line
and
throughout
paper

1" margins

States
proposal

Identifies
issue and
significance

Reason
supporting
proposal

Public Policy Proposal   3

Author is not cited in text, so name and date appear in parenthetical citation

found to reduce IOP by an average of 24% (Joy et al., 1999). This reduction of intraocular pressure helps those at risk for glaucoma and those who suffer from it.

Cites statistics

AIDS/HIV patients are another population who benefit from using marijuana. The New York AIDS Coalition reports that "among physicians specializing in AIDS/HIV, there is a widespread acknowledgement that marijuana represents a significant treatment component for those who have advanced-state HIV symptoms, as well as for those with symptoms caused by the multiple-drug therapies used to control HIV" ("Should," 2004). Marijuana is an excellent option for AIDS/HIV patients because it gives them relief from complications and pain implicit in their treatment.

Reason supporting proposal

Marijuana is not only helpful to patients, but it is also safer than many of the alternative drugs currently prescribed for treatment. It has been found to be much less addictive and to have very low withdrawal levels compared to other drugs currently on the market (Melansek, 2004). In terms of withdrawal effects an Institute of Medicine study, "Marijuana and Medicine: Assessing the Science Base," affirms these findings and states that although "withdrawal symptoms can be observed in animals, [they] appear to be mild compared to opiates or benzodiazepines, such as diazepam (Valium)" (Joy et al., 1999). Opponents of the legalization of marijuana cite the danger of addiction as a major objection. But as the chart below illustrates, this fear is overstated. This survey included 746 addiction researchers and clinicians specializing in

Cites authority

Evidence

Public Policy Proposal   4

addiction. According to their findings, cannabis is less addictive than nine other substances including caffeine, alcohol, and nicotine. Marijuana is less addictive than generally believed and is an extremely helpful alternative for those suffering from a variety of illnesses.

Statistics

It is clear that marijuana can be beneficial for treating patients with a variety of medical ailments, so why should those who turn for help face arrest? Ironically, alcohol and tobacco are known to endanger health yet are accepted as constants in our everyday lives. Meanwhile, marijuana is seen as a suspicious, unknown, dangerous, Eastern, hippy drug (Lowry, 2001). In fact, taking into account this prejudicial view, some argue that making marijuana illegal is an infringement of civil liberties, especially for people who see it as an option for healing. They see the issue as violating the Declaration of Independence and the Constitution by limiting one's ability to "pursue his own happiness as long as he does not infringe on other's rights to life and property" (Black, 1993).

Cites authority

Quotes authority

Sick individuals needing the relief marijuana offers face yet another problem. In order to obtain marijuana for their health needs, they are forced to seek their treatment in very dangerous and violent environments. Because of the illegal nature of the substance, patients must purchase it on the black market. Many times buyers do not know exactly what they are purchasing and may end up purchasing the substance with dangerously high potency effects. This has become a major problem with marijuana since the dealers seeking higher profits are

Reasons supporting proposal

Cannabis Among Least Addictive Drugs
LSD, MDMA, and cannabis were rated by addiction researchers and clinicians as significantly less addictive than nine other drugs. Crack cocaine, nicotine, and heroin were rated most addictive.

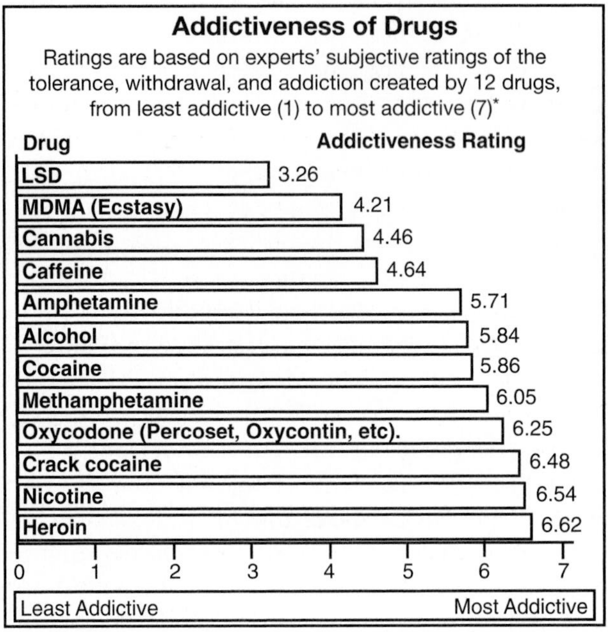

Addictiveness of Drugs
Ratings are based on experts' subjective ratings of the tolerance, withdrawal, and addiction created by 12 drugs, from least addictive (1) to most addictive (7)[*]

Drug	Addictiveness Rating
LSD	3.26
MDMA (Ecstasy)	4.21
Cannabis	4.46
Caffeine	4.64
Amphetamine	5.71
Alcohol	5.84
Cocaine	5.86
Methamphetamine	6.05
Oxycodone (Percoset, Oxycontin, etc).	6.25
Crack cocaine	6.48
Nicotine	6.54
Heroin	6.62

0   1   2   3   4   5   6   7

Least Addictive   Most Addictive

Source: Robert Gore and Mitch Earleywine, "Addiction Potential of Drugs of Abuse: A Survey of Clinicians and Researchers," Department of Psychology, University of Southern California, October 2004. The survey included 746 addiction researchers, clinicians specializing in addiction and generalist psychotherapists.

Includes chart of statistical data as supporting evidence

Fig. 1.
Marshall, P. (2005, February 11). Marijuana laws. The CQ Researcher Online, 15, 125–148. Retrieved February 12, 2005, from http://library.cqpress.com/cqresearcher/ cqresree2005021100. Document ID: cqres rre2005021100.

Public Policy Proposal   6

selling more expensive and, therefore, more
dangerously potent drugs (Block, 1993). However,
were marijuana to be made legally obtainable
from doctors and pharmacies, some of these
dangers could be eliminated.

Furthermore, if the money spent on the sale
of marijuana were controlled by the government
and drug companies, high profits would no longer
go to drug cartels and be used by drug dealers
to fund terrorism (Block, 1993). The sale of the
drug would be legal and carefully regulated by
doctors and the FDA.

Reasons
supporting
proposal

A few other options might solve the
problems that the country currently faces with
medicinal marijuana. Obviously, America is proud
of its healthcare system and cares about giving
its citizens the best possible care. In order to
help those who need marijuana to alleviate their
pain there are two possible solutions.

One way of allowing people to benefit from
the positive medical effects of marijuana
legally, is with the introduction of synthetic
drugs such as Marinol. Marinol is a result
of "pharmaceuticalization," which is the
creation of medications that are made from
derivatives of marijuana and synthetic forms
of those molecules. "Marinol is synthetic
tetrahydrocannabinol, the primary active
cannabinoid in marijuana, packed in a capsule
with sesame oil so that it cannot be smoked"
(Grinspoon, 1993). These pills allow users to
benefit from some of the same relief they
experienced with smoking marijuana.

Presents
other
positions with
quotation

However, there are a few problems with
Marinol and its relatives. First of all, many
users of the drug have complained that it does

Response to
other
position and
proposal

not work nearly as well or as fast as smoking
marijuana. One of the major reasons for this
is that the pill must be taken orally instead
of inhaled by smoking. This results in a
much slower reaction and is not as strong an
experience (Grinspoon, 1993). The second major
complaint concerning Marinol is that it is
quite expensive. It sells for about $10 a tablet
(two tablets daily must be taken), and these
tablets are not covered by health insurance
("Legalizing," 1999). This is significantly
more than marijuana would cost if it could be
prescribed by doctors.

Proposes
solution to
problem

    The second solution would be to make it
legal for doctors to prescribe marijuana to
their patients as an option for their treatment.
Since so many patients report positive effects
of the drug, this would allow them to be able
to have access to marijuana when they needed
it and have their use of the drug monitored by
their doctor. As with other prescription drugs,
it would be the doctor's responsibility to
determine when marijuana would be an effective
and necessary treatment option.

Cites
supporting
evidence with
statistics

    This issue already has a tremendous
amount of support. An astounding 85% of
Americans already support legalizing marijuana
for medicinal purposes (Stroup, 1999). In
terms of health professionals specifically,
89% of nurses and 76% of doctors support the
initiative (Grinspoon, 1993). In addition,
"many distinguished professional medical bodies,
including the American Medical Association,
the American Public Health Association and the

Use of
authority as
support

New England Journal of Medicine have publicly
supported prescriptive access to marijuana"

Public Policy Proposal   8

(Melansek, 2004). With such strong support, both from the public and medical professionals, the issue of medicinal marijuana should pass legislation to legalize it in the country.

As with other prescription drugs, medicinal marijuana should be strictly regulated and required to follow all FDA and other healthcare rules and standards. Obviously, all products would have to be cleared with the FDA and any other safety boards. Therefore, those patients who are prescribed marijuana would not have to worry about the serious issue of "lacing" or being unaware of how strong the substance is (Block, 1993).

Proposes solution to problem

It would be important that patients who are prescribed marijuana do not offend or bother other members of the community. Since marijuana would still be considered illegal for recreational use, those patients who are prescribed the substance should be required to use the drug in approved environments and in their own homes.

Proposes solution to problem

Another measure to ensure public safety would be to ban use of marijuana while driving vehicles. Although marijuana has been found to have "little effect on the skills involved in automobile driving," it does "lead to a more cautious style of driving. [Marijuana does have] a negative impact on decision time and trajectory" (Stroup & Armentano, 2002). Therefore, as with alcohol and other prescription drugs, it would be illegal to operate a motor vehicle after having smoked marijuana. Laws and repercussions would be similar to the current drunk driving laws in the country.

Proposes solution to problem

Public Policy Proposal   9

With these considerations and regulations, America and Americans would greatly benefit if marijuana were legalized for medical use. The country would be able to offer the best and most appropriate care possible for those who need marijuana to help deal with medical ailments.

Public Policy Proposal   10

References

Begin first line of each citation at the left margin. Indent all subsequent lines five spaces from the left margin

Block, W. (1993). Drug prohibition: A legal and economic analysis. *Journal of Business Ethics, 12,* 689-700.

Grinspoon, L. (2003, Summer). The shifting medical view of marijuana. *The Boston Globe,* p. 5.

Joy, J. E., Watson, S. J., & Benson, J. A. (Eds.). (1999). *Marijuana and medicine: Assessing the science base.* Washington, DC: National Academy Press.

Capitalize the first letter of titles and subtitles

Legalizing marijuana: Where there's smoke, there's medicine. (1999, December 4). *The Economist, 353,* 30-31.

Lowry, R. (2001, August 20). Weed whackers—the anti-marijuana forces and why they're wrong. *National Review, 53.*

Marshall, P. (2005, February 11). Marijuana laws. *The CO Researcher Online, 15,* 125-148. Retrieved February 12, 2005, from http://library.copress.corp/ cqresearcher/cqresrre2005021100

Melansek, A. (2004). Marijuana for medical purposes. *Debatabase.* Retrieved February 12,

Public Policy Proposal   11

    2005, from http://www.debatabase.org/
    details.asp?topicID-254

Reefer Rx: Marijuana as medicine. (2004,
    September). *Harvard Health Letter,* 5-6.

"Should marijuana be a medical option now?"
    Retrieved February 12, 2005, from
    http://www. medicalmarijuanaprocon.org/
    pop/conflicts.htm

Stroup, K. (1999). Marijuana should be legalized
    for recreational and medical purposes. In
    M. E. Williams (Ed.), *At Issue Series.* San
    Diego: Greenhaven Press.

Stroup, K., & Armentano, P. (2002, September 5).
    Legalize and regulate cannabis, Canadian
    senate committee says. Retrieved February
    13, 2005, from http://www.norml.org/
    index.cfm?Group_ID=5405

The Readings

Advertising and Consumerism

The clock radio wakes us, blaring advertisements for vitamins, banks, and automobiles. Our coffee cups announce the brand we drink, and the logos on our clothing reveal the psychology of our fashion choices. As we wait for the bus or drive our cars, billboards display lounging vacationers in exotic locations. As we read a magazine, clothing ads tell us what we should wear, cigarette ads depict a life of clean refreshment, and alcohol ads warn us to drink their product responsibly. We open the newspaper and shuffle through pages of department store advertisements. And as we sit down at our desks to work, the Internet browser flashes a banner for a camcorder, and it's not even 9:00 a.m.!

Every single day of our lives, we are bombarded with advertising images and messages. Advertising is so pervasive, few of us really notice it or consider its enormous influence on our lives. This chapter examines the many different ways advertising weaves its web of influence—how it hooks consumers, how it creates feelings of need, and how it manipulates us through words and symbols convincing us to buy.

The first section of readings, "Hooking the Consumer," addresses the ways advertisers influence our thinking to get us to buy their products. While most of us know advertising is everywhere, we may not be aware of how marketers target us. Hours of market research on the demographic structure, geographic area, age, gender, and cultural background of a consumer group are devoted to each and every product before it hits the shelf. Marketers really get to know us, and what they know may surprise you.

From luring consumers, we move to the psychology of consumer desire in "The Quest for Stuff." What drives consumerism in this country? Why do we want what we want, and is it really so bad that we want it all? Why don't we admit that we are all basically consumers at heart? The essays in this section encourage us to take a closer look at our consumer habits and the cultural and social forces that drive our desire to acquire.

The chapter closes with a group of readings exploring the language of advertising, one of the most pervasive forms of persuasion in American life. The language used in advertising is a special form of communication, one that combines words, images, and fantasies for the sole purpose of separating consumers from their money. Advertisers twist words that carry no true meanings yet still convince us that their product is better or more desirable. They use images to manipulate our most basic instincts to get us to need and want. But is this just part of the game of advertising—and do consumers really care what language or images are used to sell them products?

HOOKING THE CONSUMER

Targeting a New World
Joseph Turow

Advertisers do not pitch their marketing campaigns to a universal audience. Rather, they target specific audiences to market specific products. This "divide and conquer" approach is called target marketing. In the following article, communications professor Joseph Turow explores how the techniques of target marketing exploit and even encourage rips in the American social fabric.

Turow is a professor at the Annenberg School for Communication at the University of Pennsylvania. He is the author of many books on mass media and its structure, organization, and social functions, including *Media Today* (2002) and *Niche Envy: Marketing Discrimination in the Digital Age* (2006). The following article is excerpted from his book, *Breaking Up America: Advertisers and the New Media World* (1998).

BEFORE YOU READ ───────────────────────────

The following piece discusses how marketers use target marketing, based on demographic profiling, to sell specific products to particular groups of people. How would you describe the consumer target group to which you belong? What values define your group, and why?

AS YOU READ ───────────────────────────

How can exploiting Americans' social and cultural divisions help advertisers market their products? Is there anything unethical about this approach?

1   **"A**dvertisers will have their choice of horizontal demographic groups and vertical psychographic program types."*

2   *"Our judgment as to the enhanced quality of our subscriber base has been confirmed by the advertisers."*

3   *"Unfortunately, most media plans are based on exposure opportunities. This is particularly true for television because G.R.P. analysis is usually based on television ratings and ratings do not measure actual exposure."*

4   Most Americans would likely have a hard time conceiving the meaning of these quotations. The words would clearly be understood as English, but the jargon would seem quite mysterious. They might be surprised to learn that they have heard

a specialized language that advertisers use about them. Rooted in various kinds of research, the language has a straightforward purpose. The aim is to package individuals, or groups of people, in ways that make them useful targets for the advertisers of certain products through certain types of media.

5   Clearly, the way the advertising industry talks about us is not the way we talk about ourselves. Yet when we look at the advertisements that emerge from the cauldron of marketing strategies and strange terminology, we see pictures of our surroundings that we can understand, even recognize. The pictures remind us that the advertising industry does far more than sell goods and services through the mass media. With budgets that add up to hundreds of billions of dollars, the industry exceeds the church and the school in its ability to promote images about our place in society—where we belong, why, and how we should act toward others.

6   A revolutionary shift is taking place in the way advertisers talk about America and the way they create ads and shape media to reflect that talk. The shift has been influenced by, and has been influencing, major changes in the audiovisual options available to the home. But it most importantly has been driven by, and has been driving, a profound sense of division in American society.

7   The era we are entering is one in which advertisers will work with media firms to create the electronic equivalents of gated communities. Marketers are aware that the U.S. population sees itself marked by enormous economic and cultural tensions. Marketers don't feel, though, that it benefits them to encourage Americans to deal with these tensions head-on through a media brew of discussion, entertainment, and argumentation aimed at broadly diverse audiences. Rather, new approaches to marketing make it increasingly worthwhile for even the largest media companies to separate audiences into different worlds according to distinctions that ad people feel make the audiences feel secure and comfortable. The impact of these activities on Americans' views of themselves and others will be profound, enduring, and often disturbing.

8   The changes have begun only recently. The hallmark is the way marketers and media practitioners have been approaching the development of new audiovisual technology. Before the late 1970s, most people in the United States could view without charge three commercial broadcast stations, a public (non-commercial) TV station, and possibly an independent commercial station (one not affiliated with a network). By the mid-1990s, several independent broadcast TV stations, scores of cable and satellite television channels, videocassettes, video games, home computer programs, online computer services, and the beginnings of two-way ("interactive") television had become available to major segments of the population with an interest and a budget to match.

9   People in the advertising industry are working to integrate the new media channels into the broader world of print and electronic media to maximize the entire system's potential for selling. They see these developments as signifying not just the breakup of the traditional broadcast network domain, but as indicating a breakdown in social cohesion, as well. Advertisers' most public talk about America—in trade magazine interviews, trade magazine ads, convention speeches, and interviews for this book—consistently features a nation that is breaking up. Their vision is of a fractured

population of self-indulgent, frenetic, and suspicious individuals who increasingly reach out only to people like themselves.

10   Advertising practitioners do not view these distinctions along primarily racial or ethnic lines, though race and ethnicity certainly play a part, provoking turf battles among marketers. Rather, the new portraits of society that advertisers and media personnel invoke involve the blending of income, generation, marital status, and gender into a soup of geographical and psychological profiles they call "lifestyles."

11   At the business level, what is driving all this is a major shift in the balance between targeting and mass marketing in U.S. media. Mass marketing involves aiming a home-based medium or outdoor event at people irrespective of their background or patterns of activities (their lifestyles). Targeting, by contrast, involves the intentional pursuit of specific segments of society—groups and even individuals. The Underground [radio] Network, the Comedy Central cable channel, and *Details* magazine are far more targeted than the ABC Television Network, the Sony Jumbotron Screen on Times Square, and the Super Bowl. Yet even these examples of targeting are far from close to the pinpointing of audiences that many ad people expect is possible.

12   The ultimate aim of this new wave of marketing is to reach different groups with specific messages about how certain products tie into their lifestyles. Target-minded media firms are helping advertisers do that by building *primary media communities*. These are formed when viewers or readers feel that a magazine, TV channel, newspaper, radio station, or other medium reaches people like them, resonates with their personal beliefs, and helps them chart their position in the larger world. For advertisers, tying into those communities means gaining consumer loyalties that are nearly impossible to establish in today's mass market.

13   Nickelodeon and MTV were pioneer attempts to establish this sort of ad-sponsored communion on cable television. While they started as cable channels, they have become something more. Owned by media giant Viacom, they are lifestyle parades that invite their target audiences (relatively upscale children and young adults, respectively) into a sense of belonging that goes far beyond the coaxial wire into books, magazines, videotapes, and outdoor events that Viacom controls or licenses.

14   The idea of these sorts of "programming services" is to cultivate a must-see, must-read, must-share mentality that makes the audience feel part of a family, attached to the program hosts, other viewers, and sponsors. It is a strategy that extends across a wide spectrum of marketing vehicles, from cable TV to catalogs, from direct mailings to online computer services, from outdoor events to in-store clubs. In all these areas, national advertisers make it clear that they prefer to conduct their targeting with the huge media firms they had gotten to know in earlier years. But the giants don't always let their offspring operate on huge production budgets. To keep costs low enough to satisfy advertisers' demands for efficient targeting, much of ad-supported cable television is based on recycled materials created or distributed by media conglomerates. What makes MTV, ESPN, Nickelodeon, A&E, and other such

"program services" distinctive is not the uniqueness of the programs but the special character created by their *formats*: the flow of their programs, packaged to attract the right audience at a price that will draw advertisers.

15 But media firms have come to believe that simply attracting groups to special-ized formats is often not enough. Urging people who do not fit the desired lifestyle profile *not* to be part of the audience is sometimes also an aim, since it makes the community more pure and thereby more efficient for advertisers. So in the highly competitive media environment of the 1980s and early 1990s, cable companies aim-ing to lure desirable types to specialized formats felt the need to create "signature" materials that both drew the "right" people and signaled the "wrong" people that they ought to go away. It is no accident that the producers of certain signature pro-grams on Nickelodeon (for example, *Ren and Stimpy*) and MTV (such as *Beavis and Butt-head*) in the early 1990s acknowledge that they chase away irrelevant viewers as much as they attract desirable ones.

16 An even more effective form of targeting, ad people believe, is a type that goes beyond chasing undesirables away. It simply excludes them in the first place. Using computer models based on zip codes and a variety of databases, it is economically feasible to tailor materials for small groups, even individuals. That is already taking place in the direct mail, telemarketing, and magazine industries. With certain forms of interactive television, it is technologically quite possible to send some TV pro-grams and commercials only to neighborhoods, census blocks, and households that advertisers want to reach. Media firms are working toward a time when people will be able to choose the news, information, and entertainment they want when they want it. Advertisers who back these developments will be able to offer different product messages—and variable discounts—to individuals based on what they know about them.

17 Clearly, not all these technologies are widespread. Clearly, too, there is a lot of hype around them. Many companies that stand to benefit from the spread of target marketing have doubtless exaggerated the short time it will take to get there and the low costs that will confront advertisers once they do. Moreover, as will be seen, some marketers have been slower than others to buy into the usefulness of a media system that encourages the partitioning of people with different lifestyles.

18 Nevertheless, the trajectory is clear. A desire to label people so that they may be separated into primary media communities is transforming the way television is pro-grammed, the way newspapers are "zoned," the way magazines are printed, and the way cultural events are produced and promoted. Most critically, advertisers' interest in exploiting lifestyle differences is woven into the basic assumptions about media models for the next century—the so-called 500 Channel Environment or the future Information Superhighway.

19 For me and you—individual readers and viewers—this segmentation and tar-geting can portend terrific things. If we can afford to pay, or if we're important to sponsors who will pick up the tab, we will be able to receive immediately the news, information, and entertainment we order. In a world pressing us with high-speed concerns, we will surely welcome media and sponsors that offer to surround us with

exactly what we want when we want it. As an entirety, though, society in the United States will lose out.

20   One of the consequences of turning the U.S. into a pastiche of market-driven labels is that such a multitude of categories makes it impossible for a person to directly overlap with more than a tiny portion of them. If primary media communities continue to take hold, their large numbers will diminish the chance that individuals who identify with certain social categories will even have an opportunity to learn about others. Off-putting signature programs such as *Beavis and Butt-head* may make the situation worse, causing individuals annoyed by the shows or what they read about them to feel alienated from groups that appear to enjoy them. If you are told over and over again that different kinds of people are not part of your world, you will be less and less likely to want to deal with those people.

21   The creation of customized media materials will likely take this lifestyle segregation further. It will allow, even encourage, individuals to live in their own personally constructed worlds, separated from people and issues they don't care about or don't want to be bothered with. The desire to do that may accelerate when, as is the case in the late-twentieth-century United States, seemingly intractable antagonisms based on age, income, ethnicity, geography, and more result from competition over jobs and political muscle. In these circumstances, market segmentation and targeting may accelerate an erosion of the tolerance and mutual dependence between diverse groups that enable a society to work. Ironically, the one common message across media will be that a common center for sharing ideas and feelings is more and more difficult to find—or even to care about.

QUESTIONS FOR ANALYSIS AND DISCUSSION

1. Turow uses three quotations to begin his essay. How do these quotations contribute to the points he makes in his article? Are they an effective way to reach his audience? Explain.

2. How does packaging individuals, or groups of people, make them "useful targets" for advertisers? Give some examples of ways advertisers "package" people or groups of people.

3. According to Turow, what social impact does target marketing have on America? Do you agree with his perspective? Explain.

4. Evaluate Turow's tone in this essay. What phrases or words reveal his tone? Who is his audience? How does this tone connect to his intended audience?

5. What point is the author trying to make in this article? What is his own particular opinion of targeted marketing? Cite examples from the text in your response.

6. Why would producers of certain television programs actually want to "chase away" certain viewers? How can audience exclusion help improve a target market for advertisers? Is this practice damaging to our society? Why or why not?

Buy This 24-Year-Old and Get All His Friends Absolutely Free

Jean Kilbourne

Have you ever stopped to think about how much advertising permeates our world? You may be surprised to discover that advertising now supports almost every communication medium, from newspapers and magazines to television, radio, and the Internet. Advertising sponsors most sporting events, and even schools receive large sums from companies for their product loyalty. Products are clearly placed in television programs from reality TV hits such as *Biggest Loser* to sitcoms such as *How I Met Your Mother*. In fact, the average person views over 3,000 advertisements each and every day! In the next article, Jean Kilbourne describes the subtle ways advertisers influence consumers and how much they are willing to spend just for a chance to entice us.

Jean Kilbourne, EdD, is an expert in psychology and the media. Kilbourne explores the way advertising creates and feeds addictive mind-sets that starts in childhood and grips us throughout our adult lives. She is the author of *Deadly Persuasion: Why Women and Girls Must Fight the Addictive Power of Advertising* (1999). She has produced several award-winning documentaries, including *Killing Us Softly*, *Slim Hope*, and *Calling the Shots*. The next article is an excerpt from the first chapter of *Can't Buy Me Love: How Advertising Changes the Way We Think and Feel* (2000), a revised edition of her book, *Deadly Persuasion*.

BEFORE YOU READ

When you read a magazine or newspaper, or watch a television program, how aware are you of the products that are pitched to you? Do you think these advertisements influence you as a consumer?

AS YOU READ

What populations does the author identify as the most vulnerable to advertising, and how does she feel about the exploitation of these groups?

1   If you're like most people, you think that advertising has no influence on you. This is what advertisers want you to believe. But, if that were true, why would companies spend over $200 billion a year on advertising? Why would they be willing to spend over $250,000 to produce an average television commercial and another $250,000 to air it? If they want to broadcast their commercial during the Super Bowl, they will gladly spend over a million dollars to produce it and over one and a half million to air it. After all, they might have the kind of success that Victoria's Secret did during the 1999 Super Bowl. When they paraded bra-and-panty-clad

models across TV screens for a mere thirty seconds, one million people turned away from the game to log on to the Website promoted in the ad. No influence?

2   Ad agency Arnold Communications of Boston kicked off an ad campaign for a financial services group during the 1999 Super Bowl that represented eleven months of planning and twelve thousand "man-hours" of work. Thirty hours of footage were edited into a thirty-second spot. An employee flew to Los Angeles with the ad in a lead-lined bag, like a diplomat carrying state secrets or a courier with crown jewels. Why? Because the Super Bowl is one of the few sure sources of big audiences—especially male audiences, the most precious commodity for advertisers. Indeed, the Super Bowl is more about advertising than football: The four hours it takes include only about twelve minutes of actually moving the ball.

3   Three of the four television programs that draw the largest audiences every year are football games. And these games have coattails: twelve prime-time shows that attracted bigger male audiences in 1999 than those in the same time slots the previous year were heavily pushed during football games. No wonder the networks can sell this prized Super Bowl audience to advertisers for almost any price they want. The Oscar ceremony, known as the Super Bowl for women, is able to command one million dollars for a thirty-second spot because it can deliver over 60 percent of the nation's women to advertisers. Make no mistake: The primary purpose of the mass media is to sell audiences to advertisers. We are the product. Although people are much more sophisticated about advertising now than even a few years ago, most are still shocked to learn this.

4   Magazines, newspapers, and radio and television programs round us up, rather like cattle, and producers and publishers then sell us to advertisers, usually through ads placed in advertising and industry publications. "The people you want, we've got all wrapped up for you," declares *The Chicago Tribune* in an ad placed in *Advertising Age*, the major publication of the advertising industry, which pictures several people, all neatly boxed according to income level.

5   Although we like to think of advertising as unimportant, it is in fact the most important aspect of the mass media. It is the point. Advertising supports more than 60 percent of magazine and newspaper production and almost 100 percent of the electronic media. Over $40 billion a year in ad revenue is generated for television and radio and over $30 billion for magazines and newspapers. As one ABC executive said, "The network is paying affiliates to carry network commercials, not programs. What we are is a distribution system for Procter & Gamble." And the CEO of Westinghouse Electric, owner of CBS, said, "We're here to serve advertisers. That's our raison d'être."

6   The media know that television and radio programs are simply fillers for the space between commercials. They know that the programs that succeed are the ones that deliver the highest number of people to the advertisers. But not just any people. Advertisers are interested in people aged eighteen to forty-nine who live in or near a city. *Dr. Quinn, Medicine Woman*, a program that was number one in its time slot and immensely popular with older, more rural viewers, was canceled in 1998 because it couldn't command the higher advertising rates paid for younger, richer audiences. This is not new: the *Daily Herald*, a British newspaper with 47 million readers,

double the combined readership of *The Times, The Financial Times, The Guardian*, and *The Telegraph*, folded in the 1960s because its readers were mostly elderly and working class and had little appeal to advertisers. The target audience that appeals to advertisers is becoming more narrow all the time. According to Dean Valentine, the head of United Paramount Network, most networks have abandoned the middle class and want "very chic shows that talk to affluent, urban, unmarried, huge-disposable-income 18-to-34-year-olds because the theory is, from advertisers, that the earlier you get them, the sooner you imprint the brand name."

7   Newspapers are more in the business of selling audiences than in the business of giving people news, especially as more and more newspapers are owned by fewer and fewer chains. They exist primarily to support local advertisers, such as car dealers, realtors, and department store owners. A full-page ad in the *New York Times* says, "A funny thing happens when people put down a newspaper. They start spending money." The ad continues, "Nothing puts people in the mood to buy like a newspaper. In fact, most people consider it almost a prerequisite to any spending spree." It concludes, "Newspaper. It's the best way to close a sale." It is especially disconcerting to realize that our newspapers, even the illustrious *New York Times*, are hucksters at heart.

8   The Internet advertisers target the wealthy too, of course. "They give you Dick," says an ad in *Advertising Age* for an Internet news network. "We give you Richard." The ad continues, "That's the Senior V.P. Richard who lives in L.A., drives a BMW and wants to buy a DVD player and a kayak." Not surprisingly, there are no magazines or Internet sites or television programs for the poor or for people on welfare. They might not be able to afford the magazines or computers but, more importantly, they are of no use to advertisers.

9   This emphasis on the affluent surely has something to do with the invisibility of the poor in our society. Since advertisers have no interest in them, they are not reflected in the media. We know so much about the rich and famous that it becomes a problem for many who seek to emulate them, but we know very little about the lifestyles of the poor and desperate. It is difficult to feel compassion for people we don't know.

10   Ethnic minorities will soon account for 30 percent of all consumer purchases. No wonder they are increasingly important to advertisers. Nearly half of all Fortune 1000 companies have some kind of ethnic marketing campaign. Nonetheless, minorities are still underrepresented in advertising agencies. African-Americans, who are over 10 percent of the total workforce, are only 5 percent of the advertising industry. Minorities are underrepresented in ads as well—about 87 percent of people in mainstream magazine ads are white, about 3 percent are African-American (most likely appearing as athletes or musicians), and less than 1 percent are Hispanic or Asian. As the spending power of minorities increases, so does marketing segmentation. Mass marketing aimed at a universal audience doesn't work so well in a multicultural society, but cable television, the Internet, custom publishing, and direct marketing lend themselves very well to this segmentation. The multiculturalism that we see in advertising is about money, of course, not about social justice.

11   Many companies these days are hiring anthropologists and psychologists to examine consumers' product choices, verbal responses, even body language for deeper

meanings. They spend time in consumers' homes, listening to their conversations and exploring their closets and bathroom cabinets. Ad agency Leo Burnett's director of planning calls these techniques "getting in under the radar." Robert Deutsch, a neuroscientist and anthropologist who works for ad agency DDB Needham, likens himself to a vampire—"I suck information out of people, and they love it."

12   One new market research technique involves monitoring brain-wave signals to measure how "engaged" viewers are in what they are watching. According to the president of the company doing this research, "We are the only company in the industry reading people's thoughts and emotions. Someone's going to be a billionaire doing this. I think it will be us."

13   Through focus groups and in-depth interviews, psychological researchers can zero in on very specific target audiences—and their leaders. "Buy this 24-year-old and get all his friends absolutely free," proclaims an ad for MTV directed to advertisers. MTV presents itself publicly as a place for rebels and nonconformists. Behind the scenes, however, it tells potential advertisers that its viewers are lemmings who will buy whatever they are told to buy.

14   The MTV ad gives us a somewhat different perspective on the concept of "peer pressure." Advertisers, especially those who advertise tobacco and alcohol, are forever claiming that advertising doesn't influence anyone, that kids smoke and drink because of peer pressure. Sure, such pressure exists and is an important influence, but a lot of it is created by advertising. Kids who exert peer pressure don't drop into high schools like Martians. They are kids who tend to be leaders, whom other kids follow for good or for bad. And they themselves are mightily influenced by advertising, sometimes very deliberately as in the MTV ad. As an ad for *Seventeen* magazine, picturing a group of attractive young people, says, "Hip doesn't just happen. It starts at the source: *Seventeen*." In the global village, the "peers" are very much the same, regardless of nationality, ethnicity, culture. In the eyes of the media, the youths of the world are becoming a single, seamless, soulless target audience—often cynically labeled "Generation X," or, for the newest wave of teens, "Generation Y." "We're helping a soft drink company reach them, even if their parents can't," says an ad for newspapers featuring a group of young people. The ad continues, "If you think authority figures have a hard time talking to Generation X, you should try being an advertiser," and goes on to suggest placing ads in the television sections of newspapers.

15   Direct-marketing techniques make it possible for advertisers to customize ads for subscribers of the same magazine according to what a particular subscriber has previously bought. In 1994 the direct-marketing firm Bronner Slosberg Humphrey Inc. customized a print campaign for L. L. Bean by comparing the company's customer base to the subscription lists of about twenty national magazines. Different ads were tailored to specific customers. Thus if two *New Yorker* subscribers lived next door to each other, the same edition of the magazine could contain two different L. L. Bean ads. According to Mike Slosberg, vice-chairman of the company, "In essence, the ad becomes direct mail, and the magazine is the envelope."

16   Perhaps we are not surprised that magazines are only envelopes. But many of us had higher hopes for cable television and the Internet. However, these new

technologies have mostly become sophisticated targeting devices. "Now you can turn your target market into a captive audience," says an ad for an Internet news and information service that features a man roped into his office chair.

17 "Capture your audience," says another, featuring a bunch of eyeballs dripping in a net. This ad is selling software that "allows you to track the clicks and mouse-over activities of every single user interacting with your banner ad." Another company recently launched a massive data-collection effort, with the goal of getting at least one million consumers to fill out surveys. It will use the data to deliver ads it claims can be targeted right down to the individual. "Sorry. We can't target by shoe-size. YET," says an ad for Yahoo!, a very successful Internet company, which goes on to tell advertisers, "You're wondering . . . what do our 35 million registered users offer you? Well, information. A lot of it. About who they are. What they're interested in. What kind of job they hold. How old they are. Get the picture?" As a writer for *Advertising Age* said, "What was once a neutral platform for global communication and vast information gathering is now seen as a virtual playground for marketers seeking new and better ways to reach consumers."

18 Home pages on the World Wide Web hawk everything from potato chips to cereal to fast food—to drugs. Alcohol and tobacco companies, chafing under advertising restrictions in other media, have discovered they can find and woo young people without any problem on the Web. Indeed, children are especially vulnerable on the Internet, where advertising manipulates them, invades their privacy, and transforms them into customers without their knowledge. Although there are various initiatives pending, there are as yet no regulations against targeting children online. Marketers attract children to Websites with games and contests and then extract from them information that can be used in future sales pitches to the child and the child's family. They should be aware that this information might be misleading. My daughter recently checked the "less than $20,000" household income box because she was thinking of her allowance.

19 Some sites offer prizes to lure children into giving up the e-mail addresses of their friends too. Online advertising targets children as young as four in an attempt to develop "brand loyalty" as early as possible. Companies unrelated to children's products have Websites for children, such as Chevron's site, which features games, toys, and videos touting the importance of—surprise!—the oil industry. In this way, companies can create an image early on and can also gather marketing data. As one ad says to advertisers, "Beginning this August, Kidstar will be able to reach every kid on the planet. And you can, too."

20 Children are easily influenced. Most little children can't tell the difference between the shows and the commercials (which basically means they are smarter than the rest of us). The toys sold during children's programs are often based on characters in the programs. Recently the Center for Media Education asked the Federal Trade Commission to examine "kidola," a television marketing strategy in which toy companies promise to buy blocks of commercial time if a local broadcast station airs programs associated with their toys.

21 Perhaps most troubling, advertising is increasingly showing up in our schools, where ads are emblazoned on school buses, scoreboards, and book covers, where

corporations provide "free" material for teachers, and where many children are a captive audience for the commercials on Channel One, a marketing program that gives video equipment to desperate schools in exchange for the right to broadcast a "news" program studded with commercials to all students every morning. Channel One is hardly free, however—it is estimated that it costs taxpayers $1.8 billion in lost classroom time. But it certainly is profitable for the owners who promise advertisers "the largest teen audience around" and "the undivided attention of millions of teenagers for 12 minutes a day." Another ad for *Channel One* boasts, "Our relationship with 8.1 million teenagers lasts for six years [rather remarkable considering most of theirs last for . . . like six days]." Imagine the public outcry if a political or religious group offered schools an information package with ten minutes of news and two minutes of political or religious persuasion. Yet we tend to think of commercial persuasion as somehow neutral, although it certainly promotes beliefs and behavior that have significant and sometimes harmful effects on the individual, the family, the society, and the environment.

22 "Reach him at the office," says an ad featuring a small boy in a business suit, which continues, "His first day job is kindergarten. Modern can put your sponsored educational materials in the lesson plan." Advertisers are reaching nearly 8 million public-school students each day.

23 According to the Council for Aid to Education, the total amount corporations spend on "educational" programs from kindergarten through high school has increased from $5 million in 1965 to about $500 million today. The Seattle School Board recently voted to aggressively pursue advertising and corporate sponsorship. "There can be a Nike concert series and a Boeing valedictorian," said the head of the task force. We already have market-driven educational materials in our schools, such as Exxon's documentary on the beauty of the Alaskan coastline or the McDonald's Nutrition Chart and a kindergarten curriculum that teaches children to "Learn to Read through Recognizing Corporate Logos."

24 There are penalties for young people who resist this commercialization. In the spring of 1998 Mike Cameron, a senior at Greenbrier High School in Evans, Georgia, was suspended from school. Why? Did he bring a gun to school? Was he smoking in the boys' room? Did he assault a teacher? No. He wore a Pepsi shirt on a school-sponsored Coke day, an entire school day dedicated to an attempt to win ten thousand dollars in a national contest run by Coca-Cola.

25 Coke has several "partnerships" with schools around the country in which the company gives several million dollars to the school in exchange for a long-term contract giving Coke exclusive rights to school vending machines. John Bushey, an area superintendent for thirteen schools in Colorado Springs who signs his correspondence "The Coke Dude," urged school officials to "get next year's volume up to 70,000 cases" and suggested letting students buy Coke throughout the day and putting vending machines "where they are accessible all day." Twenty years ago, teens drank almost twice as much milk as soda. Today they drink twice as much soda as milk. Some data suggest this contributes to broken bones while they are still teenagers and to osteoporosis in later life.

26   Just as children are sold to the toy industry and junk food industry by programs, video games, and films, women are sold to the diet industry by the magazines we read and the television programs we watch, almost all of which make us feel anxious about our weight. "Hey, Coke," proclaims an ad placed by *The Ladies' Home Journal*, "want 17-1/2 million very interested women to think Diet?" It goes on to promise executives of Coca-Cola a "very healthy environment for your ads." What's being sold here isn't Diet Coke—or even *The Ladies' Home Journal*. What's really being sold are the readers of *The Ladies' Home Journal*, first made to feel anxious about their weight and then delivered to the diet industry. Once there, they can be sold again—*Weight Watchers Magazine* sells its readers to the advertisers by promising that they "reward themselves with $4 billion in beauty and fashion expenditures annually."

27   No wonder women's magazines so often have covers that feature luscious cakes and pies juxtaposed with articles about diets. "85 Ways to Lose Weight," *Woman's Day* tells us—but probably one of them isn't the "10-minute ice cream pie" on the cover. This is an invitation to pathology, fueling the paradoxical obsession with food and weight control that is one of the hallmarks of eating disorders.

28   It can be shocking to look at the front and back covers of magazines. Often there are ironic juxtapositions. A typical woman's magazine has a photo of some rich food on the front cover, a cheesecake covered with luscious cherries or a huge slice of apple pie with ice cream melting on top. On the back cover, there is usually a cigarette ad, often one implying that smoking will keep women thin. Inside the magazine are recipes, more photos of fattening foods, articles about dieting—and lots of advertising featuring very thin models. There usually also is at least one article about an uncommon disease or trivial health hazard, which can seem very ironic in light of the truly dangerous product being glamorized on the back cover.

29   In February 1999, *Family Circle* featured on its front cover a luscious photo of "gingham mini-cakes," while promoting articles entitled "New! Lose-Weight, Stay-Young Diet," "Super Foods That Act Like Medicine," and "The Healing Power of Love." On the back cover was an ad for Virginia Slims cigarettes. The same week, *For Women First* featured a chocolate cake on its cover along with one article entitled "Accelerate Fat Loss" and another promising "Breakthrough Cures" for varicose veins, cellulite, PMS, stress, tiredness, and dry skin. On the back cover, an ad for Doral cigarettes said, "Imagine getting more." *The Ladies' Home Journal* that same month offered on its cover "The Best Chocolate Cake You Ever Ate," along with its antidote, "Want to Lose 10 lbs? Re-program Your Body." Concern for their readers' health was reflected in two articles highlighted on the cover, "12 Symptoms You Must Not Ignore" and "De-Stressors for Really Crazy Workdays"—and then undermined by the ad for Basic cigarettes on the back cover (which added to the general confusion by picturing the pack surrounded by chocolate candies).

30   Dr. Holly Atkinson, a health writer for *New Woman* between 1985 and 1990, recalled that she was barred from covering smoking-related issues, and that her editor struck any reference to cigarettes in articles on topics ranging from wrinkles to cancer. When Atkinson confronted the editor, a shouting match ensued. "Holly, who

do you think supports this magazine?" demanded the editor. As Helen Gurley Brown, former editor of *Cosmopolitan*, said: "Having come from the advertising world myself, I think, 'Who needs somebody you're paying millions of dollars a year to come back and bite you on the ankle?' "

31   Today we export a popular culture that promotes escapism, consumerism, violence, and greed. Half the planet lusts for Cindy Crawford, lines up for blockbuster films like *Die Hard2* with a minimum of dialogue and a maximum of violence (which travels well, needing no translation), and dances to the monotonous beat of the Backstreet Boys. *Baywatch*, a moronic television series starring Ken and Barbie, has been seen by more people in the world than any other television show in history. And at the heart of all this "entertainment" is advertising. As Simon Anholt, an English consultant specializing in global brand development, said, "The world's most powerful brand is the U.S. This is because it has Hollywood, the world's best advertising agency. For nearly a century, Hollywood has been pumping out two-hour cinema ads for Brand U.S.A., which audiences around the world flock to see." When a group of German advertising agencies placed an ad in *Advertising Age* that said, "Let's make America great again," they left no doubt about what they had in mind. The ad featured cola, jeans, burgers, cigarettes, and alcohol—an advertiser's idea of what makes America great.

32   Some people might wonder what's wrong with this. On the most obvious level, as multinational chains replace local stores, local products, and local character, we end up in a world in which everything looks the same and everyone is Gapped and Starbucked. Shopping malls kill vibrant downtown centers locally and create a universe of uniformity internationally. Worse, we end up in a world ruled by, in John Maynard Keynes's phrase, the values of the casino. On this deeper level, rampant commercialism undermines our physical and psychological health, our environment, and our civic life and creates a toxic society. Advertising corrupts us and, I will argue, promotes a dissociative state that exploits trauma and can lead to addiction. To add insult to injury, it then co-opts our attempts at resistance and rebellion.

33   Although it is virtually impossible to measure the influence of advertising on a culture, we can learn something by looking at cultures only recently exposed to it. In 1980 the Gwich'in tribe of Alaska got television, and therefore massive advertising, for the first time. Satellite dishes, video games, and VCRs were not far behind. Before this, the Gwich'in lived much the way their ancestors had for a thousand generations. Within ten years, the young members of the tribe were so drawn by television they no longer had time to learn ancient hunting methods, their parents' language, or their oral history. Legends told around campfires could not compete with *Beverly Hills 90210*. Beaded moccasins gave way to Nike sneakers, sled dogs to gas-powered skimobiles, and "tundra tea" to Folger's instant coffee.

34   Human beings used to be influenced primarily by the stories of our particular tribe or community, not by stories that are mass-produced and market-driven. As George Gerbner, one of the world's most respected researchers on the influence of the media, said, "For the first time in human history, most of the stories about people, life,

and values are told not by parents, schools, churches, or others in the community who have something to tell, but by a group of distant conglomerates that have something to sell." The stories that most influence our children these days are the stories told by advertisers.

QUESTIONS FOR ANALYSIS AND DISCUSSION

1. According to Kilbourne, why don't advertisers want consumers to be aware of the influence of advertising? Evaluate how Kilbourne supports this assertion. How do you think advertising agencies would respond to her statement? Explain.
2. How do advertisers use "peer pressure" to target young adults? How effective is this tactic, and why?
3. Kilbourne describes how some schools make deals with advertisers in exchange for free educational materials and/or funding. How does she feel about this practice? What is your own position on the situation? Explain.
4. What mixed messages do advertisers send to women? How do these mixed messages help promote their marketing agenda?
5. How does Kilbourne's example of the influence of advertising in the Gwich'in tribe in Alaska support her points regarding the influence of advertising in our own culture? Are the examples parallel? Explain.

Consumer Angst
Paul Lutus

James Luther Adams, a Unitarian theologian, observed, "For whether a person craves prestige, wealth, security, or amusement . . . that person is demonstrating a faith, showing confidence in something. Find out what he gives his deepest loyalty to and you've found his religion." In the next essay, Paul Lutus describes consumerism as the new American religion, in which brands create loyalty and cultivate the faithful. Advertisers engender the belief in consumers that we need a product, and once we have a product, we will need additional things to maintain it or the lifestyle the product promotes. Are consumers giving their "deepest loyalty" to things they can buy? And what does that mean to our collective social "soul"?

Paul Lutus is a scientist, technologist, and author. In 1986, he was named "Scientist of the Year" by the Oregon Academy of Science. He is the author of the best-selling word processing program "Apple Writer." In articles at his website (http://www.arachnoid.com) he explores the relationship between reason and belief. This essay, posted on his website, examines the nuances of consumer culture and how advertisers get us to believe "the big lie."

BEFORE YOU READ ————————————————————————

Consider the differences between items that are advertised as things we "need" and the items we really need but are not advertised. How do marketers get us to believe we need a product?

AS YOU READ ——————————————————————————————

In this essay, Paul Lutus describes the "big lie" and the "little lies" that we must believe for consumerism to flourish. What role must the consumer play in order for advertising to be effective? How compliant are you as a consumer in buying into "the big lie"?

1   ▌n this story there are no heroes or villains, just people who believe they can buy happiness, and advertisers who support this belief. Consumerism is one of religion's modern replacements, and, like religion, it actively encourages, then exploits, dissatisfaction with everyday reality.

History

2   It is possible to examine nearly any aspect of modern society—the conduct of war, government, marriage, education—and find a similar practice, an earlier version, in history. In most cases, the seeds of the present can be seen in the past. But this is not true for consumerism, for consumerism has no parallel in early human societies.

3   The closest thing to consumerism—and this is offered only as a point of reference, not comparison—is the practice of barter. In barter, two or more individuals met and exchanged what they had for what they didn't have. Advertising either didn't exist or was very primitive, and there was no hierarchy—no natural division between producers and consumers, because everyone was both a producer and a consumer.

4   The motivation for barter was also much more basic—the point was to avoid being dead. It was very straightforward—you could trade your surplus of corn for some arrowheads, or for the services of a mercenary to guard your cornfield, or simply to avoid an untimely death. You could instead keep the corn and hope no one attacked your field, but over time it may have come to you that hiring a mercenary, or owning some arrowheads, would increase the amount of corn you actually kept for more than a few days.

The Role of Surplus

5   The key change that separates modern from traditional societies is the concept of surplus, a condition in which there is more than enough of everything to sustain the lives of all the members of a society. As it happens, people are not designed to cope

with surplus. We have many, many strategies to deal with perpetual deficit, some learned, some congenital, but surplus bewilders us.

6   As just one example, many Americans are overweight because we sit down to eat and—for reasons buried in our collective past—expect to see no more food for a week or more. Therefore, we eat much more than we should, if only our perceptions were based on current reality. Three hours later, we sit down and repeat the performance. But we never adjust to the surplus, leading many researchers to the conclusion that deficit behaviors are very deeply rooted in our characters and are not easily modified by experience.

7   This condition—a world of surplus, occupied by people programmed for deficit—is a perfect setting for modern consumerism. Modern consumerism is based on the triple premise that:

- luxuries are actually needs,
- what you already have is not satisfactory, and
- no product is so basic that advertising is superfluous.

Reactive and Proactive Consumerism

8   I define consumerism as the voluntary suspension of disbelief in the value of material goods. Suspension of disbelief is desirable when viewing a fantasy world such as a stage play or motion picture, and it is also necessary in modern shopping, and for exactly the same reason—the things on display cannot meaningfully be compared with reality.

9   Consumerism is itself divided into two subcategories, reactive consumerism and proactive consumerism. Reactive consumerism (hereinafter RC) awaits a public demand for a product and, no matter how absurd the demand, fills it. Proactive consumerism (hereinafter PC) uses advertising to create markets for products that have no natural market.

10   Before going on, I must add that PC isn't always as parasitic as it might sound on first hearing. Sometimes a perceived need is created out of nowhere, and this engineered need leads to a societal advance—a self-fulfilling prophecy, if you will. For example, education is a form of PC—it appears to convey knowledge, when in fact its real purpose is to create a lifelong taste for knowledge. But to the original target audience of young people (and, sadly, to some of their parents), the "product" being offered has no obvious purpose—an acquired taste for ideas makes young people nearly uncontrollable, rebellious, doubtful of received wisdom. Only later in life does this fondness for ideas bear fruit, at a time (in the brief and brittle lifecycle of the average human brain) when it would be nearly impossible to instill the taste anew.

11   RC can exist in times of deficit, because it only springs to life in response to voiced demand. But PC, the practice of creating a market and then serving it, can only exist in times of surplus. In RC, advertising is an adjunct, a facilitation of the basic process of producing and distributing goods. In PC, advertising is the process—everything else depends on it.

The Big Lie

12 There is one thing you absolutely must know about modern advertising. No matter how true any single advertisement is, modern advertising itself, taken as a whole, tells a lie—that you need the thing being advertised. It is a lie because consumer goods of real value do not need to be advertised—such goods are part of a natural market that flows "beneath" the PC marketplace, although as time passes these basic necessities represent a shrinking percentage of the total flow of goods.

13 When I was young, if you wanted a candy bar and you could afford a good one, you bought a Hershey's Bar (as they were called when I was a child), because they were known to be the best. But, whatever the source of this perception of quality, it certainly was not because of advertising, because Hershey Chocolate Company did not advertise before 1970. They were the best, everyone knew it, why waste the company's money asserting the obvious? Founder Milton Hershey said, "Give them quality. That's the best advertising in the world."

14 By 1970, the world had changed, and products of obvious value were being advertised alongside goods of no intrinsic worth, thus leveling the playing field and making it difficult to distinguish goods of actual worth from make-believe goods designed to fill make-believe needs. And in that year the Hershey Company began to advertise.

15 To put this another way, modern advertising spends vast sums trying to make the buying public aware of products that it also portrays as a necessity of life—an obvious contradiction. After all, how could our loyal consumer have survived to the present moment without this crucial product, to be in a position to witness its advertising?

16 The truth is, by the time an advertisement fills a time slot on your television set, or plays on the radio, or appears in print in your newspaper, chances are you already have all you need to live comfortably. The global purpose of modern advertising is to make you forget this fact. Advertising does this in two ways:

- By creating an atmosphere of dissatisfaction with everything not purchasable, or already purchased. (More on this subject below.)
- By telling lies, appealing lies, lies nearly everyone wants to hear.

17 All the little lies support the big lie—that no product is so valuable that advertising has no purpose.

The Little Lies

18 Here are some examples of the minor lies that are included in advertising to support the big lie:

- "New!" How can something be simultaneously new and absolutely essential to survival? Or, given the thesis that new is better, the advertiser should honestly list the ways that the old new product failed us, thus setting the stage for inevitable disenchantment with the new new product.

- "An exclusive offer!" This nationally televised, prime-time advertisement excludes only the dead, and those too penniless from responding to previous exclusive offers.
- "It costs more, but it is worth it." By implication, things that cost more are worth more, and by negation, things that have no price also have no value. This is an appeal to reject the entire natural world out of hand.
- "You deserve the best." A questionable premise, one intended to cloud your mind and distract you from the more practical question of whether you can afford the best, or whether the product is in fact the best.
- "Everybody has one of these." Except you. Yes—we spent 30 million dollars on a national advertising campaign to reach the last holdout—you. Now buy our $5.95 product and redeem our investment.
- "Protect your children with . . ." A pitch often seen on television. Ironically, television itself threatens your children in ways too numerous to list. There is no advertisement telling you to protect your children from TV itself. I should add that, taken as a whole, the Internet is probably worse.
- "Want to know what women really like?" ad infinitum. This class of advertising exploits the fact that men and women either do not talk to each other, or, if they do, do not understand what the other person is saying. As to the latter, when a man says, "I love your youthful appearance and spirit," he does not add, "When your youthful appearance wears off, your spirit by itself won't be able to sustain our relationship." When a woman says, "I treasure your moments of sensitivity and vulnerability," she does not add, "but you must never appear weak or indecisive. You sort it out—you're a man." These examples show we are so completely saturated by the language of advertising with a sexual angle, that we no longer remember how to speak to each other in a way that doesn't mimic advertising. And we are progressively less likely to talk to each other to sort out reality—we expect the advertisers to tell us what the other sex wants. Instead, and inevitably, we only discover what the advertiser wants.
- "This car is not for everyone." But it certainly is for the 98% of the male car-buying public our team of psychologists has identified as possessing the conceit that they are unique. You are entirely unique in the world, yet you are going to line up and choose one of the three colors this car is available in, then drive this cookie–cutter symbol of your uniqueness off into the sunset.
- "I'm not a doctor, but I play one on television." I didn't make this up. This opening pitch was followed by an endorsement for a patent medicine. This particular example shows the advertisers' contempt for the consumer's intelligence, a contempt almost always justified by subsequent events.

Products that Require Products of Their Own

19 Once advertising has delivered the product into your hands, other aspects of consumerism then come into play. These aspects rely on connections between products, real and imagined. Here are some examples:

20   *"Protect your investment in A with B."* Examples abound—I will use insurance. The entire insurance industry is based on a lie—that purchasing insurance is a better

strategy than keeping your money and personally replacing the insured item in the event of loss. The insurance schema on its surface is very simple—you pay premiums to the insurance company, in exchange for which the insurance company agrees to replace your property in the event of loss.

21 The dirty secret of the insurance business is that, on average, the insurance company has collected much more than the value of the insured property by the time it pays a claim. This is called "making a profit," a trait considered desirable in a company, and insurance companies are very profitable. The profit comes from two sources:

- Your premium payments, and
- The return on the investments made, with your money, by the insurance company.

22 Instead of paying the insurance premiums, you could invest the money as the insurance company does, and simply pay to replace the valued item in the event of a loss. On average, you would come out very far ahead using this strategy. There are two categories of consumers for which this strategy won't work:

- People who can't actually afford the insured item, who are purchasing with borrowed money (these individuals are usually required by the lender to carry insurance), and
- People who slept through economics in school.

23 But most consumers don't know this basic truth about the insurance business. Most people think buying insurance is a smart investment, the action of a mature, responsible person. It isn't—the only time insurance can be justified is if you are buying something you can't afford to replace, and then only when it is required of you. This discussion doesn't apply to liability insurance, where the potential losses are quite beyond imagining, and only the wealthiest individuals can afford to pay direct costs.

24 *"A implies B."* Virtually all consumer products, above a rudimentary level of complexity, have accessories and "enhancements." One can easily imagine a graph of products with the simplest (fewest accessories) on the left and the most complex (most accessories) at the right.

25 At the very left of our imaginary graph is a screwdriver. Not a Phillips screwdriver, just a plain old-fashioned straight-slot screwdriver. If you buy one of these carefully, you will have it decades from now. Your children will inherit it from you. From the standpoint of marketing, this is a nightmare—any number of advertising executives start up from their pillows in terror, having just imagined that screwdriver in reliable service over years and years, its original brand name slowly wearing off.

26 The reason I didn't choose a Phillips screwdriver for my example is because as time passes there are more and more "standard" Phillips screw head sizes, so even though a screwdriver is very basic, in this case you can find yourself looking for a perfect fit for a Phillips screw virtually forever. This assures our ad executive a sound sleep. By contrast, even if you wear out the tip of a standard screwdriver, you can recreate it at home with a file (okay, one possible accessory).

27   At the middle of our graph, let's put a car. A car is a virtual playground for accessories. There is nothing that someone, somewhere, hasn't considered adding to a car. Wet bars. Saunas and hot tubs. There is even a car product whose purpose I haven't been able to figure out. I don't dare name it (since I intend to ridicule it), but it is described as "satisfying" and it comes in a spray can. It has something to do with pretending your car is shinier and newer than it is. In any event, I am always suspicious of advertising where the purpose of the product is left out and the emotional effect of its use is described instead.

28   Even the most basic car, a car you might try to hide from your friends, has some accessories—certainly plastic floor protectors. Once I looked into a car at a dealership and saw the usual floor protectors, and over the protectors I spied a plastic sheet. As I gazed, I wondered if some demented consumer might allow the sheet to wear completely through, thus jeopardizing the plastic floor protectors – for shame!

29   At the right of our graph—remember, this is supposed to be the most accessorizable thing imaginable—let's put marriage. Some may object that marriage, strictly speaking, isn't a consumer item in the same sense as a house or car. But it is! Modern marriage is a packaged, advertised, promoted consumer item, in fact in some ways it is the prototype for all other consumer items, also it has the largest "tree" of dependent accessories and potential replacement items—including the marriage partner—of any product.

30   Marriage has the advantage that there is an innate desire for the product built into the buying public, therefore promoting it only makes people go crazier. And if a particular marriage fails to please, the average consumer will gullibly listen to promoters' claims that it was that particular marriage, not marriage itself, that was at fault. This degree of gullibility is present to a degree not seen in any other product except religion.

31   Now imagine our completed graph, which even the Internet cannot meaningfully contain. Product complexity and accessorizability increases from left to right. The "trees" of dependent accessories stretch upward from the baseline of the graph. At the left is our lowly screwdriver, with no essential accessories above it. At the middle is a car, with a rather impressive tree of accessories growing out of it. At the right is marriage, with a vast tree of dependent products reaching up higher than any practical finite paper size or computer graph could contain, including nearly all the items to the left of it on the graph itself. Thinking about this graph, you will realize why you almost never see an advertisement for screwdrivers.

32   *"A is replaced by B."* This is a very common pitch. A trivial change is made in the formulation of laundry soap, and suddenly you are the last holdout with a clearly inferior product. Your children will be roundly jeered from the playground. But there are more robust versions of this pitch, guaranteed to drag the majority of consumers, kicking and screaming (but still buying) into the advertiser's future, if not their own.

33   One very effective method is to tie several products together in a dependent relationship, so that, if any one of the products changes, all of them require replacement. Example: the personal computer. As time passes, incremental changes in computer hardware can be accommodated without starting over, but from time to time

an irresistible technological breakthrough comes along that sweeps all prior hardware out the door.

34   There have been two such sweeping changes so far. One was IBM's decision to introduce an "entry system" that it hoped would be a steppingstone into that company's principal business, large systems. But IBM cast such a long shadow on the computing landscape (in those bygone days) that even their deliberately crippled design became the de facto standard personal computer and eclipsed several other contenders.

35   The second change was the introduction of graphical environments such as Windows, which first required a great deal more computer power than its predecessors, and eventually obsoleted all but the most powerful systems.

36   The reason these changes swept away entire architectures was partly fashion, a theme in all of consumerism, but also because of the interdependent nature of individual computers and networks of computers. To a marketer, this gives computers a mixture of attractive and terrifying qualities. Attractive because a single change can create a huge wave of system replacements—all you have to do is figure out how to ride the wave. Terrifying because no individual—not even Bill Gates—can foresee the technological breakthrough that will trigger the next wave, or its timing.

37   Sweeping changes like this are so attractive that one sees valiant attempts to create them out of nothing. Quadraphonic sound is an example. Unfortunately, the American public rejected the thesis that they needed four speakers instead of two, and the idea died.

38   The next visible change of this kind, one supported and encouraged by the American government, is called "High-Definition Television" (HDTV). Basically it constitutes a technological scheme that will improve picture quality and flexibility, and finally replace the oldest and least satisfactory method for encoding a television picture still in use, NTSC (supposedly this stands for "Never Twice the Same Color").

39   Unfortunately for consumers and fortunately for TV manufacturers, this change will eventually require the complete replacement of every TV set, every TV camera and studio, TV transmitters, cable networks, everything. Even more interesting is that the schedule of changes is mandated by the government—beginning with a mixture of old-style and new-style broadcasting, ending with a complete replacement of NTSC programs with HDTV programs, in the communication pathways that are administered by the government. According to this schedule, about ten years from now, barring unforeseen events, the transition will be complete – all commercial broadcasting will be based on the HDTV standard. Consumers will either have new receivers or will have some sort of converter box that will allow them to see some fraction of the size and quality of the new standard's TV image.

40   With all the committees meeting around this issue, it is surprising that no one has asked if the content of TV will be improved along with the image. I think I know the answer.

41   *"B shows the folly of A."* This is a marketing position dearly to be wished for, and it doesn't happen very often. But the examples are memorable: FM radio compared to AM radio. Personal computers compared to typewriters. Calculators compared to

slide rules. Transistor radios compared to tube radios (an older example). But the majority of real-world examples are an illusory, not real, replacement of a prior product on the basis of overwhelming merit: Electric toothbrushes. Anti-lock brakes. Automotive air bags. Electric bug zappers (they don't work against mosquitoes). Sonic bug repellers (they don't work at all).

The Role of Dissatisfaction

42 I earnestly believe that some degree of dissatisfaction is innate in people, and absent our modern society, the chance that someone would fall to his knees in wonder at the sight of a wildflower is marginal. But I can say with assurance that modern advertising makes this possibility disappear entirely, for most people in most places, because in order to consume as we do, we must first be programmed to regard everyday experiences as completely unsatisfactory.

43 This aspect of marketing has a lot in common with traditional religious practices:

- The truth is hidden from view.
- Your reward lies in the hereafter.
- True happiness in only available to the initiated, the "insiders."
- Everyday reality is a sham, a waste of time, an illusion.
- We are all defective, our personal experiences have no legitimacy without the validation of priests.

44 When I was young, this kind of talk was perfect—I already held everyday experience in contempt (meaning I was already a trained consumer). Each new belief system that came along seemed more sophisticated and promising than the last, certain to show how the seemingly random events around me actually fit together into a coherent whole, a whole that I could perceive if only I underwent an initiation ritual.

45 Finally I realized that each of the belief systems I sampled were simply examples of modern product packaging and marketing: Your individual, direct experience means nothing. Join up. Get with the program. Oh, by the way, we are going to need some funds to cover our legitimate expenses in showing you the True Path to Enlightenment.

46 This doesn't mean I suddenly saw the value of direct, personal experience, but I certainly did see that the packaged version was not innately superior. For me, this was a big step forward.

47 But for most Americans, rich and poor, the packaged version is still innately superior, and this is tangible evidence of the triumph of marketing. For us, a personal view of a field of sunflowers is quite ordinary, but a painting of that same view can fetch millions. Even the paintings of sunflowers rejected by the artist, then used by his maid as rags to clean up his studio, are prized beyond any imaginable real-life scene of sunflowers. Why? Simple: the real scene cannot be packaged and marketed— it can never be "more" than an individual experience.

48 Pablo Picasso realized the importance of marketing, late in his career. At that time, he began churning out works that had as their only distinguishing characteristic

a resemblance to the works of an artist named Picasso. The subject meant nothing, the style meant everything. Pure marketing.

49   We distrust our direct experiences, and require a commentator—an authority—to interpret our experiences for us. This is why Americans believe nothing is real until it has been on television. In this sense, television is the product package, as well as a vehicle for the ultimate comment on all contemporary reality—advertising.

50   When the "pet rock" was first introduced, when a completely ordinary rock became valuable by virtue of its package and advertising, I imagine some advertiser on Madison Avenue saying, "Yes! Now we have them! They will buy absolutely anything!"

Coping Skills

51   Here are some common-sense suggestions to minimize the negative effects of consumerism in your life:

- It is very likely that most of your dissatisfactions are a carefully engineered preparation for consumerism. So examine your dissatisfactions—keep only those that, if discarded, might kill you. Toss the rest.
- The first rule of advertising: if it is advertised, it is not a necessity. So start out by saying "I don't need this product. Now, do I want it?"
- Ask yourself how much of an advertisement appeals to reason, and how much appeals to emotion. If the primary appeal is to emotion, you should expect to feel another, stronger emotion after the purchase: disappointment.
- Ask yourself if the advertisement describes a product, or instead describes you in unrealistic ways. After all, it is the real you that will be paying for the product, not the fantasy you that "deserves the very best."
- Apply common sense to advertising. If you are being offered a book that is guaranteed to make you millions and costs $39.95, you should wonder why it didn't work for the author. Real millionaires don't promote get-rich-quick schemes on late-night TV unless the actual get-rich-quick scheme is to sell millions of copies of a worthless book.
- Above all, recapture an appreciation for ordinary reality. Two reasons quickly come to mind:
  - Fields of flowers don't lie, and
  - If you postpone a walk in the flowers for long enough, the next time you check, they will be gone.

52   In my view, if a person can't sit down in a forest, look between the trees at a sunlit meadow and say, "This is all I really need," then that person is more than slightly bent. But that's only my opinion—I could be wrong.

A Closing Comment

53   In your life, how many print articles have you read that portray consumerism and advertising in this way? Chances are, very few or none. Why? Is it because the author

is spectacularly original, possibly inspired by genius? Or is it simply because television, magazines and newspapers reject this kind of writing out of hand, for fear of offending advertisers? Even though I am the author and would like you to believe the first premise, the second is actually correct—articles like this are almost never seen in print, and ideas like these are almost never aired on TV. They are deliberately excluded.

54   In the commercial publishing business and in television network programming, articles like this are tantamount to treason or suicide. Small-circulation scholarly journals are another story, but their readership is so small and specialized that they do not represent a threat to mass marketing. For various reasons the Internet, although increasingly commercial in content, is also the best source for anti-consumerist sentiment.

QUESTIONS FOR ANALYSIS AND DISCUSSION ─────────

1. What circumstances are necessary for consumerism to take root and flourish? Explain. How effective are the author's references to history in framing his argument?
2. According to Lutus, what is the "triple premise" of modern consumerism?
3. Review the author's definition of consumerism and its two subcategories. Can you think of examples of "reactive consumerism" and "proactive consumerism" in your own purchasing experience? Explain.
4. Evaluate Lutus's argument. What position does he take on consumerism and consumer culture? Identify areas of his essay that made sense to you. Did you disagree with any of his points? Explain.
5. In what ways, according to the author, is consumerism similar to traditional religious practices? Do you agree with this view? Why or why not?

Which One of These Sneakers Is Me?
Douglas Rushkoff

Brand-name products target groups of consumers—Pepsi and Levi's appeal to large, diverse populations, while Fendi or Gucci appeal to very elite ones. Brands depend on image—the image they promote, and the image the consumer believes they will project by using the product. For many teens, brands can announce membership in a particular group, value systems, personality, and personal style. As Douglas Rushkoff explains in the next essay, today's youth are more consumer and media savvy than previous generations, forcing retailers to rethink how they brand and market goods to this group. But while teens like to think that they are hip to advertising gimmicks, marketers are one step ahead of the game—a game that teens are likely to lose as they strive to "brand" themselves.

Douglas Rushkoff is a writer and columnist who analyzes, writes, and speaks about the way people, cultures, and institutions share and influence each other's values. He is the author of many books on new media and popular culture, including *Coercion: Why We Listen to What "They" Say* (2002) and *Get Back in the Box* (2005). Winner of the first Neil Postman award for Career Achievement in Public Intellectual Activity, Rushkoff also serves as advisor to the United Nations' Commission on World Culture. This essay appeared in the April 30, 2000, edition of *The London Times.*

BEFORE YOU READ

When you were in junior and senior high school, did you have particular brands to which you were most loyal? What cultural and social influences, if any, contributed to your desire for a particular brand?

AS YOU READ

What can a brand tell you about the person who uses it? Do brands "define" people? How do brands "identify" people as members of a particular group or lifestyle?

1   I was in one of those sports "superstores" the other day, hoping to find a pair of trainers for myself. As I faced the giant wall of shoes, each model categorized by either sports affiliation, basketball star, economic class, racial heritage or consumer niche, I noticed a young boy standing next to me, maybe 13 years old, in even greater awe of the towering selection of footwear.

2   His jaw was dropped and his eyes were glazed over—a psycho-physical response to the overwhelming sensory data in a self-contained consumer environment. It's a phenomenon known to retail architects as "Gruen Transfer," named for the gentleman who invented the shopping mall, where this mental paralysis is most commonly observed. Having finished several years of research on this exact mind state, I knew to proceed with caution. I slowly made my way to the boy's side and gently asked him, "what is going through your mind right now?"

3   He responded without hesitation, "I don't know which of these trainers is 'me.'" The boy proceeded to explain his dilemma. He thought of Nike as the most utilitarian and scientifically advanced shoe, but had heard something about third world laborers and was afraid that wearing this brand might label him as too anti-Green. He then considered a skateboard shoe, Airwalk, by an "indie" manufacturer (the trainer equivalent of a micro-brewery) but had recently learned that this company was almost as big as Nike. The truly hip brands of skate shoe were

too esoteric for his current profile at school—he'd look like he was "trying." This left the "retro" brands, like Puma, Converse and Adidas, none of which he felt any real affinity, since he wasn't even alive in the 70's when they were truly and non-ironically popular.

4   With no clear choice and, more importantly, no other way to conceive of his own identity, the boy stood there, paralyzed in the modern youth equivalent of an existential crisis. Which brand am I, anyway?

5   Believe it or not, there are dozens, perhaps hundreds of youth culture marketers who have already begun clipping out this article. They work for hip, new advertising agencies and cultural research firms who trade in the psychology of our children and the anthropology of their culture. The object of their labors is to create precisely the state of confusion and vulnerability experienced by the young shopper at the shoe wall—and then turn this state to their advantage. It is a science, though not a pretty one.

6   Marketers spend millions developing strategies to identify children's predilections and then capitalize on their vulnerabilities. Young people are fooled for a while, but then develop defense mechanisms, such as media-savvy attitudes or ironic dispositions. Then marketers research these defenses, develop new countermeasures, and on it goes.

7   The battle in which our children are engaged seems to pass beneath our radar screens, in a language we don't understand. But we see the confusion and despair that results. How did we get in this predicament, and is there a way out? Is it your imagination, you wonder, or have things really gotten worse? Alas, things seem to have gotten worse. Ironically, this is because things had gotten so much better.

8   In olden times—back when those of us who read the newspaper grew up—media was a one-way affair. Advertisers enjoyed a captive audience, and could quite authoritatively provoke our angst and stoke our aspirations. Interactivity changed all this. The remote control gave viewers the ability to break the captive spell of television programming whenever they wished, without having to get up and go all the way up to the set. Young people proved particularly adept at "channel surfing," both because they grew up using the new tool, and because they felt little compunction to endure the tension-provoking narratives of storytellers who did not have their best interests at heart. It was as if young people knew that the stuff on television was called "programming" for a reason, and developed shortened attention spans for the purpose of keeping themselves from falling into the spell of advertisers. The remote control allowed young people to deconstruct TV.

9   The next weapon in the child's arsenal was the video game joystick. For the first time, viewers had control over the very pixels on their monitors. The television image was demystified. Then, the computer mouse and keyboard transformed the TV receiver into a portal. Today's young people grew up in a world where a screen could as easily be used for expressing oneself as consuming the media of others. Now the media was up-for-grabs, and the ethic, from hackers to camcorder owners, was "do it yourself."

10   Likewise, as computer interfaces were made more complex and opaque—think Windows—the do-it-yourself ethic of the Internet was undone. The original Internet was a place to share ideas and converse with others. Children actually had to use the keyboard! Now, the World Wide Web encourages them to click numbly through packaged content. Web sites are designed to keep young people from using the keyboard, except to enter in their parents' credit card information.

11   But young people had been changed by their exposure to new media. They constituted a new "psychographic," as advertisers like to call it, so new kinds of messaging had to be developed that appealed to their new sensibility.

12   Anthropologists—the same breed of scientists that used to scope out enemy populations before military conquests—engaged in focus groups, conducted "trend-watching" on the streets, in order to study the emotional needs and subtle behaviors of young people. They came to understand, for example, how children had abandoned narrative structures for fear of the way stories were used to coerce them. Children tended to construct narratives for themselves by collecting things instead, like cards, bottlecaps called "pogs," or keychains and plush toys. They also came to understand how young people despised advertising—especially when it did not acknowledge their media-savvy intelligence.

13   Thus, Pokemon was born—a TV show, video game, and product line where the object is to collect as many trading cards as possible. The innovation here, among many, is the marketer's conflation of TV show and advertisement into one piece of media. The show is an advertisement. The story, such as it is, concerns a boy who must collect little monsters in order to develop his own character. Likewise, the Pokemon video game engages the player in a quest for those monsters. Finally, the card game itself (for the few children who actually play it) involves collecting better monsters—not by playing, but by buying more cards. The more cards you buy, the better you can play.

14   Kids feel the tug, but in a way they can't quite identify as advertising. Their compulsion to create a story for themselves—in a world where stories are dangerous—makes them vulnerable to this sort of attack. In marketers terms, Pokemon is "leveraged" media, with "cross-promotion" on "complementary platforms." This is ad-speak for an assault on multiple fronts.

15   Moreover, the time a child spends in the Pokemon craze amounts to a remedial lesson in how to consume. Pokemon teaches them how to want things that they can't or won't actually play with. In fact, it teaches them how to buy things they don't even want. While a child might want one particular card, he needs to purchase them in packages whose contents are not revealed. He must buy blind and repeatedly until he gets the object of his desire.

16   Meanwhile, older kids have attempted to opt out of aspiration, altogether. The "15–24" demographic, considered by marketers the most difficult to wrangle into submission, have adopted a series of postures they hoped would make them impervious to marketing techniques. They take pride in their ability to recognize when they are being pandered to, and watch TV for the sole purpose of calling out when they are being manipulated.

17   But now advertisers are making commercials just for them. Soft drink advertisements satirize one another before rewarding the cynical viewer: "image is nothing,"

they say. The technique might best be called "wink" advertising, for its ability to engender a young person's loyalty by pretending to disarm itself. "Get it?" the ad means to ask. If you're cool, you do.

18   New magazine advertisements for jeans, such as those created by Diesel, take this even one step further. The ads juxtapose imagery that actually makes no sense—ice cream billboards in North Korea, for example. The strategy is brilliant. For a media-savvy young person to feel good about himself, he needs to feel he "gets" the joke. But what does he do with an ad where there's obviously something to get that he can't figure out? He has no choice but to admit that the brand is even cooler than he is. An ad's ability to confound its audience is the new credential for a brand's authenticity.

19   Like the boy at the wall of shoes, kids today analyze each purchase they make, painstakingly aware of how much effort has gone into seducing them. As a result, they see their choices of what to watch and what to buy as exerting some influence over the world around them. After all, their buying patterns have become the center of so much attention!

20   But however media-savvy kids get, they will always lose this particular game. For they have accepted the language of brands as their cultural currency, and the stakes in their purchasing decisions as something real. For no matter how much control kids get over the media they watch, they are still utterly powerless when it comes to the manufacturing of brands. Even a consumer revolt merely reinforces one's role as a consumer, not an autonomous or creative being.

21   The more they interact with brands, the more they brand themselves.

QUESTIONS FOR ANALYSIS AND DISCUSSION

1. How does Rushkoff support his argument? Evaluate his use of supporting sources. Are there any gaps in his article? If so, identify areas where his essay could be stronger. If not, identify some of the essay's particular strengths.

2. How would you define your personal style and the image you wish to project? What products and/or brands contribute to that image? Explain.

3. In paragraph 7, Rushkoff notes that things have gotten worse because they have gotten better. What does he mean by this statement? Explain.

4. Look up the phrase "Gruen transfer" on the Internet. Were you aware of this angle of marketing practice? Does it change the way you think about how products are sold to you? Explain.

5. In order to stay in business, marketers have had to rethink how they sell products to the youth market. How have they changed to keep pace with the youth market? Explain.

6. In his conclusion, Rushkoff predicts that even media-savvy kids will still "lose" the game. Why will they fail? Explain.

Branded World: The Success of the Nike Logo
Michael Levine

In the last essay, a teenager is faced with a daunting challenge—choosing a sneaker brand that was "him." Sneakers are well known for their use of logos to distinguish brands from each other. The young man worries that choosing the wrong brand will make him look like he is "trying" or is a member of the wrong group. Clearly, he believes the expression "the clothes make the man." To him, a logo is a reflection of his identity and of the image he wishes to project.

Logos are graphic designs that represent and help market a particular brand or company. Some logos are instantly recognizable, needing no words to explain what they represent. A good example of a logo with international recognition is the image of the Olympic rings. Other logos may be more obscure and specific to particular countries or demographic groups. Chances are most senior citizens wouldn't recognize the Lugz logo or know what product was associated with it. Sometimes a logo can simply be the initial or name of the brand. Chanel is famous for its interlocking C design, and Kate Spade's name serves as her logo. Spade's logo is distinctive because of the font face used to spell her name, which is written in lowercase letters. The next piece, by public relations guru Michael Levine, examines why the brand Nike is such a successful logo.

BEFORE YOU READ

What makes you want to buy a product? Is it peer influence, cultural pressure, or social status? Do generational marketing techniques influence you?

AS YOU READ

Consider the influence of athlete endorsement for products: from sports equipment and apparel to soft drinks, watches, and automobiles. What image does the athlete project about the product? How much does the brand's logo factor into the product promotion? Do athletes sell products, or do athletes wearing brand logos sell products? Explain.

1 There are few branding tales as epic and impressive as that of Nike. Before Phil Knight made the swoosh a universally known symbol, a soft shoe you wore to play sports or run in was called a sneaker. There weren't separate sneakers for basketball, running, walking, cross training, and tennis; there were just sneakers. They were made by companies like Keds and PF Fliers, and they were usually worn by children. Professional athletes wore shoes made for their individual sports, which were either not available to the general public or were not identifiable by brand. A few companies, like Adidas, were making "tennis shoes," which adults wore when they played a sport on the weekends.

2   Now, there are "athletic shoes." They are very specific to their tasks and can be found in stores like Foot Locker and Sports Authority, classified by usage: Cross-trainers are not the same as shoes for walking, which are different from running shoes, which are not to be confused with basketball shoes. And much of that distinction can be attributed to Nike and the awe-inspiring job it has done in defining not only its own brand but the very category of product the brand helped to create.

3   "The way you build a brand is by creating a new category you can be first in," says branding guru Al Ries. "I have yet to hear anybody ever refer to Nike as a sneaker. It's only the older people who used to buy Keds who refer to Nike as a sneaker. There is an enormous difference between an athletic shoe and a sneaker. You can look at the two and say they look alike, they smell alike, they sound alike. I say no: Your typical inner-city kid isn't going to wear Keds and call it a sneaker. They want a Nike; it's a different deal." How did Nike transform the category of sports footwear into the massive $14 billion business it is today? And how did it manage to grab an astounding 45 percent of the market by the year 2000? Was it just such an obviously superior product that the public couldn't help but notice and respond to? Or was the branding of Nike so well considered and crafty that it outshone all the rest of the brands in its category, using every possible branding tactic almost perfectly?

4   Once it was associated with the active, aggressive, powerful brand Nike had assigned itself, the swoosh become an incredibly articulate mark . . .

5   I am inclined to state that the latter was the prevailing condition. Nike took what was, for its category, a revolutionary product (the waffle sole) and transformed what could have been a niche product into something that every kid in the street playing basketball had to have. Beyond that, however, Nike expanded its brand into other market segments, appealing to adults, to women, to nonathletes. And it extended its brand into products other than shoes: apparel, signature hats, shirts, shorts, and many other products that bore the suddenly familiar Nike symbol.

6   "[Nike] figured out a very simple brand visually, and they didn't deviate from it at all. They kept that message very well defined," says Howard Rubenstein, president of Rubenstein Associates, a New York publicity firm. "If you just glance at [Nike's] logo, you know what the message is."

7   The swoosh, Nike's squiggly symbol, has no intrinsic meaning in our lexicon; before the company developed it, it did not exist as a symbol communicating anything. But once it was associated with the active, aggressive, powerful brand Nike had assigned itself, the swoosh become an incredibly articulate mark, communicating the continued thrust forward of anyone who had the wherewithal to don a piece of apparel that bore the symbol.

8   Still, the swoosh wasn't the only way that Nike differentiated itself from other athletic shoe companies, and it certainly wasn't the main tool in developing that brand's identity. More than anything else, the company was probably best known in its early years for its associations with well-known sports celebrities, who never, ever appeared in public without a swoosh on at least one visible article of clothing.

9   Tiger Woods, Derek Jeter, and especially Michael Jordan were routinely seen wearing the Nike logo, and while they never necessarily said a word in a Nike advertisement, it was clear their endorsement was meant to relay a message to

consumers: "Be like (fill in the extremely famous sports celebrity). Wear Nike." The copy might have read "Just Do It," but the message was loud and clear.

10   "Nike was successful in making that [swoosh] synonymous with performance," says *Variety* publisher Charlie Koones. "Not just the performance of their shoe, but performance on a larger scale." By allying themselves with great athletes, by building a bit of a jock attitude. It's interesting to ask yourself what is the feeling that comes out of your brand promise."

11   The road for Nike has not been entirely bump free, however. Allegations that the company's products were manufactured overseas in sweatshops have dogged the brand, and there have been declines in the athletic shoe market generally in the past few years. But Nike continues on, and even if its brand is a tiny bit diminished, it is still head and shoulders above the rest of the industry.

12   "At one time, I think Nike truly was a genuine brand," says Duane Knapp, author of *The Brand Mindset*. "In others words, they were perceived by the customer as one of a kind. Maybe in some customers' minds, that's true today. They're not perfect. At this point in time, you'd have to ask their customers what's the difference between Nike and Adidas. It really doesn't matter what the executives think; it matters what the customers think. When Phil Knight invented the waffle sole, they were a genuine brand. Now that they've gotten into different things, my feeling is they've probably moved from right to left on that continuum in the customer's mind. They are not a one-of-a-kind brand anymore. That doesn't mean they're a bad brand. But every brand is moving toward being a commodity unless the company does something continually, every single day, and that is where the public relations comes in."

13   Nike's position in the athletic shoe and apparel industry is without peer, but it is true that the brand is not as strong as it once was, partially due to increased competition and partially because nothing could stay that hot. Allegations that the company used overseas sweatshops to assemble $120 athletic shoes didn't help.

14   Through it all, Nike's public relations professionals emphasized that the company was doing its best to improve conditions in its worldwide facilities, and, as it addressed the problem, it continued to thrive. While the situation is not yet completely resolved, it has not crippled Nike by any stretch of the imagination.

15   Knapp brings up two important points: First, the company has to have a strong sense of its identity from the consumer's point of view. The image company executives have is irrelevant if the consumer sees the product and the brand in a different light. Second, the brand identity and brand integrity must be reinforced in the consumer's mind every day. Not once a week, not whenever there's a sales downturn: every day. If the mission of the company is not to satisfy the customer's expectations and exceed them every time, the brand might never become a true household name, and it certainly won't last for decades like Coca-Cola, Disney, and McDonald's—and even those brands have had major stumbling points.

QUESTIONS FOR ANALYSIS AND DISCUSSION

1. Levine notes that Nike's swoosh logo has no "intrinsic meaning" beyond what it has come to represent: Nike products. Examine the clothing you are wearing and the personal items within 10 feet of you right

now. How many items bear a logo? What are they? Do they have any "intrinsic meaning"? Explain.

2. What brands do you tend to purchase and why? Are there particular logos that are associated with the brands you prefer? Explain.

3. Are you more likely to purchase a product with a prominent or prestigious logo than a "no-name" brand? Why or why not?

4. What is your college or university's logo? Is it a shield? A phrase? A mascot? How does the symbol chosen by your school reflect its values and identity? Explain.

5. Levine quotes Duane Knapp on the shifting of the Nike brand, "At one time, I think Nike truly was a genuine brand." Why does Knapp feel that Nike is not a "genuine" brand anymore? What changed? Do you agree with his assessment?

READING THE VISUAL

Brand Logos

As Douglas Rushkoff and Michael Levine describe, brand names project promise—the promise of associations and images for the target audience to identify with, and the promise regarding the qualities and particularities that make the brand manufacturer special or unique. Perhaps the highest aim of brand marketing is to create in the mind of the audience an instant association of an identifying image with the brand's manufacturer. And in the mad competition for brand recognition, that instant visual association is the logo.

Consumer critics have observed that many logos can be identified by children almost as soon as they learn to talk. Consider the logos (or icons) below and on the next page. How many do you recognize? After you have completed this exercise, ask a child between the ages of 3 and 9 to identify (either the company or what it does) as many as he or she can. Prepare a short summary of your results for broader class discussion.

RipCurl

Coach

UGG

Seven for all Mankind

Nike Swoosh

WRITING ASSIGNMENTS

1. Locate some advertisements for some popular products. Who is the audience for each advertisement? Discuss the ways the ads are, or are not, targeted to a specific demographic group. Assess how well the ads appeal to the shared lifestyle and desires of this group.

2. Write an essay in which you explore the connection between social diversification, product targeting, and audience packaging. Explore some of the reasons why the "divide and conquer" method of marketing works, and if it is an ethical approach to advertising.

3. Rushkoff notes in paragraph 11 that the youth generation "constituted a new psychographic." First, define what you think "psychographic" means in the advertising industry. What makes this generation different from previous generations of consumers? If you are part of this generation (ages 14–24), explain why you think you indeed represent a new "psychographic," or not. If you are older than this group, answer the same question based on your own experience and observation of younger consumers.

4. Advertisers might argue that corporate sponsorship in schools makes students' educational quality of life better: from supporting athletic events to outfitting a new computer lab to providing expensive scientific equipment. Is this the trade-off for sponsorship? Should schools allow companies exclusive rights to market products to students in school? Write an essay in which you support or question this practice.

5. Write an essay evaluating advertising techniques in the last half of the twentieth century. How have ads changed, and why? Has advertising become more or less ethical? creative? focused?

6. Teens and young adults covet certain brand-name clothing because they believe it promotes a particular image. What defines brand image? Is it something created by the company, or by the people who use the product? How does advertising influence the social view we hold of ourselves and the brands we use? Write an essay on the connection among advertising, image, and cultural values of what is "in," or popular, and what is not.

THE QUEST FOR STUFF

Two Cheers for Consumerism
James Twitchell

While media and social critics question the methods of advertising agencies and lament the loss of basic values in the name of consumerism, Professor James Twitchell openly embraces the media-driven world of advertising. In the next piece, Twitchell explores the joys of consumerism, and the social criticism that condemns our "quest for stuff" as materialistic and self-centered.

Twitchell is a professor of English and advertising at the University of Florida. He switched from teaching poetry to the study of mass culture and advertising after discovering that his students could complete more ad jingles than they could lines of poetry. Since then, he has written several books on the subject, including *Twenty Ads That Shook the World* (2001), *Branded World* (2005), and *Shopping for God: How Christianity Went from in Your Heart to in Your Face* (2007). This essay originally appeared in the August/September 2000 issue of *Reason Magazine.*

BEFORE YOU READ

Why is materialism so criticized, yet so wholeheartedly embraced by American society? If we are basically consumers at heart, as the next piece argues, why are we so quick to condemn advertising?

AS YOU READ

How does the perspective of the author of the next essay differ from others in this section in his attitude toward advertising? What can you surmise from his tone and use of language? How well does Twitchell convince his readers that his position is reasonable and correct?

1   Of all the strange beasts that have come slouching into the 20th century, none has been more misunderstood, more criticized, and more important than materialism. Who but fools, toadies, hacks, and occasional loopy libertarians have ever risen to its defense? Yet the fact remains that while materialism may be the most shallow of the 20th century's various isms, it has been the one that has ultimately triumphed. The world of commodities appears so antithetical to the world of ideas that it seems almost heresy to point out the obvious: Most of the world most of the time spends most of its energy producing and consuming more and more stuff. The really interesting question may be not why we are so materialistic, but why we are so unwilling to acknowledge and explore what seems the central characteristic of modern life.

2   And why is the consumer so often depicted as powerless? From Thomas Hobbes in the mid-17th century ("As in other things, so in men, not the seller but the buyer determines the price") to Edwin S. Gingham in the mid-20th century ("Consumers with dollars in their pockets are not, by any stretch of the imagination, weak. To the contrary, they are the most merciless, meanest, toughest market disciplinarians I know"), the consumer was seen as participating in the meaning-making of the material world. How and why did the consumer get dumbed down and phased out so quickly? Why has the hypodermic metaphor (false needs injected into a docile populace) become the unchallenged explanation of consumerism?

3   Much of our current refusal to consider the liberating role of consumption is the result of who has been doing the describing. Since the 1960s, the primary "readers" of the commercial "text" have been the well-tended and tenured members of the

academy. For any number of reasons—the most obvious being their low levels of disposable income, average age, and the fact that these critics are selling a competing product, "high culture" (which is also coated with its own dream values)—the academy has casually passed off as "hegemonic brainwashing" what seems to me, at least, a self-evident truth about human nature: We like having stuff.

4   In place of the obvious, they have substituted an interpretation that they themselves often call vulgar Marxism. It is supposedly vulgar in the sense that it is not as sophisticated as the real stuff, but it has enough spin on it to be more appropriately called Marxism lite. Go into almost any cultural studies course in this country and you will hear consumerism condemned: What we see in the marketplace is the result of the manipulation of the many for the profit of the few. Consumers are led around by the nose. We live in a squirrel cage. Left alone, we would read Wordsworth, eat lots of salad, and meet to discuss Really Important Subjects.

5   The idea that consumerism creates artificial desires rests on a wistful ignorance of history and human nature, on the hazy, romantic feeling that there existed some halcyon era of noble savages with purely natural needs. Once we're fed and sheltered, our needs have always been cultural, not natural. Until there is some other system to identify and satisfy those needs and yearnings, capitalism—and the culture it carries with it—will continue not just to thrive, but to triumph.

6   In the way we live now, it is simply impossible to consume objects without consuming meaning. Meaning is pumped and drawn everywhere throughout the modern commercial world, into the farthest reaches of space and into the smallest divisions of time. Commercialism is the water we all swim in, the air we breathe, our sunlight and shade. Currents of desire flow around objects like smoke in a wind tunnel.

7   This isn't to say that I'm sanguine about material culture. It has many problems that I have glossed over. Consumerism is wasteful; it is devoid of otherworldly concerns. It is heedless of the truly poor, who cannot gain access to the loop of meaningful information that is carried through its ceaseless exchanges. On a personal level, I struggle daily to keep it at bay. For instance, I fight to keep Chris Whittle's Channel One TV and all place-based advertising from entering the classroom; I contribute to PBS in the hope that they will stop slipping down the slope of commercialism (although I know better); I am annoyed that Coke has bought all the "pouring rights" at my school and is now trying to do the same to the world; and I just go nuts at Christmas.

8   But I also realize that while you don't have to like it, it doesn't hurt to understand it and our part in it. We have not been led astray. To some degree, the triumph of consumerism is the triumph of the popular will. You may not like what is manufactured, advertised, packaged, branded, and broadcast, but it is far closer to what most people want most of the time than at any other period of modern history.

9   We have not been led into this world of material closeness against our better judgment. For many of us, especially when we're young, consumerism is not against our better judgment. It is our better judgment. And this is true regardless of class or culture. We have not just asked to go this way, we have demanded. Now most of the world is lining up, pushing and shoving, eager to elbow into the mall. Woe to the government or religion that says no.

10   Getting and spending have been the most passionate, and often the most imaginative, endeavors of modern life. We have done more than acknowledge that the good life starts with the material life, as the ancients did. We have made stuff the dominant prerequisite of organized society. Things "R" Us. Consumption has become production. While this is dreary and depressing to some, as doubtless it should be, it is liberating and democratic to many more.

QUESTIONS FOR ANALYSIS AND DISCUSSION

1. In his first paragraph, Twitchell asks, "The really interesting question may not be why we are so materialistic, but why we are so unwilling to acknowledge and explore what seems the central characteristic of modern life." Answer his question drawing from information presented in this chapter and your own personal experience.
2. Why, according to Twitchell, is consumption "liberating"? Why do we, as a society, seem to want to refuse this role, but secretly embrace it?
3. What is the attitude of academia toward consumerism? How does Twitchell feel about this attitude? Because he is a professor of English, how do you think his colleagues would respond to his study of consumerism and advertising?
4. Critics of advertising assert that consumerism creates artificial desires. On what is this idea based? How does Twitchell respond to this idea?
5. Why is it impossible, according to the author, to "consume objects without consuming meaning"? Do you agree? Explain.

READING THE VISUAL

Powerful Drug Advertising

Mike Lester

QUESTIONS FOR ANALYSIS AND DISCUSSION ——————

1. What does this cartoon make fun of? What does it say about American consumer habits? Explain.
2. What social and cultural information do you need to know in order to understand the cartoon? For example, to what "pain medication" does the woman refer?
3. Would this cartoon be relevant 10 or 20 years ago? Do you think it will have relevance 10 years in the future? Why or why not?

Manufacturing Desire
Harry Flood

"Welcome to the factory floor. The product? Things that are not essential, but hard to live without. What is being supplied here is demand. Want. Craving. All you could desire. All you can imagine. Maybe more than you can handle." So reads the clip leading into Harry Flood's article on "manufacturing desire" in *Adbusters* magazine. The final decade of the twentieth century was one of the most prosperous in American history. Unemployment fell to new national lows, salaries reached new highs, and Americans with money to spend kept the economy humming. In the next article, Flood explores some of the social forces driving the "decadence" of the 1990s, what it reveals about us as consumers, and what it might foreshadow in our future.

Adbusters magazine, a nonprofit magazine published by the Adbusters Media Foundation based in Vancouver, Canada, is concerned with the ways in which commercial forces "erode our physical and cultural environment." Its articles have been featured in the *Wall Street Journal* and hundreds of other newspapers, magazines, and television and radio shows around the world. This article first appeared in the Winter 2000 issue of *Adbusters* magazine.

BEFORE YOU READ

What things do you want that money can buy? Do you want a luxury automobile? a designer wardrobe? a signature watch? What makes these items more desirable than their less expensive, but equally functional, counterparts? What makes you want these things?

AS YOU READ

How does the "culture of celebrity" contribute to our desire for decadence? Explain.

1   **"W**HY IS THIS CHILD SMILING?"** asks a recent print ad of a cute tot blissfully snoozing. "Because he has lived his whole life in the biggest bull market in history." Cue the smug nods, the flush of pride. For here, swaddled in Baby Gap and lying in a Morigeau crib, is the immaculate American kid, born in the best damn place and time there has ever been. A child wanting for nothing.

2   He will soon learn, of course, to want everything.

3   Americans are beyond apologizing for their lifestyle of scorched-earth consumerism. To the strange little cabal of moralists who have recently questioned the official program, the response has mostly been to crank up the volume and drown the doubt out. Global consumer culture? Supersize it, baby. Pile on the wattage, horsepower, silicone, cholesterol and RAM until the lights flicker, the smoke-alarms shriek and the cardiac paddles lurch to life. Give us marbled steaks and sport-utes,

please, and put it all on our tab—we're good for it. Because we are working dogs. And we have worked out the formula for millennial prosperity: keep your head down and your wallet open, and watch the economy roll. Enjoy the rollicking good times while building "the America we deserve."

4   Time was, decadence on this scale was something to fear. If one group of people was gobbling up resources out of all proportion to its needs, consuming at thirty times the rate of other groups of people, at everyone's expense, well . . . that was bad karma, to say the least. Their society was surely soft, cancerous and doomed.

5   But somehow, the First World has managed to give it all a happy spin. We have decided not to avoid decadence but to embrace it. Crave it. Buy it. Sell it. What's decadent? Ice cream with the density of plutonium, a bubblebath with a barley-flour chaser, that great new Gucci scent called "Envy." Decadence is just the celebration of universal human appetites, fully expressed—and any premium whiner who'd object to that idea must already be half-dead.

6   There's no mistaking contemporary America for Versailles-era France or Rome in the time of the Caesars. Decadence has grown up, grown cool, grown systematic in its excess. It's an indoor trout stream in the tasteful lakeside mansion of a software magnate. It's leasing, rather than owning, a fine German automobile so you can exchange it for a new one in ten months. You don't see the new deci-billionaires of Silicon Valley splashing their wealth around wantonly, like the '80s Wall Street crowd. What you see is specific, laser-guided generosity—like cutting friends and relatives into the IPO, or buying a tax-deductible painting by your boss' kid. Keeping the money in the family. The new design aesthetic, as seen in *Wallpaper* magazine, is sexily minimalist, with high design and hyperattention to every detail. Labor-intensive and expensive as hell, but worth it.

7   See how much we're grown up? Can you understand now why the rest of the world has its nose to the glass, wanting a piece of this?

8   Perhaps decadence isn't a thing but a behavior. Or maybe decadence goes deeper than a behavior, as deep as the emotion that hatched it. The Motion Picture Association of America fixes an R rating on films that include profanity, nudity, sex, violence or "decadent situations." So understanding decadence may simply involve renting a few saucy blockbuster action pictures and monitoring the responses they provoke. As the beloved stars appear on the screen, predictable thoughts materialize in the primitive hindbrain of the viewer: I want your hair. I want your money. I want to see you naked on the Internet.

9   Not every American lives a decadent life, of course. But decadence, as the marketers say, has great penetration. Those who aren't themselves trashing hotel rooms or being photographed in their swimming pools for *InStyle* magazine, end up thinking a lot about those who are—because the culture of celebrity (or the culture of "ornament," as Susan Faludi calls it) is the water we're all swimming in. Refracted through the glass of the tank, the contours of the world outside tend to distort.

10   A Canadian newspaper recently quoted a Toronto woman who had taken a leave from her law practice to stay home with the baby. She was grumbling that the family was now forced to get by on her husband's $37,000 salary. "I love to live in poverty," she said, sardonically. "It's my favorite thing in life." The story was supposed to be

about the social trend of professional women making domestic choices. But it was really about a different social trend altogether: the hyper-inflation of the concept of "enough."

11   Decadence is self-delusion on a massive scale. Like the motto of the new gadget-packed magalog Sony Style—"things that are not essential, yet hard to live without"—it's about convincing yourself of the value of this lifestyle, because to question it would force choices we're not prepared to make.

12   "How much do I deserve?" we all ask ourselves, if only implicitly. "Not just money, but adventure, sex, fizzy water, educational opportunities, time on the beach, peace of mind—the package. How much do I deserve?"

13   A thoughtful answer might be, "I don't deserve anything. The notion that some people are just naturally more entitled than others is for Calvinists, Monarchists and Donald Trump. It simply doesn't feel right to claim more than a modest reasonable allotment. If I've happened to stake a claim on a rich crook of the river, that's my good luck. The guy upstream has worked just as hard as I have. So I share."

14   But that view now seems downright un-American. "How much do I deserve? All I can cram in my mouth, brain, glove-box and daytimer," says the hard-charging capitalist. "I've earned it. And you haven't earned the right to tell me differently." That's why, when the Australian ethicist Peter Singer wonders, "What is our charitable burden?" it strikes so many Americans as unusual, controversial, bizarre. For a lot of folks, the calculation of an acceptable level of personal sacrifice is easy: It's zero. No other answer computes. I think that partly explains the extreme responses Singer evokes. He touches people in a place they don't like to be touched.

15   It's tempting to think of decadence as a personal act with personal consequences (namely, to the soul). If that were true, it would all come down to a matter of taste, and we could agree to live and let live with our own strange preoccupations. But decadence is really a political act. Americans aren't living large in a vacuum; they're living large at the expense of things and people: the growing underclass, the stability of the economy, the texture of mental environment, the planet itself. Every mile we log alone in the car, every sweat-shop-made sneaker we buy, every porn site we visit, every tobacco stock we day-trade in, is a brick in the wall of the new world we're creating. Not everyone got a vote in this process; yet everyone pays the price. Eventually, everyone pays an incredible price.

16   "In a new way, America's decadence has made it vulnerable," a friend offers. Today, all is well, so keep your eye on today. Ten years ago the average personal savings rate in North America was about ten percent. Now it's zero. "If the Dow tumbles, people literally will not be able to tolerate a diminishment in their lifestyle. You'll see consumer rage, deeper and deeper debt problems as consumption patterns hold constant but income falls." Because, the thing is, the desire doesn't go away. The manufacture of desire won't slow down, even if the manufacture of everything else does.

QUESTIONS FOR ANALYSIS AND DISCUSSION

1. According to Flood, what was America's cultural attitude toward "decadence"? How has this attitude changed, and why?

2. According to Flood, how does contemporary America compare to Versailles-era France and Imperial Rome? Explain the similarities and differences between the cultures.

3. In paragraph 10, Flood gives an example of a Toronto woman lamenting her single-family income. How does this example support his point?

4. Flood concludes his article with the ominous warning that "America's decadence has made it vulnerable." A year after he wrote this article, America entered a recession. From your own perspective, discuss whether Flood's concerns carry merit.

5. Go to the *Adbusters* website at <http://www.adbusters.com>. How would you define the political stance of this magazine? What leads you to this conclusion? How is Flood's piece compatible with the political and cultural position of the magazine?

Materialistic Values: Causes and Consequences

Tim Kasser, Richard M. Ryan, Charles E. Couchman, and Kennon M. Sheldon

We all know the impact of consumerism on our wallets. In the next essay, a team of psychologists explores the consequences of materialism and consumer culture on the individual, the community, and the world. Consumerism, and especially the insatiable materialism of American culture as a whole, is threatening to devour the resources of the planet. The authors also examine how consumptive behaviors largely driven by our personal and collective insecurities shape us and our society.

Tim Kasser is clinical psychologist and associate director of the Ecopsychology Institute, and co-author of *Ecopsychology: Restoring the Earth, Healing the Mind* (1995). The following article is an excerpt from his 2004 book, *Psychology and Consumer Culture: The Struggle for a Good Life in a Materialistic World*, written with Allen D. Kanner, a professor at Knox College. This essay, fully referenced in publication (but not in this reprint) was co-written with Richard M. Ryan and Charles E. Couchman, both professors of psychology at the University of Rochester, and Kennon M. Sheldon, a professor of psychology at the University of Missouri, Columbia.

BEFORE YOU READ ─────────────────────────

Recall a time when you experienced a decadent spending situation—either for yourself or with someone else. What motivated your spending? Did you purchase things that you needed, or simply wanted? How did you feel afterward?

AS YOU READ

What is our social attitude about people who spend a lot on items they don't really need? Do we send mixed messages that consumerism is a bad thing, but then urge consumers to keep spending?

1   *Homo sapiens* have long distinguished themselves by their use of and desire for material objects, and human social environments have long worked to support these tendencies to consume. It seems safe to say, however, that never before in humankind's history has our drive toward materialism and consumption been afforded such opportunity for expression and satisfaction. Although this can be seen in the extravagance of wealthy individuals purchasing $6,000 shower curtains and $20 million rocket excursions into outer space, more remarkable is the extent to which high levels of consumption are within reach of even the average person living in a Western society. Almost everyone in the United States owns a telephone, television set, and an automobile (U.S. Census Bureau, 2001), and the homes in which the lower middle class live have comforts like plumbing, heat, and air conditioning that far exceed those enjoyed by royalty 1,000 years ago. Consumption also plays an enormous role in most individuals' leisure activities, be it through watching commercial television, wandering the shopping malls, or surfing the Internet. And, wherever we go, our ears and eyes are bombarded with material messages encouraging us to purchase more and more.

2   Upon accepting the fact that most humans currently live in a culture of consumption, one might ask "Why? Why do we have this culture?" An economist might reply that a culture of consumption is a necessary outgrowth of the advanced capitalistic economic systems under which most Westerners live, because these systems require the production and purchase of ever-increasing amounts of goods. A historian might explain how consumer culture emerged from the industrial age or even earlier, how modern advertising developed and gained prominence, and how particular captains of capitalism changed society by the force of their wills. A political scientist might note the multiple ways in which governmental structures maintain and support the power and interest of businesses to earn money through the sale of goods and services, and how these same structures encourage consumption on the part of citizens.

3   Each of these explanations, as well as others which might be offered from other disciplines, meaningfully elucidates aspects of the culture of consumption. From a psychological perspective, however, they remain less than satisfying, for they do not consider the ways in which individual humans simultaneously create and are created by this culture. As recognized by most sociocultural and anthropological approaches, in order for some dimension of a culture to exist, it must be supported by individual human beings who follow the beliefs and practices of that culture; at the same time, the individual humans who support that aspect of culture are themselves shaped by the beliefs and practices that they have internalized. Take, for example, the particular aspect of culture known as religion. In order for any religion to exist, a reasonably large number of individuals must believe in the tenets and engage in the practices it

espouses. If everyone stopped going to its religious centers, practicing the way of life it encourages, and reading its texts, the religion would die out, as have many religions in the past. At the same time that a religion is created by its followers, its followers are shaped by the religion. When individuals believe in the ideas of the religion and engage in its practices, their identities, personalities, and behaviors are molded in particular and profound ways.

4   If we look a contemporary culture, we see that the media propagate messages to purchase items and experiences, that myths are passed on that say that America is the land of opportunity, that governments work to support capitalism, that business people make decisions on the basis of how to maximize profit, and that consumers amass debt to buy products such as sport utility vehicles and large-screen television sets. These actions can be viewed from many angles, but they must also be understood as reflecting the combined actions and beliefs of a large number of individuals who have internalized the capitalistic, consumeristic worldview. Thus, the culture of consumption is, in part, a shared worldview lodged within the psyches of the members of the culture. However, we must also recognize that living in a culture of consumption means that individuals are exposed to enormous pressures to conform to the beliefs and values of this culture. Accordingly, the worldview in a society shapes the identities and lives of its members, leading them to hold the goals and engage in the practices (e.g., watching commercial television, working for a paycheck, shopping at the mall, investing in the stock market) that support the culture.

5   In this chapter, we refer to the culture of consumption's constellation of aims, beliefs, goals, and behaviors as a *materialistic value orientation* (MVO). From our perspective, an MVO involves the belief that it is important to pursue the culturally sanctioned goals of attaining financial success, having nice possessions, having the right image (produced, in large part, through consumer goods), and having a high status (defined mostly by the size of one's pocketbook and the scope of one's possessions). We focus here on two questions: First, "What leads people to care about and 'buy into' materialistic values and consumption behavior?" And second, "What are the personal, social, and ecological consequences of having a strong MVO?"

6   We use as our point of reference a theory of materialistic values that is grounded in humanistic, existential, and organismic thought, as well as in substantial empirical data. We propose that an MVO develops through two main pathways: (a) from experiences that induce feelings of insecurity and (b) from exposure to social models that encourage materialistic values. We further show that when materialistic values become relatively central to a person's system of values, personal well-being declines because the likelihood of having experiences that satisfy important psychological needs decreases. Finally, we demonstrate that an MVO encourages behaviors that damage interpersonal and community relations, as well as the ecological health of the planet.

How Do People Become Materialistic?

7   Research suggests two main pathways toward the development of an MVO. First, experiences that undermine the satisfaction of psychological needs can cause individuals to orient toward materialism as one type of compensatory strategy intended to countermand the distressing effects of feelings of insecurity. Second, materialis-

tic models and values exert more direct influences on the development of an MVO through the processes of socialization, internalization, and modeling. In the next two sections, we review evidence supporting each of these propositions, and in the third section we show how interactions between the pathways can explain the effectiveness of advertising and the spread of materialism in previously noncapitalistic societies.

Insecurity

8 According to our model, a strong MVO is one way in which people attempt to compensate for worries and doubts about their self-worth, their ability to cope effectively with challenges, and their safety in a relatively unpredictable world. For example, large salaries and the possession of material goods may be especially valued if they represent an attempt to gain approval and acceptance that is otherwise felt to be lacking. A strong MVO may also develop in situations where people feel that wealth, possessions, image, and status enhance their likelihood of meeting basic needs for safety and sustenance (i.e., when they are seen as necessary for continued survival).

9 One primary source of insecurity, in our view, involves exposure to environments and experiences that frustrate or block the fulfillment of people's basic psychological needs, such as those for autonomy, competence, and relatedness, as well as for safety. A growing body of research suggests that individuals become more materialistic when they experience environmental circumstances that do no support such psychological needs. As reviewed below, both people's proximal interpersonal environments and their more distal socioeconomic and cultural environments are important to need fulfillment, and consequently, to the development of a strong MVO.

10 Several studies have explored the effects of family environments, showing that parental styles and practices that poorly satisfy children's needs are also associated with an increased MVO in children. For example, one study reported that late adolescents[1] focused on financial success aspirations (in comparison to self-acceptance, affiliation, or community feeling aspirations) were more likely to have mothers who made more negative and fewer positive emotional expressions about the adolescents and who described their own parenting styles as involving less warmth and democracy, along with greater control. Other studies have shown that children tend to be more materialistic when they have less frequent communication with their parents, when their parents are over-involved, highly punitive, or quite lax in the structure they provide, and when they perceive their parents as less supportive of their desires for autonomy. Each of these parental characteristics is likely to cause feelings of insecurity, which may be compensated for by the development of strong MVO.

11 Divorce is another family experience that can interrupt the satisfaction of children's psychological needs, because it often leads to decreased stability, exposure to more hostility, and increased worries about being loved, Not surprisingly, then, another study found that materialistic young adults are more likely to have divorced parents.

---

[1]Most were approximately age 18.

The authors' investigation of mediational reasons for this finding led them to conclude that "it is the diminution of interpersonal resources such as love and affection, rather than financial resources, that links family disruption and materialism," a statement quite consistent with our framework. Of course, the high rate of divorce in the United States puts many children at risk of developing materialistic values.

12   Although characteristics of one's family environment bear consistent relationships with later material values, the broader institutional and cultural structures within which individuals live can also be more or less supportive of psychological needs. To take an obvious example, blatant political oppression clearly undermines the autonomy of those who are subject to it, just as constant warfare and dire poverty undermine feelings of safety and security. Research shows that certain characteristics of one's culture and society can foster insecurities and therefore influence the extent to which people espouse an MVO.

13   The relation between economic deprivation and materialism is currently the most well-researched of these social dimensions. Researchers have shown that highly materialistic teens have experienced greater socioeconomic disadvantages, as measured by parental socioeconomic and educational status, as well as by neighborhood quality. From a broader perspective, the political scientist Inglehart has reviewed findings showing that national economic indicators can influence materialism. For example, poorer countries tend to be more materialistic than richer countries, generations raised in bad economic times are more materialistic than those raised in prosperous times, and national recessions generally increase people's materialism. Like us, Inglehart has suggested that poor economic conditions cause feelings of deprivation or insecurity and that people may compensate for these feelings by focusing on materialistic goals. Poverty alone may not lead to the adoption of materialistic goals, as seen in the case of religious novitiates who give up their possessions; as described below, however, poverty may work in combination with social modeling to produce a strong MVO.

14   In summary, then, both correlational studies and experimental manipulations of insecurity point to the same conclusion: When people experience situations that do not support the satisfaction of their basic psychological needs, the resultant feelings of insecurity may lead them to adopt a more materialistic outlook on life as a way to compensate for these feelings. Perhaps materialistic pursuits have been evolutionarily ingrained within humans as a way to feel more secure and safe (e.g., Hungry? Get food. Being attacked? Grab a club.), and this tendency is especially heightened under the current clime of cultural consumerism.

Exposure to Materialistic Models and Values

15 A second pathway to the development of materialism involves exposure to materialistic models and values. From the time they are born, people receive implicit and explicit messages endorsing the importance of money and possessions. These endorsements take the form of parental values, the materialistic lifestyles of family members and peers, and the materialistic messages frequently found in popular culture, such as in the media. People often accept such messages, take on materialistic goals, and strive to attain them, as humans have a fundamental tendency to adopt

ambient cultural and familial values and behavioral regulations, a process referred to as *internalization*.

16   Evidence suggests that children do indeed take on the materialistic values of those in their social surroundings. A 1995 study of mothers and their adolescent children showed that when mothers thought it was highly important to pursue financial success, their children generally expressed the same value. Another study assessed the extent to which people perceived their parents, peers, heroes, various other adult figures, and the local community as valuing materialist social values in comparison to values such as self-expression, belonging, aesthetic satisfaction, and quality of life. Individuals who reported growing up in a materialist social milieu were more likely to be materialistic themselves. Although additional research is required to expand on this work (especially through exploration of the influence of same-age peers), the results of these two studies do indeed suggest that people often internalize the materialistic orientations of the salient models around them.

17   Another extremely pervasive source of materialistic messages is popular culture and the media, epitomized by commercial television. Besides the sitcoms, dramas, and game shows with subtexts clearly extolling materialism (e.g., *The Price Is Right*, *Who Wants to Be a Millionaire?*), television is replete with advertisements painstakingly crafted to promote consumption. Advertisers have at their disposal many techniques designed to convince people to purchase their products. For example, they show products being used by people who are famous or extremely attractive (often both), or by someone who obtains some sort of social reward by using the product. The ads also display products amidst a level of wealth that is unattainable by the average consumer and often show idealized versions of life within the context of the advertisement. Such tactics create associations between the product and desirable outcomes and also teach consumptive behavior through modeling.

18   Given the purpose of these techniques and the ubiquitousness of these messages, it is not surprising that studies consistently show a positive correlation between television watching and materialism. This has been reported across different age groups and in samples drawn from a number of different countries. Notably, however, the causal pathway of these studies is ambiguous. Although it is certainly likely that television watching may increase an MVO, it is also possible that television may be more appealing to those with a high MVO because it may validate their worldview, present new ways to pursue materialistic goals, and help them escape from the anxiety associated with insecurity. Future research applying insights derived from the literature on television and aggression may help to untangle the relations between television and an MVO.

Effective Advertising and the Spread of Capitalism

19   Whereas the two pathways described above may each make independent contributions toward the development of an MVO, they may also interact. That is, people experiencing higher levels of insecurity may be more susceptible to the influence of environmental messages concerning the benefits of acquisitiveness, which may in turn make them feel increasingly insecure, and on and on in a vicious cycle. Below,

we briefly describe how this interaction might explain the effectiveness of advertising and the spread of capitalistic ideology.

20   Marketing expert Marsha Richins has noted that ads are often constructed to engender upward social comparisons that make viewers feel uncomfortably inferior. For example, women exposed to perfume ads with highly attractive models report less satisfaction with their own appearance. In our view, these comparisons heighten feelings of personal insecurity, which may then activate compensatory mechanisms designed to alleviate negative feelings. Although many compensatory methods may serve this purpose, the likelihood of choosing a materialistic or consumption-oriented method is increased by the fact that the ads themselves always present a very clear option for feeling better about oneself: buy the product! Moreover, compared to those who care little for materialistic pursuits, people with a strong MVO are more concerned with social comparison, are more likely to compare themselves with images of wealthy people, strongly endorse wanting to make money in order to prove that they are worthwhile people in comparison to others, and are more susceptible to normative influence, such that their buying habits are more influenced by wanting others to approve of their purchases. Each of these factors not only makes materialistic individuals more likely to be attentive to and be influenced by materialistic messages but also might maintain and reinforce the feelings of insecurity that underlie an MVO. This makes such individuals even more susceptible to the craft of advertising.

21   The interaction of forces promoting insecurity and encouraging materialism can also partially explain how capitalistic, free-market economies have been spreading to formerly communist and socialist nations and to less economically developed nations. Several factors relevant to our discussion thus far are at work here. First, as is clear from the anthropological literature, marketers intentionally attempt to foster consumeristic desires in developing countries. As television watching and advertising make their way into new markets, potential consumers are flooded with new models suggesting that viewers have not "made it" unless they own the right products. Inevitably, these messages are internalized to some degree and have the net effect of promoting materialism.

22   Second, market capitalism strikes at the heart of family structure, decreasing resources that provide for quality caretaking and breaking apart a sense of relatedness with one's extended family and community. Less attention and nurturance provided to children produces greater insecurity, which in turn increases the likelihood that they will develop an MVO. Furthermore, the breakdown of the family may lead to increased materialism, as one study reported that children of divorced parents are likely to become more materialistic than children whose parents are not divorced.

23   Finally, free-market economies lead to the concentration of wealth in relatively few hands. The disparities that arise between subgroups within a culture or between different nations have become increasingly noticeable with the spread of modern media to more and more of the world's citizens. The salience of these disparities is likely to fuel increased social comparison, which, as we have noted above, is associated with increased materialism. Furthermore, such upward social comparison is likely to increase feelings of insecurity among the poor when combined with the

dominant message that people are worthwhile to the extent that they own many prestigious goods and are financially successful. Thus, the poor, who already may be vulnerable to materialistic messages as a result of their relative lack of opportunities for need satisfaction, may be subject to yet another factor promoting an MVO.

Materialistic Values and the Welfare of Society

24 Although it is disconcerting to know that the ideology encouraged by our culture of consumption undermines the personal well-being and need satisfaction of those who accept its values, a strong MVO also leads people to engage in behaviors and hold attitudes damaging to our communities and to the world's ecological health.

25 A healthy community is based on people helping one another, on cooperation, and on mutual trust. Several pieces of evidence suggest, however, that a strong MVO is associated with less "civil" behavior. For example, an MVO tends to conflict with the desire to help the world be a better place and to take care of others, decreasing the likelihood that people oriented toward materialism will behave pro-socially. Indeed, research shows that people strongly focused on materialistic values are also lower in social interest, pro-social behavior, and social productivity and are more likely to engage in anti-social acts. That they have more manipulative tendencies and compete more than cooperate provides further evidence that an MVO undermines what is best for the whole community.

26 An MVO can also lead people to care less about environmental issues and to engage in more environmentally destructive behaviors and attitudes. Materialistic values conflict with values to protect the environment and are associated with more negative attitudes toward the environment and fewer environmentally friendly behaviors. An MVO has also been associated with increased greed and heightened consumption in simulated social dilemmas involving ecological issues.

27 In summary, the culture of consumption, as represented by an MVO, not only degrades psychological health, but spreads seeds that may lead to its own destruction. Materialistic values not only heighten our vulnerability to serious social and environmental problems, but also undermine our ability to work cooperatively in finding solutions to these problems.

Conclusion: Implications and Directions

28 Our ideas about how materialistic values are inculcated into individuals, and the data showing how an MVO diminishes personal, social, and ecological well-being, have a number of implications for theoretical, clinical and social change issues.

Theory

29 In psychology, the dominant theory behind much empirical research and clinical work is a behavioral or cognitive viewpoint, which suggests that striving for important social rewards, obtaining one's goals (whatever they may be) and integrating into society (whatever its values) are key features of psychological well-being. The evidence presented here, in contrast, shows that when people focus on obtaining

rewards, when they concern themselves with materialistic goals, and when they espouse the values of the dominant consumer culture, the result is lower well-being. From the needs-based theory we use, influenced by humanistic and organismic assumptions, these results make sense; an MVO reflects and exacerbates people's alienation from their natural strivings to grow, actualize, and connect with others. Because behavioral and cognitive perspectives typically do not contain such theoretical constructs as basic psychological needs and organismic actualization and integration, the results reviewed above are seemingly at odds with such viewpoints on humans and their well-being. Furthermore, behavioral and cognitive perspectives have few theoretical constructs to explain how feelings of insecurity might lead to the internalization of an MVO, because their viewpoints typically only acknowledge the direct roles of learning and imitation in the internalization of values, not more "dynamic" pathways.

30   We raise these theoretical points in the hope of demonstrating how the study of the culture of consumption can address academic problems of concern to theorists and researchers. That is, the material reviewed above, inspired by humanistic, organismic, and existential viewpoints, suggests the need for some important revisions to mainstream psychology's dominant paradigm concerning human motivation and well-being.

Psychology and Social Change

31 The empirical skills and strengths of psychology might be applied to counteract some of the problems inherent in the culture of consumption and in an MVO. One might even argue that psychology bears a special responsibility to do so, given that our discipline's findings have often been used to support and encourage the culture of consumption. Many theoretical ideas from psychology have been "profitably" applied to business, advertising, and education to focus people more heavily on rewards and praise and to more efficiently direct workers, students, and consumers into the channels of action desired by consumer culture.

32   Psychology must begin, therefore, by acknowledging how it has helped spread the culture of consumption and now use these same skills to slow (and, may we hope, reverse) materialism. So, rather than studying how to convince children, adolescents, and adults to purchase products and hinge their self-worth on what they own, psychologists might turn to developing media literacy programs and other types of interventions that would increase individuals' resilience in the face of advertising. Rather than focusing on the use of rewards (supposedly) to improve student creativity and worker productivity, psychologists could give more attention to understanding how grades and paychecks can actually detract from people's intrinsic interest and performance in certain activities. Rather than ignoring the detrimental impact of people's values on the environment, psychologists might begin to study how to help individuals leave smaller "ecological footprints" and live materially simpler lifestyles. And rather than supporting the dominant cultural belief that happiness and well-being are the result of increasing personal and national economic growth, psychologists might begin to educate more broadly the public that increases the GNP and even one's own salary do not equate with increases in happiness and that materialistic values actually undermine well-being.

33   Through such efforts, we may be able to weaken the hold that the capitalistic, consumeristic worldview has on both people's psyches and on the culture, and thereby improve the quality of life for humans, as well as the many other species inhabiting our planet.

QUESTIONS FOR ANALYSIS AND DISCUSSION ─────────

1. In paragraph 2, the authors ask, "Why do we have [consumer] culture?" What different views do they offer? Why do they feel these explanations are unsatisfactory from a psychological perspective?
2. How do humans create and, in turn, how are humans created by consumer culture and consumer habits? Explain.
3. Before reading this essay, had you thought about how the American "culture of consumption" exerted pressure on you to "conform to the beliefs and values of this culture"? Can you think of examples in which your core values where influenced or shaped by consumerism? Explain.
4. According to the authors, how do our materialistic values harm interpersonal and community relationships as well as the health of the planet? Explain.
5. Do you believe your consumer habits are driven, at least in part, by your insecurities? How do advertisers leverage our insecurities to drive consumer culture?
6. What does American consumption mean in a more global context? How does it affect the way other nations view the United States? How does it impact the ecosystem?

The $100 Christmas
Bill McKibben

For many of us, the December holidays are a time of gift lists and flurried shopping. Christmas sales begin the day after Thanksgiving and stores stay open until midnight on Christmas Eve, hoping to get the last dollar out of holiday shoppers. Many department stores generate almost one-third of their annual revenue during the holiday season. But is the spirit of giving getting out of hand? Has it been corrupted by advertisers weaving the "powerful dark magic" of greed? In the next essay, Bill McKibben describes how his church promoted the radical idea that people spend only $100 on gifts per family during the holidays. And he proposes that other churches, mosques, and synagogues consider making the same recommendation.

McKibben is a former staff writer for *The New Yorker* and the author of numerous books, including *Long Distance: A Year of Living Strenuously* (2000), *Enough: Staying Human in an Engineered Age* (2004), and, most recently, *Fight Global Warming Now* (2007). He wrote the following article for the November/December 1997 issue of *Mother Jones* magazine. The article later inspired a longer version of his Christmas experience, with the book *Hundred Dollar Holiday: A Case for a Joyful Christmas* (1999).

BEFORE YOU READ

How do you approach the holiday season? Do you anticipate it with excitement? stress? depression? Do you plan, decorate, and shop? Are your memories warm, lonely, comforting, happy? Explain.

AS YOU READ

How is McKibben's proposal both conservative and radical at the same time?

1   I know what I'll be doing on Christmas Eve. My wife, my 4-year-old daughter, my dad, my brother, and I will snowshoe out into the woods in late afternoon, ready to choose a hemlock or a balsam fir and saw it down—I've had my eye on three or four likely candidates all year. We'll bring it home, shake off the snow, decorate it, and then head for church, where the Sunday school class I help teach will gamely perform this year's pageant. (Last year, along with the usual shepherds and wise people, it featured a lost star talking on a cell phone.) And then it's home to hang stockings, stoke the fire, and off to bed. As traditional as it gets, except that there's no sprawling pile of presents under the tree.

2   Several years ago, a few of us in the northern New York and Vermont conference of the United Methodist Church started a campaign for what we called "Hundred Dollar Holidays." The church leadership voted to urge parishioners not to spend more than $100 per family on presents, to rely instead on simple homemade gifts and on presents of services—a back rub, stacking a cord of firewood. That first year I made walking sticks for everyone. Last year I made spicy chicken sausage. My mother has embraced the idea by making calendars illustrated with snapshots she's taken.

3   The $100 figure was a useful anchor against the constant seductions of the advertisers, a way to explain to children why they weren't getting everything on their list. So far, our daughter, Sophie, does fine at Christmas. Her stocking is exciting to her, the tree is exciting; skating on the pond is exciting. It's worth mentioning, however, that we don't have a television, so she may not understand the degree of her impoverishment. This holiday idea may sound modest. It is modest. And yet at the same time it's pretty radical. Christmas, it turns out, is a bulwark of the nation's economy. Many businesses—bookstores, for instance, where I make my living—do one-third of their volume in the months just before December 25th. And so it hits a nerve to question whether it all makes sense, whether we should celebrate the birth of a man who said we should give all that we have to the poor by showering each other with motorized tie racks.

4   It's radical for another reason, too. If you believe that our consumer addiction represents our deepest problem—the force that keeps us from reaching out to others, from building a fair society, the force that drives so much of our environmental degradation—then Christmas is the nadir. Sure, advertising works its powerful dark magic year-round. But on Christmas morning, with everyone piling downstairs to mounds of presents, consumption is made literally sacred. Here, under a tree with roots going far back into prehistory, here next to a crèche with a figure of the infant child of God, we press stuff on each other, stuff that becomes powerfully connected in our heads to love, to family, and even to salvation. The 12 days of Christmas—and in many homes the eight nights of Hanukkah—are a cram course in consumption, a kind of brainwashing.

5   When we began the $100 campaign, merchants, who wrote letters to the local papers, made it clear to us what a threatening idea it was. Newspaper columnists thought it was pretty extreme, too—one said church people should stick to religion and leave the economy alone. Another said that while our message had merit, it would do too much damage to business.

6   And he was right, or at least not wrong. If we all backed out of Christmas excess this year, we would sink many a gift shop; if we threw less lavish office parties, caterers would suffer—and florists and liquor wholesalers and on down the feeding chain. But we have to start somewhere, if we're ever to climb down from the unsustainable heights we've reached, and Christmas might as well be it.

7   When we first began to spread this idea about celebrating Christmas in a new way, we were earnest and sober. Big-time Christmas was an environmental disgrace—all that wrapping paper, all those batteries. The money could be so much better spent: The price of one silk necktie could feed a village for a day; the cost of a big-screen television could vaccinate more than 60 kids. And struggling to create a proper Christmas drives poor families into debt. Where I live, which is a poor and cold place, January finds many people cutting back on heat to pay off their bills. Those were all good reasons to scale back. But as we continued our campaign, we found we weren't really interested in changing Christmas because we wanted fewer batteries. We wanted more joy. We felt cheated by the Christmases we were having—so rushed, so busy, so full of mercantile fantasy and catalog hype that we couldn't relax and enjoy the season.

8   Our growing need to emphasize joy over guilt says a great deal about the chances for Christian radicalism, for religious radicalism in general. At its truest, religion represents the one force in our society that can postulate some goal other than accumulation. In an I-dolatrous culture, religion can play a subversive role. Churches, mosques, and synagogues almost alone among our official institutions can say, It's not the economy, stupid. It's your life. It's learning that there's some other center to the universe.

9   Having that other center can change the way we see the world around us. It's why devoted clergy and laypeople occasionally work small miracles in inner cities and prisons; it's why alcoholics talk about a Higher Power. If we're too big, then perhaps the solution lies in somehow making ourselves a little smaller.

10   You may be too late for this Christmas. You may already have bought your pile of stuff, or perhaps it's too late to broach the subject with relatives who will gather

with you for the holidays, bearing (and therefore expecting) great stacks of loot. Our local Methodist ministers begin in September, preaching a skit sermon about the coming holiday. Many in our church community now participate. So do some of our neighbors and friends around the country. None of us are under any illusions; we know that turning the focus of Christmas back to Christ is a long and patient effort, one that works against every force that consumer culture can muster. But to judge from our own holidays in recent years, it's well worth the effort. I know what we'll be doing Christmas morning: After we open our stockings and exchange our few homemade gifts, we'll go out for a hike. Following the advice of St. Francis of Assisi, who said that even the birds deserve to celebrate this happy day, we'll spread seed hither and yon—and for one morning the chickadees and the jays will have it easy. And then we'll head back inside to the warm and fragrant kitchen and start basting the turkey, shaping the rolls, mashing the potatoes.

QUESTIONS FOR ANALYSIS AND DISCUSSION

1. Is a $100 holiday possible in your family? realistic? good in principle but impossible in practice? Is it fair? Explain.
2. McKibben defines the current materialistic traditions of Christmas and Hanukkah as the result of advertisers who have exploited the spirit of these holidays and brainwashed consumers. "The 12 days of Christmas—and in many homes the eight nights of Hanukkah—are a cram course in consumption. . . ." Do you agree? Why or why not?
3. McKibben states that his daughter, Sophie, is happy with her modest gifts because she finds the entire holiday experience exciting. He comments, though, that "it's worth mentioning, however, that we don't have a television, so she may not understand the degree of her impoverishment." What connection is McKibben making between television and our desire for things? Does he have a point?
4. How did merchants react to the proposal of a $100 holiday? Why is one columnist's comment that "church people should stick to religion and leave the economy alone" ironic? Explain.

READING THE VISUAL

Bump

Adbusters magazine is a nonprofit, reader-supported, 120,000-circulation journal that provides critical commentary on consumer culture and corporate marketing agendas. Articles and issues from the magazine have been featured on MTV and PBS, the *Wall Street Journal*, *Wired*, and in hundreds of other newspapers, magazines, and television and radio shows around the world. They are "dedicated to examining the relationship between human beings and their physical and mental environment," striving to create a "world in which the economy and ecology resonate in balance." This "ad" appeared in both their magazine and on their website, at <http://www.adbusters.org>.

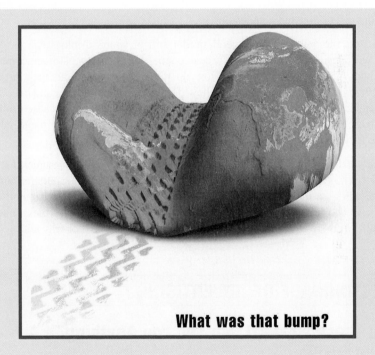

What was that bump?

QUESTIONS FOR ANALYSIS AND DISCUSSION

1. What message is *Adbusters* trying to convey with this ad? Explain.
2. What is your impression of this ad? Does it appeal to you? Why or why not? Who do you think is the intended audience?
3. Visit the <http://adbusters.org/spoofads/> website and view some of the other "ads" they have posted online. Select one and explain how *Adbusters* twists the original ad to make a point.

WRITING ASSIGNMENTS

1. In their article "Materialistic Values: Causes and Consequences," the authors theorize that the roots of materialism are deeply connected to human nature and our personal insecurities. If materialism is an important element of civilization, why do so many critics of consumerism imply that our desire for things is bad for our culture and our society?

2. With a group of classmates, make a list of at least 15 to 20 appliances and equipment that people have in their homes—refrigerators, microwave ovens, DVD players, computers, VCRs, televisions, stereos (include components), and so on. Individually, rank each item as a necessity, a desirable object, or a luxury item. For example, you may decide a refrigerator is a necessary item, but that an air conditioner is a luxury item. Compare your list with others in your group. How do the lists compare? What accounts for the discrepancies? Write an essay detailing your discussion and conclusions.

3. Access the websites for several similar soft or sports drinks, such as <http://www.pepsi.com>, <http://www.coke.com>, <http://www.gatorade.com>, and <http://www.powerade.com>. How do the websites promote their products? Who is the target audience, and how do their sites reflect this audience? What techniques do they use to sell? Write an essay evaluating how these drinks sell their products. Address the fact that the products are essentially the same. How do they convince consumers to part with their money?

4. *Adbusters* addresses the unethical ways advertisers manipulate consumers to "need" products. However, if we study ads long enough, we can determine for ourselves the ways we may be manipulated. Select several printed or television advertisements and analyze how they manipulate consumers to increase their "quest for stuff." Is there anything wrong with this manipulation? Why or why not?

THE LANGUAGE OF ADVERTISING

With These Words, I Can Sell You Anything
William Lutz

Words such as "help" and "virtually" and phrases such as "new and improved" and "acts fast" seem like innocuous weaponry in the arsenal of advertising. But not to William Lutz, who analyzes how such words are used in ads—how they misrepresent, mislead, and deceive consumers. In this essay, he alerts us to the special power of "weasel words"—those familiar and sneaky little critters that "appear to say one thing when in fact they say the opposite, or nothing at all." The real danger, Lutz argues, is how such language debases reality and the values of the consumer.

William Lutz has been called the "George Orwell of the 1990s." He teaches English at Rutgers University and is the author of several books, including *Beyond Nineteen Eighty-Four*

(1984) and *Doublespeak Defined* (1999). The following article is an excerpt from Lutz's book *Doublespeak* (1990).

BEFORE YOU READ ──────────────────────────

Consider the phrase "like magic" as it might be used in an ad—for example, "Zappo dish detergent works like magic." What does the phrase suggest at a quick glance? What does it mean upon detailed analysis? Make a list of other such words used in advertising to make "big promises."

AS YOU READ ──────────────────────────

A "weasel word" is a word so hollow it has no meaning. As you read Lutz's article, consider your own reaction to such words when you hear them. Have they ever motivated you to make a purchase?

1   One problem advertisers have when they try to convince you that the product they are pushing is really different from other, similar products is that their claims are subject to some laws. Not a lot of laws, but there are some designed to prevent fraudulent or untruthful claims in advertising. Even during the happy years of non-regulation under President Ronald Reagan, the FTC did crack down on the more blatant abuses in advertising claims. Generally speaking, advertisers have to be careful in what they say in their ads, in the claims they make for the products they advertise. Parity claims are safe because they are legal and supported by a number of court decisions. But beyond parity claims there are weasel words.

2   Advertisers use weasel words to appear to be making a claim for a product when in fact they are making no claim at all. Weasel words get their name from the way weasels eat the eggs they find in the nests of other animals. A weasel will make a small hole in the egg, suck out the insides, then place the egg back in the nest. Only when the egg is examined closely is it found to be hollow. That's the way it is with weasel words in advertising: Examine weasel words closely and you'll find that they're as hollow as any egg sucked by a weasel. Weasel words appear to say one thing when in fact they say the opposite, or nothing at all.

"Help"—The Number One Weasel Word

3   The biggest weasel word used in advertising doublespeak is "help." Now "help" only means to aid or assist, nothing more. It does not mean to conquer, stop, eliminate, solve, heal, cure, or anything else. But once the ad says "help," it can say just about anything after that because "help" qualifies everything coming after it. The trick is that the claim that comes after the weasel word is usually so strong and so dramatic that you forget the word "help" and concentrate only on the dramatic claim. You read into the ad a message that the ad does not contain. More importantly, the advertiser is not responsible for the claim that you read into the ad, even though the advertiser wrote the ad so you would read that claim into it.

4   The next time you see an ad for a cold medicine that promises that it "helps re-lieve cold symptoms fast," don't rush out to buy it. Ask yourself what this claim is really saying. Remember, "helps" means only that the medicine will aid or assist. What will it aid or assist in doing? Why, "relieve" your cold "symptoms." "Relieve" only means to ease, alleviate, or mitigate, not to stop, end, or cure. Nor does the claim say how much relieving this medicine will do. Nowhere does this ad claim it *will cure anything.* In fact, the ad doesn't even claim it will *do* anything at all. The *ad only claims* that it will aid in relieving (not curing) your cold symptoms, which are probably a runny nose, watery eyes, and a headache. In other words, this medi-cine probably contains a standard decongestant and some aspirin. By the way, what does "fast" mean? Ten minutes, one hour, one day? What is fast to one person can be very slow to another. Fast is another weasel word.

5   Ad claims using "help" are among the most popular ads. One says, "Helps keep you young looking," but then a lot of things will help keep you young looking, in-cluding exercise, rest, good nutrition, and a facelift. More importantly, this ad does-n't say the product will keep you young, only "young *looking.*" Someone may look young to one person and old to another.

6   A toothpaste ad says, "Helps prevent cavities," but it doesn't say it will actually prevent cavities. Brushing your teeth regularly, avoiding sugars in foods, and floss-ing daily will also help prevent cavities. A liquid cleaner ad says, "Helps keep your home germ free," but it doesn't say it actually kills germs, nor does it even specify which germs it might kill.

7   "Help" is such a useful weasel word that it is often combined with other action-verb weasel words such as "fight" and "control." Consider the claim, "Helps control dandruff symptoms with regular use." What does it really say? It will assist in con-trolling (not eliminating, stopping, ending, or curing) the symptoms of dandruff, not the cause of dandruff nor the dandruff itself. What are the symptoms of dandruff? The ad deliberately leaves that undefined, but assume that the symptoms referred to in the ad are the flaking and itching commonly associated with dandruff. But just shampooing with *any* shampoo will temporarily eliminate these symptoms, so this shampoo isn't any different from any other. Finally, in order to benefit from this product, you must use it regularly. What is "regular use"—daily, weekly, hourly? Using another shampoo "regularly" will have the same effect. Nowhere does this ad-vertising claim say this particular shampoo stops, eliminates, or cures dandruff. In fact, this claim says nothing at all, thanks to all the weasel words.

8   Look at ads in magazines and newspapers, listen to ads on radio and television, and you'll find the word "help" in ads for all kinds of products. How often do you read or hear such phrases as "helps stop . . . ," "helps overcome . . . ," "helps eliminate . . . ," "helps you feel . . . ," or "helps you look . . . "? If you start looking for this weasel word in advertising, you'll be amazed at how often it occurs. Analyze the claims in the ads using "help," and you will discover that these ads are really saying nothing.

9   There are plenty of other weasel words used in advertising. In fact, there are so many that to list them all would fill the rest of this book. But, in order to identify the doublespeak of advertising and understand the real meaning of an ad, you have to be aware of the most popular weasel words in advertising today.

Virtually Spotless

10 One of the most powerful weasel words is "virtually," a word so innocent that most people don't pay any attention to it when it is used in an advertising claim. But watch out. "Virtually" is used in advertising claims that appear to make specific, definite promises when there is no promise. After all, what does "virtually" mean? It means "in essence of effect, although not in fact." Look at that definition again. "Virtually" means *not in fact*. It does *not* mean "almost" or "just about the same as," or anything else. And before you dismiss all this concern over such a small word, remember that small words can have big consequences.

11 In 1971 a federal court rendered its decision on a case brought by a woman who became pregnant while taking birth control pills. She sued the manufacturer, Eli Lilly and Company, for breach of warranty. The woman lost her case. Basing its ruling on a statement in the pamphlet accompanying the pills, which stated that, "When taken as directed, the tablets offer virtually 100 percent protection," the court ruled that there was no warranty, expressed or implied, that the pills were absolutely effective. In its ruling, the court pointed out that, according to *Webster's Third New International Dictionary,* "virtually" means "almost entirely" and clearly does not mean "absolute" (*Whittington* v. *Eli Lilly and Company,* 333 F. Supp. 98). In other words, the Eli Lilly company was really saying that its birth control pill, even when taken as directed, *did not in fact* provide 100 percent protection against pregnancy. But Eli Lilly didn't want to put it that way because then many women might not have bought Lilly's birth control pills.

12 The next time you see the ad that says that this dishwasher detergent "leaves dishes virtually spotless," just remember how advertisers twist the meaning of the weasel word "virtually." You can have lots of spots on your dishes after using this detergent and the ad claim will still be true, because what this claim really means is that this detergent does not *in fact* leave your dishes spotless. Whenever you see or hear an ad claim that uses the word "virtually," just translate that claim into its real meaning. So the television set that is "virtually trouble free" becomes the television set that is not in fact trouble free, the "virtually foolproof operation" of any appliance becomes an operation that is in fact not foolproof, and the product that "virtually never needs service" becomes the product that is not in fact service free.

New and Improved

13 If "new" is the most frequently used word on a product package, "improved" is the second most frequent. In fact, the two words are almost always used together. It seems just about everything sold these days is "new and improved." The next time you're in the supermarket, try counting the number of times you see these words on products. But you'd better do it while you're walking down just one aisle, otherwise you'll need a calculator to keep track of your counting.

14 Just what do these words mean? The use of the word "new" is restricted by regulations, so an advertiser can't just use the word on a product or in an ad without meeting certain requirements. For example, a product is considered new for about

six months during a national advertising campaign. If the product is being advertised only in a limited test market area, the word can be used longer, and in some instances has been used for as long as two years.

15   What makes a product "new"? Some products have been around for a long time, yet every once in a while you discover that they are being advertised as "new." Well, an advertiser can call a product new if there has been "a material functional change" in the product. What is "a material functional change," you ask? Good question. In fact it's such a good question it's being asked all the time. It's up to the manufacturer to prove that the product has undergone such a change. And if the manufacturer isn't challenged on the claim, then there's no one to stop it. Moreover, the change does not have to be an improvement in the product. One manufacturer added an artificial lemon scent to a cleaning product and called it "new and improved," even though the product did not clean any better than without the lemon scent. The manufacturer defended the use of the word "new" on the grounds that the artificial scent changed the chemical formula of the product and therefore constituted "a material functional change."

16   Which brings up the word "improved." When used in advertising, "improved" does not mean "made better." It only means "changed" or "different from before." So, if the detergent maker puts a plastic pour spout on the box of detergent, the product has been "improved," and away we go with a whole new advertising campaign. Or, if the cereal maker adds more fruit or a different kind of fruit to the cereal, there's an improved product. Now you know why manufacturers are constantly making little changes in their products. Whole new advertising campaigns, designed to convince you that the product has been changed for the better, are based on small changes in superficial aspects of a product. The next time you see an ad for an "improved" product, ask yourself what was wrong with the old one. Ask yourself just how "improved" the product is. Finally, you might check to see whether the "improved" version costs more than the unimproved one. After all, someone has to pay for the millions of dollars spent advertising the improved product.

17   Of course, advertisers really like to run ads that claim a product is "new and improved." While what constitutes a "new" product may be subject to some regulation, "improved" is a subjective judgment. A manufacturer changes the shape of its stick deodorant, but the shape doesn't improve the function of the deodorant. That is, changing the shape doesn't affect the deodorizing ability of the deodorant, so the manufacturer calls it "improved." Another manufacturer adds ammonia to its liquid cleaner and calls it "new and improved." Since adding ammonia does affect the cleaning ability of the product, there has been a "material functional change" in the product, and the manufacturer can now call its cleaner "new," and "improved" as well. Now the weasel words, "new and improved" are plastered all over the package and are the basis for a multimillion-dollar ad campaign. But after six months the word "new" will have to go, until someone can dream up another change in the product. Perhaps it will be adding color to the liquid, or changing the shape of the package, or maybe adding a new dripless pour spout, or perhaps a _____ . The "improvements" are endless, and so are the new advertising claims and campaigns.

18   "New" is just too useful and powerful a word in advertising for advertisers to pass it up easily. So they use weasel words that say "new" without really saying it.

One of their favorites is "introducing," as in, "Introducing improved Tide," or "Introducing the stain remover." The first is simply saying, here's our improved soap; the second, here's our new advertising campaign for our detergent. Another favorite is "now," as in "Now there's Sinex," which simply means that Sinex is available. Then there are phrases like "Today's Chevrolet," "Presenting Dristan," and "A fresh way to start the day." The list is really endless because advertisers are always finding new ways to say "new" without really saying it. If there is a second edition of this book, I'll just call it the "new and improved" edition. Wouldn't you really rather have a "new and improved" edition of this book rather than a "second" edition?

Acts Fast

19 "Acts" and "works" are two popular weasel words in advertising because they bring action to the product and to the advertising claim. When you see the ad for the cough syrup that "Acts on the cough control center," ask yourself what this cough syrup is claiming to do. Well, it's just claiming to "act," to do something, to perform an action. What is it that the cough syrup does? The ad doesn't say. It only claims to perform an action or do something on your "cough control center." By the way, what and where is our "cough control center"? I don't remember learning about that part of the body in human biology class.

20 Ads that use such phrases as "acts fast," "acts against," "acts to prevent," and the like are saying essentially nothing, because "act" is a word empty of any specific meaning. The ads are always careful not to specify exactly what "act" the product performs. Just because a brand of aspirin claims to "act fast" for headache relief doesn't mean this aspirin is any better than any other aspirin. What is the "act" that this aspirin performs? You're never told. Maybe it just dissolves quickly. Since aspirin is a parity product, all aspirin is the same and therefore functions the same.

Works Like Anything Else

21 If you don't find the word "acts" in an ad, you will probably find the weasel word "works." In fact, the two words are almost interchangeable in advertising. Watch out for ads that say a product "works against," "works like," "works for," or "works longer." As with "acts," "works" is the same meaningless verb used to make you think that this product really does something, and maybe even something special or unique. But "works," like "acts," is basically a word empty of any specific meaning.

Like Magic

22 Whenever advertisers want you to stop thinking about the product and to start thinking about something bigger, better, or more attractive than the product, they use that very popular weasel word, "like." The word "like" is the advertiser's equivalent of a magician's use of misdirection. "Like" gets you to ignore the product and concentrate on the claim the advertiser is making about it. "For skin like peaches and cream" claims the ad for a skin cream. What is this ad really claiming? It doesn't

say this cream will give you peaches-and-cream skin. There is no verb in this claim, so it doesn't even mention using the product. How is skin ever like "peaches and cream"? Remember, ads must be read literally and exactly, according to the dictionary definition of words. (Remember "virtually" in the Eli Lilly case.) The ad is making absolutely no promise or claim whatsoever for this skin cream. If you think this cream will give you soft, smooth, youthful-looking skin, you are the one who has read that meaning into the ad.

23   The wine that claims "It's like taking a trip to France" wants you to think about a romantic evening in Paris as you walk along the boulevard after a wonderful meal in an intimate little bistro. Of course, you don't really believe that a wine can take you to France, but the goal of the ad is to get you to think pleasant, romantic thoughts about France and not about how the wine tastes or how expensive it may be. That little word "like" has taken you away from crushed grapes into a world of your own imaginative making. Who knows, maybe the next time you buy wine, you'll think those pleasant thoughts when you see this brand of wine, and you'll buy it. Or, maybe you weren't even thinking about buying wine at all, but now you just might pick up a bottle the next time you're shopping. Ah, the power of "like" in advertising.

24   How about the most famous "like" claim of all, "Winston tastes good like a cigarette should"? Ignoring the grammatical error here, you might want to know what this claim is saying. Whether a cigarette tastes good or bad is a subjective judgment because what tastes good to one person may well taste horrible to another. Not everyone likes fried snails, even if they are called escargot. (*De gustibus non est disputandum,* which was probably the Roman rule for advertising as well as for defending the games in the Coliseum.) There are many people who say all cigarettes taste terrible, other people who say only some cigarettes taste all right, and still others who say all cigarettes taste good. Who's right? Everyone, because taste is a matter of personal judgment.

25   Moreover, note the use of the conditional, "should." The complete claim is, "Winston tastes good like a cigarette should taste." But should cigarettes taste good? Again, this is a matter of personal judgment and probably depends mostly on one's experiences with smoking. So, the Winston ad is simply saying that Winston cigarettes are just like any other cigarette: Some people like them and some people don't. On that statement, R. J. Reynolds conducted a very successful multimillion-dollar advertising campaign that helped keep Winston the number-two-selling cigarette in the United States, close behind number one, Marlboro.

Can't It Be Up to the Claim?

26 Analyzing ads for doublespeak requires that you pay attention to every word in the ad and determine what each word really means. Advertisers try to wrap their claims in language that sounds concrete, specific, and objective, when in fact the language of advertising is anything but. Your job is to read carefully and listen critically so that when the announcer says that "Crest can be of significant value . . . ," you know immediately that this claim says absolutely nothing. Where is the doublespeak in this ad? Start with the second word.

27   Once again, you have to look at what words really mean, not what you think they mean or what the advertiser wants you to think they mean. The ad for Crest only says that using Crest "can be" of "significant value." What really throws you off in this ad is the brilliant use of "significant." It draws your attention to the word "value" and makes you forget that the ad only claims that Crest "can be." The ad doesn't say that Crest is of value, only that it is "able" or "possible" to be of value, because that's all that "can" means.

28   It's so easy to miss the importance of those little words, "can be." Almost as easy as missing the importance of the words "up to" in an ad. These words are very popular in sales ads. You know, the ones that say, "Up to 50 percent Off!" Now, what does that claim mean? Not much, because the store or manufacturer has to reduce the price of only a few items by 50 percent. Everything else can be reduced a lot less, or not even reduced. Moreover, don't you want to know 50 percent off of what? Is it 50 percent off the "manufacturer's suggested list price," which is the highest possible price? Was the price artificially inflated and then reduced? In other ads, "up to" expresses an ideal situation. The medicine that works "up to ten times faster," the battery that lasts "up to twice as long," and the soap that gets you "up to twice as clean" all are based on ideal situations for using these products, situations in which you can be sure you will never find yourself.

Unfinished Words

29   Unfinished words are a kind of "up to" claim in advertising. The claim that a battery lasts "up to twice as long" usually doesn't finish the comparison—twice as long as what? A birthday candle? A tank of gas? A cheap battery made in a country not noted for its technological achievements? The implication is that the battery lasts twice as long as batteries made by other battery makers, or twice as long as earlier model batteries made by the advertiser, but the ad doesn't really make these claims. You read these claims into the ad, aided by the visual images the advertiser so carefully provides.

30   Unfinished words depend on you to finish them, to provide the words the advertisers so thoughtfully left out of the ad. Pall Mall cigarettes were once advertised as "A longer, finer and milder smoke." The question is, longer, finer, and milder than what? The aspirin that claims it contains "Twice as much of the pain reliever doctors recommend most" doesn't tell you what pain reliever it contains twice as much of. (By the way, it's aspirin. That's right; it just contains twice the amount of aspirin. And how much is twice the amount? Twice of what amount?) Panadol boasts that "nobody reduces fever faster," but, since Panadol is a parity product, this claim simply means that Panadol isn't any better than any other product in its parity class. "You can be sure if it's Westinghouse," you're told, but just exactly what it is you can be sure of is never mentioned. "Magnavox gives you more" doesn't tell you what you get more of. More value? More television? More than they gave you before? It sounds nice, but it means nothing, until you fill in the claim with your own words, the words the advertisers didn't use. Since each of us fills in the claim differently, the ad and the product can become all things to all people, and not promise a single thing.

31   Unfinished words abound in advertising because they appear to promise so much. More importantly, they can be joined with powerful visual images on television to appear to be making significant promises about a product's effectiveness without really making any promises. In a television ad, the aspirin product that claims fast relief can show a person with a headache taking the product and then, in what appears to be a matter of minutes, claiming complete relief. This visual image is far more powerful than any claim made in unfinished words. Indeed, the visual image completes the unfinished words for you, filling in with pictures what the words leave out. And you thought that ads didn't affect you. What brand of aspirin do you use?

32   Some years ago, Ford's advertisements proclaimed "Ford LTD—700 percent quieter." Now, what do you think Ford was claiming with these unfinished words? What was the Ford LTD quieter than? A Cadillac? A Mercedes Benz? A BMW? Well, when the FTC asked Ford to substantiate this unfinished claim, Ford replied that it meant that the inside of the LTD was 700 percent quieter than the outside. How did you finish those unfinished words when you first read them? Did you even come close to Ford's meaning?

Combining Weasel Words

33   A lot of ads don't fall neatly into one category or another because they use a variety of different devices and words. Different weasel words are often combined to make an ad claim. The claim, "Coffee-Mate gives coffee more body, more flavor," uses Unfinished Words ("more" than what?) and also uses words that have no specific meaning ("body" and "flavor"). Along with "taste" (remember the Winston ad and its claim to taste good), "body" and "flavor" mean nothing because their meaning is entirely subjective. To you, "body" in coffee might mean thick, black, almost bitter coffee, while I might take it to mean a light brown, delicate coffee. Now, if you think you understood that last sentence, read it again, because it said nothing of objective value; it was filled with weasel words of no specific meaning: "thick," "black," "bitter," "light brown," and "delicate." Each of those words has no specific, objective meaning, because each of us can interpret them differently.

34   Try this slogan: "Looks, smells, tastes like ground-roast coffee." So, are you now going to buy Taster's Choice instant coffee because of this ad? "Looks," "smells," and "tastes" are all words with no specific meaning and depend on your interpretation of them for any meaning. Then there's that great weasel word "like," which simply suggests a comparison but does not make the actual connection between the product and the quality. Besides, do you know what "ground-roast" coffee is? I don't, but it sure sounds good. So, out of seven words in this ad, four are definite weasel words, two are quite meaningless, and only one has any clear meaning.

35   Remember the Anacin ad—"Twice as much of the pain reliever doctors recommend most"? There's a whole lot of weaseling going on in this ad. First, what's the pain reliever they're talking about in this ad? Aspirin, of course. In fact, any time you see or hear an ad using those words "pain reliever," you can automatically

substitute the word "aspirin" for them. (Makers of acetaminophen and ibuprofen pain relievers are careful in their advertising to identify their products as nonaspirin products.) So, now we know that Anacin has aspirin in it. Moreover, we know that Anacin has twice as much aspirin in it, but we don't know twice as much as what. Does it have twice as much aspirin as an ordinary aspirin tablet? If so, what is an ordinary aspirin tablet, and how much aspirin does it contain? Twice as much as Excedrin or Bufferin? Twice as much as a chocolate chip cookie? Remember those Unfinished Words and how they lead you on without saying anything.

36   Finally, what about those doctors who are doing all that recommending? Who are they? How many of them are there? What kind of doctors are they? What are their qualifications? Who asked them about recommending pain relievers? What other pain relievers did they recommend? And there are a whole lot more questions about this "poll" of doctors to which I'd like to know the answers, but you get the point. Sometimes, when I call my doctor, she tells me to take two aspirin and call her office in the morning. Is that where Anacin got this ad?

Read the Label, or the Brochure

37 Weasel words aren't just found on television, on the radio, or in newspaper and magazine ads. Just about any language associated with a product will contain the doublespeak of advertising. Remember the Eli Lilly case and the doublespeak on the information sheet that came with the birth control pills. Here's another example.

38   [Several years ago], the Estée Lauder cosmetics company announced a new product called "Night Repair." A small brochure distributed with the product stated that "Night Repair was scientifically formulated in Estée Lauder's U.S. laboratories as part of the Swiss Age-Controlling Skincare Program. Although only nature controls the aging process, this program helps control the signs of aging and encourages skin to look and feel younger." You might want to read these two sentences again, because they sound great but say nothing.

39   First, note that the product was "scientifically formulated" in the company's laboratories. What does that mean? What constitutes a scientific formulation? You wouldn't expect the company to say that the product was casually, mechanically, or carelessly formulated, or just thrown together one day when the people in the white coats didn't have anything better to do. But the word "scientifically" lends an air of precision and promise that just isn't there.

40   It is the second sentence, however, that's really weasely, both syntactically and semantically. The only factual part of this sentence is the introductory dependent clause—"only nature controls the aging process." Thus, the only fact in the ad is relegated to a dependent clause, a clause dependent on the main clause, which contains no factual or definite information at all and indeed purports to contradict the independent clause. The new "skincare program" (notice it's not a skin cream but a "program") does not claim to stop or even retard the aging process. What, then, does Night Repair do? According to this brochure, nothing. It only "helps," and the brochure does not say how much it helps. Moreover, it only "helps control," and then it only helps control the "signs of aging," not the aging itself. Also, it "encourages"

skin not to be younger but only to "look and feel" younger. The brochure does not say younger than what. Of the sixteen words in the main clause of this second sentence, nine are weasel words. So, before you spend all that money for Night Repair, or any other cosmetic product, read the words carefully, and then decide if you're getting what you think you're paying for.

Other Tricks of the Trade

41　Advertisers' use of doublespeak is endless. The best way advertisers can make something out of nothing is through words. Although there are a lot of visual images used on television and in magazines and newspapers, every advertiser wants to create that memorable line that will stick in the public consciousness. I am sure pure joy reigned in one advertising agency when a study found that children who were asked to spell the world "relief" promptly and proudly responded "r-o-l-a-i-d-s."

42　The variations, combinations, and permutations of doublespeak used in advertising go on and on, running from the use of rhetorical questions ("Wouldn't you really rather have a Buick?" "If you can't trust Prestone, who can you trust?") to flattering you with compliments ("The lady has taste." "We think a cigar smoker is someone special." "You've come a long way, baby."). You know, of course, how you're *supposed* to answer those questions, and you know that those compliments are just leading up to the sales pitches for the products. Before you dismiss such tricks of the trade as obvious, however, just remember that all of these statements and questions were part of very successful advertising campaigns.

43　A more subtle approach is the ad that proclaims a supposedly unique quality for a product, a quality that really isn't unique. "If it doesn't say Goodyear, it can't be Polyglas." Sounds good, doesn't it? Polyglas is available only from Goodyear because Goodyear copyrighted that trade name. Any other tire manufacturer could make exactly the same tire but could not call it "Polyglas," because that would be copyright infringement. "Polyglas" is simply Goodyear's name for its fiberglass-reinforced tire.

44　Since we like to think of ourselves as living in a technologically advanced country, science and technology have a great appeal in selling products. Advertisers are quick to use scientific doublespeak to push their products. There are all kinds of elixirs, additives, scientific potions, and mysterious mixtures added to all kinds of products. Gasoline contains "HTA," "F-130," "Platformate," and other chemical-sounding additives, but nowhere does an advertisement give any real information about the additive.

45　Shampoo, deodorant, mouthwash, cold medicine, sleeping pills, and any number of other products all seem to contain some special chemical ingredient that allows them to work wonders. "Certs contains a sparkling drop of Retsyn." So what? What's "Retsyn"? What's it do? What's so special about it? When they don't have a secret ingredient in their product, advertisers still find a way to claim scientific validity. There's "Sinarest. Created by a research scientist who actually gets sinus headaches." Sounds nice, but what kind of research does this scientist do? How do you know if she is any kind of expert on sinus medicine? Besides, this ad doesn't tell you a thing about the medicine itself and what it does.

Advertising Doublespeak Quick Quiz

Now it's time to test your awareness of advertising doublespeak. The following is a list of statements from some recent ads. Your job is to figure out what each of these ads really says.

DOMINO'S PIZZA: "Because nobody delivers better."

SINUTAB: "It can stop the pain."

TUMS: "The stronger acid neutralizer."

MAXIMUM STRENGTH DRISTAN: "Strong medicine for tough sinus colds."

LISTERMINT: "Making your mouth a cleaner place."

CASCADE: "For virtually spotless dishes nothing beats Cascade."

NUPRIN: "Little. Yellow. Different. Better."

ANACIN: "Better relief."

SUDAFED: "Fast sinus relief that won't put you fast asleep."

ADVIL: "Better relief."

PONDS COLD CREAM: "Ponds cleans like no soap can."

MILLER LITE BEER: "Tastes great. Less filling."

PHILIPS MILK OF MAGNESIA: "Nobody treats you better than MOM (Philips Milk of Magnesia)."

BAYER: "The wonder drug that works wonders."

CRACKER BARREL: "Judged to be the best."

KNORR: "Where taste is everything."

ANUSOL: "Anusol is the word to remember for relief."

DIMETAPP: "It relieves kids as well as colds."

LIQUID DRÁNO: "The liquid strong enough to be called Dráno."

JOHNSON & JOHNSON BABY POWDER: "Like magic for your skin."

PURITAN: "Make it your oil for life."

PAM: "Pam, because how you cook is as important as what you cook."

TYLENOL GEL-CAPS: "It's not a capsule. It's better."

ALKA-SELTZER PLUS: "Fast, effective relief for winter colds."

The World of Advertising

46 In the world of advertising, people wear "dentures," not false teeth; they suffer from "occasional irregularity," not constipation; they need deodorants for their "nervous wetness," not for sweat; they use "bathroom tissue," not toilet paper; and they don't dye their hair, they "tint" or "rinse" it. Advertisements offer "real counterfeit diamonds" without the slightest hint of embarrassment, or boast of goods made out of "genuine imitation leather" or "virgin vinyl."

47   In the world of advertising, the girdle becomes a "body shaper," "form persuader," "control garment," "controller," "outerwear enhancer," "body garment," or "anti-gravity panties," and is sold with such trade names as "The Instead," "The Free Spirit," and "The Body Briefer."

48   A study some years ago found the following words to be among the most popular used in U.S. television advertisements: "new," "improved," "better," "extra," "fresh," "clean," "beautiful," "free," "good," "great," and "light." At the same time, the following words were found to be among the most frequent on British television: "new," "good-better-best," "free," "fresh," "delicious," "full," "sure," "clean," "wonderful," and "special." While these words may occur most frequently in ads, and while ads may be filled with weasel words, you have to watch out for all the words used in advertising, not just the words mentioned here.

49   Every word in an ad is there for a reason; no word is wasted. Your job is to figure out exactly what each word is doing in an ad—what each word really means, not what the advertiser wants you to think it means. Remember, the ad is trying to get you to buy a product, so it will put the product in the best possible light, using any device, trick, or means legally allowed. Your own defense against advertising (besides taking up permanent residence on the moon) is to develop and use a strong critical reading, listening, and looking ability. Always ask yourself what the ad is really saying. When you see ads on television, don't be misled by the pictures, the visual images. What does the ad say about the product? What does the ad not say? What information is missing from the ad? Only by becoming an active, critical consumer of the doublespeak of advertising will you ever be able to cut through the doublespeak and discover what the ad is really saying.

QUESTIONS FOR ANALYSIS AND DISCUSSION

1. How would a copywriter for an advertising agency respond to this article? Would he or she agree with the way Lutz characterizes all advertisements as trying to trick consumers with false claims into buying a product?

2. When you see the word "new" on a product, do you think twice about buying that product? What regulations restrict use of the word "new"? How can manufacturers make a product "new" to sidestep these regulations? Do these regulations serve the interests of the advertiser or the consumer?

3. Review Lutz's "Advertising Doublespeak Quick Quiz." Choose five items and analyze them using dictionary meanings to explain what the ads are really saying.

4. What tone does Lutz use throughout the article? Is his writing style humorous, informal, or academic? What strategies does he use to involve the reader in the piece?

5. In paragraph 43, Lutz describes how manufacturers claim for their products unique properties that are not in fact unique after all. Could these claims be considered circular reasoning? Explain.

The Language of Advertising
Charles A. O'Neill

In this essay, marketing executive Charles A. O'Neill disputes William Lutz's criticism of advertising doublespeak. While admitting to some of the craftiness of his profession, O'Neill defends the huckster's language—both verbal and visual—against claims that it distorts reality. Examining some familiar television commercials and magazine ads, he explains why the language may be charming and seductive but far from brainwashing.

O'Neill is an independent marketing and advertising consultant in Boston. This essay first appeared in the textbook *Exploring Language* in 1998 and was updated for this edition in 2007.

BEFORE YOU READ

O'Neill makes several generalizations that characterize the language of advertising. Think about ads you have recently seen or read and make a list of your own generalizations about the language of advertising.

AS YOU READ

Does the fact that O'Neill is a professional advertising consultant influence your reception of his essay? Does it make his argument more or less persuasive?

1   His name was Joe Camel. On the billboards and in the magazine ads, he looked like a cartoonist's composite sketch of the Rolling Stones, lounging around in a celebrity waiting area at MTV headquarters in New York. He was poised, confident, leaning against a railing or playing pool with his friends. His personal geometry was always just right. He often wore a white suit, dark shirt, sunglasses. Cigarette in hand, wry smile on his lips, his attitude was distinctly confident, urbane.

2   He was very cool and powerful. So much so that more than 90 percent of 6-year-olds matched Joe Camel with a picture of a cigarette, making him as well known as Mickey Mouse.[1]

3   Good advertising, but bad public relations.

4   Finally, after extended sparring with the tobacco company about whether Joe really promoted smoking, the Federal Trade Commission brought the ads to an end. President Clinton spoke for the regulators when he said, "Let's stop pretending that a cartoon camel in a funny costume is trying to sell to adults, not children."

5   Joe's 23-year-old advertising campaign was stopped because it was obvious that he could turn kids into lung cancer patients. That's bad enough. But beneath the surface, the debate about Joe typifies something more interesting and broad-based: the rather uncomfortable, tentative acceptance of advertising in our society. We recognize the legitimacy—even the value—of advertising, but on some level we can't quite fully embrace it as a "normal" part of our experience.

6   At best, we view advertising as distracting. At worst, we view it as dangerous to our health and a pernicious threat to our social values. One notable report acknowledged the positive contribution of advertising (e.g., provides information, supports worthy causes, and encourages competition and innovation), then added, "In the competition to attract even larger audiences . . . communicators can find themselves pressured . . . to set aside high artistic and moral standards and lapse into superficiality, tawdriness, and moral squalor."[2]

7   How does advertising work? Why is it so powerful? Why does it raise such concern? What case can be made for and against the advertising business?

8   In order to understand advertising, you must accept that it is not about truth, virtue, love, or positive societal values. It is about money. It is about moving customers through the sales process. Sometimes the words and images are concrete; sometimes they are merely suggestive. Sometimes ads provide useful information; sometimes they convince us that we need to spend money to solve a problem we never knew we had. Ads are designed to be intrusive. We're not always pleased about the way they clutter our environment and violate our sense of private space. We're not always happy with the tactics they use to impose themselves upon us.

9   Whatever the product or creative strategy, advertisements derive their power from a purposeful, directed combination of images. These can take the form of text in a magazine or newspaper, images on television, interactive games on web pages, or mini-documentaries on YouTube. Whatever the means of expression, the combination of images is the language of advertising, a language unlike any other.

10   Everyone who grows up in the civilized world knows that advertising language is different from other languages. Read this aloud: "With Nice 'n Easy, it's color so natural, the closer he gets, the better you look." Many children would be unable to explain how this classic ad for Clairol's Nice 'n Easy hair coloring differs from "ordinary language," but they would say, "It sounds like an ad."

11   The language of advertising changes with the times. Styles and creative concepts come and go. But there are at least four distinct, general characteristics of the language of advertising that make it different from other languages. They lend advertising its persuasive power:

- The language of advertising is edited and purposeful.
- The language of advertising is rich and arresting; it is specifically intended to attract and hold our attention.

- The language of advertising involves us; in effect, *we* complete the message.
- The language of advertising is simple and direct. It holds no secrets from us.

Edited and Purposeful

12   In his famous book, *Future Shock,* Alvin Toffler describes various types of messages we receive from the world around us each day. He observed that there is a difference between normal, "coded" messages and "engineered" messages. Much of normal, human experience is "uncoded." When a man walks down a street, for example, he sees where he is going and hears random sounds. These are mental images, but they are not messages "designed by anyone to communicate anything, and the man's understanding of it does not depend directly on a social code—a set of agreed-upon signs and definitions."[3]

13   In contrast, the language of advertising is "coded." It exists in the context of our society. It is also carefully engineered and ruthlessly purposeful. When he wrote in the 1960s, Toffler estimated that the average adult was exposed to 560 advertising messages each day. Now, our homes are equipped with 400-channel, direct-broadcast satellite television, the Internet, video-streaming mobile devices, and other new forms of mass media. We're literally swimming in a sea of information. We're totally wired and wireless. We're overwhelmed by countless billboards in subway stations, stickers on light poles, 15-second spots on television, and an endless stream of spam and pop-up messages online.

Demanding Attention

14   Among the hundreds of advertising messages in store for us each day, very few will actually command our conscious attention. The rest are screened out. The people who design and write ads know about this screening process; they anticipate and accept it as a premise of their business.

15   The classic, all-time favorite device used to breach the barrier is sex. There was a time, many years ago, when advertisers used some measure of subtlety and discretion in their application of sexual themes to their mass media work. No more. Sensuality has been replaced by in-your-face, unrestrained sexuality. One is about romance and connection; the other, physical connection and emotional distance.

16   A poster promotes clothing sold by the apparel company, French Connection group, United Kingdom: (FCUK). Large type tells us, "Apparently there are more important things in life than fashion. Yeah, right." This text is accompanied by a photo of two young people in what has become a standard set up: A boy. A girl. She is pretty, in a detached, vapid sort of way. He has not shaved for 48 hours. They are sharing physical space, but there is no sense of human contact or emotion. The company name appears on the lower right hand side of the poster. The headline is intended to be ironic: "Of course there are things that are more important than fashion, but right now, who cares?" The company maintains that they are "not trying to shock people." As absurd as it may seem, this is actually the truth. This company is not in the business of selling shock. They are selling clothes. They are making a lot

of money selling clothes, because they know what motivates their teenaged customers—a desire to separate from their parents and declare their membership in the tribe of their peers.

17   Fortunately, advertisers use many other techniques to attract and hold the attention of the targeted consumer audience. The strategy may include strong creative execution, humor, or a plain, straightforward presentation of product features and customer benefits. Consider this random cross section of advertisements from popular media:

- An ad for SalesForce.com used a photo of the Dalai Lama beneath the headline, "There is no software on the path to enlightenment." (What does this mean? "Salesforce.com provides computer services, so I won't have to buy software myself.")
- An ad for Chevrolet HHR automobiles sports a headline, "We're innocent in every way like apple pie and Chevrolet—Mötley Crüe." (Another use of irony. Most readers of Rolling Stone are unlikely to consider the band to be a paragon of innocence, and by extension, neither is the car.)
- Some ads entertain us and are effective, even though they don't focus much on the product. They work because we remember them. Geico is an automobile insurance company, but they use angst-ridden cavemen and a cute little lizard—appropriately enough, a Gecko—as characters in their ads.
- Some ads tell us we have problems—real or imagined—that we'd better solve right away. Do you have dry skin or "unsightly eyebrow hairs?" (Causing the hapless reader to think, "I never really noticed, but now that they mention it. . . .").

18   Soft drink companies are in an advertising category of their own. In the archetypical version of a soft drink TV spot, babies frolic with puppies in the sunlit foreground while their youthful parents play touch football. On the porch, Grandma and Pops quietly smile as they wait for all of this affection to transform the world into a place of warmth, harmony, and joy.

19   Dr. Pepper ads say "Be you!" and feature dancers prancing around singing songs about "individuality." In Coke's ads, the singer Maya tells us this can of syrupy fizz is "real." And Pepsi has Britney Spears singing "Pepsi: for those who think young!" The message: If you are among the millions of people who see the commercial and buy the product, you will become "different." You will find yourself transformed into a unique ("Be you," "individuality," "real"), hip ("young") person.[4]

20   These "slice of life" ads seduce us into feeling that if we drink the right combination of sugar, preservatives, caramel coloring, and a few secret ingredients, we'll fulfill our yearning for a world where folks from all nations, creeds, and sexual orientations live together in a state of perfect bliss. At least for the five minutes it takes to pour the stuff down our parched, fast-food-filled throats. If you don't buy this version of the American Dream, look around. You are sure to find a product that promises to help you gain prestige in whatever posse you do happen to run with.

21   When the connection is made, the results can be very powerful. Starbucks has proven that a commodity product like coffee can be artfully changed from a mere beverage into an emotional experience.

22   Ad campaigns and branding strategies do not often emerge like Botticelli's *Venus* from the sea, flawless and fully grown. Most often, the creative strategy is developed only after extensive research. "Who will be interested in our product? How old are they? Where do they live? How much money do they earn? What problem will our product solve?" The people at Starbucks did not decide to go to China on a whim. The people at French Connection did not create their brand name simply to offend everyone who is old-fashioned enough to think that some words don't belong on billboards, T-shirts, and storefronts.

Involving

23   We have seen that the language of advertising is carefully engineered; we have discovered a few of the devices it uses to get our attention. Coke and Pepsi have entranced us with visions of peace and love. An actress offers a winsome smile. Now that they have our attention, advertisers present information intended to show us that their product fills a need and differs from the competition. Advertisers exploit and intensify product differences when they find them and invent them when they do not.

24   As soon as we see or hear an advertisement, our imagination is set in motion, and our individual fears and aspirations, quirks, and insecurities come out to play.

25   It was common not long ago for advertisers in the fashion industry to make use of gaunt, languid models. To some observers, these ads promoted "heroin chic." Perhaps only a few were substance abusers, but something was most certainly unusual about the models appearing in ads for Prada and Calvin Klein products. A young woman in a Prada ad projects no emotion whatsoever. Her posture suggests that she is in a trance or drug-induced stupor. In a Calvin Klein ad, a young man, like the woman from Prada, is gaunt beyond reason. He is shirtless. As if to draw more attention to his peculiar posture and "zero body fat" status, he is shown pinching the skin next to his navel. To some, this also suggests that he is preparing to insert a needle.

26   The fashion industry backed away from the heroin theme. Now the models look generally better fed. But they are, nonetheless, still lost in a world of ennui and isolation. In an ad by Andrew Mark NY, we see a young woman wearing little leather shorts. Her boyfriend's arm is wrapped around her, his thumb pushing ever-so-slightly below the waistband of her pants. What does he look like? He appears to be dazed. He is wearing jeans, an unzipped leather jacket. He hasn't shaved for a couple of days. We are left with the impression that either something has just happened here or is about to. It probably has something to do with sex.

27   Do these depictions of a decadent lifestyle exploit certain elements of our society—the young, insecure, or clueless? Or did these ads, and others of their ilk, simply reflect profound bad taste? Most advertising is about exploitation—the systematic, deliberate identification of our needs and wants, followed by the delivery of a carefully constructed promise that the product will satisfy them.

28   Advertisers make use of a variety of techniques and devices to engage us in the delivery of their messages. Some are subtle, making use of warm, entertaining, or

comforting images or symbols. Others, as we've seen, are about as subtle as an action sequence from Quentin Tarantino's latest movie. Although it may seem hard to believe, advertising writers did not invent sex. They did not invent our tendency to admire and seek to identify ourselves with famous people. Once we have seen a famous person in an ad, we associate the product with the person. When we buy Coke, we're becoming a member of the Friends of Maya Club. The logic is faulty, but we fall for it just the same. Advertising works, not because Maya and Britney have discriminating taste, or the nameless waif in the clothing ad is a fashion diva, but because we participate in it.

Keeping It Simple

29   Advertising language differs from other types of language in another important respect: it is simple by design. To measure the simplicity of an ad, calculate its Fog Index. Robert Gunning[5] developed this formula to determine the comparative ease with which any given piece of communication can be read. The resulting number is intended to correspond with grade level.

- Calculate the number of words in an average sentence.
- Count the number of words of three or more syllables in a typical 100-word passage, omitting words that are capitalized, combinations of two simple words, or verb forms made into three-syllable words by the addition of -ed or -es.
- Add the two figures (the average number of words per sentence and the number of three-syllable words per 100 words), then multiply the result by .4.

30   Consider the text of this ad for Geico automobile insurance:
"The Gecko speaks out." (Headline)
"I love to entertain, but I'm here to save you money on car insurance. Get a FREE rate quote. 15 minutes could save you 15% or more." (Body copy)

1. Words per sentence: 10
2. Three syllable words/100:   2
3. Subtotal: 12
4. Multiply by .4:   4.8

31   According to Gunning's scale, you should be able to comprehend this ad if you are just about to finish the 4th grade. Compare this to comic books, which typically weigh in at 6th grade level or *Atlantic Monthly*, at the 12th.

32   Why do advertisers favor simple language? The answer lies with the consumer. As a practical matter, we would not notice many of these messages if length or eloquence were counted among their virtues. Today's consumer cannot take the time to focus on anything for long, much less blatant advertising messages. Every aspect of modern life runs at an accelerated pace. Voice mail, text messaging, cellular phones, e-mail, the Internet—the world is always awake, always switched on, and hungry for more information. Time is dissected into increasingly smaller segments.

Who Is Responsible?

33 Some critics view the advertising industry as a cranky, unwelcome child of commerce—a noisy, whining, brash truant who must somehow be kept in line but can't just yet be thrown out of the house. In reality, advertising mirrors the fears, quirks, and aspirations of the society that creates it (and is, in turn, sold by it). This alone exposes advertising to parody and ridicule. The overall level of acceptance and respect for advertising is also influenced by the varied quality of the ads themselves. Critics have declared advertising guilty of other failings as well:

1. Advertising encourages unhealthy habits.
2. Advertising feeds on human weaknesses and exaggerates the importance of material things, encouraging "impure" emotions and vanities.
3. Advertising sells daydreams—distracting, purposeless visions of lifestyles beyond the reach of the majority of the people who are most exposed to advertising.
4. Advertising warps our vision of reality, implanting in us groundless fears and insecurities.
5. Advertising downgrades the intelligence of the public.
6. Advertising debases English.
7. Advertising perpetuates racial and sexual stereotypes.

34 What can be said in advertising's defense? Does it encourage free-market competition and product innovation? Sure. But the real answer is simply this: Advertising is, at heart, only a reflection of society.

35 What can we say about the charge that advertising debases the intelligence of the public? Exactly how intelligent is "the public"? Sadly, evidence abounds that the public at large is not particularly intelligent after all. Americans now get 31 percent of their calories from junk food and alcoholic beverages.[6] Michael can't read. Jessica can't write. And the entire family spends the night in front of the television, watching people eat living insects in the latest installment of a "reality" show.

36 Ads are effective because they sell products. They would not succeed if they did not reflect the values and motivations of the real world. Advertising both reflects and shapes our perception of reality. Ivory Snow is pure. Federal Express won't let you down. Absolut is cool. Sasson is sexy. Mercedes represents quality. Our sense of what these brand names stand for may have as much to do with advertising as with the objective "truth."

37 Good, responsible advertising can serve as a positive influence for change, while fueling commerce. But the obverse is also true: Advertising, like any form of mass communication, can be a force for both "good" and "bad." It can just as readily reinforce or encourage irresponsible behavior, ageism, sexism, ethnocentrism, racism, homophobia, heterophobia—you name it—as it can encourage support for diversity and social progress.

38 As Pogo once famously said, "We have met the enemy, and he is us."[7]

NOTES

1. Internet: <http://www.joechemo.org>.

2. Pontifical Council for Social Communications, "Ethics in Advertising," published 2/22/97.

3. Alvin Toffler, *Future Shock* (New York Random House, 1970), p. 146.

4. Shannon O'Neill, a graduate student at the University of New Hampshire, contributed this example and others cited here.

5. Curtis D. MacDougall, *Interpretive Reporting* (New York: Macmillan, 1968), p. 94.

6. 2000 study by the American Society for Clinical Nutrition (*Milwaukee Journal Sentinal*, 7/28/03).

7. Walt Kelly, *Pogo* cartoon (1960s); referring to the Vietnam War.

QUESTIONS FOR ANALYSIS AND DISCUSSION ———————

1. O'Neill opens his essay with a discussion of the controversial figure Joe Camel. What are your views on the Joe Camel controversy? Do you think the FTC and the former president were justified in expressing their concerns about the character? Should ads that target young people for products that are bad for them be outlawed? Explain.

2. Do you think it is ethical for advertisers to create a sense of product difference when there really isn't any? Consider advertisements for products such as gasoline, beer, or coffee.

3. In the last section of the essay, O'Neill anticipates potential objections to his defense of advertising. What are some of these objections? What effect does his anticipation of these objections have on the essay as a whole?

4. O'Neill is an advertising professional. How does his writing style reflect the advertising techniques he describes? Cite examples to support your answer.

"WAAAAASSSSSUUUP" With Advertising?

Tracy Pomerinke

When it comes to ad copy that "breaks the rules," grammarians and linguists don't speak the same language. In this essay, writer Tracy Pomerinke looks at ad copy that breaks the rules—of grammar, that is. As she explains, unimaginative and grammatically faulty language, often paired with worn-out clichés, alienate consumers and dilute our language as a whole.

The author of several essays on writing and grammar, Pomerinke is a writer based in San Antonio, Texas. This essay appeared in the 2003 online issue of *Writer's Block*.

BEFORE YOU READ ───────────────────────────────────

Think about some popular slogans for products. Has a good slogan or an effective advertising phrase encouraged you to try a product? Conversely, have you ever found yourself "turned off" by an ad slogan or phrase?

AS YOU READ ───────────────────────────────────

In this essay, Tracy Pomerinke wonders whether the corrupted grammar used in many ads harms our language as a whole, or if it simply reflects the organic nature of language. What do you think? Should language be preserved as unchangeable or flexible?

1　On a typical day, a person is exposed to between 3,000 and 5,000 advertisements. Text, images, and layout—all carefully designed to get people's attention.

2　Maybe ad execs have been reading their dictionaries. The word "advertise" comes from the root advertere, the Latin word meaning "to turn towards," so the etymology of the word suggests a directing of one's attention.

3　But in the chaos of conflicting messages—buy this, stop that, believe in this, don't do that—how can attention be focused? The quandary has put the effectiveness of ads into question. In response, the advertising industry is moving toward an emphasis on "creativity." So now it is about "the art," which often means ignoring or breaking conventions. The idea is to be different and get noticed.

4　One way to do that is through language. In 2000, the Budweiser "Whassup?" campaign generated the most attention ever, and won more awards—including The Grand Prix for TV and Cinema at Cannes—than any other advertising program in history. In the following year came "What are you doing?"—a supposed yuppie spoof of the "Whassup?" campaign. Budweiser won a Bronze Lion at Cannes, while the VP for Marketing was named Advertiser of the Year. Budweiser was able to capture all this attention by playing with grammar.

Now That They Have Our Attention . . .

5　Okay, we're looking, reading, watching, waiting—so what do these ad execs want? Ultimately, the company or organization paying the advertiser wants a person to translate that attention into something more tangible: some immediate action or some favorable disposition that will lead to some future action. The advertiser can make that happen by getting people to "turn toward" the ad so that they register its communication.

6　In *The Language of Advertising*, Angela Goddard describes the study of advertising copy as discourse—a system of language whereby readers have a "fleeting conversation" with writers of the text. But advertisers hope the conversation doesn't stop there. They want the ad to be talked about and keep being talked about.

7　Even the name for the text of an ad—copy—connotes replication and reproduction. And since ads also have to compete with each other, the sheer number of a species can serve to help its survival: more of a particular ad means more opportunity to gain people's attention, be talked about, and reproduce, which means even more opportunity to gain people's attention . . . and so it goes.

8   But ads operate within narrow limits on the time and space to do all this. Such constraints favor ad copy that mimics spoken language: sentence fragments, colloquialisms, and other verbal shortcuts.

9   For example, the "Be Cointreauversial" campaign promoted the orange-flavored alcohol by creating a new word and thus breaking the "use accepted vocabulary" rule. The reader could relate the freshly coined term to an existing word, and thereby derive meaning.

10   Another common device used in ad copy (as well as in literary prose) is to jump into a sequence in mid-action. That way, readers feel they are chance observers of something that is already occurring. Text built in such a way acquires an independent existence and assumes the status of "reality." It creates a need in the reader/audience to catch up and be informed.

11   For example, a Volkswagen ad stated, "Somewhere between tuxedo and birthday suit." This sentence fragment slogan does not specifically state the product, and so feels incomplete. This invites the reader to reconstruct the thought and thereby participate in the ad.

12   It has not always been this complicated. Language history buff Bill Bryson reminds us that "advertising" was originally more a matter of broadcasting or disseminating news. By the early 1800s, the term advertising had come to include the idea of spreading news of the availability of goods or services. The phenomenon of advertising as a tool of persuasion is a more recent product of the modern day.

Other "Cointreauversial" Examples

13   In the manner of "be careful what you wish for," some ad campaigns get more attention than they intend. Consider these cases, which provoked widespread response from grammar-concerned citizens:

> "Treat yourself well. Everyday." for Coca-Cola's Dasani mineral water.
>   After much consideration, the company claims it decided to go with the adjective option everyday rather than the adjective plus noun composition every day. See the July 2003 edition of Harper's magazine for a hilarious letter exchange.
> "Toyota. Everyday."
>   Same grammar rebellion as above. The company claimed its word usage was deliberate and the two-word every day looked awkward with the space in the middle.
> Apple Computer's "Think different" campaign.
>   Again, the company defended its choice, saying that differently would tell a person how to think. They wanted to suggest different as the thing to think about.

"Winston tastes good, like a cigarette should."

For using like rather than as, this cigarette slogan is perhaps the most commonly cited example of a grammar goof in advertising. The debate spurred spin-off commercials, in which a "Mrs. Grundy" observed that like is not a conjunction. Her remark was met with, "What do you want, good grammar or good taste?"

Nine out of Ten Grammarians Agree . . .

14   These ads all contain deviations from the standards of prescriptive, or normative, grammar. Prescriptive grammar provides guidelines for how one "ought" to speak, and its prescription is simple: good grammar means obeying rules. Do not end a sentence with a preposition, use the proper case of pronoun—we are taught these prescriptive grammar rules in school and read about them in style guides.

15   Yet these same rules, so carefully recited by teachers and delineated in manuals, are broken every day by advertisers. They may be catching our attention, but grammarians say poor grammar in ads is a corruption of the language and teaches children the improper use of words. Also, the prevalence of English globally is due in part to advertising, so these grammar errors will be the first contact that many non-English speakers have with the language.

16   Grammar classic *The Elements of Style* warns of the negative effects. The language of advertising, say Strunk and White, "profoundly influences the tongues and pens of children and adults," with its "deliberate infractions of grammatical rules and its crossbreeding of the parts of speech." The authors venture that people will want to try writing that way, but admonish, "You do so at your own peril, for it is the language of mutilation." They add "[T]he young writer had best not adopt the device of mutilation in ordinary composition, whose purpose is to engage, not paralyze, the reader's senses."

17   In general, the argument goes something like this: when a word is seen correctly written and in its proper context, it helps to strengthen a child's habit of recognition. (Indeed, parents and teachers can cite many examples of how more reading translates into better spelling. Children who read a lot see the proper spelling of words and it sticks.) On the other hand, certain cultural influences, such as advertisements, do not reinforce and, in fact, contradict the instruction a child receives in school.

18   This argument is posed by grammarians, but the phenomenon of rule breaking in popular media is not unique to language. A child watching Roadrunner outwit the Coyote is exposed to all sorts of physical law violations. In that sense, the cartoon certainly does not reinforce "correct" physics, and contradicts the principles that children learn in science class.

. . . But Do They Know Anything about Grammar?

19   In *The Language Instinct*, Montréal-born Steven Pinker, Professor of Brain and Cognitive Sciences at MIT, argues that the words "rules," "grammatical" and "ungrammatical" have very different meanings, depending on your interest in

language. To the scientist or linguist these terms are descriptive; to the layperson or grammarian, they are prescriptive.

20 Pinker uses an analogy to illustrate. A taxi can obey the laws of physics, while breaking the laws of Chicago. Similarly, a person can speak grammatically (in the systematic sense) while also speaking ungrammatically (in the non-prescriptive sense). For example, as children learn language they make all sorts of grammatical errors by breaking conventions of adult language. Yet a child's utterances do have structure, say linguists, and this early grammar gradually develops into adult grammar.

21 Likewise, ad copy is not just a random jumble of words. Advertisements may break prescriptive norms, but ads have a grammatical structure that makes them intelligible. Pinker observes that most disputes about "correct" grammar are not about grammatical logic, but questions of custom and authority. It's not that advertisers are using "bad grammar," it's just non-standard for written English.

22 Pinker, who *Publisher's Weekly* called "language's bad boy," derides grammarians for their obsession for the conventional. "When a scientist considers all the high-tech mental machinery needed to arrange words into ordinary sentences, prescriptive rules are, at best, inconsequential little decorations," he says. Imagine listening to the complex song of the humpback whale and declaring that you noticed an error! He muses, isn't the song of the humpback whale whatever the whale decides to sing?

Groovy Baby! Language Is a Lava Lamp

23 Journalist and American social critic H. L. Mencken saw language as "a man suffering incessantly from small hemorrhages, and what it needs above all else is constant transactions of new blood from other tongues. The day the gates go up, that day it begins to die." Language is indeed alive, say linguists. It will change inevitably.

24 "The use of the language determines the grammar. If usage changes, the rules change," says Anthea Fraser Gupta, a linguist at the University of Leeds, England. It seems that some grammarians are trying to resist such change. For instance, convention today says never split an infinitive, yet this is a throwback to the Latin roots of English. In Latin, it is impossible to split infinitives because an infinitive is a single word.

25 In *The Power of Babel*, John McWhorter identifies five processes of change in language. One of them is grammar: patterns of grammar that occur occasionally are generalized into rules. For example, English began like Latin with many endings to indicate plural, depending on the class of the noun. Now the ending "–s" (or "–es") is favoured. (Although, as with any rule in English, there are many exceptions.)

26 McWhorter emphasizes that while culture may appear central to the process, language change is not collapsible into the larger category of cultural change. For example, he observes, there is nothing inherently French about taking a beverage (je prends une biere) instead of drinking it. And there is nothing inherently English about "taking" a nap, while French "make" one (faire un petit somme). Most aspects of speech, says McWhorter, are not determined by culture, but by "the cumulative effect of countless millennia of transformation proceeding through structured chaos." In this way, he envisions language as a lava lamp.

Going with the Flow of Language

27 More precisely, in an article in *Nature* (27 September 2001), researchers noted that human language has a unique combination of characteristics.

1. Semantic word-to-world relations (a feature we share with other primates);
2. Complex, exact syntactic structures (similar to formal languages, such as mathematics); and
3. Openness, flexibility and ambiguity.

28 In other words, human language combines aspects of primate and mathematical language. Our words have meaning, we use them according to a system of rules, but the system has the structural resources for indefinite recombination. That means language is open enough to allow for creativity and change. These qualities of human language distinguish us from the ape and the machine.

29 It would seem that part of the joy of being human is to have this kind of freedom in the way we communicate—and grammar allows for it. Karen-Elizabeth Gordon says it well in the foreword to *Sin & Syntax*:

> I see grammar as the choreographer of our language, coordinating the movements of our baffling, flummoxed urge to express, to give voice to the ineffable. Familiarity with the rules of grammar tones our mental musculature, expands our repertoire, sets us free to dance. To break the rules consciously or go around them on purpose is a pleasure multiplied: willful violation, defiance, or deviation with a wicked glint in the eye.

They Doth Protest Too Much

30 To summarize the value of grammar: we need it to be understood. When communicating with language, thoughts are formed into certain orders to be intelligible. Grammar provides a set of rules to do just that. On this point grammarians and linguists agree.

31 But many champions of prescriptive grammar go one step farther, and are concerned about maintaining the purity of the language. They want to protect a body of clearly defined rules and try to entice others to follow the rules for the good of the language. How far will they go? Taken to the extreme, adherence to prescriptive grammar comes to the issue of censorship. If books are banned for their "harmful" effects on society, might it be good to stop children from reading *Huckleberry Finn*, so they don't pollute the acquisition of proper language with a dialect that disregards standard English conventions?

32 In the preface to an English dictionary in 1755, Dr. Samuel Johnson characterized the desire to keep the language static and pure. He said a lexicographer who imagines his dictionary can embalm the language, and thus preserve words and phrases from mutability, is like a man seeking an elixir to extend life unnaturally.

33 But unlike the life and death hi-jinx of the Roadrunner and Coyote, prescriptive grammar seems to be no laughing matter. A survey of the language reference section in a bookstore betrays a certain level of anxiety. Titles include *Painless Grammar,*

Woe Is I: A Grammarphobe's Guide, and the particularly colorful, *Deluxe Transitive Vampire: The Ultimate Handbook of Grammar for the Innocent, the Eager, and the Doomed*, which amazon.com claims can help you "exorcise" your "grammatical demons." With all these references to suffering and phobia—even blood-sucking damnation—a person might wonder: does attention to grammatical principles actually relieve angst or produce more of it?

34   One thing is certain—attention to grammatical principles can be shrewdly channeled for economic gain. The grammarians decrying advertisers for breaking language rules may not be disinterested parties. Many have a stake in our believing that the erosion of grammar indicates a decline in society. Creating the perception of a "problem," and offering a ready solution (buy their grammar guides) is a standard marketing scheme.

35   Maybe grammarians know something about advertising discourse after all.

QUESTIONS FOR ANALYSIS AND DISCUSSION ———————

1. Describe the voice you hear in this essay. How does Pomerinke balance humor and a sense of concern regarding the ineffective use of language in advertising today?
2. What is "prescriptive grammar?" What is Pomerinke's opinion of prescriptive grammar, especially in advertising? Explain.
3. Evaluate Pomerinke's title. Does it effectively draw in the reader? How does it connect to her essay and her argument? Explain.
4. Pomerinke provides several examples of ads that bend grammar rules in favor of a more effective slogan. Can you think of more examples in which advertising ignores the rules of grammar? Do you think the slogans are good ones, or does the poor grammar bother you?

BLOG IT

Flip It—Girls Fight Back Against Bad Ads
Holly Buchanan
October 22, 2007

Poor Heidi.

For months I've been squirming like a 3-year-old . . .
"Can I talk about it yet?"
"Can I talk about it yet?"
"Can I talk about it yet?"

She finally gave me the OK. What have I been so anxious to spread the word about?

"Flip It." Flip It is a series of videos <http://youtube.com/user/3iying> where girls talk about specific ads and why they don't relate to those ads. Ad Age is even talking about it.

Flip It is the brain child of Heidi Dangelmaier and the team at *3iying [An all female marketing agency specializing in marketing and design strategies for young women.]* I've been really intrigued by 3iying and some of their innovative approaches to marketing to girls 15–25. So how did Flip It come about?

Marketers targeting girls think they're doing a good job. They don't understand the extent of the disconnect that exists between girls 15–25 and the companies who are trying to reach them.

Being the super smart person she is, Heidi decided that instead of trying to tell them about the problem, she'd let the girls speak for themselves.

The result is Flip It. It started with a couple of girls around the office, but grew into a landslide of videos from girls who jumped at the chance to let marketers know just how off the mark they are.

Now, do not think this is just some bitch-fest. These girls are articulate, insightful and very specific about exactly why the ads are not relevant to them. These girls are bright, funny, and real. There is a huge amount of information and insight to be gained from these videos. View some at http://www.3iying.com.

I hope companies and marketers are listening. There is a huge disconnect between this market and the companies trying to speak to them. And it's not just girls 15–25. It's marketing to women of all ages.

3iying is not out to attack marketing—they are trying to make it better. 3iying is not in the business of flipping. We are an all-girl strategic and creative think tank that helps mass-scale brands become more relevant to girls. 3iying offers our contribution to ending this gap. We cannot do it alone. The new millennium girls reflect a consumer shift that will lead generations to come. Their mindset cannot be ignored if we wish to keep our client's brands alive and powerful and stop wasting their money.

Here's to more marketing to women that is relevant, insightful, fun and uplifting. Heidi Dangelmaier and the girls at 3iying—you rock.

Mo Says:

October 22nd, 2007 at 9:21 pm

Two words, VICTORIA'S SECRET.

I just got their new catalogue for Christmas and it is utterly disgusting. After taking a gender studies class focusing on female sexuality in advertising, I have found this catalogue to be the worst of any advertisement I have ever seen. It's gross and is being marketed to extremely young girls through their "PINK" line.

Check it out if you can. Someone needs to do something. This company is over sexualizing our youth and giving them a terribly skewed outlook on what it means to be a woman.

Penelope Says:

November 30th, 2007 at 8:53 pm

Thanks Holly for bringing these to our attention. You would think by listening to some of these poignant testimonials that there are a lot of creatives out there who have never seen a teenage girl—let alone spoken with one. It also brings home the fact that we need niche agencies that are wholly focused on Youth or other hugely important demographic segments—way to go 3iying.

YOU SAY:

After viewing some of the flipped ads and commentary on the 3iying website, add your own blog comment.

Sample Ads and Study Questions

The following section features recently published magazine advertisements. Diverse in content and style, some ads use words to promote the product, while others depend on emotion, name recognition, visual appeal, or association. They present a variety of sales pitches and marketing techniques.

Corresponding to each ad is a list of questions to help you analyze how the ad works its appeal to promote a product. When studying the advertisements, approach each as a consumer, an artist, a social scientist, and a critic with an eye for detail.

ACLU

1. Who is featured in the picture? How does this image play upon our cultural and historical expectations and twist them?
2. Who is the ACLU? What mission do they support? Does this ad motivate you to take action? Why or why not?
3. Apply the Fog Index from Charles A. O'Neill's article "The Language of Advertising" to the blurb at the bottom of the page. What is the grade level of the language? What does this tell you about the intended purchasing audience?
4. Who do you think is the target audience for this advertisement? How do you think a young adult would respond to it? a married man? a politician or government worker? a teenage girl? a lawyer? Explain.

DENTYNE

1. What is happening in this ad? How do the people in the ad "sell" the product? Does the product have any relationship to the people and what they are doing? Explain.
2. How would this ad be different if a woman were pictured pulling the gum out of a man's pocket?
3. Who is the audience for this ad? How old do the woman and man look in the ad? How are they dressed? Does the ad appeal equally to men as well as women?
4. If you were leafing through a magazine and saw this ad, would you stop to examine it? Why or why not? In what sort of magazine would you expect to see this ad?
5. Review the tagline featured in the ad "Everybody wants a piece." What are the multiple interpretations of this line? Where does the tagline appear? Would the tagline work as well if it were placed in the upper left corner of the ad? Why or why not?

GAP RED

1. Would you know what this ad was promoting if the company name was not located at top-right section of the ad? Would there be any ambiguity about what was being "sold" in the advertisement? How much does this ad depend on name and image recognition? Explain.
2. Where would you expect to see an ad like this and why? If you were an advertising executive, where would you place this ad? How would you target your public? Explain.
3. This ad uses the tagline "ADMI(RED)" How does the typeface work with the tagline and its message? Explain.
4. This ad promotes a nonprofit campaign that depends a great deal on knowledge of popular culture. Visit the website http://www .gapinc.com/red/ that explains the RED project. After viewing the site, discuss how the man in the ad supports the cause and how his celebrity can help promote the message and the product.

JIMMY CHOO ────────────────────────────────

1. Examine this advertisement carefully. What is happening in this ad? How does it sell the product? Can you tell what product the ad promotes?

2. How does the desert setting and mountains and cracked earth contribute to the image? Do these elements tap into audience expectations about the product? Are they confusing? Entertaining? Explain.

3. Would you know what this ad was selling if there were no brand name mentioned in the ad? Explain.

4. If you were leafing through a magazine and saw this ad, would you stop to read it? Why or why not?

5. In January 2007, Dolce & Gabbana pulled an ad that depicted an image that could have been interpreted as promoting violence against women. Could this ad be viewed similarly? Why or why not?

NATIONAL HEALTH SERVICE (UK) ———————————————

1. The National Health Service (NHS) is the publicly funded health care system of England. Does the fact that this ad comes from a health agency influence your reception of its message or point? Why or why not?

2. In what ways does the young woman in the photograph represent her generation? Do you agree with this representation? Explain.

3. Unlike ads that warn of the health risks of smoking and threat to others, this ad tries a more personal approach. Why do you think the

* "Fag" is British slang for a cigarette.

NHS opted for this tactic? Is it effective? Does it carry more impact than a warning that cigarettes are harmful to health? Explain.

4. Who is the target audience for this ad? Where would you expect to see it? Would it be as effective in the United States as in European countries?

5. If you were reading a magazine or walking by a billboard and saw this image, would you stop and look at it? Would it make an impression on you? Why or why not?

HEIRESS ———————————————————————————————

1. In what ways does the young woman in the photograph represent the product? Who is she? How essential is it to the product's success that viewers recognize the woman?
2. Who is the likely target audience for this ad? In what magazines would you expect to see it? Is it an effective ad? Explain.
3. Analyze the young woman's position in the ad and her pose. Would this ad be more effective if she were facing forward? Why or why not?
4. What lifestyle does the ad promote? What is the product's implied promise? Explain.

WRITING ASSIGNMENTS

1. You are an advertising executive. Select one of the products featured in the sample ads section and write a new advertising campaign for it. Do you tap into popular consciousness? Do you use "weasel words"? How do you hook your audience, and how do you create a need for the product? Defend your campaign to your supervisors by explaining the motivation behind your creative decisions.

2. Write a paper in which you consider advertising strategies. Support your evaluation with examples of advertising campaigns with which you are familiar. Make an argument for or against particular campaigns. Are they appropriate? Do they exploit emotions? Are they opportunistic? You may draw support from the articles written by William Lutz, Tracy Pomerinke, and Charles A. O'Neill.

3. In his essay, William Lutz highlights some marketing ploys that he finds particularly annoying and ineffective. Identify some commercials or advertisements that especially annoyed you. Why exactly did they bother you? Try to locate any cultural, linguistic, social, or intellectual reasons behind your annoyance or distaste. How do these commercials compare to the marketing criticisms expressed in essays featured in this section?

4. The authors in this section give many examples of language use and abuse from companies such as Calvin Klein, Camel cigarettes, Eli Lilly, and Volkswagon. Examine a few of these companies' marketing campaigns in detail. Write an essay that compares the language in these ads to the language the authors describe. Discuss whether you find any of the ads or marketing efforts particularly effective.

Gender Matters

In the past century, we have witnessed enormous changes in the roles of women and men at home, in the workplace, and in society. Traditional ways of defining the self in terms of gender have been challenged and irrevocably altered. The essays in this chapter examine how these changes have affected men and women as they continue to redefine themselves, their relationships with each other, and their relationships with society.

Perceptions of gender begin at an early age, and it seems as if children face social and cultural pressures their parents' generation never experienced. The first section, "Fitting In," takes a look at the way society influences our perceptions of gender and our expectations of ourselves and of the opposite sex. We live in a society obsessed with image—a society seemingly more driven by the cultivation of the body and how we clothe it than in personal achievement. In fact, so powerful is the influence of image that other terms of self-definition are difficult to identify. Men and women confront challenges related to body image and self-perception daily. From where does all the body-consciousness pressure come? Why are so many young people seemingly at war with their bodies? And how do cultural perceptions of beauty influence our view of what it means to be male or female?

The readings in the next section, "A Brave New World," explore the ways society influences our perceptions of gender and impacts our culture as a whole. The conflicts in the Middle East remind us that we still live in a world where gender roles are clearly defined—even mandated by government and religion. As we examine gender roles and cultural influences closer to home, we see that men and women must navigate a sometimes confusing social landscape.

Most college-age men and women were born after the "sexual revolution" and the feminist movements of the 1960s and 1970s. But it is these movements that have shaped the way men and women behave today and how they view themselves and each other, evaluate opportunity, and envision the future. Some people claim that things have become more complicated, and not for the better. Others can't imagine a culture where a woman couldn't pursue a business or medical career without facing tremendous obstacles, or a society in which a man staying at home to raise his children was considered an oddity. In addition to exploring cultural influences on gender, the section also addresses whether feminism has—or hasn't—changed the way women perceive themselves.

FITTING IN

Saplings in the Storm
Mary Pipher

With the onset of adolescence, children are faced with a multitude of gender-related issues. In addition to dealing with physical and emotional changes, many adolescents must try to adapt to shifting social roles. Changing social expectations can be overwhelming, says psychologist Mary Pipher, especially for girls. In this excerpt taken from the introduction to her best-selling book *Reviving Ophelia* (1995), Pipher is concerned that girls may be losing their true selves in an effort to conform to what they believe society expects from them.

Psychologist and family therapist Pipher is the author of several best-selling books, including *The Shelter of Each Other* (1997) and *Another Country: Navigating the Emotional Terrain of Our Elders* (1999), which examines the difficulties older adults face in American culture. Her special area of interest is how American culture influences the mental health of its people. She has written articles for *Time Magazine, Hope, Psychotherapy Networker, The Journal of Family Life*, and many other publications. Her most recent book is *Writing to Change the World*, which describes how to write to effect social change.

BEFORE YOU READ ————————————————————

Did the way you fit into your social groups change when you reached adolescence? If so, in what ways? What do you think accounts for such changes?

AS YOU READ ————————————————————

According to Pipher, what social constraints do girls alone face with the onset of adolescence? Why do these cultural pressures exist?

1   When my cousin Polly was a girl, she was energy in motion. She danced, did cartwheels and splits, played football, basketball and baseball with the neighborhood boys, wrestled with my brothers, biked, climbed trees and rode horses. She was as lithe and as resilient as a willow branch and as unrestrained as a lion cub. Polly talked as much as she moved. She yelled out orders and advice, shrieked for joy when she won a bet or heard a good joke, laughed with her mouth wide open, argued with kids and grown-ups and insulted her foes in the language of a construction worker.

2   We formed the Marauders, a secret club that met over her garage. Polly was the Tom Sawyer of the club. She planned the initiations, led the spying expeditions and hikes to haunted houses. She showed us the rituals to become blood "brothers" and taught us card tricks and how to smoke.

3   Then Polly had her first period and started junior high. She tried to keep up her old ways, but she was called a tomboy and chided for not acting more ladylike. She was excluded by her boy pals and by the girls, who were moving into makeup and romances.

4   This left Polly confused and shaky. She had temper tantrums and withdrew from both the boys' and girls' groups. Later she quieted down and reentered as Becky Thatcher. She wore stylish clothes and watched from the sidelines as the boys acted and spoke. Once again she was accepted and popular. She glided smoothly through our small society. No one spoke of the changes or mourned the loss of our town's most dynamic citizen. I was the only one who felt that a tragedy had transpired.

5   Girls in what Freud called the latency period, roughly age six or seven through puberty, are anything but latent. I think of my daughter Sara during those years—performing chemistry experiments and magic tricks, playing her violin, starring in her own plays, rescuing wild animals and biking all over town. I think of her friend Tamara, who wrote a 300-page novel the summer of her sixth-grade year. I remember myself, reading every children's book in the library of my town. One week I planned to be a great doctor like Albert Schweitzer. The next week I wanted to write like Louisa May Alcott or dance in Paris like Isadora Duncan. I have never since had as much confidence or ambition.

6   Most preadolescent girls are marvelous company because they are interested in everything—sports, nature, people, music and books. Almost all the heroines of girls' literature come from this age group—Anne of Green Gables, Heidi, Pippi Longstocking and Caddie Woodlawn. Girls this age bake pies, solve mysteries and go on quests. They can take care of themselves and are not yet burdened with caring for others. They have a brief respite from the female role and can be tomboys, a word that conveys courage, competency and irreverence.

7   They can be androgynous, having the ability to act adaptively in any situation regardless of gender role constraints. An androgynous person can comfort a baby or change a tire, cook a meal or chair a meeting. Research has shown that, since they are free to act without worrying if their behavior is feminine or masculine, androgynous adults are the most well-adjusted.

8   Girls between seven and eleven rarely come to therapy. They don't need it. I can count on my fingers the girls this age whom I have seen: Coreen, who was physically abused; Anna, whose parents were divorcing; and Brenda, whose father killed himself. These girls were courageous and resilient. Brenda said, "If my father didn't want to stick around, that's his loss." Coreen and Anna were angry, not with themselves, but rather at the grown-ups, whom they felt were making mistakes. It's amazing how little help these girls needed from me to heal and move on.

9   A horticulturist told me a revealing story. She led a tour of junior-high girls who were attending a math and science fair on her campus. She showed them side oats grama, bluestem, Indian grass and trees—redbud, maple, walnut and willow. The

younger girls interrupted each other with their questions and tumbled forward to see, touch and smell everything. The older girls, the ninth-graders, were different. They hung back. They didn't touch plants or shout out questions. They stood primly to the side, looking bored and even a little disgusted by the enthusiasm of their younger classmates. My friend asked herself, What's happened to these girls? What's gone wrong? She told me, "I wanted to shake them, to say, 'Wake up, come back. Is anybody home at your house?'"

10   Recently I sat sunning on a bench outside my favorite ice-cream store. A mother and her teenage daughter stopped in front of me and waited for the light to change. I heard the mother say, "You have got to stop blackmailing your father and me. Every time you don't get what you want, you tell us that you want to run away from home or kill yourself. What's happened to you? You used to be able to handle not getting your way." The daughter stared straight ahead, barely acknowledging her mother's words. The light changed. I licked my ice-cream cone. Another mother approached the same light with her preadolescent daughter in tow. They were holding hands. The daughter said to her mother, "This is fun. Let's do this all afternoon."

11   Something dramatic happens to girls in early adolescence. Just as planes and ships disappear mysteriously into the Bermuda Triangle, so do the selves of girls go down in droves. They crash and burn in a social and developmental Bermuda Triangle. In early adolescence, studies show that girls' IQ scores drop and their math and science scores plummet. They lose their resiliency and optimism and become less curious and inclined to take risks. They lose their assertive, energetic and "tomboyish" personalities and become more deferential, self-critical and depressed. They report great unhappiness with their own bodies.

12   Psychology documents but does not explain the crashes. Girls who rushed to drink in experiences in enormous gulps sit quietly in the corner. Writers such as Sylvia Plath, Margaret Atwood and Olive Schreiner have described the wreckage. Diderot, in writing to his young friend Sophie Volland, described his observations harshly: "You all die at 15."

13   Fairy tales capture the essence of this phenomenon. Young women eat poisoned apples or prick their fingers with poisoned needles and fall asleep for a hundred years. They wander away from home, encounter great dangers, are rescued by princes and are transformed into passive and docile creatures.

14   The story of Ophelia, from Shakespeare's *Hamlet*, shows the destructive forces that affect young women. As a girl, Ophelia is happy and free, but with adolescence she loses herself. When she falls in love with Hamlet, she lives only for his approval. She has no inner direction; rather she struggles to meet the demands of Hamlet and her father. Her value is determined utterly by their approval. Ophelia is torn apart by her efforts to please. When Hamlet spurns her because she is an obedient daughter, she goes mad with grief. Dressed in elegant clothes that weigh her down, she drowns in a stream filled with flowers.

15   Girls know they are losing themselves. One girl said, "Everything good in me died in junior high." Wholeness is shattered by the chaos of adolescence. Girls become fragmented, their selves split into mysterious contradictions. They are sensitive and tenderhearted, mean and competitive, superficial and idealistic. They are

confident in the morning and overwhelmed with anxiety by nightfall. They rush through their days with wild energy and then collapse into lethargy. They try on new roles every week—this week the good student, next week the delinquent and the next, the artist. And they expect their families to keep up with these changes.

16   My clients in early adolescence are elusive and slow to trust adults. They are easily offended by a glance, a clearing of the throat, a silence, a lack of sufficient enthusiasm or a sentence that doesn't meet their immediate needs. Their voices have gone underground—their speech is more tentative and less articulate. Their moods swing widely. One week they love their world and their families, the next they are critical of everyone. Much of their behavior is unreadable. Their problems are complicated and metaphorical—eating disorders, school phobias and self-inflicted injuries. I need to ask again and again in a dozen different ways, "What are you trying to tell me?"

17   Michelle, for example, was a beautiful, intelligent seventeen-year-old. Her mother brought her in after she became pregnant for the third time in three years. I tried to talk about why this was happening. She smiled a Mona Lisa smile to all my questions. "No, I don't care all that much for sex." "No, I didn't plan this. It just happened." When Michelle left a session, I felt like I'd been talking in the wrong language to someone far away.

18   Psychology has a long history of ignoring girls this age. Until recently adolescent girls haven't been studied by academics, and they have long baffled therapists. Because they are secretive with adults and full of contradictions, they are difficult to study. So much is happening internally that's not communicated on the surface.

19   Simone de Beauvoir believed adolescence is when girls realize that men have the power and that their only power comes from consenting to become submissive adored objects. They do not suffer from the penis envy Freud postulated, but from power envy.

20   She described the Bermuda Triangle this way: Girls who were the subjects of their own lives become the objects of other's lives. "Young girls slowly bury their childhood, put away their independent and imperious selves and submissively enter adult existence." Adolescent girls experience a conflict between their autonomous selves and their need to be feminine, between their status as human beings and their vocation as females. De Beauvoir says, "Girls stop being and start seeming."

21   Girls become "female impersonators" who fit their whole selves into small, crowded spaces. Vibrant, confident girls become shy, doubting young women. Girls stop thinking, "Who am I? What do I want?" and start thinking, "What must I do to please others?" This gap between girls' true selves and cultural prescriptions for what is properly female creates enormous problems. To paraphrase a Stevie Smith poem about swimming in the sea, "they are not waving, they are drowning." And just when they most need help, they are unable to take their parents' hands.

22   This pressure disorients and depresses most girls. They sense the pressure to be someone they are not. They fight back, but they are fighting a "problem with no name." One girl put it this way: "I'm a perfectly good carrot that everyone is trying to turn into a rose. As a carrot, I have good color and a nice leafy top. When I'm carved into a rose, I turn brown and wither."

23   Adolescent girls are saplings in a hurricane. They are young and vulnerable trees that the winds blow with gale strength. Three factors make young women vulnerable to the hurricane. One is their developmental level. Everything is changing— body shape, hormones, skin and hair. Calmness is replaced by anxiety. Their way of thinking is changing. Far below the surface they are struggling with the most basic of human questions: What is my place in the universe, what is my meaning?

24   Second, American culture has always smacked girls on the head in early adolescence. This is when they move into a broader culture that is rife with girl-hurting "isms," such as sexism, capitalism and lookism, which is the evaluation of a person solely on the basis of appearance.

25   Third, American girls are expected to distance from parents just at the time when they most need their support. As they struggle with countless new pressures, they must relinquish the protection and closeness they've felt with their families in childhood. They turn to their none-too-constant peers for support.

26   Parents know only too well that something is happening to their daughters. Calm, considerate daughters grow moody, demanding and distant. Girls who loved to talk are sullen and secretive. Girls who liked to hug now bristle when touched. Mothers complain that they can do nothing right in the eyes of their daughters. Involved fathers bemoan their sudden banishment from their daughters' lives. But few parents realize how universal their experiences are. Their daughters are entering a new land, a dangerous place that parents can scarcely comprehend. Just when they most need a home base, they cut themselves loose without radio communications.

27   Most parents of adolescent girls have the goal of keeping their daughters safe while they grow up and explore the world. The parents' job is to protect. The daughters' job is to explore. Always these different tasks have created tension in parent-daughter relationships, but now it's even harder. Generally parents are more protective of their daughters than is corporate America. Parents aren't trying to make money off their daughters by selling them designer jeans or cigarettes, they just want them to be well adjusted. They don't see their daughters as sex objects or consumers but as real people with talents and interests. But daughters turn away from their parents as they enter the new land. They befriend their peers, who are their fellow inhabitants of the strange country and who share a common language and set of customs. They often embrace the junk values of mass culture.

28   This turning away from parents is partly for developmental reasons. Early adolescence is a time of physical and psychological change, self-absorption, preoccupation with peer approval and identity formation. It's a time when girls focus inward on their own fascinating changes.

29   It's partly for cultural reasons. In America we define adulthood as a moving away from families into broader culture. Adolescence is the time for cutting bonds and breaking free. Adolescents may claim great independence from parents, but they are aware and ashamed of their parents' smallest deviation from the norm. They don't like to be seen with them and find their imperfections upsetting. A mother's haircut or a father's joke can ruin their day. Teenagers are furious at parents who say the wrong things or do not respond with perfect answers. Adolescents claim not to hear their parents, but with their friends they discuss endlessly all parental attitudes.

With amazing acuity, they sense nuances, doubt, shades of ambiguity, discrepancy and hypocrisy.

30   Adolescents still have some of the magical thinking of childhood and believe that parents have the power to keep them safe and happy. They blame their parents for their misery, yet they make a point of not telling their parents how they think and feel; they have secrets, so things can get crazy. Most parents feel like failures during this time. They feel shut out, impotent and misunderstood. They often attribute the difficulties of this time to their daughters and their own failings. They don't understand that these problems go with the developmental stage, the culture and the times.

31   Parents experience an enormous sense of loss when their girls enter this new land. They miss the daughters who sang in the kitchen, who read them school papers, who accompanied them on fishing trips and to ball games. They miss the daughters who liked to bake cookies, play Pictionary and be kissed good-night. In place of their lively, affectionate daughters they have changelings—new girls who are sadder, angrier and more complicated. Everyone is grieving.

32   Fortunately adolescence is time-limited. By late high school most girls are stronger and the winds are dying down. Some of the worst problems—cliques, a total focus on looks and struggles with parents—are on the wane. But the way girls handle the problems of adolescence can have implications for their adult lives. Without some help, the loss of wholeness, self-confidence and self-direction can last well into adulthood. Many adult clients struggle with the same issues that overwhelmed them as adolescent girls. Thirty-year-old accountants and realtors, forty-year-old homemakers and doctors, and thirty-five-year-old nurses and schoolteachers ask the same questions and struggle with the same problems as their teenage daughters.

33   Even sadder are the women who are not struggling, who have forgotten that they have selves worth defending. They have repressed the pain of their adolescence, the betrayals of self in order to be pleasing. These women come to therapy with the goal of becoming even more pleasing to others. They come to lose weight, to save their marriages or to rescue their children. When I ask them about their own needs, they are confused by the question.

34   Women often know how everyone in their family thinks and feels except themselves. They are great at balancing the needs of their coworkers, husbands, children and friends, but they forget to put themselves into the equation. They struggle with adolescent questions still unresolved: How important are looks and popularity? How do I care for myself and not be selfish? How can I be honest and still be loved? How can I achieve and not threaten others? How can I be sexual and not a sex object? How can I be responsive but not responsible for everyone?

35   Before I studied psychology, I studied cultural anthropology. I have always been interested in that place where culture and individual psychology intersect, in why cultures create certain personalities and not others, in how they pull for certain strengths in their members, in how certain talents are utilized while others atrophy from lack of attention. I'm interested in the role cultures play in the development of individual pathology.

36   For a student of culture and personality, adolescence is fascinating. It's an extraordinary time when individual, developmental and cultural factors combine in

ways that shape adulthood. It's a time of marked internal development and massive cultural indoctrination.

37   An analysis of the culture cannot ignore individual differences in women. Some women blossom and grow under the most hostile conditions while others wither after the smallest storms. And yet we are more alike than different in the issues that face us. The important question is, Under what conditions do most young women flower and grow?

38   Adolescent clients intrigue me as they struggle to sort themselves out. But these last few years my office has been filled with girls—girls with eating disorders, alcohol problems, posttraumatic stress reactions to sexual or physical assaults, sexually transmitted diseases (STDs), self-inflicted injuries and strange phobias, and girls who have tried to kill themselves or run away. A health department survey showed that 40 percent of all girls in my midwestern city considered suicide last year. The Centers for Disease Control in Atlanta reports that the suicide rate among children age ten to fourteen rose 75 percent between 1979 and 1988. Something dramatic is happening to adolescent girls in America, something unnoticed by those not on the front lines.

39   At first I was surprised that girls were having more trouble now. After all, we have had a consciousness-raising women's movement since the sixties. Women are working in traditionally male professions and going out for sports. Some fathers help with the housework and child care. It seems that these changes would count for something. And of course they do, but in some ways the progress is confusing. The Equal Rights Amendment was not ratified, feminism is a pejorative term to many people and, while some women have high-powered jobs, most women work hard for low wages and do most of the "second shift" work. The lip service paid to equality makes the reality of discrimination even more confusing.

40   Many of the pressures girls have always faced are intensified in the 1990s. Many things contribute to this intensification: more divorced families, chemical addictions, casual sex and violence against women. Because of the media, which Clarence Page calls "electronic wallpaper," girls all live in one big town—a sleazy, dangerous tinsel town with lots of liquor stores and few protected spaces. Increasingly women have been sexualized and objectified, their bodies marketed to sell tractors and toothpaste. Soft-and hard-core pornography are everywhere. Sexual and physical assaults on girls are at an all-time high. Now girls are more vulnerable and fearful, more likely to have been traumatized and less free to roam about alone. This combination of old stresses and new is poison for our young women.

41   Parents have unprecedented stress as well. For the last half-century, parents worried about their sixteen-year-old daughters driving, but now, in a time of driveby shootings and car-jackings, parents can be panicked. Parents have always worried about their daughters' sexual behavior, but now, in a time of date rapes, herpes and AIDS, they can be sex-phobic. Traditionally parents have wondered what their teens were doing, but now teens are much more likely to be doing things that can get them killed.

42   I am saying that girls are having more trouble now than they had thirty years ago, when I was a girl, and more trouble than even ten years ago. Something new is

happening. Adolescence has always been hard, but it's harder now because of cultural changes in the last decade. The protected place in space and time that we once called childhood has grown shorter. There is an African saying, "It takes a village to raise a child." Most girls no longer have a village.

QUESTIONS FOR ANALYSIS AND DISCUSSION ─────

1. What does Pipher mean when she says that girls "disappear mysteriously into the Bermuda Triangle" in early adolescence? Why do you think she uses this analogy repeatedly?
2. How do girls change with the onset of adolescence? To what extent are these changes physical and to what extent are they cultural? Do you think girls must make sacrifices to "fit in"? Explain.
3. What is the benefit of androgyny to girls? Can the same benefits be applied to boys?
4. Pipher's essay focuses on what happens to girls when they reach adolescence. Do you think she feels boys face similar issues? Do you think Pipher thinks society is harder on girls than on boys? Explain.
5. Is audience important to the success of this essay? Why or why not? How could this essay apply to issues that face both men and women?
6. Place Pipher's essay in different historical contexts. For example, do you think the problems she describes faced girls in the 1930s or the 1950s? Are the underlying social pressures facing teenage girls the same today? Explain.

─────────────

The Bully in the Mirror
Stephen S. Hall

The expression goes "vanity, thy name is woman," and most people think of body obsessive behavior as a female trait. Women still account for 90 percent of cosmetic surgical procedures, and roughly the same number is true for teenagers being treated for eating disorders. But boys are becoming just as obsessed with their bodies, say psychiatrists Harrison Pope, Katharine Phillips, and Roberto Olivardia. Their research reveals a disturbing trend—teenage boys are spending more time in the gym in quest of steroid-boosted buff bodies. Cultural messages reinforce this viewpoint, from the action heroes they play with as children, to the images they view on television, to the peer pressure they receive at school. In America today, young men are constantly faced with "the bully in the mirror."

Stephen S. Hall is a science writer and author of several books, including *Merchants of Immortality: Chasing the Dream of Human Life Extension* (2003) and *Size Matters: How Height Affects the Health, Happiness, and Success of Boys and the Men They Become* (2006), which describes the topic of male body image and shows how physical size during childhood affects our psychology, social status, relationships, and income as adults. He is a contributing writer to *Discover* and *New York Times Magazine,* in which this article first appeared on August 22, 1999.

BEFORE YOU READ ————————————————————————————

What is the "perfect" male physique? What does it look like? Is your image influenced by outside forces, such as the media, your gender, or your age? How do the real men you know compare to the image you have in your mind?

AS YOU READ ————————————————————————————————

The young man featured in this article, Alexander, comments that people judge others on physical appearance. What do you want people to notice about you? How do your feelings compare to those Alexander expresses in this article?

1   On an insufferably muggy afternoon in July, with the thermometer pushing 90 degrees and ozone alerts filling the airwaves, Alexander Bregstein was in a foul mood. He was furious, in fact, for reasons that would become clear only later. Working on just three hours of sleep, and having spent the last eight hours minding a bunch of preschool kids in his summer job as a camp counselor, Alexander was itching to kick back and relax. So there he was, lying on his back in the weight room of his gym, head down on an incline bench, earphones pitching three-figure decibels of the rock band Finger Eleven into his ears as he gripped an 85-pound weight in each hand and then, after a brief pause to gather himself, muscled them into the air with focused bursts of energy. Each lift was accompanied by a sharp exhalation, like the quick, short stroke of a piston.

2   The first thing you need to know about Alexander is that he is 16 years old, bright, articulate and funny in that self-deprecating and almost wise teen-age way. However, about a year ago, Alexander made a conscious decision that those weren't the qualities he wanted people to recognize in him, at least not at first. He wanted people to see him first, and what they see these days are thick neck muscles, shoulders so massive that he can't scratch his back, a powerful bulge in his arms and a chest that has been deliberately chiseled for the two-button look—what Alexander now calls "my most endearing feature." He walks with a kind of cocky gravity-testing bounce in his step that derives in part from his muscular build but also from the confidence of knowing he looks good in his tank top and baggy shorts. As his spotter, Aaron Anavim, looked on, Alexander lifted the 85-pound weights three more times, arms quivering, face reddening with effort. Each dumbbell, I realized as I watched, weighed more than I did when I entered high school.

3   Another half-dozen teen-agers milled around the weight room, casting glances at themselves and one another in the mirror. They talked of looking "cut," with sharp definition to their muscles, and of developing "six-packs," crisp divisions of the

abdominals, but of all the muscles that get a workout in rooms like these, the most important may be the ones that move the eyes in restless sweeping arcs of comparison and appraisal. "Once you're in this game to manipulate your body," Alexander said, "you want to be the best," likening the friendly competition in the room to a form of "whipping out the ruler." While we talked between sets of Alexander's 90-minute routine, his eyes wandered to the mirror again and again, searching for flaws, looking for areas of improvement. "The more you lift," he admitted, "the more you look in the mirror."

4   In this weight room, in a gym in a northern New Jersey suburb, the gym rats have a nickname for Alexander: Mirror Boy. That's a vast improvement over the nicknames he endured at school not long ago. "I know it sounds kind of odd to have favorite insults," he told me with a wry smile, munching on a protein bar before moving on to his next set of lifts, "but Chunk Style always was kind of funny." And kind of appropriate. Until recently, Alexander carried nearly 210 pounds on a 5-foot-6 frame, and when I asked if he was teased about his weight, he practically dropped a dumbbell on my feet. "Oh! Oh, man, was I teased? Are you kidding?" he said in his rapid, agreeable patter. "When I was fat, people must have gone home and thought of nothing else except coming in with new material the next day. They must have had study groups just to make fun of people who were overweight." He even got an earful at home. "My parents—God bless them, but they would make comments all the time. My father would say, 'If you eat all that, you'll be as big as a house.' And I'm, like: 'Dad, it's a little late for that. What am I now? A mobile home?'"

5   The day of reckoning came in April 1998, during a spring-break vacation in Boca Raton, Fla. As his family was about to leave its hotel room to go to the beach, Alexander, then 15, stood in front of a mirror and just stared at the spectacle of his shirtless torso. "I remember the exact, like, moment in my mind," he said. "Everything about that room is burned into my head, every little thing. I can tell you where every lamp was, where my father was standing, my mother was sitting. We were about to go out, and I'm looking in this mirror—me, with my gut hanging over my bathing suit—and it was, like: Who would want to look at this? It's part of me, and I'm disgusted! That moment, I realized that nobody was giving me a chance to find out who I was because of the way I looked." And so Alexander decided to do something about it, something drastic.

6   There is a kind of timeless, archetypal trajectory to a teen-ager's battle with body image, but in most accounts the teen-ager is female and the issue is anorexia or bulimia. As any psychologist knows, however, and as any sufficiently evolved adult male could tell you, boys have body-image problems, too. Traditionally, they have felt pressure to look not thin, but rather strong and virile, which increasingly seems to mean looking bulked up and muscular, and that is why I was interested in talking to Alexander.

7   No one can quite cite any data, any scientific studies proving that things are different, but a number of psychologists with whom I spoke returned to the same point again and again: the cultural messages about an ideal male body, if not new, have grown more insistent, more aggressive, more widespread and more explicit in recent years.

8   Since roughly 90 percent of teen-agers who are treated for eating disorders are female, boys still have a way to go. Young girls have suffered greatly from insecurity about appearance and body image, and the scientific literature on anorexia and related body-image disorders depicts a widespread and serious health problem in adolescent females. But to hear some psychologists tell it, boys may be catching up in terms of insecurity and even psychological pathology. An avalanche of recent books on men and boys underlines the precarious nature of contemporary boyhood in America. A number of studies in the past decade—of men, not boys—have suggested that "body-image disturbances," as researchers sometimes call them, may be more prevalent in men than previously believed and almost always begin in the teen-age years. Katharine Phillips, a psychiatrist at the Brown University School of Medicine, has specialized in "body dysmorphic disorder," a psychiatric illness in which patients become obsessively preoccupied with perceived flaws in their appearance—receding hairlines, facial imperfections, small penises, inadequate musculature. In a study of "30 cases of imagined ugliness," Phillips and colleagues described a surprisingly common condition in males whose symptoms include excessive checking of mirrors and attempts to camouflage imagined deformities, most often of the hair, nose and skin. The average age of onset, Phillips says, is 15.

9   Two years ago, Harrison G. Pope Jr., of Harvard Medical School, and his colleagues published a modest paper called "Muscle Dysmorphia: An Underrecognized Form of Body Dysmorphic Disorder" in a relatively obscure journal called *Psychosomatics*. The study described a group of men and women who had become "pathologically preoccupied" by their body image and were convinced that they looked small and puny, even though they were bulging with muscles. The paper got a lot of attention, and it led to an even more widely publicized study earlier this year from the same lab reporting how male action-figure toys like G.I. Joe and the "Star Wars" characters have bulked up over the years.

10   When you visit the office of Harrison (Skip) Pope, in a grim institutional building on the rolling grounds of McLean Hospital in Belmont, Mass., the first thing you notice are the calipers hanging on the wall—partly as objets d'art, but partly as a reminder that what we subjectively consider attractive can sometimes yield to objective measurement. Pope, after all, was one of the scientists who devised what might be called the Buff Equation, or: $FFMI = W \times (1 - BF/100) \times h - 2 + 6.1 \times (1.8 - H)$.

11   The formula is ostensibly used to calculate a person's Fat-free Mass Index; it has sniffed out presumed steroid use by Mr. America winners, professional bodybuilders and men whose unhealthy preoccupation with looking muscular has induced them to use drugs.

12   Pope is a wiry, compact psychiatrist who can squat 400 pounds in his spare time. ("You can reach me pretty much all day except from 11 A.M. to 2 P.M.," he told me, "when I'm at the gym.") I had gone to see him and his colleague Roberto Olivardia not only because they were the lead authors on the G.I. Joe study, but also because their studies of body-image disorders in slightly older postadolescent men may be the best indicator yet of where male body-image issues are headed.

13   Shortly after I arrived, Olivardia emptied a shopping bag full of male action dolls onto a coffee table in the office. The loot lay in a heap, a plastic orgy of superhero

beefcake—three versions of G.I. Joe (Hasbro's original 1964 version plus two others) and one G.I. Joe Extreme, Luke Skywalker and Han Solo in their 1978 and mid-90's versions, Mighty Morphin Power Rangers, Batman, Superman, Iron Man and Wolverine. The inspiration for the whole study came from an adolescent girl. Pope's 13-year-old daughter, Courtney, was surfing the Web one night, working on a school project on how Barbie's body had radically changed over the years, and Pope thought to himself, There's got to be the male equivalent of that.

14   Once Pope and Olivardia gathered new and "vintage" action figures, they measured their waist, chest and biceps dimensions and projected them onto a 5-foot-10 male. Where the original G.I. Joe projected to a man of average height with a 32-inch waist, 44-inch chest and 12-inch biceps, the more recent figures have not only bulked up, but also show much more definition. Batman has the equivalent of a 30-inch waist, 57-inch chest and 27-inch biceps. "If he was your height," Pope told me, holding up Wolverine, "he would have 32-inch biceps." Larger, that is, than any bodybuilder in history.

15   Now let it be said that measuring the styrene hamstrings of G.I. Joe does not represent 20th-century science at its most glorious. But Pope says it's a way to get at what he calls "evolving American cultural ideals of male body image." Those ideals, he maintains, create "cultural expectations" that may contribute to body-image disorders in men. "People misinterpreted our findings to assume that playing with toys, in and of itself, caused kids to develop into neurotic people as they grew up who abused anabolic steroids," Pope said. "Of course that was not our conclusion. We simply chose the toys because they were symptomatic of what we think is a much more general trend in our society."

16   Leaving such extreme pathology aside, the point remains that a boy's body image is shaped, if not determined, by the cruelest, most unforgiving and meanest group of judges imaginable: other boys. And even if you outgrow, physically and emotionally, the body image that oppressed you as an adolescent, it stays with you in adult life as a kind of subdermal emotional skin that can never be shed, only incorporated into the larger person you try to become. I think that's what Garry Trudeau, the formerly small cartoonist, had in mind when he described life as a tall adult as that of a "recovering short person."

17   It was during his sophomore year, getting "the daylights pounded out of him" in wrestling and gaining even more weight, that Alexander began what he calls, with justification, his "drastic transformation." He started by losing 30 pounds in one month. For a time, he consumed only 900 calories a day, and ultimately got down to 152 pounds. He began to lift weights seriously, every day for three months straight. He started to read magazines like *Flex* and *Men's Fitness*. He briefly dabbled with muscle-building supplements like creatine. He got buff, and then beyond buff.

18   By the time his junior year in high school began, Alexander had packaged his old self in a phenomenally new body, and it has had the desired effect. "My quality of social life changed dramatically when I changed my image," he said. He still maintained friendships with the guys in the computer lab, still programmed, still played Quake with dozens of others. But he worked out at the gym at least five times a week. He shifted his diet to heavy protein. He pushed himself to lift ever-heavier

weights. Until an injury curtailed his season, he brought new strength to his wrestling. Still, he wasn't satisfied. When I asked him if he ever felt tempted to try steroids during his effort to remake his physical image, he denied using them, and I believe him. But he wasn't coy about the temptation.

19 "When someone offers you a shortcut," he replied, "and it's a shortcut you want so bad, you're willing to ignore what it might be doing to your insides. I wanted to look better. Who cares if it's going to clog up my kidneys? Who cares if it'll destroy my liver? There was so much peer pressure that I didn't care."

20 Alexander was especially pleased by the good shape he was in—although he didn't care for aerobics, his resting heart rate was low, he ran a mile under six minutes and seemed to have boundless energy. But fitness was only part of what he was after. As he put it: "No one's looking for a natural look, of being thin and in shape. It's more of looking toward a level beyond that." He added that "guys who work out, especially guys who have six-packs and are really cut up, are the ones girls go after."

21 To be honest, I was a little dubious about this until I spoke with an admittedly unscientific sampling of teen-age girls. It turned out that they not only agreed with the sentiment, but also spoke the same lingo. "If you're going swimming or something like that, girls like the stomach best," said Elizabeth, a 14-year-old. "Girls like it if they have a six-pack, or if they're really ripped, as they say. That's the most important thing. And arms too."

22 "But not too much," added her friend Kate, also 14. "You don't like it if the muscles are too huge."

23 "It changes your perspective on them if they have a flabby stomach," Elizabeth continued. "And the chest is important too."

24 After Alexander finished his workout that hot July day, we stopped to get something to drink at the gym's cafe. "I feel pretty good right now," Alexander admitted, "and I was furious when I went in there." It turned out that the night before, he had a conversation with a girl that took a decidedly unsatisfying turn at the end.

25 At a time when the collective amount of American body fat is enough to stretch the jaws of Skip Pope's calipers from coast to coast, when so many adults amble about like fatted calves and so many children are little more than couch potatoes in training, it's hard to find fault with disciplined, drug-free efforts by teen-age boys to add a bit of muscle; weight lifting is not a sport with shortcuts, and it has become an essential adjunct to contemporary athletic performance. But there is a psychological side to all this heavy lifting that may be as unhealthy and undermining on the inside as it seems fit on the outside. And it resides not in that telltale mirror, but in how we see ourselves.

26 "I look in the mirror and I don't see what other people see," Alexander told me. "I look in the mirror, and I see my flaws. People go, 'Oh, you're narcissistic.' I go, 'No, I was looking at how uneven my pecs are,' although I know that in reality, they're, like, a nanometer off. And I have three friends who do exactly the same thing. They look and they go, 'Look how uneven I am, man!' And I go: 'What are you talking about! They look pretty even to me.' It's not narcissism—it's lack of self-esteem."

27   I'm not so worried about kids like Alexander—he clearly has demonstrated both the discipline to remake his appearance and the psychological distance not to take it, or himself, too seriously. But there will be many other boys out there who cannot hope to match the impossibly raised bar of idealized male body image without resorting to the physically corrosive effects of steroids or the psychologically corrosive effects of self-doubt. Either way, the majority of boys will be diminished by chasing after the golden few.

28   Moreover, this male preoccupation with appearance seems to herald a dubious, regressive form of equality—now boys can become as psychologically and physically debilitated by body-image concerns as girls have been for decades. After all, this vast expenditure of teen-age male energy, both psychic and kinetic, is based on the premise that members of the opposite sex are attracted to a retro, rough-hewn, muscular look, and it's a premise that psychologists who study boys have noticed, too. "While girls and women say one thing, some of them continue to do another," Pollack says. "Some of them are still intrigued by the old male images, and are attracted to them."

29   Because he's a perceptive kid, Alexander recognizes how feckless, how disturbing, how crazy this all is. "I tell you, it's definitely distressing," he said, "the fact that as much as girls get this anorexic thing and they're going through these image things with dolls and stuff, guys are definitely doing the same." True, he admitted, his social life has never been better. "But in a way it depresses me," he said, before heading off to a party, "that I had to do this for people to get to know me."

QUESTIONS FOR ANALYSIS AND DISCUSSION

1. Alexander states that he suffered from cruel comments about his weight for most of his life. Even his parents would make comments about his weight. What motivated Alexander to change his physique? Is it an extreme response, or a reasonable one? Does Alexander think he is better off now? Does Hall? Explain.
2. Alexander comments that he had an epiphany in a hotel room when he was 15: "I realized that nobody was giving me a chance to find out who I was because of the way I looked." What is ironic about this statement? Is the "ripped" Alexander the real person? Explain.
3. In your opinion, do the "jacked-up" muscles on action figures influence the way boys feel about their own bodies? If possible, go to a toy store or online and examine some of these figures. Do they reflect, as Pope claims, "evolving American cultural ideals of male body image"?
4. What cultural messages tell boys that steroid use is permissible? Describe some of the ways children receive these messages.
5. Analyze the author's use of statistics, facts, and supporting information to reinforce the points he makes in his essay. Do his conclusions seem reasonable based on the data he cites? Why or why not?

READING THE VISUAL
NEDA Ad and BOD Ad

Adolescence can be a period of great self-consciousness and insecurity. Some young people—especially teenage girls—may suffer from eating disorders such as anorexia nervosa or bulimia due to distorted self-perception. The person they see in the mirror is drastically different from physical reality. In 2004, the National Eating Disorders Association (NEDA) launched the "Get Real" awareness campaign to portray how distorted the self-image of someone suffering from an eating disorder can be. The campaign ran ads in several fashion and popular magazines, including *InStyle* and *People*. This print ad was created for NEDA by Porter Novelli, a public relations firm known for health care promotional campaigns.

The second ad is for BOD body spray, a popular fragrance by Parfums de Coeur, only one of several that have hit the market in the last two years. The sprays, aimed at teens, present the wearer as a desirable sex object, wanted for his "BOD." Rather than depicting real people, the ad features idealized drawings of three attractive women around a single chiseled man in the center. Fragrance "flavors" include "Rock Hard" and "Really Ripped Abs."

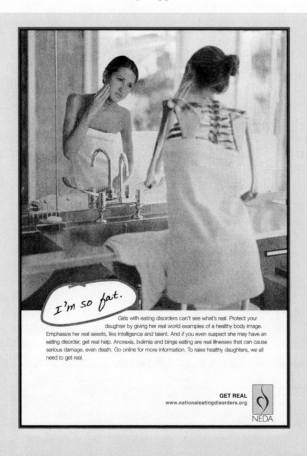

I'm so fat.

Girls with eating disorders can't see what's real. Protect your daughter by giving her real world examples of a healthy body image. Emphasize her real assets, like intelligence and talent. And if you even suspect she may have an eating disorder, get real help. Anorexia, bulimia and binge eating are real illnesses that can cause serious damage, even death. Go online for more information. To raise healthy daughters, we all need to get real.

GET REAL
www.nationaleatingdisorders.org

NEDA

QUESTIONS FOR ANALYSIS AND DISCUSSION

1. These two ads are both aimed at teens. What does each assume about the viewer? How does each ad use social constructions of body image to make its point? Explain.
2. What social and cultural influence could the "BOD" ad have on young men? Do you think that teens project that they will look like the man in the ad if they use the product?
3. Both of these ads use exaggerated depictions of the body to get their point across. Evaluate each depiction and how it tries to reach its young audience.
4. If you were leafing through a magazine and saw either one of these ads, would you stop to read or examine it? What catches your eye? How long do you think you would spend looking at the ad? Longer than average, or less?
5. What is happening in the NEDA photo? What is the young woman thinking? What does she see, and what do we see?

What I Think About the Fashion World
Liz Jones

Are thin models part of a fashion conspiracy, or are they merely reflective of what the public wants to see? For many young women, the perfect beauty is defined by fashion models: tall, thin, long limbed, and with sculpted features. In a culture in which women are often measured by how they look, the pressure to be thin can be great. In this article, Liz Jones gives her perspective on the fashion industry's influence on female body image.

Jones is the former editor of the British edition of *Marie Claire*, a women's fashion magazine. While editor of *Marie Claire*, she shocked the fashion world by featuring two covers, one featuring a thin Pamela Anderson and one with a voluptuous Sophie Dahl, then a size 12. Many fashion critics spoke out against Jones for using the magazine to "forward her own agenda," but consumers voted with their pocketbooks by buying more issues with the Dahl cover. This article was first published in *YOU* magazine, a supplement of *The London Daily Mail*, on April 15, 2001. Jones is currently the fashion editor for the *Daily Mail*.

BEFORE YOU READ

Try to picture your version of the perfect female body. What does it look like? Is your image influenced by outside forces, such as the media, your gender, or your age? How do real women you know compare to the image in your mind?

AS YOU READ

In your opinion, is the fashion industry's use of extremely thin models harmful? In your opinion, has mass media created unrealistic expectations of beauty? Explain.

1 For four weeks last month I sat in the front row of catwalk shows in London, Milan, Paris and New York watching painfully thin models walking up and down inches from my nose.

2 Kate Moss, the original "superwaif," was looking positively curvaceous compared to the current bunch of underweight teenagers.

3 For those used to the fashion industry there was nothing unusual about the shows at all. But for me it was the end; it was then that I decided to resign as editor of *Marie Claire* magazine.

4 I had reached the point where I had simply had enough of working in an industry that pretends to support women while it bombards them with impossible images of perfection day after day, undermining their self-confidence, their health and hard-earned cash.

5   My decision to quit was partly precipitated by the failure of a campaign I started a year ago to encourage magazines, designers and advertisers to use models with more realistic, representative body images. Then I could not have anticipated the extraordinarily hostile reaction to my fairly innocuous suggestions from fellow editors and designers. A year later I have come to realize the sheer terrorism of the fashion industry and accept that, alone, I cannot change things.

6   But in the spring last year I was full of optimism that we could change. I believed wholeheartedly that we could stop magazines and advertisers using underweight girls as fashion icons. I had already banned diets and slimming advice from our pages but after meeting Gisele, the Brazilian supermodel credited with bringing "curves to the catwalk," and discovering that she is a tiny size 8, I decided to challenge the status quo.

7   We decided to publish two covers for the same edition—one featuring Sophie Dahl, a size 12; the other, Pamela Anderson, a minute size 6—and we asked readers to choose between the skinny, cosmetically enhanced "perfection," or a more attainable, but still very beautiful curvy woman. Sophie Dahl won by an overwhelming majority.

8   But you would think that we had declared war. The reaction was staggering. Newspapers, radio and TV stations were largely behind us. They welcomed the opportunity to demystify the closed and cliquey world of fashion. Our covers were in the national press for weeks—even making headlines in the *New York Post*. I had requests from universities here and abroad wanting to include our experiment in their college courses. Documentaries were made in the US and Germany. The response from readers was unprecedented. We received 4,000 letters in two weeks.

9   However, the very people from whom I had expected the most support—my fellow female editors—were unanimous in their disapproval.

10   I was invited to speak at the Body Image Summit set up by Tessa Jowell, Minister for Women, in June 2000 to debate the influence of media images on rising problems of anorexia and bulimia among women. One suggestion was that a group—consisting of editors, designers, young women readers and professionals who treat women with eating disorders—should get together on a regular basis to monitor the industry, bring in guidelines on using girls under a certain body size and weight and discuss ways the industry could evolve. My job was to gather these people: not one single other editor agreed to take part.

11   Instead most of them were hostile and aggressive. Jo Elvin, then editor of *New Woman*, accused *Marie Claire* of "discriminating against thin women." (As if there aren't enough role models in the media for thinness, from Jennifer Aniston to Gwyneth Paltrow to American supermodel Maggie Rizer.) Another fashion editor made the point that there had always been skinny women—look at Twiggy, for example. Jasper Conran absurdly suggested we should be looking at obesity as a serious health problem instead of anorexia and bulimia. I didn't bother to point out that people with obesity were not usually put on magazine covers as fashion icons.

12   The next day, after the summit, I received a fax, signed by nearly all the other editors of women's magazines and some model agencies, stating that they would not be following any initiative to expand the types of women featured in their

magazines—one of the topics up for discussion at the summit was how to introduce more black and Asian women onto the pages of Britain's glossies.

13   When I read the list of names, I felt like giving up the fight there and then. I was isolated, sickened to my stomach that something so positive had been turned into a petty catfight by women I respected and admired. They were my peers, friends and colleagues I sat next to in the front row of the fashion shows. They were also the most important, influential group of women in the business, the only people who could change the fashion and beauty industry. Why were they so reluctant to even think about change?

14   Like me, they had sat at the summit while a group of teenage girls, black, Asian and white, some fat, some thin, had berated us all for what we were doing to their lives. I had found it moving to listen to these young women, brave enough to come and talk in front of all these scary high profile people. Anyway, to me, it made good business sense to listen to them and address their concerns: why alienate your readers? I could see those teenagers turning away from magazines because we seemed hopelessly outmoded, old fashioned, unattainable. But I was clearly alone.

15   The other editors seemed to revel in the chance to counter attack. Alexandra Shulman, editor of *Vogue*, denounced the whole campaign as a promotional tool for *Marie Claire* and said that suggestions of an agreement to set up a self-regulatory body within the industry was "totally out of order." Debbie Bee, then editor of *Nova*—a supposedly cutting edge fashion magazine for young women—asserted in her editorial the following month that magazines didn't cause anorexia as readers were intelligent enough to differentiate between an idealized model and real life.

16   Fiona McIntosh, editor of *Elle*, published a cover picture of Calista Flockhart with the caption, "I'm thin, so what?" She accused me of "betraying the editors' code." Frankly, I didn't even know there was a code; only one, surely, to put your readers first.

17   Some model agencies blacklisted the magazine. Storm, who represents Sophie Dahl and who you would have thought would have been happy that one of their models was being held up as an example of healthy gorgeousness, told us that we could no longer book any of their girls. Several publicists from Hollywood, reacting both to the cover and a feature called "Lollipop ladies" about women in Hollywood whose heads are too big for their tiny bodies, wrote to me saying their stars would not be gracing our covers—ever.

18   I had clearly put my head too far above the parapet. I realized that far from being the influential trendsetters I had thought, magazine editors are more often ruled by fear—and advertisers. No one feels that they can afford to be different. They are happy to settle, instead, for free handbags and relentless glamour.

19   To be honest, it would have been very easy to give up then. Every time the contacts of a fashion shoot landed on my desk with a model whose ribs showed, whose bony shoulders and collar bone could have cut glass, whose legs were like sticks, we could have published them anyway and said, "oh well, we tried." But we didn't. We threw them out, set up a reshoot, and eventually, slowly, agencies started to take us seriously and would only send girls with curves in all the right places.

20   I cannot deny the campaign got the magazine talked and written about. The choice of covers got the readers involved and made them have a little bit of power

for a change; they got to choose who they wanted on the cover. The Sophie Dahl cover started to sell out, and readers would phone me, frantic, saying, "I could only buy the Pamela Anderson cover, but I want you to register my vote for Sophie." It could never have been a scientific exercise—subscribers to the magazine had to take pot luck; but still they would phone up saying, "No, I wanted Sophie!"

21 But I was dismayed by accusations that this was just another way to boost sales. I suffered from anorexia from the age of 11 until my late twenties and understand first hand the damaging effect of a daily diet of unrealistically tiny role models gracing the pages of the magazines that I was addicted to. Although it did not cause my illness, the images definitely perpetuated the hatred I had for my own body.

22 I agree with Debbie Bee of *Nova* that young women are intelligent enough to be able to tell the difference between a model and real life but the effects are often subliminal. One piece of research we did at *Marie Claire* was to ask a group of intelligent professional women about their bodies, then let them browse a selection of magazines for an hour, before asking them again. Their self-esteem had plummeted.

23 Never before have we been bombarded with so many images of perfection: more and more glossies on the shelves, web sites, digital satellite channels, more and more channels showing music videos 24 hours a day. New technology is also removing the images we see of women even further from reality. Just try finding a cover on the shelves this month where the star has not had her spots removed, the dark circles under her eyes eradicated, the wrinkles smoothed and her waist trimmed. It is common practice nowadays to "stretch" women whose legs aren't long enough. One men's magazine currently on the shelves, so the industry gossip has it, has put one star's head on another woman's body—apparently, her original breasts weren't "spherical enough."

24 So women have been conditioned to go to the gym and diet, or if they don't, to feel guilty about it, but that still won't achieve "cover girl" perfection because you can't be airbrushed in real life. I've seen the models close up: believe me, lots of them have varicose veins, spots, appendectomy scars and, yes, cellulite. Only the 16 year olds don't have fine lines.

25 So did I achieve anything with my campaign? I believe so. One newspaper conducted a survey of high street and designer shops and proved how women over size 12 were not being catered for. Stores are now providing a broader range of sizes.

26 In the subsequent issue, we published naked pictures of eight ordinary women, and asked readers to fill in a questionnaire telling us honestly how they feel about the women in the photographs, and about their own bodies. Interestingly, of the respondents so far, all the women say their boyfriends find the size 16 woman the most attractive. The results will be made into a Channel 4 documentary in the autumn.

27 In the next issue, my final edition as editor, we have on our cover three young women, all a size 12, curvy, imperfect, but very beautiful all the same. On the shoot, it was apparent that Suzanne, Myleene and Kym from Hear'Say were all happy in their own skin. For now. On the Popstars[1] program, Nasty Nigel had told the girls

---

[1]The British equivalent to the television program "American Idol."

they should go on a diet. "Christmas is over," he said to Kym, "but the goose is still fat." How long before the girls start feeling paranoid about their bodies, under the constant pressure of fame, is anybody's guess.

28   In Britain an estimated 60,000 people, most of them young women, suffer from eating disorders while far greater numbers have an unhealthy relationship with food. Many of them take up smoking or eat diet pills to keep their weight below a certain level. Of all psychiatric disorders, anorexia has the most fatalities—it is very hard to recover from. I refuse to conform to an industry that could, literally, kill.

29   It's time for the industry—the photographers, the editors, the casting directors, designers and the advertisers—to wake up and allow women to just be themselves. From the phone calls and letters I received at *Marie Claire*, I know that women are fed up with feeling needlessly bad about their wobbly bits.

30   I only hope that my successor listens to them.

QUESTIONS FOR ANALYSIS AND DISCUSSION

1. By running the two covers, Jones sought to discover whether women wanted perfection and aspiration or something more realistic and attainable. What did sales of the June 2000 cover reveal? Based on your own observations, how do you think American women would have reacted to the same experiment?

2. How did other fashion magazine editors react to Jones's *Marie Claire* covers? What do you think their reaction reveals about the fashion industry?

3. Debbie Bee of *Nova*, another British fashion magazine, argues that young women are "intelligent enough to be able to tell the difference between a model and real life." How does Jones test this theory? What does she discover?

4. Evaluate how well Jones supports her viewpoint in this essay. Does she provide supporting evidence? Is she biased? Does she provide a balanced perspective, or does she slant her data? Explain.

5. Jones is a former editor for a major fashion magazine. Does the fact that she held this position and was willing to risk her career for this issue influence your opinion of her essay or her points? Why or why not?

Men's Magazines and Gender Construction
David Gauntlett

The last decade has witnessed an explosion of magazines for men—from *FHM* and *Maxim*, to *Men's Health* and *Stuff*. Most women's fashion and lifestyle magazines feature female fashion models or celebrities. Interestingly, so do the covers of men's magazines—which often sport scantily clad young women. What messages do these magazines project about women, and how do they influence men's personal identities and how they relate to the opposite sex? The next piece is an excerpt from a media studies text by British lecturer David Gauntlett that explores the different types of masculinities promoted by various men's magazines and assesses their potential impact. Because the men's magazine trend is an export from Great Britain, Gauntlett is in a unique position to evaluate the medium from both sides of the Atlantic.

Gauntlett is a lecturer at the Institute of Communications Studies at the University of Leeds in England. He is the author of several books on the media, including *TV Living* (1999) and *Web.Studies* (2000). He also maintains a popular website on media theory, gender and identity, http://www.theory.org.uk. The following article is an excerpt from his most recent book, *Media, Gender, and Identity, An Introduction* (2005).

BEFORE YOU READ

What magazines do you enjoy reading? Are they geared toward a male or female audience? Why do you read them? Do they help you figure out who you are and how you relate to your friends, family, and significant others?

AS YOU READ

Have you ever considered the way a magazine is written as gendered—that is, that the language and style the writers use is geared to a male or female audience? Does knowing this change your view of these magazines? Why or why not?

1   The men's magazine market is relatively new. It's not that men never bought magazines in the past, [but most] were dedicated to a particular hobby or interest. There were also the "top shelf" pornography magazines such as *Playboy*, *Penthouse*, and *Men Only*. But there was not really a general "men's interests" magazine to parallel the numerous women's titles. Publishers were aware of the gap in the market but felt that men would not want to read general "lifestyle" material—glossy magazines were seen as rather feminine products, and "real men" didn't need a magazine to tell them how to live.

2   The men's market as we know it today really took off with the launch of *Loaded* in 1994. Loaded is widely recognized as the cornerstone of the modern British "lad" culture, and for years now UK journalists have regularly used "*Loaded* reader" as shorthand for a kind of twenty-something, beer-drinking, football loving, sex-obsessed male stereotype. However, sales of the less macho *FHM (For Him Magazine)* overtook those of *Loaded* in 1996, and it now sells almost twice as many copies each month. Further titles, *Maxim* and *Men's Health*, were launched in 1995, and both sold well. Since then, publishers have sought to make the men's market even bigger and broader, with varying degrees of success. Overall, though, the

expansion of this area has been incredible, and unusually, these British inventions have crossed the Atlantic: *Maxim* and *FHM* have broken open a significant market for young men's lifestyle magazines in the USA.

3   All of the men's lifestyle magazines cover aspects of men's lives today, which previous literature for men (the hobby and special-interest magazines) did not discuss. They all include reviews of films, music, video games and books (except *Men's Health*). But the magazines otherwise differ quite a lot: *Loaded* celebrates watching football with a few beers for example, but the *Men's Health* reader would forgo the drink, and play the game himself. [And] *FHM* encourages quality sex.

4   The new men's magazines have been given predictably rough treatment by some cultural critics. Pro-feminist and left-wing writers often seem to see the provocative picture of a scantily-clad woman on the cover and assume that the meaning of the entire magazine can be "read off" from that image alone—it's a sexist repositioning of soft-porn, and that's all there is to be said. Even those who glance inside are quick to judge. For example, Andrew Sullivan (2000) writing in the *New Republic*, dismisses contemporary men's magazines as plain "dumb." He has evidence from one issue of *Maxim*:

> The June issue features a primer of penis size ("How It's Really Hangin") and a moronic guide to becoming a millionaire (Rule #4: "Ditch your loser friends").

5   Sullivan's smug rejection of these features ignores the humor and self-consciousness that riddle these magazines. Articles such as the one on becoming

a millionaire are meant to be read as humorous, jokily aspirational but fundamentally silly; to sneer at the quality of their advice is to miss the point. Meanwhile, it would be wrong to see the penis article as a restatement of phallic dominance; on the contrary, surely a very un-macho cloud of insecurity hangs over the male audience for articles on penis size. It is difficult to imagine a masculine archetype like Clint Eastwood settling down to study *Maxim*'s guide to how he measures up in the trouser department.

6   The most perceptive and sensitive analysis of the new men's magazines and their readers has been produced by the research team of Peter Jackson, Nate Stevenson and Kate Brooks. These researchers thankfully do not assume a moral superiority to the magazines or their readers and do not try to "prove" that that the magazines are mere trash, enjoyed by a large audience of mindless fools. Instead, they take the huge growth of men's magazines to be a cultural phenomenon worthy of serious consideration, which should be able to tell us something about men and masculinity today. In the following sections I will discuss some of the points made by Jackson, Stevenson and Brooks, while also making my own argument that the magazines really show men to be insecure and confused in the modern world, and seeking help and reassurance even if this is (slightly) suppressed by a veneer of irony and heterosexual lust.

7   Jackson et al. rightly note that men's magazines usually address the reader as a "friend," of the same status as the magazine journalists themselves. The tone is generally "friendly and ironic." The irony is uses as a kind of defensive shield: the writers anticipate that many men may reject serious articles on relationships, or advice about sex, health or cooking, and so douse their pieces with humor, silliness, and irony to "sweeten the pill." This use of irony is no secret. As publishers launched *FHM* in South Africa, their marketing blurb proudly explained:

> Before FHM, conventional wisdom had it that women read magazines from an introspective point of view, seeking help and advice for, and about, themselves. Men on the other hand, read magazines about things like sports, travel, science, business, and cars. FHM realizes that men will read magazines about themselves if you give them the information in the right context: irreverent, humorous, and never taking itself too seriously. The articles in FHM, although highly informative, are written tongue-in-cheek. The fashion is accessible, the advice humorous and empathetic. (www.natmags.com, 1999)

8   Jackson et al. note that the magazines "are careful to avoid talking down to their readers, and their focus group interviews confirm that men like to feel that they are flicking through the magazines and not taking them too seriously, which they believe is in contrast to women who read the magazine advice 'religiously.'" In fact, research on female magazine readers indicates that they too like to treat their magazines lightly and with little commitment, but the fact remains that male readers seem to be extremely wary of being told what to do—they like to feel they know best already—which is why humor and irony have to be deployed.

9   The fact that humor and irony is required in the magazines does not, of course, show that today's men do not "really" want to read articles and advice about relationships,

sex, health or other "personal" matters. After all, the magazines could easily forget about these areas altogether and focus on cars and guns and white-water rafting. So we have to conclude that many men *want* articles like this, but do not want others—or even perhaps themselves—to think that they *need* them. The humor of the lifestyle articles means that they can be read "for a laugh" although, I would argue, men are at the same time quietly curious to pick up information about relationships and sex, and what is considered good or bad practice in these areas. It's difficult to prove this assertion, by definition, because men are not eager to admit this curiosity.

10   Irony provides a "protective layer," then, between lifestyle information and the readers, so that men don't have to feel patronized or inadequate. But irony has other functions too. Jackson et al. assert that one of these is "to subvert political critique"—in other words, feminists or others who criticize the contents of the magazines can be said to be "missing the joke," making their complaints redundant. This is true, but I would say that irony is not used in order to provide a "get out clause" against critics. Although the sexism of some of the less popular magazines can sometimes appear genuine, in *FHM* and its imitators, I would say that it is the irony which is genuine. The *FHM* writer, and their projected reader, do actually know that women are as good as men, or better; the put-downs of women—such as jokey comments about their supposed incompetence with technology—are knowingly ridiculous, based on the assumptions that it's silly to be sexist (and therefore is funny, in a silly way), and that men are usually just as rubbish as women.

11   The idea that the underlying assumptions of these magazines are more anti-sexist than sexist may not always be true, of course, and is optimistic; and it is always possible for readers to read the sexist jokes literally. But I would say that the "sexist jokiness" of *FHM* is based on thoroughly non-sexist assumptions—the intended laugh, more often than not, is about the silliness of being sexist, rather than actual sexism because, in the world of *FHM*, men are aware, however quietly embarrassedly, that it's only fair to treat women and men as equals in the modern world, and that sexism is idiotic.

12   Having said that, it has to be admitted that many *FHM* readers may be sexist, in one way or another, and their reading of *FHM* may not challenge their sexism and many indeed support it. That's sadly true. At the same time, though, *FHM* consistently teaches men to treat their girlfriends nicely, to try to be considerate, and to give satisfaction, both sexually and in more general terms. It also teaches men various domestic skills—even if the justification is that it will "impress your lady." You could even say that *FHM*'s general project is to create a man who is competent in the home and kitchen, skilled in the bedroom, not overly dependent on his partner, healthy, interested in travel, able to buy his own fashionable clothes, a good laugh and a pleasure to live with. Based on this list, we have the kind of man that feminists would surely prefer to have around. The pictures of beautiful members of the opposite sex wearing little clothing, and the emphasis on sex rather than relationships, don't fit within this thesis, of course, although we can at least point out that several women's magazines contain that same kind of material today too.

Fear of Intimacy?

13   Another theme in the arguments of Jackson, Stevenson and Brooks is the idea that men's magazines reflect a "fear" of intimacy or commitment. They say that the magazines which emerged in the 1990s were focused—amongst other things—on "obsessive forms of independence (read: fear of commitment and connection)" and are a "celebration of autonomy and a fear of dependence." Later we are again told that they are "a desperate defense of masculine independence."

14   This all makes being independent sound like a psychotic tendency, and some kind of macho neurosis. But women's magazines filled hundreds of pages, over *years*, telling women how to be independent, and it's a message they still carry. And that's fine: the message that you shouldn't depend on a partner for your happiness is widely seen as being a very good one. Being a "dependent" person is not ideal, and if we think that's true for women, it's true for men too. Calling it a "fear of dependence" is Jackson et al.'s sneaky way of making it sound like a product of dumb macho psychology, but the received wisdom from women's magazines and self-help books is that being wary of becoming dependent is eminently sensible. We can also note that feminism used to criticize men for being too dependent on their female partners, sapping women's energies by selfishly expecting women to tend to their emotional, sexual and domestic needs. That was a valid criticism. But now if we criticize men for being maddeningly independent—as if men are selfishly *refusing* to rely on women for emotional support—it starts to get a bit silly.

15   To be fair, though, although Jackson et al. don't exactly explain *why* they view the promotion of independence as a bad thing in men's magazines, we can infer that they are concerned that the magazines encourage men to be *too* self-contained—the kind of man who couldn't express himself fully within a relationship, perhaps, and who was unable to give love and share his life with someone. We can agree that that would not be good; but do the magazines really encourage men to be excessively insular and unexpressive? Not really. The "new" feature of many of the top men's magazines, as we've noted, is that they are full of relationship tips, from *FHM* explaining the difference between physical lust and emotional attachment to a reader concerned that his nice girlfriend isn't his ideal physical type (August 2001), *Maxim* advising on tactful ways to impress a woman (July 2001), and *Men's Health* discussing how to keep a partner interested (August 2001), to all of these magazines offering sex advice and asking famous females what makes them happy in a relationship. There can be no escape from these magazines' emphasis on being a decent, considerate and attentive boyfriend.

16   The enormously successful *Maxim* does sometimes seem to embrace the idea that women are eager to "trap" men into a long-term relationship or marriage, and this, of course, is an irritating slice of sexism. The view that a person should not be tied too hastily into an imperfect relationship, however, especially when young, is a perfectly reasonable one. Without wanting to defend the dim sexism of some articles in *Maxim*, the advice itself isn't terrible. And we can note that after feminists went to such lengths to argue that marriage was a patriarchal system which

trapped women into an unhappy life of exploitation and lack of freedom, it seems (again) a bit odd for us to start complaining that men's magazines are not in favour of marriage or similar tight commitments.

17   In general, there does not seem to be evidence for a "fear of intimacy" in men's magazines; there is a *fear of anything that might stop you enjoying yourself*, which includes boring mates, the police, illnesses and partners that do things that prevent you from having a good time. Positive relationships are not to be feared, though, and the all-powerful *FHM*, as we've said, is full of advice about how to keep your girlfriend happy.

Men and Women as Clear and Opposite Identities

18   Finally, Jackson et al. argue that in men's magazines, "men and women are [represented as] polar opposites in terms of their sexual identities and desires," and suggest that the magazines' model of "new lad" masculinity "acts as a means of enforcing boundaries between men and women." They go on to say:

> The accompanying fear seems to be that, unless men and women are rigidly rendered apart, this would introduce a small grain of uncertainty within the representation of masculine identity, thereby threatening to undermine it all together. . . . "New laddism," as we have seen, leaves no room for doubt, questioning, ambiguity or uncertainty.

Again, this looks like quite a good argument on paper, but doesn't match up with the actual content of the magazines—especially as these points are made in relation to *FHM* in particular. As I have already argued and illustrated, the magazines do *not* assume that their readers have a fixed and ready-to-wear masculine identity—if they did, they would not fill so many pages with advice on how to achieve some basic competences in life. *FHM* in particular is quietly brimming with the "doubt, questioning, ambiguity [and] uncertainty" which Jackson et al. say is absent. In the late 1990s, when Jackson et al. were looking at the magazines, even the *covers* of *FHM* were riddled with anxiety: "Fat? Boring? Crap in bed? Does this sound familiar to anyone?" (February 1998), "Look at the state of you!" (February 1998), "Am I gay?" (February 1999), "Is your love life just a hollow sham?" (April 1999), "Are you going mental?" (April 1999), and "Does your penis horrify women?" (July 1999) are typical examples.

19   As for the idea that women and men are shown to be "polar opposites" sexually—Jackson et al. note an implication in a few articles that while men are perennially eager for sex, women "would always prefer a candle-lit bath"—this doesn't apply to most articles in most of the magazines, which generally assume that women will be eager and willing partners in sexual activities—especially if men deploy the pleasurable techniques suggested. Meanwhile, it's true that the magazines do often joke about general supposed "differences" between women and men, although this can be at the expense of either sex. I would also repeat my suggestion that the magazines don't *really* think that the differences are fundamental, and that the "sexist jokiness" is based on an understanding that men and women are not

very different *really*—an idea underlined by the fact that men's and women's magazines are becoming increasingly similar in very obvious ways.

In general it seems most appropriate to see men's magazines as reflecting a frequently imperfect attempt to find positions for the ideas of "women" and "men" in a world where it's pretty obvious that the sexes are much more the same than they are different. The magazines sometimes discuss men and women as if they were different species, but this is a way of making sense of reality, rather than reality itself, and readers (hopefully) understand this.

Summary

20   In this discussion I have argued against the view that men's lifestyle magazines represent a reassertion of old-fashioned masculine values, or a "backlash" against feminism. While certain pieces in the magazines might support such an argument, this is not their primary purpose or selling point. Instead, I have suggested, their existence and popularity shows men rather insecurely trying to find their place in the modern world, seeking help regarding how to behave in relationships, and advice on how to earn the attention, love and respect of women and the friendship of other men. At the same time, the magazines may raise some anxieties—about fitness of the body, say, or whether the reader is sufficiently "one of the boys." The discourses of masculinity which the magazines help to circulate can therefore, unsurprisingly, be both enabling and constraining. Nevertheless, the playfulness of the magazines and their (usually) cheerful, liberal attitude to most things—apart from the occasional nasty sting of homophobia—suggests that some fluidity of identities is invited. Furthermore, the humour and irony found throughout these publications doesn't hide a strong macho agenda, but conceals the nervousness of boys who might prefer life to be simpler, but are doing their best to face up to modern realities anyway.

QUESTIONS FOR ANALYSIS AND DISCUSSION ──────

1. What does the popularity of men's magazines tell us about men and masculinity today? Why are these magazines so popular? Do you think they would have found a market if they had been introduced 20 or 30 years ago? Why or why not?
2. Why do many articles in men's magazines assume an ironic or sarcastic tone? Explain.
3. In paragraph 6, Gauntlett argues that men's "magazines really show men to be insecure and confused in the modern world." How well does he defend his argument? Do you agree with his view?
4. What differences exist between how men and women read magazines? Why is understanding these differences important to how they are marketed?
5. How are men's magazines helping to define men's personal self-image and how they relate to women and the world today? Explain.

6. Gauntlett argues, "I would say that the 'sexist jokiness' of *FHM* is based on thoroughly non-sexist assumptions—the intended laugh, more often than not, is about the silliness of being sexist, rather than actual sexism because, in the world of *FHM*, men are aware, however quietly embarrassedly, that it's only fair to treat women and men as equals in the modern world, and that sexism is idiotic." What is the "world" of *FHM*? Do you think that readers of this magazine would agree with Gauntlett's conclusion?

In the Combat Zone
Leslie Marmon Silko

Safety experts warn women not to walk alone at night, to park where it is well-lit, and to avoid areas that could conceal muggers or rapists. Self-defense classes for women stress avoidance tactics rather than ways to confront violence actively. This approach, says Leslie Marmon Silko, creates a cultural consciousness of women as victims and targets. In this essay, Silko relates how her childhood hunting experiences helped empower her in a society that tends to view women as prey.

A recipient of a MacArthur Foundation Fellowship, Silko is one of America's best-known Native American writers. A former professor of English and creative writing, she is the author of many short stories, essays, poetry, plays, articles, and books, including *Almanac of the Dead* (1991) and *Gardens in the Dunes* (1999).

BEFORE YOU READ ────────────────

Have you ever found yourself planning your activities based on personal safety? For example, did you do without something because you were afraid of going to the store at night by yourself? Or have you skipped taking a shortcut when it was dark out? If not, why don't you fear these situations?

AS YOU READ ────────────────

Note Silko's references to hunting throughout the essay. How does the theme of hunting unify the piece?

1 Women seldom discuss our wariness or the precautions we take after dark each time we leave the apartment, car, or office to go on the most brief errand. We take for granted that we are targeted as easy prey by muggers, rapists, and serial killers. This is our lot as women in the United States. We try to avoid going anywhere alone after dark, although economic necessity sends women out night after night.

We do what must be done, but always we are alert, on guard and ready. We have to be aware of persons walking on the sidewalk behind us; we have to pay attention to others who board an elevator we're on. We try to avoid all staircases and deserted parking garages when we are alone. Constant vigilance requires considerable energy and concentration seldom required of men.

2   I used to assume that most men were aware of this fact of women's lives, but I was wrong. They may notice our reluctance to drive at night to the convenience store alone, but they don't know or don't want to know the experience of a woman out alone at night. Men who have been in combat know the feeling of being a predator's target, but it is difficult for men to admit that we women live our entire lives in a combat zone. Men have the power to end violence against women in the home, but they feel helpless to protect women from violent strangers. Because men feel guilt and anger at their inability to shoulder responsibility for the safety of their wives, sisters, and daughters, we don't often discuss random acts of violence against women.

3   When we were children, my sisters and I used to go to Albuquerque with my father. Sometimes strangers would tell my father it was too bad that he had three girls and no sons. My father, who has always preferred the company of women, used to reply that he was glad to have girls and not boys, because he might not get along as well with boys. Furthermore, he'd say, "My girls can do anything your boys can do, and my girls can do it better." He had in mind, of course, shooting and hunting.

4   When I was six years old, my father took me along as he hunted deer; he showed me how to walk quietly, to move along and then to stop and listen carefully before taking another step. A year later, he traded a pistol for a little single shot .22 rifle just my size. He took me and my younger sisters down to the dump by the river and taught us how to shoot. We rummaged through the trash for bottles and glass jars; it was great fun to take aim at a pickle jar and watch it shatter. If the Rio San Jose had water running in it, we threw bottles for moving targets in the muddy current. My father told us that a .22 bullet can travel a mile, so we had to be careful where we aimed. The river was a good place because it was below the villages and away from the houses; the high clay riverbanks wouldn't let any bullets stray. Gun safety was drilled into us. We were cautioned about other children whose parents might not teach them properly; if we ever saw another child with a gun, we knew to get away. Guns were not toys. My father did not approve of BB guns because they were classified as toys. I had a .22 rifle when I was seven years old. If I felt like shooting, all I had to do was tell my parents where I was going, take my rifle and a box of 12 shells and go. I was never tempted to shoot at birds or animals because whatever was killed had to be eaten. Now, I realize how odd this must seem; a seven-year-old with a little .22 rifle and a box of ammunition, target shooting alone at the river. But that was how people lived at Laguna when I was growing up; children were given responsibility from an early age.

5   Laguna Pueblo people hunted deer for winter meat. When I was thirteen I carried George Pearl's saddle carbine, a .30–30, and hunted deer for the first time. When I was fourteen, I killed my first mule deer buck with one shot through the heart.

6   Guns were for target shooting and guns were for hunting, but also I knew that Grandma Lily carried a little purse gun with her whenever she drove alone to Albuquerque or Los Lunas. One night my mother and my grandmother were driving the

fifty miles from Albuquerque to Laguna down Route 66 when three men in a car tried to force my grandmother's car off the highway. Route 66 was not so heavily traveled as Interstate 40 is now, and there were many long stretches of highway where no other car passed for minutes on end. Payrolls at the Jackpile Uranium Mine were large in the 1950s, and my mother or my grandmother had to bring home thousands from the bank in Albuquerque to cash the miners' checks on paydays.

7   After that night, my father bought my mother a pink nickel-plated snub-nose .22 revolver with a white bone grip. Grandma Lily carried a tiny Beretta as black as her prayer book. As my sisters and I got older, my father taught us to handle and shoot handguns, revolvers mostly, because back then, semiautomatic pistols were not as reliable—they frequently jammed. I will never forget the day my father told us three girls that we never had to let a man hit us or terrorize us because no matter how big and strong the man was, a gun in our hand equalized all differences of size and strength.

8   Much has been written about violence in the home and spousal abuse. I wish to focus instead on violence from strangers toward women because this form of violence terrifies women more, despite the fact that most women are murdered by a spouse, relative, fellow employee, or next-door neighbor, not a stranger. Domestic violence kills many more women and children than strangers kill, but domestic violence also follows more predictable patterns and is more familiar—he comes home drunk and she knows what comes next. A good deal of the terror of a stranger's attack comes from its suddenness and unexpectedness. Attacks by strangers occur with enough frequency that battered women and children often cite their fears of such attacks as reasons for remaining in abusive domestic situations. They fear the violence they imagine strangers will inflict upon them more than they fear the abusive home. More than one feminist has pointed out that rapists and serial killers help keep the patriarchy in place.

9   An individual woman may be terrorized by her spouse, but women are not sufficiently terrorized that we avoid marriage. Yet many women I know, including myself, try to avoid going outside of their homes alone after dark. Big deal, you say; well yes, it is a big deal since most lectures, performances, and films are presented at night; so are dinners and other social events. Women out alone at night who are assaulted by strangers are put on trial by public opinion: Any woman out alone after dark is asking for trouble. Presently, for millions of women of all socioeconomic backgrounds, sundown is lockdown. We are prisoners of violent strangers.

10   Daylight doesn't necessarily make the streets safe for women. In the early 1980s, a rapist operated in Tucson in the afternoon near the University of Arizona campus. He often accosted two women at once, forced them into residential alleys, then raped each one with a knife to her throat and forced the other to watch. Afterward the women said that part of the horror of their attack was that all around them, everything appeared normal. They could see people inside their houses and cars going down the street—all around them life was going on as usual while their lives were being changed forever.

11   The afternoon rapist was not the only rapist in Tucson at that time; there was the prime-time rapist, the potbellied rapist, and the apologetic rapist all operating in Tucson in the 1980s. The prime-time rapist was actually two men who invaded

comfortable foothills homes during television prime time when residents were preoccupied with television and eating dinner. The prime-time rapists terrorized entire families; they raped the women and sometimes they raped the men. Family members were forced to go to automatic bank machines, to bring back cash to end the ordeal. Potbelly rapist and apologetic rapist need little comment, except to note that the apologetic rapist was good looking, well educated, and smart enough to break out of jail for one last rape followed by profuse apologies and his capture in the University of Arizona library. Local papers recounted details about Tucson's last notorious rapist, the red bandanna rapist. In the late 1970s this rapist attacked more than twenty women over a three-year period, and Tucson police were powerless to stop him. Then one night, the rapist broke into a midtown home where the lone resident, a woman, shot him four times in the chest with a .38 caliber revolver.

12   In midtown Tucson, on a weekday afternoon, I was driving down Campbell Avenue to the pet store. Suddenly the vehicle behind me began to weave into my lane, so I beeped the horn politely. The vehicle swerved back to its lane, but then in my rearview mirror I saw the small late-model truck change lanes and begin to follow my car very closely. I drove a few blocks without looking in the rearview mirror, but in my sideview mirror I saw the compact truck was right behind me. OK. Some motorists stay upset for two or three blocks, some require ten blocks or more to recover their senses. Stoplight after stoplight, when I glanced into the rearview mirror I saw the man—in his early thirties, tall, white, brown hair, and dark glasses. This guy must not have a job if he has the time to follow me for miles—oh, ohhh! No beast more dangerous in the U.S.A. than an unemployed white man.

13   At this point I had to make a decision: do I forget about the trip to the pet store and head for the police station downtown, four miles away? Why should I have to let this stranger dictate my schedule for the afternoon? The man might dare to follow me to the police station, but by the time I reach the front door of the station, he'd be gone. No crime was committed; no Arizona law forbids tailgating someone for miles or for turning into a parking lot behind them. What could the police do? I had no license plate number to report because Arizona requires only one license plate, on the rear bumper of the vehicle. Anyway, I was within a block of the pet store where I knew I could get help from the pet store owners. I would feel better about this incident if it was not allowed to ruin my trip to the pet store.

14   The guy was right on my rear bumper; if I'd had to stop suddenly for any reason, there'd have been a collision. I decide I will not stop even if he does ram into the rear of my car. I study this guy's face in my rearview mirror, six feet two inches tall, 175 pounds, medium complexion, short hair, trimmed moustache. He thinks he can intimidate me because I am a woman, five feet five inches tall, 140 pounds. But I am not afraid, I am furious. I refuse to be intimidated. I won't play his game. I can tell by the face I see in the mirror this guy has done this before; he enjoys using his truck to menace lone women.

15   I keep thinking he will quit, or he will figure that he's scared me enough; but he seems to sense that I am not afraid. It's true. I am not afraid because years ago my father taught my sisters and me that we did not have to be afraid. He'll give up when I turn into the parking lot outside the pet store, I think. But I watch in my rearview

mirror; he's right on my rear bumper. As his truck turns into the parking lot behind my car, I reach over and open the glove compartment. I take out the holster with my .38 special and lay it on the car seat beside me.

16   I turned my car into a parking spot so quickly that I was facing my stalker who had momentarily stopped his truck and was watching me. I slid the .38 out of its holster onto my lap. I watched the stranger's face, trying to determine whether he would jump out of his truck with a baseball bat or gun and come after me. I felt calm. No pounding heart or rapid breathing. My early experience deer hunting had prepared me well. I did not panic because I felt I could stop him if he tried to harm me. I was in no hurry. I sat in the car and waited to see what choice my stalker would make. I looked directly at him without fear because I had my .38 and I was ready to use it. The expression on my face must have been unfamiliar to him; he was used to seeing terror in the eyes of the women he followed. The expression on my face communicated a warning: if he approached the car window, I'd kill him.

17   He took a last look at me and then sped away. I stayed in the car until his truck disappeared in the traffic of Campbell Avenue.

18   I walked into the pet store shaken. I had felt able to protect myself throughout the incident, but it left me emotionally drained and exhausted. The stranger had only pursued me—how much worse to be battered or raped.

19   Years before, I was unarmed the afternoon that two drunken deer hunters threatened to shoot me off my horse with razor-edged hunting crossbows. I was riding a colt on a national park trail near my home in the Tucson Mountains. These young white men in their late twenties were complete strangers who might have shot me if the colt had not galloped away erratically bucking and leaping—a moving target too difficult for the drunken bow hunters to aim at. The colt brought me to my ranch house where I called the county sheriff's office and the park ranger. I live in a sparsely populated area where my nearest neighbor is a quarter-mile away. I was afraid the men might have followed me back to my house so I took the .44 magnum out from under my pillow and strapped it around my waist until the sheriff or park ranger arrived. Forty-five minutes later, the park ranger arrived—the deputy sheriff arrived fifteen minutes after him. The drunken bow hunters were apprehended on the national park and arrested for illegally hunting; their bows and arrows were seized as evidence for the duration of bow hunting season. In southern Arizona that is enough punishment; I didn't want to take a chance of stirring up additional animosity with these men because I lived alone then; I chose not to make a complaint about their threatening words and gestures. I did not feel that I backed away by not pressing charges; I feared that if I pressed assault charges against these men, they would feel that I was challenging them to all-out war. I did not want to have to kill either of them if they came after me, as I thought they might. With my marksmanship and my .243 caliber hunting rifle from the old days, I am confident that I could stop idiots like these. But to have to take the life of another person is a terrible experience I will always try to avoid.

20   It isn't height or weight or strength that make women easy targets; from infancy women are taught to be self-sacrificing, passive victims. I was taught differently. Women have the right to protect themselves from death or bodily harm. By becoming strong and potentially lethal individuals, women destroy the fantasy that we are sitting ducks for predatory strangers.

21   In a great many cultures, women are taught to depend upon others, not themselves, for protection from bodily harm. Women are not taught to defend themselves from strangers because fathers and husbands fear the consequences themselves. In the United States, women depend upon the courts and the police; but as many women have learned the hard way, the police cannot be outside your house twenty-four hours a day. I don't want more police. More police on the street will not protect women. A few policemen are rapists and killers of women themselves; their uniforms and squad cars give them an advantage. No, I will be responsible for my own safety, thank you.

22   Women need to decide who has the primary responsibility for the health and safety of their bodies. We don't trust the State to manage our reproductive organs, yet most of us blindly trust that the State will protect us (and our reproductive organs) from predatory strangers. One look at the rape and murder statistics for women (excluding domestic incidents) and it is clear that the government FAILS to protect women from the violence of strangers. Some may cry out for a "stronger" State, more police, mandatory sentences, and swifter executions. Over the years we have seen the U.S. prison population become the largest in the world, executions take place every week now, inner-city communities are occupied by the National Guard, and people of color are harassed by police, but guess what? A woman out alone, night or day, is confronted with more danger of random violence from strangers than ever before. As the U.S. economy continues "to downsize," and the good jobs disappear forever, our urban and rural landscapes will include more desperate, angry men with nothing to lose.

23   Only women can put a stop to the "open season" on women by strangers. Women are TAUGHT to be easy targets by their mothers, aunts, and grandmothers who themselves were taught that "a women doesn't kill" or "a woman doesn't learn how to use a weapon." Women must learn how to take aggressive action individually, apart from the police and the courts. . . . Those who object to firearms need trained companion dogs or collectives of six or more women to escort one another day and night. We must destroy the myth that women are born to be easy targets.

QUESTIONS FOR ANALYSIS AND DISCUSSION

1. Why, according to Silko, do women live in a state of fear? What measures must they take to prevent personal harm? What effect does this mentality have on society as a whole?

2. How does a gun equalize the differences between men and women? Do you agree with Silko's father's comment that she and her sisters should never be afraid because a gun "equalized all differences of size and strength" (paragraph 7)?

3. Silko points out that "more than one feminist has pointed out that rapists and serial killers help keep the patriarchy in place" (paragraph 8). How do acts of violence against women maintain the "patriarchy"? What is the patriarchy?

4. Crime experts say that most rapes are motivated by a desire for power and not really for sex. Apply this fact to the rapists Silko describes in paragraphs 10 and 11.

5. In paragraph 21, Silko comments that in many cultures, "women are not taught to defend themselves from strangers because fathers and husbands fear the consequences themselves." What does she mean? Does this statement apply to American society? Explain.
6. How does Silko's story of her trip to the pet store support her argument? Explain.
7. Throughout the essay, Silko makes references to hunting. Explore the multifaceted levels of this hunting theme.

He's a Laker; She's a "Looker"
Jennifer L. Knight and Traci A. Giuliano

Are female athletes taken less seriously than male athletes? Are they judged more on their looks than on their abilities? Is their competition devalued by the media? In the next essay, Jennifer L. Knight and Traci A. Giuliano explain how the media perpetuates stereotypes that serve to trivialize women's sports. The time has come, they explain, for the media to present balanced coverage of female athletes and to stop promoting outdated stereotypes. Only then, they argue, will the public begin to see female athletes as great competitors first, and as women second.

Southwestern University alumnus Jennifer Knight graduated with her PhD from Rice University in 2004. Traci Giuliano, her former teacher and collaborator on several research papers, is an associate professor of psychology at Southwestern University. "He's a Laker; She's a 'Looker': The Consequences of Gender-Stereotypical Portrayals of Male and Female Athletes by the Print Media" appeared in the August 2001 issue of the interdisciplinary journal *Sex Roles*. Their research was also featured in the June 2002 issue of *Allure* magazine. Their entire paper, including their extensive references omitted here for space, appears online at <http://www.southwestern.edu/academic/bwp/pdf/2002bwp-knight_giuliano.pdf.>

BEFORE YOU READ ─────────────────────────

Do we hold female athletes to different standards than male athletes? Is it important for a female athlete to "look good" in addition to playing well?

AS YOU READ ─────────────────────────

Knight and Giuliano note that female sports figures are judged more on their attractiveness than on their athletic prowess. Do you think the media indeed gives more "face time" to a female athlete judged to be beautiful— say, Anna Kournikova—than to one who is known for her abilities alone, such as Martina Navratilova? Does the media do the same thing to male athletes? Explain.

1   In an era in which men's professional sport is becoming characterized by multi-million dollar contracts, player's union lockouts, illegal steroid use, and an individualistic mentality, disgruntled sports fans are increasingly turning to women's professional sport for entertainment. Indeed, leagues such as the Women's National Basketball Association (WNBA), the Ladies' Professional Golf Association (LPGA), the Women's Pro Softball League (WPSL), the Women's Pro Tennis Tour (WTA), and the Women's United Soccer Association (WUSA) are a welcome sign for fans searching for team-oriented play, affordable seats, and accessible sports stars (Wulf, 1997). In addition to the burgeoning field of women's professional sport, the Olympic Games have also been a showcase for successful female athletes. In the 1996 Atlanta Games, U.S. women's teams earned gold medals in gymnastics, soccer, softball, and basketball (with the softball and basketball teams reclaiming their titles at the 2000 Sydney Games). Their Winter counterparts in the 1998 Nagano Games also fared well, with the first-place women's hockey team and with individual stars Picabo Street, Tara Lipinski, and Christine Witty securing victories.

2   Female athletes competing at the interscholastic and intercollegiate levels have also made great strides. The Title IX court decision of 1972 requires all federally-funded programs, including athletics, to provide equal treatment and opportunity for participation for men and women. The implication for sports programs was that high schools and public universities subsequently were required to spend equivalent amounts of time and money for male and female athletes' scholarships, recruitment, facilities, supplies, travel, and services (Curtis & Grant, 2001). In part because of these improved opportunities, girls and women's involvement in sport has reached an all-time high. Whereas in 1971, only 1 in 27 girls participated in high school athletics, over 1 in 3 participated in 1997 (Women's Sports Foundation, 1998).

3   Although women's participation in professional, Olympic, intercollegiate, and interscholastic sport has reached unprecedented highs, research shows that media coverage of female athletes still lags behind that of men's (Tuggle & Owen, 1999). For example, women were featured on the cover of *Sports Illustrated* a scant 4 times out of 53 issues in 1996 (Women's Sports Foundation, 1997). A longitudinal study of *Sports Illustrated* feature articles from the mid 1950s to the late 1980s also revealed that the popular sport magazine allots far fewer column inches and photographs per article for women's sport as compared to men's (Salwen & Wood, 1994). A similar pattern was exhibited in television coverage of the Olympics, both in 1992 (Higgs & Weiller, 1994) and in 1996, purportedly "the year of women's sports" (Eastman & Billings, 1999). Even coverage of collegiate and high school sport is gender biased—boys receive more and longer articles than do girls (Sagas, Cunningham, Wigley, & Ashley, 2000). In effect, this "symbolic annihilation" (Gerbner, 1972) of women's sport by the media conveys the inaccurate idea that women's sport is inferior to and not as noteworthy as men's sport.

4   Coverage of women's sport is inferior to that of men's not only in quantity but in quality as well (Duncan & Messner, 2000). Sport commentators and writers often allude or explicitly refer to a female athlete's attractiveness, emotionality, femininity, and heterosexuality (all of which effectively convey to the audience that her stereotypical gender role is more salient than her athletic role), yet male athletes are

depicted as powerful, independent, dominating, and valued (Sabo & Jansen, 1992). Because competitively participating in sports is inconsistent with society's prescribed female role, the media coverage of female athletes seems to be trying to protect female athletes from rejection (or, more cynically, giving the public what they think it "wants") by emphasizing other aspects of their "femaleness," such as their attractiveness (Kane, 1996). For instance, although Gabrielle Reese, Anna Kournikova, Katarina Witt, and Jan Stephenson are all exceptional athletes, the media often focus on their attractiveness, a problem that is much less common for male athletes. In effect, the media tend to represent female athletes as women first (i.e., through focusing on their hair, nails, clothing, and attractiveness) and as athletes second; however, male athletes for the most part are portrayed solely in terms of their athleticism (Boutilier & San Giovanni, 1983).

5   This trivialization of women athletes is consistent with schema theory, which proposes that people have implicit cognitive structures that provide them with expectancies when processing information (Fiske & Taylor, 1991). One of the most socially constructed and dichotomous stereotypes is that of gender (Burn, O'Neal, & Nederend, 1996). Gender schema theory argues that people are socialized (e.g., through parents, teachers, peers, toys, and the popular media) into believing that gender differences are significant and worth maintaining (Bem, 1981). Although there is actually more variability within than between the sexes, the concept of distinct and exclusive gender differences persists nonetheless (Martin, 1987).

6   When people do violate our well-ingrained schemas (as would a female truck driver or a male secretary), they are consequently perceived more negatively than are people who are schema-consistent (Knight, Giuliano, & Sanchez-Ross, 2001). It may be, then, that men are readily portrayed by the media as athletes first because being an athlete is consistent with the traditional male role (Coakley & White, 1992). However, for women, being an athlete contradicts the conventional female role, and thus media coverage emphasizes other aspects of their "femaleness" (such as their attractiveness). Consequently, the narratives of male athletes are free to focus on their athletic accomplishments, whereas the portrayals of female athletes focus on aspects of their femininity, possibly to make these female athletes appear more gender-role consistent.

7   The trivialization of women's sport by the media is well established, but researchers have yet to empirically investigate how differential portrayals of male and female athletes affect the public's view of the athletes. Although researchers have speculated as to how people's beliefs might be influenced by biased coverage (Fasting, 1999), there is a dearth of research on the actual consequences of these differential portrayals as well as on the extent to which the media can truly influence people's perceptions of athletes. In addition, members of the media argue that they simply provide coverage that "the public wants," yet this also remains to be substantiated by empirical research. In other words, to what end the media merely reflects or actively refracts public opinion is still unknown. As such, the purpose of the present investigation was to address these previously unanswered questions in the sport literature.

8   To explore how gender-consistent and inconsistent portrayals of athletes affect people's perceptions, [we designed] a hypothetical Olympic profile in which the focal

point of the article was either a male or female athlete's physical attractiveness (a typically female portrayal) or athleticism (a typically male portrayal).

9   In general, we predicted that female athletes described as attractive would be perceived more positively (e.g., as more likable, more dedicated to sports, and more heroic) than female athletes who were not described in such a manner, because being attractive "softens" the perceived gender-role inconsistency of a female athlete. Conversely, [we expected] male athletes described as attractive to be perceived more negatively than would males not described as such, because the gender schema for male athletes leads people to expect that a man's athleticism, rather than his physical attractiveness, should be the focus of a magazine article.

10   Furthermore, [we expected] the results to be qualified by the gender of the participant. Because women typically are more accepting of schema-inconsistency (Greendorfer, 1993) and of female athletes in general (Nixon, Maresca, & Silverman, 1979), three-way interactions were expected such that male participants would perceive gender-typical behavior (i.e., articles about attractive female athletes and athletic male athletes) positively, whereas female participants would be more likely to value atypical, out-of-role behavior (i.e., articles about athletic female athletes or attractive male athletes).

Method

Participants

11   Data were collected from 92 predominantly White undergraduate students (40 men, 52 women) at a small liberal arts university in the Southwest. Participants were recruited primarily from introductory psychology and economics classes and were given extra credit in their courses for completing the study. Additional participants were recruited from the men and women's Division III soccer teams at the university, and they were given small prizes as incentives.

Design and Materials

12   [. . .] Because newspaper and magazine articles rarely just describe physical attributes, a picture of the hypothetical athlete was included in the article. [. . .] In the article emphasizing the athlete's physical attractiveness, the athlete was described as "becoming known as much for his [her] incredible body as for his [her] powerful strokes," as being one of *People Magazine*'s "Fifty Most Beautiful People in the World," and as having recently signed a modeling contract to make a "Wet and Wild" calendar for Speedo swimwear after the Olympics. By contrast, in the article that focused on the athlete's athleticism, he or she was described as "becoming known both for his [her] incredible speed and his [her] powerful strokes," as being one of *Sports Illustrated*'s "Fifty Up-and-Coming Athletes," and as having recently signed a contract to model for a Speedo promotional calendar. [. . .]

Procedure

13   Potential participants were approached and told that the current study was "an investigation of people's perceptions of Olympic athletes." After agreeing to complete

the questionnaire, participants read a hypothetical newspaper account about an athlete (who ostensibly had competed in the 1996 Summer Olympic Games) and then made judgments in response to the coverage and the athlete involved. All participants saw identical profiles, except that the first names (i.e., the gender) and type of coverage (i.e., attractive- or athletic-focused) varied according to each of the four specific experimental conditions.

14   After reading four profiles (three additional hypothetical profiles were included as part of a separate investigation) and completing the corresponding response sheets, participants recorded their answers to demographic questions (e.g., age, gender, athletic status, and the amount of time they spend following sports through the media) and other personality measures, including the Bem Sex-Role Inventory (Bem, 1974) and the Sex-Role Egalitarian Scale (Beere, King, Beere, & King, 1984). Upon completion of the questionnaire, participants were told that the article was hypothetical, thanked for their participation, and dismissed.

Results

15   [. . .] As expected, female athletes depicted in terms of their attractiveness were seen as more attractive than those depicted in terms of their athleticism only; by contrast, there was no difference in the perceived attractiveness of male athletes described as attractive or as athletic.

16   Additionally, there were several main effects of the focus of the article. Athletes whose coverage focused on their attractiveness were viewed as less talented than were athletes who were described in an athletic manner. Athletes described as attractive were also seen as less aggressive than athletes described as athletic. Furthermore, athletes portrayed as attractive were viewed as less heroic than were athletes portrayed as athletic. Finally, when attractiveness was the focus of the article, people liked the article less than when the coverage focused on the athlete's athletic ability.

Discussion

17   The results of the present study confirm that people's perceptions of athletes are influenced by the gender of the athlete and by the type of media coverage provided in the article. Interestingly, although the same picture was used in each condition, a female athlete whose attractiveness was the main focus of an article was perceived to be more physically attractive than was a female athlete whose athletic accomplishments were the focus of an article. However, the same pattern was not found with male athletes. Previous research has demonstrated that people have weaker schemas for ideal athletes than for ideal persons because the general public has fewer experiences (and thus, fewer cognitive associations) with the very specific category of "an ideal athlete" as opposed to the broader category of "an ideal person" (Martin & Martin, 1995). It follows that perhaps the schema for a female athlete is not as strong as that for a male athlete (because of less "mere exposure" through their "symbolic annihilation" by the media; Gerbner, 1972), and thus people's perceptions (especially of attractiveness it seems) of a female athlete are more malleable and open to alteration. As such, this study

implies that people are more apt to rely on peripheral information (such as the angle provided by the type of coverage) to form impressions of a female athlete.

18   Regardless of athlete gender, however, focusing on attractiveness to the exclusion of athletic ability had striking consequences on how athletes were perceived. Interestingly, our results indicate that male athletes are also affected by trivializing coverage; however, since men are rarely portrayed by the media in terms of their attractiveness (as female athletes often are), this marginalizing coverage seems to predominantly affect female athletes. Because of this negative effect on impressions of female and male athletes, the media need to be cognizant of (a) the damage that focusing on athletes' attractiveness can have on people's perceptions, (b) the fact that people might prefer articles that focus on an athlete's athleticism more than ones that focus on attractiveness, and (c) the reality that they do not merely reflect public opinion; they, in fact, can actively shape it.

19   Interestingly, participant gender was not a significant factor in ratings of the athlete or the article—a finding contrary to some previous research (Fisher, Genovese, Morris, & Morris, 1977), but consistent with other research (Michael, Gilroy, & Sherman, 1984). Perhaps this heralds a change in men's attitudes toward female athletes. Although women have traditionally been more accepting than men of female athletes (Nixon, Maresca, & Silverman, 1979), with the accomplishments of female athletes at the professional, Olympic, college, and high school levels, men might now be more aware and, hence, more accepting of women's sport.

20   An examination of the open-ended responses further confirmed what the quantitative data revealed. For example, one female participant shrewdly noted about the female athlete whose coverage centered on her attractiveness, "If I were her, I would be offended that this article talked more about my physical appearance than my talent—a typical attitude towards women. They can't resist talking about your appearance." A male participant similarly remarked, "If this was done in an edition of *Cosmopolitan* I might have liked it, but it told me nothing about her as an athlete." Yet another male participant said, "I wonder what her priorities are . . . is she using the 'swimming thing' to parlay a sweet modeling career?" Open-ended responses about male athletes portrayed as attractive revealed that they, too, were perceived in a negative light. A female participant wrote that this athlete was "a snobby rich kid who is a good swimmer and is used to everyone telling him how great he is." Another female participant remarked, "The article gave no mention of sports or athletic profile, only appearance. When speaking of an athlete in an Olympic sport, that is disconcerting."

21   There were several limitations of the present study, most notably that the kind of methodology used (i.e., "effects" research) cannot truly simulate the long term consequences of the media as a tool of socialization (Lewis, 1991). Although this kind of research does have certain limitations, other researchers have recognized its potential theoretical and practical value. For instance, in their research involving "face-ism," Archer and his colleagues took a qualitative finding (i.e., that pictures of women in the media often feature their entire body, whereas photographs of men usually only feature their heads) and experimentally determined through a quantitative methodology that this pattern results in men appearing smarter and in women appearing objectified (Archer, Iritani, Kimes, & Barrios, 1983). In a similar vein,

the current research has shown the negative impressions and effects that can occur from articles which focus exclusively on an athlete's attractiveness. It is through this process of triangulation and examining the same phenomenon from different paradigms and disciplinary perspectives that we will begin to be able to truly understand social patterns and their potential effect on society.

22   Another potential limitation was that some of the conditions within the study lacked external validity (i.e., male athletes are seldom depicted in terms of their attractiveness). Although articles such as these are rarely found in the print media, it was important to include them in the present study so that it could be empirically determined how gender-atypical portrayals of male and female athletes affect people's perceptions. That is, a conscious decision was made to trade internal for external validity in the present case. Finally, participants were not asked to report their race, and thus, the race of the participant was not taken into account in analyses. Although the majority of participants were White, previous research shows that White and Black participants weigh certain characteristics differently when evaluating the attractiveness of White and Black individuals (Hebl & Heatherton, 1998). Diverse audiences (in terms of age, socioeconomic status, education level, sexual orientation, and political orientation) might also differ with regards both to how much they like articles that focus on male and female athletes' attractiveness and athleticism and to their subsequent impressions of the athletes.

23   Opportunities are rife for future quantitative research in the area of gendered portrayals in the sport media. For example, the photographs selected for inclusion in the present study were both of White targets. Because people have different expectations and schemas for Black female athletes, the results from the present study might not generalize to athletes of other races. For instance, it traditionally is more acceptable for minority and working-class female athletes to participate in gender-inappropriate sports (e.g., basketball, soccer, hockey) than for White and middle-class female athletes because of the former group's more dynamic perceptions of femininity (Cahn, 1994). As such, further research is necessary to investigate the potential interactions among participant race, participant gender, athlete race, and athlete gender (Gissendaner, 1994).

24   In a broader scope, more experimental quantitative research should be conducted to empirically verify what descriptive qualitative studies have been reporting all along—that female athletes receive trivializing coverage from the media. For instance, "gender marking" (i.e., qualifying athletic contests and teams for women as though men's contests are the norm or standard) is very prevalent in television coverage of female athletes (Kane, 1996). Sports writers and commentators often use gendered labels to describe games in which female athletes participate (e.g., the "Women's Final Four"), yet male athletic contests are not referred to in these gendered terms (e.g., the "Final Four" rather than the "Men's Final Four"). Although researchers have speculated that this type of coverage marginalizes female athletes by making them appear to be "the other" rather than the norm, research has yet to empirically demonstrate the consequences of gender marking. Exploring how these and other types of gender-stereotypical portrayals affect both male and female athletes is an important next step in the sport literature.

25   In the meantime, the present study provides an empirical perspective to the burgeoning psychological and sociological fields that study the media, sport, and gender. At no other time in history have women had as much personal encouragement (Weiss & Barber, 1995) or as many opportunities to participate in sport (Women's Sport Foundation, 1998) as they do now, yet coverage of women's sport still lags behind men's coverage in both quantity and quality. The media need to be cognizant of the effects of their trivializing and marginalizing coverage and of the fact that this type of coverage may not be "what the public wants" after all. Hopefully, with a sustained and diligent commitment from the media, sport will be viewed as an unconditionally acceptable and beneficial activity for women.

QUESTIONS FOR ANALYSIS AND DISCUSSION —————

1. According to Knight and Giuliano, what role does the media play in conveying the idea that women's sports are inferior to men's sports? Explain.
2. What is "schema theory"? How does schema theory connect to the trivialization of women athletes and women's sports?
3. How do Knight and Giuliano support their argument that coverage of female athletes is not only unequal but also actually reinforces stereotypes that in turn serve to further trivialize women's sports in general? Evaluate their research and methods. How convincing is their argument? Explain.
4. Visit a sports-themed website such as ESPN.com or pick up a copy of a sports-themed publication such as *Sports Illustrated* or *Sporting News* and critically evaluate its content for gender bias. What is the ratio of male to female sports coverage? article length? Are female athletes described differently than male athletes? In addition to analyzing the text, examine the photographs accompanying the stories for any differences in the photographic portrayal of male and female athletes.

Self-Made Man
Norah Vincent

For almost a year and a half, journalist Norah Vincent lived undercover as a man to see what life was like on the other side of the gender divide. At 5 feet 10 inches and 155 pounds, Vincent passed as a medium-build man she renamed Ned. Attired with a buzz cut, men's clothes, a tight-fitting sports bra, new muscles built up at the gym, and some padding in a jock strap, she also sought the help of makeup artist Ryan McWilliams and Juilliard voice teacher Kate Maré to learn how to look and sound like a man. Her experiences are detailed in her book, *Self-Made Man*. What follows is an excerpt from her introduction to her book, in which Vincent explains the difference between walking down the street as a woman and walking down the same street as a man.

Vincent was formerly a syndicated columnist and is currently a freelance writer. In 2003, she took a leave from her job as a weekly columnist for the *Los Angeles Times*. Her essays, columns, and reviews have also appeared in newspapers across the nation, including the *New Republic*, the *New York Times*, the *New York Post*, the *Washington Post*, and the *Baltimore Sun*. The following is an excerpt from her acclaimed and controversial book, *Self-Made Man* (2005).

BEFORE YOU READ

Consider how you behave around members of the opposite sex. Are you relaxed? on guard? Do you act differently? Do you treat members of the opposite sex differently than your own? If so, in what ways, and why?

AS YOU READ

Vincent is shocked by how differently she feels walking down the street dressed as a man rather than as a woman. Have you ever experienced a similar situation in which how you dressed and acted influenced the people around you?

1   Seven years ago, I had my first tutorial in becoming a man.

2   The idea for a book came to me then, when I went out for the first time in drag. I was living in the East Village at the time, undergoing a significantly delayed adolescence, drinking and drugging a little too much, and indulging in all the sidewalk freak show opportunities that New York City has to offer.

3   Back then I was hanging around a lot with a drag king whom I had met through friends. She used to like to dress up and have me take pictures of her in costume. One night she dared me to dress up with her and go out on the town. I'd always wanted to try passing as a man in public, just to see if I could do it, so I agreed enthusiastically.

4   She had developed her own technique for creating a beard whereby you cut half inch chunks of hair from unobtrusive parts of your own head, cut them into smaller pieces, and then more or less glopped them onto your face with spirit gum. Using a small round freestanding mirror on her desk, she showed me how to do it in the dim, greenish light of her cramped studio apartment. It wasn't at all precise and it wouldn't have passed muster in the daylight, but it was good enough for the stage, and it would work well enough for our purposes in dark bars at night. I made myself a goatee and mustache, and a pair of baroque sideburns. I put on a baseball cap, loose-fitting jeans and a flannel shirt. In the full-length mirror I looked like a frat boy—sort of.

5   She did her thing—which was more willowy and soft, more like a young hippie guy who couldn't really grow much of a beard—and we went out like that for a few hours.

6   We passed, as far as I could tell, but I was too afraid to really interact with anyone, except to give one guy brief directions on the street. He thanked me as "dude"

and walked on. Mostly though, we just walked the streets of the Village scanning people's faces to see if anyone took a second or third look. But no one did. And that, oddly enough, was the thing that struck me the most about that evening. It was the only thing of real note that happened. But it was significant.

7   I had lived in that neighborhood for years, walking its streets where men lurk outside of bodegas, on stoops and in doorways much of the day. As a woman, you couldn't walk down those streets invisibly. You were an object of desire or at least semi-prurient interest to the men who waited there, even if you weren't pretty—that, or you were just another piece of pussy to be put in its place. Either way, their eyes followed you all the way up and down the street, never wavering, asserting their dominance as a matter of course. If you were female and you lived there, you got used to being stared down, because it happened every day and there wasn't anything you could do about it.

8   But that night in drag, we walked by those same stoops and doorways and bodegas. We walked right by those same groups of men. Only this time they didn't stare. On the contrary, when they met my eyes they looked away immediately and concertedly and never looked back. It was astounding, the difference, the respect they showed me by not looking at me, by purposely not staring.

9   That was it. That was what had annoyed me so much about meeting their gaze as a woman, not the desire, if that was ever there, but the disrespect, the entitlement. It was rude, and it was meant to be rude, and seeing those guys looking away deferentially when they thought I was male, I could validate in retrospect the true hostility of their former stares.

10   But that wasn't quite all there was to it. There was something more than plain respect being communicated in their averted gaze, something subtler, less direct. It was more like a disinclination to show disrespect. For them, to look away was to decline a challenge, to adhere to a code of behavior that kept the peace among human males in certain spheres just as surely as it kept the peace and the pecking order among male animals. To look another male in the eye and hold his gaze is to invite conflict, either that or a homosexual encounter. To look away is to accept the status quo, to leave each man to his tiny sphere of influence, the small buffer of pride and poise that surrounds and keeps him.

11   I surmised all of this the night it happened, but in the weeks and months that followed I asked most of the men I knew whether I was right, and they agreed, adding usually that it wasn't something they thought about anymore, if they ever had. It was just something you learned or absorbed as a boy, and by the time you were a man, you did it without thinking.

12   After the whole incident had blown over, I started thinking that if in such a short time in drag I had learned such an important secret about the way males and females communicate with each other, and about the unspoken codes of male experience, then couldn't I potentially observe much more about the social differences between the sexes if I passed as a man for a much longer period of time? It seemed true, but I wasn't intrepid enough yet to do something that extreme. Besides it seemed impossible, both psychologically and practically, to pull it off. So I filed the information away in my mind for a few more years and got on with other things.

13   Then, in the winter of 2003, while watching a reality television show on the A&E network, the idea came back to me. In the show, two male and two female con-

testants set out to transform themselves into the opposite sex—not with hormones or surgeries, but purely by costume and design. The women cut their hair. The men had theirs extended. Both took voice and movement lessons to try to learn how to speak and behave more like the sex they were trying to become. All chose new wardrobes, personas and names for their alter egos. The bulk of the program focused on the outward transformations, though the point at the end was to see who could pass in the real world most effectively. Neither of the men really passed, and only one of the women stayed the course. She did manage to pass fairly well, though only for a short time and in carefully controlled circumstances.

14 But, as in most reality television programs, especially the American ones, nobody involved was particularly introspective about the effect their experiences had had on them or the people around them. It was clear that the producers didn't have much interest in the deeper sociologic implications of passing as the opposite sex. It was all just another version of an extreme make-over. Once the stunt was accomplished—or not—the show was over.

15 But for me, watching the show brought my former experience in drag to the forefront of my mind again and made me realize that passing in costume in the daylight could be possible with the right help. I knew that writing a book about passing in the world as a man would give me the chance to explore some of the unexplored territory that the show had left out, and that I had barely broached in my brief foray in drag years before.

16 I was determined to give the idea a try.

QUESTIONS FOR ANALYSIS AND DISCUSSION

1. What change in behavior does Vincent experience when she walks down the street dressed as a man? How does the experience make her feel?
2. If you are female, have you ever experienced the "disrespect, the entitlement" of male gazes as you walked along the street? If you are male, have you engaged in this sort of behavior? If so, describe the feelings behind it as candidly as you can.
3. Why does Vincent feel the reality program that switched genders lacked substance? Explain.
4. What irritates Vincent the most about the gaze of the men on the doorsteps in her neighborhood? Explain.

WRITING ASSIGNMENTS

1. Write a detailed description of your ideal male image, or ideal female image (what you desire or what you would most like to look like yourself). Now record the personality traits you would want in this person. How does your description compare with the conclusions drawn by the psychologists in this section? Did outside cultural forces influence your description? Explain.

2. Several of the authors in this section attribute youth's desire to act, dress, and look a certain way to media pressure. Write an essay discussing whether this is

true or not true. Support your perspective using examples from the authors, and your own experiences and observations.

3. Is it harder to grow up male or female in America today? Using information from the articles in this section, as well as outside resources, write an essay explaining which gender faces the greatest and most daunting challenges, and why. Will this situation grow worse? Offer suggestions to help ease the gender-related challenges children face growing up in today's culture.

4. Write an essay in which you consider your own sense of cultural conditioning. Do you feel your behavior has been conditioned by sex-role expectations? In what ways? Is there a difference between the "real" you and the person you present to the world? If there is a difference, is it the result of cultural pressure? Explain.

5. Write an essay examining the role advertising has had on feminism and on our perceptions of male and female social roles and how we fit in as men and as women in the new millennium.

A BRAVE NEW WORLD?

Where the Boys Aren't
Melana Zyla Vickers

Before the 1970s, most college campuses—with the exception of women's colleges—were dominated by men. In 1972, Title IX, now known as the Patsy T. Mink Equal Opportunity in Education Act, ensured that "No person in the United States shall, on the basis of sex, be excluded from participation in, be denied the benefits of, or be subjected to discrimination under any education program or activity receiving Federal financial assistance." This act allowed women equal access to a college education. By the 1980s, a noticeable gender shift rippled through college campuses across the country. More women were enrolling in college than men. Where have the boys gone? In the next essay, columnist Melana Zyla Vickers explores the new gender gap on college campuses.

Vickers is senior fellow at the Independent Women's Forum in Washington, D.C., and a columnist for TechCentralStation.com. She is a former member of the *USA Today* editorial board. She covers national security issues, foreign affairs, and global economics issues, among other topics. Her articles have appeared in many political publications and newspapers, including the *Asian Wall Street Journal*, the *Far Eastern Economic Review*, and *The Globe and Mail*. This article was published in *The Weekly Standard* on January 2, 2006.

BEFORE YOU READ

What is the ratio of male to female students at your institution and in your classroom? Is it fairly equal? Do you notice a "gender gap" on campus?

AS YOU READ

Before Title IX, women could be excluded from college enrollment merely because they were female. Has a form of reverse gender discrimination emerged on college campuses? Can Title IX be applied in reverse to balance the gender distribution on campus?

1   Here's a thought that's unlikely to occur to twelfth-grade girls as their college acceptances begin to trickle in: After they get to campus in the fall, one in four of them will be mathematically unable to find a male peer to go out with.

2   At colleges across the country, 58 women will enroll as freshmen for every 42 men. And as the class of 2010 proceeds toward graduation, the male numbers will dwindle. Because more men than women drop out, the ratio after four years will be 60-40, according to projections by the Department of Education.

3   The problem isn't new—women bachelor's degree-earners first outstripped men in 1982. But the gap, which remained modest for some time, is widening. More and more girls are graduating from high school and following through on their college ambitions, while boys are failing to keep pace and, by some measures, losing ground.

4   Underperformance in education is no longer a problem confined to black males, Hispanic males, or even poor whites. In 2004, the nation's middle-income, white undergraduate population was 57 percent female. Even among white undergraduates with family incomes of $70,000 and higher, the balance tipped in 2000 to 52 percent female. And white boys are the only demographic group whose high school dropout rate has risen since 2000. Maine, a predominantly white state, is at 60-40 in college enrollment and is quickly reaching beyond it. There are now more female master's degree-earners than male, and in 10 years there will be more new female Ph.D.s, according to government projections. American colleges from Brown to Berkeley face a man shortage, and there's no end in sight.

5   Yet few alarm bells are ringing. In the early 1970s, when the college demographics were roughly reversed at 43 percent female and 57 percent male, federal education laws were reformed with the enactment in 1972 of Title IX, a provision that requires numerical parity for women in various areas of federally funded schooling. Feminist groups pushed the Equal Rights Amendment through the House and Senate. Universities opened women's studies departments. And the United Nations declared 1975 the International Year of the Woman. The problem was structural, feminists never tired of repeating: A system built by men, for men, was blocking women's way.

6   Today's shortage of men, by contrast, is largely ignored, denied, or covered up. Talk to university administrators, and few will admit that the imbalance is a problem, let alone that they're addressing it. Consider the view of Stephen Farmer, director of undergraduate admissions at the University of North Carolina-Chapel Hill, where this year's enrollment is only 41.6 percent male. "We really have made no attempt to balance the class. We are gender blind in applications, very scrupulously so."

7   Why the blind devotion to gender-blindness? Because affirmative action for men is politically incorrect. And at universities receiving federal funding like UNC, it's also illegal. "My understanding of Title IX is that an admissions process that advantages men would be very difficult to defend," Farmer says.

8   The recent history at the University of Georgia, with its male enrollment of 42 percent, explains the situation further. In 2001, a federal appeals court struck down the university's use of gender and race criteria to try to boost its black, male numbers in undergraduate admissions. Three white women sued the school after being rejected, arguing they'd have gotten into the University of Georgia if they had been black men. The appeals court agreed with a lower court's finding that the admissions process in place at the time violated Title VI (race equity) and Title IX (gender equity) by "intentionally discriminating against them based on race and gender."

9   It didn't even take a court ruling to cause Brandeis University, which is 46 percent male, to abandon its lame effort to attract more men. A few years ago it offered free baseball caps to the first 500 male undergraduate applicants. Brandeis's new dean of admissions, Gil Villanueva, says "things were looking pretty low on the male end and so people said let's give it a shot and see what happens." Evidently not much—the promotion was never repeated. Says Villanueva, "We have no special recruitment plan for males. We are very much gender blind." He says the administrators won't worry about the gender balance unless "all of a sudden our applicant pool is 75 percent female."

10   Boston University, 40.8 percent male at the undergraduate level, shows even less official concern. The imbalance is a national trend that begins with fewer men graduating from high school and applying to college, says spokesman Colin Riley. "We can't do something about the pool if they're not applying."

11   BU's position wasn't always so passive. In the mid-'90s, then-president John Silber sought to take a few small steps to address the shortfall of males. He told staff that BU's publicity materials ought to be gender-neutral, and that an ROTC publicity photo showing a woman ought to show a man, because ROTC at the university was predominantly male. Asked this month about Silber's minor intervention, university spokesman Riley tried to downplay it, saying "most places would be impressed" to have a woman in the ROTC photo. He added that the gender ratio is not "discerned as a problem. We certainly don't view it as such." Interesting, then, that BU doesn't publicize the sex breakdown of its student body on its website.

12   Richard Nesbitt, admissions director at Williams College, which is just 52 percent female, sees things differently. "If we got to 60-40, that would set off some alarm bells because we would like to have a 50-50 split," he says, adding balance is desirable "in terms of the social atmosphere and so forth."

13   Nesbitt says Williams's past as an all-men's college, plus strong math and science departments and athletics programs, helps keep the male numbers higher than the average. A few other formerly all-male schools, such as Princeton, actually have male majorities. But while the situation isn't yet alarming for such schools as Williams, Nesbitt calls it "alarming in terms of what's happening in our society."

14   The Department of Education doesn't appear to agree. The home of Title IX enforcement continues to be so preoccupied with advancing women that a recent

50-page study called Gender Differences in Participation and Completion of Under-graduate Education focuses not on the shortfall of men that's evident in practically every data point, but on tiny subpopulations of women who still have "risk charac-teristics," such as those entering university after age 29. And the department still spends money on studies such as Trends in Educational Equity of Girls and Women: 2004, while ignoring the eye-popping trends for boys and men.

15   The neglect has extended to the press as well, though there are a few signs that the blackout may be ending. The *Chronicle of Higher Education*, the bible of col-lege and university news, has hardly touched the issue. *EdWeek*, while it has done better, still devotes less ink to the current gender gap than it does to women. And a recent piece in the *Washington Post* is an encouraging sign. As for state governments, inquiries around the country have turned up only a single public body studying the problem, a commission in Maine that is due to publish a study of boys' underper-formance in education in January. It's true that President Bush mentioned boys' troubles in the 2005 State of the Union, but his aim was to "keep young people out of gangs, and show young men an ideal of manhood that respects women and rejects violence." Only a few business groups have looked at young men's academic perfor-mance, as have a handful of private researchers and authors.

16   Yet the trends are grave. Women outstrip men in education despite that there are 15 million men and 14.2 million women aged 18–24 in the country. Kentucky col-leges enroll at least 67 first-year women for every 50 men. Delaware has 74 first-year women for every 50 men.

17   The gender gap is even more palpable within the colleges themselves, because women and men gravitate to different majors. While a split in preferences has al-ways been the case, the gender imbalance in the overall college makes departments so segregated that campus life just ain't what it used to be. In North Carolina's pub-lic and private universities, a typical psychology class has four women for every man. In education, the ratio is five to one. The English and foreign language depart-ments are heavily female as well.

18   The consequences go far beyond a lousy social life and the longer-term reality that many women won't find educated male peers to marry. There are also academic consequences, and economic ones.

19   Only a few fields, such as business and the social sciences, show men and women signing up at comparable rates. Math, computers, engineering, and the physical sci-ences continue to be male-dominated (in North Carolina, for example, engineering is 79 percent male), and the total number of graduates in these economically essential fields is often stagnant or declining. Thus, between 1992 and 2002, when the number of bachelor's degree-earners in California's public university system grew by 11 percent, the number of engineering bachelor's degrees shrank by 8 percent. California's private universities fared better, but the gap is still striking: bachelor's degrees grew by 41 per-cent overall, while bachelor's degrees in engineering grew only 27 percent.

20   It seems the education system is favoring quantity over quantitative skills. The result? American companies and research organizations that need to employ graduates in quantitative fields have to turn to foreigners. Already, an astounding 40 percent of all the master's degrees awarded by American institutions in science,

engineering, and information technology go to foreign students, as do 45 percent of all Ph.D.s in those fields, according to a study of the gender gap in education by the Business Roundtable in Washington, D.C.

21   The answer that education experts keep recycling is that American girls need to be encouraged to go into quantitative fields. After all, if there's one thing Harvard president Larry Summers taught the nation, it's that questioning women's aptitude for science is an absolute no-no. But surely some reflection is needed on whether science, mathematics, and engineering wouldn't be more attractive to American boys if more of them were encouraged to discover, at an early age, whether they have strengths in those fields and were warmly encouraged to pursue them in their schooling.

22   We're certainly not seeing any such encouragement these days. While much of the gender imbalance in higher education results from girls' advancing through high school and into university in greater proportions than boys, there are a few categories of boys who are stuck or losing ground. The high school dropout rate for white boys hovers around 7 percent, at a time when girls—black, white, and Hispanic—are making annual progress in cutting their dropout numbers, as are black and Hispanic boys. (To be sure, the Hispanic boys' high school dropout rate remains astonishingly high, and contributes to the overall college imbalance: 26.7 percent in 2003, a rate not seen since the early 1970s among black boys and girls.)

23   Young men also drop out of college more readily than young women do. And even in affluent, educated, white suburbs, fewer twelfth-grade boys make plans to attend college than girls do, according to a study by the Boston Private Industry Council. Unfortunately, a student who defers college enrollment increases his odds of never attending. All of this makes the pool of applicants to college predominantly female, and the pool of enrollees more female as well.

24   What is going on? Schools are not paying enough attention to the education of males. There's too little focus on the cognitive areas in which boys do well. Boys have more disciplinary problems, up to 10 percent are medicated for Attention Deficit Disorder, and they thrive less in a school environment that prizes what Brian A. Jacob of Harvard's Kennedy School of Government calls "noncognitive skills." These include the ability to pay attention in class, to work with others, to organize and keep track of homework, and to seek help from others. Where boys and girls score comparably on cognitive skills, boys get worse grades in the touchy-feely stuff. Perhaps not coincidentally, boys reportedly enjoy school less than girls do, and are less likely to perceive that their teachers support them, according to studies of Hispanic dropouts.

25   Harvard's Jacob is one of the few scholars to have studied the gender gap in higher education. His statistical analysis suggests it is boys' lack of skill in these noncognitive areas that is the principal cause of the gap. Other factors, which include young men choosing to go into the military or winding up in prison, account for only about one-sixth of the spread, according to his calculations.

26   Plain old economics is at work as well. Consider that among Hispanic boys, the wage gap between high school dropouts and high school graduates is much smaller than for whites and blacks. Hispanic boys may figure that high college tuition and four more years of touchy-feely classroom work is less appealing than a job and an immediate income. The economic draw of the workplace holds great sway over male college dropouts as well. A "need to work" accounted for fully 28 percent of

male dropouts' reasons for leaving college, but only 18 percent of women dropouts' reasons, according to a Department of Education study. The men were also more likely than women to report academic problems and dissatisfaction with classes as their reasons for leaving.

27   Whatever the precise combination of causes, the imbalance on today's campuses can only be harmful in its social and economic effects. In a rational world, the Bush administration would take a serious look at whether continued enforcement of Title IX is keeping men away from college. At a minimum, the federal Department of Education would follow the example of the state of Maine and mine its statistics for detailed information about boys. Only then would researchers be equipped to address the problem.

28   Even now, almost two decades after the failure of the effort to ratify the Equal Rights Amendment, the culture is still in thrall to feminist orthodoxy. The Bush administration declined to do battle against Title IX three years ago, essentially preserving the status quo when college sports teams sued for reforms. Meanwhile, the myopic bureaucrats at the Department of Education are unlikely to take their heads out of the sand unless forced to: As if prompted by the imminent release of Maine's report on how to help boys catch up, the National Center for Education Statistics led its website on December 1 with a colorful chart displaying the sex breakdown at a single high school—one in Bangor, where it just happens that boys outnumber girls.

QUESTIONS FOR ANALYSIS AND DISCUSSION ─────

1. In this essay, what accounts for the imbalance of men to women ratios at many institutions of higher learning?
2. According to Vickers, what problems will eventually rise due to the male/female imbalance in colleges and universities?
3. What examples does Vickers use to show that the government and other institutions are not reacting to the male/female imbalance in higher education appropriately?
4. Do you think the government should intervene to balance gender distribution on campus? If so, what steps could the government take to correct the problem?
5. In your opinion, are the institutions of higher education discriminating against males when they are "gender blind in applications"?

The New Girl Order
Kay S. Hymowitz

Young women today are marrying later, are having children later, and, as many pursue meaningful careers, have more disposable income than ever before. Across the globe, women are changing the cultural landscape and challenging long-held traditional gender roles. Do such changes represent a positive shift, or could they have negative implications in the long run? As Kay S. Hymowitz discusses in the next essay, the Carrie Bradshaw lifestyle is showing up in unexpected places, with unintended consequences.

Hymowitz is a contributing editor of *City Journal* and the William E. Simon Fellow at the Manhattan Institute. She has written for many major publications, including the *New York Times*, the *Washington Post*, the *Wall Street Journal*, the *New Republic*, and *New York Newsday*. The author of several books on family dynamics and society, her most recent books are *Liberation's Children: Parents and Kids in a Postmodern Age* (2003) and *Marriage and Caste in America* (2006). This essay was first published in the autumn 2007 issue of *City Journal*.

BEFORE YOU READ

Why are young adults waiting longer than ever to get married and have children? What are your own plans for marriage and family?

AS YOU READ

Is Hymowitz supportive or critical of "the New Girl Order" she describes? Identify areas in her essay that reveal her point of view on this topic.

1   **A**fter my Los Airlines flight from New York touched down at Warsaw's Frédéric Chopin Airport a few months back, I watched a middle-aged passenger rush to embrace a waiting younger woman—clearly her daughter. Like many people on the plane, the older woman wore drab clothing and had the short, square physique of someone familiar with too many potatoes and too much manual labor. Her Poland-based daughter, by contrast, was tall and smartly outfitted in pointy-toed pumps, slim-cut jeans, a cropped jacket revealing a toned midriff (Yoga? Pilates? Or just a low-carb diet?), and a large, brass-studded leather bag, into which she dropped a silver cell phone.

2   Yes: Carrie Bradshaw is alive and well and living in Warsaw. Well, not just Warsaw. Conceived and raised in the United States, Carrie may still see New York as a spiritual home. But today you can find her in cities across Europe, Asia, and North America. Seek out the trendy shoe stores in Shanghai, Berlin, Singapore, Seoul, and Dublin, and you'll see crowds of single young females (SYFs) in their twenties and thirties, who spend their hours working their abs and their careers, sipping cocktails, dancing at clubs, and (yawn) talking about relationships. *Sex and the City* has gone global; the SYF world is now flat. Is this just the latest example of American cultural imperialism? Or is it the triumph of planetary feminism? Neither. The globalization of the SYF reflects a series of stunning demographic and economic shifts that are pointing much of the world—with important exceptions, including Africa and most of the Middle East—toward a New Girl Order. It's a man's world, James Brown always reminded us. But if these trends continue, not so much.

3   Three demographic facts are at the core of the New Girl Order. First, women—especially, but not only, in the developed world—are getting married and having

kids considerably later than ever before. According to the UN's *World Fertility Report*, the worldwide median age of marriage for women is up two years, from 21.2 in the 1970s to 23.2 today. In the developed countries, the rise has been considerably steeper—from 22.0 to 26.1. Demographers get really excited about shifts like these, but in case you don't get what the big deal is, consider: in 1960, 70 percent of American 25-year-old women were married with children; in 2000, only 25 percent of them were. In 1970, just 7.4 percent of all American 30- to 34-year-olds were unmarried; today, the number is 22 percent. That change took about a generation to unfold, but in Asia and Eastern Europe the transformation has been much more abrupt. In today's Hungary, for instance, 30 percent of women in their early thirties are single, compared with 6 percent of their mothers' generation at the same age. In South Korea, 40 percent of 30-year-olds are single, compared with 14 percent only 20 years ago.

4   Nothing-new-under-the-sun skeptics point out, correctly, that marrying at 27 or 28 was once commonplace for women, at least in the United States and parts of northern Europe. The cultural anomaly was the 1950s and 60s, when the average age of marriage for women dipped to 20—probably because of post-Depression and postwar cocooning. But today's single 27-year-old has gone global—and even in the West, she differs from her late-marrying great-grandma in fundamental ways that bring us to the second piece of the demographic story. Today's aspiring middle-class women are gearing up to be part of the paid labor market for most of their adult lives; unlike their ancestral singles, they're looking for careers, not jobs. And that means they need lots of schooling.

5   In the newly global economy, good jobs go to those with degrees, and all over the world, young people, particularly women, are enrolling in colleges and universities at unprecedented rates. Between 1960 and 2000, the percentages of 20-, 25-, and 30-year-olds enrolled in school more than doubled in the U.S., and enrollment in higher education doubled throughout Europe. And the fairer sex makes up an increasing part of the total. The majority of college students are female in the U.S., the U.K., France, Germany, Norway, and Australia, to name only a few of many places, and the gender gap is quickly narrowing in more traditional countries like China, Japan, and South Korea. In a number of European countries, including Denmark, Finland, and France, over half of all women between 20 and 24 are in school. The number of countries where women constitute the majority of graduate students is also growing rapidly.

6   That educated women are staying single is unsurprising; degreed women have always been more likely to marry late, if they marry at all. But what has demographers taking notice is the sheer transnational numbers of women postponing marriage while they get diplomas and start careers. In the U.K., close to a third of 30-year-old college-educated women are unmarried; some demographers predict that 30 percent of women with university degrees there will remain forever childless. In Spain—not so long ago a culturally Catholic country where a girl's family would jealously chaperone her until handing her over to a husband at 21 or so—women now constitute 54 percent of college students, up from 26 percent in 1970, and the average age of first birth has risen to nearly 30, which appears to be a world record.

7   Adding to the contemporary SYF's novelty is the third demographic shift: urbanization. American and northern European women in the nineteenth and early twentieth centuries might have married at 26, but after a long day in the dairy barn or cotton mill, they didn't hang out at Studio 54 while looking for Mr. Right (or, as the joke has it, Mr. Right for Now). In the past, women who delayed marriage generally lived with their parents; they also remained part of the family economy, laboring in their parents' shops or farms, or at the very least, contributing to the family kitty. A lot of today's bachelorettes, on the other hand, move from their native village or town to Boston or Berlin or Seoul because that's where the jobs, boys, and bars are—and they spend their earnings on themselves. By the mid-1990s, in countries as diverse as Canada, France, Hungary, Ireland, Portugal, and Russia, women were out-urbanizing men, who still tended to hang around the home village. When they can afford to, these women live alone or with roommates. The Netherlands, for instance, is flush with public housing, some of it reserved for young students and workers, including lots of women. In the United States, the proportion of unmarried twentysomethings living with their parents has declined steadily over the last 100 years, despite sky-high rents and apartment prices. Even in countries where SYFs can't afford to move out of their parents' homes, the anonymity and diversity of city life tend to heighten their autonomy. Belgians, notes University of Maryland professor Jeffrey Jensen Arnett, have coined a term—"hotel families"—to describe the arrangement.

8   Combine these trends—delayed marriage, expanded higher education and labor-force participation, urbanization—add a global media and some disposable income, and voilà: an international lifestyle is born. One of its defining characteristics is long hours of office work, often in quasi-creative fields like media, fashion, communications, and design—areas in which the number of careers has exploded in the global economy over the past few decades. The lifestyle also means whole new realms of leisure and consumption, often enjoyed with a group of close girlfriends: trendy cafés and bars serving sweetish coffee concoctions and cocktails; fancy boutiques, malls, and emporiums hawking cosmetics, handbags, shoes, and $100-plus buttock-hugging jeans; gyms for toning and male-watching; ski resorts and beach hotels; and, everywhere, the frustrating hunt for a boyfriend and, though it's an ever more vexing subject, a husband.

9   The SYF lifestyle first appeared in primitive form in the U.S. during the seventies, after young women started moving into higher education, looking for meaningful work, and delaying marriage. Think of ur-SYF Mary Richards, the pre-Jordache career girl played by Mary Tyler Moore, whose dates dropped her off—that same evening, of course—at her apartment door. By the mid-nineties, such propriety was completely passé. Mary had become the vocationally and sexually assertive Carrie Bradshaw, and cities like New York had magically transformed into the young person's pleasure palace evoked by the hugely popular TV show *Sex and the City*. At around the same time, women in Asia and in post-Communist Europe began to join the SYF demographic, too. Not surprisingly, they also loved watching themselves, or at least Hollywood versions of themselves, on television. *Friends, Ally McBeal,* and *Sex and the City* became global favorites. In repressive places like Singapore and China, which banned SATC, women passed around pirated DVDs.

10   By the late 1990s, the SYF lifestyle was fully globalized. Indeed, you might think of SYFs as a sociological Starbucks: no matter how exotic the location, there they are, looking and behaving just like the American prototype. They shop for shoes in Kyoto, purses in Shanghai, jeans in Prague, and lip gloss in Singapore; they sip lattes in Dublin, drink cocktails in Chicago, and read lifestyle magazines in Kraków; they go to wine tastings in Boston, speed-dating events in Amsterdam, yoga classes in Paris, and ski resorts outside Tokyo. "At the fashionable Da Capo Café on bustling Kolonaki Square in downtown Athens, Greek professionals in their 30s and early 40s luxuriate over their iced cappuccinos," a *Newsweek International* article began last year. "Their favorite topic of conversation is, of course, relationships: men's reluctance to commit, women's independence, and when to have children." Thirty-seven-year-old Eirini Perpovlov, an administrative assistant at Associated Press, "loves her work and gets her social sustenance from her *parea*, or close-knit group of like-minded friends."

11   Sure sounds similar to this July's *Time* story about Vicky, "a purposeful, 29-year-old actuary who . . . loves nothing better than a party. She and her friends meet so regularly for dinner and at bars that she says she never eats at home anymore. As the pictures on her blog attest, they also throw regular theme parties to mark holidays like Halloween and Christmas, and last year took a holiday to Egypt." At the restaurant where the reporter interviews them, Vicky's friends gab about snowboarding, iPods, credit-card rates, and a popular resort off the coast of Thailand. Vicky, whose motto is "work hard, play harder," is not from New York, London, or even Athens; she's from the SYF delegation in Beijing, China, a country that appears to be racing from rice paddies to sushi bars in less than a generation—at least for a privileged minority.

12   With no children or parents to support, and with serious financial hardship a bedtime story told by aging grandparents, SYFs have ignited what *The Economist* calls the "Bridget Jones economy"—named, of course, after the book and movie heroine who is perhaps the most famous SYF of all. Bridget Jonesers, the magazine says, spend their disposable income "on whatever is fashionable, frivolous, and fun," manufactured by a bevy of new companies that cater to young women. In 2000, Marian Salzman—then the president of the London-based Intelligence Factory, an arm of Young & Rubicam—said that by the 1990s, "women living alone had come to comprise the strongest consumer bloc in much the same way that yuppies did in the 1980s."

13   SYFs drive the growth of apparel stores devoted to stylish career wear like Ann Taylor, which now has more than 800 shops in the United States, and the international Zara, with more than 1,000 in 54 countries. They also spend paychecks at the Paris-based Sephora, Europe's largest retailer of perfumes and cosmetics, which targets younger women in 14 countries, including such formerly sober redoubts as Poland and the Czech Republic. The chain plans to expand to China soon. According to *Forbes*, the Chinese cosmetics market, largely an urban phenomenon, was up 17 percent in 2006, and experts predict a growth rate of between 15 and 20 percent in upcoming years. Zara already has three stores there. The power of the SYF's designer purse is also at work in the entertainment industry. By the mid-1990s, "chick lit," a contemporary urban version of the Harlequin romance with the SYF as

heroine, was topping bestseller lists in England and the United States. Now chick lit has spread all over the world. The books of the Irish writer Marian Keyes, one of the first and most successful chick-litterateurs, appear in 29 languages. *The Devil Wears Prada* was an international hit as both a book (by Lauren Weisberger) and a movie (starring Meryl Streep). Meantime, the television industry is seeking to satisfy the SYF's appetite for single heroines with *Sex and the City* clones like *The Marrying Type* in South Korea and *The Balzac Age* in Russia.

14   Bridget Jonesers are also remaking the travel industry, especially in Asia. A 2005 report from MasterCard finds that women take four out of every ten trips in the Asia-Pacific region—up from one in ten back in the mid-1970s. While American women think about nature, adventure, or culture when choosing their travel destinations, says MasterCard, Asian women look for shopping, resorts, and, most of all, spas. Female travelers have led to what the report calls the "spa-ification of the Asian hotel industry." That industry is growing at a spectacular rate—200 percent annually.

15   And now the maturing Bridget Jones economy has begun to feature big-ticket items. In 2003, the Diamond Trading Company introduced the "right-hand ring," a diamond for women with no marital prospects but longing for a rock. ("Your left hand is your heart; your right hand is your voice," one ad explains.) In some SYF capitals, women are moving into the real-estate market. Canadian single women are buying homes at twice the rate of single men. The National Association of Realtors reports that in the U.S. last year, single women made up 22 percent of the real-estate market, compared with a paltry 9 percent for single men. The median age for first-time female buyers: 32. The real-estate firm Coldwell Banker is making eyes at these young buyers with a new motto, "Your perfect partner since 1906," while Lowe's, the home-renovation giant, is offering classes especially for them. SYFs are also looking for wheels, and manufacturers are designing autos and accessories with them in mind. In Japan, Nissan has introduced the Pino, which has seat covers festooned with stars and a red CD player shaped like a pair of lips. It comes in one of two colors: "milk tea beige" and pink.

16   Japan presents a striking example of the sudden rise of the New Girl Order outside the U.S. and Western Europe. As recently as the nation's boom years in the 1980s, the dominant image of the Japanese woman was of the housewife, or *sengyoshufu*, who doted on her young children, intently prepared older ones for the world economy, and waited on the man of the house after his 16-hour day at the office. She still exists, of course, but about a decade ago she met her nemesis: the Japanese SYF. Between 1994 and 2004, the number of Japanese women between 25 and 29 who were unmarried soared from 40 to 54 percent; even more remarkable was the number of 30- to 34-year-old females who were unmarried, which rocketed from 14 to 27 percent. Because of Tokyo's expensive real-estate market, a good many of these young single women have shacked up with their parents, leading a prominent sociologist to brand them "parasite singles." The derogatory term took off, but the girls weren't disturbed; according to *USA Today*, many proudly printed up business cards bearing their new title.

17   The New Girl Order may represent a disruptive transformation for a deeply traditional society, but Japanese women sure seem to be enjoying the single life. Older singles who can afford it have even been buying their own apartments. One of them,

37-year-old Junko Sakai, wrote a best-selling plaint called *The Howl of the Loser Dogs*, a title that co-opts the term *makeinu*—"loser"—once commonly used to describe husbandless 30-year-olds. "Society may call us dogs," she writes, "but we are happy and independent." Today's Japanese SYFs are world-class shoppers, and though they must still fight workplace discrimination and have limited career tracks—particularly if they aren't working for Westernized companies—they're somehow managing to earn enough yen to keep the country's many Vuitton, Burberry, and Issey Miyake boutiques buzzing. Not so long ago, Japanese hotels wouldn't serve women traveling alone, in part because they suspected that the guests might be spinsters intent on hurling themselves off balconies to end their desperate solitude. Today, the losers are happily checking in at Japanese mountain lodges, not to mention Australian spas, Vietnamese hotels, and Hawaiian beach resorts.

18   And unlike their foreign counterparts in the New Girl Order, Japanese singles don't seem to be worrying much about finding Mr. Right. A majority of Japanese single women between 25 and 54 say that they'd be just as happy never to marry. Peggy Orenstein, writing in the *New York Times Magazine* in 2001, noted that Japanese women find American-style sentimentality about marriage puzzling. Yoko Harruka, a television personality and author of a book called *I Won't Get Married*—written after she realized that her then-fiancé expected her to quit her career and serve him tea—says that her countrymen propose with lines like, "I want you to cook miso soup for me for the rest of my life." Japanese SYFs complain that men don't show affection and expect women to cook dinner obediently while they sit on their duffs reading the paper. Is it any wonder that the women prefer Burberry?

19   Post-Communist Europe is also going through the shock of the New Girl Order. Under Communist rule, women tended to marry and have kids early. In the late eighties, the mean age of first birth in East Germany, for instance, was 24.7, far lower than the West German average of 28.3. According to Tomáš Sobotka of the Vienna Institute of Demography, young people had plenty of reasons to schedule an early wedding day. Tying the knot was the only way to gain independence from parents, since married couples could get an apartment, while singles could not. Furthermore, access to modern contraception, which the state proved either unable or unwilling to produce at affordable prices, was limited. Marriages frequently began as the result of unplanned pregnancies. And then the Wall came down. The free market launched shiny new job opportunities, making higher education more valuable than under Communist regimes, which had apportioned jobs and degrees. Suddenly, a young Polish or Hungarian woman might imagine having a career, and some fun at the same time. In cities like Warsaw and Budapest, young adults can find pleasures completely unknown to previous generations of singles. In one respect, Eastern European and Russian SYFs were better equipped than Japanese ones for the new order. The strong single woman, an invisible figure in Japan, has long been a prominent character in the social landscape of Eastern Europe and Russia, a legacy, doubtless, of the Communist-era emphasis on egalitarianism (however inconsistently applied) and the massive male casualties of World War II.

20   Not that the post-Communist SYF is any happier with the husband material than her Japanese counterpart is. Eastern European gals complain about men overindulged by widowed mothers and unable to adapt to the new economy.

According to *The Economist*, many towns in what used to be East Germany now face *Frauenmangel*—a lack of women—as SYFs who excelled in school have moved west for jobs, leaving the poorly performing men behind. In some towns, the ratio is just 40 women to 100 men. Women constitute the majority of both high school and college graduates in Poland. Though Russian women haven't joined the new order to the same extent, they're also grumbling about the men. In Russian TV's *The Balzac Age*, which chronicles the adventures of four single thirtysomething women, Alla, a high-achieving yuppie attorney, calls a handyman for help in her apartment. The two—to their mutual horror—recognize each other as former high school sweethearts, now moving in utterly different social universes. There's much to admire in the New Girl Order—and not just the previously hidden cleavage. Consider the lives most likely led by the mothers, grandmothers, great-grandmothers, and so on of the fashionista at the Warsaw airport or of the hard-partying Beijing actuary. Those women reached adulthood, which usually meant 18 or even younger; married guys from their village, or, if they were particularly daring, from the village across the river; and then had kids—end of story, except for maybe some goat milking, rice planting, or, in urban areas, shop tending. The New Girl Order means good-bye to such limitations. It means the possibility of more varied lives, of more expansively nourished aspirations. It also means a richer world. SYFs bring ambition, energy, and innovation to the economy, both local and global; they simultaneously promote and enjoy what author Brink Lindsey calls "the age of abundance." The SYF, in sum, represents a dramatic advance in personal freedom and wealth.

21 But as with any momentous social change, the New Girl Order comes with costs—in this case, profound ones. The globalized SYF upends centuries of cultural traditions. However limiting, those traditions shaped how families formed and the next generation grew up. So it makes sense that the SYF is partly to blame for a worldwide drop in fertility rates. To keep a population stable, or at its "replacement level," women must have an average of at least 2.1 children. Under the New Girl Order, though, women delay marriage and childbearing, which itself tends to reduce the number of kids, and sometimes—because the opportunity costs of children are much higher for educated women—they forgo them altogether. Save Albania, no European country stood at or above replacement levels in 2000. Three-quarters of Europeans now live in countries with fertility rates below 1.5, and even that number is inflated by a disproportionately high fertility rate among Muslim immigrants. Oddly, the most Catholic European countries—Italy, Spain, and Poland—have the lowest fertility rates, under 1.3. Much of Asia looks similar. In Japan, fertility rates are about 1.3. Hong Kong, according to the CIA's *World Factbook*, at 0.98 has broken the barrier of one child per woman.

22 For many, fertility decline seems to be one more reason to celebrate the New Girl Order. Fewer people means fewer carbon footprints, after all, and thus potential environmental relief. But while we're waiting for the temperature to drop a bit, economies will plunge in ways that will be extremely difficult to manage—and that, ironically, will likely spell the SYF lifestyle's demise. As Philip Longman explains in his important book *The Empty Cradle*, dramatic declines in fertility rates

equal aging and eventually shriveling populations. Japan now has one of the oldest populations in the world—one-third of its population, demographers predict, will be over 60 within a decade. True, fertility decline often spurs a temporary economic boost, as more women enter the workforce and increase income and spending, as was the case in 1980s Japan. In time, though, those women—and their male peers—will get old and need pensions and more health care. And who will pay for that? With fewer children, the labor force shrinks, and so do tax receipts. Europe today has 35 pensioners for every 100 workers, Longman points out. By 2050, those 100 will be responsible for 75 pensioners; in Spain and Italy, the ratio of workers to pensioners will be a disastrous *one-to-one*. Adding to the economic threat, seniors with few or no children are more likely to look to the state for support than are elderly people with more children. The final irony is that the ambitious, hardworking SYF will have created a world where her children, should she have them, will need to work even harder in order to support her in her golden years.

23   Aging populations present other problems. For one thing, innovation and technological breakthroughs tend to be a young person's game—think of the young Turks of the information technology revolution. Fewer young workers and higher tax burdens don't make a good recipe for innovation and growth. Also, having fewer people leads to declining markets, and thus less business investment and formation. Where would you want to expand your cosmetics business: Ireland, where the population continues to renew itself, or Japan, where it is imploding?

24   And finally, the New Girl Order has given birth to a worrying ambivalence toward domestic life and the men who would help create it. Many analysts argue that today's women of childbearing age would have more kids if only their countries provided generous benefits for working mothers, as they do in Sweden and France. And it's true that those two countries have seen fertility rates inch up toward replacement levels in recent years. But in countries newly entering the New Girl Order, what SYFs complain about isn't so much a gap between work and family life as a chasm between their own aspirations and those of the men who'd be their husbands (remember those Japanese women skeptical of a future cooking miso soup). Adding to the SYF's alienation from domesticity is another glaring fact usually ignored by demographers: the New Girl Order is fun. Why get married when you can party on?

25   That raises an interesting question: Why are SYFs in the United States—the Rome of the New Girl Order—still so interested in marriage? By large margins, surveys suggest, American women want to marry and have kids. Indeed, our fertility rates, though lower than replacement level among college-educated women, are still healthier than those in most SYF countries (including Sweden and France). The answer may be that the family has always been essential ballast to the individualism, diversity, mobility, and sheer giddiness of American life. It helps that the U.S., like northwestern Europe, has a long tradition of "companionate marriage"—that is, marriage based not on strict roles but on common interests and mutual affection. Companionate marriage always rested on the assumption of female equality. Yet countries like Japan are joining the new order with no history of companionate relations, and when it comes to adapting to the new order, the cultural cupboard is bare.

A number of analysts, including demographer Nicholas Eberstadt, have also argued that it is America's religiousness that explains our relatively robust fertility, though the Polish fertility decline raises questions about that explanation. It's by no means certain that Americans will remain exceptional in this regard. The most recent census data show a "sharp increase," over just the past six years, in the percentage of Americans in their twenties who have never married. Every year sees more books celebrating the SYF life, boasting titles like *Singular Existence* and *Living Alone and Loving It*. And SYFs will increasingly find themselves in a disappointing marriage pool. The *New York Times* excited considerable discussion this summer with a front-page article announcing that young women working full-time in several cities were now outearning their male counterparts. A historically unprecedented trend like this is bound to have a further impact on relations between the sexes and on marriage and childbearing rates.

26   Still, for now, women don't seem too worried about the New Girl Order's downside. On the contrary. The order marches on, as one domino after another falls to its pleasures and aspirations. Now, the *Singapore Times* tells us, young women in Vietnam are suddenly putting off marriage because they "want to have some fun"—and fertility rates have plummeted from 3.8 children in 1998 to 2.1 in 2006.

27   And then there's India. "The Gen Now bachelorette brigade is in no hurry to tie the knot," reports the *India Tribune*. "They're single, independent, and happy." Young urbanites are pushing up sales of branded apparel; Indian chick lit, along with *Cosmopolitan* and *Vogue*, flies out of shops in Delhi and Mumbai. Amazingly enough, fertility rates have dropped below replacement level in several of India's major cities, thanks in part to aspirant fashionistas. If in India—*India!*—the New Girl Order can reduce population growth, then perhaps nothing is beyond its powers. At the very least, the Indian experiment gives new meaning to the phrase "shop till you drop."

QUESTIONS FOR ANALYSIS AND DISCUSSION

1. How does Hymowitz describe "the New Girl Order"? What cultural icons does she refer to in her description?
2. What warning does Hymowitz give if the New Girl Order continues unchecked?
3. According to Hymowitz, what is a "hotel family" or a "parasite single"? Do you see versions of this in the United States? Explain.
4. Hymowitz asks, "Why are SYFs [Single Young Females] in the United States . . . still so interested in marriage?" Answer this question from your own perspective. How does the marriage culture in the United States different from the marriage culture in other countries, such as Japan?
5. How do the points Hymowitz raises in her essay connect to points made by Melana Zyla Vickers in her article "Where the Boys Aren't"? Analyze and discuss the possible cause/effect connections between the two essays.

READING THE VISUAL

Asking for Directions

Don Reilly

This cartoon by Don Reilly first appeared in *The New Yorker* magazine.

"Because my genetic programming prevents me from stopping to ask directions—that's why!"

QUESTIONS FOR ANALYSIS AND DISCUSSION

1. It has been a long-held adage that men don't stop to ask for directions. Is it self-reliance? independence? Or are men simply unwilling to admit that they need help? What social impressions may influence their reluctance? Explain.

2. Are women more likely to stop and ask for directions or other assistance? Or more importantly, why does this stereotype exist?

3. In the cartoon, the man tells the woman that it is his "genetic programming" that prevents him from stopping. How do you think the authors in this section would respond to this cartoon?

4. Explain why, in your opinion, the cartoon is—or isn't—true. Is this an American comedic situation, or does is it hold true for other cultures? Show this cartoon to some international students and ask for their reactions. Report your results in class for discussion.

Soldiers Ahead
Holly Yeager

Over a relatively short period of time, the American military has witnessed tremendous changes in its culture. Many questions remain, however. Should women be allowed to participate in armed combat? Would they pose a distraction, and thus a danger to the men fighting next to them? Are they less physically able to fight? What happens when they are captured by the enemy? Are they better negotiators? In this next essay, Holly Yeager describes the female face of the military today—and that face, she explains, no longer wears Montezuma Red lipstick.

Holly Yeager, a Washington journalist, was until recently the U.S. politics correspondent for *The Financial Times*. She previously covered the Pentagon for the Hearst newspaper group and Defense Daily and now writes frequently about women's issues. This essay appeared in the summer 2007 issue of the *Wilson Quarterly*.

BEFORE YOU READ

What is your personal viewpoint on women in the military? Should women be allowed to join field artillery units? If there were a draft, should women be included? Explain why or why not.

AS YOU READ

What objections do people traditionally have with women in the military or participating in ground combat? In light of today's technology, are the concerns expressed 30 years ago less applicable? Why or why not?

1   When Dymetra Bass was a drill sergeant, she had no trouble proving her mettle to the fresh Army recruits she pushed through basic training at Fort Leonard Wood in Missouri. "Every private would tell me, the meanest drill sergeants were the women drill sergeants," she says with a touch of pride. "We had to be so tough because people come from all walks of life. Some people, women have never told them what to do before."

2   Bass enlisted in 1989, right after high school, where she had been a cheerleader, and she arrived with an essential drill sergeant's tool: a booming voice. She also knew how to keep her soldiers motivated. "I like control, so it was easy for me. I like being in the front. I like leading. I believe in leading by example."

3   But things changed when Bass moved to Fort Sill, Oklahoma, in 1999 as part of the first group of female drill sergeants assigned to train new members of field artillery units—one of the few areas still closed to women. "It was the drill sergeants who couldn't accept us, because they were artillery, and then you bring these women in here to teach these civilians how to be soldiers, and teach them combat skills. . . . They didn't believe it could be done, or done the right way."

4   Bass had no background in artillery, but that didn't matter. Her job was to do basic training. But her male colleagues still worried that the women wouldn't be able to carry their load and that to pick up the slack, men would always have to run with the fastest group and demonstrate the most demanding drills, such as scurrying under barbed wire and using a rope to maneuver across water. "We had to prove ourselves a lot more," Bass says.

5   Female leaders up and down the U.S. military's chain of command—from non-commissioned officers such as Bass, who deal most directly with troops, to two and three-star generals and admirals—talk about having to prove themselves, again and again. But slowly, and rather quietly, more and more women have been doing just that. Women make up 14.4 percent of enlisted personnel and 15.9 percent of the officer corps in the 1.4-million-strong active-duty U.S. military, according to the most recent Defense Department figures. That is a marked increase from the 1.6 percent of the military that was female in 1973, when the draft ended and new recruitment goals for women were set.

6   The war in Iraq has been a major test of women's new role in the military, and they seem to have performed well in the field. Women are now permitted to serve in more than 90 percent of military occupations; though they are still barred from jobs or units whose main mission is direct ground combat. But the fluid lines of conflict in Iraq have put the units in which women serve, such as military police, supply, and support, in the line of fire, challenging traditional ideas about what constitutes a "combat" position. "Women are fighting, they are in the streets and on the patrols," says Pat Foote, a retired Army brigadier general. "They are running the convoys, getting shot at and shooting back." The war's death toll reflects this battlefield reality: As of early June 2007, the nearly 3,500 U.S. service members who had lost their lives in Operation Iraqi Freedom included more than 70 women.

7   "Critics speculated a lot about what would happen if we let women in these jobs," notes Lory Manning, a retired Navy captain who directs the Women in the Military project at the Women's Research & Education Institute in Washington, D.C. "[They speculated that] the men couldn't do their jobs, that everyone would be pregnant, that they'd be so busy having sex that they couldn't do anything else. "We now have units under fire with men and women in them," Manning says. "We have experience of women firing weapons. They don't fall to emotional bits."

8   Nor has the American public fallen to bits. The sometimes dramatic footage of women on the front-lines, of women returning home to military hospitals, even the too-good-to-be-true story of the capture and rescue of Jessica Lynch, have prompted little popular outcry against women's role in the war, and little evidence that the public is somehow less willing to tolerate their suffering than that of men. And while Lynndie England drew public attention and outrage for her role in the Abu Ghraib prison scandal, advocates of women in the military say critics have been on the lookout for any systemic failure of women to perform well in Iraq—and have found little to point to. Instead, just as the invasion of Panama and the Persian Gulf War led to reviews of women's role in the military—and expansions of the positions open to them—Iraq will likely prompt another reconsideration. Any increase in their combat role would improve women's opportunities at the top of the

command structure, where their numbers are small today in part because of their lack of combat experience.

9   More important than how uniformed women and the public have reacted is how America's armed services have fared. After more than 30 years of experience with women in leadership positions and in the ranks, what may be most surprising is how little the rise of women has actually affected the American military. Make no mistake, the armed services have experienced enormous changes, including the incorporation of both devastating new killing technologies and more family friendly personnel policies. But just as women's distinctive contribution to the forging of today's highly effective fighting force is hard to identify, so is it difficult to say what part they have played in enhancing some of the military's "softer" features.

10   Technological advances, new thinking from outside the military, changes in the attributes of senior leaders, and the demands of the all-volunteer force have resulted in adjustments in the way the military is led. Women as well as men have had to change. "It used to be that you ordered somebody to do something," says Darlene Iskra, a retired Navy officer who runs a leadership training program for young Navy and Marine Corps officers at the University of Maryland. "Now, it's more that you ask them to do it, but they understand it's an order, or you have meetings and ask people's opinions, ask for their input, and help them to own the solution, rather than dictating."

11   That shift to a more collaborative approach—which some may attribute to the growing role of women—is in part explained by the fact that new technology has given junior officers more access to information, which used to be the purview of age and experience. "Women have in some measure changed the culture, but the access to information, and the horizontal nature of how information is managed and controlled . . . came at about the same time," Vice Admiral Ann Rondeau says. In addition, because of the war in Iraq, "the average junior officer in the military today has more operational experience in war than the average senior officer." As young officers bring their real-life experience and information to the table, "I think there is a move toward collaboration that would normally be seen as a feminine leadership trait," Rondeau says. She prefers to see this tendency as a democratic product of the speed with which information flows.

12   A 2004 study of four Army divisions that had just returned from tours in Iraq found that most leaders had strong technical and tactical skills. What set the best leaders apart was interpersonal skills. The study, headed by Walter F. Ulmer Jr., a retired Army general and leadership specialist, identified what it called the "Big 12"—a set of behaviors exhibited by officers best able to achieve operational excellence and motivate good soldiers to stay in the Army. At the top of the list: keeps cool under pressure; clearly explains missions, standards, and priorities; sees the big picture, provides context and perspective. The ability to make "tough, sound decisions on time" was also among the most prized skills. Despite the growing value of collaboration, military leaders know better than most that, ultimately, hard choices need to be made—sometimes with lives hanging in the balance—and only one person can be in charge. The study did not say that the decider shouldn't be a woman.

13   Today's general acceptance of women on the battlefield is a far cry from the skepticism—and sometimes outright hostility—that greeted the opening of the services

to women after the end of the Vietnam War. Faced with manpower shortages when the draft ended in 1973 and expecting that the Equal Rights Amendment would be enacted, Pentagon officials set aggressive goals for recruiting women and started changing the rules that governed the jobs female service members were allowed to do. American women already had a long military history, but it was a history that had largely seen them confined to separate branches such as the WAVES and WAAC, which called on women to enlist during World War II in order to "free a man to fight." Now women were to be integrated into regular service units. Could they really carry heavy packs on their backs? What would happen if they got pregnant? Would military wives put up with their presence in the ranks?

14   A question posed in a 1976 study by the U.S. Army Research Institute for the Behavioral and Social Sciences provided a gauge of prevailing attitudes: "What percentage of women will it take to degrade unit performance?" But the results of a three-day field exercise with units ranging from all-male to 35 percent female, and a follow-up study the next year, surprised nearly everyone. "When properly trained and led, women are proving to be good soldiers in the field, as well as in garrison," the Army concluded. A research brief titled Military Readiness: Women Are Not a Problem, published by RAND in 1997, showed that the tone had shifted a little in 20 years. It found that gender integration in military units "had a relatively small effect on readiness, cohesion, and morale," but that a unit's leadership, training, and workload had a much deeper influence.

15   In the heat of the 1970s debate, researchers' findings that women would not wreck the joint did little to cool the fury of traditionalists. Perhaps the most dramatic statement of opposition—one that still rankles some women in uniform—came from James Webb, a decorated ex-Marine who would go on to become secretary of the Navy in the Reagan administration and get elected to the Senate from Virginia as a Democrat in 2006. Webb, a Naval Academy graduate, took particular offense at the decision to admit women to the service academies beginning in 1976. In an emotional 1979 screed in *The Washingtonian* titled "Women Can't Fight," Webb argued that women were unsuited to be military leaders and unfit for the trenches. "There is a place for women in our military, but not in combat," he wrote. "And their presence at institutions dedicated to the preparation of men for combat command is poisoning that preparation. By attempting to sexually sterilize the Naval Academy environment in the name of equality, this country has sterilized the whole process of combat leadership training, and our military forces are doomed to suffer the consequences."

16   Such public declarations against women in the military are rare today. During his Senate campaign, Webb apologized for any "hardship" his article had caused and said he was "completely comfortable" with the role women play in the military. But on-the-record comfort does not mean the question is settled. The day I met Bass, she said that one of the officers in her command had told her in casual conversation earlier in the day that he did not think women belonged anywhere near combat, because he would be so concerned about protecting them that he would be distracted from his own duties.

17   International comparisons don't offer much useful guidance about how to integrate women into the armed services. The United States has more women in the military than

any other country. Those with the fewest barriers to women in combat, such as Sweden and Norway, also have small forces with fundamentally different missions. In Israel, women are automatically conscripted into the armed forces, but many receive exemptions for religious or family reasons. Some ground combat units include women, and an army commission is currently studying whether infantry, armor, and special forces should be opened to women. The Israeli military's highest echelons still include no female officers. In the United States, one of the main complaints of critics is differing physical standards for men and women. (To get a perfect score on the Army fitness test, a 22-year-old man must do 75 push-ups, 80 sit-ups, and run two miles in 13 minutes. Women soldiers must do 46 push-ups, 80 sit-ups, and run two miles in 15:38).

18   The promotion system is another sore spot. Boards that meet each year to consider which officers from each service will be promoted make their decisions based on the information they find in a file about each candidate, including work history, training, honors, performance evaluations, any disciplinary action—often a photograph. They are also given equal opportunity goals, designed to ensure that the number of women and minorities promoted in each group of officers reflects that group's representation in the promotable pool. Such guidelines urge board members not to penalize candidates because they lack certain job experiences, such as combat assignments, if they were barred from such positions. But race and gender are not the only concerns. The promotion boards are pulled in many other directions as well, needing to keep a balance between, say, helicopter and fixed-wing pilots. Most analyses find the promotion system to be widely accepted by men and women within the military.

19   For many of the women who entered the military in the 1970s and are senior officers today, it is simply the access to that merit system, the chance to succeed or fail based on their own performance without first being discounted by others and denied opportunities because of their gender, that may be the biggest change they have seen.

20   Despite that opportunity, and their larger numbers, women face a "brass ceiling," with only the thinnest representation at the highest ranks. The limited range of combat-related jobs open to women until the 1990s meant that many lack the experience that is highly valued in promotion decisions. At the same time, the arc of a military career is long, and because the service academies only opened their doors to women in 1976, the cohort of female officers with both those top credentials are only now in position to use them to help push their careers to the highest levels.

21   In the face of such institutional limits to advancement, it can be difficult to understand why so many women entered the military in the 1970s and '80s. Many say they did so because they wanted the chance to serve their country, just like men, and to explore interesting career paths. But there was something else. Vice Admiral Rondeau, one of just five female officers with three stars currently serving in the U.S. military and frequently mentioned as a candidate to become the first four-star woman in the country's history, explains: "There were glass ceilings. There were prejudices. There were barriers. But . . . there was equal pay for equal work."

22   Even as they prove themselves and parry occasional resistance to their presence, some women have brought their personal—and sometimes decidedly

feminine—approaches to this most masculine of institutions. While none would argue that they are fundamentally changing the culture around them, they are finding different ways to lead.

23   Barbara Bell, a Navy captain who graduated from the Naval Academy in 1983, says it took many years in uniform before she came to a simple realization: "I recognize that I'm different. I recognize that I stick out, and I'm not going to fight it," she says with a smile. Bell, a pilot who now works in acquisitions, recently told an audience that included young servicewomen that she tries hard to establish a respectful office environment and to pay attention to the work-life balance for her staff and herself. Most days she leaves work by 4:30 to pick up her 7-year-old son.

24   While many senior women in uniform say they had few female role models and mentors, their ascendance is beginning to change that, too. The mere presence of more women in the senior officer grades has made a difference. "It just helps everyone to know what the art of the possible is, and that they can continue to move up the ranks," says Lieutenant General Ann E. Dunwoody, deputy chief of staff of the Army.

25   Bass—now a first sergeant, the top enlisted soldier working at the National Defense University in Washington, D.C.—says that when she was in Iraq in 2005, she and her unit's commander, also a woman, "did things a little differently." Sitting in her office at Fort McNair, she pointed to a photograph of a young female soldier. When Bass and her commander got the news that the soldier had been killed on duty, "we woke everyone up—it was at night—so they wouldn't wake up to it [in the morning], so they could deal with it."

26   After addressing them in formation, Bass stayed with her soldiers, talking to them, listening to them cry, trying to let them know that she understood their sadness and, at the same time, that their work had to continue. "I think we were more nurturing, which also motivated the troops to do well, and when they had problems, they knew they could come into our offices and talk to us, compared to the male first sergeants, who were so hard." There is growing evidence that the military is putting new emphasis on just the kind of interpersonal skills Bass displayed.

27   Day-to-day standards for behavior have also changed. Pinups are gone from barracks walls and dirty language has been cleaned up. "It's definitely had an impact on the social culture of the military, which used to be one of the great boys' clubs of the world," says Phillip Carter, a military analyst and former Army officer. "It's not just this Spartan legion of men. Now it's much more like society at large."

28   For all that, it is hard to find anyone, male or female, in or out of uniform, who would assert that the ascendance of women to leadership positions has fundamentally changed martial culture. "The military is still not just overwhelmingly male, but its ways of doing things are still very male," says Mady Segal, a sociology professor at the University of Maryland whose work focuses on women in the military. Top leaders go to the service academies, where traditional culture is reinforced. Even though about 20 percent of new students are women, they must make difficult adjustments. But perhaps more important in maintaining the military's ethos than tradition and machismo, haircuts and push-ups, is the fact that much of what the military does is determined by its well-defined mission to be ready, as the Army field manual puts it, "to fight and win the Nation's wars."

29   Successful women in the military are well aware of that basic fact, and many say they did not arrive with a desire to change the institution. "You are joining an institution that has doctrine, that has tradition, and you either appreciate it and come to love that aspect of the institution, or at some point you say, 'No, this really isn't where I want to be in life,' and you go back to civilian life," says Rear Admiral Michelle Howard, who graduated from the Naval Academy in 1982, a member of the third class to include women.

30   The strength of that tradition does not mean that the organization has not changed since the 1970s. But while those changes—in management style, family-friendliness, and other areas—may be seen as a shift toward what management gurus call a more "feminine" approach to leadership, they reflect other factors at work—most important, the demands of attracting, and retaining, the all-volunteer force. Younger people in all walks of life are less willing to sacrifice everything for their careers, and are more concerned with preserving their lives outside work. As in the corporate world, military leaders have recognized the need for policies to protect investments in careers and training with benefits for families, as well as for soldiers themselves. But the prospect of losing skilled professionals—in an organization that wants its leadership to be as diverse as its enlisted corps—is in some ways more troubling for the military. As Howard explains, "We don't have the luxury of a corporation, of hiring in someone with this skill set. . . . So then the issue becomes, how do we retain this talent?"

31   Recent research indicates that the departure of female officers, largely due to such issues of work-life balance, poses a particular challenge to the Pentagon. A study published early this year of officers at several career points by the Government Accountability Office found that "all services encountered challenges retaining female officers." The difference was most marked in the Navy, with its increasingly long spells of duty at sea, where continuation rates among female officers with four or five years of service averaged nine percentage points lower than those of male officers.

32   A 2005 report from the Army Research Institute found that the gap between male and female Army officers who said they intended to stay in the service until retirement age had held relatively steady over 10 years. In a 1995 survey, 66 percent of male officers and 51 percent of female officers said they planned to stay; in 2004, the numbers were 69 and 53 percent, respectively.

33   Male and female officers agree that women face special challenges in pursuing military careers, but they differ over the reasons, according to a 2001 RAND report. Male officers offered researchers three main explanations: "Women are inherently less capable, physically and mentally, to perform a military job and lead troops," in the study's words, and the ban on women in combat jobs has kept them from occupations with the greatest opportunities for advancement. The men also said that male superiors fear that they will find themselves unable to refute an unwarranted charge of sexual harassment and therefore hold back from interactions, such as mentoring, with female subordinates.

34   Female officers said their chances to perform and the recognition they received were "diminished by expectations that they are less capable," according to the study.

Female officers reported "difficulties forming peer and mentor relationships," and said they "receive fewer career-enhancing assignments." They also cited a conflict between work demands and family responsibilities, and a lack of consensus on the appropriate role for women in the military. The female officers said sexual harassment leads to an uncomfortable working environment for women who are harassed, and they agreed that male fears of harassment charges had inhibited interactions between men and women.

35   Officers of both sexes cited the amount of time they spent away from their families and the enjoyment they got from their jobs as the most important factors influencing their decision about whether to leave the Army. But family issues appear to have a special effect on women officers. In the research institute study, time away from family was listed as the most important reason by 43 percent of women planning to leave, and 27 percent of men. One reason for the difference is that female officers are much more likely than their male peers to be married to another person in the military, who can't easily follow when a new posting comes along. Another study, conducted in 1997 by the Army Research Institute, found that 80 percent of male officers were married, but just seven percent of them had wives in the military. Among female officers, 58 percent were married, and more than half of their spouses were also in the military.

36   For women in the military, there are plenty of easy reminders of how much things have changed. Female Marines in the 1940s were strongly encouraged to wear lipstick, but it had to match the red cord on their winter caps—a requirement that prompted Elizabeth Arden to make Montezuma Red for just that purpose. As recently as 1989, when Bass enlisted, it was assumed that women would remain far away from combat zones. "When I first came in the Army," she says, "my supervisor told me, 'If you're firing your weapon, the war is over.' "

37   Of course, this sort of vision of slow, steady, and accepted progress for women is not the only way to look at the recent past. In 1990, Darlene Iskra, the now-retired naval officer who provides leadership training to recently commissioned Navy and Marine personnel, became the first woman to command a Navy vessel. She remembers the stack of congratulatory messages that awaited her when she arrived at her ship, the USS Opportune, and the way her male colleagues showed new respect when she wore her command pin. But 10 years later, something had changed: "The reason I got out was because I felt like an ensign again. They just did not respect me. It was awful."

38   Elaine Donnelly, president of the Center for Military Readiness, a non-profit advocacy group, complains that career-minded female officers have been behind the decades-long push to open more jobs to women, and that the changes have come at the cost of dangerous "double standards involving women." A case in point, she said, was the treatment of Lamar Owens Jr., a former star quarterback at the Naval Academy, who was accused of rape by a female classmate. Owens and the classmate were both drinking and ended up in bed together. He said their sex was consensual; she said she was raped.

39   Owens was acquitted of the charge but dismissed from the academy and ordered to repay the cost of his education after being found guilty of conduct unbecoming

an officer. His accuser admitted to breaking academy rules but was granted immunity as a witness and permitted to remain enrolled.

40   But even Donnelly, perhaps the most outspoken conservative critic of the Pentagon's gender policies, doesn't directly call for a rollback of women's role in the military. As a practical matter, it is hard to see how the Army and other branches could be staffed without a significant complement of women—and some politicians in both parties are calling for an expansion of troop strength.

41   Does all this mean that it is only a matter of time until women are fully integrated into the armed services leadership? New technology, fresh attention to inclusive leadership styles, and societal attitudes all favor a greater role for women in the top ranks.

42   Deeper changes in military culture, however, are likely to be difficult. Along with the physiological fact that most women cannot develop the upper body strength thought to be needed in traditional warfare, general questions about their fitness for the most direct combat assignments remain. Lory Manning, of the Women's Research & Education Institute, says that the issue of women in combat will still be politically sensitive, but she expects it to be re-examined after the Iraq war. She singles out the "co-location rule," which prohibits women with non-combat jobs, such as medics and mechanics, from being based with combat units, as one that will likely be changed formally after the war. "Sheer necessity made it go away" in Iraq. But Manning does not foresee a sweeping removal of the remaining bans on direct combat.

43   The career of Erin Morgan, who graduated from West Point in May and is now a second lieutenant in the Army Intelligence Corps, is off to a promising start, with wide opportunities and the open doors that a degree from the academy can secure. But a few weeks before graduation, she said that women still do not have an easy time fitting in. "Soldiering is a masculine trait, something that separates the men from the women and the men from the boys," she says. "That is something that cadets still struggle with."

44   Amid the constant reminders of great warriors of the past embodied in statues and paintings at West Point, Morgan saw depictions of Douglas MacArthur, George Patton, Dwight Eisenhower, and other fabled generals. But she was only able to find one woman: Joan of Arc, whose image is part of the mess hall mural.

QUESTIONS FOR ANALYSIS AND DISCUSSION

1. In what ways has technology opened up the armed forces to women?
2. How does women's role in the military encourage Americans to re-assess their views of men and women and gender roles?
3. How are women in the armed forces changing the culture of the military? What challenges do both men and women in the military face when addressing the changing culture of this institution?
4. At the beginning of this essay, you were asked to consider your own opinion regarding women in the military. After reading this article, has your opinion altered in any way? Why or why not?

Homeward Bound
Linda Hirshman

The next reading addresses the "mommy-wars debate" concerning women who "opt-out" of work in favor of staying at home to care for their children. Prompted to write after reading a story in the *New York Times* describing the trend, Women's Studies Professor Linda Hirshman argues against what she believes to be the fallacies of "choice feminism" in which women can choose to stay at home or work outside of it. Hirshman contends that this is no choice at all, because it removes women from positions of power and spheres of political and social influence. Her article set off a firestorm of controversy. In a follow-up article, Hirshman said, "even though I knew the Greeks made Socrates drink poison, the reaction to my judgment took me by surprise." Are young women making a mistake when they leave work for at-home motherhood? Or is this choice an example of how far women have come?

Hirshman is a lawyer and well-known feminist. She is a retired professor of philosophy and Women's Studies at Brandeis University. She has written for a variety of periodicals, including *Glamour, Tikkun, Ms.*, and the *Boston Globe.* She is the author of several books, including *The Woman's Guide to Law School* (1999), *Hard Bargains: The Politics of Sex* (1999), and *Get to Work: A Manifesto for Women of the World* (2006), in which she expands the argument that follows. Hirshman's essay appeared in the *American Prospect* on November 21, 2005.

BEFORE YOU READ

In your opinion and experience, are women socially pressured to stay at home? Do men want them to stay home once children enter the picture?

AS YOU READ

What does Hirshman mean that the "real glass ceiling is at home"? What is the "glass ceiling"? Explain.

The Truth about Elite Women

1 Half the wealthiest, most-privileged, best-educated females in the country stay home with their babies rather than work in the market economy. When in September *The New York Times* featured an article exploring a piece of this story, "Many Women at Elite Colleges Set Career Path to Motherhood," the blogosphere went ballistic, countering with anecdotes and sarcasm. *Slate*'s Jack Shafer accused the *Times* of "weasel-words" and of publishing the same story—essentially, "The Opt-Out Revolution"—every few years, and, recently, every few weeks. A month after the flap, the *Times*' only female columnist, Maureen Dowd, invoked the elite-college article in her contribution to the *Times*' running soap, "What's a Modern Girl to Do?" about

how women must forgo feminism even to get laid. The colleges article provoked such fury that the *Times* had to post an explanation of the then-student journalist's methodology on its Web site.

2   There's only one problem: There is important truth in the dropout story. Even though it appeared in *The New York Times*.

3   I stumbled across the news three years ago when researching a book on marriage after feminism. I found that among the educated elite, who are the logical heirs of the agenda of empowering women, feminism has largely failed in its goals. There are few women in the corridors of power, and marriage is essentially unchanged. The number of women at universities exceeds the number of men. But, more than a generation after feminism, the number of women in elite jobs doesn't come close.

4   Why did this happen? The answer I discovered—an answer neither feminist leaders nor women themselves want to face—is that while the public world has changed, albeit imperfectly, to accommodate women among the elite, private lives have hardly budged. The real glass ceiling is at home.

5   Looking back, it seems obvious that the unreconstructed family was destined to re-emerge after the passage of feminism's storm of social change. Following the original impulse to address everything in the lives of women, feminism turned its focus to cracking open the doors of the public power structure. This was no small task. At the beginning, there were male juries and male Ivy League schools, sex-segregated want ads, discriminatory employers, harassing colleagues. As a result of feminist efforts—and larger economic trends—the percentage of women, even of mothers in full- or part-time employment, rose robustly through the 1980s and early '90s.

6   But then the pace slowed. The census numbers for all working mothers leveled off around 1990 and have fallen modestly since 1998. In interviews, women with enough money to quit work say they are "choosing" to opt out. Their words conceal a crucial reality: the belief that women are responsible for child-rearing and home-making was largely untouched by decades of workplace feminism. Add to this the good evidence that the upper-class workplace has become more demanding and then mix in the successful conservative cultural campaign to reinforce traditional gender roles and you've got a perfect recipe for feminism's stall.

7   People who don't like the message attack the data. True, the *Times* based its college story on a survey of questionable reliability and a bunch of interviews. It is not necessary to give credence to Dowd's book, from which her *Times Magazine* piece was taken and which seems to be mostly based on her lifetime of bad dates and some e-mails from fellow *Times* reporters, to wonder if all this noise doesn't mean something important is going on in the politics of the sexes.

8   What evidence is good enough? Let's start with you. Educated and affluent reader, if you are a 30- or 40-something woman with children, what are you doing? Husbands, what are your wives doing? Older readers, what are your married daughters with children doing? I have asked this question of scores of women and men. Among the affluent-educated-married population, women are letting their careers slide to tend the home fires. If my interviewees are working, they work largely part time, and their part-time careers are not putting them in the executive suite.

9 Here's some more evidence: During the '90s, I taught a course in sexual bargaining at a very good college. Each year, after the class reviewed the low rewards for child-care work, I asked how the students anticipated combining work with child-rearing. At least half the female students described lives of part-time or home-based work. Guys expected their female partners to care for the children. When I asked the young men how they reconciled that prospect with the manifest low regard the market has for child care, they were mystified. Turning to the women who had spoken before, they said, uniformly, "But she chose it."

10 Even Ronald Coase, Nobel Prize–winner in economics in 1991, quotes the aphorism that "the plural of anecdote is data." So how many anecdotes does it take to make data? I—a 1970s member of the National Organization for Women (NOW), a donor to EMILY's List, and a professor of women's studies—did not set out to find this. I stumbled across the story when, while planning a book, I happened to watch Sex and the City's Charlotte agonize about getting her wedding announcement in the "Sunday Styles" section of The *New York Times*. What better sample, I thought, than the brilliantly educated and accomplished brides of the "Sunday Styles," circa 1996? At marriage, they included a vice president of client communication, a gastroenterologist, a lawyer, an editor, and a marketing executive. In 2003 and 2004, I tracked them down and called them. I interviewed about 80 percent of the 41 women who announced their weddings over three Sundays in 1996. Around 40 years old, college graduates with careers: Who was more likely than they to be reaping feminism's promise of opportunity? Imagine my shock when I found almost all the brides from the first Sunday at home with their children. Statistical anomaly? Nope. Same result for the next Sunday. And the one after that.

11 Ninety percent of the brides I found had had babies. Of the 30 with babies, five were still working full time. Twenty-five, or 85 percent, were not working full time. Of those not working full time, 10 were working part time but often a long way from their prior career paths. And half the married women with children were not working at all.

12 And there is more. In 2000, Harvard Business School professor Myra Hart surveyed the women of the classes of 1981, 1986, and 1991 and found that only 38 percent of female Harvard MBAs were working full time. A 2004 survey by the Center for Work-Life Policy of 2,443 women with a graduate degree or very prestigious bachelor's degree revealed that 43 percent of those women with children had taken a time out, primarily for family reasons. Richard Posner, federal appeals-court judge and occasional University of Chicago adjunct professor, reports that "the [*Times*] article confirms—what everyone associated with such institutions [elite law schools] has long known: that a vastly higher percentage of female than of male students will drop out of the workforce to take care of their children."

13 How many anecdotes to become data? The 2000 census showed a decline in the percentage of mothers of infants working full time, part time, or seeking employment. Starting at 31 percent in 1976, the percentage had gone up almost every year to 1992, hit a high of 58.7 percent in 1998, and then began to drop—to 55.2 percent in 2000, to 54.6 percent in 2002, to 53.7 percent in 2003. Statistics just released showed further decline to 52.9 percent in 2004. Even the percentage of working

mothers with children who were not infants declined between 2000 and 2003, from 62.8 percent to 59.8 percent.

14   Although college-educated women work more than others, the 2002 census shows that graduate or professional degrees do not increase work-force partici- pation much more than even one year of college. When their children are infants (under a year), 54 percent of females with graduate or professional degrees are not working full time (18 percent are working part time and 36 percent are not work- ing at all). Even among those who have children who are not infants, 41 percent are not working full time (18 percent are working part time and 23 percent are not working at all).

15   Economists argue about the meaning of the data, even going so far as to con- tend that more mothers are working. They explain that the bureau changed the definition of "work" slightly in 2000, the economy went into recession, and the falloff in women without children was similar. However, even if there wasn't a falloff but just a leveling off, this represents not a loss of present value but a loss of hope for the future—a loss of hope that the role of women in society will con- tinue to increase.

16   The arguments still do not explain the absence of women in elite workplaces. If these women were sticking it out in the business, law, and academic worlds, now, 30 years after feminism started filling the selective schools with women, the elite workplaces should be proportionately female. They are not. Law schools have been graduating classes around 40-percent female for decades—decades during which both schools and firms experienced enormous growth. And, although the legal pop- ulation will not be 40-percent female until 2010, in 2003, the major law firms had only 16-percent female partners, according to the American Bar Association. It's im- portant to note that elite workplaces like law firms grew in size during the very years that the percentage of female graduates was growing, leading you to expect a higher female employment than the pure graduation rate would indicate. The Harvard Busi- ness School has produced classes around 30-percent female. Yet only 10.6 percent of Wall Street's corporate officers are women, and a mere nine are Fortune 500 CEOs. Harvard Business School's dean, who extolled the virtues of interrupted ca- reers on *60 Minutes*, has a 20-percent female academic faculty.

17   It is possible that the workplace is discriminatory and hostile to family life. If firms had hired every childless woman lawyer available, that alone would have been enough to raise the percentage of female law partners above 16 percent in 30 years. It is also possible that women are voluntarily taking themselves out of the elite job competition for lower status and lower-paying jobs. Women must take responsibility for the consequences of their decisions. It defies reason to claim that the falloff from 40 percent of the class at law school to 16 percent of the partners at all the big law firms is unrelated to half the mothers with graduate and professional degrees leav- ing full-time work at childbirth and staying away for several years after that, or possibly bidding down.

18   This isn't only about day care. Half my *Times* brides quit before the first baby came. In interviews, at least half of them expressed a hope never to work again. None had realistic plans to work. More importantly, when they quit, they were already

alienated from their work or at least not committed to a life of work. One, a female MBA, said she could never figure out why the men at her workplace, which fired her, were so excited about making deals. "It's only money," she mused. Not surprisingly, even where employers offered them part-time work, they were not interested in taking it.

The Failure of Choice Feminism

19 What is going on? Most women hope to marry and have babies. If they resist the traditional female responsibilities of child-rearing and householding, what Arlie Hochschild called "The Second Shift," they are fixing for a fight. But elite women aren't resisting tradition. None of the stay-at-home brides I interviewed saw the second shift as unjust; they agree that the household is women's work. As one lawyer-bride put it in explaining her decision to quit practicing law after four years, "I had a wedding to plan." Another, an Ivy Leaguer with a master's degree, described it in management terms: "He's the CEO and I'm the CFO. He sees to it that the money rolls in and I decide how to spend it." It's their work, and they must do it perfectly. "We're all in here making fresh apple pie," said one, explaining her reluctance to leave her daughters in order to be interviewed. The family CFO described her activities at home: "I take my [3-year-old] daughter to all the major museums. We go to little movement classes."

20 Conservatives contend that the dropouts prove that feminism "failed" because it was too radical, because women didn't want what feminism had to offer. In fact, if half or more of feminism's heirs (85 percent of the women in my *Times* sample), are not working seriously, it's because feminism wasn't radical enough: It changed the workplace but it didn't change men, and, more importantly, it didn't fundamentally change how women related to men.

21 The movement did start out radical. Betty Friedan's original call to arms compared housework to animal life. In *The Feminine Mystique* she wrote, "[V]acuuming the living room floor—with or without makeup—is not work that takes enough thought or energy to challenge any woman's full capacity. . . . Down through the ages man has known that he was set apart from other animals by his mind's power to have an idea, a vision, and shape the future to it . . . when he discovers and creates and shapes a future different from his past, he is a man, a human being."

22 Thereafter, however, liberal feminists abandoned the judgmental starting point of the movement in favor of offering women "choices." The choice talk spilled over from people trying to avoid saying "abortion," and it provided an irresistible solution to feminists trying to duck the mommy wars. A woman could work, stay home, have 10 children or one, marry or stay single. It all counted as "feminist" as long as she chose it. (So dominant has the concept of choice become that when Charlotte, with a push from her insufferable first husband, quits her job, the writers at Sex and the City have her screaming, "I choose my choice! I choose my choice!")

23 Only the most radical fringes of feminism took on the issue of gender relations at home, and they put forth fruitless solutions like socialism and separatism. We know the story about socialism. Separatism ran right into heterosexuality and

reproduction, to say nothing of the need to earn a living other than at a feminist bookstore. As feminist historian Alice Echols put it, "Rather than challenging their subordination in domestic life, the feminists of NOW committed themselves to fighting for women's integration into public life."

24   Great as liberal feminism was, once it retreated to choice the movement had no language to use on the gendered ideology of the family. Feminists could not say, "Housekeeping and child-rearing in the nuclear family is not interesting and not socially validated. Justice requires that it not be assigned to women on the basis of their gender and at the sacrifice of their access to money, power, and honor."

25   The 50 percent of census answerers and the 62 percent of Harvard MBAs and the 85 percent of my brides of the *Times* all think they are "choosing" their gendered lives. They don't know that feminism, in collusion with traditional society, just passed the gendered family on to them to choose. Even with all the day care in the world, the personal is still political. Much of the rest is the opt-out revolution.

What Is to Be Done?

26   Here's the feminist moral analysis that choice avoided: The family—with its repetitious, socially invisible, physical tasks—is a necessary part of life, but it allows fewer opportunities for full human flourishing than public spheres like the market or the government. This less-flourishing sphere is not the natural or moral responsibility only of women. Therefore, assigning it to women is unjust. Women assigning it to themselves is equally unjust. To paraphrase, as Mark Twain said, "A man who chooses not to read is just as ignorant as a man who cannot read."

27   The critics are right about one thing: Dopey *New York Times* stories do nothing to change the situation. Dowd, who is many things but not a political philosopher, concludes by wondering if the situation will change by 2030. Lefties keep hoping the Republicans will enact child-care legislation, which probably puts us well beyond 2030. In either case, we can't wait that long. If women's flourishing does matter, feminists must acknowledge that the family is to 2005 what the workplace was to 1964 and the vote to 1920. Like the right to work and the right to vote, the right to have a flourishing life that includes but is not limited to family cannot be addressed with language of choice.

28   Women who want to have sex and children with men as well as good work in interesting jobs where they may occasionally wield real social power need guidance, and they need it early. Step one is simply to begin talking about flourishing. In so doing, feminism will be returning to its early, judgmental roots. This may anger some, but it should sound the alarm before the next generation winds up in the same situation. Next, feminists will have to start offering young women not choices and not utopian dreams but solutions they can enact on their own. Prying women out of their traditional roles is not going to be easy. It will require rules—rules like those in the widely derided book *The Rules*, which was never about dating but about behavior modification.

29   There are three rules: Prepare yourself to qualify for good work, treat work seriously, and don't put yourself in a position of unequal resources when you marry.

30   The preparation stage begins with college. It is shocking to think that girls cut off their options for a public life of work as early as college. But they do. The first pitfall is the liberal-arts curriculum, which women are good at, graduating in higher numbers than men. Although many really successful people start out studying liberal arts, the purpose of a liberal education is not, with the exception of a miniscule number of academic positions, job preparation.

31   So the first rule is to use your college education with an eye to career goals. Feminist organizations should produce each year a survey of the most common job opportunities for people with college degrees, along with the average lifetime earnings from each job category and the characteristics such jobs require. The point here is to help women see that yes, you can study art history, but only with the realistic understanding that one day soon you will need to use your arts education to support yourself and your family. The survey would ask young women to select what they are best suited for and give guidance on the appropriate course of study. Like the rule about accepting no dates for Saturday after Wednesday night, the survey would set realistic courses for women, helping would-be curators who are not artistic geniuses avoid career frustration and avoid solving their job problems with marriage.

32   After college comes on-the-job training or further education. Many of my *Times* brides—and grooms—did work when they finished their educations. Here's an anecdote about the difference: One couple, both lawyers, met at a firm. After a few years, the man moved from international business law into international business. The woman quit working altogether. "They told me law school could train you for anything," she told me. "But it doesn't prepare you to go into business. I should have gone to business school." Or rolled over and watched her husband the lawyer using his first few years of work to prepare to go into a related business. Every *Times* groom assumed he had to succeed in business, and was really trying. By contrast, a common thread among the women I interviewed was a self-important idealism about the kinds of intellectual, prestigious, socially meaningful, politics-free jobs worth their incalculably valuable presence. So the second rule is that women must treat the first few years after college as an opportunity to lose their capitalism virginity and prepare for good work, which they will then treat seriously.

33   The best way to treat work seriously is to find the money. Money is the marker of success in a market economy; it usually accompanies power, and it enables the bearer to wield power, including within the family. Almost without exception, the brides who opted out graduated with roughly the same degrees as their husbands. Yet somewhere along the way the women made decisions in the direction of less money. Part of the problem was idealism; idealism on the career trail usually leads to volunteer work, or indentured servitude in social-service jobs, which is nice but doesn't get you to money. Another big mistake involved changing jobs excessively. Without exception, the brides who eventually went home had much more job turnover than the grooms did. There's no such thing as a perfect job. Condoleezza Rice actually wanted to be a pianist, and Gary Graffman didn't want to give concerts.

34   If you are good at work you are in a position to address the third undertaking: the reproductive household. The rule here is to avoid taking on more than a fair share of the second shift. If this seems coldhearted, consider the survey by the Center

for Work-Life Policy. Fully 40 percent of highly qualified women with spouses felt that their husbands create more work around the house than they perform. According to Phyllis Moen and Patricia Roehling's *Career Mystique,* "When couples marry, the amount of time that a woman spends doing housework increases by approximately 17 percent, while a man's decreases by 33 percent." Not a single *Times* groom was a stay-at-home dad. Several of them could hardly wait for Monday morning to come. None of my *Times* grooms took even brief paternity leave when his children were born.

35   How to avoid this kind of rut? You can either find a spouse with less social power than you or find one with an ideological commitment to gender equality. Taking the easier path first, marry down. Don't think of this as brutally strategic. If you are devoted to your career goals and would like a man who will support that, you're just doing what men throughout the ages have done: placing a safe bet.

36   In her 1995 book, "Kidding Ourselves: Babies, Breadwinning and Bargaining Power," Rhona Mahoney recommended finding a sharing spouse by marrying younger or poorer, or someone in a dependent status, like a starving artist. Because money is such a marker of status and power, it's hard to persuade women to marry poorer. So here's an easier rule: Marry young or marry much older. Younger men are potential high-status companions. Much older men are sufficiently established so that they don't have to work so hard, and they often have enough money to provide unlimited household help. By contrast, slightly older men with bigger incomes are the most dangerous, but even a pure counterpart is risky. If you both are going through the elite-job hazing rituals simultaneously while having children, someone is going to have to give. Even the most devoted lawyers with the hardest-working nannies are going to have weeks when no one can get home other than to sleep. The odds are that when this happens, the woman is going to give up her ambitions and professional potential.

37   It is possible that marrying a liberal might be the better course. After all, conservatives justified the unequal family in two modes: "God ordained it" and "biology is destiny." Most men (and most women), including the liberals, think women are responsible for the home. But at least the liberal men should feel squeamish about it.

38   If you have carefully positioned yourself either by marrying down or finding someone untainted by gender ideology, you will be in a position to resist bearing an unfair share of the family. Even then you must be vigilant. Bad deals come in two forms: economics and home economics. The economic temptation is to assign the cost of child care to the woman's income. If a woman making $50,000 per year whose husband makes $100,000 decides to have a baby, and the cost of a full-time nanny is $30,000, the couple reason that, after paying 40 percent in taxes, she makes $30,000, just enough to pay the nanny. So she might as well stay home. This totally ignores that both adults are in the enterprise together and the demonstrable future loss of income, power, and security for the woman who quits. Instead, calculate that all parents make a total of $150,000 and take home $90,000. After paying a full-time nanny, they have $60,000 left to live on.

39   The home-economics trap involves superior female knowledge and superior female sanitation. The solutions are ignorance and dust. Never figure out where

the butter is. "Where's the butter?" Nora Ephron's legendary riff on marriage begins. In it, a man asks the question when looking directly at the butter container in the refrigerator. "Where's the butter?" actually means butter my toast, buy the butter, remember when we're out of butter. Next thing you know you're quitting your job at the law firm because you're so busy managing the butter. If women never start playing the household-manager role, the house will be dirty, but the realities of the physical world will trump the pull of gender ideology. Either the other adult in the family will take a hand or the children will grow up with robust immune systems.

40   If these prescriptions sound less than family-friendly, here's the last rule: Have a baby. Just don't have two. Mothers' Movement Online's Judith Statdman Tucker reports that women who opt out for child-care reasons act only after the second child arrives. A second kid pressures the mother's organizational skills, doubles the demands for appointments, wildly raises the cost of education and housing, and drives the family to the suburbs. But cities, with their Chinese carryouts and all, are better for working mothers. It is true that if you follow this rule, your society will not reproduce itself. But if things get bad enough, who knows what social consequences will ensue? After all, the vaunted French child-care regime was actually only a response to the superior German birth rate.

Why Do We Care?

41   The privileged brides of the *Times*—and their husbands—seem happy. Why do we care what they do? After all, most people aren't rich and white and heterosexual, and they couldn't quit working if they wanted to.

42   We care because what they do is bad for them, is certainly bad for society, and is widely imitated, even by people who never get their weddings in the *Times*. This last is called the "regime effect," and it means that even if women don't quit their jobs for their families, they think they should and feel guilty about not doing it. That regime effect created the mystique around "The Feminine Mystique," too.

43   As for society, elites supply the labor for the decision-making classes—the senators, the newspaper editors, the research scientists, the entrepreneurs, the policy-makers, and the policy wonks. If the ruling class is overwhelmingly male, the rulers will make mistakes that benefit males, whether from ignorance or from indifference. Media surveys reveal that if only one member of a television show's creative staff is female, the percentage of women on-screen goes up from 36 percent to 42 percent. A world of 84-percent male lawyers and 84-percent female assistants is a different place than one with women in positions of social authority. Think of a big American city with an 86-percent white police force. If role models don't matter, why care about Sandra Day O'Connor? Even if the falloff from peak numbers is small, the leveling off of women in power is a loss of hope for more change. Will there never again be more than one woman on the Supreme Court?

44   Worse, the behavior tarnishes every female with the knowledge that she is almost never going to be a ruler. Princeton President Shirley Tilghman described the elite colleges' self-image perfectly when she told her freshmen last year that they

would be the nation's leaders, and she clearly did not have trophy wives in mind. Why should society spend resources educating women with only a 50-percent return rate on their stated goals? The American Conservative Union carried a column in 2004 recommending that employers stay away from such women or risk going out of business. Good psychological data show that the more women are treated with respect, the more ambition they have. And vice versa. The opt-out revolution is really a downward spiral.

45   Finally, these choices are bad for women individually. A good life for humans includes the classical standard of using one's capacities for speech and reason in a prudent way, the liberal requirement of having enough autonomy to direct one's own life, and the utilitarian test of doing more good than harm in the world. Measured against these time-tested standards, the expensively educated upper-class moms will be leading lesser lives. At feminism's dawning, two theorists compared gender ideology to a caste system. To borrow their insight, these daughters of the upper classes will be bearing most of the burden of the work always associated with the lowest caste: sweeping and cleaning bodily waste. Not two weeks after the Yalie flap, the *Times* ran a story of moms who were toilet training in infancy by vigilantly watching their babies for signs of excretion 24-7. They have voluntarily become untouchables.

46   When she sounded the blast that revived the feminist movement 40 years after women received the vote, Betty Friedan spoke of lives of purpose and meaning, better lives and worse lives, and feminism went a long way toward shattering the glass ceilings that limited their prospects outside the home. Now the glass ceiling begins at home. Although it is harder to shatter a ceiling that is also the roof over your head, there is no other choice.

QUESTIONS FOR ANALYSIS AND DISCUSSION ————

1. Hirshman argues that when women leave the workforce, they not only put their own careers at risk but also jeopardize the economic and political power of all women who seek to achieve in high-status jobs. Do you agree or disagree with her argument? Does the "conundrum" of "opting out" put all women at risk? Why or why not?

2. Summarize Hirshman's study of the *New York Times* brides. What did she discover? What conclusions did she draw from the data? Do her conclusions have merit? Does this group of women accurately represent the female body-politic of the United States? Explain.

3. Why does Hirshman object to young women "opting out" of careers in favor of stay-at-home motherhood?

4. Evaluate Hirshman's recommendations for young women. Do you agree with her plan? Do you think her plan will be received differently by young women than by young men?

5. One reason Hirshman's article elicited such an angry response was women who had elected to stay at home negatively reacted to her assertion one could not "flourish" taking care of a home and children. Respond to her argument with your own viewpoint.

BLOG IT

Do Violent Words Beget Violent Deeds?
Posted by Rod Van Mechele
March 17, 2004

Is boy-bashing, good, clean fun, damaging to self-esteem, or does it promote violence? http://www.backlash.com/content/gender/2004/rodvanmechelen031704a.html

Get a life!

My, how times have changed. Just a few years ago, programs to sensitize boys to the plight of girls were making big headlines. Not that long ago, there was a story about a six-year-old boy who was labeled a lecherous harasser for kissing one of the girls . . . on the cheek. He was suspended and sent home for that. Last year, however, we began to see T-shirts urging girls to attack boys.

> *Yes, it's true. The latest trend in fashion apparel for teenage girls is a direct jab at their male counterparts: T-shirts that carry slogans like "Boys are stupid—throw rocks at them," "Boys are goobers—drop anvils on their heads" and "Boys lie—make them cry."—Jane Ganahl, Chronicle Staff Writer, Will you please shut up and get a life, already?, San Francisco Chronicle, Sunday, February 22, 2004*

Yet, had the shoe been on the other foot, or, in this case, the shirt on the other gender, we can only imagine the screeching from feminists as they sallied forth to quash yet another example of patriarchal badness. And that, as Warren Farrell, author of several books, including *Father and Child Reunion*, has long taught, is the measure of sexism: if it's funny about one sex but unacceptable about the opposite sex, then it's sexist.

Equalitarians attacked

With this view in mind, equalitarians, such as Glenn Sacks, started to campaign against the "Boys are Stupid" products. "As parents, we suffer along with our children," wrote Sacks. "Perhaps this explains why the campaign has struck such a chord—in the past week over 300 newspapers and television and radio stations have carried stories about it." Ironically, some of the harshest critics of Sacks' campaign have been men:

> *Other critics, mostly men, deride me as unmanly. I confess this attitude puzzles me. These men often grumble about TV commercials in which men are portrayed as idiots and clowns, and they read their kids*

bedtime stories from children's books where fathers—the few left in modern children's literature—are similarly depicted. Yet many of these men seem to be struck by cultural amnesia the moment somebody finally decides to do something about male-bashing.—Glenn Sacks, Why I Launched the Campaign Against 'Boys are Stupid' Products, February 4, 2004

Reasonably, some may question the fuss. As the old chant goes, "sticks and stones may break my bones, but words can never hurt me . . . unless I'm a victim-feminist." Since boys are not victim-feminists, what should a few humorous slogans matter? Perhaps because violent words can beget violence. Will they matter when girls start throwing rocks? Will they matter when these girls grow up to become batterers?

No parenting expert interviewed suggests that mean-spirited slogans on clothing will destroy a young man's sense of self-worth. They do worry, however, that derogatory and sexist messages contribute to creating a hostile atmosphere.

"If we said that about blacks or Jews or Norwegians even, you'd be stoned immediately," (Armin Brott, author and "Ask Mr. Dad" columnist) says.— Monique Beeler, Boy bashing: Some say girl power movement may have gone too far, Alameda-Times Star, January 21, 2004

"Well, so what?" Feminists might retort. "Men have battered women for millennia, a little payback won't hurt them!" Feminists did write and say such things 10 years ago, but they were eventually silenced by the mounting resistance to their sexist remarks. But despite this they still snarl comments like that in unguarded moments of anger, and amongst themselves. And we might respond by pointing out that, while women are far more likely to be injured from domestic violence, because, in general, men are physically capable of far greater violence than women, women are slightly more likely to initiate domestic violence, so, sadly, there is already parity.

Of course, the feminist retort to this is that this is sexist nonsense based on a relatively few studies, while the government and law enforcement statistics prove that, by a wide margin, women are overwhelmingly the victims, and men are overwhelmingly the perpetrators, of domestic violence:

Exact statistics shift from study to study, but results over three decades of investigation by governmental agencies, social service organizations, and women's health researchers consistently confirm that women are the overwhelming majority of victims of domestic violence—and that men who are victimized are most often assaulted not by women but by other men.— Jennifer L. Pozner, Not All Domestic Violence Studies Are Created Equal, Extra!, November/December 1999

What Pozner and other feminists ignore is that the government and law enforcement studies are based on crime statistics, where most of the victims are women, because, to this day, men are still far less likely to report themselves as victims of domestic violence, as the stigma from doing so would be roughly equivalent to a woman in the 1960s reporting that she had been raped.

Violent Grrlz

But what if the violence begins before puberty? Children can be cruel. Aren't these T-shirts encouraging girls to do more than taunt the boys? Isn't it a call to commit acts of violence? Ridiculous, says Ganahl, who sees it as a liberating joke celebrating that "today's high school girls have come into their 'power'."

> It might not be great manners, but this is the kind of crowing that comes with knowing you've gained ground. Cut these young women a little slack, and have a sense of humor. And I swear, no one will hit you with a rock.—Jane Ganahl, Chronicle Staff Writer, Will you please shut up and get a life, already?, San Francisco Chronicle, Sunday, February 22, 2004

Assuming even half of the complaints modern feminists have leveled against the American male were true, she might have a point. But the uncomfortable truth today's feminists refuse to acknowledge is that, from the right to vote to the birth control pill to equal rights in virtually every bastion of society, all women's victories have been handed to them by men. And what men have given, the sexism of feminists may persuade them to take away.

YOU BLOG IT:

Write your own response to this blog posting.

Revisionist Feminism

Susan Faludi and Karen Lehrman

The next article is the beginning of a multiletter dialogue between feminist writers Susan Faludi and Karen Lehrman featured in *Slate MSN*, in which the two women discuss the meaning of "real feminism." Faludi objects to the "revisionist feminists" who seem to feel that feminism denies them their femininity. Lehrman responds by explaining that the leftist political agenda of conventional feminism has clouded the goals of the movement and has alienated both men and women.

Faludi is the author of the critically acclaimed books *Backlash: The Undeclared War Against American Women* (1991) and *Stiffed: The Betrayal of the American Man* (1998). Her articles have appeared in many journals and magazines, including *Newsweek* and *Esquire*. Karen Lehrman is the managing editor of *Consumer's Research* magazine and the author of *The Lipstick Proviso: Woman, Sex & Power in the Real World* (1997).

BEFORE YOU READ

Look up the word "feminism" in the dictionary. Does the definition surprise you? Does American society seem to have a different understanding of what feminism means? Explain.

AS YOU READ

Do Faludi and Lehrman enter this dialogue on feminism in order to reach an understanding or middle ground? What evidence is there, if any, on either side of their discussion of an attempt to reach a consensus or at least an understanding of the other's point of view?

Dear Karen,

1   I enter into this conversation with you about feminism with some misgivings. Not because I don't want to talk to you. It's just that I suspect it will be like a phone conversation where the connection's so bad neither party can hear the other through the static. I say this because in my experience, there's no getting through to the group of "feminists" (and I use that word with heavy quotation marks and highly arched brows) who are your sister travelers. I mean the group that maintains that an "orthodoxy" of "reigning feminists" (your terms) torments the American female population with its highhanded fiats, its litmus tests of "proper" feminist behavior, its regulatory whip seeking to slap the femininity out of the American girl. Christina Hoff Sommers, Katie Roiphe, Laura Ingraham, Danielle Crittenden, and the rest of the inside-the-Beltway "revisionist feminists" (as the media would have it) condemn

feminism for its "excesses" over and over on the *New York Times* and *Washington Post* op-ed pages and the major TV talk shows (while complaining they are viciously "silenced" by the "reigning" feminists, who hardly ever get an airing in the aforementioned forums).

2   And you, too, Karen. Your own book-length addition to this chorus repeats the argument that feminism has turned women off by denying them the right to display and revel in their feminine beauty and sexuality. You then adorn that old can of "revisionist" contents with a fancy new label, *The Lipstick Proviso*, which you define as "women don't have to sacrifice their individuality, or even their femininity—whatever that means to each of them—in order to be equal."

3   For the longer version of my response to the "revisionists" and their charges against feminism, please see "I'm Not a Feminist But I Play One on TV." For the shorter version, to your book specifically, here 'tis:

4   Earth to Karen! Do you read me? . . . 'Cuz back on planet Earth, feminists don't "reign" and they certainly don't stop women at checkpoints to strip them of their "individuality" by impounding their lipstick (though what a pathetic "individuality" that must be if it depends on the application of Revlon to achieve it). Bulletin from the front: I wear lipstick, and I've spotted it on other feminists, too. I've watched, in fact, legions of "militant" feminists apply makeup brazenly in public ladies' rooms, and no femi-Nazi police swooped down and seized their compacts. And you know why? Because lipstick is not what feminism is about.

5   What's clear in your book is you feel gypped by feminism. You feel the feminists of the '60s and '70s made a promise to your generation of women that they didn't keep. Let us assume you are sincere, and I have no reason—in your case—to think otherwise. But why do you feel so betrayed? Maybe the answer lies in your definition of feminism. You write in your book that "as a young woman eager to escape the confines of a traditional household," you embraced feminism, which, you believed, "was going to turn all women into liberated women, into women who would unfailingly exhibit serene confidence, steely resolve, and steadfast courage. Unburdened by the behavioral and sartorial restrictions of traditional femininity, we would all want to trek alone through the wilds of Indonesia, head IBM, run for president." You then go on to lament, "Yet it doesn't seem as though the first generation of women to come of age with feminism . . . has metamorphosed en masse into briefcase-toting, world-wandering Mistresses of the Universe."

6   Now here's the problem: Your definition of feminism is gleaned not from '70s feminism but from '70s advertising. In that decade, Madison Avenue and Hollywood and the fashion industry and mass media all saw a marketing opportunity in "women's lib" and they ran with it. Feminism as reinterpreted through television commercials for pantyhose and marketing manuals for Dress for Success bow ties would do just what advertising is supposed to do: Inflame your hungers and your anxieties, then offer to mollify them with a product that makes ludicrously inflated promises. So just as Hanes tried to convince shoppers that slipping on a pair of pantyhose would turn them into raving beauties with a million suitors, so the faux-feminism of Consumer America tried to convince a younger generation of women

that "liberation" led to Banana Republicesque treks in the Himalayas and starring roles in the executive penthouse suite. All young women had to do to get that liberation was smoke Virginia Slims. As Christopher Lasch (that raving liberal!) wrote prophetically in 1979 in *The Culture of Narcissism,* "The advertising industry thus encourages the pseudo-emancipation of women, flattering them with its insinuating reminder, 'You've come a long way, baby,' and disguising the freedom to consume as genuine autonomy."

7   Now you are trying to reclaim that promise, proclaiming in your book that women have the "right" to liberate themselves via the marketplace. You champion women's right to express themselves through makeup, lingerie, cosmetic surgery, aerobics classes, and corsets. You even say that "entering a wet T-shirt contest" can be a "liberating" act for some women.

8   But, but, but . . . you are mad at the wrong folks. Feminists never promised you a rose garden in Lotusland, the consumer culture did. Feminism, unlike advertising, is not about gulling you into believing you could win the sweepstakes. Feminism is and always has been about women acting in the world as full-fledged citizens, as real participants in the world of ideas and policy and history. That doesn't have anything to do with wearing lipstick or not wearing lipstick or even about making obscene amounts of money. It's about insisting on the right of women to dignity, a living wage, meaningful work, and active engagement in the public arena. As for lipstick: For most women who work in the cruddy lower reaches of American employment, the problem isn't being denied the "right" to wear makeup and lingerie; it's about the right not to be forced to dress and act the way their male bosses demand. You may recall that flight attendants in the '60s fought one of the earliest battles of feminism's second wave so that male corporate bosses could no longer fire them over their weight, age, dress, or marital status. (Stewardesses were also, by the way, required to wear girdles—and didn't consider it liberating when their supervisors conducted company-mandated "touch checks.") Feminism, real feminism, is about freeing women to be genuine individuals—and recognizing that such individuality doesn't come in one size only or out of a bottle.

9   You propose that we cleanse feminism of political content and even "abolish" the term "women's movement." "This next wave" of feminism, you say, "needs to be primarily devoted to developing our emotional independence." Well, we certainly are in an "emotional" era. That's because we are steeped in a consumer culture where emotional manipulation is the name of the game and political analysis interferes with the Big Sell and so is discouraged. Now you are asking that feminism junk the politics and join in on the consumerizing of the American female public. Well, you can ask. You can cheerlead for that all you like, of course. And I'm sure a lot of powerful institutions will be only too glad to enable your cheerleading for their own selfish ends. But you can't call what you're asking for feminism, or progress. You can't say we've come a long way when you are still championing our "right" to stand on the stage in a wet T-shirt and be called baby.

10   . . . Am I getting through, or does this all sound like static on the line?
Sincerely,
Susan

Dear Susan,

11   Well, I think there would be much less static between us if you had read my book more carefully, did not take my words out of context, and did not lump me in with women with whom I clearly have little in common. I also think we'd have a much better connection if you'd drop the sneery, condescending tone you always seem to adopt when writing about women with whom you disagree. I respect you, I'd probably even like you if we met under slightly less fraught circumstances. Yes, I disagree with some of your philosophical and political views. But those views don't make you any less of a feminist. As long as you believe that women should have the same rights, opportunities, and responsibilities as men, you can have whatever political agenda, lifestyle, or wardrobe you wish.

12   Unfortunately, you don't seem to feel the same way about me or millions of other women. You say that "feminism, real feminism, is about freeing women to be genuine individuals—and recognizing that such individuality doesn't come in one size only or out of a bottle." But much of what you've written on the subject—in your book, magazine articles, and already in this dialogue—would indicate that you don't really mean it. And the same, I'm afraid, is true about most of the other self-appointed spokeswomen for feminism.

13   You each appear to believe that, to be allowed to use the term feminist, a woman has to adhere to a well-defined leftist political agenda, consisting of, at the very least, affirmative action, nationally subsidized day care, and "pay equity" (formerly known as comparable worth). In your *Ms.* article, you call a handful of women who happen to disagree with you politically (myself included) "pod" or "pseudo" feminists. You say that we're right-wing misogynists or pawns of right-wing misogynists. Perhaps most curiously, you imply that we're also racist. In 1992, the National Organization for Women tried to start a "women's party," offering a distinctly leftist "women's agenda." During the last election, NOW president Patricia Ireland said women should vote only for "authentic" female candidates, Gloria Steinem called Texas Republican Sen. Kay Bailey Hutchinson a "female impersonator," and Naomi Wolf described the foreign-policy analysis of Jeane Kirkpatrick as being "uninflected by the experiences of the female body." The desire to enforce political conformity is even worse in academia. Many women's-studies professors regularly judge texts and opinions in terms of their agreement with the orthodox political agenda. (For an honest "insider" account, check out *Professing Feminism*, by Daphne Patai and Noretta Koertge.)

14   Fortunately, all women don't think alike, and as far as feminism is concerned they certainly don't have to. The only items on the real feminist agenda are equal rights and opportunities, a society capable of accepting the widest array of women's choices, and women strong and independent enough to make rational ones. This in no way means that feminists should "junk the politics." It means that feminism is a moral ideal; how women achieve it is a matter of political debate.

15   It's true that some of the women you mention above and in your *Ms.* article do oppose abortion rights, do deny that discrimination exists, and do believe that it is a woman's God-given duty to have children and stay home with them—all anti-feminist

notions. Some have minimized the very real problems of sexual harassment and date rape, and seem far more interested in self-promotion than in the future of feminism. Yet the surveys suggest that the vast majority of women—and men—who have criticized the women's movement in recent years do believe in women's essential equality and are simply unhappy with the fact that feminism has turned into an orthodoxy, that it now means precisely the opposite of what it was intended to mean—namely, freedom.

16   Feminist theorists have gotten much better at not explicitly stating that women need to follow a certain lifestyle or dress code to be a feminist. But an implicit criticism of more traditional choices is still quite apparent. In *Backlash*, for instance, you blame the fact that women are still primarily clustered in the "pink ghetto" or low- to mid-level management positions entirely on discrimination. Some of it surely is discrimination, and some of it is due to the fact that women are still working their way up. But much of the explanation can be found in the choices of women themselves. The vast majority of women—even young women with college degrees who have grown up with nearly every option open to them—still prefer to give their families higher priority than their careers. According to the Women's Education and Research Institute (hardly a bastion of conservative thought), employed mothers are significantly more likely than fathers to want to stay at their current levels of responsibility and to trade job advancement to work part time, work at home, or have control over their work schedules. Four-fifths of mothers who work part time do so by choice.

17   The larger problem is that most feminist theorists still refuse to acknowledge that there appear to be significant biological differences between the sexes. They still seem to believe that equality with men has to mean sameness to men, that until all aspects of traditional femininity are abolished, women will not be free. Thankfully, this is far from necessary. Women, on average, may always have a stronger need than men to nurture, a need that will at times eclipse their desire for power. Restructuring the corporate world to better accommodate two-career families may certainly help women to deal with these conflicting goals, but I don't think they will ever disappear. We may not like the choices many women continue to make, but not only are they really none of our business, there's precious little we could do about them if they were.

18   Biology also still seems to be turning up in courtship (the desire of the vast majority of women to want men to pursue them), sex (the ambivalence most women have toward casual sex), and beauty (the energy most women give toward making themselves attractive). As you well know, I do not say anywhere in the book that women have to wear lipstick to be feminist or even feminine. I use lipstick as a metaphor for all of the traditionally feminine behaviors that feminist theorists have at some point condemned as being degrading and exploitative—from being a mother to staying home full time with one's children to wearing miniskirts and makeup. In *Backlash*, you implicitly argue that the desire of many women to buy feminine or sexy clothing and indulge in cosmetic products and services is wholly the result of manipulation by the beauty and fashion industries. You call women's desire for sexy lingerie "fashion regression," and argue that happy and confident women don't care

about clothes. Actually, I think the desire of most women to not hide their sexuality is a sign of progress, evidence that many women now feel they no longer have to renounce a fundamental aspect of themselves in order to make a symbolic point.

19   I do not feel "gypped" by feminism. On the contrary, feminism has offered me the opportunity to live my life in a way that was considered reprehensible just 40 years ago. What I do feel is that the feminist revolution is not complete, and it's incomplete in ways that differ from the orthodox feminist line. There's still more political work to be done, to be sure, especially involving the issues of rape and domestic violence. But there's also much personal work to be done. This is a major theme of my book, yet for some reason you have chosen to purposefully misread what I wrote about it. Where do I say anything about "the consumerizing of the American female public"?

20   Of course the advertising industry exploited feminism; that's their job. But that has nothing to do with what I'm talking about. I use the term emotional independence to refer to self-development, which was a prominent part of feminist theorizing and activism in the early days of the Second Wave. Actually, it's not that surprising that you chose to ignore what I was saying and turn the focus back on how society has victimized women. Feminists have unfortunately been doing that for the past 20 years, which may partly explain why women lag so far behind in their emotional development. While enormous attention has been paid to how the "patriarchy" mistreats women, little has been written about how women mistreat themselves. Even focusing on how women should take responsibility for their problems is often dismissed as naive, sexist, or "blaming the victim."

21   (By the way, you also took my point about "entering a wet T-shirt contest" completely out of context. As you well know, I was actually saying that just because women now have the freedom to do something doesn't mean it's the most rational thing to do. "Only each woman can decide if her actions are self-destructive and thus unfeminist," I wrote, "What is self-destructive for one woman—entering a wet T-shirt contest, for instance, or being a full-time housewife—may be liberating for another.")

22   It's true that the orthodoxy is breaking up, and other feminist voices are finally being heard. But that's no thanks to you, Susan. I think you have focused more energy on stifling dissent than perhaps any other feminist writer. In your book, you castigate Susan Brownmiller, Betty Friedan, and Erica Jong for having the gall to suggest that the women's movement's refusal to acknowledge biological differences between the sexes is hurtful to women. You can't blame the media for the fact that two-thirds of women still don't call themselves feminists. The media may very well highlight the extremes, but it has also given Gloria Steinem, Naomi Wolf, Patricia Ireland, and yourself plenty of space and air time to alienate the majority of women through your restrictive view of feminism.

23   Feminism—real feminism—deserves to be respected and honored. Every woman today should proudly call herself a feminist. But that is not going to happen until prominent feminist writers such as yourself admit to a couple of things. One, that a Republican housewife who annually has her face lifted and daily greets her husband at the door wearing only heels can be a feminist if she knows her mind, follows her desires, and believes that every woman has the right to do the same. Two, that the

notion of sisterhood is false, outdated, and sexist. Women don't "owe" each other anything: They don't have to like each other, agree with each other, vote for each other, or hire each other for feminism to succeed.

24   Three, the notion of a "women's movement" has outlived its usefulness. Men must be just as aware and involved as women—on both a personal and political level—for feminism to work. Four, women can act differently from men. Even if that means that Congress, corporate boards, and CEOs will never be 50 percent female, as long as women are making their choices freely, feminism will not be undermined. And finally, each woman is fundamentally unique. No assumptions can be made about her politics, values, goals, and beliefs.

25   Instead of fighting about whether or not feminism has turned into an orthodoxy, I think it would be far more useful if this dialogue—as well as the larger feminist debate—were focused on the complexities that women must deal with today. For instance, how does the corporate world learn to judge women strictly on their merits yet recognize the obvious differences—e.g., that women are the only ones who get pregnant? How do we help women deal with their ambivalence toward responsibility and power? How do we help women develop the strength and independence to demand boyfriends who don't abuse them, and raises that they deserve? These are tough questions, and I'd really like to know what you think about them.

Sincerely,
Karen

QUESTIONS FOR ANALYSIS AND DISCUSSION ————

1. Why does Faludi express "misgivings" about entering into a conversation on feminism with Lehrman? What tone does she set for the dialogue? How does Lehrman respond to this tone?
2. Summarize Faludi's argument. What is her definition of "real feminism"? Why does she object to "revisionist feminism"? Explain.
3. Summarize Lehrman's argument. What is her definition of "real feminism"? Why does she object to Faludi and other "self-appointed spokeswomen for feminism"? Explain.
4. In what ways has consumer culture clouded the goals of feminism? How has advertising exploited feminism? Explain.
5. On what points do Faludi and Lehrman agree? If you were the moderator of this dialogue, how would you use these points of agreement to help them reach a consensus?

WRITING ASSIGNMENTS

1. Write an essay exploring the effects of the perception of women as homemakers and mothers in the media. Some of the areas of your exploration might draw from television, film, art, advertising, newspapers, music, and other popular media. How do media representations of women enforce (or refute) the perception of women as mothers and homemakers rather than professionals?

2. Consider the ways Hollywood influences our cultural perspectives of gender and identity. Write an essay exploring the influence, however slight, film and television have had on your own perceptions of gender. If you wish, interview other students for their opinion on this issue, and address some of their points in your essay.

3. Linda Hirshman's essay elicited angry responses across the blogosphere. Read a few entries from various blogs addressing the controversy. Write an essay summarizing the controversy and refer to other comments on blog entries surrounding the reaction to Hirshman's article.

4. Thirty years ago, men were expected to earn more than women. Do we still hold such beliefs? Poll your classmates to find out their opinions regarding income status. Do men feel that they should earn more? Would they feel less masculine if their girlfriends or wives earned more then they did? Do women look for higher incomes when they consider a partner? Analyze your results and write an argument that draws conclusions from your survey and its connection to feminism in the twenty-first century.

5. In your own words, define the terms "masculine" and "feminine." You might include library research on the origins of the words or research their changing implications over the years. Develop your own definition for each word, and then discuss with the rest of the class how you arrived at your definitions.

CHAPTER 12

Spotlight on America

American consciousness was forever changed on September 11, 2001. While the United States and the world reeled from the shock, Americans were faced with the reality that their concept of safety and security would never be the same. In response to this threat to our security and freedom, the executive branch of American government emerged as more powerful than ever—beginning and extending a war in Iraq that many Americans now challenge and many countries around the world question. This chapter explores some of the issues facing America and how it fits during a time when terrorism is a daily threat and international opinion is at an all-time low.

Signs that our lives have changed are everywhere. For some people, checking the "terrorist alert" level is as common as checking the weather. The media, for better or worse, provides daily updates on terrorist activity here and abroad. Subway loudspeakers encourage riders to keep an eye out for suspicious or unattended packages. Airports warn travelers to arrive at least two hours in advance of their flights in order to clear security. Armed guards may check car trunks before vehicles are allowed to park in private and public garages. Most stadiums and sports arenas no longer allow fans to carry a bag larger than a fanny pack. Is this the price we must pay for security?

The first section examines terrorism, the American War in Iraq, and how our lives have changed since 9/11. The next section considers some different views of America—from America and other countries. How can America restore its place in world opinion? Does it matter? What will be America's place in a world irrevocably changed by the events of 9/11?

THE AMERICAN WAR IN IRAQ

Terrorism and the Media
The Council on Foreign Relations

Is the press inadvertently playing into the hands of terrorists by reporting on their activities and giving them extensive media coverage? If terrorists could not count on the press to bring kidnappings, beheadings, and even suicide bombings into the public eye, would such activities be less frequent? less violent? The fact sheet that follows, prepared by the Council on Foreign Relations, explains how terrorists depend on publicity and may be prompted to enact horrific acts of violence in order to shock viewers and draw attention to their causes.

This fact sheet, prepared by the Council on Foreign Relations, draws on interviews with Brigitte Nacos, lecturer in political science at Columbia University; Paul McMasters, First Amendment ombudsman for the Freedom Forum; and Henry Jenkins, director of the Comparative Media Studies program at the Massachusetts Institute of Technology. It also draws on Bruce Hoffman, *Inside Terrorism* (1998); Walter Laqueur, *The Age of Terrorism* (1987); Brigitte Nacos, *Terrorism and the Media* (1994); Nacos, *Mass Mediated Terrorism* (2002); and David L. Paletz and Alex P. Schmid, eds., *Terrorism and the Media* (1992).

BEFORE YOU READ ─────────────────────────

How much attention do you give to press coverage on terrorist acts, such as kidnappings, beheadings, and suicide bombings? Explain.

AS YOU READ ─────────────────────────

Do you think the press should reduce the amount of coverage it gives to terrorist activity, or does this violate the public's right to know? Is there a balance between providing information and not giving terrorists the publicity they crave? What do you think?

Are terrorists interested in publicity?

1   Intensely. The scholar Brian Jenkins declared in 1974 that "terrorism is theatre," and terrorists themselves have long seen it much the same way. Narodnaya Volya, the late-19th-century Russian anarchist group, conceived of its violent activities as "propaganda by deed." Ever since, terrorists have tailored their attacks to maximize publicity and get their messages out through all available channels. Experts say the attacks on the World Trade Center and the Pentagon, for example, were designed to provide billions of television viewers with pictures symbolizing U.S. vulnerability, and they prompted extensive reporting on al-Qaeda and its Islamist agenda.

2   However, some experts say that the nature of terrorism may now be changing. Jenkins has famously said that terrorists want a lot of people watching, not a lot of people dead. But the emergence of religious terror groups with apocalyptic outlooks and the availability of weapons of mass destruction may indicate that inflicting mass casualties has supplanted publicity as the primary goal of some terrorist campaigns.

Is modern terrorism tailored to the media?

3   Yes. Terrorists want governments and the public to pay attention, and the media provide the conduit. Experts say terrorism is calculated violence, usually against symbolic targets, designed to deliver a political or religious message. Beyond that, terrorists' goals might also include winning popular support, provoking the attacked country to act rashly, attracting recruits, polarizing public opinion, demonstrating their ability to cause pain, or undermining governments.

Do terrorists try to attract media attention?

4   Yes, and terrorists say they design their operations accordingly. Timothy McVeigh, who was convicted of the 1995 Oklahoma City bombing that killed 168 people, said he chose the Murrah Federal Building as a target because it had "plenty of open space around it, to allow for the best possible news photos and television footage." The Italian leftist Red Brigades liked to stage attacks on Saturdays to make it into the Sunday newspapers, which had a higher circulation. And the Palestinian group Black September took Israeli athletes hostage at the 1972 Munich Olympics because television sets worldwide were already tuned in to the games and the concentrated foreign press would amplify the story. Terrorist groups study the media carefully, and some groups have their own media operations; the Colombian leftists of the FARC, for example, put out their own radio broadcasts, and many groups have promotional Web sites.

Does media attention help terrorists?

5   Experts disagree. The old saying that any publicity is good publicity has often been applied to terrorism; even when an assassin misses or a bomb doesn't go off, an attack can raise awareness about the terrorists' cause. Terrorism, which garners a disproportionately large share of news coverage, can also move neglected issues to the top of the political agenda—as a series of attacks in the 1970s and 1980s did for the cause of Palestinian nationalism. Terrorism can also provoke policy debates and public discussion by highlighting both the terrorists' radical views and the visceral anger of terrorism's victims and their families.

6   But other experts doubt that media coverage really helps terrorists. Attacks can spin out of control or have unintended consequences; too much slaughter can alienate potential supporters and sympathizers; terrorist activities have different meanings for different audiences; and even when terrorists' attack plans work, they cannot necessarily control how their actions are covered or perceived. Finally, being

saddled with the pejorative label "terrorist" focuses attention on a group's methods, not its message, and can delegitimize its cause in the public eye.

Why do the media cover terrorist attacks?

7   Because terrorist attacks are news, journalists say. Many terrorism scholars have identified a symbiotic relationship between terrorists, who want attention, and news organizations, which want dramatic stories to boost readership or ratings. Most news organizations, while aware that terrorist groups are manipulating them, want to report on major events without becoming a platform for terrorists. Critics say live television news is particularly susceptible to becoming an unwitting partner in the theater of terrorism.

Can media coverage shape the outcome of a terrorist incident?

8   Yes, in various ways. Experts say sustained coverage of a hijacking sometimes protects hostages' lives by building international sympathy for their plight. But it can also prolong a hostage situation since terrorists may hold out until the publicity—and therefore the attention—fades. When an unfolding attack is covered on television, a lull in real-time developments can make it seem like a government isn't responding to an attack and lead to pressure on officials to resolve the situation, perhaps prematurely, with dangerous consequences. Media coverage can also disrupt or prevent counterterrorist operations. It can tell hijackers how their attack is proceeding and even tip them off to a rescue attempt. But it can also lead to arrests. The decision by major U.S. newspapers to publish the antimodern political manifesto of the Unabomber, a lone serial mail bomber who eluded FBI investigators for 17 years, brought about his identification and capture.

Do terrorist groups ever target the media?

9   Yes; experts say targeting the media can help to attract attention or shape coverage. Anthrax-laden letters were mailed to several newsrooms; Islamist militants in Pakistan linked to al-Qaeda lured the *Wall Street Journal* reporter Daniel Pearl to an interview only to abduct and kill him; and intelligence reports said that al-Qaeda was scouting the Prague headquarters of Radio Free Europe as a target. Earlier terrorists in Beirut killed or kidnapped foreign correspondents whose coverage they considered unsympathetic—Associated Press reporter Terry Anderson spent seven years as a hostage in Lebanon—and the Basque separatist group ETA killed a Spanish editor whose newspaper published an antiterrorist manifesto.

Do democracies ever try to control media coverage of terrorism?

10   Yes. In the 1980s, for example, Britain banned the broadcasting of statements by members of terrorist organizations or their supporters, following then Prime Minister Margaret Thatcher's argument that the surest way to stop terrorism was to cut off "the oxygen of publicity." Democracies that do not regulate press coverage of terrorism sometimes ask media organizations to voluntarily hold back—either for national security reasons or to deny terrorists an outlet for their political views. Following the September 11 attacks, for example, the Bush administration asked

U.S. networks not to air videos of Osama bin Laden because the government said they might contain coded messages with instructions for future attacks. Other U.S. officials have said that coverage of homeland-security vulnerabilities, from nuclear power plants to cyberterrorism, has been a boon for terrorists planning future attacks.

11   News organizations say that they carefully consider whether to interview terrorists or broadcast footage of their activities and that they prefer to establish their own guidelines for covering terrorist activity rather than bowing to government censorship or pressure. They also say that the Bush administration has never demonstrated that bin Laden videos do contain coded messages, and that reporting on homeland-security vulnerabilities brings attention to these situations and encourages the government to fix them. However, critics argue that many news organizations focus more on profits than public service.

Do new forms of media change terrorists' behavior?

12   Yes. Experts say terrorists have learned to adapt their methods and messages as the media have evolved. Hijacking passenger airplanes, for example, became a common terrorist strategy only after the launch of the first international television satellite, which allowed viewers worldwide to watch hijackings as real-time dramas. More recently, al-Qaeda's strategy of not claiming responsibility for attacks—unlike earlier generations of terrorists—helps perpetuate insecurity and drive media coverage. The growth of satellite networks such as the Arabic cable news network al-Jazeera and of the video capabilities of the World Wide Web let terrorists make video recordings—for example, ones showing the murder of Daniel Pearl or Palestinian suicide bombers' last testaments—that can be seen even if CNN and the BBC decide not to show them.

How do terrorists use the Internet?

13   Terrorists have learned to use the Internet for secret communications among themselves, facilitating planning and fund-raising, and they have promotional Web sites. However, experts say that information flow on the World Wide Web is hard to predict or control, and the Internet isn't yet a way to reach everyone at once, as carrying out a spectacular televised attack is. However, rumors spread via the Internet sometimes filter up into other media.

QUESTIONS FOR ANALYSIS AND DISCUSSION ———————

1. In your opinion, does media attention help terrorists? Express your own point of view, supporting it with examples based on personal observation.
2. In what ways are religious terror groups reshaping traditional terrorist attacks? What makes their terrorism different? Explain.
3. What is the "symbiotic" relationship between news organizations and terrorist groups? How does each depend on the other?
4. Former British prime minister Margaret Thatcher argued that the way to stop terrorism was to "cut off the oxygen of publicity." Is such a resolution possible in a media-driven society? How do you think the public would react to such a policy?

READING THE VISUAL

Support Our Troops

Barry Blitt

Source: *Atlantic,* Nov. 2007, p. 54

QUESTIONS FOR ANALYSIS AND DISCUSSION ──────

1. What is happening in this political cartoon? What is the unexpected twist?
2. Based on this cartoon, what message is the artist trying to convey? What is his "argument"?
3. Who is the target audience for this cartoon? In what ways might it connect with multiple audiences—including those who oppose, and those who support, the war in Iraq?

News Judgment and Jihad

Mark Bowden

The previous piece discussed how terrorists use the media for publicity and to spread the message of their cause to a wide audience. In the next essay, veteran journalist Mark Bowden calls on news media to put a stop to all the grisly publicity. While he concedes that the beheading of hostages is newsworthy, he objects to putting coverage of such atrocities on the front page of every newspaper. Editors have a responsibility to balance news on importance, not simply on the drama factor. Failure to curtail the coverage, he fears, could encourage terrorists to "come up with something more awful."

Bowden is the author of several bestselling books, including *Black Hawk Down: A Story of Modern War*, which was turned into a film directed by Ridley Scott in 2001. He has won numerous awards and has written for *Men's Journal*, *Sports Illustrated*, and *Rolling Stone*. Bowden's most recent work is *Guests of the Ayatollah: The First Battle in America's War with Militant Islam* (2006). This article was published in the December 2004 issue of *The Atlantic Monthly*.

BEFORE YOU READ

Look at the headlines of several major newspapers. What gets a headline? What news is covered on the front page? Then read the rest of the first section of the newspaper. Were the stories that grabbed the headlines the most important? or the most likely to catch a reader's eye? Explain.

AS YOU READ

How does Bowden use his experience as a journalist and an editor to support his argument that editors and producers should exercise better judgment in covering terrorist acts in the media? Does his background add credibility to his point of view? Explain.

1   As I write this, three more Western workers have been kidnapped and beheaded by insurgents in Iraq. The pattern is by now sadly familiar. Foreigners are taken hostage. Videotapes are released of the captives kneeling before their masked, armed captors, and demands are made. As the deadline approaches, new videotapes are released of the captives pleading with their governments, often tearfully, to meet the kidnappers' demands. Then comes video of the grisly beheadings.

2   The first time this happened, it was horrifying and startling. Now it has become horrifying and predictable. Yet many of America's newspapers and TV networks continue to treat these criminal atrocities as the most important news of the day. Newspapers play the wrenching stories on the front page, often above the fold, and the networks feature them prominently, often as lead news items. Good taste has, thank goodness, banished the videos of the beheadings to obscure regions of

the Internet, where those who must see such things can find them, but editors and producers have yet to display any equivalent exercise of judgment.

3   It is time for American journalism to voluntarily adopt more sensible and prudent standards for covering all acts of terror. When I started working as a newspaper reporter, thirty years ago, editors at least claimed to weigh the relative importance of a day's stories before deciding where to run them in the newspaper. Most sober papers, like the *New York Times*, prided themselves on resisting sensationalism. The steady erosion of this standard has long concerned traditionalists. In today's news world whatever grabs the most attention leads. In general I have no problem with this: people can usually sort out for themselves how the Scott Peterson murder trial stacks up against uranium enrichment in Iran, and nowadays they can readily get more information about either. What disturbs me is the way terrorists use sensationalism to vastly amplify their message. They know that horror and drama capture the media's attention, so they manufacture them. This is why instead of merely executing their victims, they cut off their heads on camera and broadcast the videos. When that gets old, which it will, they will come up with something even more awful.

4   Must we help them? Granted, the murder of a worker or a soldier allied with the American war effort in Iraq is newsworthy. It speaks to the danger of the place, and to the pain and difficulty of subduing the continuing insurgency. But the emphasis on the recent beheadings has largely been driven by the availability of appalling video. The news business is not a monolith (fortunately), and it has no governing body and no way of imposing or enforcing rules. But shouldn't editors and producers weigh the public interest along with news and shock value? Would some larger journalistic principle be lost if they decided to deny these killers center stage?

5   There is plenty of precedent for self-restraint in presenting the news. Most newspapers and networks voluntarily withhold the names of rape victims or juveniles charged with crimes. Newspapers routinely withhold the names of sources and restrict quotations from children. Responsible people have long advocated that television networks withhold tallies and projections on Election Day until polling places on the West Coast have closed. Over the years reputable news organizations have even withheld advance knowledge of U.S. military actions, in order to preserve the element of surprise.

6   Leading the news with acts of terrorism is often both journalistically unwarranted and—assuming that decent people everywhere would like to see such acts cease—tragically self-defeating. In a democracy, policy is ultimately set by the people, so anybody can alter it by scaring enough of them. Theoretically, a handful of depraved and determined men with a video camera can make the strongest army in the world back down. But to prevail they need journalism's help—and until the world's media stop giving it to them, they will continue killing and videotaping.

7   Most deaths, at home or abroad, have little real significance beyond the immediate personal tragedy—and, sadly, there is no shortage of that in the world. The slaying of a soldier or a foreign worker in Iraq has a certain local impact: it frightens those in the vicinity and is likely to prompt improvements in security procedures. But it doesn't significantly alter the facts on the ground. The occupying army still controls the same neighborhoods and roads, and still vastly outnumbers and outguns

those who oppose it. This past September, in the same week that two Americans were beheaded, more than 3,000 people were killed in Haiti by Tropical Storm Jeanne. On average more than a hundred Americans are killed every day in auto accidents. None of these deaths is any less final than a beheading—an act that makes political sense only if it can be made to influence public policy. But graphic news coverage, tearful vigils with family members, high-visibility funerals, commentary, and analysis can make any tragedy influential.

8   Without a doubt, the recent beheadings in Iraq were newsworthy and deserved to be widely reported. The American press should never be in the business of censoring or burying bad news, or of becoming a propagandist for the government or military. It is also true that as such sadistic acts have frightened us, they have better acquainted us with the nature of the insurgency. Sensible people recoil. One might argue that giving such stories prominence isolates violent Islamist extremism, which, like the *Ebola* virus, is too deadly to spread all that far.

9   But those beheadings were not the most important events in the world on the days they occurred. Nor were they even the most important developments in the region, where American soldiers and volunteers for the Iraqi police force continued to be targeted, and where officials were wrestling over when to hold national elections. The beheadings led the news in so many places strictly because they were so terrible and because they were on videotape, a medium that so vividly conveys the horror.

10   They led because the cold men behind them wanted them to. I think we should consider the consequences of continually giving those men their way.

QUESTIONS FOR ANALYSIS AND DISCUSSION

1. What is Bowden's argument in this essay? Identify specific lines from his essay that reveal his thesis and his position.
2. Why, according to Bowden, is leading the news with stories on acts of terrorism "tragically self-defeating"? Explain.
3. Is the issue of extensive media coverage for acts of terrorism an ethical one? political? both?
4. Bowden observes that while the violent beheadings of hostages at the hands of Islamic extremists is indeed news, it isn't necessarily headline news. Do you agree? Why or why not?

Words in a Time of War
Mark Danner

Mark Danner has written about foreign affairs and politics for two decades, covering Latin America, Haiti, the Balkans, and the Middle East. He is a former staff writer at *The New Yorker* and currently teaches at the University of California at Berkeley and at Bard College. He is the author of many books, most recently *The Secret Way to War: The Downing Street Memo and the Iraq War's Buried History* (2006). Danner delivered this commencement address to graduates of the Department of Rhetoric at Zellerbach Hall, University of California, Berkeley, on May 10, 2007. This speech was posted online on May 31, 2007, as part of the "Moral Dispatch" series appearing in *The Nation.*

BEFORE YOU READ

Look up the definition of "rhetoric." What does it mean? Why would we want to study rhetoric, and how might it apply to our understanding of current issues and political questions today?

AS YOU READ

Consider the influence of words and how words "construct" reality. Why is critical thinking more important than ever in a culture where politicians can claim to "create" reality through what they tell the public?

1   When my assistant greeted me, a number of weeks ago, with the news that I had been invited to deliver the commencement address to the Department of Rhetoric, I thought it was a bad joke. There is a sense, I'm afraid, that being invited to deliver The Speech to students of Rhetoric is akin to being asked out for a romantic evening by a porn star: Whatever prospect you might have of pleasure is inevitably dampened by performance anxiety—the suspicion that your efforts, however enthusiastic, will inevitably be judged according to stern professional standards. A daunting prospect.

2   The only course, in both cases, is surely to plunge boldly ahead. And that means, first of all, saluting the family members gathered here, and in particular you, the parents.

3   Dear parents, I welcome you today to your moment of triumph. For if a higher education is about acquiring the skills and knowledge that allow one to comprehend and thereby get on in the world—and I use "get on in the world" in the very broadest sense—well then, oh esteemed parents, it is your children, not those boringly practical business majors and pre-meds your sanctimonious friends have sired, who have chosen with unerring grace and wisdom the course of study that will best guide them in this very strange polity of ours. For our age, ladies and gentlemen, is truly the Age of Rhetoric.

4   Now I turn to you, my proper audience, the graduating students of the Department of Rhetoric of 2007, and I salute you most heartily. In making the choice you have, you confirmed that you understand something intrinsic, something indeed . . . intimate about this age we live in. Perhaps that should not surprise us. After all, you have spent your entire undergraduate years during a time of war—and what a very strange wartime it has been.

5   When most of you arrived on this campus, in September 2003, the rhetorical construction known as the War on Terror was already two years old and that very real war to which it gave painful birth, the war in Iraq, was just hitting its half-year

mark. Indeed, the Iraq War had already ended once, in that great victory scene on the USS Abraham Lincoln off the coast of San Diego, where the President, clad jauntily in a flight suit, had swaggered across the flight deck and, beneath a banner famously marked "Mission Accomplished," had declared: "Major combat operations in Iraq have ended. In the battle of Iraq, the United States and our allies have prevailed."

6   Of the great body of rich material encompassed by my theme today—"Words in a Time of War"—surely those words of George W. Bush must stand as among the era's most famous, and most rhetorically unstable. For whatever they may have meant when the President uttered them on that sunny afternoon of May 1, 2003, they mean something quite different today, almost exactly four years later. The President has lost control of those words, as of so much else.

7   At first glance, the grand spectacle of May 1, 2003 fits handily into the history of the pageantries of power. Indeed, with its banners and ranks of cheering, uniformed extras gathered on the stage of that vast aircraft carrier—a stage, by the way, that had to be turned in a complicated maneuver so that the skyline of San Diego, a few miles off, would not be glimpsed by the television audience—the event and its staging would have been quite familiar to, and no doubt envied by, the late Leni Riefenstahl (who, as filmmaker to the Nazis, had no giant aircraft carriers to play with). Though vast and impressive, the May 1 extravaganza was a propaganda event of a traditional sort, intended to bind the country together in a second precise image of victory—the first being the pulling down of Saddam's statue in Baghdad, also staged—an image that would fit neatly into campaign ads for the 2004 election. The President was the star, the sailors and airmen and their enormous dreadnought props in his extravaganza.

8   However ambitiously conceived, these were all very traditional techniques, familiar to any fan of Riefenstahl's famous film spectacular of the 1934 Nuremberg rally, *Triumph of the Will*. As trained rhetoricians, however, you may well have noticed something different here, a slightly familiar flavor just beneath the surface. If ever there was a need for a "disciplined grasp" of the "symbolic and institutional dimensions of discourse"—as your Rhetoric Department's website puts it—surely it is now. For we have today an administration that not only is radical—unprecedentedly so—in its attitudes toward rhetoric and reality, toward words and things, but is willing, to our great benefit, to state this attitude clearly.

9   I give you my favorite quotation from the Bush Administration, put forward by the proverbial "unnamed Administration official" and published in the *New York Times* magazine by the fine journalist Ron Suskind in October 2004. Here, in Suskind's recounting, is what that "unnamed Administration official" told him:

> The aide said that guys like me were 'in what we call the reality-based community,' which he defined as people who 'believe that solutions emerge from your judicious study of discernible reality.' I nodded and murmured something about enlightenment principles and empiricism. He cut me off. 'That's not the way the world really works anymore,' he continued. 'We're an empire now, and when we act, we create our own reality. And while you're studying that reality—judiciously, as you will—we'll act again, creating other new realities,

which you can study too, and that's how things will sort out. We're history's actors. . . . and you, all of you, will be left to just study what we do.'

10   I must admit to you that I love that quotation; indeed, with your permission, I would like hereby to nominate it for inscription over the door of the Rhetoric Department, akin to Dante's welcome above the gates of Hell, "Abandon hope, all ye who enter here."

11   Both admonitions have an admirable bluntness. These words from "Bush's Brain"—for the unnamed official speaking to Suskind seems to have been none other than the selfsame architect of the aircraft-carrier moment, Karl Rove, who bears that pungent nickname—these words sketch out with breathtaking frankness a radical view in which power frankly determines reality, and rhetoric, the science of flounces and folderols, follows meekly and subserviently in its train. Those in the "reality-based community"—those such as we—are figures a mite pathetic, for we have failed to realize the singular new principle of the new age: Power has made reality its bitch.

12   Given such sweeping claims for power, it is hard to expect much respect for truth; or perhaps it should be "truth"—in quotation marks—for, when you can alter reality at will, why pay much attention to the idea of fidelity in describing it? What faith, after all, is owed to the bitch that is wholly in your power, a creature of your own creation?

13   Of course I should not say "those such as we" here, for you, dear graduates of the Rhetoric Department of 2007, you are somewhere else altogether. This is, after all, old hat to you; the line of thinking you imbibe with your daily study, for it is present in striking fashion in Foucault and many other intellectual titans of these last decades—though even they might have been nonplussed to find it so crisply expressed by a finely tailored man sitting in the White House. Though we in the "reality-based community" may just now be discovering it, you have known for years the presiding truth of our age, which is that the object has become subject and we have a fanatical follower of Foucault in the Oval Office. Graduates, let me say it plainly and incontrovertibly: George W. Bush is the first Rhetoric-Major President.

The Dirtied Face of Power

14   I overstate perhaps, but only for a bit of—I hope—permitted rhetorical pleasure. Let us gaze a moment at the signposts of the history of the present age. In January 2001, the Rhetoric Major President came to power after a savage and unprecedented electoral battle that was decided not by the ballots of American voters—for of these he had 540,000 fewer than his Democrat rival—but by the votes of Supreme Court Justices, where Republicans prevailed five to four, making George W. Bush the first President in more than a century to come to the White House with fewer votes than those of his opponent.

15   In this singular condition, and with a Senate precisely divided between parties, President Bush proceeded to behave as if he had won an overwhelming electoral victory, demanding tax cuts greater and more regressive than those he had outlined in the campaign. And despite what would seem to have been debilitating political weakness, the President shortly achieved this first success in "creating his own

reality." To act as if he had overwhelming political power would mean he had over-whelming political power.

16   This, however, was only the overture of the vast symphonic work to come, a work heralded by the huge, clanging, echoing cacophony of 9/11. We are so embed-ded in its age that it is easy to forget the stark, overwhelming shock of it: Nineteen young men with box cutters seized enormous transcontinental airliners and brought those towers down. In an age in which we have become accustomed to two, three, four, five suicide attacks in a single day—often these multiple attacks from Baghdad don't even make the front pages of our papers—it is easy to forget the blunt, scathing shock of it, the impossible image of the second airliner disappearing into the great office tower, almost weirdly absorbed by it, and emerging, transformed into a great yellow and red blossom of flame, on the other side; and then, half an hour later, the astonishing flowering collapse of the hundred-story structure, trans-forming itself, in a dozen seconds, from mighty tower to great plume of heaven-reaching white smoke.

17   The image remains, will always remain, with us; for truly the weapon that day was not box cutters in the hands of nineteen young men, nor airliners at their com-mand. The weapon that day was the television set. It was the television set that made the image possible, and inextinguishable. If terror is first of all a way of talking—the propaganda of the deed, indeed—then that day the television was the indispens-able conveyer of the conversation: the recruitment poster for fundamentalism, the only symbolic arena in which America's weakness and vulnerability could be dra-matized on an adequate scale. Terror—as Menachem Begin, the late Israeli prime minister and the successful terrorist who drove the British from Mandate Palestine, remarked in his memoirs—terror is about destroying the prestige of the imperial regime; terror is about "dirtying the face of power."

18   President Bush and his lieutenants surely realized this and it is in that knowl-edge, I believe, that we can find the beginning of the answer to one of the more in-triguing puzzles of these last few years: What exactly lay at the root of the almost fanatical determination of Administration officials to attack and occupy Iraq? It was, obviously, the classic "over-determined" decision, a tangle of fear, in the form of those infamous weapons of mass destruction; of imperial ambition, in the form of the neoconservative project to "remake the Middle East"; and of realpolitik, in the form of the "vital interest" of securing the industrial world's oil supplies.

19   In the beginning, though, was the felt need on the part of our nation's leaders, men and women so worshipful of the idea of power and its ability to remake reality itself, to restore the nation's prestige, to wipe clean that dirtied face. Henry Kissinger, a confidant of the President, when asked by Bush's speechwriter why he had sup-ported the Iraq War, responded: "Because Afghanistan was not enough." The radical Islamists, he said, want to humiliate us. "And we need to humiliate them." In other words, the presiding image of The War on Terror—the burning towers collapsing on the television screen—had to be supplanted by another, the image of American tanks rumbling proudly through a vanquished Arab capital. It is no accident that Secretary of Defense Donald Rumsfeld, at the first "war cabinet" meeting at Camp David the Saturday after the 9/11 attacks, fretted over the "lack of targets" in Afghanistan and

wondered whether we "shouldn't do Iraq first." He wanted to see those advancing tanks marching across our television screens, and soon.

20   In the end, of course, the enemy preferred not to fight with tanks, though they were perfectly happy to have us do so, the better to destroy these multi-million dollar anachronisms with so-called IEDs, improvised explosive devices, worth a few hundred bucks apiece. This is called asymmetrical warfare and one should note here with some astonishment how successful it has been these last half dozen years. In the post-Cold War world, after all, as one neo-conservative theorist explained shortly after 9/11, the United States was enjoying a rare "uni-polar moment." It deployed the greatest military and economic power the world has ever seen. It spent more on its weapons, its Army, Navy, and Air Force, than the rest of the world combined.

21   It was the assumption of this so-called preponderance that lay behind the philosophy of power enunciated by Bush's Brain and that led to an attitude toward international law and alliances that is, in my view, quite unprecedented in American history. That radical attitude is brilliantly encapsulated in a single sentence drawn from the National Security Strategy of the United States of 2003: "Our strength as a nation-state will continue to be challenged by those who employ a strategy of the weak using international fora, judicial processes and terrorism." Let me repeat that little troika of "weapons of the weak": international fora (meaning the United Nations and like institutions), judicial processes (meaning courts, domestic and international), and . . . terrorism. This strange gathering, put forward by the government of the United States, stems from the idea that power is, in fact, everything. In such a world, courts—indeed, law itself—can only limit the power of the most powerful state. Wielding preponderant power, what need has it for law? The latter must be, by definition, a weapon of the weak. The most powerful state, after all, makes reality.

Asymmetric Warfare and Dumb Luck

22   Now, here's an astonishing fact: Fewer than half a dozen years into this "uni-polar moment," the greatest military power in the history of the world stands on the brink of defeat in Iraq. Its vastly expensive and all-powerful military has been humbled by a congeries of secret organizations fighting mainly by means of suicide vests, car bombs and improvised explosive devices—all of them cheap, simple, and effective, indeed so effective that these techniques now comprise a kind of ready-made insurgency kit freely available on the Internet and spreading in popularity around the world, most obviously to Afghanistan, that land of few targets.

23   As I stand here, one of our two major political parties advocates the withdrawal—gradual, or otherwise—of American combat forces from Iraq and many in the other party are feeling the increasing urge to go along. As for the Bush Administration's broader War on Terror, as the State Department detailed recently in its annual report on the subject, the number of terrorist attacks worldwide has never been higher, nor more effective. True, Al Qaeda has not attacked again within the United States. They do not need to. They are alive and flourishing. Indeed, it might even be said that they are winning. For their goal, despite the rhetoric of the Bush Administration, was not simply to kill Americans but, by challenging the United States in this spectacular

fashion, to recruit great numbers to their cause and to move their insurgency into the heart of the Middle East. And all these things they have done.

24   How could such a thing have happened? In their choice of enemy, one might say that the terrorists of Al Qaeda had a great deal of dumb luck, for they attacked a country run by an Administration that had a radical conception of the potency of power. At the heart of the principle of asymmetric warfare—Al Qaeda's kind of warfare—is the notion of using your opponents' power against him. How does a small group of insurgents without an army, or even heavy weapons, defeat the greatest conventional military force the world has ever known? How do you defeat such an army if you don't have an army? Well, you borrow your enemy's. And this is precisely what Al Qaeda did.

25   Using the classic strategy of provocation, the group tried to tempt the superpower into its adopted homeland. The original strategy behind the 9/11 attacks—apart from humbling the superpower and creating the greatest recruiting poster the world had ever seen—was to lure the United States into a ground war in Afghanistan, where the one remaining superpower (like the Soviet Union before it) was to be trapped, stranded, and destroyed. It was to prepare for this war that Osama bin Laden arranged for the assassination, two days before 9/11—via bombs secreted in the video cameras of two terrorists posing as reporters—of the Afghan Northern Alliance leader, Ahmed Shah Massood, who would have been the United States' most powerful ally.

26   Well aware of the Soviets' Afghanistan debacle—after all, the US had supplied most of the weapons that defeated the Soviets there—the Bush Administration tried to avoid a quagmire by sending plenty of air support, lots of cash, and, most important, very few troops, relying instead on its Afghan allies. But if bin Laden was disappointed in this, he would soon have a far more valuable gift: the invasion of Iraq, a country that, unlike Afghanistan, was at the heart of the Middle East and central to Arab concerns, and, what's more, a nation that sat squarely on the critical Sunni-Shia divide, a potential ignition switch for Al Qaeda's great dream of a regional civil war. It is on that precipice that we find ourselves teetering today.

27   Critical to this strange and unlikely history were the Administration's peculiar ideas about power and its relation to reality—and beneath that a familiar imperial attitude, if put forward in a strikingly crude and harsh form: "We're an empire now and when we act we create our own reality." Power, untrammeled by law or custom; power, unlimited by the so-called weapons of the weak, be they international institutions, courts, or terrorism—power can remake reality. It is no accident that one of Karl Rove's heroes is President William McKinley, who stood at the apex of America's first imperial moment, and led the country into a glorious colonial adventure in the Philippines that was also meant to be the military equivalent of a stroll in the park and that, in the event, led to several years of bloody insurgency—an insurgency, it bears noticing, that was only finally put down with the help of the extensive use of torture, most notably water-boarding, which has made its reappearance in the imperial battles of our own times.

28   If we are an empire now, as Mr. Rove says, perhaps we should add, as he might not, that we are also a democracy, and therein, Rhetoric graduates of 2007, lies the rub. A democratic empire, as even the Athenians discovered, is an odd beast, like one of those mythological creatures born equally of lion and bird, or man and horse.

If one longs to invade Iraq to restore the empire's prestige, one must convince the democracy's people of the necessity of such a step. Herein lies the pathos of the famous weapons-of-mass-destruction issue, which has become a kind of synecdoche for the entire lying mess of the past few years. The center stage of our public life is now dominated by a simple melodrama: Bush wanted to invade Iraq; Bush told Americans that Iraq had weapons of mass destruction; Iraq did not have such weapons. Therefore Bush lied, and the war was born of lies and deception.

29   I hesitate to use that most overused of rhetorical terms—irony—to describe the emergence of this narrative at the center of our national life, but nonetheless, and with apologies: It is ironic. The fact is that officials of the Bush administration did believe there were weapons of mass destruction in Iraq, though they vastly exaggerated the evidence they had to prove it and, even more, the threat that those weapons might have posed, had they been there. In doing this, the officials believed themselves to be "framing a guilty man"; that is, like cops planting a bit of evidence in the murderer's car, they believed their underlying case was true; they just needed to dramatize it a bit to make it clear and convincing to the public. What matter, once the tanks were rumbling through Baghdad and the war was won? Weapons would be found, surely; and if only a few were found, who would care? By then, the United States military would have created a new reality.

30   I have often had a daydream about this. I see a solitary Army private—a cook perhaps, or a quartermaster—breaking the padlock on some forgotten warehouse on an Iraqi military base, poking about and finding a few hundred, even a few thousand, old artillery shells, leaking chemicals. These shells—forgotten, unusable—might have dated from the time of the first Gulf War, when Iraq unquestionably possessed chemical munitions. (Indeed, in the 1980s, the United States had supplied targeting intelligence that helped the Iraqis use them effectively against the Iranians.) And though now they had been forgotten, leaking, unusable, still they would indeed be weapons of mass destruction—to use the misleading and absurd construction that has headlined our age—and my solitary cook or quartermaster would be a hero, for he would have, all unwittingly, "proved" the case.

31   My daydream could easily have come to pass. Why not? It is nigh unto miraculous that the Iraqi regime, even with the help of the United Nations, managed so thoroughly to destroy or remove its once existing stockpile. And if my private had found those leaky old shells what would have been changed thereby? Yes, the Administration could have pointed to them in triumph and trumpeted the proven character of Saddam's threat. So much less embarrassing than the "weapons of mass destruction program related activities" that the administration still doggedly asserts were "discovered." But, in fact, the underlying calculus would have remained: that, in the months leading up to the war, the Administration relentlessly exaggerated the threat Saddam posed to the United States and relentlessly understated the risk the United States would run in invading and occupying Iraq. And it would have remained true and incontestable that—as the quaintly fact-bound British Foreign Secretary put it eight months before the war, in a secret British cabinet meeting made famous by the so-called Downing Street Memo—"the case [for attacking Iraq] was thin. Saddam was not threatening his neighbors and his WMD capability was less than that of Libya, North Korea or Iran."

32   Which is to say, the weapons were a rhetorical prop and, satisfying as it has been to see the administration beaten about the head with that prop, we forget this underlying fact at our peril. The issue was never whether the weapons were there or not; indeed, had the weapons really been the issue, why could the Administration not let the UN inspectors take the time to find them (as, of course, they never would have)? The administration needed, wanted, had to have, the Iraq war. The weapons were but a symbol, the necessary casus belli, what Hitchcock called the Maguffin—that glowing mysterious object in the suitcase in Quentin Tarantino's *Pulp Fiction*: that is, a satisfyingly concrete object on which to fasten a rhetorical or narrative end, in this case a war to restore American prestige, project its power, remake the Middle East.

33   The famous weapons were chosen to play this leading role for "bureaucratic reasons," as Paul Wolfowitz, then Deputy Secretary of Defense and until quite recently the unhappy President of the World Bank, once remarked to a lucky journalist. Had a handful of those weapons been found, the underlying truth would have remained: Saddam posed nowhere remotely near the threat to the United States that would have justified running the enormous metaphysical risk that a war of choice with Iraq posed. Of course, when you are focused on magical phrases like "preponderant power" and "the uni-polar moment," matters like numbers of troops at your disposal—and the simple fact that the United States had too few to sustain a long-term occupation of a country the size of Iraq—must seem mundane indeed.

Imperial Words and the Reality-Based Universe

34   I must apologize to you, Rhetoric Class of 2007. Ineluctably, uncontrollably, I find myself slipping back into the dull and unimaginative language of the reality-based community. It must grate a bit on your ears. After all, we live in a world in which the presumption that we were misled into war, that the Bush officials knew there were no weapons and touted them anyway, has supplanted the glowing, magical image of the weapons themselves. It is a presumption of great use to those regretful souls who once backed the war so fervently, not least a number of Democratic politicians we all could name, as well as many of my friends in the so-called liberal punditocracy who now need a suitable excuse for their own rashness, gullibility, and stupidity. For this, Bush's mendacity seems perfectly sized and ready to hand.

35   There is, however, full enough of that mendacity, without artificially adding to the stockpile. Indeed, all around us we've been hearing these last many months the sound of ice breaking, as the accumulated frozen scandals of this Administration slowly crack open to reveal their queasy secrets. And yet the problem, of course, is that they are not secrets at all: One of the most painful principles of our age is that scandals are doomed to be revealed—and to remain stinking there before us, unexcised, unpunished, unfinished.

36   If this Age of Rhetoric has a tragic symbol, then surely this is it: the frozen scandal, doomed to be revealed, and revealed, and revealed, in a never-ending torture familiar to the rock-bound Prometheus and his poor half-eaten liver. A full three years ago, the photographs from Abu Ghraib were broadcast by CBS on Sixty

Minutes II and published by Seymour Hersh in *The New Yorker*; nearly as far back I wrote a book entitled *Torture and Truth*, made up largely of Bush Administration documents that detailed the decision to use "extreme interrogation techniques" or—in the First President of Rhetoric's phrase—"an alternative set of procedures" on prisoners in the War on Terror.

37   He used this phrase last September in a White House speech kicking off the 2006 midterm election campaign, at a time when accusing the Democrats of evidencing a continued softness on terror—and a lamentable unwillingness to show the needed harshness in "interrogating terrorists"—seemed a winning electoral strategy.

38   And indeed Democrats seemed fully to agree, for they warily elected not to filibuster the Military Commissions Act of last October, which arguably made many of these "alternative sets of procedures" explicitly legal. And Democrats did win both houses of Congress, a victory perhaps owed in part to their refusal to block Bush's interrogation law. Who can say? What we can say is that if torture today remains a "scandal," a "crisis," it is a crisis in that same peculiar way that crime or AIDS or global warming are crises: that is, they are all things we have learned to live with.

39   Perhaps the commencement address to the Department of Rhetoric at the University of California at Berkeley is not the worst of places to call for a halt to this spinning merry-go-round. I know it will brand me forever a member of the reality-based community if I suggest that the one invaluable service the new Democratic Congress can provide all Americans is a clear accounting of how we came to find ourselves in this present time of war: an authorized version, as it were, which is, I know, the most pathetically retrograde of ideas.

40   This would require that people like Mr. Wolfowitz, Mr. Rumsfeld, and many others be called before a select, bipartisan committee of Congress to tell us what, in their view, really happened. I squirm with embarrassment putting forward such a pathetically unsophisticated notion, but failing at least the minimally authorized version that Congress could provide, we will find ourselves forever striving—by chasing down byways like the revelation of the identity of Valerie Plame, or the question of whether or not George Tenet bolstered his slam dunk exclamation in the Oval Office with an accompanying Michael Jordan-like leap—to understand how precisely decisions were made between September 11, 2001 and the invasion of Iraq eighteen months later.

41   Don't worry, though, Rhetoric graduates: such a proposal has about it the dusty feel of past decades; it is as "reality-based" as can be and we are unlikely to see it in our time. What we are likely to see is the ongoing collapse of our first Rhetoric-Major President, who, with fewer than one American in three now willing to say they approve of the job he is doing, is seeing his power ebb by the day. Tempting as it is, I will urge you not to draw too many overarching conclusions from his fate. He has had, after all, a very long run—and I say this with the wonder that perhaps can only come from having covered both the 2000 and 2004 election campaigns, from Florida, and the Iraq War.

42   I last visited that war in December, when Baghdad was cold and grey and I spent a good deal of time drawing black Xs through the sources listed in my address book, finding them, one after another, either departed or dead. Baghdad

seemed a sad and empty place, with even its customary traffic jams gone, and the periodic, resonating explosions attracting barely glances from those few Iraqis to be found on the streets.

43   How, in these "words in a time of war," can I convey to you the reality of that place at this time? Let me read to you a bit of an account from a young Iraqi woman of how that war has touched her and her family, drawn from a newsroom blog. The words may be terrible and hard to bear, but—for those of you who have made such a determined effort to learn to read and understand—this is the most reality I could find to tell you. This is what lies behind the headlines and the news reports and it is as it is.

> We were asked to send the next of kin to whom the remains of my nephew, killed on Monday in a horrific explosion downtown, can be handed over. . . .
>
> So we went, his mum, his other aunt and I . . . When we got there, we were given his remains. And remains they were. From the waist down was all they could give us. "We identified him by the cell phone in his pants' pocket. If you want the rest, you will just have to look for yourselves. We don't know what he looks like." [. . .]
>
> We were led away, and before long a foul stench clogged my nose and I retched. With no more warning we came to a clearing that was probably an inside garden at one time; all round it were patios and rooms with large-pane windows to catch the evening breeze Baghdad is renowned for. But now it had become a slaughterhouse, only instead of cattle, all around were human bodies. On this side; complete bodies; on that side halves; and everywhere body parts.
>
> We were asked what we were looking for; "upper half," replied my companion, for I was rendered speechless. "Over there." We looked for our boy's broken body between tens of other boys' remains; with our bare hands sifting them and turning them.
>
> Millennia later we found him, took both parts home, and began the mourning ceremony.

44   The foregoing were words from an Iraqi family, who find themselves as far as they can possibly be from the idea that, when they act, they create their own reality—that they are, as Bush's Brain put it, "history's actors." The voices you heard come from history's objects and we must ponder who the subjects are, who exactly is acting upon them.

45   The car bomb that so changed their lives was not set by Americans; indeed, young Americans even now are dying to prevent such things. I have known a few of these young Americans. Perhaps you have as well, perhaps they are in the circles of your family or of your friends. I remember one of them, a young lieutenant, a beautiful young man with a puffy, sleepy face, looking at me when I asked whether or not he was scared when he went out on patrol—this was October 2003, as the insurgency was exploding. I remember him smiling a moment and then saying with evident pity for a reporter's lack of understanding. "This is war. We shoot, they shoot. We shoot, they shoot. Some days they shoot better than we do." He was patient in his answer, smiling sleepily in his young beauty, and I could tell he regarded me as from another world, a man who could never understand the world in which he lived. Three days after our interview, an explosion near Fallujah killed him.

46 Contingency, accidents, the metaphysical ironies that seem to stitch history together like a lopsided quilt—all these have no place in the imperial vision. A perception of one's self as "history's actor" leaves no place for them. But they exist and it is invariably others, closer to the ground, who see them, know them, and suffer their consequences.

47 You have chosen a path that will let you look beyond the rhetoric that you have studied and into the heart of those consequences. Of all people you have chosen to learn how to see the gaps and the loose stitches and the remnant threads. Ours is a grim age, this Age of Rhetoric, still infused with the remnant perfume of imperial dreams. You have made your study in a propitious time, oh graduates, and that bold choice may well bring you pain, for you have devoted yourselves to seeing what it is that stands before you. If clear sight were not so painful, many more would elect to have it. Today, you do not conclude but begin: today you commence. My blessings upon you, and my gratitude to you for training yourself to see. Reality, it seems, has caught up with you.

QUESTIONS FOR ANALYSIS AND DISCUSSION

1. How does Danner's introduction to the graduates and his feelings about delivering this commencement speech set the tone of the essay? Judging by his words, what sort of professor do you think he is? Identify other comments and words in his essay that reveal his personal style and tone.

2. Analyze Danner's summary of the statement made by an "unnamed Administration official" in paragraph 9. What is this individual saying about government, its influence, and the people? What does Danner mean when he paraphrases, "power has made reality its bitch"?

3. Why did Danner choose to discuss this topic as a commencement speech? Why would his points matter to this group of graduates? Could it be delivered to other majors? Why or why not?

4. What is television's role in constructing perception and the American people's understanding of our political system and sociocultural reality?

5. According to Danner, why is the study of rhetoric especially important during a time of war? Explain.

Why Study War?

Victor Davis Hanson

Military history teaches us about honor, sacrifice, and the inevitability of conflict.

Victor Davis Hanson is a conservative military historian, columnist, political essayist, and former classics professor, best known as a scholar of ancient warfare as well as a commentator on modern warfare. Hanson is currently Senior Fellow at the Hoover Institution and Fellow in California Studies at the Claremont Institute. Hanson writes two weekly columns, one for *National Review* and one syndicated by Tribune Media Services, and has been published in many journals and newspapers, including the *New York Times*, the *Wall Street Journal*, the *American Spectator*, and the *Weekly Standard*. In 2007, he was awarded the National Humanities Medal. The author of many books, his most recent work is *War Like No Other: How the Athenians and Spartans Fought the Peloponnesian War* (2005). This essay appeared in the Summer 2007 issue of *City Journal*.

BEFORE YOU READ

What are American students taught about war? What do you recall from your grade-school studies about war?

AS YOU READ

Why does Hanson feel that Americans should improve their basic understanding of the military and its knowledge of war? Explain.

1   Try explaining to a college student that Tet was an American military victory. You'll provoke not a counterargument—let alone an assent—but a blank stare: Who or what was Tet? Doing interviews about the recent hit movie *300*, I encountered similar bewilderment from listeners and hosts. Not only did most of them not know who the *300* were or what Thermopylae was; they seemed clueless about the Persian Wars altogether.

2   It's no surprise that civilian Americans tend to lack a basic understanding of military matters. Even when I was a graduate student, 30-some years ago, military history—understood broadly as the investigation of why one side wins and another loses a war, and encompassing reflections on magisterial or foolish generalship, technological stagnation or breakthrough, and the roles of discipline, bravery, national will, and culture in determining a conflict's outcome and its consequences—had already become unfashionable on campus. Today, universities are even less receptive to the subject.

3   This state of affairs is profoundly troubling, for democratic citizenship requires knowledge of war—and now, in the age of weapons of mass annihilation, more than ever.

4   I came to the study of warfare in an odd way, at the age of 24. Without ever taking a class in military history, I naively began writing about war for a Stanford classics dissertation that explored the effects of agricultural devastation in ancient Greece, especially the Spartan ravaging of the Athenian countryside during the Peloponnesian War. The topic fascinated me. Was the strategy effective? Why assume that ancient armies with primitive tools could easily burn or cut trees, vines, and grain on thousands of acres of enemy farms, when on my family farm in Selma, California, it took me almost an hour to fell a mature fruit tree with a sharp modern ax? Yet even if the invaders couldn't starve civilian populations, was the destruction still harmful psychologically? Did it goad proud agrarians to come out and fight?

And what did the practice tell us about the values of the Greeks—and of the generals who persisted in an operation that seemingly brought no tangible results?

5   I posed these questions to my prospective thesis advisor, adding all sorts of further justifications. The topic was central to understanding the Peloponnesian War, I noted. The research would be interdisciplinary—a big plus in the modern university—drawing not just on ancient military histories but also on archaeology, classical drama, epigraphy, and poetry. I could bring a personal dimension to the research, too, having grown up around veterans of both world wars who talked constantly about battle. And from my experience on the farm, I wanted to add practical details about growing trees and vines in a Mediterranean climate.

6   Yet my advisor was skeptical. Agrarian wars, indeed wars of any kind, weren't popular in classics Ph.D. programs, even though farming and fighting were the ancient Greeks' two most common pursuits, the sources of anecdote, allusion, and metaphor in almost every Greek philosophical, historical, and literary text. Few classicists seemed to care any more that most notable Greek writers, thinkers, and statesmen—from Aeschylus to Pericles to Xenophon—had served in the phalanx or on a trireme at sea. Dozens of nineteenth-century dissertations and monographs on ancient warfare—on the organization of the Spartan army, the birth of Greek tactics, the strategic thinking of Greek generals, and much more—went largely unread. Nor was the discipline of military history, once central to a liberal education, in vogue on campuses in the seventies. It was as if the university had forgotten that history itself had begun with Herodotus and Thucydides as the story of armed conflicts.

7   What lay behind this academic lack of interest? The most obvious explanation: this was the immediate post-Vietnam era. The public perception in the Carter years was that America had lost a war that for moral and practical reasons it should never have fought—a catastrophe, for many in the universities, that it must never repeat. The necessary corrective wasn't to learn how such wars started, went forward, and were lost. Better to ignore anything that had to do with such odious business in the first place.

8   The nuclear pessimism of the cold war, which followed the horror of two world wars, also dampened academic interest. The postwar obscenity of Mutually Assured Destruction had lent an apocalyptic veneer to contemporary war: as President Kennedy warned, "Mankind must put an end to war, or war will put an end to mankind." Conflict had become something so destructive, in this view, that it no longer had any relation to the battles of the past. It seemed absurd to worry about a new tank or a novel doctrine of counterinsurgency when the press of a button, unleashing nuclear Armageddon, would render all military thinking superfluous.

9   Further, the sixties had ushered in a utopian view of society antithetical to serious thinking about war. Government, the military, business, religion, and the family had conspired, the new Rousseauians believed, to warp the naturally peace-loving individual. Conformity and coercion smothered our innately pacifist selves. To assert that wars broke out because bad men, in fear or in pride, sought material advantage or status, or because good men had done too little to stop them, was now seen as antithetical to an enlightened understanding of human nature. "What difference does it make," in the words of the much-quoted Mahatma Gandhi, "to the dead, the

orphans, and the homeless whether the mad destruction is wrought under the name of totalitarianism or the holy name of liberty and democracy?"

10   The academic neglect of war is even more acute today. Military history as a discipline has atrophied, with very few professorships, journal articles, or degree programs. In 2004, Edward Coffman, a retired military history professor who taught at the University of Wisconsin, reviewed the faculties of the top 25 history departments, as ranked by U.S. News and World Report. He found that of over 1,000 professors, only 21 identified war as a specialty. When war does show up on university syllabi, it's often about the race, class, and gender of combatants and wartime civilians. So a class on the Civil War will focus on the Underground Railroad and Reconstruction, not on Chancellorsville and Gettysburg. One on World War II might emphasize Japanese internment, Rosie the Riveter, and the horror of Hiroshima, not Guadalcanal and Midway. A survey of the Vietnam War will devote lots of time to the inequities of the draft, media coverage, and the antiwar movement at home, and scant the air and artillery barrages at Khe Sanh.

11   Those who want to study war in the traditional way face intense academic suspicion, as Margaret Atwood's poem "The Loneliness of the Military Historian" suggests:

> Confess: it's my profession
> that alarms you.
> This is why few people ask me to dinner,
> though Lord knows I don't go out of my
>   way to be scary.

Historians of war must derive perverse pleasure, their critics suspect, from reading about carnage and suffering. Why not figure out instead how to outlaw war forever, as if it were not a tragic, nearly inevitable aspect of human existence? Hence the recent surge of "peace studies" (see "The Peace Racket").

12   The university's aversion to the study of war certainly doesn't reflect public lack of interest in the subject. Students love old-fashioned war classes on those rare occasions when they're offered, usually as courses that professors sneak in when the choice of what to teach is left up to them. I taught a number of such classes at California State University, Stanford, and elsewhere. They'd invariably wind up overenrolled, with hordes of students lingering after office hours to offer opinions on the battles of Marathon and Lepanto.

13   Popular culture, too, displays extraordinary enthusiasm for all things military. There's a new Military History Channel, and Hollywood churns out a steady supply of blockbuster war movies, from *Saving Private Ryan* to *300*. The post–Ken Burns explosion of interest in the Civil War continues. Historical reenactment societies stage history's great battles, from the Roman legions' to the Wehrmacht's. Barnes and Noble and Borders bookstores boast well-stocked military history sections, with scores of new titles every month. A plethora of websites obsess over strategy and tactics. Hit video games grow ever more realistic in their reconstructions of battles.

14   The public may feel drawn to military history because it wants to learn about honor and sacrifice, or because of interest in technology—the muzzle velocity of a Tiger Tank's 88mm cannon, for instance—or because of a pathological need to

experience violence, if only vicariously. The importance—and challenge—of the academic study of war is to elevate that popular enthusiasm into a more capacious and serious understanding, one that seeks answers to such questions as: Why do wars break out? How do they end? Why do the winners win and the losers lose? How best to avoid wars or contain their worst effects?

15   A wartime public illiterate about the conflicts of the past can easily find itself paralyzed in the acrimony of the present. Without standards of historical comparison, it will prove ill equipped to make informed judgments. Neither our politicians nor most of our citizens seem to recall the incompetence and terrible decisions that, in December 1777, December 1941, and November 1950, led to massive American casualties and, for a time, public despair. So it's no surprise that today so many seem to think that the violence in Iraq is unprecedented in our history. Roughly 3,000 combat dead in Iraq in some four years of fighting is, of course, a terrible thing. And it has provoked national outrage to the point of considering withdrawal and defeat, as we still bicker over up-armored Humvees and proper troop levels. But a previous generation considered Okinawa a stunning American victory, and prepared to follow it with an invasion of the Japanese mainland itself—despite losing, in a little over two months, four times as many Americans as we have lost in Iraq, casualties of faulty intelligence, poor generalship, and suicidal head-on assaults against fortified positions.

16   It's not that military history offers cookie-cutter comparisons with the past. Germany's World War I victory over Russia in under three years and her failure to take France in four apparently misled Hitler into thinking that he could overrun the Soviets in three or four weeks—after all, he had brought down historically tougher France in just six. Similarly, the conquest of the Taliban in eight weeks in 2001, followed by the establishment of constitutional government within a year in Kabul, did not mean that the similarly easy removal of Saddam Hussein in three weeks in 2003 would ensure a working Iraqi democracy within six months. The differences between the countries—cultural, political, geographical, and economic—were too great.

17   Instead, knowledge of past wars establishes wide parameters of what to expect from new ones. Themes, emotions, and rhetoric remain constant over the centuries, and thus generally predictable. Athens's disastrous expedition in 415 BC against Sicily, the largest democracy in the Greek world, may not prefigure our war in Iraq. But the story of the Sicilian calamity does instruct us on how consensual societies can clamor for war—yet soon become disheartened and predicate their support on the perceived pulse of the battlefield.

18   Military history teaches us, contrary to popular belief these days, that wars aren't necessarily the most costly of human calamities. The first Gulf War took few lives in getting Saddam out of Kuwait; doing nothing in Rwanda allowed savage gangs and militias to murder hundreds of thousands with impunity. Hitler, Mao, Pol Pot, and Stalin killed far more off the battlefield than on it. The 1918 Spanish flu epidemic brought down more people than World War I did. And more Americans—over 3.2 million—lost their lives driving over the last 90 years than died in combat in this nation's 231-year history. Perhaps what bothers us about wars, though, isn't just their horrific lethality but also that people choose to wage them—which makes them seem avoidable, unlike a flu virus or a car wreck, and their tolls unduly

grievous. Yet military history also reminds us that war sometimes has an eerie utility: as British strategist Basil H. Liddell Hart put it, "War is always a matter of doing evil in the hope that good may come of it." Wars—or threats of wars—put an end to chattel slavery, Nazism, fascism, Japanese militarism, and Soviet Communism.

19   Military history is as often the story of appeasement as of warmongering. The destructive military careers of Alexander the Great, Caesar, Napoleon, and Hitler would all have ended early had any of their numerous enemies united when the odds favored them. Western air power stopped Slobodan Milošević's reign of terror at little cost to NATO forces—but only after a near-decade of inaction and dialogue had made possible the slaughter of tens of thousands. Affluent Western societies have often proved reluctant to use force to prevent greater future violence. "War is an ugly thing, but not the ugliest of things," observed the British philosopher John Stuart Mill. "The decayed and degraded state of moral and patriotic feeling which thinks that nothing is worth war is much worse."

20   Indeed, by ignoring history, the modern age is free to interpret war as a failure of communication, of diplomacy, of talking—as if aggressors don't know exactly what they're doing. Speaker of the House Nancy Pelosi, frustrated by the Bush administration's intransigence in the War on Terror, flew to Syria, hoping to persuade President Assad to stop funding terror in the Middle East. She assumed that Assad's belligerence resulted from our aloofness and arrogance rather than from his dictatorship's interest in destroying democracy in Lebanon and Iraq, before such contagious freedom might in fact destroy him. For a therapeutically inclined generation raised on Oprah and Dr. Phil—and not on the letters of William Tecumseh Sherman and William Shirer's Berlin Diary—problems between states, like those in our personal lives, should be argued about by equally civilized and peaceful rivals, and so solved without resorting to violence.

21   Yet it's hard to find many wars that result from miscommunication. Far more often they break out because of malevolent intent and the absence of deterrence. Margaret Atwood also wrote in her poem: "Wars happen because the ones who start them/think they can win." Hitler did; so did Mussolini and Tojo—and their assumptions were logical, given the relative disarmament of the Western democracies at the time. Bin Laden attacked on September 11 not because there was a dearth of American diplomats willing to dialogue with him in the Hindu Kush. Instead, he recognized that a series of Islamic terrorist assaults against U.S. interests over two decades had met with no meaningful reprisals, and concluded that decadent Westerners would never fight, whatever the provocation—or that, if we did, we would withdraw as we had from Mogadishu.

22   In the twenty-first century, it's easier than ever to succumb to technological determinism, the idea that science, new weaponry, and globalization have altered the very rules of war. But military history teaches us that our ability to strike a single individual from 30,000 feet up with a GPS bomb or a jihadist's efforts to have his propaganda beamed to millions in real time do not necessarily transform the conditions that determine who wins and who loses wars.

23   True, instant communications may compress decision making, and generals must be skilled at news conferences that can now influence the views of millions

worldwide. Yet these are really just new wrinkles on the old face of war. The impro-vised explosive device versus the up-armored Humvee is simply an updated take on the catapult versus the stone wall or the harquebus versus the mailed knight. The long history of war suggests no static primacy of the defensive or the offensive, or of one sort of weapon over the other, but just temporary advantages gained by particular strategies and technologies that go unanswered for a time by less adept adversaries.

24 So it's highly doubtful, the study of war tells us, that a new weapon will emerge from the Pentagon or anywhere else that will change the very nature of armed conflict—unless some sort of genetic engineering so alters man's brain chemistry that he begins to act in unprecedented ways. We fought the 1991 Gulf War with daz-zling, computer-enhanced weaponry. But lost in the technological pizzazz was the basic wisdom that we need to fight wars with political objectives in mind and that, to conclude them decisively, we must defeat and even humiliate our enemies, so that they agree to abandon their prewar behavior. For some reason, no American general or diplomat seemed to understand that crucial point 16 years ago, with the result that, on the cessation of hostilities, Saddam Hussein's supposedly defeated generals used their gunships to butcher Kurds and Shiites while Americans looked on. And because we never achieved the war's proper aim—ensuring that Iraq would not use its petro-wealth to destroy the peace of the region—we have had to fight a second war of no-fly zones, and then a third war to remove Saddam, and now a fourth war, of counterinsurgency, to protect the fledgling Iraqi democracy.

25 Military history reminds us of important anomalies and paradoxes. When Sparta invaded Attica in the first spring of the Peloponnesian war, Thucydides recounts, it expected the Athenians to surrender after a few short seasons of rav-aging. They didn't—but a plague that broke out unexpectedly did more damage than thousands of Spartan ravagers did. Twenty-seven years later, a maritime Athens lost the war at sea to Sparta, an insular land power that started the conflict with scarcely a navy. The 2003 removal of Saddam refuted doom-and-gloom critics who predicted thousands of deaths and millions of refugees, just as the subsequent messy four-year reconstruction hasn't evolved as anticipated into a quiet, stable democracy—to say the least.

26 The size of armies doesn't guarantee battlefield success: the victors at Salamis, Issos, Mexico City, and Lepanto were all outnumbered. War's most savage moments—the Allied summer offensive of 1918, the Russian siege of Berlin in the spring of 1945, the Battle of the Bulge, Hiroshima—often unfold right before hostili-ties cease. And democratic leaders during war—think of Winston Churchill, Harry Truman, and Richard Nixon—often leave office either disgraced or unpopular.

27 It would be reassuring to think that the righteousness of a cause, or the bravery of an army, or the nobility of a sacrifice ensures public support for war. But military history shows that far more often the perception of winning is what matters. Citi-zens turn abruptly on any leaders deemed culpable for losing. "Public sentiment is everything," wrote Abraham Lincoln. "With public sentiment nothing can fail. With-out it nothing can succeed. He who molds opinion is greater than he who enacts laws." Lincoln knew that lesson well. Gettysburg and Vicksburg were brilliant

Union victories that by summer 1863 had restored Lincoln's previously shaky credibility. But a year later, after the Wilderness, Spotsylvania, Petersburg, and Cold Harbor battles—Cold Harbor claimed 7,000 Union lives in 20 minutes—the public reviled him. Neither Lincoln nor his policies had changed, but the Confederate ability to kill large numbers of Union soldiers had.

28   Ultimately, public opinion follows the ups and downs—including the perception of the ups and downs—of the battlefield, since victory excites the most ardent pacifist and defeat silences the most zealous zealot. After the defeat of France, the losses to Bomber Command, the U-boat rampage, and the fall of Greece, Singapore, and Dunkirk, Churchill took the blame for a war as seemingly lost as, a little later, it seemed won by the brilliant prime minister after victories in North Africa, Sicily, and Normandy. When the successful military action against Saddam Hussein ended in April 2003, over 70 percent of the American people backed it, with politicians and pundits alike elbowing each other aside to take credit for their prescient support. Four years of insurgency later, Americans oppose a now-orphaned war by the same margin. General George S. Patton may have been uncouth, but he wasn't wrong when he bellowed, "Americans love a winner and will not tolerate a loser." The American public turned on the Iraq War not because of Cindy Sheehan or Michael Moore but because it felt that the battlefield news had turned uniformly bad and that the price in American lives and treasure for ensuring Iraqi reform was too dear.

29   Finally, military history has the moral purpose of educating us about past sacrifices that have secured our present freedom and security. If we know nothing of Shiloh, Belleau Wood, Tarawa, and Chosun, the crosses in our military cemeteries are just pleasant white stones on lush green lawns. They no longer serve as reminders that thousands endured pain and hardship for our right to listen to what we wish on our iPods and to shop at Wal-Mart in safety—or that they expected future generations, links in this great chain of obligation, to do the same for those not yet born. The United States was born through war, reunited by war, and saved from destruction by war. No future generation, however comfortable and affluent, should escape that terrible knowledge.

30   What, then, can we do to restore the study of war to its proper place in the life of the American mind? The challenge isn't just to reform the graduate schools or the professoriate, though that would help. On a deeper level, we need to reexamine the larger forces that have devalued the very idea of military history—of war itself. We must abandon the naive faith that with enough money, education, or good intentions we can change the nature of mankind so that conflict, as if by fiat, becomes a thing of the past. In the end, the study of war reminds us that we will never be gods. We will always just be men, it tells us. Some men will always prefer war to peace; and other men, we who have learned from the past, have a moral obligation to stop them.

QUESTIONS FOR ANALYSIS AND DISCUSSION

1. Answer the question Hanson poses in his title—"why study war?"
2. According to Hanson, what accounts for the general disinterest in war studies by most Americans today?
3. Why does Hanson include Margaret Atwood's poem, "The Loneliness of the Military Historian" in his essay? Read the entire poem (it can

be found online at http://www.poetryfoundation.org/archive/poem.
html?id=177286). What is Atwood saying about war and the war
historian? How does her poem connect to Hanson's argument?

4. Summarize Hanson's argument. What is his call to action? What does he
hope to change by writing this essay? Who does he hope to influence?

5. Evaluate this quote from Hanson's essay by the British philosopher
John Stuart Mill. "War is an ugly thing, but not the ugliest of things. The
decayed and degraded state of moral and patriotic feeling which thinks
that nothing is worth war is much worse." What does Mill mean? From
your own perspective, do you agree or disagree with his statement?

Fear and Trembling in the Age of Terror
Robert J. Lewis

America's "war on terror" has sparked debate over the appropriate balance between freedom and security. Many Americans find themselves facing a quandary—how do we balance
our personal freedoms with our desire to be safe? Can we protect the personal rights and
freedoms that we hold dear without sacrificing national security? In the next essay, Robert J.
Lewis asks the tough question of whether we are inadvertently letting terrorists win. By giving up our freedoms, he argues, we admit that we are afraid, and willing to let terrorists direct how we will live our lives.

Lewis is editor of *Arts and Opinion*, a Canadian Web magazine about arts, culture, and
politics. He is also a columnist for All About Jazz, a website produced by jazz fans for jazz
fans. This editorial appeared in *Arts and Opinion* in 2006.

BEFORE YOU READ

In this article, Robert J. Lewis examines how our concepts of safety and
security have been changed forever by the events of September 11. In what
ways did your personal perceptions change because of what happened
that day?

AS YOU READ

When you travel by plane, do you feel inconvenienced by the new rules
and regulations imposed on passengers, or do you feel safer flying because of them?

1   "I'm sorry, sir, but you can't take that on board," said the security official in a
benign, narcosis inducing baritone, a voice he's been obliged to use ever since the
London terrorist plot was uncovered. His manner was so ingratiating, for a second
I thought he was a close friend. How are the wife and kids, I almost asked.

2   They couldn't have chosen a better person to work the security x-ray machine at Pierre Trudeau International Airport in Montreal. He was referring to my mini vial of contact lens liquid which I would later use to float my lenses during the eight-hour flight. I considered shaking the daylights out of the bottle to reassure him that it wasn't nitroglycerin. "I usually don't wear lenses when I fly," I explained. "What can I say?" his sympathetic eyes seemed to reply. "Next time you had better pack them in your luggage." The long table behind him was overflowing with containers of all shapes and sizes, which now included my lens liquid vial.

3   Since the disruption of the terrorist plot in London and implementation of new regulations interdicting all liquids, gels etc. in hand luggage, my thoughts had been turning criminal, plotting ways to get my two teaspoons worth of Bausch & Lomb past security. I considered crotching it, or parking the vial in my mouth for the inspection, a strategy that wouldn't survive the first question and answer sequence. But law-abiding person that I am, I overruled my wicked designs and thought with a little bit of luck and common sense, they would let it go. So much for that.

4   September terrorist bombings in resort towns in Turkey have all but shut down a once thriving tourist industry, costing the country millions in revenues; the same in Israel and Egypt and wherever terrorism is a reality on the ground. Terrorism has cost the world billions of dollars to which we add time lost worrying and wondering about what is happening to our world.

5   Terrorism works and its working effects are cumulative. Contrary to conventional wisdom, the terrorists do have a goal: to remake the world in their own image, to make us as unfree as them. Which makes every terrorist event a success because it is not so much the damage it inflicts but the fact and production of the event we are not able to prevent that rips into and embeds itself in the psyche like an unexploded bullet.

6   Since terrorism is not going to go away, the question we must ask is do we allow ourselves to be held hostage by the constant threat of it and resign ourselves to the gradual erosion of freedoms that have defined the Western spirit, or do we decide to live with terrorism on our terms—and not theirs?

7   So far, we've been playing by their rules, in part because we have failed to offer sufficient thought to the gross disconnect that has peripheralized the sacrifice of tens of thousands of men and women who have fought to the death for the sake of the freedoms and liberties we enjoy—and obscenely take for granted. There comes a time when the beliefs and founding principles of every nation and its politics are put to the test, and I believe we are at this crossroads moment. Just as deserts are encroaching on what was once arable land, terrorism is eating away at our freedoms. The question both of these unrelated events ask is whether there exists the political will to reverse them. Perhaps the solution is as simple as learning to think outside the box, to recontextualize terrorism so that it corresponds to a value commensurate with the warped and debased project that it is. If we can live with the fact that thousands of soldiers have sacrificed their lives for the cause of freedom, surely we can learn to live with terrorist events that in and of themselves should be no more noteworthy than a plane crash, bridge collapse, or ferry sinking, which are serious enough, but do not impact on our way of life.

8   In North America we love our alcohol. We discovered how much so during pro-hibition when millions of decent, law-abiding citizens resorted to breaking the laws of the land for the sake of their booze. Every year on our North American highways 50,000 people, many of whom are under the influence, are killed in motor vehicle ac-cidents, while 250,000 more are injured, many of them seriously. Billions of dollars and tears are spent burying the dead, attending to the injured, supporting for life those who can no longer support themselves. That's how much we love our automobiles.

9   But don't we love our freedom more than our A & A (alcohol and autos)? If on Jan. 1st of the new year we won't bat an eyelash at the thought that 50,000 people are going to be killed in alcohol related automobile accidents, we should be at least as blasé at the thought that only 2,000 of us will lose our lives in terrorist related incidents over the course of the year. For those of us who don't want our phones tapped, our IDs rigged with personal information that leave us vulnerable to the greedy and exploitive, who don't want to bother worrying about contact lens liquid restrictions, having to remove our bras and shoes at security check points, what words to avoid in our e-mails for fear of triggering an investigation or getting put on someone's list, and in general, the grad-ual legislative erosion of freedoms upon which our way of life is founded, 2,000 deaths is a small price to pay compared to the 50,000 who will die on the road.

10   The hard fact of the matter is that it's not yet unconscionable that the world's 1,000 worst terrorists are methodically refashioning the world in their own image by out-thinking us, by making us fear, tremble and genuflect to their agenda. Since terrorism is not science, but psychology, where the cause can produce any number of contingent effects, why are we allowing ourselves to be affected exactly as they would have it? Which makes terrorism a war of wills, and all land-based counter-terrorist wars red herrings.

11   If the mentally tougher terrorist mind is to be undone, we will have to will ourselves to rethink the meaning of terrorism in order to assign it its due value in relation to what is due to our hard earned freedoms. Less than that, we have signed on to a blueprint of a world where terrorism will one day no longer be necessary because it will have rendered us as unfree as the terrorists themselves.

QUESTIONS FOR ANALYSIS AND DISCUSSION ───────

1. What freedoms are you willing to give up in the name of national and personal security?
2. Evaluate Lewis's argument that giving up our freedoms is worse than losing 2,000 people per year to terrorism. Do you agree?
3. According to the article, terrorism does work. What examples does Lewis use to prove that terrorism is working on Americans today? How is the United States allowing terrorists to "win"? Do you agree or disagree with his assessment? Explain.
4. Lewis states, "terrorism [is] a war of wills, and all land-based counter-terrorist wars red herrings." What is a red herring? Explain why Lewis believes that the war in Iraq is a red herring.
5. Why does Lewis begin his essay with an anecdote about airport secu-rity, and how does this anecdote relate to the main point of his essay?

WRITING ASSIGNMENTS

1. Several of the writers in this section comment that terrorism is aimed at the cultural ideals and political ideology of the United States. Write an essay in which you explore these ideals. Why would the people of other countries find these ideals threatening? Do Americans force their ideology on others? If so, in what ways?

2. How has terrorism affected your life since September 11, 2001? Have you been inconvenienced at airports? Have you considered your vacation destination more carefully? Are you more vigilant in public spaces? Write an essay on the personal impact of terrorism on ordinary Americans, drawing from information provided in this chapter and your own observations and experience.

3. Write a paper exploring the connection between the media and terrorism. Is the media helping terrorists by giving them extensive coverage? Does it help encourage even more violent acts of terrorism? In your opinion, should the media report on terrorist threats or activity? Explain.

4. Just about everyone has an opinion as to whether the United States should be in Iraq. Explain why you think the United States now, or at any time, should or should not be fighting in Iraq or other countries in the Middle East. When is it appropriate for the United States to intervene?

OUTSIDE LOOKING IN—VIEWS OF THE UNITED STATES

Pell-Mell
Tom Wolfe

Unlike European social systems that historically were based on aristocracy and class, the American social system, at least in theory, supported the idea that anyone, regardless of their background, had a chance at success. The American tradition of "all men are created equal" promotes the idea that, rather than be born to one's station, any American with drive, ambition, intelligence, and fortitude can reach the highest office in government, or attain the highest level of business success. In the next essay, novelist Tom Wolfe describes the history behind the "American idea" and shows how this way of life has made the United States "the freest, most open country in the world."

Tom Wolfe is a journalist of many nonfiction books and the novelist of several best-selling works of fiction, including the critically acclaimed *Bonfire of the Vanities* (1987), which was later made into a motion picture starring Tom Hanks and Melanie Griffith. His most recent book is *I Am Charlotte Simmons* (2004). In November 2007, *The Atlantic* ran a series of essays by novelists, politicians, artists, and others reflecting on the future of the "American idea." This essay appeared as part of that series.

When we refer to the "American idea," what do we mean? Create your own definition of the "American idea."

How does the tone of Wolfe's essay shift? What do you think accounts for this tone shift?

1   Since you asked . . . the American idea was born at approximately 5 p.m. on Friday, December 2, 1803, the moment Thomas Jefferson sprang the so-called pell-mell on the new British ambassador, Anthony Merry, at dinner in the White House. Oh, this was no inadvertent faux pas. This was faux pas aforethought. Jefferson obviously loved the prospect of dumbfounding the great Brit and leaving him speechless, furious, seething, so burned up that smoke would start coming out of his ears. And all that the pell-mell did.

2   Jefferson had already tenderized the ambassador three days earlier. Merry was the first foreign diplomat to take up residence in Washington. Accompanied by Secretary of State James Madison, he shows up at the White House wearing a hat with a swooping plume, a ceremonial sword, gold braid, shoes with gleaming buckles—in short, the whole aristocratic European ambassadorial getup—for his formal introduction to the president of the United States. He is immediately baffled. Jefferson doesn't come to greet him in the grand reception hall. Instead, Merry and Madison have to go looking for him . . . Bango! All at once they bump into the American head of state in some tiny tunnel-like entryway to his study. What with three men and a sword in it all at once, the space is so congested that Merry has to back himself and his sword out of it just to have room to shake hands. When he shakes hands, he's stunned, appalled: The president of the United States is a very Hogarth of utter slovenliness from his head . . . to his torso, clad in a casual workaday outfit thrown together with a complete indifference to appearances and a negligence so perfectly gross, it has to have been actually studied . . . down to his feet, which are stuffed, or mostly stuffed, into a pair of down-at-the-heels slippers, literally slippers and literally worn down at the heels in a way that is sheer Gin Lane. "Utter slovenliness," "negligence actually studied," "indifference to appearances," and "down at the heels" were Merry's own words in the first of what would become a regular jeremiad of complaints and supplications to Lord Hawkesbury, the foreign secretary, all but coming right out and begging him to break off relations with the United States to protest such pointed insults toward His Majesty's representative. Merry was ready to bail out . . . and his wife, a notably not-shy woman née Elizabeth Death (yes), even more so.

3   The introductory insult was on November 29. Merry and his wife were invited to dinner at the White House on the fateful day, December 2. Merry accepted . . . warily . . . under the impression that he and his wife would be the guests of honor

and that this would be Jefferson's opportunity to make up for his lapse in protocol. The Merrys arrived at 4:30. Along with the other guests, they were assembled for a reception in a drawing room across the hall from the dining room. The Merrys were left flabbergasted and aghast when Jefferson ignored Mrs. Merry and gave his arm to Dolley Madison, who often served as White House hostess for the widowed president. James Madison gave his arm to an already furious Mrs. Merry. The dining room seems to have had a single large, round table. Jefferson took a seat and gave Dolley Madison the ladies' seat of honor on his right. James Madison didn't give Elizabeth Death Merry the seat on the president's other side, however. That went to the Spanish ambassador's wife. The already insulted Mrs. Merry, guest of honor presumptive, took it like a kick in the shin when Madison showed her to an obviously back-of-the-pack seat.

4   Meantime, her husband's dignity was taking an even worse beating. He was part of an undifferentiated haunch-to-paunch herd of the titled, the untitled, the eminences, and the not-muches entering the doorway. They had no choice but to take their seats pell-mell . . . any seat—first come, first served. Literally pell-mell referred to a confused, disorderly crowd in a headlong rush, and that was exactly what it felt like to His Majesty's Ambassador Merry. An outrageous insult was now in progress, but he had only two choices: take a seat or make a scene. So he headed for a chair next to the Spanish ambassador's wife. But before he could get to it, some crude savage who bore the title "Congressman" lunged past him and took it for himself.

5   Foreign dignitaries, even the Spanish ambassador, were flashing loaded glances at each other—these Americans—savages!—and muttering behind the backs of their hands. Merry and his wife vowed never to dine at the White House again—and never did. They did accept an invitation from Secretary of State Madison, who had been the good guy in Jefferson's good-guy/bad-guy team—only to get pell-melled all over again chez Madison. For a time, at least, they refused all invitations from Jefferson's Cabinet members, too. In due course they officially protested their treatment. But Jefferson had such an aristocratic bearing and presence, was from such a prominent family—in America they didn't come any better than the Randolphs of Virginia—was so filthy land-rich, so learned—he spoke Latin as well as French and could read classical Greek as easily as Plato and Aristotle ever did—was so sophisticated and urbane, in fact so cosmopolitan—he had been ambassador to France at the court of Louis XVI—no one could very well write him off as one of . . . "these Americans."

6   In addition to being seven or eight other species of the genus Genius, Jefferson proved to be a psychological genius at least a century before all the -ology adjectives entered the English language. He realized that you could write every conceivable radical new freedom into a constitution—freedom of the press and freedom from the heavy hand of an official state religion were very radical notions 218 years ago—and install a democracy with foolproof guarantees, and that still wouldn't be enough to save Americans from the plight of the masses of Europe. After a thousand years or more of rule by kings who were believed to possess divine rights and by hereditary aristocrats believed to possess demigodly rights at least, ordinary citizens in Europe had been irreparably damaged psychologically and would never recover

from it. They had lived their lives as if the fix were in, as if there would forever be a certain class of people above them who were predestined to dominate government, industry, all influential forms of intellectual life, and, needless to say, society.

7   Even today, in the 21st century, an era of political democracies throughout the West, the great mass of ordinary citizens in Europe remain resigned to their ordinariness because they still feel the presence of "that certain class," that indefinable but nevertheless eternal status stratum forever destined to be their superiors. In England, France, Italy, Germany, rare are the parents who urge their children to live out their dreams and rise as far above their station as they possibly can. As a result, such dreams, if any, don't last long. Only in America do visitors to other people's homes routinely ask their hosts' children, "What do you want to be when you grow up?" In every other country on Earth the question would seem fatuous, since it implies that the child might have a world of choices.

8   Fortunately for America, as Jefferson saw it, British aristocracy had never taken root here in the colonies. Most British toffs didn't have the faintest urge to depart their country estates and London clubs, their coaches-and-four, their tailors, valets, butlers, ballrooms, peruke-makers, and neck-cloth launderers for a wilderness full of painted bow-and-arrow-bearing aborigines . . . and no desirable women, unless one were a rather twisted toff who had a thing for granola girls with honest calves and forearms and hands thick as a blacksmith's from hoeing the corn and black-eyed peas. From the very beginning of his political career, Jefferson was determined to make sure no aristocracy, European- or American-born, would ever be established here. Aristocracy literally means rule by the best, but he knew the proper word was plutocracy, rule by the rich, in this case big landowners who maintained their lordly, demigodly, hereditary rank only by passing their estates down generation after generation—intact—courtesy of the law of entail and the right of primogeniture. As soon as the Revolution was won, Jefferson launched a successful campaign to abolish both. Too bad he couldn't have lived another hundred years to see just how efficient his strategy was. In America, rare is the plutocrat whose family wields power and influence beyond the second generation. One need only think of the Vanderbilts, Goulds, Astors, Carnegies, and Mellons. Where are they now? On the letterheads of charitable solicitations, at best. They don't even rise to the eminence of gossip-column boldface any longer. The rare ones have been the Bushes, who have wielded power—a lot of it—into the third generation, and the Rockefellers, who have made it into the fourth . . . by a thread, the thread being Senator Jay Rockefeller of West Virginia. But the odds are 2-to-5—you'll have to bet $5 to win $2—that within 10 years the last, best hope of even these exceptional families' next generations will be to start climbing the white cliffs of the disease-charity letterheads.

9   Jefferson created a radically new frame of mind. In a thousand different ways he obliterated the symbols and deferential manners that comprise aristocracy's cardiovascular system. Led by Jefferson, America became a country in which every sign of aristocratic pretensions was systematically uprooted and destroyed. The round table where the Merrys suffered their intolerable humiliation? It has been recorded that Jefferson insisted on round tables for dining because they had no head and no foot, removing any trace of the aristocratic European custom of silently

ranking dinner guests by how close to the head of the table they sat. "That certain class" does not exist here psychologically.

10   Jefferson's pell-mell gave America a mind-set that has never varied. In 1862, 36 years after Jefferson's death, the government began the process of settling our vast, largely uninhabited western territories. Under the terms of the Homestead Act, they gave it away by inviting people, anybody, to head out into the open country and claim any plot they liked—Gloriously pell-mell! First come, first served! Each plot was 160 acres, and it was yours, free! By the time of the first Oklahoma Land Rush, in 1889, it had become a literal pell-mell—a confused, disorderly, headlong rush. People lined up on the border of the territory and rushed out into all that free real estate at the sound of a starter gun. Europeans regarded this as more lunacy on the part of . . . these Americans . . . squandering a stupendous national asset in this childish way on a random mob of nobodies. They could not conceive of the possibility that this might prove to be, in fact, a remarkably stable way of settling the West, of turning settlers into homeowners with a huge stake in making the land productive . . . or that it might result, as the British historian Paul Johnson contends, in "the immense benefits of having a free market in land—something which had never before occurred at any time, anywhere in the world." So long as you had made certain required improvements, after five years you could sell all or part of your 160 acres to other people, any other people. It's hard to be absolutely sure, but where else in the world could ordinary citizens go out and just like that—how much you want for it?—buy themselves a piece of land?

11   The Jefferson frame of mind, product of one of the most profound political insights of modern history, has had its challenges in the two centuries since the night Jefferson first sprang the pell-mell upon the old European aristocratic order. But today the conviction that America's limitless freedom and opportunities are for everyone is stronger than ever. Think of just one example from the late 20th century: Only in America could immigrants of many colors from a foreign country with a foreign language and an alien culture—in this case, Cubans—take political control pell-mell via the voting booth of a great metropolis—Miami—in barely more than one generation.

12   America remains, as it has been from the very beginning, the freest, most open country in the world, encouraging one and all to compete pell-mell for any great goal that exists and to try every sort of innovation, no matter how far-fetched it may seem, in order to achieve it. It is largely this open invitation to ambition that accounts for America's military and economic supremacy and absolute dominance in science, medicine, technology, and every other intellectual pursuit that can be measured objectively. And it is absolute.

13   Yet from our college faculties and "public intellectuals" come the grimmest of warnings. The government has assumed Big Brother powers on the pretext of protecting us from Terror, and the dark night of fascism is descending upon America. As Orwell might have put it, only an idiot or an intellectual could actually believe that.

1. What examples does Tom Wolfe use in "Pell-Mell" to argue that "America's limitless freedom and opportunities are for everyone"? Can you think of any examples in your experience that would counteract this assertion?
2. Why is the phrase "pell-mell" significant? How does it relate to Wolfe's views of the history of our country's freedom of opportunity and pursuit of happiness?
3. What motivated Thomas Jefferson to treat Ambassador Merry and his wife as "nobodies"? Do you think he was right? Why or why not?
4. Do you agree with Wolfe's claim that there is no true American plutocracy except perhaps for the Bushes and Rockefellers and that even their families will one day cease to be anything more than "letterhead"? Did Wolfe leave out any other families that may be viewed as "American Aristocracy"? Do you think it is impossible for the United States to become a plutocracy?
5. What stereotypes did Europeans have of Americans following the Revolutionary War? How did Thomas Jefferson's background upset the stereotype of the "savage American"? Do stereotypes of Americans and American life still exist in Europe? Explain.

Dear Mr. President
Joe Rothstein

It seems as if Americans are not the most popular people, or government, in the world right now. In the next essay, political strategist Joe Rothstein tells of a popular song from the United States that is making quite a political statement in Europe. The song, by the American popular artist Pink, reflects both the sentiments of its author, as well as of many Europeans today.

Rothstein is the editor of *U.S. Politics Today* and is a long-time national political strategist based in Washington, D.C. He also is adjunct professor of political science at George Washington University's graduate school for political management and a member of both the International Association of Political Consultants and the National Press Club in Washington, D.C. This commentary appeared in *U.S. Politics Today* on November 6, 2007.

The press has noted that American public policy and Americans in general are often not widely respected in other countries, especially in Europe. What accounts for this attitude? Is it justified, or biased, or a bit of both? Explain.

AS YOU READ

In the song that follows, the artist speaks directly to the President of the United States. What would you say to the president if you had the chance?

1   'm traveling in Europe. And everywhere I go I hear Pink's song, "Dear Mr. President.".

2   In France. In Germany. In the Czech Republic. Everywhere.

3   It's constantly on the radio. You hear it in small shops. People talk about it. Young and old. The song has captured the continent.

4   If you're not familiar with "Dear Mr. President," here are the lyrics:

> *Dear Mr. President*
> *Come take a walk with me*
> *Let's pretend we're just two people and*
> *You're not better than me*
> *I'd like to ask you some questions if we can speak honestly*
>
> *What do you feel when you see all the homeless on the street*
> *Who do you pray for at night before you go to sleep*
> *What do you feel when you look in the mirror*
> *Are you proud*
>
> *How do you sleep while the rest of us cry*
> *How do you dream when a mother has no chance to say goodbye*
> *How do you walk with your head held high*
> *Can you even look me in the eye*
> *And tell me why*
>
> *Dear Mr. President*
> *Were you a lonely boy*
> *Are you a lonely boy*
> *Are you a lonely boy*
> *How can you say*
> *No child is left behind*
> *We're not dumb and we're not blind*
> *They're all sitting in your cells*
> *While you pave the road to hell*
>
> *What kind of father would take his own daughter's rights away*
> *And what kind of father might hate his own daughter if she were gay*
> *I can only imagine what the first lady has to say*
> *You've come a long way from whiskey and cocaine*
>
> *How do you sleep while the rest of us cry*
> *How do you dream when a mother has no chance to say goodbye*
> *How do you walk with your head held high*
> *Can you even look me in the eye*

Let me tell you bout hard work
Minimum wage with a baby on the way
Let me tell you bout hard work
Rebuilding your house after the bombs took them away
Let me tell you bout hard work
Building a bed out of a cardboard box
Let me tell you bout hard work
Hard work
Hard work
You don't know nothing bout hard work
Hard work
Hard work
Oh

How do you sleep at night
How do you walk with your head held high
Dear Mr. President
You'd never take a walk with me
Would you

5 What does it mean that this song's so popular in Europe? What does it mean?

6 You decide. I just report.

QUESTIONS FOR ANALYSIS AND DISCUSSION ─────

1. What is the overall message of the song "Dear Mr. President" by Pink? Interpret the song in your own words.
2. In what ways does Pink question President George W. Bush on a personal level? On a political level? What opinion of him does she convey to her listeners?
3. What is Joe Rothstein's reasoning for not giving his own answer to why Pink's song is popular in Europe? What accounts for the popularity of this song abroad? How do you think Rothstein feels about the song's message? About hearing it as an American in Europe?
4. Author and conservative talk show host, Laura Ingraham, in her book *Shut Up & Sing* has commented that popular entertainers should not delve into politics. In particular, Ingraham criticizes the Dixie Chicks for speaking out against President Bush. Do you agree or disagree with Ingraham that singers such as Pink and the Dixie Chicks should not make political statements but just entertain? Explain.

BLOG IT

Does Europe Really Hate Us?
Posted by Corrina Collins
May 14, 2007

On the heels of the election of Nicolas Sarkozy to the Presidency of France, the *Washington Post* published a commentary <http://www.washingtonpost.com/wp-dyn/content/article/2007/05/11/AR2007051102069_pf.html> on May 13, 2007. According to the William Drozdiak, author of "4 Myths About America-Bashing in Europe":

> While President Bush is held in low esteem in many world capitals, the fact that the new leaders of "Old Europe" could win with pro-America platforms suggests that Yankee phobia may not be as toxic or universal as some pundits, mainly on the American left, claim.

> Why has U.S. stature in the world eroded? Opinion polls cite widespread dismay with the Iraq war, our dog-eat-dog social model and the arrogance of an imperial superpower that places itself above international law. But behind the surveys about "why they hate us" lies a reservoir of goodwill waiting to be tapped among foreigners who would prefer to see the United States succeed rather than fail.

Drozdiak goes on to discuss the following myths:

1. The French hate us.
2. Europeans look down on the American way of life.
3. "Old Europe" no longer matters because China and India are the future.
4. Europe loves only Democrats.

I have known and presently know several Europeans. Very few of them harbor any ill will toward the United States. Indeed, although most of them lean to the left, they love America, particularly the freedom of speech which we Americans take for granted. Furthermore, several of my European friends have, in the past few years, expressed the wish to immigrate to the United States.

Under the fourth myth discusssed in the article, Drozdiak makes the point that Europeans' perceptions of former United States Presidents changed after those Presidents left office. For example, many Europeans derided Ronald Reagan as just a Hollywood actor and ignorant of foreign affairs; however, thanks to Reagan's success in helping to bring down the Soviet Empire, he is today considered a visionary. The converse is true of Jimmy Carter, applauded when he held office but held in low regard today.

Ultimately, every nation acts, or should act, in its own best interests. Isolationism is impossible and even undesirable in today's world. Nevertheless, just as an individual cannot live his life to please someone else, so a nation should not measure itself by how other countries perceive that nation. As goes the variation of these words attributed to Abraham Lincoln,

> *You can please all the people some of the time, and some of the people all the time, but you cannot please all the people all the time.*

YOU SAY:

Add your own blog comment.

READING THE VISUAL

Anti-American Graffiti

Jayanta Shaw/Reuters/Corbis

QUESTIONS FOR ANALYSIS AND DISCUSSION

1. What message does the image on the wall convey? How does it make you feel?
2. Where would you expect to see an image like this? Would your reaction to the image be different if you saw it in New York City or Los Angeles or on a wall in Paris or London?
3. How does graffiti reflect the sentiments of the artist and his/her community? How does it serve as an "argument" for or against a particular cause? Explain.

BBC OPINION POLL

The USA's role in the world was discussed in a unique global television debate hosted by the BBC. The debate revealed the results of a ground-breaking, international survey of attitudes that will capture popular prejudices and convictions about America. Under discussion was America's relations with other countries post–September 11, the country's cultural legacy, and what the future holds for the world's only superpower. The program also revealed that *News Online* readers voted Homer Simpson as the Greatest American in history. What follows is the thread of responses to the June 2003 online opinion poll. The answers may surprise you.

BEFORE YOU READ

Based on media reports and your own experience, what responses would you expect these questions to elicit?

AS YOU READ

What differences do respondents make between Americans themselves and American government?

What Do You Think of America?

Q. What do you think of America? Who is the greatest American? What is the USA's best, and worst, contribution to the world?

With so much of the world living in poverty, under the shadow of autocratic governments, it is easy to see why America is the target of so much hate. Jealousy is a powerful emotion.
LP, Egham, UK

If we compare the actions of the US (especially foreign policy) with the historical actions of the European imperialists, we cannot say they are any worse. But, when we compare their actions and policies with the ideals they preach, they are their own enemy.
David C, London, UK

America is still the leader of the western world and the champion of democracy, which could have perished if not for the sacrifices made by the US. My regret is that the American people needed and deserved a more ethical administration to lead them in the aftermath of 9/11.

Ken, UK, England

I suppose that since America is such a young country, we shouldn't be surprised that they're now so gung-ho about making the kind of foreign policy mistakes that we in "Old Europe" were making 250 years ago.

Stuart W, UK

I came to the USA three years ago from the Philippines. It was not an easy transition. I found Americans to be too direct and rude. At first I associated with only other Filipino immigrants but eventually I met a wonderful American man and recently married him. I was also able to get a great job doing the same thing I was doing in the Philippines but making unbelievable money ($100,000/yr). Since I have married and began working with Americans, I have begun to see the admirable traits. Americans are ambitious, funny, sympathetic, and smart. People here are also opinionated. My husband is well-educated and we have well-educated friends. The view that Americans are ignorant is puzzling to me.

Maria C, USA (Ex-Philippines)

The average American doesn't support critics or other ways of thinking. The US has nothing to do with the great tolerant democracy we used to know. Politicians there exploit their patriotism. They are totally misinformed but believed they are better informed than the rest of the world. And I think they have a special vision of their own history. By becoming ignorant Americans are becoming dangerous. The fear we have of them is nothing to do with jealousy.

Luc, France

America doesn't realise how nationalistic it is and that universals like freedom and liberty have many different interpretations within different cultural contexts.

Katherine Barlow, United Kingdom

Everyone loves to hate the winner if they are not a part of the same team. It is amazing how many NY Yankee hats you see on people's heads no matter what country you are in. Perhaps the bitterness needs to end and everyone should learn from American perseverance. Americans aren't perfect but neither is anyone else. Anyone that thinks Americans are too aggressive might want to consider the fact that it has only taken 200 plus years of existence to get where they are as a superpower. I say hats-off this July 4th and a pat on the back.

Mike, UK

America: a wonderful country full of genuinely nice people who are controlled and ruled by some exceptionally greedy individuals.

John Neal, UK

America seems to have no political left as a counter-balance. It has centre right (Democrats) and neo-Conservative (Republican). This combined with Christian Conservatism means that opposing views can be listened to but never taken into account when making important decisions. Too many people in power think too similarly to the others in power. e.g. only one person voted against the war in Afghanistan in the Senate.

Rahul, UK

America? Greatest country in the world. Took me in when I was cast-off by my own country as an undesirable. Now on my way to becoming a millionaire. Love the country, people, culture, energy, and most of all the HOPE. Thank you America for giving me an opportunity at life. God Bless You Always.

Note to the BBC: Homer Simpson was the creation of a Canadian—he likened the character to his dad. So Homer's a Canadian. Who's having the last laugh here?

Shah, USA

The USA's only real contributions to the rest of the world are McDonalds and war. I can very well do without both.

Steve, UK

Nice place, shame about the guns.

Joe Horvath, Australia

The USA is a very patriotic nation, and can be a generous one. The goals of the American Revolution have changed the world. The current US regime may be too trigger happy, but Sept 11 traumatized America, and has girded the Americans with a stronger national feeling.

Keith, Canada

I thank America. People have short memories. Brave Americans have fought for freedom for three hundred years. Americans died to free Europe. Americans died to stop the Japanese invading Australia & New Zealand. America is not perfect but without their ingenuity & fearlessness the rest of us would be enslaved, be-headed & worse. Go for it Mr President! You have my unqualified support. Use the big one if you have to. Better the "mushroom" appears above the axis of evil than in New York or Los Angeles. I can handle the fall-out if you can.

Deniz Ronaldo, Australia

I am an aged American expatriate and ex-patriot. I grew up in a country that held high ideals and made honest efforts to live up to them. I have for years now watched that country degrade its own moral fibre. Finally we see those ideals dead in the water. What could be more heart-breaking to those of us who deeply loved our country, what could be more terrifying to the whole world!

Caty Green, France

America is a great nation and I feel privileged to be allied with them. Besides the UK, the US are the driving force of a group of nations who would tackle dictators and terrorists head on instead of fussing around asking them to leave nicely. Long live the US.

John, England

America is not the world's only superpower. China has been a superpower for many years and will overtake America in the next decade.

Sam, UK

America as a country is representative of many western nations whose only knowledge of the rest of the world is TV. I don't blame 'em but surely they are missing a lot. I wish they'd care to listen, travel and see the rest of the world.

Lawrence gwakisa, Tanzania

It's a pity that the American dream isn't still a reality.

Martin, UK

America is a land of the brain washed public who can see no wrong in what is done in their name. If only the American people can look around and see that they need the world more then the world needs them.

Abdul, Egypt

People in Iran love America and if you ask anyone on the street they'll tell you they want to go to America. If only Iranians could be liberated from their regime as easy as the Iraqis were liberated from theirs.

Amir Kirkolofti, Iran

I never have hated America or ordinary Americans, but I am not at all pleased with the government of President Bush. When they disregarded the U.N. and attacked Iraq, after bombing Afghanistan to the stone age. Actually the US is using Al-Qaeda as an excuse and wants to attack other countries by saying that the governments of these countries are aiding Al-Qaeda, and they don't even bother to give any evidence for it.

Farrukh Ismail, Pakistan

It is a great country and an amazing land. Meanwhile it is also the land of manic political ideas and political and military leaders with surreal concepts of the world. I am deeply convinced, that the majority of Americans do not deserve the image their leaders have earned them.

Dobrin Banov, Switzerland

It is time the US stops and thinks what they want for the future, because all empires in the past suddenly disappeared without a trace. Wake up North America!

JC, Brazil

You can't compare America to the British Empire 100 years ago. We were bar-baric then and we didn't even pretend to have anyone else's interests in mind.

Dave Gerrelli, England

The US makes me uneasy. I'm sure their heart is mostly in the right place and liberals there will always prevent excesses, but the general thrust under this president looks too selfish. The world needs a liberal president willing to work with the UN if we are not to go back to "power blocks" and the danger they cause.

Phil, Scotland

Americans can be fantastic at the individual level, but its foreign policy is predicated on the misapprehension that the rest of the world should share the same political and economic values. As for the benign USA, for almost every positive act of foreign intervention, one can highlight when its adventures have had less than benign consequences.

Mike, Australia

We need America, but America must realise that it needs us in equal measure. It is a young nation compared to the others. Some old nations could be thought of as being senile and so in need of the exuberance of the USA. However, how many of us now wish that we had listened a little more to our older relatives and friends when we were young?

Phil Petravich, UK

The USA is the lesser of two evils. It is by no means perfect. It exploits a lot of the world for its own benefit. But it also does a huge amount of good. Without the USA much of the world that is free and democratic at the moment would not be. I don't believe The US is bent on world domination. They want to remain the super power and keep everyone in line but they certainly do not want to be "ruling" countries that they see as problematic.

Brad, Australia

America embodies the misuse of power. It is responsible for the Middle-East conflict, the war on Iraq and the US unjust policies in the Arab and Islamic world. The US foreign policy has succeeded in creating hatred and wrath among the Arab masses due to the utter bias toward Israel.

George Nasser, Bethlehem, Palestine

America is a dream country for many people in Africa. What makes me angry is the same people who wait at the gate of the American embassy to get a visa complain how they hate America. So why do they want to go there? It is not right to Love its resources and hate its policies at the same time. You have to choose one. Either be in America and abide by the rules and regulations or don't dream to go there.

But still they dream to be there because it is the only country where you can earn your bread without fear of any thing. How can any one hate the land of opportunity? We have to also understand America like any other Nation which has its own programme and objectives that it wants to see in the world in line with its National advantage. So what is the problem with that?? Any way, I love America and Americans.

Neftegnaw, Ethiopia

QUESTIONS FOR ANALYSIS AND DISCUSSION

1. What distinctions do respondents make between "ordinary Americans" and the U.S. political system? Explain.
2. Select one or two of these responses and reply in your own words with a reasoned, supportable argument.
3. What misconceptions—as well as insights—do the international respondents have about the United States?
4. Did any of these postings surprise you? If so, which one(s) and why?
5. In general, what accounts for Americans' perception that people in other countries do not care for Americans or America? What generalizations exist? What truths and misconceptions exist? Explain.

WRITING ASSIGNMENTS

1. In the first essay in this section, novelist Tom Wolfe wrote about the "American idea" as part of *The Atlantic* magazine's 150th anniversary issue (November 2007) that invited poets, inventors, businesspeople, jurists, politicians, artists, and others to contribute short essays on the American idea, its future, and the greatest challenges it faces. Write your own essay on the American idea. What is it, and what does it promise? What challenges does it face today? You may draw on outside research, essays in this section, and your own viewpoint.

2. Several authors in this section note that many countries hold the United States in low regard. Write an essay in which you explore this phenomenon. Should the United States be concerned about how other countries—and the citizens of other countries—feel about it? Why or why not?

3. What does it mean to be a "superpower"? Research the origins of this phrase and write an essay on (1) whether the United States still fits the definition of superpower and (2) whether it is likely to remain one. Alternatively, you may wish to write about whether the concept of superpower countries has relevancy today and in the future.

4. What challenges does American world policy face in the next ten years? From your viewpoint, identify the social, political, intellectual/cultural issues that our leadership should consider as we forge our way through the next decade. Explain why you think the issues you highlight are important.

CHAPTER 13

In God We Trust?

The concept of the freedom of religion is in principle as old as the Constitution it-self. However, different religious and secular groups have interpreted the phrase in vastly different ways, and it has only been over the last 50 years or so that the is-sue has received great national attention. At the center of the debate is the wording of the First Amendment:

> Congress shall make no law respecting an establishment of religion, or pro-hibiting the free exercise thereof; or abridging the freedom of speech, or of the press; or the right of the people peaceably to assemble, and to petition the Gov-ernment for a redress of grievances.

Beyond the immediate legality of the separation of church and state is the con-nected issue that expressions of religious belief are unacceptable in any civic arena—such as at political events, public greens, and in schools. Some towns, in an effort to include many faiths, have holiday displays that include Jewish symbols as well as Christian ones. But what happens when atheists, who do not believe in God at all, claim they are offended by such symbols? Does "under God" have any place in the Pledge of Allegiance? Should all mentions of religion be barred from the nation's courtrooms? What about the president's inaugural address? This chapter explores some of the many questions regarding the separation of church and state, how we balance religion and civic life, and the intersection of faith and the public sphere in American life.

Since 1947, stemming from a ruling related to *Everson v. Board of Education*, the U.S. judicial system has used the phrase "separation of church and state" to jus-tify decisions on the constitutionality of the interaction between the state and mat-ters of religion. Opponents of a strict separation between church and state (the phrase actually comes from a letter written by Thomas Jefferson to the Danbury Baptist Association in 1802 rather than the Constitution) argue that the founders wished to ensure that the new U.S. government did not establish a national religion, similar to that of the Church of England. Their intention was not to establish a strict separation of church and state, just to prevent one religion from trumping another.

Supporters of literal separation claim that the clause ensures that no one is forced to accept the religious beliefs of another.

Government support of any religious cause represents an endorsement of that religion and its belief system, and so violates the spirit of the Constitution. What did the founders mean when they wrote the Constitution? And are their intentions relevant to how we interpret the First Amendment?

The debate over evolution is certainly not new, but it was not until 1925 that the issue appeared in a courtroom. That year, the Scopes "monkey trial" brought the debate into public discourse, with the legendary trial lawyer Clarence Darrow challenging William Jennings Bryan, the fundamentalist Christian and staunch opponent of evolution. Darrow challenged a Tennessee law that forbade the teaching, in any state-funded educational establishment in Tennessee, of "any theory that denies the story of the Divine Creation of man as taught in the Bible, and to teach instead that man has descended from a lower order of animals." The trial highlighted what happens when religion and science collide in public schoolrooms.

Almost 60 years later the U.S. Supreme Court ruled that creationism should not be taught in public schools directly in the 1987 case of *Edwards v. Aguillard*. The most recent debate concerns the teaching of "intelligent design"—which many critics claim is just a reshaping of creationism. Also at issue is the idea of promoting evolution as "another theory" on how life began, and that it should have equal weight with other theories, including religious ones.

Debate over evolution often centers on how it fits into religious explanations of human life, and its lack of compatibility to the literal interpretation of the creation stories of the Bible and the Qur'an. In the United States, the tension between the scientific community with religious teachings focuses on public education and the separation of church and state. Should evolution be taught to children whose parents oppose the science on religious grounds? Should alternative theories to evolution be taught as well, even if they are based on religious texts? The second part of this chapter explores the current debate on evolution and the political and social nuances connected to the issue.

CHURCH AND STATE

The Wall That Never Was
Hugh Heclo

Is religion a necessary part of American life? Should it have any role in civic life? While the principles of the separation of church and state are deeply valued and protected, it seems that many Americans—over half the population, in fact—would like to see religion's influence in American society grow. In the next essay, Hugh Heclo explains that the "wall" between church and state is not a constitutional principle. Moreover, it has only been over the last 50 years or so that the separation of church and state has become a matter of heated public debate for the courts to decide. Heclo argues that religion has traditionally played a role in public affairs, and will continue to do so, because cultural ideology will support it, even if society is unaware it is doing so.

Hugh Heclo is a professor at George Mason University and formerly taught government at Harvard University. His book *Modern Social Politics* (1974) received the Woodrow Wilson award offered by the American Political Science Association for the best book published in the United States on government, politics, or international affairs. In 2001, he was appointed to the 12-member Academic Advisors Council serving the Library of Congress. His most recent publication is *Christianity and American Democracy*, with Mary Jo Bane, Michael Kazin, and Alan Wolfe (2007). This essay was published in the Winter 2003 issue of the *Wilson Quarterly*.

BEFORE YOU READ ————————————————————

Heclo notes that despite the opinion that church and state should be separate, both in America and in a global context, most modern political conflicts have their root in a religious cause or disagreement. Consider this statement. Try to identify as many international issues and conflicts as you can. Does Heclo's observation ring true? Why or why not?

AS YOU READ ————————————————————

How does Heclo's essay provide a framework to explain the current trend in which religion seems to be playing a more prominent role in politics and modern culture? Do you think this is an isolated movement, or one of larger, more lasting implications?

1   A hundred years ago, advanced thinkers were all but unanimous in dismissing religion as a relic of mankind's mental infancy. What's being dismissed today is the idea that humanity will outgrow religion. Contrary to the expectations of Sigmund Freud, Max Weber, John Dewey, and a host of others, religion has not become a mere vestige of premodern culture. If anything, Americans at the dawn of the 21st century are more willing to contemplate a public place for religion than they have been for the past two generations. But what does it mean for religion to "reenter the public square"? What good might it do there—and what harm?

2   Mention religion and public policy in the same breath these days, and what will most likely spring to mind are specific controversies over abortion, school prayer, the death penalty, and stem cell research. All are issues of public choice that arouse the religious conscience of many Americans. They are also particular instances of a larger reality: the profound, troubled, and inescapable interaction between religious faith and government action in America.

3   For most of American history, the subject of religion and public policy did not need much discussion. There was a widespread presumption that a direct correspondence existed, or should exist, between Americans' religious commitments and their government's public-policy choices. When the oldest of today's Americans were born (which is to say in the days of Bryan, McKinley, and Theodore Roosevelt), the "public-ness" of religion was taken for granted, in a national political culture dominated by Protestants. It was assumed that America was a Christian nation and should

behave accordingly. Of course, what that meant in practice could arouse vigorous disagreement—for example, over alcohol control, labor legislation, child welfare, and foreign colonization. Still, dissenters had to find their place in what was essentially a self-confident Protestant party system and moralistic political culture.

4   Those days are long past. During the 20th century, religion came to be regarded increasingly as a strictly private matter. By mid-century, Supreme Court decisions were erecting a so-called wall of separation between church and state that was nationwide and stronger than anything known in the previous practice of the individual states' governments. National bans on state-mandated prayer (1962) and Bible reading in public schools (1963) soon followed. In 1960, presidential candidate John F. Kennedy was widely applauded for assuring a convocation of Baptist ministers that his Catholic religion and his church's teachings on public issues were private matters unrelated to actions he might take in public office. Intellectual elites in particular were convinced that the privatization of religion was a natural accompaniment of modernization in any society.

5   But even as Kennedy spoke and Supreme Court justices wrote, strong crosscurrents were at work. Martin Luther King, Jr., and masses of civil rights activists asserted the very opposite of a disconnection between religious convictions and public-policy claims. King's crusade against segregation and his larger agenda for social justice were explicitly based on Christian social obligations, flowing from belief in the person of Jesus Christ. So, too, in antinuclear peace movements of the time atheists such as Bertrand Russell were probably far outnumbered by liberal religious activists. After the 1960s, the United States and many other countries witnessed a political revival of largely conservative fundamentalist religious movements. These, according to prevailing academic theories, were supposed to have disappeared with the steam engine. The horror of September 11, 2001, showed in the most public way imaginable that modernization had not relegated religion to an isolated sphere of private belief. On the contrary, religious convictions could still terrorize, as they could also comfort a nation and inspire beautiful acts of compassion.

6   It is nonetheless true that during much of the 20th century the dominant influences in American national culture—universities, media and literary elites, the entertainment industry—did move in the predicted secularist direction. What at mid-century had been mere embarrassment with old-fashioned religious belief had, by century's end, often become hostility to an orthodox Christianity that believed in fundamental, revealed truth. Noting that the inhabitants of the Indian subcontinent are the most religious society in the world and the inhabitants of Sweden the most secularized, sociologist Peter Berger has said, provocatively, that America might usefully be thought of as an Indian society ruled by a Swedish elite.

7   In contemporary discussions of religion and public affairs, the master concept has been secularization. The term itself derives from the Latin word saeculum, meaning "period of time" or "age" or "generation." The idea of the secular directs our attention to the place and time of this world rather than to things religious and beyond time. It supposes a demarcation between the sacred and the profane. The social sciences of the 19th century developed theories of secularization that dominated much of 20th-century thinking. In the disciplines' new scientific view of society, all human activities

were to be analyzed as historical phenomena, rooted in particular places and times. Religion was simply another human activity to be understood historically, an evolutionary social function moving from primitive to higher forms.

8   The idea of secularization became tightly bound up with intellectuals' understanding of modernization. As the 20th century dawned, the secularization that religious traditionalists condemned, leading modernists of the day saw as a benign and progressive evolution of belief systems. Secular political organizations had already gone far in taking over the social functions (welfare and education, for example) of medieval religious institutions. As society modernized, science and enlightened humanitarianism would provide a creed to displace religion's superstitions, and religion would retreat to private zones of personal belief. Policymaking would deal with worldly affairs in a scientific manner, indifferent to religious faith. Public religion was something humanity would outgrow. Religion in the modern state would go about its private, one-on-one soul work; public life would proceed without passionate clashes over religious truth.

9   The foregoing, in very crude terms, is what came to be known as the secularization thesis. To be modern meant to disabuse the mind of religious superstitions (about miracles, for example) and recognize the psychological needs that prompt humankind to create religious commitments in the first place. Modern society might still call things sacred, but it was a private call. In public life, the spell of enchantment was broken—or soon would be.

10   But something happened on the way to privatizing religion in the 20th century. For about the first two-thirds of the century, secularization seemed to prevail as a plausible description of public life. Then, in the final third, the picture changed considerably. Religion re-engaged with political history and refused to stay in the private ghetto to which modernity had consigned it. Witness the Islamic Revolution in Iran, the role of the Catholic Church in communist Eastern Europe, and the growth of the Religious Right in the United States. Of this resurgence of public religion, the sociologist José Casanova has observed: "During the entire decade of the 1980s it was hard to find any serious political conflict anywhere in the world that did not show behind it the not-so-hidden hand of religion. . . . We are witnessing the 'de-privatization' of religion in the modern world."

11   This "going public" of religion, moreover, was not an expression of new religious movements or of the quasi-religions of modern humanism. Rather, it was a reentry into the political arena of precisely those traditional religions—the supposedly vestigial survivals of an unenlightened time—that secular modernity was supposed to have made obsolete.

12   Three powerful forces make this a particularly important time to take stock of the new status of religion in public life. The first is the ever-expanding role of national policy in Americans' mental outlook. During the 20th century, struggles over federal policy increasingly defined America's political and cultural order. In other words, conceptions of who we are as a people were translated into arguments about what Washington should do or not do. The abortion debate is an obvious example, but one might also consider our thinking about race, the role of women, crime, free speech, economic security in old age, education, and our relationship

with the natural environment. After the 1950s, academics, and then the public, began to make unprecedented use of the term *policy* as a conceptual tool for understanding American political life. But the entire century nourished and spread the modern syndrome of "policy-mindedness"—an addiction to the idea that everything preying on the public mind requires government to do or to stop doing something. It's a notion that allows almost any human activity to be charged with public relevance—from the design of toilets to sexual innuendo in the workplace (filigrees of environmental policy and civil rights policy, respectively). Like it or not, our cultural discussions and decisions are now policy-embedded. And this in turn inevitably implicates whatever religious convictions people may have.

13   The juggernaut of today's scientific applications is a second development that now compels us to think hard about religion in the public square. Technological advances have brought our nation to a point where momentous public choices are inescapable. To be sure, scientific knowledge has been accumulating over many generations. But in the latter years of the 20th century, much of modern society's earlier investment in basic research led to technological applications that will affect human existence on a massive scale. For example, though the human egg was discovered in 1827, the DNA structure of life did not become known until the middle of the 20th century. Since then, sweeping applications of that accumulated knowledge have cascaded with a rush. By 1978, the first human baby conceived in vitro had been born. By the 1990s, the first mammals had been cloned, the manipulation of genes had begun, and the first financial markets for human egg donors had developed. These and other scientific advances are forcing far-reaching decisions about the meaning of life forms, about artificial intelligence and reconstitution of the human brain, and even about the reconstruction of matter itself.

14   These choices at the microlevel have been accompanied by technology's challenge to human destiny at the macrolevel. It was also in the mid-20th century that mankind became increasingly conscious that it held Earth's very life in its own contaminating hands. At the onset of the 1960s, Rachel Carson did much to overturn generations of unbridled faith in scientific progress when she publicized the first dramatic charges about humankind's disastrous impact on the environment in *Silent Spring*. By the end of the 1960s, people saw the first pictures from space of the fragile Earth home they share. The first Earth Day and the blossoming of the modern environmental movement soon followed. The point is not simply that issues such as ozone depletion, species extinction, global warming, and the like have not been thought about until now. It's that people have never before had to deal with them as subjects of collective decision-making—which is to say, as public-policy choices.

15   Our modern technological condition thus represents a double historical climacteric. Today's citizens must manage the first civilization with both the outward reach to bring all human societies within a common global destiny and the inward reach to put the very structures of life and matter into human hands. For more than 2,000 years, philosophers could talk abstractly about the problem of being and the nature of human existence. For 21st-century citizens, the problem of being is an ever-unfolding agenda of public-policy choices. The extent to which ethics leads or lags the scientific juggernaut will now be measured in the specific policy decisions our democratic political

systems produce. And the decisions are saturated with religious and cultural implications about what human beings are and how they should live.

16   Even as the policy choices are forcing citizens into a deeper search for common understandings, doubts about a shared cultural core of American values are pushing in precisely the opposite direction. Those doubts are the third challenge to religion in the public square. Thanks to the homogenization produced by mass markets throughout the 50 states, 20th-century America experienced a marked decline in traditional geographic and class differences. But with the uniformity in material culture has come a greater insistence on and acceptance of variation in the realm of nonmaterial meanings and values. The widespread use of phrases such as "identity politics," "culture wars," "inclusiveness," and "political correctness" reflects the extent to which affirmations of diversity have supplanted earlier assumptions about a cultural core. "Multiculturalism" is a label for a host of changes in mental outlook, group self-consciousness, and educational philosophy. And with Muslims almost as numerous as Presbyterians in today's America, multiculturalism is more than faddish academic terminology. It's true that self-identified Christians still outnumber all other faith categories of Americans by 8 to 1 (in 2001, 82 percent of the population reported themselves to be Christian, 10 percent non-Christian, and 8 percent nonbelievers). But the Christianity in the figures is often purely nominal, with little orthodox content. The cultural indicators show that, by and large, America is well on its way to becoming a post-Christian, multireligion society of personally constructed moral standards.

17   These, then, are three developments that compel attention to the interrelations between religion and public policy: A vast and powerful political society is defining itself to an ever greater extent through self-conscious policy decisions about what to do and what not to do; a technological imperative is driving that society's policy agenda to raise ever more profound questions about the nature of life and the sustainability of our earthly existence; and an increasingly fragmented sense of cultural identity is taking hold among the self-governing people who are called upon to make and oversee these collective decisions.

18   In light of these developments, how are we to think about "public religion" in our self-proclaimed democratic world superpower (so much for Christian humility)? Ordinary Americans continue to profess a devotion to religion far greater than is found in other developed nations. At the beginning of the 21st century, some 90 percent of Americans say they believe in God and pray at least once a week. Sixty percent attend religious services at least once a month, and 43 percent do so weekly. Nonbelief is a distinctly minority position; it's also a hugely unpopular position. Large majorities of Americans claim that they would vote for a presidential candidate who was female (92 percent), black (95 percent), Jewish (92 percent), or homosexual (59 percent)— but only 49 percent say they would do so for a candidate who was an atheist.

19   In the summer of 2002, a political firestorm greeted a federal appellate court's decision that the words "under God" (which Congress added to the Pledge of Allegiance in 1954) violated the constitutional separation of church and state. As the hapless Ninth Circuit Court backed off, delaying the decision's effect, polls showed that 87 percent of Americans supported keeping God in the pledge, and that 54 percent

favored having government promote religion. These figures reflect a significant shift: After declining sharply between the mid-1960s and late 1970s, the proportion of Americans who say religion is very important to them grew to roughly two out of three by 2001. Seventy percent of Americans want to see religion's influence on American society grow, and an even larger proportion, including two-thirds of Americans aged 17 to 35, are concerned about the moral condition of the nation. (And yet, by general agreement, the common culture has become more coarse and salacious. One may well wonder who's left to be making the popular culture so popular.)

20   However, the meaning of religious belief has also been changing in recent decades. A great many Americans find that the search for spirituality is more important to them than traditional religious doctrines, confessional creeds, or church denominations. Although most Americans say they want religion to play a greater public role so as to improve the moral condition of the nation, only 25 percent say that religious doctrines are the basis for their moral judgments about right and wrong. Even among born-again Christians, fewer than half say that they base their moral views on specific teachings of the Bible. To claim that there are absolute moral truths (a view rejected by three out of four American adults at the end of the 20th century), or that one religious faith is more valid than another, is widely regarded as a kind of spiritual racism. The new cornerstone of belief is that moral truths depend on what individuals choose to believe relative to their particular circumstances. Human choice has become the trump value and judgmentalism the chief sin. Thus, three-fourths of that large majority of Americans who want religion to become more influential in American society say that it does not matter to them which religion becomes more influential. Similarly, between 80 and 90 percent of Americans identify themselves as Christians, though most of them dismiss some of the central beliefs of Christianity as it has traditionally been understood. Father Richard John Neuhaus, editor of the journal *First Things*, recently summed up the situation: "To say that America is a Christian nation is like saying it's an English-speaking nation. There are not many people who speak the language well, but when they are speaking a language poorly, it is the English language they are speaking."

21   What all this means for the intertwining of religious faith and the politics of government policymaking is something of a mystery. It's mysterious because Americans both want and distrust religious convictions in the public arena. Thus, more than 60 percent want elected officials to compromise rather than to vote their religious beliefs, even on life-and-death issues such as abortion and capital punishment. And though Americans have become more open in recent decades to having religion talked about in the public arena, 70 percent of them also think that when political leaders talk about their faith, they're just saying what people want to hear. Most people surveyed are willing to have religious leaders speak out more on public issues, but they also don't care much whether they do so or not. In the spring of 2001, when President Bush's faith-based initiatives were being publicized, three-quarters of Americans expressed strong support for the idea that faith-based groups should receive government funds to provide social services. But that same proportion opposed having government-funded religious groups hire only people who shared their beliefs. This amounts to support for religion as long as religion does

not really insist on believing anything. Then again, most Americans opposed funding American Muslim or Buddhist groups, and they regarded even Mormon groups as marginal.

22   So never mind thinking outside the box. When it comes to religion—their own or others'—in the public square, today's Americans have trouble thinking seriously even inside the box. The wonderfully rich history of religion and democracy in modern America has been ignored and even suppressed in public-school textbooks and university curricula, both of which were largely purged of "God talk" after the mid-20th century. The sowing of traditional religious information in the school system has been so sparse that one national researcher on the topic has called younger cohorts of Americans a "seedless" generation. A less polite term for their religiously lobotomized view of culture would be heathen. Here is crooked timber indeed for building a framework to support the culture-shaping interactions between religion and public policy.

23   When Americans do think, however imprecisely, about religion and public decision-making, what do they commonly have in mind? Their predominant notion is probably of "a wall of separation between church and state." Most citizens would be surprised to learn that the phrase is not in the Constitution; it comes from a church building here, a government building there, distinctly separate institutions. And that, Americans have long believed, is as it should be. But even casual observation reveals that there's more going on in that square. Perched atop the ostensible wall of separation between the structures of church and state, we watch a public forum where religion and politics are anything but separate. There are not two kinds of people in the forum, some of them religious and some political. There are only citizens. And as they interact, they express themselves both religiously and politically. Religious, nonreligious, and antireligious ideas are all at work in their heads when they define problems and choose measures to deal with them collectively, as a people. Religious and irreligious ideas commingle in programs enacted in behalf of this or that vision of a good social order. Church and state, religion and politics, and ideas and social action are crosscutting elements whose presence, even if poorly articulated, we often sense in the public square.

24   To put it another way, the major interactions between religion and public policy occur across three domains. The first is institutional and focuses on the way organized structures of religion and government impinge on one another—and together impinge on society. This institutional perspective comes most naturally to Americans because it's encoded in their nation's constitutional understanding of itself. The bland phrase "separation of church and state" conceals what was the most audacious and historically unique element of America's experiment in self-government: the commitment to a free exercise of religion. In this institutional domain, one encounters, for example, groups claiming infringement on the unfettered exercise of their religious liberties and disputes over government sponsorship of religious organizations. Less obviously, it is where one also finds religious and public agencies jostling against one another as they pursue, for example, education and welfare policies.

25   The second domain where religion and public policy connect can be called behavioral. Here the term simply means that religious attachments move people to

act in public ways (e.g., to vote, to organize within the community, to engage in other political activities). There's a direct, though paradoxical, link between the first and second domains. The distancing between religious and government institutions has allowed religion in America to be an immense resource for the nation's politics. Alexis de Tocqueville concluded that his American informants were correct in believing that the main reason religion held great sway over their country was the separation of church and state. He wrote, "by diminishing the apparent power of religion one increased its real strength." Since his visit in 1831, Americans in religious associations have created and sustained public movements to promote slavery's abolition, women's rights, prison and asylum reform, child welfare and worker protection, mothers' pensions, liquor regulation, racial desegregation, and civil rights legislation. (Such associations have also been an important source of less savory causes, such as anti-Catholic and anti-Jewish laws.) And citizens moved to more routine political action through religious affiliations have done much to shape America's party system and election outcomes.

26   The third domain connecting religion and public policy is more difficult to describe, but one senses that something important is missing if we take account only of organized institutions and politically relevant behaviors. For lack of a better term, we might call the third domain philosophical. It reflects broad policy outlooks on the social order. At this intersection, ideas and modes of thought are expressed in programmatic courses of action. It's the realm in which people operate when they speak about culture wars in the schools, the work ethic in welfare, or the need for moral clarity in foreign policy. It's the basis on which some people cringe and others rejoice.

QUESTIONS FOR ANALYSIS AND DISCUSSION ───────

1. Heclo notes that at the turn of the twentieth century most U.S. citizens "assumed that America was a Christian nation and should behave accordingly." How did this assumption change during the twentieth century? What do you think caused a shift in thinking? Explain.

2. What did sociologist Peter Berger (paragraph 6) mean when he said America might be considered "an Indian society ruled by a Swedish elite"? How does "the intellectual elite" view religion?

3. What role has the concept of secularization played in the discussion of religion and public affairs? How did the principles of secularization shift during the last half of the twentieth century?

4. Based on his writing alone, can you tell how Heclo feels about the separation of church and state and the role of religion in civic life?

5. Why does Heclo feel now is an especially important time to "take stock of the new status of religion in public life"? To what trends should we be paying attention? How could these trends impact the future of the concept of separation between church and state? Explain.

6. Why, according to Heclo, is multiculturalism more than "faddish academic terminology"? What is multiculturalism? In your opinion, what influence, if any, has multiculturalism had on the issue of church and state?

Why We're Not One Nation "Under God"

David Greenberg

In June of 2002, Alfred Goodwin issued an unpopular ruling declaring the recitation of the Pledge of Allegiance in public schools unconstitutional. Goodwin was deciding a lawsuit brought by Michael Newdow, who filed the lawsuit on behalf of his daughter "because I am an atheist and this offends me." The Senate was so outraged by Goodwin's decision that it passed a resolution 99–0 expressing full support for the Pledge of Allegiance and voted 99–0 to recodify the "under God" language in the pledge. Goodwin stayed his decision even before an appeal was filed. In June of 2004, the Supreme Court overturned the decision but did so on a technicality that Newdow did not have the right to represent his daughter, leaving the issue wide open for future lawsuits. Should the Pledge of Allegiance be changed? Should "under God" be dropped? And would it surprise you to learn that these two words were not part of the original pledge? In this essay, historian David Greenberg explores the history of the Pledge of Allegiance, and how this history might just solve the problem.

Greenberg teaches at Rutgers University in the department of Journalism and Media Studies and History. His first book, *Nixon's Shadow: The History of an Image* (2003) won the American Journalism History Award. He is currently at work on a biography of Calvin Coolidge for the American Presidents Series. Greenberg has written for many scholarly and popular publications, including *The New York Times*, *The Washington Post*, *The Atlantic Monthly*, *The New Yorker*, and *Daedalus*. He is a regular contributor to the online magazine *Slate*, where he writes the "History Lesson" column and other occasional reviews and essays. This essay was posted on June 28, 2002, on *Slate*.

BEFORE YOU READ

What do the words "under God" in the Pledge of Allegiance mean? Do they refer to a specific deity or endorse a particular faith? Do the words violate the separation of church and state as outlined in the First Amendment?

AS YOU READ

Greenberg observes that the original Pledge of Allegiance was "meant as an expression of patriotism, not religious faith." Do you think the Pledge of Allegiance is an expression of faith? Why or why not?

1   **P**oor Alfred Goodwin! So torrential was the flood of condemnation that followed his opinion—which held that it's unconstitutional for public schools to require students to recite "under God" as part of the Pledge of Allegiance—that the beleaguered appellate-court judge suspended his own ruling until the whole 9th Circuit Court has a chance to review the case. Not one major political figure summoned the

courage to rebut the spurious claims that America's founders wished to make God a part of public life. It's an old shibboleth of those who want to inject religion into public life that they're honoring the spirit of the nation's founders. In fact, the founders opposed the institutionalization of religion. They kept the Constitution free of references to God. The document mentions religion only to guarantee that godly belief would never be used as a qualification for holding office—a departure from many existing state constitutions. That the founders made erecting a church-state wall their first priority when they added the Bill of Rights to the Constitution reveals the importance they placed on maintaining what Isaac Kramnick and R. Laurence Moore have called a "godless Constitution." When Benjamin Franklin proposed during the Constitutional Convention that the founders begin each day of their labors with a prayer to God for guidance, his suggestion was defeated.

2   Given this tradition, it's not surprising that the original Pledge of Allegiance—meant as an expression of patriotism, not religious faith—also made no mention of God. The pledge was written in 1892 by the socialist Francis Bellamy, a cousin of the famous radical writer Edward Bellamy. He devised it for the popular magazine *Youth's Companion* on the occasion of the nation's first celebration of Columbus Day. Its wording omitted reference not only to God but also, interestingly, to the United States:

3   "I pledge allegiance to my flag and the republic for which it stands, one nation indivisible, with liberty and justice for all."

4   The key words for Bellamy were "indivisible," which recalled the Civil War and the triumph of federal union over states' rights, and "liberty and justice for all," which was supposed to strike a balance between equality and individual freedom. By the 1920s, reciting the pledge had become a ritual in many public schools.

5   Since the founding, critics of America's secularism have repeatedly sought to break down the church-state wall. After the Civil War, for example, some clergymen argued that the war's carnage was divine retribution for the founders' refusal to declare the United States a Christian nation, and tried to amend the Constitution to do so.

6   The efforts to bring God into the state reached their peak during the so-called "religious revival" of the 1950s. It was a time when Norman Vincent Peale grafted religion onto the era's feel-good consumerism in his best-selling *The Power of Positive Thinking*; when Billy Graham rose to fame as a Red-baiter who warned that Americans would perish in a nuclear holocaust unless they embraced Jesus Christ; when Secretary of State John Foster Dulles believed that the United States should oppose communism not because the Soviet Union was a totalitarian regime but because its leaders were atheists.

7   Hand in hand with the Red Scare, to which it was inextricably linked, the new religiosity overran Washington. Politicians outbid one another to prove their piety. President Eisenhower inaugurated that Washington staple: the prayer breakfast. Congress created a prayer room in the Capitol. In 1955, with Ike's support, Congress added the words "In God We Trust" on all paper money. In 1956 it made the same four words the nation's official motto, replacing "E Pluribus Unum." Legislators introduced Constitutional amendments to state that Americans obeyed "the authority and law of Jesus Christ."

8   The campaign to add "under God" to the Pledge of Allegiance was part of this movement. It's unclear precisely where the idea originated, but one driving force was the Catholic fraternal society the Knights of Columbus. In the early '50s the Knights themselves adopted the God-infused pledge for use in their own meetings, and members bombarded Congress with calls for the United States to do the same. Other fraternal, religious, and veterans clubs backed the idea. In April 1953, Rep. Louis Rabaut, D-Mich., formally proposed the alteration of the pledge in a bill he introduced to Congress.

9   The "under God" movement didn't take off, however, until the next year, when it was endorsed by the Rev. George M. Docherty, the pastor of the Presbyterian church in Washington that Eisenhower attended. In February 1954, Docherty gave a sermon—with the president in the pew before him—arguing that apart from "the United States of America," the pledge "could be the pledge of any country." He added, "I could hear little Moscovites [sic] repeat a similar pledge to their hammer-and-sickle flag with equal solemnity." Perhaps forgetting that "liberty and justice for all" was not the norm in Moscow, Docherty urged the inclusion of "under God" in the pledge to denote what he felt was special about the United States.

10   The ensuing congressional speechifying—debate would be a misnomer, given the near-unanimity of opinion—offered more proof that the point of the bill was to promote religion. The legislative history of the 1954 act stated that the hope was to "acknowledge the dependence of our people and our Government upon . . . the Creator . . . [and] deny the atheistic and materialistic concept of communism." In signing the bill on June 14, 1954, Flag Day, Eisenhower delighted in the fact that from then on, "millions of our schoolchildren will daily proclaim in every city and town . . . the dedication of our nation and our people to the Almighty." That the nation, constitutionally speaking, was in fact dedicated to the opposite proposition seemed to escape the president.

11   In recent times, controversies over the pledge have centered on the wisdom of enforcing patriotism more than on its corruption from a secular oath into a religious one. In the 1988 presidential race, as many readers will recall, George Bush bludgeoned Democratic nominee Michael Dukakis for vetoing a mandatory-pledge bill when he was governor of Massachusetts, even though the state Supreme Court had ruled the bill unconstitutional. Surely one reason for the current cravenness of Democratic leaders is a fear of undergoing Dukakis' fate in 2002 or 2004 at the hands of another Bush.

12   The history of the pledge supports Goodwin's decision. The record of the 1954 act shows that, far from a "de minimis" reference or a mere "backdrop" devoid of meaning, the words "under God" were inserted in the pledge for the express purpose of endorsing religion—which the U.S. Supreme Court itself ruled in 1971 was unconstitutional. Also according to the Supreme Court's own rulings, it doesn't matter that students are allowed to refrain from saying the pledge; a 2000 high court opinion held that voluntary, student-led prayers at school football games are unconstitutionally "coercive," because they force students into an unacceptable position of either proclaiming religious beliefs they don't share or publicly protesting.

13   The appeals court decision came almost 40 years to the day after the Supreme Court decision in *Engel v. Vitale*. In that case, the court ruled it unconstitutional for

public schools to allow prayer, even though the prayer was non-denominational and students were allowed to abstain from the exercise. When asked about the unpopular decision, President John F. Kennedy replied coolly that he knew many people were angry, but that the decisions of the court had to be respected. He added that there was "a very easy remedy"—not a constitutional amendment but a renewed commitment by Americans to pray at home, in their churches, and with their families.

QUESTIONS FOR ANALYSIS AND DISCUSSION

1. Were you surprised to learn that the original pledge made no mention of God? Do you think that restoring the original pledge could be the solution to the argument that the pledge violates the separation of church and state? Why or why not?
2. What does Greenberg mean "It's an old shibboleth of those who want to inject religion into public life that they're honoring the spirit of the nation's founders"? What is a shibboleth? Explain.
3. What official references to God were added during the 1950s? What motivated this movement? Do you think that social attitudes have changed sufficiently to drop these references? Why or why not?
4. Write an argument in which you either advocate to keep the pledge as it is, drop the words "under God," or drop the pledge entirely.
5. What is the author's position on the issue of "under God" in the Pledge of Allegiance? Identify statements in his essay in which he reveals his position. How does he use history to support his viewpoint? Explain.
6. How do you think Greenberg would respond to Heclo's essay, and vice versa? As fellow historians, on what points do you think they would agree and disagree?

READING THE VISUAL

Religious Membership in the United States

The U.S. Census Bureau does not ask questions related to faith or religion as part of the census. The Glenmary Research Center, a Catholic organization, publishes *Religious Congregations and Membership in the United States.* The last compilation of data provided the foundation for this map in 2000. Detailed information on how they gathered and complied this data is available on their website at http://www.glenmary.org.

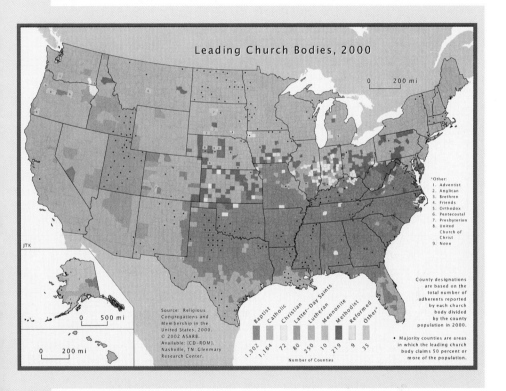

QUESTIONS FOR ANALYSIS AND DISCUSSION

1. Where do you fall on this map? Does the data on the map match your current comprehension of religious concentrations in the United States? Does any of the data surprise you? Explain.

2. This data was gathered from participating religious bodies. How does this knowledge influence your critical assessment of the map?

3. In your opinion, should the U.S. Census include information about religious affiliation as an optional part of its survey? Why or why not?

God of Our Fathers

Walter Isaacson

Many arguments in favor of retaining references to "God" in government-directed areas of civic life cite the "intentions of the founding fathers" when the United States was an infant nation. However, drafts of the Declaration of Independence and of the Constitution indicate that religious references (such as "God," "Creator," and "Providence") were added later. The conspicuous lack of references to God in a culture that was highly religious could be significant. In the next essay, editor and historian Walter Isaacson explores the "God of our Fathers," and how they might feel about the fury over the issue of church and state.

Isaacson is former chairman and CEO of CNN and President and CEO of the Aspen Institute, an international education and leadership organization. He is the author of *Einstein: His Life and Universe* (2007), *Benjamin Franklin: An American Life* (2003), and *Kissinger: A Biography* (1992). He is a regular columnist for *Time* magazine. In December 2007, he was appointed by President George W. Bush to the chairman of the U.S.-Palestinian Public-Private Partnership, which seeks to create economic and educational opportunities in the Palestinian territories. This essay was published in the July 5, 2004, issue of *Time* magazine.

BEFORE YOU READ

Should the intentions of the Founding Fathers—such as Jefferson, Washington, Adams, Franklin, Hancock—be considered when courts decide issues connected to the separation of church and state? Why or why not?

AS YOU READ

What does the crafting of the Declaration of Independence reveal about the possible religious intentions of the Founding Fathers?

1 Whenever an argument arises about the role that religion should play in our civic life, such as the dispute over the phrase "under God" in the Pledge of Allegiance or the display of the Ten Commandments in an Alabama courthouse, assertions about the faith of the founders are invariably bandied about. It's a wonderfully healthy debate because it causes folks to wrestle with the founders and, in the process, shows how the founders wrestled with religion.

2 The only direct reference to God in the Declaration of Independence comes in the first paragraph, in which Thomas Jefferson and his fellow drafters of that document—including Benjamin Franklin and John Adams—invoke the "laws of nature and of nature's god." (The absence of capitalization was the way Jefferson wrote it, though the final parchment capitalizes all four nouns.) The phrase "nature's god" reflected Jefferson's deism—his rather vague Enlightenment-era belief, which he

shared with Franklin, in a Creator whose divine handiwork is evident in the wonders of nature. Deists like Jefferson did not believe in a personal God who interceded directly in the daily affairs of mankind.

3   In his first rough draft of the Declaration, Jefferson began his famous second paragraph: "We hold these truths to be sacred and undeniable." The draft shows Franklin's heavy printer's pen crossing out the phrase with backslashes and changing it to "We hold these truths to be self-evident." Our rights derive from nature and are secured "by the consent of the governed," Franklin felt, not by the dictates or dogmas of any particular religion. Later in that same sentence, however, we see what was likely the influence of Adams, a more doctrinaire product of Puritan Massachusetts. In his rough draft, Jefferson had written, after noting that all men are created equal, "that from that equal creation they derive rights inherent & inalienable." By the time the committee and then Congress finished, the phrase had been changed to "that they are endowed by their Creator with certain unalienable Rights." For those of us who have toiled as editors, it is wonderful to watch how ideas can be balanced and sharpened through the editing process (and also how even giants have trouble knowing whether the word is inalienable or unalienable). The final version of the sentence weaves together a respect for the role of the Almighty Creator with a belief in reason and rationality.

4   The only other religious reference in the Declaration comes in the last sentence, which notes the signers' "firm reliance on the protection of divine Providence." Most of the founders subscribed to the concept of Providence, but they interpreted it in different ways. Jefferson believed in a rather nebulous sense of "general Providence," the principle that the Creator has a benevolent interest in mankind. Others, most notably those who followed in the Puritan footsteps of Cotton Mather, had faith in a more specific doctrine, sometimes called "special Providence" which held that God has a direct involvement in human lives and intervenes based on personal prayer.

5   In any event, that phrase was not in Jefferson's original draft or the version as edited by Franklin and Adams. Instead, it was added by Congress at the last minute. Like the phrase "under God" in the Pledge, it got tucked into a resounding peroration and somewhat broke up the rhythm: ". . . for the support of this Declaration, with a firm reliance on the protection of divine Providence, we mutually pledge to each other our Lives, our Fortunes and our sacred Honor."

6   In the Constitution, the Almighty barely makes an appearance, except in the context of noting that it was written in "the Year of our Lord," 1787. (Jefferson was ambassador to France at the time, so he missed the convention.) The one clear proclamation on the issue of religion in the founding documents is, of course, the First Amendment. It prohibits the establishment of a state religion or any government interference in how people freely exercise their beliefs. It was Jefferson, the original spirit behind the Virginia Statute for Religious Freedom, who emphasized that this amounted to a wall between two realms. "I contemplate with sovereign reverence," he wrote after becoming President, "that act of the whole American people which declared that their legislature should 'make no law respecting an establishment of religion, or prohibiting the free exercise thereof,' thus building a wall of separation between church & State."

7   Colonial America had seen its share of religious battles, in which arcane theological disputes like the one over antinomianism caused Puritans to be banished from Massachusetts and have to go establish colonies like Rhode Island. The founders, however, were careful in their debates and seminal documents to avoid using God as a political wedge issue or a cause of civic disputes. Indeed, that would have appalled them. Instead they embraced a vague civic religion that invoked a depersonalized deity that most people could accept. "Religion is a subject on which I have ever been most scrupulously reserved," Jefferson once wrote. "I have considered it as a matter between every man and his Maker, in which no other, and far less the public, had a right to intermeddle." So it is difficult to know exactly what the founders would have felt about the phrase "under God" in the Pledge of Allegiance or about displaying the Ten Commandments. It is probable, however, that they would have disapproved of people on either side who used the Lord's name or the Ten Commandments as a way to divide Americans rather than as a way to unite them.

QUESTIONS FOR ANALYSIS AND DISCUSSION ─────────

1. Why does Isaacson feel that arguments about the intentions of the Founding Fathers' feelings regarding the separation of church and state stimulate "wonderfully healthy debate"? Why is such debate, in his opinion, important? Explain.

2. Did Isaacson's essay on the crafting of the Declaration of Independence and the Constitution influence your own opinions on the issue of the separation of church and state? Why or why not?

3. Isaacson observes, "the founders, however, were careful in their debates and seminal documents to avoid using God as a political wedge issue or a cause of civic disputes." Imagine that the Founding Fathers were able to witness the current controversies regarding church and state—religion in schools, the Ten Commandments in courthouses, "under God" in the Pledge, "in God we trust" on currency, or nativity scenes on town greens. Based on the information in this essay, write a short response to these issues from their point of view.

4. Do you think the intentions of the Founding Fathers have any relevance today? Does it matter what they were thinking when they wrote the Constitution? Why or why not?

───

Public Prayers on State Occasions Need Not Be Divisive or Generic
Charles Haynes

In January 2005, Michael Newdow, dubbed "America's least favorite atheist" by *Time* magazine, filed a lawsuit to try to prevent George W. Bush from placing his hand on the Bible or engaging in public prayer at his second inauguration. Newdow had gained fame with his

2004 lawsuit charging that the "under God" wording included in the Pledge of Allegiance violated the establishment clause of the U.S. Constitution. Attorneys representing Bush argued that prayers have been widely accepted at inaugurals for more than 200 years and that Bush's decision to have a minister recite the invocation was a personal choice the court had no power to prevent. A U.S. district judge determined that Newdow had no legal basis to pursue his claim because he could not show he would suffer any injury from hearing a prayer. While Newdow lost his bid to bar "all Christian religious acts" from the January 20 inauguration, his lawsuit raises questions about how we legislate the separation of church and state. Is it possible for a politician to be religious upon state occasions, but not alienate people who do not share his or her beliefs? Charles Haynes proposes some solutions.

Haynes is a senior scholar at the First Amendment Center, where he directs the center's First Amendment educational program in schools and addresses issues concerning religious liberty in American public life. He is the author of *Religion in American History: What to Teach and How* (1990) and *Finding Common Ground: A First Amendment Guide to Religion and Public Education.* He is co-author of *Religion in American Public Life: Living with Our Deepest Differences* (2001). His weekly column on religious liberty appears in newspapers nationwide.

BEFORE YOU READ

Do you think public prayer at state or public events is appropriate? If so, what kind of prayer do you think is acceptable? Should prayer be inclusive, without any religious preference, or may it be a prayer representing the religion of the person of honor, such as the president at an inauguration?

AS YOU READ

Have you ever attended a public event, such as an inauguration, a sporting event, a benefit, or a building dedication, in which a prayer was included as part of the program? If so, what was the nature of the prayer? How did you feel about it? Did you participate? Did anyone look uncomfortable?

1   The debate over the prayers offered at President Bush's inauguration is yet another reminder of just how diverse and contentious America has become in the 21st century.

2   Prayers at inaugural ceremonies are nothing new, of course. The practice dates back to the day George Washington took the oath of office. And the Supreme Court has indicated that a prayer on such occasions is constitutional.

3   But we've just been through a long and bitter campaign full of charges and counter-charges about the influence of the "religious right" on George W. Bush. Now that the election is finally over, every symbolic gesture by the president is scrutinized for possible hidden messages and motives.

4   Why did these particular prayers spark debate? Because both ministers chosen to pray were evangelical Protestants, and both prayed in the name of Jesus Christ.

5   One writer criticized the prayers as "divisive, sectarian and inappropriate." Other commentators complained that millions of Americans were made to feel like "outsiders" at an official event.

6   On the other side of the argument are those who say that it is completely appropriate for the president to select clergy who share his faith. Besides, they point out, his inaugural address stressed unity and struck a note of inclusiveness by mentioning "churches, synagogues and mosques" as examples of faith communities working for the common good.

7   As this debate reveals, finding the "right" prayer for these occasions is a difficult, if not hopeless, task.

8   Some people propose general, non-sectarian prayers (common at many public events these days). While this approach has the advantage of being most inclusive, it still leaves out the growing number of Americans with no religious preference.

9   Moreover, many people of faith disparage generic prayers as meaningless addresses "to whom it may concern." In many religious traditions, how you pray and in whose name you pray determine whether or not the prayer is authentic and meaningful.

10   Since it's difficult to imagine any newly-elected president eliminating the tradition of opening and closing the inauguration with prayer, is there a way to pray that is genuine and yet somehow speaks to our nation's expanding diversity?

11   At the risk of making all sides mad, let me weigh in with two modest suggestions for public prayer at important state events.

12   First, why not consider the alternative offered by a number of religious leaders such as Bishop Krister Stendahl, former head of Harvard Divinity School, and Elder Dallin Oaks of the Mormon Church? They accept invitations to pray at public events on the condition that they be allowed to pray in ways that are authentic within their respective traditions. But they are careful to say "I," not "we" (e.g., "I pray in the name of Jesus").

13   I prefer this approach because it protects the integrity of religious traditions without assuming that we all share the same faith.

14   Second, it would be a civil and inclusive gesture for those leading the prayers— as well as for an incoming president—to acknowledge that we are a nation of many peoples and faiths.

15   It might be enough to simply say that although we have different beliefs (and prayers), under the First Amendment we share a commitment to uphold the right of every citizen to choose in matters of faith.

16   If there's going to be a religious message at inaugurations, let it be authentic. And let it be accompanied by a religious-liberty message reminding America that there are no "official prayers" in the land of the free.

QUESTIONS FOR ANALYSIS AND DISCUSSION ─────

1. Haynes observes that following Bush's election, "every symbolic gesture is scrutinized for possible hidden messages and motives." Are George W. Bush's actions and words subjected to greater inspection than other modern presidents? If so, why do people watch him more closely? Do you think he could have "hidden motives"?

2. Haynes admits that his two suggestions for prayer at public events risk "making all sides mad." What objections could both sides have to his solutions? What do you think of his suggestions? Explain.

3. Why are the pronouns "I" and "we" so important to consider when engaging in publicly led prayer? Explain.

4. Can you think of additional solutions to the issue of public prayer other than what Haynes suggests? If you think that public prayer is unacceptable under any circumstances, explain your point of view and how you would justify its removal to people who prefer to include prayer at state or public events.

READING THE VISUAL

Church and State

USA TODAY/CNN/Gallup Poll

In September 2003, USA Today/CNN/Gallup conducted a survey on public opinion regarding the separation of church and state. The results presented on page 585 are based on telephone interviews conducted September 19–21 with 1,003 adults over the age of 18. Among other findings, the survey reported that 77 percent of the subjects polled disapproved of the decision by the U.S. District Court to have the Ten Commandments monument removed from the rotunda of the Alabama Justice Building, and 90 percent approved of nondenominational school prayer at public events such as graduations.

QUESTIONS FOR ANALYSIS AND DISCUSSION

1. On what issues connected to church and state do Americans seem to overwhelmingly agree? On which do they seem sharply divided? What do you think accounts for the areas of agreement and division? Explain.

2. Based on this poll, do Americans treat all religions equally, or favor one over others? Explain.

3. Answer each question in this poll expressing your own viewpoint. Include one or two sentences for each response explaining why you answered the way you did.

4. Conduct your own poll using the questions drafted by *USA Today*. Interview at least 30 people for their viewpoints. Do the opinions expressed in the poll mirror what you have heard yourself on campus? Analyze the data.

Please say whether you approve or disapprove of each of the following:

The use of federal funds to support social programs like day care and drug rehabilitation run by Christian religious organizations

Approve	Disapprove	No opinion
64%	34%	2%

The inscription "In God We Trust" on U.S. coins

Approve	Disapprove	No opinion
90%	8%	2%

A non-denominational prayer as part of the official program at a public school ceremony such as a graduation or a sporting event

Approve	Disapprove	No opinion
78%	21%	1%

Display of a monument to the Ten Commandments in a public school or government building

Approve	Disapprove	No opinion
70%	29%	1%

Display of a monument with a verse from the Koran, the holy book of the Islamic religion, in a public school or government building

Approve	Disapprove	No opinion
33%	64%	3%

If you walked into a public school classroom and the teacher's desk had a Bible on it, would you consider that to be a good thing, or a bad thing?

Good Thing	Bad thing	Doesn't matter	No opinion
71%	18%	9%	2%

Do you think a monument to the Ten Commandments in a courthouse sends a message that the justice system gives special considerations to Jews and Christians over those who belong to other religions, or does it not send that message?

Yes, it does	No, it does not	No opinion
25%	73%	2%

In your opinion, which comes closer to your view of why some people file lawsuits opposing such things as prayer in schools or displays of religious symbols in government buildings – they are trying to turn the United States into a godless society, or they are trying to protect themselves and others from having religion forced onto them?

Turn the United States into a godless society	Protect themselves	No opinion
31%	62%	7%

Which comes closest to your opinion about displays of religion in public places or government buildings – it is acceptable to display only Christian symbols, as long as symbols of other religions are also displayed, or it is unacceptable to display any religious symbols at all?

Acceptable to display only Christian symbols	Acceptable to display symbols of all religions	Unacceptable	No opinion
10%	58%	29%	3%

Which comes closest to your view – government can promote the teachings of a religion without harming the rights of people who do not belong to that religion, or any time government promotes the teachings of a religion, it can harm the rights of people who do not belong to that religion?

Can promote without harming	Can harm any time it promotes	No opinion
40%	54%	6%

For results based on the total sample of National Adults, one can say with 95% confidence that the margin of sampling error is ± 3 percentage points. In addition to sampling error, question wording and practical difficulties in conducting surveys can introduce error or bias into the findings of public opinion polls.

What Happy Holidays?
Cathy Young

With the holiday decorations come the controversies. It is the season to argue about Christmas trees and menorahs on public greens, Santa Clauses on school property, and nativity scenes inside municipal rotaries. Do such public displays of religious celebrations oppress citizens who do not believe in the religions represented? Are cities and towns abusing the separation of church and state? Or do restrictions on such displays curtail citizens' rights to religious expression? In the next essay, Cathy Young discusses the issue of the separation of church, state . . . and holiday decorations.

Cathy Young is a columnist for the *Detroit News*. Her articles also appear regularly in *Reason* magazine and the *Jewish World Review*. She is the author of *Ceasefire! Why Women and Men Must Join Forces to Achieve True Equality* (1999) and the cofounder of the Women's Freedom Network. This article was published in *Reason Online* on December 28, 2004.

BEFORE YOU READ

Consider how the issue of public expressions of religion during the holiday season has changed over the last 20 years from your own personal experience. Do you think it is a good thing this issue has received so much attention recently, or is it much ado about nothing?

AS YOU READ

In your opinion, does a public square that features a holiday display convey the message to people who do not celebrate the holiday that "they do not belong"? Why or why not?

1   Peace on Earth? Forget it. Nowadays, Christmas is a battlefield in the culture wars. "It's beginning to look a lot like Christmas" has come to mean that there are endless arguments about nativity scenes, Santa Claus and reindeer on public property, Christmas carols in public schools, and the greeting "Merry Christmas" vs. "Happy Holidays."

2   "Arguments" is, perhaps, too polite a term. These days, we can't argue about anything without name-calling, hyperbole, paranoia, and crude stereotyping. Christmas is no exception. One side sees a satanic peril in a store clerk's "Happy Holidays" greeting; the other sees a theocratic menace in a Christmas carol sung at a school concert.

3   On one side, we get lurid tales of political correctness run amok, of nothing less than a secularist crusade to expunge all traces of Christmas and Christianity itself from the public square. On the other side, we get counterclaims of a politically motivated hysteria about a mythical war on Christmas, with the ulterior motive of shoving the religious right's social values down everybody's throats.

4 The excesses of multicultural sensitivity do exist. In my home state of New Jersey, the South Orange-Maplewood school district banned even instrumental versions of Christmas carols from school holiday concerts. (One Jewish student who plays in a high school band in Maplewood told the Associated Press the ban was "silly.") New York City's public schools bizarrely permit menorah displays, which supposedly have a secular element, but not nativity scenes. In some towns, there have been attempts to banish even recognized secular festive symbols such as the Christmas tree and Santa from public grounds.

5 The hysteria about "Christmas under attack" is equally real, and equally silly. At the conservative website Townhall.com, one Dr. Donald May thunders that the new grinches want Americans to "accept the abolition of Christmas, close down our churches, and remove the crosses from our cemeteries." Fox News talk show host Bill O'Reilly refers, with a straight face, to "the media forces of darkness" attacking "the defenders of Christmas" (such as O'Reilly himself). He also warns that "the traditions of Christmas are under fire by committed secularists, people who do not want any public demonstration of spirituality."

6 Let's put things in perspective. Even the most far-reaching efforts to stamp out religious expression in "the public square" affect only government property. No one is seeking to stop churches from displaying nativity scenes on their front lawns or homeowners from putting up religiously themed decorations. If some private businesses such as stores decide to stick to secular holiday displays and salutations, that's their choice.

7 "Season's Greetings" and "Happy Holidays" may come across as bland and politically correct. But as James Lileks documents on his blog, the shift toward such nonsectarian greetings actually began in America in the 1950s, not as an attack on religion but in acknowledgment of an increasingly diverse society. At a recent press conference, President Bush wished everyone "Happy holidays" twice and never mentioned Christmas. He must be in on the left-wing plot.

8 Those Americans who don't celebrate Christmas obviously have to be tolerant of the vast majority who do; but they also have a right to a public square which does not loudly tell them they don't belong. It's worth noting, too, that quite a few non-Christian Americans celebrate Christmas as a cultural tradition, and being inclusive toward them is a good thing. Meanwhile, many Christians are genuinely concerned about the secularization and commercialization of the holiday. But for those who truly want to "put Christ back into Christmas," the answer is in giving more time and attention to religious and charitable activities, not in demanding more Christian symbolism at the place where you shop. Macy's is not a temple.

9 Of course, the battle over Christmas isn't just over Christmas; it's part of the larger divide between liberal secularists and religious conservatives. Passions over such issues as same-sex marriage, abortion, and the teaching of evolution in schools are played out in clashes over crèches. On all those issues, there is precious little effort by either side to understand the other, and precious little respect for the other side's beliefs.

10 And so the Christmas wars are likely to continue, even though politicizing a religious holiday is surely just as bad as commercializing it. Dr. May's column at Townhall.com ends with the exhortation, "Merry Christmas to all, and to all a good fight." To this, one can only say: God help us, everyone.

QUESTIONS FOR ANALYSIS AND DISCUSSION ──────

1. Young states "these days, we can't argue about anything without name-calling, hyperbole, paranoia, and crude stereotyping. Christmas is no exception." What sort of "name calling" and "crude stereotyping" is associated with the Christmas season? Explain.
2. What is Young's position on the "culture wars" over the holiday season? Does she present a balanced perspective on the issue?
3. What is the underlying issue over the "battle over Christmas"? To what broader issues does it connect? Explain.
4. Young observes that the "hysteria about 'Christmas under attack' is equally real and equally silly." How can it be both? Is Christmas indeed under attack? By whom? Do you agree that the "hysteria" is "silly"? Why or why not?
5. Is this issue likely to have a resolution that pleases everyone? If so, propose a solution you think would work. If not, explain why you believe the issue to be at an impasse.

Deck the Halls?
Bridget Samburg

> In post-election America 2004, differences over holiday decorations in public spaces, including schools and in front of town halls, have taken on heightened significance. Bridget Samburg interviews a Massachusetts lawyer and a professor of American Jewish history for their perspective on the issue.
>
> Bridget Samburg is a correspondent for the *Boston Globe*, in which this interview appeared on December 12, 2004.

BEFORE YOU READ ──────────────────────────────

What public holiday displays, if any, does your own home town erect? Are they on the town green or in front of the town hall? on public or school property? Do you think towns should or should not erect holiday displays on public or municipal property?

AS YOU READ ──────────────────────────────────

In this interview, a Jewish professor explains why he feels that religion in the schools promotes tolerance and prepares students for the diversity of the real world. What do you think? Is it better to expose children to different religions and beliefs, or would such exposure subject them to "conflicting messages"?

1 It's holiday time again, and we've unpacked the dancing Santas, red-nosed rein-deers, and big, shiny menorahs. But is it appropriate for them, kitschy and other-wise, religious and secular to be displayed in town squares, city halls, and public schools? Should such celebrations stay in private homes, or are they good for the community, if not an integral part of American tradition? Where some see an entan-glement of government and religion, others see an opportunity to revel in our coun-try's diversity. In any case, the post-election climate raises the temperature around these issues.

2 Melissa McWhinney is a lawyer who lives in Somerville, Massachusetts, and Jonathan Sarna is a professor of American Jewish history at Brandeis University.

3 **McWhinney:** There is a difference between decorating on generalized government property versus decorating in schools because children are more vulnerable to con-flicting messages.

4 **Sarna:** While I think it is inappropriate to decorate for Christmas to the exclusion of Hanukkah, Kwanzaa, and other holidays, the notion that we have children from different cultural and religious backgrounds and that we recognize those back-grounds is legitimate. We are paying a huge price for the total removal of religion from schools. Helping youngsters understand diversity would be better for the schools and better for the youngsters.

5 **McWhinney:** It's essential that children learn about diversity. However, it tends to be pitted as a contest: "If I want to have my Christmas tree, how big a menorah do I need so I can get what I want?"

6 **Sarna:** Schools should be the arena where we work out peacefully those kinds of issues, so that we are well trained when we deal with them in society at large.

7 **McWhinney:** People who object to the denial to have Christmas parties in the schools are doing it because they remember how nice life was in the second grade. It's legally a problem, and it's culturally a problem. Winter decorations are fine. Crèches are out. Christmas trees play strongly on people's emotional sensitivities. I would prefer not to see them at all.

8 **Sarna:** The tension that we face is a larger tension about what the relationship of religion and state should be in America. We agree that the notion of a triumphant Chris-tianity in society or in the classroom is inappropriate. Separationism in an extreme has turned out to neither work nor to reflect the kind of society most Americans want.

9 **McWhinney:** How do you compromise with the Christmas carols? What do you do with kids for whom this is a problem religiously?

10 **Sarna:** Any student should be allowed to bow out.

11 **McWhinney:** It's a small minority who actually bows out, but I think it's a larger minority who wishes they could.

12 **Sarna:** We respect the rights of children and their parents to make a variety of decisions.

13 **McWhinney:** I admire the families who stand up to it, but it puts them in a tremendous conflict situation, which is unnecessary. It's a question of the endorsement, the support, and the celebration with public funding that is of concern. There are some school districts that are not interested in this discussion and defend their right to do things as they always have.

14 **Sarna:** I'm arguing for a middle ground that would celebrate the religious diversity of the country.

15 **McWhinney:** What would be in your town square?

16 **Sarna:** A wide array of religious symbols: a Christmas tree, a menorah, symbols of other communities.

17 **McWhinney:** Everyone's symbol cannot stand in the public square. There is simply not enough room. I don't think it's possible to draw the line in a reasonable manner, which is why I would prefer that all these things retreat to the home and church. What I do in my home may be very different than what I expect to see at a town hall. To have my tax money spent on the promotion of what I consider a religious expression or endorsement of a particular religion does concern me.

18 **Sarna:** In some ways, that's what makes America great: that we do recognize various religious traditions, and we are not trying to create the sense that you are Christian at home or a Jew at home—and just a human being when you leave your home.

19 **McWhinney:** I don't think people are being asked to leave their religion at home. That's exactly why it's a problem to have Christmas parties at school. The Jewish kids, the Muslim kids, the Buddhist kids are who they are at school. How can they be asked to participate in a Christmas party?

20 **Sarna:** The goal should be to work very hard to preserve a religiously pluralistic America. I have faith in the American people that they are religiously tolerant, and given the opportunity to recognize and even venerate a full spectrum of world religions, they will do so.

21 **McWhinney:** I think they are religiously tolerant as long as you don't come along and mess with Christmas.

22 **Sarna:** The Supreme Court has approved the notion of religious diversity in the public square. It's about time we moved past these discussions and figure out how we can best carry out that ruling.

QUESTIONS FOR ANALYSIS AND DISCUSSION

1. Samburg notes that the "post-election climate raises the temperature around" the issues of holiday displays in the public arena. What is the "post-election climate"? Why does it bring these issues to the forefront? Explain.

2. McWhinney argues that religious symbols and holidays must be kept out of schools "because children are more vulnerable to conflicting messages." What conflicting messages are children likely to experience with Christmas trees, menorahs, or carols in school? Respond to her claim with your own viewpoint and personal experience.

3. Sarna observes, "separationism in an extreme has turned out to neither work nor to reflect the kind of society most Americans want." In what ways has "separationism" failed? Should the majority ("most Americans") decide this issue? Why or why not?

4. Evaluate the following statements made by McWhinney:

   a. "Everyone's symbol cannot stand in the public square. There is simply not enough room."

   b. "People who object to the denial to have Christmas parties in the schools are doing it because they remember how nice life was in the second grade."

   c. "It's a small minority who actually bow out, but I think there's a larger minority who wishes they could."

   How do these statements support McWhinney's argument that religion should have no place in schools or public spaces?

5. Do you think McWhinney and Sarna would ever reach a consensus on this issue with further discussion? Why or why not?

WRITING ASSIGNMENTS

1. In the opening paragraph of his essay, Hugh Heclo wonders what it might mean for religion to "reenter the public square." He asks, "What good might it do there—and what harm?" Write an essay in which you answer his question. Refer to some of the issues in this section, as well as the concept of religion and civic life in general.

2. Do you think there is any room for religion in the public sphere? Who should decide what the rules are and determine the level of separation between church and state? Include public expressions of religion such as prayer in schools and at state occasions, swearing on the Bible in court or featuring the Ten Commandments on state property, Congressional prayer, and religious holiday displays on public lands. Write an essay presenting your position on this issue and support it with information from this chapter as well as outside research.

3. You are a judge asked to determine whether "In God We Trust" on U.S. currency is a violation of the First Amendment. Look up the history of this phrase at the U.S. Treasury's website <http://www.treas.gov> (type in the phrase in the website's search bar). Make a ruling on the issue supporting your position on other church and state decisions.

4. Review the language of the First Amendment of the Constitution and present your own interpretation of its wording. You may include the history of the

Constitution, the background of the Founding Fathers, and the spirit of the document in your response.

5. Write a research paper on the role religion plays in other nations' governments. For example, how does religion intersect with state in a European nation such as England, Sweden, or France? Or in a Middle Eastern nation such as Iraq or Jordan? Alternatively, you may prepare a research paper exploring the validity of Hugh Heclo's observation that most major political conflicts have a religious foundation. Research the conflict and its background. Can there ever be a true separation between church and state? Why or why not?

WHAT'S WRONG WITH DARWIN?

The Courtship of Charles Darwin
Edward J. Larson

Controversy over whether scientific or biblical explanations of life's origins should be taught in our public schools emerged over 80 years ago. Today, evolutionists and creationists are engaged in a nationwide legal battle. On the one hand, evolutionists maintain that the principles put forth by Charles Darwin, including natural selection, make up a scientific theory that is supported by tons of data and visible evidence. On the other hand are the creationists, some of whom support not only the belief that God made the world—a concept embraced by many scientists who also believe in evolution—but also that the earth is only as old as the Bible records, about 10,000 years. Do alternative theories—especially religiously based ones—belong in the nation's schoolbooks? And who decides?

Edward J. Larson is the Russell Professor of History and Talmadge Professor of Law at the University of Georgia. He is the author of five books, including *Summer for the Gods: The Scopes Trial and America's Continuing Debate Over Science and Religion*, which received the 1998 Pulitzer Prize for history. His most recent book is *Evolution: The Remarkable History of a Scientific Theory*. This essay first appeared in the April 2005 issue of *Science & Spirit* magazine.

BEFORE YOU READ ————————————————————————

Should public schools be forced to teach both evolution and creationism? Is this contradictory to the mandate separation of church and state or a way to compromise a controversial subject?

AS YOU READ ————————————————————————

How does Larson's essay give us the "evolution" of creationism in public schools? Explain.

1   It's May, eighty years to the month after John Scopes was indicted for teaching evolution in Dayton, Tennessee, and I'm less than fifty miles away, lecturing to students at one of the South's premier private prep schools. In their biology classes, these students are learning the theory of evolution in preparation for attending top universities. Many of them do not believe the theory, though, and a few of them are thoroughly versed in the challenges that anti-evolutionists regularly raise against it. On the whole, these elite students are more suspicious of Darwinism now than Scopes' small town students were in 1925, but at least they have a working knowledge of the subject.

2   When speaking at colleges and universities around the country, I frequently ask students what they learned about organic origins in high school. Most of them tell me that evolution was touched on only lightly, if at all. Even fewer report receiving any creationist instruction. Mine is an unscientific survey, to be sure, but it accords with what others find: Our human origin is fast becoming the third rail of high school biology.

3   The American controversy over creation and evolution is primarily fought in our public high school biology classes. Virtually no one disputes teaching the theory of evolution in public colleges and universities, or using public funding to support evolutionary research in agriculture or medicine. It is the minds of American high school students at stake.

4   Anti-evolutionists typically ask to eliminate Darwinism (or at least what they call "macroevolution") from the science curriculum, or demand it be taught as just a "theory" and balanced with arguments against it or for special creation. In truth, the source of their concern lies in religion, not science. It goes back to the 1920s, when teenagers first began attending high school in great numbers. The transformation in American education wrought by urbanization, industrialization, and compulsory school-attendance laws made the allegedly irreligious impact of teaching evolution a divisive issue that remains today.

5   Religion addresses the great questions of life. Why are we here? Where did we come from? Where are we going? To the extent that science addresses these questions, it treads on holy ground. But more than any other concept in science, the theory of organic evolution—particularly as applied to humans—awakens a resistance among those who feel it directly threatens their religious convictions.

6   Tension has long existed between religious and scientific ways of understanding the origins of life, individual species, and humanity. From the time of the ancient Greeks, philosophers and scientists contemplating origins have recognized two alternatives: Either the various species were specially created in some way, or they evolved from pre-existing species. The former view tends to stress the importance of a divine creator, while the latter view de-emphasizes or eliminates a creator. Both views have religious implications.

7   With the rise of Christianity, special creation dominated Western thought. For centuries, mainstream science—or "natural history," as it was called—supported this view of origins. Species appear fixed, early natural historians observed, and breed true to form. They do not evolve. Even more critically, as European natural historians came to appreciate the delicate balance in nature and within each living

thing, many of them saw it not only as evidence of a creator's existence, but also as evidence of that creator's loving character and purpose. Particularly in the Protestant realms of Britain and northern Europe, where science gained cultural authority during the 1600s and 1700s, natural history became the handmaiden of natural theology.

8   Beginning in the eighteenth century, Enlightenment skeptics in France revived evolutionary thinking. Some deists and atheists argued that species must have evolved from pre-existing species, but they failed to propose a plausible means of evolutionary development. So when Charles Darwin published his theory of evolution by natural selection in 1859, he transformed the terms of this debate by supplying a logical explanation for how species evolve. Every offspring naturally differs from its parents and siblings, Darwin argued. A purely naturalistic struggle for existence selects the fittest of these offspring to survive and propagate their beneficial variations. In this manner, new species gradually evolve from pre-existing ones, each delicately adapted to its environment without the intervening hand of God.

9   Most biologists quickly accepted Darwin's theory as an explanation for the origin of biological species, but some conservative Christians objected to its atheistic implications. Some traditional scientists—most notably, in America, the great Harvard zoologist Louis Agassiz—promptly challenged the very notion of biological evolution by arguing that highly complex individual organs (such as the eye) and ecologically dependent species (such as bees and flowers) cannot evolve through the sort of minute, random steps envisioned by Darwin. To survive, each modification must be beneficial, Agassiz reasoned, but complex organs and organic relationships only work as a whole; they could not develop in steps. Instead, he proposed, complex organisms reflect intelligent design and thus testify both to the divine in nature and the nurturing character of the designer. Although the scientific community largely converted to Darwin's new theory, due to its ability to explain other natural phenomena that appear utterly senseless under a theory of design or creation (such as the fossil record, rudimentary organs, comparative morphology, and the geographic distribution of similar species), religious opponents, often invoking the earlier scientific arguments against evolution, remained.

10   Three levels of religious opposition to Darwinism are still apparent today. In a narrow sense, any theory of evolution conflicts with a literal reading of the Genesis account, which declares that God specially created each kind of living thing in six days. Accepting Genesis as literally true inclines believers to accept special creationism in biology and to reject modern geologic theories that claim the Earth has been changing and evolving for millions of years. In a broader sense, the natural theology of Darwin's theory troubles many theists. What sort of God would create living things through random change mutations and a hateful struggle for existence? God could still use evolutionary processes operating over eons to develop the current diversity of life, these critics acknowledge, but the total exclusion of God from any role in the origin of life strikes religious believers as presumptuous, if not preposterous.

11   None of these concerns constitutes a scientific objection to the neo-Darwinian synthesis that currently dominates Western biological thought, and none of these

concerns has translated into a compelling scientific alternative to neo-Darwinian theory. Virtually all biologists accept the view that current species evolved over time from pre-existing species, with many of these scientists seeing little or no role for God in the process. In contrast, most Americans profess to believe in some form of creationist view of origins, with many of them opting for special creation over theistic evolution as God's means of inception. In a democracy with compulsory education and public schools, this rift plays out every day in high school biology classes across the country: Parents, students, teachers, and taxpayers informed by the dominant scientific view of origins insist that the biology curriculum stress evolution, while many of those committed to a biblical view want some place for creation in the science classroom.

12   The American controversy over creation and evolution in the classroom first gained traction in the 1920s, when the aging political orator William Jennings Bryan launched a nationwide crusade to ban the teaching of human evolution in public schools that culminated in the passage of Tennessee's 1925 anti-evolution statute and the trial of Scopes for violating that law. With Bryan joining the prosecution, and legendary trial lawyer Clarence Darrow leading Scopes' defense, the trial became a media event that polarized the nation. And when Scopes lost and the law was upheld, restrictions similar to Dayton's statute soon appeared in other Southern states and various localities, some of them remaining on the books until 1968 when the U.S. Supreme Court finally ruled in *Epperson v. Arkansas* that they violated the Establishment Clause for having a solely religious, rather than secular, purpose.

13   In his day, Bryan never called for the inclusion of creationism in the science classroom because even he viewed it as a religious, rather than a scientific, doctrine. But with the publication of *The Genesis Flood* in 1961, Virginia Tech engineering professor Henry Morris gave believers scientific-sounding arguments supporting the biblical account of a six-day creation within the past 10,000 years. The book spawned a movement within American fundamentalism, with Morris as its Moses leading the faithful into a promised land where science proved religion.

14   This so-called "scientific creationism" spread through the missionary work of Morris' Institute for Creation Research, or ICR. The emergence of the religious right carried it into politics during the 1970s. Within two decades of the publication of *The Genesis Flood*, three states and dozens of local school districts had mandated "balanced treatment" for young-Earth creationism along with evolution in public school science courses.

15   It took another decade before the Supreme Court unraveled those mandates as unconstitutional in *Edwards v. Aguillard*, which voided Louisiana's creationism law. Scientific creationism was nothing but religion dressed up as science, the high court decreed in 1987, and therefore, like other forms of religious instruction, was barred from public school classrooms by the Establishment Clause. But by this time, conservative Christians, from California to Maine, were entrenched in local and state politics and deeply concerned about science education.

16   Then along came University of California law professor Phillip Johnson. He was no young-Earth creationist, but he was an evangelical Christian with an

uncompromising faith in God. His target became the philosophical belief and methodological practice within science that supposes material entities subject to physical laws account for everything in nature. Whether called "naturalism" or "materialism," such a philosophy or method excludes God from science laboratories and classrooms. "The important thing is not whether God created all at once [as scientific creationism holds] or in stages [as theistic evolution maintains]," Johnson asserted. "Anyone who thinks that the biological world is a product of a pre-existing intelligence . . . is a creationist in the most important sense of the word. By this broad definition, at least eighty percent of Americans, including me, are creationists." If public schools cannot teach scientific creationism because it promotes the tenets of a particular religion, then at least scientific dissent from Darwinism or evidence of "intelligent design" in nature should be permissible.

17   In a series of books published by Christian presses over the past fifteen years, Johnson has argued that science education should not automatically exclude supernatural explanations for natural phenomena. "Question the sufficiency of Darwinism to explain life" and "Teach the controversy over evolutionary naturalism in the classroom" are his post-*Aguillard* pleas that now reverberate through school board meetings and state legislative hearings.

18   Hundreds of thousands of Johnson's books have been sold, and it is no wonder that his kind of arguments now show up whenever objections are raised against teaching evolution in public schools. They were apparent in the U.S. Senate in 2001 when Pennsylvania Senator Rick Santorum, a prominent conservative Catholic, introduced an amendment to an education bill, proposing that "where biological evolution is taught, the curriculum should help students to understand why the subject generates so much continuing controversy."

19   This language, which Johnson helped frame and which singles out evolutionary theory as uniquely controversial, did not make it into the bill that was signed into law. A weaker version, in which evolution is presented as merely an example of a topic that might generate controversy, eventually became part of the conference report for that legislation. Still, similar proposals have surfaced as stand-alone bills in more than a dozen state legislatures during the past five years. State and local school boards offer an alternative avenue of attack, with several of them imposing restrictions on teaching evolution or opening the door to creationist instruction. Indeed, as *Science & Spirit* went to press, debates raged in school boards and courtrooms from Topeka, Kansas, to Cobb County, Georgia, and Dover, Pennsylvania, to name just a few battlegrounds.

20   Hearkening back to a pre-Darwinian era in natural history, Lehigh University biochemistry professor Michael Behe, a devout Catholic and another popular authority on intelligent design, or ID, challenges Darwinist explanations for complex organic processes by reviving traditional arguments for design based on evidence of nature's irreducible complexity. Behe, like Johnson, does not argue for the "young Earth" of creation science, but he does propound that intelligent design, rather than random chance, is apparent in nature. ID divorced from biblical creationism, Behe and Johnson argue, should be a fit subject for public school education. With this argument, they have expanded the tent of people willing to challenge

the alleged Darwinist hegemony in the science classroom beyond those persuaded by Morris' argument for a young Earth.

21   Some observers have labeled ID as "the new creationism," but in its basic approach, it is much older than scientific creationism. Indeed, design theorists follow a venerable intellectual tradition associated with the likes of British theologian William Paley, French zoologist Georges Cuvier, and even William Jennings Bryan— all of whom saw an orderly creation testifying to its creator and none of whom relied strictly on the Bible to reach that conclusion. Like their intellectual forebears, proponents of ID represent various religious perspectives and reach out beyond fundamentalists to evangelical Protestants and conservative Catholics. Together with scientific creationists, they reject methodological naturalism in science and object to teaching Darwinism as fact. Although ID has yet to gain the mass following of scientific creationism, its partisans now play a pivotal role in the controversy surrounding the teaching of evolution.

22   Yet the bedrock for anti-evolutionism in the United States remains the biblical literalism of the Protestant fundamentalist movement, in which there is typically greater concern about the Earth's age, to which the Bible speaks, than about such intellectual abstractions as scientific naturalism. In *The Genesis Flood*, for example, Morris stresses the theological significance of utter fidelity to the entire biblical narrative. Thus, when Genesis says that God created the universe in six days, he maintains, it must mean six twenty-four-hour days; when it says that God created humans and all animals on the sixth day, then dinosaurs must have lived alongside early man; and when it gives a genealogy of Noah's descendants, believers can use it to date the flood to between 5,000 and 7,000 years ago.

23   Despite judicial rulings against the incorporation of scientific creationism into the public school biology curriculum, vast numbers of Americans continue to accept biblical creationism of the sort espoused by Morris and the ICR. Fifty years after its initial publication, *The Genesis Flood* (now in its forty-fourth printing) continues to sell well in Christian bookstores, but is now only one on a shelf full of such books. Christian radio and television blanket the nation with creationist broadcasts and cablecasts, such as Ken Ham's "Answers . . . with Ken Ham," which is now heard on more than 500 radio stations in forty-eight states. Although still relatively small in absolute terms, the number of students receiving their primary and secondary education at home or in Christian academies has risen steadily over the past twenty-five years, with many such students learning their biology from creationist textbooks. At the post-secondary level, Bible institutes and Christian colleges continue to grow in number and size, with at least some of them offering degrees in biology and science education in a creation-friendly environment.

24   All of this creationist activity is nearly invisible outside the churches and religious communities where it occurs. While the secular media largely lost interest in scientific creationism once *Aguillard* squelched efforts to introduce it into public education, biblical creationists turned inward to entrench their views within America's vibrant conservative Christian subculture. There they flourish, virtually inaccessible to evolutionists.

25   This has not stopped some evolutionists from striking back, however. While most evolutionary biologists either ignore religion altogether or find it somehow compatible with their science, a few of them have taken a Darrowesque dislike to Christianity. British sociobiologist, zoologist, and science writer Richard Dawkins leads this pack.

26   In *The Blind Watchmaker*, published to great acclaim in the midst of legal wrangling over Louisiana's creationism law, Dawkins takes aim at what he calls "redneck" creationists and "their disturbingly successful fight to subvert American education and textbook publishing." Focusing on the philosophical heart of creationism rather than simple biblical literalism, Dawkins challenges the very notion of purposeful design in nature, which he calls "the most influential of the arguments for the existence of a God." In a legendary articulation of this argument in 1802, the theologian Paley compared living things to mechanical watches; just as the intricate workings of a watch betray its maker's purposes, Paley reasoned, so too the even more intricate complexity of organisms and of individual organs (such as the eye) proves the existence of a purposeful creator. Not so, Dawkins counters: "Natural selection, the blind, unconscious, automatic process which Darwin discovered, and which we now know is the explanation for the existence and apparently purposeful form of all life, has no purpose. . . . It is the blind watchmaker." Banishing the argument for design, Dawkins writes: "Darwin made it possible to be an intellectually fulfilled atheist."

27   Taking a more diplomatic approach, organized science has sought to defuse the controversy by affirming the compatibility of modern evolutionary naturalism and a personal belief in God. The National Academy of Sciences, or NAS, a self-selecting body of the nation's premier scientists, asserted as much in a glossy brochure distributed to schoolteachers during the 1980s in reaction to the creation science movement. In 1998, the NAS mass-produced a new booklet reasserting that while science is committed to methodological naturalism, it does not conflict with religion; it simply represents a separate way of knowing. "Science," the booklet states, "is limited to explaining the natural world through natural causes. Science can say nothing about the supernatural. Whether God exists or not is a question about which science is neutral."

28   The 9,000-member National Association of Biology Teachers took a similar tack. In a position statement initially adopted in 1995 in opposition to the creation science movement and always controversial among theists, the association defined evolution as "an unsupervised, impersonal, unpredictable, and natural process of temporal descent with gradual modification," which is a fair depiction of modern Darwinian theory. In 1997, responding to heightened sensitivity to the atheistic implications of Darwinism, the association's executive committee voted to delete the words "unsupervised" and "impersonal" from the statement. The group's executive director explained that "To say that evolution is unsupervised is to make a theological statement," and theological statements exceed the bounds of science.

29   The *New York Times* called it "a startling about-face." To Dawkins, the decision represented "a cowardly flabbiness of the intellect," while Johnson dismissed it as rank hypocrisy. If they agree on nothing else, Dawkins and Johnson acknowledge that

Darwinism and Christianity are at war—and, with their writings and talks, they help to stir popular passions over biology education, much as Darrow and Bryan once did. The fruit of their labors can be seen in pending lawsuits and current legislation.

30   That, in brief, is where the creation-evolution teaching controversy stands today—making front-page news once again, eighty years after a little town in Tennessee made headlines by prosecuting John Scopes. It resurfaces periodically in countless Daytons throughout the United States, over everyday episodes of science teachers either defying or deifying Darwin. Such acts generate lawsuits and legislation precisely because religion continues to matter greatly in America. Public opinion surveys invariably find that more than ninety percent of Americans believe in God—just as they have found since polling on such matters began in the 1950s. A recent survey indicated that more than three-quarters of all Americans believe in miracles, while another found that nearly half of those surveyed believe that "God created human beings pretty much in their present form at one time within the last 10,000 years or so" and that four-fifths of the rest believe that God actively guided the evolutionary process that produced humans. Three out of five Americans now say religion is "very important" in their lives. It troubles them that science does not affirm their faith and outrages some when biology textbooks seem to deny it.

31   As a diverse people, Americans have learned to seek middle ground whenever possible. As a species, however, humans instinctively respond to stirring oratory. Darrow and Bryan mastered that craft and used it in Dayton to enlist their legions. Dawkins and Johnson have followed in those footsteps, tapping into a cultural divide that deeply troubles this national house of ours and offers us no middle ground. And as we all know, either from the Bible or a Broadway classic, "He that troubleth his own house shall inherit the wind." That wind has sporadically touched off maelstroms over the past eighty years, sorely testing our tradition of tolerance. And if history is any guide, dark clouds remain on the horizon.

QUESTIONS FOR ANALYSIS AND DISCUSSION

1. How is the title, "The Courtship of Charles Darwin," significant to the essay's main point? How does the title reflect the controversy over Darwin, evolution, and creationism?

2. Larson describes how the debate over evolution and the public school system has sought "middle ground" for over 80 years. Is middle ground possible? Do you think it is likely that Americans will ever reach a compromise on this subject that satisfies the majority? Why or why not?

3. According to Larson, what may account for the increasing popularity of Christian colleges and Christian academies?

4. What is "Intelligent Design" (ID)? Do you agree or disagree with the theory? Are science and religion mutually exclusive?

5. Why are Americans so frustrated by the evolution versus creation debate? What is at stake intellectually, socially, and religiously?

Remove Stickers, Open Minds

Kenneth R. Miller

In the academic school year of 2004–2005, Georgia's Cobb County Board of Education required stickers to be pasted into biology textbooks, stating that "evolution is a theory, not a fact, regarding the origin of living things. The material should be approached with an open mind, studied carefully, and critically considered." After complaints from parents and teachers, a federal judge ordered the school system to remove stickers from the textbooks, saying that such disclaimers were an unconstitutional endorsement of religion. "By denigrating evolution, the school board appears to be endorsing the well-known prevailing alternative theory, creationism or variations thereof, even though the sticker does not specifically reference any alternative theories." The next piece is an editorial by biology professor Kenneth Miller discussing the argument and the verdict.

Miller is a professor of biology at Brown University and coauthor of *Biology* (2002). He is particularly known for his opposition to creationism, including the Intelligent Design movement, and has written a book on the subject, *Finding Darwin's God: A Scientist's Search for Common Ground Between God and Evolution* (2000), in which he furthers the argument that a belief in God and evolution are not mutually exclusive. This editorial appeared in the *Boston Globe* on January 22, 2005.

BEFORE YOU READ

If you took biology in high school, how much time, if any, did you spend on the theory of evolution? Were you taught any other views, such as Intelligent Design? Explain.

AS YOU READ

Miller explains, "evolution is both a theory and a fact." How can it be both? How does he support this statement?

1 ▌sn't evolution a theory? Of course it is. So why did a federal district court judge last week [January 2005] order a board of education in Georgia to remove stickers from biology textbooks that seemed to tell students that evolution was just a theory? Is this a case of censorship? Is a closed-minded scientific establishment trying to keep evidence against evolution out of the classroom? Is a federal court telling educators that evolution is now federally protected dogma?

2 The answer is far simpler. The judge simply read the sticker and saw that it served no scientific or educational purpose. Once that was clear, he looked to the reasons for slapping it in the textbooks of thousands of students, and here the record was equally clear. The sticker was inserted to advance a particular set of religious beliefs—exactly the argument advanced by the parents of six students in the district who sued the Cobb County Board of Education to get the stickers removed.

3   So what's wrong with telling students that evolution is a theory? Nothing. But the textbook they were using already described evolution as a theory, and I ought to know. Joseph Levine and I wrote the biology book Cobb County's high school students are using. Chapter 15 is titled "Darwin's Theory of Evolution." Hard to be clearer than that. So why did the Cobb County Board of Education slap a warning label inside a book that already refers to evolution as a theory? Cooper hit correctly when he wrote that "by denigrating evolution, the school board appears to be endorsing the well-known prevailing alternative theory, creationism or variations thereof, even though the sticker does not specifically reference any alternative theories."

4   Exactly. What the sticker said was that "Evolution is a theory, not a fact, regarding the origin of living things." The problem with that wording is that evolution is both a theory and a fact. It is a fact that living things in the past were different from living things today and that the life of the past changed, or evolved, to produce the life of the present. Recent news reports the discovery of a new mammalian fossil in China that has a small dinosaur in its stomach. This fossil is a fact—clear evidence that some early mammals were able to prey upon dinosaurs, at least little ones. And it is just one of millions of fossils that support the fact that life has changed over time, the fact of evolution.

5   How did that change take place? That's exactly the question that evolutionary theory attempts to answer. Theories in science don't become facts—rather, theories explain facts. Evolutionary theory is a comprehensive explanation of change supported by the facts of natural history, genetics, and molecular biology.

6   Is evolution beyond dispute? Of course not. In fact, the most misleading part of the sticker was its concluding sentence: "This material should be approached with an open mind, studied carefully, and critically considered." Think about that. The sticker told students that there was just one subject in their textbooks that had to be approached with an open mind and critically considered. Apparently, we are certain of everything in biology except evolution. That is nonsense. What that sticker should have told students is what our textbook makes clear: *Everything* in science should be approached with critical thinking and an open mind.

7   The forces of anti-evolution will pretend that the sticker case is an example of censorship and that the sinister forces of science have converged on classrooms to prevent honest and open examination of a controversial idea.

8   There is great irony in such charges. As conservative icon Alan Bloom pointed out in his landmark book "The Closing of the American Mind," one of the worst forms of intellectual intolerance is to promote a false equivalence between competing ideas. Acting as though all ideas (or all theories) have equal standing actually deprives students of a realistic view of how critical analysis is done. That's as true in science as it is in the cultural conflicts.

9   Judge Cooper saw this point clearly: "While evolution is subject to criticism, particularly with respect to the mechanism by which it occurred, the sticker misleads students regarding the significance and value of evolution in the scientific community." Does it ever. In reality, evolution is a powerful and hard-working theory used at the cutting edge of scientific inquiry in developmental biology, genome analysis,

drug discovery, and scientific medicine. To pretend otherwise is to shield students from the reality of how science is done.

10   What the removal of the sticker will do is not to close a window but to open one that will let students see a science of biology in which all theories, not just one, are the result of constant, vigorous, critical analysis. A science in which evolution is at the centerpiece of a 21st-century revolution in our understanding of the grandeur and majesty of life.

11   So, what should be done with those stickers, now pasted into thousands of textbooks? I'd pass along a suggestion I received from a science teacher in Cobb County itself: Glue an American flag on top of each and every one of them.

QUESTIONS FOR ANALYSIS AND DISCUSSION ───────

1. In this article, the author describes how a conservative school board challenged evolution by putting a sticker in biology textbooks. How much control should school boards have over what is taught in the classroom? Who should decide what is taught in public schools? What if a majority of parents, for example, object to evolution?

2. Miller explains that, despite the reasoned wording, the stickers placed in the Cobb County biology textbooks were really challenging evolution and supporting a religious viewpoint. Do you agree with his assessment? Explain.

3. What credentials does Miller bring to his argument? Does he adequately describe the opposing viewpoint?

4. Review paragraph 8 in which Miller paraphrases Alan Bloom. How does Bloom's comment support Miller's argument?

The Crusade Against Evolution
Evan Ratliff

The initial challenge against Darwinian evolutionary theory was made by "creationists" who support the idea that God created the planet and all life forms about 10,000 years ago. After creationism failed in the American classroom, a new challenger emerged, "Intelligent Design." This theory was first described in print by William Paley in 1802. Paley writes, "Every indication of contrivance, every manifestation of design, which existed in [a] watch, exists in the works of nature; with the difference, on the side of nature, of being greater or more, and that in a degree which exceeds all computation." So goes the idea of the master watchmaker—that our planet and the life that inhabits it is simply too complex a thing to have happened randomly. In the next essay, Evan Ratliff describes how ID is influencing school boards across the country. Do the ID advocates deserve a place at the table? Or are they just masking creationism with a new label?

Evan Ratliff is a contributing editor to *Wired* magazine. He is the coauthor of *Safe: The Race to Protect Ourselves in a Newly Dangerous World* (2005), a book on the science and technology of antiterrorism. A freelance journalist, his work has appeared in *The New Yorker*, *Outside*, *The New York Times Magazine*, and other publications. This article was published in the October 2004 issue of *Wired*.

BEFORE YOU READ

If you were a parent, would you want your child to be taught evolution? Would you want other theories or ideas, even religious ones, taught as well? Why or why not?

AS YOU READ

What is the difference between creationism and Intelligent Design theory? Are they the same thing? Different? Explain.

1   On a spring day two years ago, in a downtown Columbus auditorium, the Ohio State Board of Education took up the question of how to teach the theory of evolution in public schools. A panel of four experts—two who believe in evolution, two who question it—debated whether an antievolution theory known as intelligent design should be allowed into the classroom.

2   This is an issue, of course, that was supposed to have been settled long ago. But 140 years after Darwin published *On the Origin of Species*, 75 years after John Scopes taught natural selection to a biology class in Tennessee, and 15 years after the US Supreme Court ruled against a Louisiana law mandating equal time for creationism, the question of how to teach the theory of evolution was being reopened here in Ohio. The two-hour forum drew chanting protesters and a police escort for the school board members. Two scientists, biologist Ken Miller from Brown University and physicist Lawrence Krauss from Case Western Reserve University two hours north in Cleveland, defended evolution. On the other side of the dais were two representatives from the Discovery Institute in Seattle, the main sponsor and promoter of intelligent design: Stephen Meyer, a professor at Palm Beach Atlantic University's School of Ministry and director of the Discovery Institute's Center for Science and Culture, and Jonathan Wells, a biologist, Discovery fellow, and author of *Icons of Evolution*, a 2000 book castigating textbook treatments of evolution. Krauss and Miller methodically presented their case against ID. "By no definition of any modern scientist is intelligent design science," Krauss concluded, "and it's a waste of our students' time to subject them to it."

3   Meyer and Wells took the typical intelligent design line: Biological life contains elements so complex—the mammalian blood-clotting mechanism, the bacterial flagellum—that they cannot be explained by natural selection. And so, the theory goes, we must be products of an intelligent designer. Creationists call that creator God, but proponents of intelligent design studiously avoid the G-word—and never point to the Bible for answers. Instead, ID believers speak the language of science to argue that Darwinian evolution is crumbling.

4   The debate's two-on-two format, with its appearance of equal sides, played right into the ID strategy—create the impression that this very complicated issue could be seen from two entirely rational yet opposing views. "This is a controversial subject," Meyer told the audience. "When two groups of experts disagree about a controversial subject that intersects with the public-school science curriculum, the students should be permitted to learn about both perspectives. We call this the 'teach the controversy' approach."

5   Since the debate, "teach the controversy" has become the rallying cry of the national intelligent-design movement, and Ohio has become the leading battle-ground. Several months after the debate, the Ohio school board voted to change state science standards, mandating that biology teachers "critically analyze" evolutionary theory. This fall, teachers will adjust their lesson plans and begin doing just that. In some cases, that means introducing the basic tenets of intelligent design. One of the state's sample lessons looks as though it were lifted from an ID textbook. It's the biggest victory so far for the Discovery Institute. "Our opponents would say that these are a bunch of know-nothing people on a state board," says Meyer. "We think it shows that our Darwinist colleagues have a real problem now."

6   But scientists aren't buying it. What Meyer calls "biology for the information age," they call creationism in a lab coat. ID's core scientific principles—laid out in the mid-1990s by a biochemist and a mathematician—have been thoroughly dismissed on the grounds that Darwin's theories can account for complexity, that ID relies on misunderstandings of evolution and flimsy probability calculations, and that it proposes no testable explanations.

7   As the Ohio debate revealed, however, the Discovery Institute doesn't need the favor of the scientific establishment to prevail in the public arena. Over the past decade, Discovery has gained ground in schools, op-ed pages, talk radio, and congressional resolutions as a "legitimate" alternative to evolution. ID is playing a central role in biology curricula and textbook controversies around the country. The institute and its supporters have taken the "teach the controversy" message to Alabama, Arizona, Minnesota, Missouri, Montana, New Mexico, and Texas.

8   The ID movement's rhetorical strategy—better to appear scientific than holy—has turned the evolution debate upside down. ID proponents quote Darwin, cite the Scopes monkey trial, talk of "scientific objectivity," then in the same breath declare that extraterrestrials might have designed life on Earth. It may seem counterintuitive, but the strategy is meticulously premeditated, and it's working as planned. The debate over Darwin is back, and coming to a 10th-grade biology class near you.

9   At its heart, intelligent design is a revival of an argument made by British philosopher William Paley in 1802. In *Natural Theology*, the Anglican archdeacon suggested that the complexity of biological structures defied any explanation but a designer: God. Paley imagined finding a stone and a watch in a field. The watch, unlike the stone, appears to have been purposely assembled and wouldn't function without its precise combination of parts. "The inference," he wrote, "is inevitable, that the watch must have a maker." The same logic, he concluded, applied to biological structures like the vertebrate eye. Its complexity implied design.

10   Fifty years later, Darwin directly answered Paley's "argument to complexity." Evolution by natural selection, he argued in *Origin of Species*, could create the appearance of design. Darwin—and 100-plus years of evolutionary science after him—seemed to knock Paley into the dustbin of history.

11   In the American public arena, Paley's design argument has long been supplanted by biblical creationism. In the 1970s and 1980s, that movement recast the Bible version in the language of scientific inquiry—as "creation science"—and won legislative victories requiring "equal time" in some states. That is, until 1987, when the Supreme Court struck down Louisiana's law. Because creation science relies on biblical texts, the court reasoned, it "lacked a clear secular purpose" and violated the First Amendment clause prohibiting the establishment of religion. Since then, evolution has been the law of the land in US schools—if not always the local choice.

12   Paley re-emerged in the mid-1990s, however, when a pair of scientists reconstituted his ideas in an area beyond Darwin's ken: molecular biology. In his 1996 book *Darwin's Black Box*, Lehigh University biochemist Michael Behe contended that natural selection can't explain the "irreducible complexity" of molecular mechanisms like the bacterial flagellum, because its integrated parts offer no selective advantages on their own. Two years later, in *The Design Inference*, William Dembski, a philosopher and mathematician at Baylor University, proposed that any biological system exhibiting "information" that is both "complex" (highly improbable) and "specified" (serving a particular function) cannot be a product of chance or natural law. The only remaining option is an intelligent designer—whether God or an alien life force. These ideas became the cornerstones of ID, and Behe proclaimed the evidence for design to be "one of the greatest achievements in the history of science."

13   The scientific rationale behind intelligent design was being developed just as antievolution sentiment seemed to be bubbling up. In 1991, UC Berkeley law professor Phillip Johnson published *Darwin On Trial*, an influential antievolution book that dispensed with biblical creation accounts while uniting antievolutionists under a single, secular-sounding banner: intelligent design. In subsequent books, Johnson presents not just antievolution arguments but a broader opposition to the "philosophy of scientific materialism"—the assumption (known to scientists as "methodological materialism") that all events have material, rather than supernatural, explanations. To defeat it, he offers a strategy that would be familiar in the divisive world of politics, called "the wedge." Like a wedge inserted into a tree trunk, cracks in Darwinian theory can be used to "split the trunk," eventually overturning scientific materialism itself.

14   That's where Discovery comes in. The institute was founded as a conservative think tank in 1990 by longtime friends and former Harvard roommates Bruce Chapman—director of the census bureau during the Reagan administration—and technofuturist author George Gilder. "The institute is futurist and rebellious, and it's prophetic," says Gilder. "It has a science and technology orientation in a contrarian spirit." In 1994, Discovery added ID to its list of contrarian causes, which included everything from transportation to bioethics. Chapman hired Meyer, who studied origin-of-life issues at Cambridge University, and the institute signed

Johnson—whom Chapman calls "the real godfather of the intelligent design movement"—as an adviser and adopted the wedge.

15   For Discovery, the "thin end" of the wedge—according to a fundraising document leaked on the Web in 1999—is the scientific work of Johnson, Behe, Dembski, and others. The next step involves "publicity and opinion-making." The final goals: "a direct confrontation with the advocates of material science" and "possible legal assistance in response to integration of design theory into public school science curricula."

16   Step one has made almost no headway with evolutionists—the near-universal majority of scientists with an opinion on the matter. But that, say Discovery's critics, is not the goal. "Ultimately, they have an evangelical Christian message that they want to push," says Michael Ruse, a philosopher of science at Florida State. "Intelligent design is the hook."

17   It's a lot easier to skip straight to steps two and three, and sound scientific in a public forum, than to deal with the rigor of the scientific community. "It starts with education," Johnson told me, referring to high school curricula. "That's where the public can have a voice. The universities and the scientific world do not recognize freedom of expression on this issue." Meanwhile, like any champion of a heretical scientific idea, ID's supporters see themselves as renegades, storming the gates of orthodoxy. "We all have a deep sense of indignation," says Meyer, "that the wool is being pulled over the public's eyes."

18   The buzz phrase most often heard in the institute's offices is *academic freedom.* "My hackles go up on the academic freedom issue," Chapman says. "You should be allowed in the sciences to ask questions and posit alternative theories."

19   None of this impresses the majority of the science world. "They have not been able to convince even a tiny amount of the scientific community," says Ken Miller. "They have not been able to win the marketplace of ideas."

20   And yet, the Discovery Institute's appeals to academic freedom create a kind of catch-22. If scientists ignore the ID movement, their silence is offered as further evidence of a conspiracy. If they join in, they risk reinforcing the perception of a battle between equal sides. Most scientists choose to remain silent. "Where the scientific community has been at fault," says Krauss, "is in assuming that these people are harmless, like flat-earthers. They don't realize that they are well organized, and that they have a political agenda."

21   Taped to the wall of Eugenie Scott's windowless office at the National Center for Science Education on the outskirts of Oakland, California, is a chart titled "Current Flare-Ups." It's a list of places where the teaching of evolution is under attack, from California to Georgia to Rio de Janeiro. As director of the center, which defends evolution in teaching controversies around the country, Scott has watched creationism up close for 30 years. ID, in her view, is the most highly evolved form of creationism to date. "They've been enormously effective compared to the more traditional creationists, who have greater numbers and much larger budgets," she says.

22   Scott credits the blueprint laid out by Johnson, who realized that to win in the court of public opinion, ID needed only to cast reasonable doubt on evolution. "He said, 'Don't get involved in details, don't get involved in fact claims,'" says Scott.

"'Forget about the age of Earth, forget about the flood, don't mention the Bible.'"
The goal, she says, is "to focus on the big idea that evolution is inadequate. Intelligent design doesn't really explain anything. It says that evolution can't explain things. Everything else is hand-waving."

23   The movement's first test of Johnson's strategies began in 1999, when the Kansas Board of Education voted to remove evolution from the state's science standards. The decision, backed by traditional creationists, touched off a fiery debate, and the board eventually reversed itself after several antievolution members lost reelection bids. ID proponents used the melee as cover to launch their own initiative. A Kansas group called IDNet nearly pushed through its own textbook in a local school district.

24   Two years later, the Discovery Institute earned its first major political victory when US senator Rick Santorum (R-Pennsylvania) inserted language written by Johnson into the federal No Child Left Behind Act. The clause, eventually cut from the bill and placed in a nonbinding report, called for school curricula to "help students understand the full range of scientific views" on topics "that may generate controversy (such as biological evolution)."

25   As the institute was demonstrating its Beltway clout, a pro-ID group called Science Excellence for All Ohioans fueled a brewing local controversy. SEAO—consisting of a few part-time activists, a Web site, and a mailing list—began agitating to have ID inserted into Ohio's 10th-grade-biology standards. In the process, they attracted the attention of a few receptive school board members.

26   When the board proposed the two-on-two debate and invited Discovery, Meyer and company jumped at the opportunity. Meyer, whom Gilder calls the institute's resident "polymath," came armed with the Santorum amendment, which he read aloud for the school board. He was bringing a message from Washington: Teach the controversy. "We framed the issue quite differently than our supporters," says Meyer. The approach put pro-ID Ohioans on firmer rhetorical ground: Evolution should of course be taught, but "objectively." Hearing Meyer's suggestion, says Doug Rudy, a software engineer and SEAO's director, "we all sat back and said, Yeah, that's the way to go."

27   Back in Seattle, around the corner from the Discovery Institute, Meyer offers some peer-reviewed evidence that there truly is a controversy that must be taught. "The Darwinists are bluffing," he says over a plate of oysters at a downtown seafood restaurant. "They have the science of the steam engine era, and it's not keeping up with the biology of the information age."

28   Meyer hands me a recent issue of *Microbiology and Molecular Biology Reviews* with an article by Carl Woese, an eminent microbiologist at the University of Illinois. In it, Woese decries the failure of reductionist biology—the tendency to look at systems as merely the sum of their parts—to keep up with the developments of molecular biology. Meyer says the conclusion of Woese's argument is that the Darwinian emperor has no clothes.

29   It's a page out of the antievolution playbook: using evolutionary biology's own literature against it, selectively quoting from the likes of Stephen Jay Gould to illustrate natural selection's downfalls. The institute marshals journal articles discussing

evolution to provide policymakers with evidence of the raging controversy surrounding the issue.

30   Woese scoffs at Meyer's claim when I call to ask him about the paper. "To say that my criticism of Darwinists says that evolutionists have no clothes," Woese says, "is like saying that Einstein is criticizing Newton, therefore Newtonian physics is wrong." Debates about evolution's mechanisms, he continues, don't amount to challenges to the theory. And intelligent design "is not science. It makes no predictions and doesn't offer any explanation whatsoever, except for 'God did it.'"

31   Of course Meyer happily acknowledges that Woese is an ardent evolutionist. The institute doesn't need to impress Woese or his peers; it can simply co-opt the vocabulary of science—"academic freedom," "scientific objectivity," "teach the controversy"—and redirect it to a public trying to reconcile what appear to be two contradictory scientific views. By appealing to a sense of fairness, ID finds a place at the political table, and by merely entering the debate it can claim victory. "We don't need to win every argument to be a success," Meyer says. "We're trying to validate a discussion that's been long suppressed."

32   This is precisely what happened in Ohio. "I'm not a PhD in biology," says board member Michael Cochran. "But when I have X number of PhD experts telling me this, and X number telling me the opposite, the answer is probably somewhere between the two."

33   An exasperated Krauss claims that a truly representative debate would have had 10,000 pro-evolution scientists against two Discovery executives. "What these people want is for there to *be* a debate," says Krauss. "People in the audience say, Hey, these people sound reasonable. They argue, 'People have different opinions, we should present those opinions in school.' That is nonsense. Some people have opinions that the Holocaust never happened, but we don't teach that in history."

34   Eventually, the Ohio board approved a standard mandating that students learn to "describe how scientists continue to investigate and critically analyze aspects of evolutionary theory." Proclaiming victory, Johnson barnstormed Ohio churches soon after notifying congregations of a new, ID-friendly standard. In response, anxious board members added a clause stating that the standard "does not mandate the teaching or testing of intelligent design." Both sides claimed victory. A press release from IDNet trumpeted the mere inclusion of the phrase *intelligent design*, saying that "the implication of the statement is that the 'teaching or testing of intelligent design' is permitted." Some pro-evolution scientists, meanwhile, say there's nothing wrong with teaching students how to scrutinize theory. "I don't have a problem with that," says Patricia Princehouse, a professor at Case Western Reserve and an outspoken opponent of ID. "Critical analysis is exactly what scientists do."

35   The good feelings didn't last long. Early this year, a board-appointed committee unveiled sample lessons that laid out the kind of evolution questions students should debate. The models appeared to lift their examples from Wells' book *Icons of Evolution*. "When I first saw it, I was speechless," says Princehouse.

36   With a PhD in molecular and cell biology from UC Berkeley, Wells has the kind of cred that intelligent design proponents love to cite. But, as ID opponents enjoy pointing out, he's also a follower of Sun Myung Moon and once declared that

Moon's prayers "convinced me that I should devote my life to destroying Darwinism." *Icons* attempts to discredit commonly used examples of evolution, like Darwin's finches and peppered moths. Writing in *Nature*, evolutionary biologist Jerry Coyne called *Icons* stealth creationism that "strives to debunk Darwinism using the familiar rhetoric of biblical creationists, including scientific quotations out of context, incomplete summaries of research, and muddled arguments."

37 　　After months of uproar, the most obvious *Icons*-inspired lessons were removed. But scientists remain furious. "The ones they left in are still arguments for special creation—but you'd have to know the literature to understand what they are saying. They've used so much technical jargon that anybody who doesn't know a whole lot of evolutionary biology looks at it and says 'It sounds scientific to me, what's the matter with it?'" says Princehouse. "As a friend of mine said, it takes a half a second for a baby to throw up all over your sweater. It takes hours to get it clean."

38 　　As Ohio teachers prepare their lessons for the coming year, the question must be asked: Why the fuss over an optional lesson plan or two? After all, both sides agree that the new biology standards—in which 10 evolution lessons replace standards that failed to mention evolution at all—are a vast improvement. The answer: In an era when the government is pouring billions into biology, and when stem cells and genetically modified food are front-page news, spending even a small part of the curriculum on bogus criticisms of evolution is arguably more detrimental now than any time in history. Ironically, says Ohio State University biology professor Steve Rissing, the education debate coincides with Ohio's efforts to lure biotech companies. "How can we do that when our high school biology is failing us?" he says. "Our cornfields are gleaming with GMO corn. There's a fundamental disconnect there."

39 　　Intelligent design advocates say that teaching students to "critically analyze" evolution will help give them the skills to "see both sides" of all scientific issues. And if the Discovery Institute execs have their way, those skills will be used to reconsider the philosophy of modern science itself—which they blame for everything from divorce to abortion to the insanity defense. "Our culture has been deeply influenced by materialist thought," says Meyer. "We think it's deeply destructive, and we think it's false. And we mean to overturn it."

40 　　It's mid-July, and the Ohio school board is about to hold its final meeting before classes start this year. There's nothing about intelligent design on the agenda. The debate was settled months ago. And yet, Princehouse, Rissing, and two other scientists rise to speak during the "non-agenda" public testimony portion.

41 　　One by one, the scientists recite their litany of objections: The model lesson plan is still based on concepts from ID literature; the ACLU is considering to sue to stop it; the National Academy of Sciences opposes it as unscientific. "This is my last time," says Rissing, "as someone who has studied science and the process of evolution for 25 years, to say I perceive that my children and I are suffering injuries based on a flawed lesson plan that this board has passed."

42 　　During a heated question-and-answer session, one board member accuses the scientists of posturing for me, the only reporter in the audience. Michael Cochran challenges the scientists to cite any testimony that the board hadn't already heard

"ad infinitum." Another board member, Deborah Owens-Fink, declares the issue already closed. "We've listened to experts on both sides of this for three years," she says. "Ultimately, the question of what students should learn is decided in a democracy, not by any one group of experts."

43   The notion is noble enough: In a democracy, every idea gets heard. But in science, not all theories are equal. Those that survive decades—centuries—of scientific scrutiny end up in classrooms, and those that don't are discarded. The intelligent design movement is using scientific rhetoric to bypass scientific scrutiny. And when science education is decided by charm and stage presence, the Discovery Institute wins.

QUESTIONS FOR ANALYSIS AND DISCUSSION

1. According to Ratliff, how do ID believers "speak the language of science" to argue against Darwin? Why does he feel that this language is fundamentally flawed?
2. In paragraph 12, William Dembski is paraphrased: "any biological system exhibiting 'information' that is both 'complex' (highly improbable) and 'specified' (serving a particular function) cannot be a product of chance or natural law. The only remaining option is an intelligent designer." Drawing from the rhetorical chapters in this textbook describing the nuances of arguments, evaluate the validity and logic of his position.
3. What is the author's opinion on the evolution debate? Identify phrases and words that reveal his position on the issue.
4. Why are biologists "exasperated" by the willingness of school boards to allow ID to be taught in the classroom? What was decided by the Ohio board? Why did "both sides" claim victory? In your opinion, was one side more victorious?
5. Ratliff concludes his essay with the statement, "in a democracy, every idea gets heard. But in science, not all theories are equal." Respond to his conclusion with your own opinion.

BLOG IT

Evolution Beats Intelligent Design in Florida
Posted by Brandon Keim
December 27, 2007

http://blog.wired.com/wiredscience/2007/12/evolution-beats.html

Members of a Florida county school board who last month wanted a classroom balance between evolution with intelligent design have quietly reversed their positions.

Shortly before Thanksgiving, four members of the Polk County School Board said they didn't support Florida's proposed science education guidelines, which designate evolution as a fundamental concept that every student should understand.

Wired Science covered the controversy, which came hot on the heels of a Texas education official's firing for telling people about a lecture critical of intelligent design. A new battle appeared to have broken out between proponents of evolution—the scientifically observed and accepted explanation for the development of life on Earth—and intelligent design, a religiously-inspired account of life's origins as being too complicated and coincidental to be explained by anything but divine intervention.

Barely a month later, reports the *Tampa Tribune*, "the controversy is dying with a whimper," with school board officials insisting that their personal belief in intelligent design shouldn't be taught to kids as science.

What happened? You can start with the Church of the Flying Spaghetti Monster [http://www.venganza.org]. The satirical religious Web site asserts that an omnipotent, airborne clump of spaghetti intelligently designed all life with the deft touch of its "noodly appendage." Adherents call themselves Pastafarians. They deluged Polk school board members with e-mail demanding equal time for Flying Spaghetti Monsterism's version of intelligent design.

"They've made us the laughingstock of the world," said Margaret Lofton, a school board member who supports intelligent design. She dismissed the e-mail as ridiculous and insulting.

The *Tribune* also credits attention generated by science bloggers, who took a locally reported story and made it national. And make no mistake—this was, and is, a national story. If evolution and intelligent design were forced to share classroom credibility in Florida, it would be that much easier for a similarly diluted curriculum to pass in Texas, which is embarking on its own curricula revisions.

If Texas wanted scientifically bankrupt textbooks, then textbook manufacturers would provide them—and other states would buy them, too.

So chalk one up for science, and remember: just because you believe in God doesn't mean you can't believe in evolution.

YOU SAY:

Add your own opinion. You may wish to review the letter mentioned in Keim's posting at http://www.venganza.org.

Does Darwinism Devalue Human Life?

Richard Weikart

In the next essay, Richard Weikart describes how Darwinism has been used by some intellectuals, politicians, and even students to question objective morality and justify abortion, euthanasia, infanticide, and genocide. Can one hold the principles of Darwin as valid and still value human life?

Weikart is a professor of history at California State University, Stanislaus. He is the author of *From Darwin to Hitler: Evolutionary Ethics, Eugenics and Racism in Germany* (2004). This article, based on one of Weikart's lectures, first appeared in *The Human Life Review* in the Spring 2004 issue.

BEFORE YOU READ ───────────────────────────

When scientists refer to Darwinism, what do they mean? Define the term in your own words. After you finish reading this essay, review your definition and compare it with the one put forth by the author.

AS YOU READ ──────────────────────────────

Can human beings behold an objective morality without the constructs of religious belief? Can you live by a code of ethics that exists outside of religious principles? Why or why not?

1   A number of years ago two intelligent students surprised me in a class discussion by defending the proposition that Hitler was neither good nor evil. Though I kept my composure, I was horrified. One of the worst mass murderers in history wasn't evil? How could they believe this? How could they justify such a view?

2   They did it by appealing to Darwinism. Their pronouncement on Hitler occurred while we were discussing James Rachels' book, *Created from Animals: The Moral Implications of Darwinism* (Oxford University Press, 1990). Darwinism, these students informed us, undermined all morality. This was not the first time I had heard such a view. In fact, at that time I was in the beginning phases of a research project on the history of evolutionary ethics, and I had already reviewed the work of some scientists and social scientists who believed that Darwinism undermined human rights and equality.

3   Before reading Rachels' book, however, I hadn't thought much about whether or not Darwinism devalued human life itself. Rachels, a philosopher at the University of Alabama, Birmingham, best known for his contributions to the euthanasia debate, argues that Darwinism undermines the Judeo-Christian belief in the sanctity of human life. The title of his book comes from an observation Darwin makes in his 1838 notebooks, "Man in his arrogance thinks himself a great work, worthy of the interposition of a deity. More humble and, I believe, true to consider him created

from animals." Rachels assumes the truth of Darwinism and uses it as a springboard to justify euthanasia, infanticide (for disabled babies), abortion, and animal rights. Stimulated by his book, I continued my research on evolutionary ethics, but now with two new questions in mind: Does Darwinism undermine the Judeo-Christian under-standing of the sanctity of human life? Does it weaken traditional proscriptions against killing the sick and the weak?

4   As I read more about the development of evolutionary ethics, I discovered that many scientists, social thinkers, and especially physicians in late nineteenth and early twentieth-century Germany did indeed use Darwinian arguments to devalue human life. In the second edition of his popular book, *The Natural History of Creation* (1870), Ernst Haeckel, the leading Darwinist in Germany, became the first German scholar to seriously propose that disabled infants be killed at birth. Darwin-ists were in the forefront of the eugenics movement, which often taught that disabled people and non-Europeans were inferior to healthy Europeans. They argued that Darwinism implied human inequality, since biological variation has to occur to drive the process of evolution. Haeckel even suggested that Darwinism was an "aristo-cratic" process, favoring an aristocracy of talent (not the traditional landed aristoc-racy, for which Haeckel had no sympathy). Since Darwinism provided a naturalistic explanation for the origin of ethics, many of its adherents dismissed human rights as a chimera.

5   Darwin expressed incredulity when critics assailed him for undermining moral-ity. In his *Autobiography*, however, Darwin rejected the idea of objective moral stan-dards, stating that one "can have for his rule of life, as far as I can see, only to follow those impulses and instincts which are the strongest or which seem to him the best ones."[1] Friedrich Hellwald, an influential ethnologist, promoted a Darwinian view of social evolution in his major work, *The History of Culture* (1875). Hellwald was quite radical in exalting the Darwinian process of the struggle for existence above all moral considerations. "The right of the stronger," he insisted, "is a natural law."[2] He clari-fied this idea further:

> In nature only One Right rules, which is no right, the right of the stronger, or violence. But violence is also in fact the highest source of right, in that without it no legislation is thinkable. I will in the course of my portrayal easily prove that even in human history the right of the stronger has fundamentally retained its validity at all times.[3]

This Darwinian undermining of human rights would be fateful for the Judeo-Christian vision of the sanctity of human life.

6   Besides stressing human inequality, Haeckel and many of his fellow Darwinists devalued human life by criticizing Judeo-Christian conceptions of humanity as "anthropocentric." Rather than being created in the image of God, they argued, humans were descended from simian ancestors. They blurred the distinctions be-tween humans and animals, alleging that characteristics that had been traditionally considered uniquely human—rationality, morality, religion, etc.—were also present in animals to some degree. In Darwin's own words, the difference between humans and animals is quantitative, not qualitative.

7   Darwin's explanation that all human characteristics that previously had been associated with the human soul were not qualitatively distinct from animals also undermined the traditional Judeo-Christian conception of body-soul dualism, which endued humans with greater moral and spiritual significance than other organisms.[4] Many Darwinists understood the implications of this, including Haeckel, who founded the Monist League in 1906 specifically to combat all dualistic religions and philosophies, especially Christianity (but also Kantianism). One prominent member of the Monist League, August Forel, a world famous psychiatrist at the University of Zurich, described his initial encounter with Darwinism as a kind of conversion experience. He explained that Darwinism had convinced him that body-soul dualism was no longer tenable and that humans have no free will. Based on his view that heredity accounts for almost all character traits (and most mental illness), Forel became one of the most influential figures in the German eugenics movement, preaching the need to eliminate "inferior" races and handicapped infants, and recruiting Alfred Ploetz, who founded the world's first eugenics organization and journal.

8   Another element of Darwinism that contributed to the devaluing of human life was its stress on the struggle for existence. Based on the Malthusian population principle, Darwin pointed out that offspring are produced at much higher levels than can survive. Therefore multitudes necessarily perish in the struggle for existence. While Malthus saw this tendency toward overpopulation as the cause of misery and poverty, Darwin explained that it was really beneficial. In the conclusion of *The Origin of Species*, Darwin wrote, "Thus, from the war of nature, from famine and death, the most exalted object which we are capable of conceiving, namely, the production of the higher animals, directly follows."[5] For Darwin death—even mass death—was not only inevitable, necessary. As Adrian Desmond explained in his biography of T. H. Huxley (the foremost Darwinian biologist in late nineteenth-century Britain, who earned the nickname, "Darwin's bulldog"), "only from death on a genocidal scale could the few progress."[6] Hellwald expressed the same idea in *The History of Culture*, claiming that evolutionary progress would occur as the "fitter" humans "stride across the corpses of the vanquished; that is natural law."[7]

9   Indeed, many leading Darwinists in the late nineteenth and early twentieth centuries claimed that in order to foster evolutionary progress, the less valuable elements of humanity, generally defined as the disabled and those of non-European races, had to be eliminated. They feared that Judeo-Christian and humanitarian ethics, together with the advances of modern civilization—especially medicine and hygiene—would produce biological degeneration, since the weak and sick would be allowed to reproduce. Though many focused on methods to restrict reproduction, a surprising number of leading Darwinists—and not only Haeckel and Forel—actually promoted killing the "unfit" as a means to bring biological progress. Racial extermination and infanticide were integral components of their Darwinian program for biological rejuvenation.

10   In retrospect, the connection between these Darwinian ideas and Hitler's ideology are obvious. Interestingly, however, when I began my research on evolutionary ethics, Hitler was not even on my radar screen. I was wary of connecting Darwin and Hitler because of Daniel Gasman's failed attempt to draw a direct

line from Haeckel to Hitler in *The Scientific Origins of National Socialism*, a book with which most historians rightly find fault. However, the title of my book— *From Darwin to Hitler: Evolutionary Ethics, Eugenics, and Racism in Germany* (Palgrave Macmillan, 2004)—indicates that I made the connection nonetheless, though in quite a different manner from Gasman. Indeed, the more I studied books and articles on evolutionary ethics by German scientists, physicians, and social thinkers, the more I discovered that I could not avoid the parallels between German Darwinist discourse and Hitler's ideology. This should not come as a complete surprise, however, since just about all of Hitler's biographers have noted the strong social Darwinist elements in his ideology, as Ian Kershaw does recently in his magisterial two-volume biography.

11   Hitler was strongly influenced by the Darwinian ideology of the eugenics movement, and his writings and speeches clearly reflect it. In *Mein Kampf* Hitler asserted that his philosophy by no means believes in the equality of races, but recognizes along with their differences their higher or lower value, and through this knowledge feels obliged, according to the eternal will that rules this universe, to promote the victory of the better, the stronger, and to demand the submission of the worse and weaker. It embraces thereby in principle the aristocratic law of nature and believes in the validity of this law down to the last individual being. It recognizes not only the different value of races, but also the different value of individuals. But by no means can it approve of the right of an ethical idea existing, if this idea is a danger for the racial life of the bearer of a higher ethic.[8]

12   Thus Hitler justified his racial views by appealing to Darwinian science. Because Hitler's racial views were so obviously flawed, some scholars call Hitler's views pseudo-scientific or a "vulgar" form of Darwinism. However, this is to judge Hitler by later standards of scientific thought. Many leading scientists and physicians embraced eugenics and scientific racism in Hitler's day, and indeed Fritz Lenz, the first professor of eugenics at a German university, crowed in 1933 that he had formulated the essentials of Nazi ideology even before Hitler began his political career.

13   Hitler's genocidal program was not the only adverse consequence of Darwinism's devaluing of human life, and Germany was not the only country impacted. Much work on the history of the eugenics movement in the United States, Britain, and elsewhere suggests that scientific and medical elites in many parts of the world imbibed the Darwinian devaluing of human life. Though it did not lead to genocide in these countries, it did lead to other injustices, such as the compulsory sterilization of thousands of people classified as "less fit," based on their hereditary condition (sometimes based on very tenuous evidence, leading to many cases of misdiagnosis). Social Darwinist and eugenics ideology also played an important role in the budding movement to legalize abortion in the early twentieth century.

14   Further, recent confirmation of my findings about the Darwinian devaluing of human life have come from Ian Dowbiggin's and Nick Kemp's important new studies on the history of the euthanasia movements in the United States and Britain, respectively. Both emphasize the role of Darwinism in paving the way ideologically for euthanasia. According to Dowbiggin, "The most pivotal turning point in the

early history of the euthanasia movement was the coming of Darwinism to America."[9] This held true in Britain, as well, for Kemp informs us: "While we should be wary of depicting Darwin as the man responsible for ushering in a secular age we should be similarly cautious of underestimating the importance of evolutionary thought in relation to the questioning of the sanctity of human life."[10] The worldview of most early euthanasia advocates was saturated with Darwinian ideology, and they forthrightly used Darwinian ideas to combat the Judeo-Christian concept of the sanctity of human life.

15   Thus, historical evidence from the late nineteenth and early twentieth centuries overwhelmingly supports the thesis that Darwinism devalued human life. Whatever one thinks philosophically about this issue—and, of course, some Darwinists are embarrassed by the link and try to deny it—historically Darwinism has contributed to a devaluing of human life, thereby providing impetus for euthanasia, infanticide, and abortion.

16   The question now emerges: Is this all just of historical interest? Haven't we learned a lesson from Nazism not to use social Darwinism to devalue humans? Haven't we abandoned biological racism and rabid anti-Semitism, integral components of Nazi ideology?

17   Yes, indeed, we have learned much from the Nazi past, and I don't think it is fair to compare our present situation with Nazi Germany, as though they are completely the same. We don't live in a murderous dictatorship, and racism is on the defensive, at least in academic circles. For this we can be thankful. Still, in some respects, I wonder if we have learned enough, especially when I see big-name Darwinists, evolutionary psychologists, and bioethicists using Darwinism today to undermine the sanctity of human life. Whether Darwinism does actually devalue human life or not, there are certainly many people who think it does, and they are not intellectual featherweights.

18   First of all, the position that Rachels stakes out on issues of life and death are strikingly similar to that of the Australian bioethicist, Peter Singer, whose appointment a few years ago to a chair in bioethics at Princeton University stirred up vigorous controversy. Singer is renowned—or notorious, depending on one's point of view—for promoting the legitimacy of infanticide for handicapped babies and voluntary euthanasia, as well as for defending animal rights. Darwinism plays a key role in Singer's philosophy, underpinning his views on life and death. Singer claims that Darwin "undermined the foundations of the entire Western way of thinking on the place of our species in the universe." It stripped humanity of the special status that Judeo-Christian thought had conferred upon it. Singer complains that even though Darwin "gave what ought to have been its final blow" to the "human-centred view of the universe," the view that humans are special and sacred has not yet vanished. Singer is now laboring to give the sanctity-of-life ethic its deathblow.[11]

19   Singer and Rachels are not the only prominent philosophers arguing that Darwinism undermines the sanctity of human life. In *Darwin's Dangerous Idea* the materialist philosopher Daniel Dennett argues that Darwinism functions like a "universal acid," destroying traditional forms of religion and morality. In confronting the issue of biomedical ethics, Dennett asks, "At what 'point' does a human life begin

or end? The Darwinian perspective lets us see with unmistakable clarity why there is no hope at all of discovering a telltale mark, a saltation in life's processes, that 'counts.'" Because of this, Dennett argues, there are "gradations of value in the ending of human lives," implying that some human lives have more value than others. After using his Darwinian acid to dissolve the sanctity-of-life ethic, Dennett wonders, "Which is worse, taking 'heroic' measures to keep alive a severely deformed infant, or taking the equally 'heroic' (if unsung) step of seeing to it that such an infant dies as quickly and painlessly as possible?" *Darwin's Dangerous Idea* is apparently especially toxic to disabled infants.[12]

20 　　The evolutionary psychologist Steven Pinker, a professor of psychology at Harvard University, also draws connections between Darwinism and infanticide. After some high-profile cases of infanticide occurred in 1997, Pinker wrote an article purporting to explain its evolutionary origins. Since Pinker believes "that nurturing an offspring that carries our genes is the whole point of our existence," of course he tries to explain infanticide as a behavior that somehow confers reproductive advantage. He argues that a "new mother will first coolly assess the infant and her current situation and only in the next few days begin to see it as a unique and wonderful individual." (This is outrageously speculative; no new mother I have ever met has "coolly assessed" her infant, and it seems to me that those who commit infanticide are not "coolly assessing" the survival prospects for their infant, either—more likely they are desperate.) According to Pinker, the mother's love for her infant will grow in relation to the "increasing biological value of a child (the chance that it will live to produce grandchildren)." Pinker specifically denies that infants have a "right to life," so, even though he doesn't completely condone infanticide, he thinks we should not be too harsh on mothers killing their children.[13] Pinker's view of infanticide is by no means unusual among evolutionary psychologists. In a leading textbook on evolutionary psychology, *Evolution and Human Behavior: Darwinian Perspectives on Human Nature* (2000), John Cartwright provides basically the same Darwinian explanation for infanticide as Pinker's.

21 　　What do Darwinian biologists have to say about all this? Some think Singer and company are on the right track. In 2001 Richard Dawkins, probably the most famous Darwinian biologist in the world today, made an impassioned plea for using genetic engineering to create an Australopithecine (whose fossil remains are allegedly an ancestor to the human species). Producing such a "missing link" would, according to Dawkins, provide "positive ethical benefits," since it would demolish the "double standard" of those guilty of "speciesism." Dawkins specifically claims that producing such an organism would demonstrate the poverty of the pro-life position, because it would show that humans are not different from animals. In the midst of this acerbic attack on the sanctity of human life, Dawkins expresses the hope that he will be euthanized if he is ever "past it," whatever that means (some people already think that Dawkins is "past it," but fortunately for Dawkins, I suspect that most of them still uphold the sanctity-of-life ethic that Dawkins rejects).[14]

22 　　Edward O. Wilson, the Pulitzer-Prize-winning pioneer of sociobiology and Harvard professor whose entire view of human nature revolves around Darwinism, also exemplifies this devaluing of human life, though he is more subtle about it.

In his book *Consilience* (1998) he argues that his empiricist world view "has destroyed the giddying theory that we are special beings placed by a deity in the center of the universe in order to serve as the summit of Creation for the glory of the gods." In one passage in his autobiography he compares humans to ants, informing us that we humans are too numerous on the globe, while ants are in a proper population balance. "If we were to vanish today," Wilson explains, "the land environment would return to the fertile balance that existed before the human population explosion." But if ants were to disappear, thousands of species would perish as a result. The implication seems to be: ants are more valuable than humans, and biodiversity takes precedence over human life.

23   Many biologists, of course, disagree with Singer and Dawkins. From the late nineteenth century to today they have assured us that Darwinism has no implications for morality. They allege that those trying to apply Darwinism to morality are committing the "naturalistic fallacy" by deriving "ought" from "is." Darwin's friend and defender, Thomas Henry Huxley, vigorously opposed the attempts of his contemporaries to seek ethical guidance in natural evolutionary processes. More recently, Steven Jay Gould often butted heads with evolutionary psychologists, arguing that morality was a separate realm from biology. In his view Darwinism has nothing to say about how humans should act.

24   Gould, however, did not really divorce science and morality as much as he claimed. While vociferously arguing that Darwinian science on the one hand and religion and morality on the other are "non-overlapping magisteria," separated as far as the east is from the west, he persisted in drawing conclusions from his Darwinian science that are suspiciously laden with religious and moral implications. In *Wonderful Life: The Burgess Shale and the Nature of History* (1989), the whole point of his book is to use the Burgess Shale—a fossil-laden outcropping of rock in Canada teeming with many extinct, ancient forms of life—as an example of the contingency of history, to demonstrate that there is no real purpose to human existence. "Wind back the tape of life to the early days of the Burgess Shale; let it play again from an identical starting point, and the chance becomes vanishingly small that anything like human intelligence would grace the replay." His view of the contingency of human creation in the evolutionary process clearly affects the way he views the nature and status of humanity, for he informs us that "biology shifted our status from a simulacrum of God to a naked, upright ape." The closing words of this book are remarkable for someone who claims to keep science and religion in non-overlapping compartments:

> And so, if you wish to ask the question of the ages—why do humans exist?—a major part of the answer, touching those aspects of the issue that science can treat at all, must be: because Pikaia [a Burgess shale chordate] survived the Burgess decimation. This response does not cite a single law of nature; it embodies no statement about predictable evolutionary pathways, no calculation of probabilities based on general rules of anatomy or ecology. The survival of Pikaia was a contingency of "just history." I do not think that any "higher" answer can be given, and I cannot imagine that any resolution could be more fascinating. We are the offspring of history, and must establish our own paths in

this most diverse and interesting of conceivable universes—one indifferent to our suffering, and therefore offering us maximal freedom to thrive, or to fail, in our own chosen way. [15]

25   Does Gould really think this conclusion has no religious or moral implications? Does he really believe that his claim that biology demotes humans from the image of God to a naked ape is a purely scientific statement that has no bearing on moral issues, such as abortion and euthanasia?

26   In light of all this, does Darwinism really devalue human life? I think I have shown conclusively that historically Darwinism has indeed devalued human life, leading to ideologies that promote the destruction of human lives deemed inferior to others. Those on the forefront in promoting abortion, infanticide, euthanasia, and racial extermination often overtly based their views on Darwinism. Also, as I have shown in this essay, those favoring a Darwinian dismantling of the sanctity-of-life ethic have a good deal of intellectual firepower, and the idea is becoming rather widespread in academic circles today. There are, of course, various religious and philosophical moves that one can make to evade these conclusions, and some Darwinists have in the past and will continue in the future vigorously to oppose such developments (for this we can be thankful), construing them as faulty extrapolations by overzealous Darwinian materialists. However, it seems to me that there is an inherent logic in the move by Darwinists to undermine the sanctity-of-life ethic, which makes it so alluring that I doubt it will ever disappear as long as Darwinism is ascendant. In any case, it is certainly safe to say that in modern society Darwinism has contributed mightily to the erosion of the sanctity-of-life ethic. Darwinism really is a matter of life and death.

NOTES

1. Charles Darwin, *Autobiography* (NY: Norton, 1969), 94.

2. Friedrich Hellwald, *Culturgeschichte in ihrer natürlichen Entwicklung bis zur Gegenwart* (Augsburg, 1875), quote at 27, see also 278, 569.

3. Ibid, 44-45.

4. On the connection between dualism and bioethics, see J. P. Moreland and Scott Rae, *Body and Soul: Human Nature and the Crisis in Ethics* (Downers Grove, IL, 2000).

5. Darwin, *The Origin of Species* (London: Penguin, 1968), 459.

6. Adrian Desmond, *Huxley: From Devil's Disciple to Evolution's High Priest* (Reading, MA, 1997), 271.

7. Hellwald, *Culturgeschichte in ihrer natürlichen Entwicklung*, 58, 27; "Der Kampf ums Dasein im Menschen- und Völkerleben," *Das Ausland* 45 (1872): 105.

8. Adolf Hitler, *Mein Kampf*, 2 vols. in 1 (Munich, 1943), 420-1. Emphasis is mine.

9. Ian Dowbiggin, *A Merciful End: The Euthanasia Movement in Modern America* (Oxford, 2003), 8.

10. N. D. A. Kemp, *'Merciful Release': The History of the British Euthanasia Movement* (Manchester, 2002), 19. For more information on Dowbiggin's and Kemp's works, see my review essay, "Killing Them Kindly: Lessons from the Euthanasia Movement," in *Books and Culture: A Christian* Review (Jan./Feb. 2004), 30-31.

11. Peter Singer, *Writings on an Ethical Life* (New York, 2000), 77-78, 220-21.

12. Daniel Dennett, *Darwin's Dangerous Idea: Evolution and the Meanings of Life* (NY, 1995), ch. 18.

13. Steven Pinker, "Why They Kill Their Newborns," *The New York Times Sunday Magazine* (November 2, 1997).

14. Richard Dawkins, "The Word Made Flesh," *The Guardian* (December 27, 2001).

15. Stephen Jay Gould, *Wonderful Life: The Burgess Shale and the Nature of History* (NY, 1989), quotes at 14, 323; for his views on the compartmentalization of science and religion, see "Nonoverlapping Magisteria," *Natural History* 106 (March 1997): 16-22.

QUESTIONS FOR ANALYSIS AND DISCUSSION

1. According to the Darwinian principles, why do the strong need to eliminate the weak? How does this argument extend to Hitler? Explain.

2. Aside from genocide, in what other ways, according to Weikart, does Darwinism devalue human life?

3. Weikart explains that Darwinism puts forth the idea that "some human lives have more value than others." Who, then, chooses which human life is more valuable, and how does one go about making such an assessment?

4. Weikart writes about the evolutionary psychologist Steven Pinker who thinks "we should not be too harsh on mothers killing their children." (See essay in Chapter 7.) What evidence does Pinker use to explain his assertion? How does Pinker's statement connect to the points Weikart makes regarding Darwinism? Explain.

5. Do you agree with evolutionary biologist Steven Jay Gould that morality is in a separate realm from biology? Why or why not?

A New Theology of Celebration
Francis S. Collins

In this editorial, a renowned biologist reflects on the current battle between atheists and fundamentalist Christians. On the one hand, many atheists claim that intelligent people must reject religion as unreasonable and illogical. On the other hand, fundamentalist religious groups are forcing believers to agree that the world is 10,000 years old and any other interpretation is a rejection of their religious faith. Collins, himself a religious convert, describes his vision for a new theology in which faith and science cooperate and happily co-exist. Is his vision nothing more than wishful thinking?

Francis S. Collins is a physician-geneticist who is most widely known for his leadership of the Human Genome Project that identified the genetic blueprint of Homo sapiens. Collins's commitment to providing free access to genomic information made the data immediately available to the scientific community, propelling research in many areas of science and medicine. He is the author of *The Language of God: A Scientist Presents Evidence for Belief* (2006) in which he explains why he considers scientific discoveries an "opportunity to worship." This editorial appeared in the September/October 2007 issue of *Science & Spirit* magazine.

BEFORE YOU READ ─────────────────────────────

Is religious faith and acceptance of science compatible? Why or why not?

AS YOU READ ─────────────────────────────

Consider how Collins frames his argument. How does he define and identify the issue and controversy? How does he persuade readers to understand his point of view?

1   have often been accused of being optimistic. In the early days of the Human
     Genome Project, some very wise people predicted that this audacious project
would end in failure. But as the leader of the effort from 1993 until its conclusion in
2003 (ahead of schedule and under budget, no less), I never doubted that the best
and brightest minds that were recruited to work on this historic project would prevail. And they did.

2   So my faith in the ability of science to answer questions about nature paid off.
But that is not the most important area where faith is part of my life. After spending
my young years as an atheist, I became convinced through reading the logical arguments of C.S. Lewis and the words of the Bible that belief in God was more plausible
than atheism. After two years of struggle, I became a Christian at age twenty-seven.
Since then, my faith in God has been the rock on which I stand, a means to answer
critical questions on which science remains silent: What is the meaning of life? Is
there a God? Do our concepts of right and wrong have any real foundation? What
happens after we die?

3   As one of a large number of scientists who believe in God, I find it deeply troubling to watch the escalating culture wars between science and faith, especially in
America. A spate of angry books by atheists, many of them using the compelling
evidence of Darwin's theory of evolution as a rhetorical club over the heads of
believers, argues that atheism is the only rational choice for a thinking person. Some
go so far as to label religious faith as the root of all evil and insinuate that parents
who teach their children about religion are committing child abuse.

4   Partially in response to these attacks, believers, especially evangelical Christians,
have targeted evolution as godless and incompatible with the truths of the Bible.
Many Americans see Earth as less than 10,000 years old, a "young Earth" belief that
clashes with mountains of data from cosmology, physics, chemistry, geology, paleon-
tology, anthropology, biology, and genetics. Intelligent Design, which proposes that
evolution is insufficient to account for complexity, enjoys wide support in the church
despite rejection in the scientific community.

5   What a sad situation. Are we not all seeking the truth? That is what God calls us
to. It seems unlikely that God, the author of all creation, is threatened by what science is teaching us about the awesome complexity and grandeur of His creation.
Can God be well served by lies about nature, no matter how noble the intentions of
those who spread them?

6 The current circumstance is not tenable over the long run. Despite their claims to hard-nosed objectivity, atheists have gone wildly outside the evidence by declaring God imaginary. They are proposing an impoverished perspective that will not satisfy most of their intended converts. For their part, fundamentalists who demand acceptance of a unilateral interpretation of Genesis are making that a litmus test for true faith, which wise theologians over the centuries have not found necessary.

7 Could we not step back from the unloving rhetoric of these entrenched positions and seek a path towards truth? If science is a way of uncovering the details of God's creation, then it may actually be a form of worship. Did not God, in giving us the intelligence to ask and answer questions about nature, expect us to use it? We should be able to learn about God in the laboratory as well as in the cathedral.

8 The shrill voices at the extremes of this debate have had the microphone for too long. Although they will no doubt continue to rail against each other, the rest of us should find ways to bring together scientists who are open to spiritual truths, theologians who are ready to embrace scientific findings about the universe, and pastors who know the real concerns and needs of their flocks. Together, in a loving and worshipful attitude, we could formulate a new and wondrous natural theology. This kind of theology celebrates God as the creator, embraces His majestic universe from the far-flung galaxies to the "fearfully and wonderfully made" nature of humanity, and accepts and incorporates the marvelous things that God has given us the chance to discover through science.

9 If we make a serious and prayerful attempt to do this together, perhaps in a few years this new "celebration theology" could eliminate the conflict between science and faith. God didn't start the conflict. We did. I may sound unrealistic, even a bit of a Pollyanna, by proposing that we could draw this unnecessary battle to a close. But, I remind you, I have often been accused of being optimistic.

QUESTIONS FOR ANALYSIS AND DISCUSSION

1. Why does Collins open his editorial with a reference to his leadership of the Human Genome Project? Does this detailing his background help his argument? Why or why not?
2. Collins explains that the current debate over evolution has become so polarized that meaningful debate has become impossible. What problems does he identify, and what solutions does he offer?
3. Collins writes this editorial from the perspective of a believing Christian. Identify areas of his essay that reveal his religious stance.
4. Collins identifies himself as a convert to Christianity, but could his argument and his points appeal to people of other religious faiths? to atheists? to fundamentalists? Why or why not?

WRITING ASSIGNMENTS

1. Much of the debate over evolution versus creationism is that one cannot accept one theory without rejecting the other. Where do you stand on this topic? Do

you think there is a middle ground? Why or why not? Write an essay expressing your viewpoint and referencing points made by other authors in this section.

2. In "Remove Stickers, Open Minds," Judge Cooper ruled that the stickers placed in biology textbooks were misleading to students. If you had been the judge ruling on this case, what decision would you have made? Defend your decision with a reasoned explanation, drawing from this essay and any others in this section.

3. Richard Weikart is shocked when students claim that they cannot determine if Hitler was evil because Darwinian principles preclude them from making such judgments. Review their position and respond with your own point of view.

4. Before reading this chapter, did you already have an opinion on the theories of evolution and creationism and the controversy concerning both topics? Did any of the essays in this section influence your current point of view or help you to form one? Why or why not?

CHAPTER 14

Campus Experience

Campus Rights and Responsibilities

For many students, college offers both an opportunity to learn about the world and a chance to exercise the personal freedoms and responsibilities of adulthood, when words and actions matter. But despite many new freedoms, a college campus is not truly the "real world." Campus policies often aim to control student behavior. Administrators may impose restrictions on students' right to assemble, implement speech codes, and enforce rules of behavior. At the same time, universities pledge to deliver a meaningful education and to prepare students for the challenges of adulthood. This chapter examines issues connected to the role of the university, and personal rights and freedoms on campus.

The first section of this chapter explores the role of the university—what does higher education owe to students? From the minute you take your PSAT as a junior in high school, the questions abound: Does everyone have the right to a college education? Should everyone go? Is today's college curriculum preparing students for the real world? Do the liberal arts matter? And what should students expect after graduation? Great jobs? or a lifetime of hard work? Does college prepare students to compete in a new world economy and to think for themselves?

The next section in this chapter considers the multiple sides of campus free speech. The U.S. citizen's right to freedom of expression is based on a short passage in the First Amendment to the Constitution: "Congress shall make no law . . . abridging the freedom of speech, or of the press." With these simple words, the writers of the Constitution created one of the pillars of our democratic system of government— the right to the free exchange of ideas, beliefs, and political debate. But are college campuses truly a haven for the exchange of ideas and free expression, or are some ideas more acceptable than others? And what happens if you express an unpopular point of view? Most students support their right to express themselves without fear of government reprisal. However, administrators on many campuses are imposing limits on the right to free expression when the exercise of that right imposes hardship or pain on others. How should administrators respond when free expression runs counter to community and university values? Are campus speech codes appropriate, or are they a violation of free speech? And who decides what is acceptable?

Many students arrive on campus eager to learn and equally eager to party. The final section in this chapter explores the issue of personal responsibility on campus. If college students are truly adults, do they need college administrators acting *in loco parentis*—controlling what they decide to do outside the classroom? With personal freedom comes responsibility. Are students expecting college to be an educational experience that will prepare them for the real world, or are they expecting merely a fun time? The readings in this section consider the nuances of college life— what students might expect and what the university expects in return.

THE ROLE OF THE UNIVERSITY

Diversity: The Value of Discomfort
Ronald D. Liebowitz

> In the next essay, Middlebury College president Ronald D. Liebowitz explains that college is not, and should not be, a sterile environment in which one is never challenged. Diversity of students and diversity of points of view encourage real-world experiences in which people must work together. There is value in discomfort because it encourages us to be critical thinkers and to challenge ourselves and the people around us to reach consensus—even if we don't always agree with each other.
>
> Liebowitz is the 16th president of Middlebury College. Recognized as an authority on Russian economic and political geography, Liebowitz has authored scholarly articles related to Soviet and Russian regional economic policy. The following essay was first delivered as the baccalaureate address to the class of 2007 at Middlebury College on May 26, 2007.

BEFORE YOU READ ──────────────────────────

How diverse is your campus population—both among students and faculty? How much is the diversity on campus connected to your regional location and college mission?

AS YOU READ ──────────────────────────

What were the "culture wars"? Do they still exist, in whole or in part, on college campuses today?

1   Good afternoon. On behalf of the faculty and staff of the College, I extend a warm welcome to the parents and families of our graduating seniors, and of course to members of the class of 2007, as well.

2   Both this baccalaureate service and commencement are joyous occasions celebrating an important transition in the lives of our graduates. Today's service is an

occasion to reflect on what our graduating seniors have already done, on the experience and the accomplishments of the past four years, and what those years have meant to them and to this College community.

3   Let me begin, therefore, by telling you a few things about the Middlebury Class of 2007. There are 643 graduates in this class, 287 men and 356 women. Some 365 of you are graduating with honors, and 65 were elected to Phi Beta Kappa. The most popular majors for your class were economics, chosen by 92 students, and English, chosen by 74, and 135 of you majored in two subjects. About 77 percent of you— 497 students—studied at least one foreign language, and 62 percent—405 students— studied abroad for at least one semester in 48 countries. Members of your class have earned three Watson Fellowships for research abroad, two Fulbright Scholarships, and a Keasbey Scholarship to study at Oxford University.

4   Your class has been characterized by an exceptional spirit of volunteerism. Collectively, approximately 70 percent of you contributed to the community through volunteer and service-learning projects, as well as through pro bono consulting work. Some of you have served on local fire departments and rescue squads; traveled to New Orleans in the wake of hurricane Katrina to assist in the rebuilding effort; served as Big Brothers or Big Sisters to local children; worked with the John Graham Community Shelter, providing meals and companionship to the homeless; and shared your expertise with local businesses and regional economic development groups based on what you learned in economics and geography courses.

5   Largely because of your energy, leadership, and dedication, Middlebury has been recognized by the Carnegie Foundation for its "community engagement" and by the Princeton Review, which named Middlebury as one of its "colleges with a conscience" for fostering social responsibility and public service. I am enormously proud of all that you have done to bring positive changes to our community, our country, and our world.

6   I am also truly impressed by the imagination and scholarship of this class. These qualities were vividly demonstrated last month at our first College-wide symposium recognizing student research and creativity. About 60 members of your class participated in that symposium, where students presented the results of research on subjects ranging from solar power to social entrepreneurship to religious life at Middlebury. This symposium, which is going to be an annual event, exemplifies the spirit of intellectual risk-taking, independent thought, and a passion for learning that should characterize the best of a liberal arts education.

7   You've had impressive success in the arts, as well. For example, a number of members of this class belonged to the cast and crew that staged last year's remarkable production of The Bewitched, which was presented at the Kennedy Center in Washington as one of four finalists in the American College Theatre Festival. In addition, a member of your class relied on her work in the arts to become one of the winners of the Kathryn Wasserman Davis 100 Projects for Peace national fellowship program. She will use the study of architecture to analyze the border crossings between Israel and the West Bank and Gaza Strip, exploring how such crossings may be reconceived as points of connection rather than of division.

8   In athletics, too, you have excelled. Your class includes 30 athletes who have earned All American honors in intercollegiate sports and 50 who earned all-NESCAC

academic honors. You helped to win 25 NESCAC championships and eight national titles for Middlebury over the past four years in intercollegiate sports, and this spring our rugby club won its first national championship.

9   There is yet one more notable thing about this class that I would like to mention. You have helped to make Middlebury a more diverse and inclusive place than it was four years ago—which brings me to the theme I particularly want to discuss this afternoon. Your class is statistically the most diverse, and the most international, ever to graduate from Middlebury. That has certainly affected—and I would say it has greatly improved—the education you have received here.

10   Why? In a nutshell: since so much of what you learn in college you learn from your fellow students, the broader the range of backgrounds and perspectives those students represent, the broader and richer the education one is likely to receive. Because of the residential and human-intensive nature of your Middlebury education, little of what you do that is related to your studies is done in solitude. You are always bouncing ideas off of classmates, roommates, hall-mates, housemates, teammates, or fellow members of student organizations.

11   The human-intensive nature of learning at liberal arts colleges was energized by the Civil Rights and other social movements of the 1960s. Formerly underrepresented groups began attending American colleges and universities in significantly greater numbers, and the breadth of learning experiences changed radically. The changes, at first, were by dint of the kinds of discussions that were taking place on a meaningful scale in the classroom. Those discussions, whether about a classical work of literature or an interpretation of some historical event, included new perspectives that had previously been absent from the classroom, and no doubt forced some people to rethink their opinions.

12   Over time, the fruits of a broadened scope of discussion extended to the curriculum and the faculty with similar results: a bigger tent of ideas within which to teach and learn. But that bigger tent brought intellectual conflict and discomfort. The so-called "culture wars" were an expression of the tension created by the challenge and inclusion of new interpretations of the curriculum. Some degree of conflict was inevitable given the new and vastly different perspectives that had been previously excluded from, or were, at best, on the margins of the academy. Through these changes, the academy became a richer, but also a more polarized, environment for learning.

13   Since the 1960s, small, rural liberal arts colleges have not experienced as rapid and extensive a change in the composition of their student bodies as public institutions or schools located in urban areas. Yet, many have changed quite significantly, especially with the arrival, more recently, of international students, many of whom come from the developing world.

14   I cite, for example, the changes that have taken place here at Middlebury since 1980. In 1980, less than 5 percent of the student population was either an American student of color or an international student . . . that is less than 1 in 20 students. Our incoming class, the Class of 2011, will be approximately 32 percent American students of color and international. Twenty-seven years ago it was 1 in 20; today, it is 1 in 3. In addition, the change in the percentage of students on need-based financial aid is noteworthy because a student body with greater socioeconomic diversity is essential

to our students' exposure to a variety of perspectives. In 1980, the percentage was 24 percent, while for the incoming class this September, the percentage is 47 percent: the highest ever.

15   This change in the composition of the student body reflects, in part, the changing demographics of the United States. But more than that, it reflects the College's deliberate effort to provide the richest learning environment for students. The College's recently approved strategic plan has as its highest priority increasing access to Middlebury for the very strongest students by continuing to meet the full need of all admitted students, increasing the grant portion of our financial aid packages, and reducing the amount of debt a student will incur during four years at the College.

16   The strategic planning committee believed that, by removing some of the financial barriers to studying at Middlebury, the College would more easily matriculate students from rural areas, from developing countries, and from inner cities. The student body, as a result, would be more ethnically, racially, and socio-economically diverse. There would no doubt be a greater diversity of ideas coming from students with such varied backgrounds, which would once again energize the classroom with frequent exchanges rooted in our students' vastly different life experiences.

17   It is no longer a cliché to say that "the local is the global and the global the local." In fact, it should go without saying that all of you who are graduating tomorrow will no longer be competing with young men and women predominantly from your hometowns, from a particular region of this country, or even from the United States. In all likelihood, the majority of you will be trying to get a job, pursue a project, or secure a spot in a leading graduate or professional school that will bring you in direct competition with young people from . . . you name it: Shanghai, Tokyo, Madrid, Buenos Aires, Johannesburg, Dehli, or Berlin. Even those of you determined to do something independently, outside of official structures or institutions, will soon learn that you are now part of a global network, and the sooner you adapt to what this means, the easier you will discover how to succeed within that network.

18   In other words, it is no longer adequate to understand only one's own culture, no matter how dominant that culture may seem; or one's political and economic system, no matter how much others claim to want to copy it; or a single approach to solving problems, no matter how sure you are that your approach is the best. To succeed in the 21st century—which means to be engaged in the world in a way that allows you to make a difference, to fulfill a sense of achievement, and to allow you to be true to yourself because you know who you are—you need to be multi-cultural, multi-national, and multi-operational in how you think. And you can only be multi-cultural, multi-national, and multi-operational if you feel comfortable with the notion of difference. And that is why we seek diversity.

19   But greater diversity means change, and change on college campuses is almost always difficult. Few 18 to 22 year olds are skilled in inviting or tolerating perspectives that are vastly different from than their own. Frankly, the same goes for 30-, 40-, and 50-something-year-old academics. Even though a campus may become more diverse in terms of the numbers of underrepresented groups present, the level of engagement can still be inconsequential if those representing different viewpoints are not encouraged and supported to express them. If an institution is not prepared

to make space, figuratively speaking, for previously excluded groups, and support their presence on campus, its diversity efforts cannot succeed. And if the wariness about discomfort is stronger than the desire to hear different viewpoints because engaging difference is uncomfortable, then the quest for diversity is hollow no matter what the demographic statistics on a campus reflect.

20   In order for the pursuit of diversity to be intellectually defensible and valuable to those seeking a first-rate education, it needs to result in deliberation. It cannot simply facilitate the exchange of one orthodoxy or point of view for another. The best liberal arts education requires all voices, those of the old order as much as those of the new, and even those in between, to be subjected to the critical analysis that is supposed to make the academy a distinctive institution in society.

21   I know first hand of several incidents during your four years at the College that speak directly to the challenges of ensuring that a diverse spectrum of opinions can be voiced and considered within our academic community. To name just a few: the protest against the College's policy allowing military recruitment on campus; the complaints about the College's judicial procedures that were triggered by the suspension of an African-American student; the reaction to the College's decision to accept an endowed professorship in honor of a conservative former chief justice of the United States Supreme Court; and most recently, the rash of hateful homophobic graffiti and the resulting discussions about offensive stereotyping and free speech on a college campus.

22   Several of these issues were discussed at faculty meetings or in several large forums on campus. Though the depth of engagement at these gatherings may not have reached the level that many who were passionate about the issues would have liked, students and faculty did express themselves in ways that didn't happen on this campus 20, 15, or even 10 years ago. Issues were brought up by students and faculty that raised the collective consciousness of those in attendance, and, in some cases, had an impact on College policies and procedures.

23   The reaction to one gathering, in particular, was as instructive as the issues about which we learned at the open forum. Following a meeting in McCullough social space that was called to address several racial incidents on campus, I received a number of e-mails from students in which they apologized on behalf of their fellow students, whom the e-mail writers believed were disrespectful in how they engaged me. I found the e-mails—and there were a good number of them—surprising, because I found the meeting, which was attended by 300 students, more civil than I expected it to be, and in no case do I recall any student expressing their concerns in ways that I would consider disrespectful. Was it uncomfortable? Yes, for sure. Were the students disrespectful? I don't think so. But being uncomfortable, as many of us were made to feel that day, is a good thing; it needs to be part of one's education.

24   Similarly, this year's open discussions about homophobic graffiti and other anti-gay acts on campus did not delve as deeply into the root causes of such unacceptable stereotyping and the vicious treatment of individuals as one might expect given the incidents in question. Yet, the reactions to what was said at the open meetings created discomfort among those who were accused of contributing to homophobia on campus. The accusation—stereotyping recruited athletes as homophobic—highlights, once again, the challenges that greater diversity and openness bring to an academic community. Was the stereotyping of a single group a productive way to engage this important topic?

25   What emerged from our discussions of the homophobic incidents, at least thus far, is hardly what one might call neat and tidy. There was, however, much learned beginning with a far greater awareness of the bigotry that exists here as it does in society at-large, and that we have considerable work to do if we truly aspire to be a community that welcomes diversity and wishes to learn from it. We also witnessed how easy it can be for some members of an aggrieved group to fall into the same kind of stereotyping from which they themselves have suffered. Diversity sure can be messy.

26   The controversy surrounding the acceptance by the College of an endowed professorship in American history and culture in honor of William Rehnquist is one more example of the complexities that come with an increasingly diverse community. Because the former chief justice was conservative, and was on the side of several court decisions that ran counter to the positions held by several underrepresented groups on campus, there was a genuine feeling on the part of some that honoring Mr. Rehnquist was a repudiation of their presence on campus and a sign that the College did not value diversity. They felt, in their words, "invisible and disrespected" as a result of the College accepting the professorship. Though one can understand this perspective, especially given the history of underrepresented groups here and on other campuses, it is unfortunate that the Chief Justice's accomplishments and reputation as a brilliant jurist by liberal and conservative constitutional scholars alike were lost in the opposition to his politics.

27   Ironically, the stance taken by those who believed it was wrong to honor the Chief Justice because of his position on particular court cases undermines the very thing the protestors support most passionately—diversity. Some couched their protests in the name of the goals of liberal education, arguing that the ultimate goal should be about "advancing" social change. I do not share in that narrow definition of liberal education, especially liberal education in and for the 21st century. Rather, liberal education must be first and foremost about ensuring a broad range of views and opinions in the classroom and across campus so that our students can question routinely both their preconceived and newly developed positions on important matters. Such deliberation will serve as the best foundation for enabling our graduates to contribute to the betterment of society.

28   In writing on the College's alumni online listserv about the Rehnquist controversy and the reported opposition of some to President Clinton speaking at tomorrow's Commencement ceremony, an alumnus from the Class of 2001 offered this perspective:

> "I always thought that the benefit of a place like Middlebury was that it opened your mind and helped you become more informed by allowing (or, forcing) you to interact with, listen to, and learn from people [with] different opinions— even if that meant welcoming those you disagree with onto your own turf."

29   I hope those of you in the audience who are graduating tomorrow have given, and will continue to give, this topic some thought. For sure, diversity is intellectually and socially challenging; it forces you to engage issues more broadly than you might otherwise. It often creates unintended consequences; and it surely can make one uncomfortable. But some discomfort, amidst all that is comfortable about college life, is the best preparation for a successful entry into our increasingly complex global world.

30   We have today few if any institutions that can claim a monopoly on how best to make the world a better, more tolerant, and just place. Talented, thoughtful, and well-educated individuals like yourselves, who have been made to feel uncomfortable and understand difference, are more likely than others to figure out how to discern right from wrong, acceptable from unacceptable behavior, and know the difference between ethical and unethical conduct.

31   As you leave college, the most important kind of confidence you must feel is the confidence that your education has prepared you to make sound judgments and to act on them. I believe because you have been exposed to diverse ideas, opinions, and people over the course of the past four years, and have been made to feel uncomfortable at times, you will discover that confidence and draw upon it so that it will serve you well in exercising your judgment and claiming your place in the wider world.

QUESTIONS FOR ANALYSIS AND DISCUSSION ──────

1. According to Middlebury College president Ronald Liebowitz, what value does diversity add to a college education? What challenges does it present as well?
2. Liebowitz cites several examples of issues raised during the graduates' four years at Middlebury. How do these examples support his theme of the importance of diversity on campus? Why is it important to permit and even support the expression of unpopular points of view? Do you agree?
3. Liebowitz notes, "It is no longer a cliché to say that 'the local is the global and the global the local.' " What does he mean? Explain this statement and connect it to your own college experience.
4. Liebowitz leads his speech with a description of the graduates and their accomplishments. How does this introduction connect to the theme of his speech?
5. In October 2006, Middlebury College established the Justice William H. Rehnquist Professorship of American History and Culture—a controversial chair that met with some protest. Who was Rehnquist? Why did some students and faculty object to the creation of the professorship? What does Liebowitz say about the controversy, and the decision to create the professorship, despite the dispute?

Who Should Get Into College?
John H. McWhorter

In 2003, the Supreme Court sided with the University of Michigan's admissions officers on the right to use race-based admission policies, which often involve different sets of admission criteria for minority students. Most of the arguments for and against race-based admissions hinge on fairness, with supporters claiming that inequalities in education put black students at disadvantage and detractors claiming that such policies are unfair to white students as well as blacks. Following the Supreme Court's decision, then-Justice Sandra Day O'Connor noted her hope that "25 years from now the use of racial preferences will no longer be necessary." In the next essay, John H. McWhorter challenges the practice of race-based admission policies. He says that not only are they unnecessary today but also they're actually hurting the people they're supposed to help.

McWhorter is a senior fellow at the Manhattan Institute, where he addresses issues on race, ethnicity, and culture for the institute's Center for Race and Ethnicity. He also writes a regular column in the *New York Sun*. He is the author of many books on language and culture, including *The Power of Babel: A Natural History of Language* (2002), *Doing Our Own Thing: The Degradation of Language in Music in America* (2003), and most recently, *Winning the Race: Beyond the Crisis in Black America* (2006). This essay appeared in the Spring 2003 issue of *City Journal*.

BEFORE YOU READ

What is your opinion of race-based admission policies? Do they help promote diversity on campus? Do they protect minority admissions? Are they necessary in a country where the quality of high schools is so varied? Or do they do more harm than good?

AS YOU READ

What does "diversity" mean to McWhorter? What does it mean to you? Why is it important for colleges to embrace diversity on campus?

1　For many years now, elite colleges—taking their cue from the Supreme Court's 1978 Bakke decision—have justified racial preferences in admissions by saying that they are necessary to ensure campus "diversity." Get rid of preferences, "diversity" fans say, and top colleges will become minority-free enclaves; the spirit of segregation will be on the march again. The losers won't just be the folks with the brown pigmentation, now exiled from the good schools, but all those white students who now will never get to know the unique perspective of people of color.

2　Nonsense on all counts. Correctly understood, diversity encompasses the marvelous varieties of human excellence and vision in a modern civilization—from musical genius to civic commitment to big-brained science wizardry. People who recognize the folly of racial preferences are no more opposed to diversity in this sense than critics of "gangsta" rap are opposed to music. What they do reject is the condescending notion that a diverse campus demands lower admissions standards for brown students, and that, in 2003 America, brown students need crutches to make it.

3　With the Supreme Court about to decide a case that could overturn Bakke and require colorblind admissions, once and for all, it's a good time to describe what a post-affirmative-action admissions policy at a top school should look like—and explain why it would be fully compatible with minority success and real diversity.

4   The raison d'être of the nation's selective universities, at least from the standpoint of the public interest, is to forge a well-educated, national elite. Thus, our postpreferences approach to admissions must be meritocratic. But few people would want schools simply to choose students with the very best SAT scores and grades, and call it a day. The image of elite campuses populated solely by 1,600-SAT-scoring Ken Lays or Sam Waksalls, of whatever color, is unappealing.

5   Back in the early 1980s, at Simon's Rock Early College in Massachusetts, a smattering of my classmates fell into the 1,600 category. But thankfully, the school's administrators grasped that that kind of achievement represents only one of the forms of excellence that smart young people can bring to campus life. The school worked hard to attract a lively mix of students, who vastly enriched my years on campus. My cello playing, for example, took on new depth, because I had the opportunity to play with a brilliant musician whose talents on piano and violin scaled near-professional heights. A roommate was a splendid stage performer, and marinating (unwillingly at first) in his favorite music and historical anecdotes opened up a universe of vintage American popular music and theater that has been part of my life ever since.

6   At school, I also met my first Mennonite and my first white Southerner—there is no better way to get past a native sense of an accent as "funny," I discovered, than living with someone who speaks with one. There were other blacks among the school's 300 or so students, too. Most, like me, were middle-class kids, but there was one guy who had grown up in crumbling Camden, New Jersey. This student gave a lesson in one form of cultural "blackness" to his white classmates—he had real "street" cred. But far more important, after a rocky start and some coaching, he also proved he could do the schoolwork on the high level the school demanded.

7   This was real diversity—the full panoply of human variation, not just the tiny, superficial sliver of it represented by skin pigmentation. And Simon's Rock fostered it without surrendering academic standards.

8   Since my undergraduate days, however, elite universities have come to mean something much different when they speak of "diversity": having as many brown faces on campus as possible, regardless of standards. The origin of the current notion of "diversity," Peter Wood shows in his masterful *Diversity: The Invention of a Concept*, was Justice Lewis Powell's opinion for the court in Bakke. Though strict racial quotas were unconstitutional, Powell argued, schools could still use race as an "important element" in admissions in order to create a "diverse" campus that would enhance the quality of all students' educational experiences by exposing them to minority "opinions."

9   Powell's argument was, in Wood's terms, a "self-contradictory mess." How, after all, does one make race an "important" factor in admissions while avoiding quotas? It was also dishonest, in that it wasn't at bottom about broadening white students' horizons but providing a rationale for admitting blacks and Hispanics much less qualified than other applicants. The decision has encouraged the Orwellian mindset by which the University of Michigan Law School can defend its admissions process, 234 times more likely to admit black applicants than similarly credentialed whites, as an expression of "diversity," not the obvious quota system it really is.

10   Even on its own terms, Powell's "diversity" argument is demeaning and offensive to minorities. What would be a black "opinion" on French irregular verbs? Or systolic

pressure? The "black" views that most interest diversity advocates, of course, are those that illumine social injustice. But in my experience, white and Asian students are at least as likely to voice such PC opinions—often picked up in multiculturalism workshops when they first hit campus.

11   Diversity supporters sometimes reverse themselves 180 degrees and say that race preferences are necessary to show white students that there's no such thing as a "black" viewpoint. "By seeing firsthand that all black or Hispanic students in their classes do not act or think alike," argues Jonathan Alger, counsel for the American Association of University Professors, "white students can overcome learned prejudices." One can only hope that a warm corner of hell awaits anyone who would subject a race to lowered standards for a reason so callow.

12   Black students understandably can find this whole diversity regime repugnant and even racist. "Professor McWhorter," students have asked me, "what about when I am called on for my opinion as a black person in class? Is it fair that I have to deal with that burden?" A continent away, the undergraduate-written Black Guide to Life at Harvard insists: "We are not here to provide diversity training for Kate or Timmy before they go out to take over the world." Indeed, students in general are skeptical of the value of "diversity": a recent survey by Stanley Rothman and Seymour Martin Lipset of 4,000 students at 140 campuses shows that the more that racial "diversity" is emphasized on a campus, the less enthusiastic students are about the quality of education a school offers. What's more, Rothman and Lipset found that such "diversity"-focused schools had more reports of discrimination, not less.

13   The dismal failure of the "diversity" experiment of the last two decades offers an important lesson for a post-affirmative-action admissions policy. Even as we seek diversity in the worthy, Simon's Rock sense, we must recognize that students need to be able to excel at college-level studies. Nobody wins, after all, when a young man or woman of whatever color, unprepared for the academic rigors of a top university, flunks out, or a school dumbs down its curriculum to improve graduation rates. The problem, then, is to find some way to measure a student's potential that still leaves administrators enough leeway to ensure that campus life benefits from a rich variety of excellences and life experiences.

14   As it turns out, we have—and use—the measure: the Scholastic Aptitude Test. James Conant invented the SAT as a meritocratic tool to smoke out talented individuals from the wide range of life circumstances in American society, not just the WASP elite who made up the vast majority of Ivy League student bodies in the pre-SAT era. Nowadays, a creeping fashion dismisses the SAT as culturally biased, claiming that it assesses only a narrow range of ability and is irrelevant to predicting students' future performance. But while it is true that the SAT is far from perfect—if it were, students wouldn't be able to boost their scores by taking SAT preparatory classes—the exam really does tend to forecast students' future success, as even William Bowen and Derek Bok admit in their valentine to racial preferences, *The Shape of the River*. In their sample of three classes from 1951 to 1989 at 28 selective universities, Bowen and Bok show that SAT scores correlated neatly with students' eventual class ranks.

15   For gauging student potential in the humanities, the verbal SAT, or SATV, seems particularly useful. Rutgers University English professor William Dowling compared

the grades of kids in one of his classes over the years with how they did on the verbal test. "What I found," Dowling notes, "was that the SATV scores had an extraordinarily high correlation with final grades, and that neither, in the many cases where I had come to know my students' personal backgrounds, seemed to correlate very well with socio-economic status." The reason, Dowling thinks, is painfully obvious: having a strong command of English vocabulary, usually gained through a lifelong habit of reading, is hardly irrelevant to how one engages advanced reading material. As Dowling argues, a student of any socioeconomic background who can't answer correctly a relatively hard SAT question like this one—"The traditional process of producing an oil painting requires so many steps that it seems _____ to artists who prefer to work quickly: (A) provocative (B) consummate (C) interminable (D) facile (E) prolific"—will be fated to frustration at a selective university, at least in the humanities.

16   My own experience reinforces Dowling's. I've taught students who, though intelligent, possessed limited reading vocabularies and struggled with the verbal portion of the SAT. I have never known a single one of these students to reach the top ranks in one of my classes. "I think I understand what Locke is saying," one student told me in frustration while preparing for a big exam. But Locke isn't Heidegger—his prose, while sophisticated, is clear as crystal. This student confessed that he was "no reader" and possessed only a "tiny vocabulary." Without the vocabulary, he was at sea. Conversely, my textaholic students are usually the stars, gifted at internalizing material and interpreting it in fresh ways—and this is especially true of students immersed in high literature.

17   A post-preferences admissions policy, then, must accept that below a certain cut-off point in SAT scores, a student runs a serious risk of failing to graduate. As Thomas Sowell, among others, has shown, placing minorities in schools that expect a performance level beyond what they have been prepared to meet leads to disproportionate dropout rates—41 percent of the black students in Berkeley's class of 1988, to take one typical example, did not complete their education, compared with 16 percent of whites. Many of these students may have flourished at slightly less competitive schools. Moreover, when minority students attend schools beyond their level, note Stephen Cole and Elinor Barber in Increasing Faculty Diversity, poor grades often deter them from pursuing graduate degrees, contributing to the dearth of black Ph.D.s. Black and minority students overwhelmed on a too-demanding campus can succumb, too, to the bluster of seeing themselves as "survivors" in a racist country—becoming part of an embittered minority rather than proud members of a national elite. To prevent this kind of damage, the SAT can supply us with the rough parameters within which our admissions search for different kinds of merit—diversity, rightly understood—will proceed. All this makes the recent efforts by the affirmative-action claque to get rid of the SAT misguided in the extreme.

18   Within our SAT range, and once in a while even a bit outside it, there will be plenty of room for judgment calls. Grades, extracurricular activities, and character will all be key. An applicant with a high GPA and a 1,480 SAT who plays the trumpet like Clifford Brown or who gives every indication of being a unique and charismatic individual may deserve admission over an applicant with a 1,600 SAT but no real interests and the individuality of a spoon. Our top universities seek to create a

national elite, so geographical diversity will be important too: our admissions policy will seek a mix of students from all parts of the nation. As long as there is no coterie of students whose grades and test scores would have excluded them from consideration if they were white (or Asian), basic standards of excellence prevail.

19   And certainly, our admissions procedure won't immediately disqualify a student who is clearly bright and engaged, but whose test scores happen to fall slightly below the official cut-off, or whose GPA took a hit from one bad year, or who matured into a super student only late in his high school career. Fervent recommendation letters, attesting to leadership or virtue or strength of character, a flabbergastingly good writing sample, a demonstrated commitment to a calling—all will be significant in deciding whether to admit students whose grades and test scores put them on the borderline or slightly below.

20   Our admissions policy will be colorblind, but it won't ignore the working class and the poor (many of whom, as a practical matter, will be blacks or Hispanics). Of course, it's more likely that affluent children, growing up in print-rich homes, will score within our SAT parameters and have the tippy-top grades. But there have always been kids from hardscrabble backgrounds who show academic promise—by nature, by chance, or thanks to the special efforts of parents or other adults. Abraham Lincoln teaching himself to write on the back of a shovel, civil rights activist Fannie Lou Hamer growing up dust poor in the Mississippi Delta loving books—American history records many examples. Disadvantaged students of this stamp will sometimes get the nod in our admissions procedure over well-off applicants whose scores might be more impressive—provided that the disadvantaged kids' SAT scores are within our range (or close to it). That disadvantaged students have shown academic promise may be just a result of good genes, but it's often a sign of good character—a virtue that selective universities should recognize and cultivate.

21   The University of California at Berkeley, where I teach, is already on the right track here. Not so long ago, the admissions committee I sat on matter-of-factly chose middle-class brown students, essentially "white" culturally, over equally deserving white students. I felt tremendous discomfort over the practice. Since California voted in a 1997 referendum, led by anti-preferences activist Ward Connerly, to ban the use of race in admissions, things have changed. Berkeley still assesses students on grades and scores, of course, but instead of race, it now considers the "hardships" that young men and women may have overcome while excelling at school. We recently gave fellowships, for example, to two needy white students who had shown sterling promise. I felt fundamentally right about these fellowships. "This is a racially blind process," emphasizes Calvin Moore, chair of Berkeley's faculty committee on admissions.

22   The idea of a "racially blind process" makes today's "diversity" fans shudder, since they believe that it will lead to a tragic re-segregation of the best American universities and thus of American society. I'm sorry, but this is manipulative melodrama. In an America several decades past the Civil Rights Act, where far more black families are middle class than are poor, many black students will be ready for the top schools without dragging down the bar of evaluation.

23   For proof, consider the University of Washington. In 1998, the year before Washington State outlawed racial preferences in a citizen referendum (also led by

Connerly), the school counted 124 African-American students in its freshman class. Two years after the ban, there were 119. Before Texas banned preferences in its schools in 1996, the University of Texas enrolled 266 black freshmen. After the ban and the debut of a new system that admits the top 10 percent of every high school in the state regardless of race, the number actually bounced, to 286. (The "top 10 percent" approach has serious problems, including treating huge discrepancies in school quality as if they did not exist, but it's better than what it replaced.) If this is re-segregation, bring it on.

24   The kind of colorblind admissions process I have outlined would likely just reshuffle the minority presence at selective schools, not reduce it. In Virginia, where racial preferences remain entrenched, black students currently make up 7.9 percent of the student body at the highly competitive University of Virginia Law School, 9.3 percent at the slightly less selective William and Mary Law School, and just 1.7 percent at the less elite, but still fine, George Mason Law School. George Mason's "diversity" deficit results from black students getting in to the more selective schools at a higher percentage than their dossiers would suggest in the absence of affirmative action. Bar preferences, and the number of black students at George Mason would rise; the overall number of blacks getting legal training in the three schools would probably remain the same.

25   What would be so bad about that? It's doubtful that the black students at George Mason's yearly commencement ceremony, feting their accomplishments as their parents beam beside them, worry that they will soon be on the street, selling pencils. In fact, nothing better underscores the progress made by black Americans than the prevalence in the affirmative-action camp of the bizarre notion that admission to a solid second-tier university somehow represents a tragic injustice.

26   Exactly this type of resorting took place after the end of preferences in California's schools. The state's flagship universities, Berkeley and UCLA, did see an initial plunge in the number of black freshmen. But minority presence rose at the same time at most state campuses. And minority admissions at the two top schools have gone up every year following the initial drop-off. Having watched this whole process play out at Berkeley, I can confidently say that the black student community is far from a lonely remnant of what it was in the "good old days" of affirmative action. Berkeley still boasts a thriving black community—the same African-American student groups, the same black dorm floors, the same African-American studies and ethnic studies departments.

27   Moreover, the minority presence at the flagships may have taken a bigger initial hit than the ban required. Immediately after the ban, black activists at the two schools lustily proclaimed their campuses "anti-black," doubtless discouraging some black students from applying—minority applications dropped off sharply for a spell. At UC Berkeley in 1998, the minority admissions office staff actually told some black students, already accepted to the "racist" school, to enroll elsewhere. One of the motivations for writing my book *Losing the Race* was hearing a black student working in admissions casually say that she distrusted black applicants who did well enough in high school not to need preferences, since such students would not be committed to Berkeley's black community—as if it were somehow not "authentically black" to be a top student. No show lasts forever, however, and after the crowd crying "racism" had its fun and went home, minority applications have steadily climbed.

28   Most important of all, California's black students have started to do better now that they are going to schools that their academic background has prepared them to attend. As University of California at San Diego law professor Gail Heriot notes, before the preferences ban, 15 percent of the college's black freshmen undergraduates, compared with just 4 percent of whites, had GPAs below 2.0, which put them in academic jeopardy; only one black student had a GPA of 3.5 or better, compared with 20 percent of whites. The next year, after the outlawing of campus affirmative action, 20 percent of black freshmen reached the 3.5 or higher GPA level (compared with 22 percent of their white classmates), while black frosh with GPAs below 2.0 fell to 6 percent (about the same as all other racial groups). High freshmen dropout rates fell precipitously.

29   It's true that, with or without racial preferences, blacks will not make up as high a proportion of the student population at our better schools as they do of the overall population. But to worry unduly about this is ahistorical bean counting. Given the relatively short time since the nation rejected segregation, and the internal cultural factors that can hobble a group and keep it from seizing opportunities, it should surprise no one that our selective college campuses do not yet "look like America." But give it time. That's not a rhetorical statement, either: since the banning of racial preferences in California, there has been a 350 percent rise in the number of black teens taking calculus in preparation for college. Challenge people, and they respond.

30   Informed observers believe that the Supreme Court, in agreeing to decide two suits brought against the University of Michigan for reverse discrimination in its admissions, may be set to abolish all use of race in admissions, and move the nation toward the colorblind ideal that motivated the original civil rights movement. Especially in light of the stereotypes that blacks have labored under in this country, saddling black people with eternally lowered standards is immoral. We spent too much time suffering under the hideously unjust social experiments of slavery and segregation to be subjected to further social engineering that benefits the sentiments of liberal elites instead of bettering the conditions and spirits of minorities. Unfortunately, even some conservatives remain uncomfortable with this colorblind possibility: the Bush administration's amicus brief in the case, though it views the Michigan admissions policy as an unconstitutional quota system, still contemplates school officials "taking race into account."

31   It's time to step up to the plate. My years on college campuses have taught me that even those willing to acknowledge the injustices of preferences in private uphold the "diversity" party line in public—something Bakke allows them to do. "John, I get where you're coming from," a genial professor once told me, "but I reserve my right to be guilty." Indeed, 25 years of Bakke show that, in practice, even a hint that race can be "a" factor in admissions will give college administrators, ever eager to Do the Right Thing, the go-ahead to continue fostering a second-tier class-within-a-class of "spunky" minorities on their campuses.

32   Justice Powell's Bakke opinion cited an amicus brief for "diversity" submitted by Harvard, Stanford, Columbia, and the University of Pennsylvania. The brief described how these schools had traditionally aimed to compose their classes with a mixture of "students from California, New York and Massachusetts; city dwellers and farm boys; violinists, painters and football players; biologists, historians and classicists; potential stockbrokers, academics and politicians." It's a wonderful, noble goal,

this diversity—and we don't need to treat any group of citizens as lesser beings to accomplish it.

QUESTIONS FOR ANALYSIS AND DISCUSSION ─────────

1. Summarize McWhorter's argument against race-based admission policies. Include in your summary his position and his supporting evidence.
2. McWhorter admits that diversity on campus adds value to a college education. What does McWhorter feel "diversity" means? How does his definition compare with Ronald Liebowitz's concept of diversity described in the previous essay? Explain.
3. McWhorter, who is himself black, writes on many issues connected to race and ethnicity. Does the fact that McWhorter is black and expressing this opinion against race-based admissions lend more credibility to his argument? Why or why not?
4. McWhorter points out that the original purpose of the SAT was to level the field for students from all socioeconomic backgrounds. How convincing is McWhorter's argument that the SAT still serves its purpose well?
5. Why are so many administrators adamant about maintaining race-based admissions? Explain.
6. In this essay, McWhorter makes his case for "colorblind" admissions. Present your own viewpoint on this issue, responding specifically to McWhorter's supporting evidence and your own from outside research and your personal perspective as a college student.

───

What's Wrong with Vocational School?
Charles Murray

Are too many Americans going to college? Unlike students in Europe and Asia, over 70 percent of high school graduates intend to pursue some form of higher education, partially because many businesses have made a college degree a requirement for even entry-level office jobs. But are too many students trying to go to college? Are we making unreasonable demands of students and undervaluing the "vocational" trades? In the next essay, Charles Murray discusses how the pressure to go to college hurts less-gifted students as well as the extremely bright ones.

Murray is a scholar at the American Enterprise Institute, a conservative think tank in Washington, D.C. He is perhaps best known for his controversial book *The Bell Curve* (1994), co-authored with Richard Hermstein, which discusses the role of IQ in American society. Widely published, his most recent book is *In Our Hands: A Plan to Replace the Welfare State* (2006). His writing has appeared in *The New Republic*, *Commentary*, and the *National Review*, among others. This essay was the second in a three-part series of op-ed articles examining education in the United States published by the *Wall Street Journal* the week of January 17, 2007.

Much of the argument in the next essay hinges on the value of IQ. What is IQ? Do you think one's IQ should influence the decision of whether to pursue higher education?

Is vocational school, as Murray suggests, indeed considered "second class"? What accounts for this judgment? How can this attitude hurt the United States in the long run?

1 My topic yesterday was education and children in the lower half of the intelligence distribution. Today I turn to the upper half, people with IQs of 100 or higher. Today's simple truth is that far too many of them are going to four-year colleges. Begin with those barely into the top half, those with average intelligence. To have an IQ of 100 means that a tough high-school course pushes you about as far as your academic talents will take you. If you are average in math ability, you may struggle with algebra and probably fail a calculus course. If you are average in verbal skills, you often misinterpret complex text and make errors in logic.

2 These are not devastating shortcomings. You are smart enough to engage in any of hundreds of occupations. You can acquire more knowledge if it is presented in a format commensurate with your intellectual skills. But a genuine college education in the arts and sciences begins where your skills leave off.

3 In engineering and most of the natural sciences, the demarcation between high-school material and college-level material is brutally obvious. If you cannot handle the math, you cannot pass the courses. In the humanities and social sciences, the demarcation is fuzzier. It is possible for someone with an IQ of 100 to sit in the lectures of Economics 1, read the textbook, and write answers in an examination book. But students who cannot follow complex arguments accurately are not really learning economics. They are taking away a mishmash of half-understood information and outright misunderstandings that probably leave them under the illusion that they know something they do not. (A depressing research literature documents one's inability to recognize one's own incompetence.) Traditionally and properly understood, a four-year college education teaches advanced analytic skills and information at a level that exceeds the intellectual capacity of most people.

4 There is no magic point at which a genuine college-level education becomes an option, but anything below an IQ of 110 is problematic. If you want to do well, you should have an IQ of 115 or higher. Put another way, it makes sense for only about 15% of the population, 25% if one stretches it, to get a college education. And yet more than 45% of recent high school graduates enroll in four-year colleges. Adjust that percentage to account for high-school dropouts, and more than 40% of all persons in their late teens are trying to go to a four-year college—enough people to absorb everyone down through an IQ of 104.

5 No data that I have been able to find tell us what proportion of those students really want four years of college-level courses, but it is safe to say that few people who are intellectually unqualified yearn for the experience, any more than someone who is athletically unqualified for a college varsity wants to have his shortcomings exposed at practice every day. They are in college to improve their chances of making a good living. What they really need is vocational training. But nobody will say so, because "vocational training" is second class. "College" is first class.

6 Large numbers of those who are intellectually qualified for college also do not yearn for four years of college-level courses. They go to college because their parents are paying for it and college is what children of their social class are supposed to do after they finish high school. They may have the ability to understand the material in Economics 1 but they do not want to. They, too, need to learn to make a living—and would do better in vocational training.

7 Combine those who are unqualified with those who are qualified but not interested, and some large proportion of students on today's college campuses—probably a majority of them—are looking for something that the four-year college was not designed to provide. Once there, they create a demand for practical courses, taught at an intellectual level that can be handled by someone with a mildly above-average IQ and/or mild motivation. The nation's colleges try to accommodate these new demands. But most of the practical specialties do not really require four years of training, and the best way to teach those specialties is not through a residential institution with the staff and infrastructure of a college. It amounts to a system that tries to turn out televisions on an assembly line that also makes pottery. It can be done, but it's ridiculously inefficient.

8 Government policy contributes to the problem by making college scholarships and loans too easy to get, but its role is ancillary. The demand for college is market-driven, because a college degree does, in fact, open up access to jobs that are closed to people without one. The fault lies in the false premium that our culture has put on a college degree. For a few occupations, a college degree still certifies a qualification. For example, employers appropriately treat a bachelor's degree in engineering as a requirement for hiring engineers. But a bachelor's degree in a field such as sociology, psychology, economics, history or literature certifies nothing. It is a screening device for employers. The college you got into says a lot about your ability, and that you stuck it out for four years says something about your perseverance. But the degree itself does not qualify the graduate for anything. There are better, faster and more efficient ways for young people to acquire credentials to provide to employers.

9 The good news is that market-driven systems eventually adapt to reality, and signs of change are visible. One glimpse of the future is offered by the nation's two-year colleges. They are more honest than the four-year institutions about what their students want and provide courses that meet their needs more explicitly. Their time frame gives them a big advantage—two years is about right for learning many technical specialties, while four years is unnecessarily long.

10 Advances in technology are making the brick-and-mortar facility increasingly irrelevant. Research resources on the Internet will soon make the college library unnecessary. Lecture courses taught by first-rate professors are already available on CDs and DVDs for many subjects, and online methods to make courses interactive

between professors and students are evolving. Advances in computer simulation are expanding the technical skills that can be taught without having to gather students together in a laboratory or shop. These and other developments are all still near the bottom of steep growth curves. The cost of effective training will fall for everyone who is willing to give up the trappings of a campus. As the cost of college continues to rise, the choice to give up those trappings will become easier.

11   A reality about the job market must eventually begin to affect the valuation of a college education: The spread of wealth at the top of American society has created an explosive increase in the demand for craftsmen. Finding a good lawyer or physician is easy. Finding a good carpenter, painter, electrician, plumber, glazier, mason—the list goes on and on—is difficult, and it is a seller's market. Journeymen craftsmen routinely make incomes in the top half of the income distribution while master craftsmen can make six figures. They have work even in a soft economy. Their jobs cannot be outsourced to India. And the craftsman's job provides wonderful intrinsic rewards that come from mastery of a challenging skill that produces tangible results. How many white-collar jobs provide nearly as much satisfaction?

12   Even if forgoing college becomes economically attractive, the social cachet of a college degree remains. That will erode only when large numbers of high-status, high-income people do not have a college degree and don't care. The information technology industry is in the process of creating that class, with Bill Gates and Steve Jobs as exemplars. It will expand for the most natural of reasons: A college education need be no more important for many high-tech occupations than it is for NBA basketball players or cabinetmakers. Walk into Microsoft or Google with evidence that you are a brilliant hacker, and the job interviewer is not going to fret if you lack a college transcript. The ability to present an employer with evidence that you are good at something, without benefit of a college degree, will continue to increase, and so will the number of skills to which that evidence can be attached. Every time that happens, the false premium attached to the college degree will diminish.

13   Most students find college life to be lots of fun (apart from the boring classroom stuff), and that alone will keep the four-year institution overstocked for a long time. But, rightly understood, college is appropriate for a small minority of young adults—perhaps even a minority of the people who have IQs high enough that they could do college-level work if they wished. People who go to college are not better or worse people than anyone else; they are merely different in certain interests and abilities. That is the way college should be seen. There is reason to hope that eventually it will be.

QUESTIONS FOR ANALYSIS AND DISCUSSION

1. Why does Murray feel that too many students are going to college? Why does he think this harms many students?

2. Murray's essay generated much controversy. He was accused of being "elitist" and of ignoring the benefits of a wider college-educated society. What do you think? Is he being elitist, or is he expressing a truth that is uncomfortable to hear and why?

3. This essay was written as part of a series for the *Wall Street Journal*. Does the content match the presumed audience? What assumptions

based on readership does Murray make? Identify specific words/phrases/ideas in his essay that demonstrate how he writes to his audience.

4. Do you think that colleges are indeed "dumbing down" curricula to accommodate a broader range of students with lower abilities? Why or why not?

5. How, according to Murray, does government contribute to the problem of college over-enrollment? Explain.

6. Evaluate Murray's tone in paragraph 11 addressing the benefits of craftsmen. Do you agree that more value should be attributed to vocational trades so that students will be enticed to pursue careers in masonry and carpentry? Explain.

How to Get a College Education
Jeffrey Hart

Most students arrive at college ready to learn. But what happens if they arrive completely unequipped to handle the coursework assigned because they lack a foundation in literature and history? As professor Jeffrey Hart describes, many of today's freshmen cannot discuss many issues because they don't understand the basics. In this essay, Hart discusses the challenges some students face and explains how these students can still get an outstanding college education.

Jeffrey Hart is professor emeritus of English at Dartmouth College. He has served as a contributing writer to the *National Review* and currently writes columns for King Features Syndicate. His writings have appeared in many journals, including the *American Conservative*, the *Washington Monthly*, and the *Wall Street Journal*. He is the author of *Smiling Through the Cultural Catastrophe: Toward the Revival of Higher Education* (2001) and *Making of America Conservative* (2005). This essay was first published by *The National Review Online* on September 29, 2006.

BEFORE YOU READ

How well prepared do you feel you are to tackle a college curriculum? What courses and information do you think you need to know, and what do you expect to learn?

AS YOU READ

What does Hart's use of language and his style of writing reveal about his own education? What expectations does he have of his audience (and of his students)?

1 It was in the fall term of 1988 that the truth burst in upon me like something had gone terribly wrong in higher education. It was like the anecdote in Auden where the guest at a garden party, sensing something amiss, suddenly realizes that there is a corpse on the tennis court.

2 As a professor at Dartmouth, my hours had been taken up with my own writing, and with teaching a variety of courses—a yearly seminar, a yearly freshman composition course (which—some good news—all senior professors in the Dartmouth English Department are required to teach), and courses in my eighteenth-century specialty. Oh, I knew that the larger curriculum lacked shape and purpose, that something was amiss; but I deferred thinking about it.

3 Yet there does come that moment.

4 It came for me in the freshman composition course. The students were required to write essays based upon assigned reading—in this case, some Frost poems, Hemingway's *In Our Time, Hamlet*. Then, almost on a whim, I assigned the first half of Allan Bloom's surprise best-seller *The Closing of the American Mind*. When the time came to discuss the Bloom book, I asked them what they thought of it.

5 They hated it.

6 Oh, yes, they understood perfectly well what Bloom was saying: that they were ignorant, that they believed in clichés, that their education so far had been dangerous piffle and that what they were about to receive was not likely to be any better.

7 No wonder they hated it. After all, they were the best and the brightest, Ivy Leaguers with stratospheric SAT scores, the Masters of the Universe. Who is Bloom? What is the University of Chicago, anyway?

8 So I launched into an impromptu oral quiz.

9 Could anyone (in that class of 25 students) say anything about the Mayflower Compact?

10 Complete silence.

11 John Locke?

12 Nope.

13 James Madison?

14 Silentia.

15 Magna Carta? The Spanish Armada? The Battle of Yorktown? The Bull Moose party? Don Giovanni? William James? The Tenth Amendment?

16 Zero. Zilch. Forget it.

17 The embarrassment was acute, but some good came of it. The better students, ashamed that their first 12 years of schooling had mostly been wasted (even if they had gone to Choate or Exeter), asked me to recommend some books. I offered such solid things as Samuel Eliot Morison's *Oxford History of the United States*, Max Farrand's *The Framing of the Constitution*, Jacob Burckhardt's *The Civilization of the Renaissance in Italy*. Several students asked for an informal discussion group, and so we started reading a couple of Dante's Cantos per week, Dante being an especially useful author because he casts his net so widely—the ancient world, the (his) modern world, theology, history, ethics.

18 I quickly became aware of the utter bewilderment of entering freshmen. They emerge from the near-nullity of K-12 and stroll into the chaos of the Dartmouth

curriculum, which is embodied in a course catalogue about as large as a telephone directory.

19   Sir, what courses should I take? A college like Dartmouth—or Harvard, Princeton, etc.—has requirements so broadly defined that almost anything goes for degree credit. Of course, freshmen are assigned faculty "advisors," but most of them would rather return to the library or the Bunsen burner.

20   Thus it developed that I began giving an annual lecture to incoming freshmen on the subject, "What Is a College Education? And How to Get One, Even at Dartmouth."

21   One long-term reason why the undergraduate curriculum at Dartmouth and all comparable institutions is in chaos is specialization. Since World War II, success as a professor has depended increasingly on specialized publication. The ambitious and talented professor is not eager to give introductory or general courses. Indeed, his work has little or nothing to do with undergraduate teaching. Neither Socrates nor Jesus, who published nothing, could possibly receive tenure at a first-line university today.

22   But in addition to specialization, recent intellectual fads have done extraordinary damage, viz.:

- So-called Post-Modernist thought ("deconstruction," etc.) asserts that one "text" is as much worth analyzing as any other, whether it be a movie, a comic book, or Homer. The lack of a "canon" of important works leads to course offerings in, literally, anything.
- "Affirmative Action" is not just a matter of skewed admissions and hiring, but also a mentality or ethos. That is, if diversity is more important than quality in admissions and hiring, why should it not be so in the curriculum? Hence the courses in things like Nicaraguan Lesbian Poetry.
- Concomitantly, ideology has been imposed on the curriculum to a startling degree. In part this represents a sentimental attempt to resuscitate Marxism, with assorted Victim Groups standing in for the old Proletariat; in part it is a new Identity Politics in which being Black, Lesbian, Latino, Homosexual, Radical Feminist, and so forth takes precedence over any scholarly pursuit. These Victimologies are usually presented as "Studies" programs outside the regular departments, so as to avoid the usual academic standards. Yet their course offerings carry degree credit.

23   On an optimistic note, I think that most or all of Post-Modernism, the Affirmative Action/Multicultural ethos, and the Victimologies will soon pass from the scene. The great institutions have a certain sense of self-preservation. Harvard almost lost its Law School to a Marxist faculty faction, but then cleaned house. Tenure will keep the dead men walking for another twenty years or so, but then we will have done with them.

24   But for the time being, what these fads have done to the liberal-arts and social-sciences curriculum since around 1968 is to clutter it with all sorts of nonsense, nescience, and distraction. The entering student needs to be wary lest he waste his time and his parents' money and come to consider all higher education an outrageous fraud. The good news is that the wise student can still get a college education today, even at Dartmouth, Harvard, Yale, and Princeton.

25   Of course the central question is one of telos or goal. What is the liberal-arts education supposed to produce? Once you have the answer to this question, course selection becomes easy.

26   I mean to answer that question here. But first, I find that undergraduates and their third-mortgaged parents appreciate some practical tips, such as:

27   Select the "ordinary" courses. I use ordinary here in a paradoxical and challenging way. An ordinary course is one that has always been taken and obviously should be taken—even if the student is not yet equipped with a sophisticated rationale for so doing. The student should be discouraged from putting his money on the cutting edge of interdisciplinary cross-textuality.

28   Thus, do take American and European history, an introduction to philosophy, American and European literature, the Old and New Testaments, and at least one modern language. It would be absurd not to take a course in Shakespeare, the best poet in our language. There is art and music history. The list can be expanded, but these are areas an educated person should have a decent knowledge of—with specialization coming later on.

29   I hasten to add that I applaud the student who devotes his life to the history of China or Islam, but that too should come later. America is part of the narrative of European history.

30   If the student should seek out those "ordinary" courses, then it follows that he should avoid the flashy come-ons. Avoid things like Nicaraguan Lesbian Poets. Yes, and anything listed under "Studies," any course whose description uses the words "interdisciplinary," "hegemonic," "phallocratic," or "empowerment," anything that mentions "keeping a diary," any course with a title like "Adventures in Film."

31   Also, any male professor who comes to class without a jacket and tie should be regarded with extreme prejudice unless he has won a Nobel Prize.

32   All these are useful rules of thumb. A theoretical rationale for a liberal-arts education, however, derives from that telos mentioned above. What is such an education supposed to produce?

33   A philosophy professor I studied with as an undergraduate had two phrases he repeated so often that they stay in the mind, a technique made famous by Matthew Arnold.

34   He would say, "History must be told."

35   History, he explained, is to a civilization what memory is to an individual, an irreducible part of identity.

36   He also said, "The goal of education is to produce the citizen." He defined the citizen as the person who, if need be, could re-create his civilization.

37   Now, it is said that Goethe was the last man who knew all the aspects of his civilization (I doubt that he did), but that after him things became too complicated. My professor had something different in mind. He meant that the citizen should know the great themes of his civilization, its important areas of thought, its philosophical and religious controversies, the outline of its history and its major works. The citizen need not know quantum physics, but he should know that it is there and what it means. Once the citizen knows the shape, the narrative, of

his civilization, he is able to locate new things—and other civilizations—in relation to it.

38   The narrative of Western civilization can be told in different ways, but a useful paradigm has often been called "Athens and Jerusalem." Broadly construed, "Athens" means a philosophical and scientific view of actuality and "Jerusalem" a spiritual and scriptural one. The working out of Western civilization represents an interaction—tension, fusion, conflict—between the two.

39   Both Athens and Jerusalem have a heroic, or epic, phase. For Athens, the Homeric poems are a kind of scripture, the subject of prolonged ethical meditation. In time the old heroic ideals are internalized as heroic philosophy in Socrates, Plato, and Aristotle.

40   For Jerusalem, the heroic phase consists of the Hebrew narratives. Here again, a process of internalization occurs, Jesus internalizing the Mosaic Law. Socrates is the heroic philosopher, Jesus the ideal of heroic holiness, both new ideals in their striking intensity.

41   During the first century of the Christian Era, Athens and Jerusalem converge under the auspices of Hellenistic thought, most notably in Paul and in John, whose gospel defined Jesus by using the Greek term for order, Logos.

42   Athens and Jerusalem were able to converge, despite great differences, because in some ways they overlap. The ultimate terms of Socrates and Plato, for example, cannot be entirely derived from reason. The god of Plato and Aristotle is monotheistic, though still the god of the philosophers. Yet Socrates considers that his rational universe dictates personal immortality.

43   In the Hebrew epic, there are hints of a law prior to the Law of revelation and derived from reason. Thus, when Abraham argues with God over the fate of Sodom and Gomorrah, Abraham appeals to a known principle of justice which God also assumes.

44   Thus Athens is not pure reason and Jerusalem not pure revelation. Both address the perennial question of why there is something rather than nothing.

45   From the prehistoric figures in Homer and in Genesis—Achilles, Abraham— the great conversation commences. Thucydides and Virgil seek order in history. St. Augustine tries to synthesize Paul and Platonism. Montaigne's skepticism would never have been articulated without a prior assertion of cosmic order. Erasmus believed Christianity would prevail if only it could be put in the purest Latin. Shakespeare made a world, and transcended Lear's storm with that final calmed and sacramental Tempest. Rousseau would not have proclaimed the goodness of man if Calvin had not said the opposite. Dante held all the contradictions together in a total structure—for a glorious moment. Katlca could not see beyond the edges of his nightmare, but Dostoyevsky found love just beyond the lowest point of sin. The eighteenth-century men of reason knew the worst, and settled for the luminous stability of a bourgeois republic.

46   By any intelligible standard the other great civilization was China, yet it lacked the Athens-Jerusalem tension and dynamism. Much more static, its symbols were the Great Wall and the Forbidden City, not Odysseus/Columbus, Chartres, the Empire State Building, the love that moves the sun and the other stars.

47   When undergraduates encounter the material of our civilization—that is, the liberal arts—then they know that they are going somewhere. They are becoming citizens.

QUESTIONS FOR ANALYSIS AND DISCUSSION

1. Does Hart's background as a professor make him an expert on this issue? Why or why not? How much does his argument rely on the reader's acceptance of his authority on this issue?

2. Take the impromptu quiz Hart poses to his students. How many of the things he cites did you know at least something about? Do not look up any of the items on the list before answering the question.

The Mayflower Compact	*The Battle of Yorktown*	*Tenth Amendment*
John Locke	*The Bull Moose Party*	*James Madison*
The Magna Carta	*Don Giovanni*	
The Spanish Armada	*William James*	

3. Based on your responses to question 2 and learning their subsequent answers (your instructor will provide answers, but you can look them up in advance), how relevant do you think the issues on the list are to your ability to get a good college education? Explain.

4. According to the author, how has specialization harmed the undergraduate curriculum? Explain.

5. What are the "victimologies"? In Hart's opinion, how are such courses harming students' college educations?

What a College Education Buys
Christopher Caldwell

It seems as if a high school diploma isn't what it used to be. More and more high school graduates are pursuing college degrees, as more businesses demand that applicants hold at least a bachelor's degree. What can students expect from an undergraduate degree today? If more students attend college, broadening the student body, is a bachelor's degree what it was 20 years ago? Or is a college degree what a high school diploma was a generation ago? In the next essay, author Christopher Caldwell asks what all of these college graduates are actually getting for their money.

Caldwell is a senior editor at *The Weekly Standard*. He is a regular contributor to the *Financial Times* and *Slate*. His essays and reviews appear in the *New York Times*, the *Wall Street Journal*, and the *Washington Post*. This essay appeared in the *New York Times's* "The Way We Live Now" column on February 25, 2007.

BEFORE YOU READ

Should everyone get a college education? Why might college be unsuitable for some?

AS YOU READ

Who is Christopher Caldwell's intended audience? Identify areas of his essay in which he makes assumptions of his audience.

1   How important is college to Americans? Put it this way: When Philip Zelikow, the State Department counselor who worked often on Israel-Palestine issues, resigned in November, he cited "some truly riveting obligations to college bursars." That's how important college is—it's more important than peace in the Middle East.

2   The Democrats' promise to make college more affordable for the middle class was a no-lose gambit. It pleased everybody. When the new majority voted to halve the interest rate on federally guaranteed student loans, 124 Republicans joined them. "I just think that we need more of our kids going to school," said Representative Roscoe Bartlett, a Maryland Republican. But given that 45 percent of U.S. high-school graduates already enroll in four-year colleges, how dire can this "need" be?

3   Certain influential Americans have begun to reassert the old wisdom that a college education is one of those things, like sky diving and liverwurst, that are both superb and not for everybody. Not long ago, the conservative social scientist Charles Murray wrote a three-part series in the *Wall Street Journal* in which he attacked the central assumption behind President George Bush's No Child Left Behind initiative. The idea that "educators already know how to educate everyone and that they just need to try harder" is a costly wrong impression, he wrote. Not all schoolchildren have the intellectual capacity to reach "basic achievement" levels. In college, similar limitations apply. The number of Americans with the brains to master the most challenging college classes, Murray argued, is probably closer to 15 percent than to 45.

4   Of course, part of the reason Americans think everyone should go to college is for its non-educational uses. Anyone can benefit from them. Colleges are the country's most effective marriage brokers. They are also—assuming you don't study too hard—a means of redistributing four years' worth of leisure time from the sad stub-end of life to the prime of it. (Just as youth shouldn't be wasted on the young, retirement shouldn't be wasted on the old.)

5   But the price of college long ago outstripped the value of these goods. The most trustworthy indicator that an American college education is something worthwhile is that parents nationwide—and even worldwide—are eager to pay up to $180,000 to get one for their children. This is a new development. A quarter-century ago, even the top Ivy League schools were a bargain at $10,000 a year, but they received fewer applications than they do now. Presumably, college is steadily more expensive because its benefits are steadily more visible. In 1979, according to the economists Frank Levy and Richard Murnane, a 30-year-old college graduate earned 17 percent more than a 30-year-old high-school grad. Now the gap is over 50 percent.

6   These numbers don't tell us much about how people get educated at a typical American college. You can go to college to get civilized (in the sense that your thoughts about your triumphs and losses at the age of 55 will be colored and deepened by an encounter with Horace or Yeats at the age of 19). Or you can go there to get qualified (in the sense that Salomon Brothers will snap you up, once it sees your B.A. in economics from M.I.T.). Most often, parents must think they are paying for the latter product. Great though Yeats may be, 40-some-odd thousand seems a steep price to pay for his acquaintance. The timeless questions that college provokes—like "What the hell are you going to do with a degree in

English?"—must get shouted across dinner tables with increasing vehemence as college costs rise inexorably.

7   But the education kids are rewarded for may not be the same education their parents think they are paying for. Economists would say that a college degree is partly a "signaling" device—it shows not that its holder has learned something but rather that he is the kind of person who could learn something. Colleges sort as much as they teach. Even when they don't increase a worker's productivity, they help employers find the most productive workers, and a generic kind of productivity can be demonstrated as effectively in medieval-history as in accounting classes.

8   Moreover, if you're not planning on becoming, say, a doctor, the benefits of diligent study can be overstated. In recent decades, the biggest rewards have gone to those whose intelligence is deployable in new directions on short notice, not to those who are locked into a single marketable skill, however thoroughly learned and accredited. Most of the employees who built up, say, Google in its early stages could never have been trained to do so, because neither the company nor the idea of it existed when they were getting their educations. Under such circumstances, it's best not to specialize too much. Something like the old ideal of a "liberal education" has had a funny kind of resurgence, minus the steeping in Western culture. It is hard to tell whether this success vindicates liberal education's defenders (who say it "teaches you how to think") or its detractors (who say it camouflages a social elite as a meritocratic one).

9   Maybe college cannot become much more accessible. The return on college degrees must eventually fall as more people get them, and probably not everyone wants one. In France, people often refer to their education as a "formation." The word implies that an increase in your specialized capabilities is bought at a price in flexibility and breadth of knowledge. In most times and places, this bitter trade-off is worth it. But for the past few years at least, the particular advantage of an American degree has been that it doesn't qualify you to do anything in particular.

QUESTIONS FOR ANALYSIS AND DISCUSSION ────────

1. Why does Caldwell warn against specializing during the undergraduate years?
2. Why did you choose to get a college degree? Did you choose your major "to get qualified" or "to get civilized"? Explain.
3. In Caldwell's essay, which examples are used to show the various benefits of a college education? Do you agree or disagree with these "benefits"? Explain.
4. What is the plan behind George Bush's "No Child Left Behind" initiative? In Caldwell's words it is that "educators already know how to educate everyone and that they just need to try harder." Do you agree with this interpretation? Explain.
5. Caldwell references Charles Murray's essay, featured earlier in this section. Do you think he agrees with Murray's assessment and conclusions? Explain.

WRITING ASSIGNMENTS

1. John McWhorter notes that although many admissions officers dislike the idea of race-based admissions in principle, they still believe they are necessary for a diverse campus. Assume the role of a college admissions officer and create a list of the academic standards, abilities, grades, and qualities you believe should be used to admit students to the college you currently attend. Explain why you think your standards and measures are important factors in the admissions process. Finally, explain the role race plays, or does not play, in your admission policies.

2. Jeffrey Hart mentions the bewilderment of college freshmen upon embarking on a college curriculum. Describe your own experience as a new freshman. What guidance did you receive? How confident were you on your course selection? How happy are you with your current course load? Do you think you feel comfortable, or confused, as Hart describes in his essay?

3. Write an essay on what a college education means to you. Include what skills, knowledge, and abilities you feel a college education should confer after four years of study.

4. Write an essay in which you address the importance of a foundation in the liberal arts—specifically in history, literature, and philosophy—on a college education. Alternatively, you could write about why such subjects are no longer important to a good college education.

5. Design a college core curriculum that every student must take before graduation, regardless of their major. Select 12 courses to be taken over the four-year time span of the average bachelor's degree. You may be general in your selection ("Western Civilization I & II") or very specific ("Gender and Power in Modern America"). After compiling your curriculum, share your list with other students in class to see which courses were chosen in common, and which ones were different. If your college or university has a core curriculum, compare your final list with that outlined in your student handbook.

STUDENTS' RIGHTS AND RESPONSIBILITIES

Welcome to the Fun-Free University
David Weigel

Until the 1960s, the concept of colleges applying the principles of *in loco parentis*—acting in the place of a parent—was a generally accepted practice. But many students of the 1960s objected to controls that they felt were unfair violations of their rights as adults. For almost 30 years, colleges allowed students to assume personal responsibility for their actions, but in the wake of alcohol-related student deaths, unhealthy habits, and even medical conditions leading to suicide, many colleges are rethinking their "hands off" approach. Is the return of *in loco parentis* killing student freedom?

David Weigel is an associate editor of *Reason* magazine, where he regularly writes on politics. Previously, Weigel served as an editorial assistant at *USA Today's* editorial page and as a reporter for *Campaigns & Elections*. His articles have appeared in the *Los Angeles Times, Money, The Politico, The American Spectator, The American Conservative,* and *The American Prospect*, among other publications. Weigel wrote this essay in October 2004 for *Reason Online*, following his 2004 graduation from Northwestern University.

BEFORE YOU READ

What rights and privileges do you expect to enjoy as a college student? Do you expect to be treated completely as an adult? Or do you expect the school to ensure certain protections and safeguards as part of your college experience? If so, what is the balance between safety and personal responsibility?

AS YOU READ

How does the history of *in loco parentis* inform the current trend adopted by many colleges and universities to curtail student drinking on campus and enact other policies to ensure student safety?

1   In April 1968, student activists at Columbia University schemed to take over the dean's office as a protest against the Vietnam War and plans to build a new gym. More than 700 students were arrested, and the uprising won national attention. But the school's buttoned-up administrators hadn't wanted to involve the police, and the rioters eventually were allowed to graduate. The mayor of New York, John Lindsay, even arrived in December to address the students and applaud "the urgent, authentically revolutionary work of this generation."

2   How much of that revolution has carried over to the Columbia of 2004? Registered students who occupy a building would get a dialogue with administrators, but the school wouldn't shy from expulsion. According to Ricardo Morales, the school's crime prevention specialist since 1983, nonstudent radicals wouldn't make it into the campus buildings. "If you want to bring a friend over," Morales explains, "you bring him to the lobby and swipe your ID cards. The guest leaves a piece of ID. If he wants to stay for a few days, you can apply for a guest pass."

3   Even when they're not keeping their borders sealed so tight, college administrators have been adopting harsh measures in response to unapproved student behavior. Last fall, students at Southern Methodist University saw their "affirmative action bake sale," a bit of political theater in which prices were determined by the races of buyers, shut down by the student center. They had failed to register with the university as a "protest" or to go to the officially designated "protest zone," on the south stairs outside of the Hughes-Trigg Student Center.

4   Many college administrators throughout the country are taking great pains to keep their students under tight control. Yet in the late 1960s and '70s, whether colleges could rein in students was an open question. Previously, America's universities

had operated under the doctrine of *in loco parentis* ("in the place of a parent"). By the start of the '70s, thanks to a series of legal rulings and cultural shifts, courts and colleges were tossing out that policy, and universities that had been dealing with students as wards struggled to find a new approach.

5   That didn't last. *In loco parentis* has been rejuvenated and returned. Administrators have tapped into the devaluation of personal responsibility illustrated by smoking bans and fast food lawsuits, coupling it with bullish political correctness. The resulting dearth of individual liberties on campuses would have seemed impossible to college students of 25 years ago.

Save the Children

6   In 1969 Sheldon Steinbach arrived at the American Council on Education, the catchall coordinating body for universities, just in time to weather the worst of the campus revolts. Elite schools such as Berkeley, Columbia, and Cornell were acquiescing to radical students and opening up their internal judicial processes. Students won seats on some boards of trustees. Administrators appeared to have lost their grip.

7   "The basic liberal arts education began to crumble," Steinbach says. "That's what it looked like. When the war ended, we could consolidate, sit back, and look at how to save the system."

8   An unexpected boon arrived in 1974, the year of the Kent State decision *Scheuer* v. *Rhodes*. Sens. John Warner (R-Va.) and James Buckley (Conservative-N.Y.) sponsored the Family Educational Rights and Privacy Act (FERPA) in the hope of empowering parents to keep tabs on their kids' academics. Committees amended the bill into a codification of student privacy rights, and Steinbach got a crack at it before FERPA moved on to the Senate. When the bill passed, parents could peek into the records of their children until their 18th birthday, at which point those rights transferred to the student. But FERPA created exceptions: Schools could release records to providers of financial aid and to "appropriate officials in cases of health and safety emergencies." If a student was hit with a subpoena or legal charge, the school could peek into his criminal records. Yet college administrators and their advisers, Steinbach included, kept the champagne corked. It wasn't immediately clear what effect the law would have, outside of giving parents annual notice of their new rights.

9   Meanwhile, concern about the state of campuses was spreading. In March 1977, I ran a hand-wringing exposé titled "The End of Expulsion?," which gave the supposed academic apocalypse some context: "In just ten years, most of the rules that once governed student life *in loco parentis* have simply disappeared. Even serious scholastic offenses, such as cheating and plagiarism, seldom incur the harsh penalties that were once automatic. Most college administrators admit that they lean over backward to avoid expelling students." The irksome rites of passage that had been mandatory—core curricula, single-gender dorms, class attendance—fell away.

10   In the 1979 case *Bradshaw* v. *Rawlings*, the U.S. Court of Appeals for the 3rd Circuit spelled out the universities' weakness. When a Delaware Valley College sophomore three years under the Pennsylvania drinking age hitched a ride from a drunk driver and was injured in a car crash, he sued the school. The court shrugged

him off. "The modern American college is not an insurer of the safety of its students," it said. "Rights formerly possessed by college administrations have been transferred to students." Expectations were pointless, because "beer drinking by college students is a common experience. That this is true is not to suggest that reality always comports with state law and college rules. It does not."

11   The court's decision reflected the way students lived: They had a new relationship with their deans, who should treat them like the young adults they were.

Just Say No

12   University administrators immediately started wringing their hands over the "kids will be kids" philosophy of *Bradshaw* v. *Rawlings*. When one of their wards was arrested, injured, or killed, whether a lawsuit resulted or not, the school felt a blow to its prestige and sense of community. Unchecked hedonism and recklessness among students increasingly free to skip classes or make their own schedules were perceived as a threat to the institution's reputation.

13   Brett Bokolow, manager of the National Center for Higher Education Risk Management (NCHERM), estimates that colleges have been seeking formulas to keep students out of actionable situations for 20 years. In the 1980s, they were increasingly finding themselves liable for providing services or sponsoring events that involved alcohol. After only a few legal wounds, schools sought methods to put the responsibility for drinking or drug use on the backs of students and fraternities and sororities. Two weapons fell into their laps.

14   As the Department of Education opened for business in 1980, an increasing number of students were turning to government aid and loans to pay for their college bills. From 1970 to 1980, federal aid to college students soared from $600 million to $4.5 billion. In 1978 Congress had passed legislation that entitled all college students to federally insured loans. Suddenly, colleges had leverage to punish students for misusing their leisure time. If they were getting money from taxpayers, they were treated like any other employee found partying on the job. Since students were making use of their loans every minute of the academic year, all of their fun was suspect, and much of the adult behavior that vexed administrators was happening on the public dime.

15   Colleges became willing and able to shift some burden to Greek organizations, which had grown again after a marked falloff in the Vietnam era. Many schools created incentives for fraternities and sororities to go dry, or at least disincentives for them to stay wet. In one typical action in 1988, Rutgers University, which had just banned bringing kegs into dorms, responded to a student's death by embargoing all Greek events. In 1997, after first-year student Scott Kreuger drank himself to death at a pledge event, MIT banned freshmen from fraternities. More responsibility was shifted to fraternity and sorority members. By the mid-'90s, universities had become so strict that they were rarely found liable for student sins. Instead of threatening to punish their kids if they came home late, schools simply took away the car keys. If kids somehow got themselves into trouble, it was a police matter.

16   Colleges found the rest of their arsenal in 1987, when Congress threatened to withhold federal transportation money from states that allowed anyone below the age

of 21 to buy alcohol, with the result that 21 became the de facto national drinking age. Across the country, the harshness many schools had formerly applied only to drug offenses began to apply to drinking as well, and the war on fraternities was ramped up. Finally, in 1998 FERPA was amended to make one provision clearer: Colleges could sidestep their students' wishes and inform parents whenever a drug or alcohol law was broken. Before that, less than 20 percent of schools had informed parents of such violations. Afterward, most of them did so.

17   In 2001 *The Chronicle of Higher Education* reviewed this phone-home policy and found great success. Reporters spotlighted the story of a University of Delaware freshman who pledged to quit drinking after police stopped him on the street for a Breathalyzer test. After he was caught, his parents began bringing him home each weekend and lecturing him on his mistakes. The student stopped drinking, but not because he worried about the effects of booze. If he was caught again, he would be suspended for a year.

Back in Control

18   Four decades after *in loco parentis* started to stagger, college students would be hard pressed to name their new personal liberties. When administrators crack down, they will almost always at least provide a reason. But today's students may be punished just as hard as their predecessors—often harder. They've discovered that social engineers have a hard time turning down the opportunity to control things.

19   The expanding control over college students has had repercussions in the rest of America. Campuses are proving grounds for make-nice public programs. They've provided laboratories to test speech codes and small, designated "free speech zones" for protests. (Such zones marginalize and effectively silence dissent, which is one reason they've been adopted by the major political parties for their national conventions.) The stiffening of campus law also illustrates the trend toward greater control of adults' personal behavior.

20   *In loco parentis* could be overturned only once. After 1974, students should have had an arsenal of new rights. But parents never stopped believing that universities were responsible for shaping their kids, and schools have nervously assumed that too much freedom will bring about the system's collapse.

21   It won't. College students will drink, despair, play loose with hygiene, make dirty jokes. Before *in loco parentis* made its comeback, they were thriving. Meanwhile, the changes that really worried academics in the 1970s—demands for new disciplines, shrinking core curricula—are settling into permanence. It's the most enjoyable effect of the '60s student revolts that's being whittled away.

QUESTIONS FOR ANALYSIS AND DISCUSSION

1. Do you think *in loco parentis* has a place on modern college campuses? Why or why not? Support your perspective on this issue with examples to back up personal viewpoints.

2. What did the decision of *Bradshaw* v. *Rawlings* reveal about administrators' views of student personal responsibility in the 1970s? Do you think a court today would make a similar pronouncement? Why or why not?

3. Weigel observes, "Four decades after *in loco parentis* started to stagger, college students would be hard pressed to name their new personal liberties. . . . They've discovered that social engineers have a hard time turning down the opportunity to control things." What are your personal liberties? Are any indeed new? Have any liberties enjoyed by your predecessors 10 or 20 years ago been revoked?

4. What does Weigel think of the resurrection of *in loco parentis* on college campuses? Identify specific areas where he makes his viewpoint clear.

Parental Notification: Fact or Fiction
Joel Epstein

In 1998, Congress amended Section 444 of the General Education Provisions Act by adding *Sec. 952: Alcohol or Drug Possession Disclosure:* "Nothing in this Act or the Higher Education Act of 1965 shall be construed to prohibit an institution of higher education from disclosing, to a parent or legal guardian of a student, information regarding any violation of any Federal, State, or local law, or of any rule or policy of the institution, governing the use or possession of alcohol or a controlled substance, regardless of whether that information is contained in the student's education records, if (a) the student is under the age of 21; and (b) the institution determines that the student has committed a disciplinary violation with respect to such use or possession." Since the passage of this provision, some college administrators are warning students that their parents will be contacted if they are caught drinking alcohol or if they are deemed intoxicated by campus security. Should administrators notify parents of students' alcohol violations? Would notification reduce alcohol abuse? Joel Epstein explores both sides of this question in the next essay.

Joel Epstein, J.D., is associate director and senior attorney with the U.S. Department of Education's Higher Education Center for Alcohol and Other Drug Prevention. The center is based at Education Development Center, Inc., in Newton, Massachusetts. This article appeared in the *Prevention File* journal, Vol. 14, No. 2, published by The Silver Gate Group, an organization that prepares reports on topics regarding public health and safety for professional and public audiences.

BEFORE YOU READ

Have you ever been in a situation, such as at a party, concert, or sporting event, in which either you or the people around you became unruly because of excessive alcohol consumption? How did college administrators respond? Were parents notified?

AS YOU READ

In this essay, first-year student Jessica Kirshner is quoted as saying that alcohol is "just a way of life." What role does alcohol play in your student life? In your roommates' and friends' lives? How would your college experience be different if there were no alcohol at all? Explain.

1   It happens every weekend. A son or daughter, away at college for the first time, drinks him- or herself into a drunken stupor at an off-campus bar. Around 3:00 A.M. two less-intoxicated friends help their roommate, hardly able to stand, onto the Happy Bus, the local college shuttle, where they join nine other similarly inebriated undergraduates for the bumpy ride back to campus. This trip is an uneventful one. No major fights ensue and none of the dozen heavily besotted souls on this outing lose it on the way back to their dorm room.

2   Upon staggering off the bus at the college student union, several of the more intoxicated students are approached by campus police. What's happening here? Quickly the drunk and underage students are advised that they are being charged with violating the school's policy against underage drinking. The students are written up and told that under a newly enacted disciplinary policy their parents will be notified that the students have been charged with violating the school policy and state law.

3   Can a school really confront high-risk student drinking in this manner? Laws aimed at curtailing college student drinking and drug use was one of several major legislative initiatives passed during the 105th Congress. At first glance, these laws appear to represent important developments in the evolving attitude of the public toward student drinking and drug use and disorder. But some people question the conviction with which the new approaches will be embraced and the debate rages on about whether student privacy rights prohibit approaches like parental notification. Indeed, Section 952, Alcohol or Drug Possession Disclosure, of the Higher Education Act, is still being widely debated both on- and off-campus.

4   Signed into law in October 1998, the law clearly permits schools to disclose to parents violations of not only local, state, and federal laws but also school policies and rules governing the use or possession of alcohol or controlled substances. The parental notification amendment came about largely as a result of the efforts of Jeffrey Levy, the father of a college student killed in 1997 in an alcohol-related traffic crash. Levy lobbied hard for the proposal after his 20-year-old son, a student at Radford University in Virginia, was killed while riding as a passenger in a car driven by a drunk driver.

5   Appointed to a Virginia attorney general's task force on college drinking, Levy encouraged the task force to act forcefully with respect to parental notification. The other members of the task force listened. One of the group's leading recommendations was the parental notification idea and eventually the task force persuaded Virginia Senator John W. Warner to introduce legislation in the U.S. Senate. As enacted, the law permits but does not require schools to notify parents of a student's alcohol or other drug violation. [. . .]

A Student's View

6   Opinions vary widely however as to whether schools should notify parents of their child's alcohol or drug violation. Jessica Kirshner, a first-year student at Harvard University, thinks maybe at a certain point parents should be notified, but not if the

violation is just an isolated incident. "Perhaps after repeated incidents or if the incident is serious enough that the student has to be hospitalized, but otherwise I do not believe parents need to be notified," says Kirshner.

7   In Cambridge and Boston, undergraduates witness a great deal of drinking by underage students. "It permeates campus life," explains Kirshner. "Underage students definitely need fake IDs. Bars are conscious that these students are underage, but if the student has an ID to show at the door, they're in."

8   As for local enforcement efforts, Kirshner adds, "I know that liquor stores in Cambridge have 'Cops in Shops,' so it's a deterrent, but there are other ways to get around that."

9   One of the most common ways underage students obtain beer and liquor is simply by having of-age students purchase the alcohol. And a lot of the time students don't even have to buy it, "it's just around."

10   A close observer of campus alcohol policy, Kirshner is not aware of any disciplinary incidents this year at Harvard involving alcohol that resulted in parents being notified.

11   "I have seen underage students who got drunk at campus parties sent before the disciplinary board, but I have not seen any expulsions. Typically they get put on probation. It doesn't look good for the time being but assuming there is no subsequent violation, the charge gets taken off the student's record by the end of the term," Kirshner said. In her view, students are little concerned about underage drinking, and parental notification is not even on their radar. She adds, "I don't know if underage drinking would be considered a right of passage, it's just something to do."

12   As for the types of drinking taking place among underage students, "it tends to depend on the venue. Around the dorms it's not binge drinking or heavy drinking. Heavy drinking sitting around your room is not 'socially acceptable.' But once you get out in the bars, there it is heavier," explains Kirshner.

Who's Responsible?

13   Before passage of the federal parental notification law, officials at most schools across the country had refused to tell parents about student drug and alcohol violations, citing the Family Educational Rights and Privacy Act (FERPA), also known as the Buckley Amendment, a 1974 law on the privacy of student records. Nonetheless, some parents had for years argued that they have a right to be alerted to their children's life-threatening habits. Now the new law is causing many school administrators to rethink their position on parental notification, although a few schools, including Virginia's Radford University had changed their policy even before Congress acted.

14   Today, many university administrators believe that both students and their parents need to take more accountability and responsibility for their actions. But before the recent media focus on the problem of high-risk student drinking, most parents had little sense of the scope of the problem. Those who did know, more often than not saw it as the aberrant behavior of someone else's son or daughter.

15   While Jeffrey Levy views the parental notification amendment as an important first step, he remains skeptical about the willingness of most schools to take meaningful

steps to address the heavy drinking that has become a way of life for too many college students. Levy fears that many universities will now simply make the empty promise that they have a notification policy in place. The bereaved father suspects that even at many of those schools that adopt a parental notification policy, no or few notifications will be made.

16   "What we had hoped for was a clear statement that schools will notify parents when their son or daughter has been involved in aggressive or binge drinking. Instead, at most colleges a report will only be made if there is evidence of a legal or disciplinary violation . . ." [Many campus police and school administrators would not even consider apprehending heavily intoxicated students as described in the fictional scenario above], explains Levy.

17   Advocates of parental notification warn that students know exactly what is going on. They fear that by not having a strong parental notification policy in place and by failing to say, "I will not tolerate abusive or binge drinking on my campus," schools may be sending the message that nothing has changed.

18   Levy says: "If the notifications were going out, the students would know about it and on most campuses the students can tell you that they do not."

19   Levy has had a hard time finding out how many notifications are actually being made. He says, "I've also spoken to many parents and I've never met a parent who had been notified."

20   A notable exception to what Levy has observed is the experience of the University of Delaware, which last year sent letters to the parents of 1,414 students who had violated the school's disciplinary rules. According to Timothy F. Brooks, Delaware's dean of students, most of these letters reported a student's alcohol or drug violation. Brooks notes that student recidivism has declined precipitously since Delaware enacted its three-strikes policy and initiated the practice of parental notification.

21   Parental notification advocates however are not persuaded by the exception to the general rule. Explains Levy, "A lot of schools have a three-strikes policy, but how many kids wander around campus drunk out of their minds and still there is no action. There's a big difference between, 'Oh, I had one too many to drink,' and 'I'm going to get wasted.' I can accept the first, I can't and I don't think any parent can accept the second. The whole attitude 'I'm going to open up the door, pick up a glass and drink as much as I can, as fast as I can, with the prime purpose of getting wasted,' that is different from the intention of going out to have fun. . . . The failure to stand up to that is unacceptable. Parents don't know about this and in failing to notify them, universities are not helping either the students or their parents."

22   In Levy's experience university presidents want this problem to go away, but they do not want to be seen by students as the heavy. He predicts that on most campuses, for parental notification to be triggered the student will have to have violated a state law, or campus policy which mirrors state law. The catch is, most college officials believe they must catch the student in the act of drinking and much campus drinking has been pushed off-campus or underground. For all intents and purposes, there are no laws against public intoxication on campus.

23   "The sight of two sober students carrying a passed-out student into the dorm should trigger a college to say, 'you are in violation of my policy.' But it doesn't. I want

to see more colleges stand up and say, 'Binge or problem drinking is against our policy,'" says Levy.

24   Advocates of parental notification will have to look carefully at campuses where problems continue and critically scrutinize how many parental notifications there have been.

25   Robert Metcalf, counsel to the Attorney General of Virginia and a prime mover behind the parental notification amendment, is the first to admit the new law is not a silver bullet.

26   "It doesn't force colleges to do anything," notes Metcalf. "It should be called the drunkenness in the sunshine amendment. The way the system was colleges were reluctant to go after students who were clearly violating the law. This new law is just one of a number of methods schools can now use to address the problem. The law removes an artificial barrier that some schools used in the past to not notify parents. Now they can. In Virginia, the development of policy is still at the school level. We just hope that they adopt the amendment approach."

27   With passage of the parental notification law many more schools are now considering adopting a policy of parental notification. Not surprisingly, Virginia and District of Columbia schools have been among the first to take advantage of parental notification. Recently, Virginia Tech, where two students died last year in alcohol-related incidents, became the first major Virginia college to make use of the new federal law. Effective in spring 1999, the new policy will permit the notification of parents of underage students sanctioned for alcohol or drug violations on and off campus.

28   Virginia Tech's new policy is also noteworthy because it forges a partnership with the local police who will notify the school if students are caught off campus with alcohol or drugs. The new collaborative approach will mean students may face both campus disciplinary penalties and public prosecution. In Washington, D.C., both American University and George Washington University are also reviewing their parental notification policies.

29   In considering adopting a parental notification policy, schools need to remember what the amendment is not. Schools should know that the amendment does not impose any affirmative obligation on the institution to inform parents of the disciplinary violation. Rather, it specifically states that such action does not violate FERPA or the Higher Education Act. Basically, it's all up to the schools.

QUESTIONS FOR ANALYSIS AND DISCUSSION

1. Epstein comments that the laws passed as a result of Section 952 "appear to represent important developments in the evolving attitude of the public toward student drinking and drug use and disorder." What does he mean by "evolving attitude"? How has the attitude toward student drinking changed in recent years, and why?

2. What position does the author take on the issue of student drinking? Identify two statements in his essay that may be interpreted as revealing a position on this issue.

3. Do you think college administrators have the right to contact parents when the parents' underage children are caught drinking? Do you think that notification would reduce drinking? Would knowing that this could happen to you curtail your own drinking habits? Why or why not?
4. Epstein presents the student perspective of Jessica Kirshner and administrator Jeffrey Levy. Do these two perspectives present the issue in a balanced way? Whose perspective do you agree with more, and why?

READING THE VISUAL

NASULGC/Anheuser-Busch Spring Break Ad

The National Association of State Universities and Land-Grant Colleges (NASULGC) teamed up with Anheuser-Busch to educate students about the "true view" of typical college drinking behavior. Trying to dispel the stereotype perpetuated by movies such as the film classic *Animal House,* the campaign attempted to promote more responsible drinking behavior among college students. Full-page ads and radio spots profiled the "social norms" theme, asserting that the majority of college students do not engage in excessive, or high-risk, consumption of alcohol. Featured on the next page is one of the ads from this campaign providing some interesting statistics.

QUESTIONS FOR ANALYSIS AND DISCUSSION ————

1. If you were reading a newspaper or saw this ad featured on a poster on campus, would you stop and read it? Would it influence your attitude toward alcohol consumption? Why or why not?

2. This campaign was inspired by the assumption that college students are likely to follow peer-behavior. How much, if at all, are your drinking habits influenced by your peers? Are you more likely to drink when others are doing so? Do you drink more when your friends do? Explain.

3. This ad is done in the form of a true or false test. Why do you think the advertisers chose this format? How does it connect to the audience and the subject matter? Explain.

4. The sixth question on the "test" was distinguished from the others by appearing in red. Why do you think this question was highlighted? Visit the Core Institute's Library, the source of this data, and review their reports on college drinking at <http://www.siu.edu/~coreinst/> and click on the "Library" tab. Is Anheuser-Busch skewing the data? What is the source for this statistic? Are they telling the whole story? Explain.

5. This ad was featured in a campaign designed to encourage responsible drinking. In your opinion, do the facts listed in the ad help promote responsible drinking? Do they dispel any myths students are likely to have about their peer group's alcohol consumption habits? Explain.

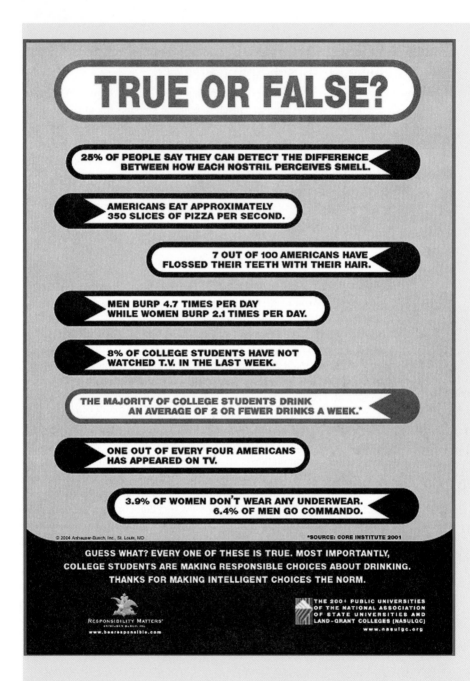

"In Loco Parentis": Invasions of Privacy or Moral Formation?

Joanna K. M. Bratten

During the 1960s, many colleges and universities eased the rules and restrictions on student behavior previously governed by schools acting *in loco parentis*. Before this time, students were expected to sleep in their dorms—often by 10:00 p.m. They were not allowed to entertain guests of the opposite sex, drink, smoke, or engage in other "immoral behavior." Some schools—often religious ones—kept in place the rules governing student conduct along moral and religious lines. In the next essay, Joanna K. M. Bratten, a graduate of a Catholic university, discusses the lines between violating school rules and students' right to privacy.

Joanna Bratten graduated from Franciscan University of Steubenville in 1997. This essay was printed in the *University Concourse*, an independent journal of opinion published at Franciscan University, Ave Maria University, and related Catholic institutions of higher learning on April 12, 1999, when Bratten was a PhD student at the University of St. Andrews in Scotland.

BEFORE YOU READ

What are your expectations of your privacy rights as a college student? Is it ever acceptable for university administrators to regulate what a student chooses to do on his or her own time? off campus? Why or why not?

AS YOU READ

In your opinion, do colleges have the right to determine what is "moral" behavior? Explain.

1   A couple of years ago a 23 year-old student of Thomas Aquinas College was expelled for breaking the college rule prohibiting its unmarried students to spend nights outside their dormitories, unless first granted permission in writing. Not only did she repeatedly commit this violation, but compounded it, by spending these nights in her boyfriend's off-campus apartment, in flagrant disregard of the school commitment to basic Christian moral principles. After warnings, which went unheeded, TAC took action and expelled her. She responded by suing the college for violation of privacy.

2   From a legal and moral perspective her case appeared to have little merit. TAC's policy on the matter was well documented, the student was fully aware of the policy and of the consequences of violating it, and she had been given fair notice. TAC had every right, in these circumstances, to do what it did. And indeed, the suit was eventually dropped. Still, the case has opened up a whole can of worms by invoking the concept of student "privacy." What should a college or university regard as "private" in the lives of its students?

3   As Susan Fischer recently pointed out, the purpose of a university is to educate the whole person. Education cannot be restricted to a classroom; most university students mature not only intellectually but emotionally and—especially at universities such as Franciscan University and TAC—spiritually, even morally. But should the moral life be taught outside of a class in Christian Moral Principles or Ethics? And if so, how? This is where the debate begins.

4   Many universities, even Catholic universities, allow their students to "learn the hard way," leaving them free to dabble in petty—and not so petty—vices during their formative college years. Many students, living for four years or more in such an environment find themselves entrapped for the rest of their lives by vicious habits developed in college. Some universities go too far in the opposite direction, making incoming students sign contracts upon arrival which state that they will not smoke, drink, or even date while they are students at that institution. What happens to a young person in such a situation is perhaps best left to the imagination. Obviously, neither end of the spectrum is the best way for a university to help its students mature emotionally and morally. But where is the golden mean?

5   An educational institution such as TAC seems to have all the best motives in demanding that its unmarried students live on campus and not spend unapproved nights off campus. By restricting the freedom of the students, they hope to instill in them a very clear knowledge of how best to behave as a human person, made in the likeness of God. "Sleeping-over" regularly at one's boy/girlfriend's is a practice which any "dynamically orthodox" Catholic university would wish to discourage in its students. However, is it meet that an academic institution act in loco parentis to ensure that such practices do not occur? Or is it indeed a violation of an individual's privacy when an academic institution insists on keeping an omnipresent eye upon his or her behavior?

6   Without condoning premarital sex or other such "private" sins, I would like to argue that a university should not require itself to expel a student for fornication. TAC, not having expelled the student in question for this moral offense, is quite in the right in expelling the student for violation of university policy, but is that policy altogether fair in the first instance? Compared to the policies of private institutions such as Bob Jones University, alluded to earlier, TAC's policy seems to offer enough room for its students to live, move, breathe and sin. But when each individual student—as an individual and as a student—is considered, such a strict policy might do more harm than good.

7   The best parents learn early on that if a young person is forbidden to do something and is given a pat answer as to why this thing should not be done, more often than not the child goes right ahead and does it, getting hurt in the process. But if a parent explains why a thing is not the best choice and can point out reasonable alternatives and then lets the child go forth and put his own judgments to work, sooner or later the child will come around and see the issue as the parent sees it. I think students can be looked at similarly.

8   In the best of all possible worlds all college students would be reasonable enough to learn to behave in a manner which becomes a true student, a true seeker of truth. In this utopia of sorts students could be expelled for only two reasons: failure to meet academic standards and violation of any university policy which damages other students, staff, faculty, or the reputation of the university itself. But, as Voltaire

has wryly reminded us, we are not living in the best of all possible worlds. The moral and intellectual waste land which is our world today sends students into college who are in need of not only education, but complete reformation on a moral and spiritual level. So, many universities are forced to tighten their grip on the personal lives of their students, just to prevent the entire institution from being sucked into the flow of post-modern materialistic amorality.

9   It is rather a fruitless inquiry to ask if universities have the right to attempt to reform the moral lives of their students and invade their privacy. It would seem that restricting the actions of the students would prevent all those little sins at midnight which keep the students from jaunting down the straight and narrow, yet we must acknowledge the fact that these college students are, like it or not, adults. As adults they should be given the freedom to make adult choices, some of which may be personally detrimental. And above all, if college students are not treated like adults and given at least one chance to prove their capacity to make rational, healthy choices, they will never have the room or the motivation to grow.

10   Privacy is a word which is flung around with little discretion in this day and age, particularly in the abortion debate, and other "rights" debates. In this particular context, however, privacy should be regarded as not so much the right of the individual to do whatever he wants to himself, but as the right of the individual to be permitted to exercise his own judgment within reason. If a student is suspected of being suicidal, or suspected of substance abuse to an extremely dangerous degree, then perhaps the university powers-that-be do have the right, as fellow human beings, to investigate and help the student as they can. But this is a very different sort of intervention than preventing a student from sleeping off campus when he chooses.

11   Perhaps the best answer to the problems which our colleges and universities face is found in the family, in the rebuilding of the family. We know that if children went through moral formation in the home, academic institutions would not have to worry about amorality running rampant. But since the family has deteriorated as far as it has, we must be realistic and determine how to treat the problems as we can. It is generally found that it is best to give a person too much room to act than too little room. God is generous enough to have granted us free will; only by exercising our free will can we ever learn why we were given it.

QUESTIONS FOR ANALYSIS AND DISCUSSION ──────

1. Bratten observes that when a young person is forbidden from doing something, he or she will go out of their way to do it. Do you agree with her statement? Have you acted this way yourself? Explain.
2. Bratten describes the case of a young woman's expulsion from Thomas Aquinas College for breaking school rules. In your opinion, do you think the student should have been expelled? Why or why not?
3. What is the author's position on the issue of *in loco parentis* and rules guiding student behavior?
4. Evaluate Bratten's closing paragraph. How does it connect to her argument? Do you agree?

In Re: Loco Parents
Margaret Gutman Klosko

The departure for college stirs many pangs of fear in the hearts of parents. They worry whether their children will fit in and be happy, safe, and supported. They hope their children study, enjoy their chosen majors, and achieve academic success. But are today's parents too involved in the lives of their college-bound children? In the next essay, former college administrator Margaret Gutman Klosko explains why parents must learn to step aside and let their children become the adults parents want them to be.

Margaret Gutman Klosko is a writer based in Virginia who dealt with anxious mothers and fathers when she worked at the University of Virginia. Here, she offers her advice to parents like her, with children in college. This essay appeared in the April 18, 2006, issue of *Inside Higher Ed.*

BEFORE YOU READ

How involved are your parents in your college experience? Did they help you choose a school? a major? Have they intervened in college disputes or issues? Do you discuss your college experiences with them regularly? Do you ever find them intrusive? Explain.

AS YOU READ

How does Gutman Klosko establish her credibility on this issue? Explain.

1   I am a baby-boom parent with children in college. We baby-boomers, now in our pre-dotage, have become infamous on college campuses—again—this time for noisily hovering over our children as they try to make their ways in the world (see Wikpedia on "helicopter parents"). From my own bleak experience—both professional and personal—I can say with confidence that our children become adults not because of our involvement in their lives, but in spite of it.

2   Penny Rue, the University of Virginia's dean of students, calls us "benign dictators." We, who reacted against the enforced age hierarchy of our own dictatorial parents, have become instead oppressors whose rule is based on the illusion that we and our children are peers, Rue says. And the illusion is so strong, that our children are fooled into not claiming the birthright that we claimed at their age: personal autonomy.

3   This embrace of dependence is not surprising given the attitudes of contemporary college students toward their parents. At the University of Maryland at College Park, James M. Osteen, the assistant vice president for student affairs, writes, "I find that students and their parents generally have a much closer relationship in recent years as compared to earlier decades. Students are very likely to list their parents

as significant role models; whereas in the past students might name people like Gandhi, Martin Luther King or Mother Theresa."

4   It is sweet and fine for your 5 year old to think of you as sainted and heroic, but for your 20 year old to have the same attitude should be worrying. Why don't we hear self-help sages speaking of the problem of arrested development any more?

5   Rue and Osteen see the positive side of parental involvement. Both judge today's parental role as student advocates to be an invitation to college-parent partnerships that can benefit students. But they also recognize the dangers: Both Osteen and Rue note that with parents handling everything from roommate problems to purchasing airplane tickets, students cannot develop a sense of mastery and the confidence necessary to live on one's own. Such parental behavior deprives young people of their identities as autonomous and competent adults.

6   I learned my own necessary lesson about meddling in my children's education probably too late, after a critical period of development—when the second of my three children was in sixth grade. Before that, I would regularly become concerned and then incensed about some way or other schools were failing my children. So caught up in tilting at windmills, I did not devote a moment's attention to the big picture—to problems of other students, teachers, schools, or to my children's educational needs beyond small and preoccupying slights.

7   This is how I learned my lesson: My child, a superior sort of girl, of course, seemed not to be doing any work, while at the same time was receiving good grades. At a teacher conference I complained/boasted that my daughter was not doing any work and getting good grades. I suppose I imagined that with the complaint, her brilliance would be more appreciated, and she would get the special attention that as an exceptional person she deserved. Sure enough, it got her more attention immediately. Her grades plummeted. She became discouraged. And until she enrolled in college and had only herself to please, she never again studied for a test or did a lick of homework. To this day, this is the story my children tell their friends to describe the sort of person their mother is. There is no living it down.

8   As a parent of two in college and one in graduate school, I get involved only in questions of spelling. They may beg me to advise about conditional clauses, but I stand firm. I do listen to complaints about roommates, but have learned that in this area as in most issues of personal relationships it is best to listen only.

9   If other parents would fail earlier in their micro-management careers, college educators would not have to grin and bear helpful advice from over-bearing parents who threaten to bury student affairs offices under ship-loads of constructive criticism. Student affairs professional regularly remark to novices, "You see all those students walking around with cell phones? They are not talking to friends. They are talking to their mothers."

10   And what are these students telling their parents? What they want to hear: that the people who run colleges don't know half as much as their parents do and that life on campus is hell. And then their parents get on their mobile phones and call administrators who, if they weren't chained to their desks would run screaming from their shabby little offices each time a call from a parent were announced.

11   I've looked at life from both sides now—as a parent and as a college administrator. These calls can generate a lot of negative emotion—raising blood pressure of both parents and college administrators. The number of these calls increase exponentially every year. The U.S. Census Bureau reports that in 2003, 16.6 million students were enrolled in college. I imagine that 16.6 million cell phones transmitting the troubled chatter of parents and children about what is going wrong in college must surely be capable of unbalancing the music of the spheres.

12   When I worked in a college president's office, I often took calls from irate parents. I sometimes thought I felt the universe skipping a beat as they described the woes of their children in college: not being able to get into a popular (gut) class; wet, slippery floors in the bathroom; having to go to class in the snow/wind/rain; having an electrical box mounted outside their dorm room (which was sending out dangerous electrical waves); poor grades on tests studied for; having to study for tests over Thanksgiving break; having too short a Thanksgiving/Christmas/Summer break; administrators not doing something about hurt feelings caused by not being offered a place in a fraternity; not doing something about roommates having sex; not being allowed to cheat on exams; the president getting too tough on those who assault others, etc., etc.

13   Some parents would call already angry. Some would become angry when they realized that no matter how much they wanted it, changing the university was going to take longer than 24 hours. They became angrier and angrier as they were transferred from one office to another. The political science department would get calls from parents complaining about fully enrolled courses out of which their children were closed out. The department would pass the calls on to the provost's office, which would pass it along to the president's office. What did I do? I told these parents to write to their legislators about getting more funding for public universities. I pitied the next person they would talk to after getting off the phone with me.

14   Sometimes I think that my generation doesn't much care about what we are trying to control. It is the existential act of exerting control that is important to us. Not going gently into that good night makes us forget ultimate truths. We may have short memories, but those we plague with our demands do not. Student affairs officers shake their heads and remember that baby boomers in their own youths had demonstrated for increased personal freedom, and had gotten rid of the college practice of *in loco parentis*. Now for their children, irony of ironies, they are demanding that it be put back.

15   In our 45–60 years we have been promiscuous and irrational in many of the issues we have raised our voices about. We got the U.S. out of Vietnam and, 30 years later, into Iraq. We started the sexual revolution, and now we vote for anti-birth control and anti-abortion politicians. We rejected our elders' assertion of control over our lives and we put chokeholds on the lives of our children.

16   The time has come to think about the consequences of indiscriminately throwing our considerable middle-aged weight around. It seems to me we have to face some facts. First of all, we need to let our children grow up. Second, we need to realize that we can't stop the world from turning, that the generation we bred will replace us, and that they need to be prepared to do so. Most of all, we need to grow up, grow old, shut up, and step aside.

QUESTIONS FOR ANALYSIS AND DISCUSSION ————

1. What are "helicopter parents"? Do you have helicopter parents or know someone who does? In your opinion, are such parents helpful, or do they hinder students' ability to become full-fledged adults?
2. How does Gutman Klosko's title connect to her theme and the theme of this section?
3. What experience prompted Gutman Klosko to stop being a "helicopter parent" herself?
4. How has Gutman Klosko's experience as a college administrator influenced her view of parental involvement in student affairs? Evaluate the examples she cites, and provide your own view as to whether parents should or should not be involved in such issues.

WRITING ASSIGNMENTS

1. One of the most pressing issues regarding student behavior is binge drinking. Binge drinking is defined as four drinks in a row for females, and five or six drinks in a row for males. Discuss this definition with your peers and determine whether you feel that it is realistic. Then discuss the seriousness of the issue of drinking at your own campus. What reputation does your school have? Is it considered a "party school" or a "drinking school?" Is it a dry campus? Research the issue of drinking on your campus and write a short essay exploring the issue as it relates specifically to your campus.

2. Bratten describes the balance between following university rules and students' right to privacy. Write an essay in which you explore this concept.

3. It seems as if the biggest issue regarding student rights and responsibilities is connected to their consumption of alcohol. Prepare a short questionnaire on college student drinking habits at your school and administer the survey to at least 50 college students from different majors and years. When writing your survey, think about the data you wish to collect. For example, do you want to determine whether some majors are more likely to drink? Is drinking more common among fraternity members? seniors or freshmen? Should college administrators implement measures to curtail college students' drinking? After administering the survey, collect the data and discuss the results. Prepare a short report analyzing the information you gathered.

4. Review your student handbook and summarize your student rights and responsibilities. Do you agree with your college's rules and regulations? Write an essay in which you agree or disagree, in whole or in part, with the rules and regulations guiding student conduct.

5. Research the history of *in loco parentis*. If possible, see if you can find out more about your own college's rules and regulations guiding student behavior 20 or 40 years ago. How have things changed? Do you think things are better now? worse? Explain.

Family and Relationships

The American family has always been in a state of transition, deeply influenced by the social and economic landscape. How we envision the concept of family is based largely on our personal history and the values we share. Many of our ideas regarding the "traditional family" are based on models generations old, touted by politicians and perpetuated by media archetypes. However, the role the American family plays as a social and moral barometer is undeniable. A nationwide poll conducted by the *Los Angeles Times* reported that 78 percent of respondents felt dissatisfied with today's moral values, with half of this group identifying divorce as a key problem.

Many sociologists tell us that our vision of family is not based on reality, but on social ideals and media images. Television programs from the 1950s and 1960s rerun illusions of seemingly perfect families: polite children, neat and orderly homes, strong moral values, happy marriages, and social harmony. Such images may make us feel that our own families fall short of the ideal mark. Stepfamilies, same-sex relationships, divorce, single-parent households, and extended families force us to redefine, or at least reexamine, our traditional definitions of family. This chapter considers several multifaceted aspects of family: marriage, divorce, single parenthood, and even same-sex marriage.

We open the chapter with an examination of how our vision of the perfect family may be based on a media-constructed ideal. Despite the fact that almost half of all marriages end in divorce, we still tend to hold this family structure as the most desirable. Is the institution of marriage a failing concept? Do we scapegoat single parents, especially single mothers, as the source of many social ills? If roughly half of all marriages fail, why is divorce still stigmatized? And what influence, if any, has the conservative, and often religious, right had on the politics of marriage?

The next section explores the issue of gay marriage. Much of the debate hinges on how we define marriage—is it a partnership between two loving, consenting adults, or a sanctified or legal union between a man and a woman? Many arguments circle around the issue of love—if two people love each other, goes the argument, they should be allowed to marry. Opponents to this view contend that marriage is about more than love—it has traditionally been a legal and social bond between a man and a woman, foremost to support the upbringing of children. To redefine this definition of marriage, they argue, would be to undermine the institution itself and threaten the American family.

WHAT ABOUT MARRIAGE?

The Future of Marriage in America
The National Marriage Project

Divorce has become an American way of life. Before they reach the age of 18, nearly half of all children will see their parents' marriage terminate. What does this fact reveal about American attitudes toward marriage? In the next article, the National Marriage Project examines the current and shifting view of marriage in our society. Essay author David Popenoe argues that long-term trends point to the gradual weakening of marriage as the primary social institution of family life. More Americans today are living together, marrying at older ages or not at all, and rearing children outside of marriage. He attributes this weakening of marriage to a broad cultural shift away from religion and social traditionalism and toward faith in personal independence and tolerance for diverse lifestyles. Is the concept of marriage outdated?

The National Marriage Project at Rutgers University defines its mission as follows: "to strengthen the institution of marriage by providing research and analysis that informs public policy, educates the American public, and focuses attention on a problem of enormous scope and consequence." David Popenoe, professor of social and behavioral sciences at Rutgers University, codirects the project with Barbara Dafoe Whitehead, a sociologist who writes extensively on issues related to marriage and the family. Popenoe is the author of *Disturbing the Nest* (1988), *Life Without Father* (1996), and most recently, *War Over the Family* (2005). This essay appears as part of the National Family Project 2007 report. References for this article appear at http://www.marriage.rutgers.edu.

BEFORE YOU READ

The next article addresses American attitudes toward marriage. What is your personal opinion of marriage and divorce? Is marriage an archaic institution, no longer practical in today's society?

AS YOU READ

Is marriage a life goal for you? Do you think you should be married before deciding to have a family? Do you think women's improved economic role outside the home has influenced their feelings about marriage?

1 **A**lmost a decade ago, in our first annual State of Our Unions Report in 1999, the lead essay was "What's Happening to Marriage." The picture we painted was hopeful, if not especially optimistic. Marriage, we reported, "is weakening but it is

too soon to write its obituary." In this, our ninth annual report to the nation, I want to summarize what has been happening to marriage in recent years and peer into the future. One question in particular is compelling: Is marriage in America headed in the direction of the European nations, where it is an even weaker social institution than in the United States? Or are we, as in other areas of our national life—such as our higher level of religious participation and belief—the great exception to the seemingly entrenched trends of the developed, Western societies? This raises, in turn, another intriguing question: Is America still a single nation in family terms, or are we becoming more divided by region and class?

Marriage and Family Trends of the Past Decade

2   There can be no doubt that the institution of marriage has continued to weaken in recent years. Whereas marriage was once the dominant and single acceptable form of living arrangement for couples and children, it is no longer. Today, there is more "family diversity": Fewer adults are married, more are divorced or remaining single, and more are living together outside of marriage or living alone. [The most recent data are available in the second half of this report.] Today, more children are born out-of-wedlock (now almost four out of ten), and more are living in stepfamilies, with cohabiting but unmarried adults, or with a single parent. This means that more children each year are not living in families that include their own married, biological parents, which by all available empirical evidence is the gold standard for insuring optimal outcomes in a child's development.

3   In the late 1990s quite a bit was written about a "marriage and family turnaround," or a reversal of the many family weakening trends. Most negative family trends have slowed appreciably in recent years; they have not continued in the dramatically swift trajectory upward that prevailed in the 1970s and 1980s. Much of this may be due simply to the slowing of social trends as they "mature." The only major family trend that has actually reversed direction is divorce. After rising steeply, beginning around 1965, the divorce rate has dropped gradually since the early 1980s, apparently mainly the result of adults becoming better educated and marrying at a later age. Other possible reasons for the decreasing divorce rate are the rise of non-marital cohabitation and a decline in second and subsequent marriages. Divorcees, for example, have become more likely to cohabit rather than remarry, thus avoiding remarriages that have always had a disproportionately high risk of divorce.

The Marriage Gap

4   One surprising development of recent years is the growth of a marriage and divorce "gap" between differently educated segments of the population. People who have completed college (around a quarter of the population) tend to have significantly higher marriage and lower divorce rates compared to those with less education. Among those married in the early 1990s, for example, only 16.5 percent of college-educated women were divorced within ten years, compared to 46 percent for high school dropouts. Indeed, most of the recent divorce rate decline has been among the college educated; for those with less than a high school education, the divorce rate actually has been rising. (1)

5   The weakening of marriage and the resultant growth of family diversity thus is found much more prominently among those with less education and associated lower incomes. The underlying reason for this may be as simple as the fact that the personality and social characteristics enabling one to complete college are similar to those that foster today's long-term marriages. Or, that delayed entry into the adult world of work and childbearing, and the increase in income and knowledge that college typically fosters, better allows mature values and financial security to undergird choice of partner and family life. Whatever the reasons, this marriage and divorce gap has been a major contributor to the growing economic inequality in America.

6   Some expect the marriage gap to grow larger in the future because children tend to follow the family behavior of their parents. Children of the educated and financially comfortable are better socialized to marry successfully and to contain childbearing within marriage, whereas children of the lower classes often do not have this advantage. But it is doubtful that this gap will have much effect on the over-all drift of marriage in America. The increase in the college-educated portion of the population has been slowing appreciably. And the fertility of college-educated women has dropped. Twenty-four percent of college-educated women aged 40–44 were childless in 2004, compared to only 15 percent of women that age who didn't finish high school. (2) On a national scale, the continuation of this fertility discrepancy could seriously counteract any beneficial family effects of higher education.

The European Direction

7 No matter how weak it has become, however, compared to other modern nations marriage remains at the center of American life. About 85 percent of Americans are expected to marry sometime in their lives, compared to less than 70 percent in a number of European nations. Only ten percent of Americans in an international survey agreed that "marriage is an out-dated institution," compared to 26 percent in the UK and 36 percent in France. (3) Only about ten percent of American couples are cohabiting outside of marriage, compared to almost one third in Sweden. And our commercial wedding industry certainly has become huge. Yet an overriding question is whether marriage and family trends in every modern society are headed in a common direction. In other words, is there a set of family trends endemic to modern (urban, industrial, democratic, and still mostly Western) societies that supercedes economic, cultural, and even religious differences among regions and nations? If so, the current family system in the United States is not an exception but merely a laggard; we will gradually be swept up in the tide.

8   Up to now, the pacesetters in most contemporary marriage and family trends—all moving in the direction of a non-marriage culture—have been the nations of Northwestern Europe, especially the Nordic countries. They have the latest age at first marriage, the lowest marriage and highest non-marital cohabitation rates, and the largest number of out-of-wedlock births. The nations in Southern Europe such as Spain, Italy and Greece, with less cohabitation and fewer out-of-wedlock births, tend to look more like the United States. Family traditionalism remains stronger in

these southern nations, and young people live longer in their childhood homes, often until they marry, rather than living independently or in cohabiting unions. The United Kingdom and the Anglo-settler nations, Canada, Australia and New Zealand, typically stand somewhere in between the two extremes.

9   But with respect to each of the dominant family trends of recent decades the other modern nations have been moving, albeit at varying speeds and not without some temporary lapses, in the Northwest European direction. The percentage of people getting married has been going down, the number of people cohabiting outside of marriage has been increasing, and the out-of-wedlock birth percentage has been skyrocketing. Between the early to mid 1990s and the early 2000s, for example, the marriage rate dropped twelve percent in Italy, 14 percent in Spain, 22 percent in Canada, 28 percent in New Zealand and 24 percent in the United States. At the same time, the non-marital cohabitation percentage (of all couples) climbed 23 percent in Italy and Australia, 53 percent in the United Kingdom, and 49 percent in the United States. The nonmarital birth rate jumped 24 percent in the United States, 48 percent in the United Kingdom, 96 percent in Italy, and a whopping 144 percent in Spain. (4)

10   In one major respect the United States has long been the pacesetter and not the laggard. For generations, we have had the highest divorce rate. Yet even this is now changing. The U.S. rate has been dropping for several decades, while the divorce rate in many European nations has stayed the same or been climbing. The number of divorces per one thousand married women in the United Kingdom in 2002 was 14.4, not too far from the United States rate of 18.4. In the past, the incidence of family breakup was closely aligned with the incidence of divorce, but this is no longer the case. Because more people now cohabit in place of marrying, when a co-habiting couple breaks up it is not registered as a divorce would be. Unfortunately, we have no standard reporting system for the breakup of cohabiting couples, but all empirical studies show that cohabiting couples breakup at a much higher rate than married couples. While only ten percent of American couples cohabit, some 20 percent of British couples do. So if we are considering total family breakup, it is likely the case that Britain plus a number of other European nations now surpass us.

11   There is one other important respect in which America has been in the vanguard of family trends—we have the highest percentage of mother-only families. Many European nations have a much higher percentage of out-of-wedlock births than we do, but the great majority of these births are to unmarried but cohabiting couples. In America, much more often, children are born to a lone mother with the father not in residence and often out of the child's life. Nearly half of all extramarital births in America were of this nature in 2001, according to the latest available data. (5) One reason is our relatively high percentage of births to teenagers, 80 percent of which are non-marital and more than half of those to lone mothers; another is that 70 percent of all unwed births to African Americans are to lone mothers.

12   However, the gap in mother-only families between the United States and other nations of the West is also in the process of diminishing. Being born to a lone mother is only one route to living in a mother-only family. Another route is through the break-up of parents after the child is born, which is far more common among

parents who cohabit compared to those who marry. With parental break-up rates in other nations climbing rapidly, thanks largely to increased non-marital cohabitation, many of these nations are catching up with us in the alarming statistic of mother-only families. Even by the early 1990s, according to the calculations of several scholars, New Zealand had caught up with the United States with nearly 50 percent of children expected to experience single parenting by age 15, and the figure for Canada and five European countries exceeded 33 percent. (6) These percentages would probably be much higher if they were recalculated today using more recent data.

13   So if we are moving in the direction of the more negative family trends of other modern nations, and they are moving in the direction of our negative trends, where does this leave us? Aren't we all in a common basket, destined to witness an institution of marriage that is ever weakening? Before considering this, let us first have a look at the possibility that America is becoming increasingly bifurcated into two distinct cultures. Could it be that only one part of America is moving in a European family direction?

The American Red-Blue Divide

14   The recent family trends in the Western nations have been largely generated by a distinctive set of cultural values that scholars have come to label "secular individualism." It features the gradual abandonment of religious attendance and beliefs, a strong leaning toward "expressive" values that are preoccupied with personal autonomy and self-fulfillment, and a political emphasis on egalitarianism and the tolerance of diverse lifestyles. An established empirical generalization is that the greater the dominance of secular individualism in a culture, the more fragmented the families. The fundamental reason is that the traditional nuclear family is a somewhat inegalitarian group (not only between husbands and wives but also parents and children) that requires the suppression of some individuality and also has been strongly supported by, and governed by the rules of, orthodox religions. As a seeming impediment to personal autonomy and social equality, therefore, the traditional family is an especially attractive unit for attacks from a secular individualistic perspective.

15   On average, America has been moving in the direction of secular individualism, as can be seen in the general drift of our family trends. But the "on average" covers up some very substantial variations, some of which account for why, looked at internationally, we are a nation with relatively conservative family values. A recent National Cultural Values Survey (7) found that American adults usefully can be split into three groups, based on the degree to which they have embraced secular individualism, ranging from the Orthodox to the Progressives, with Independents in the middle. The survey found 31 percent of the population in the religiously Orthodox category, 17 percent in the secular Progressive category, and 46 percent as Independents. The Orthodox category is far larger than one finds in Western Europe and the other Anglo nations, and the Progressive category (i.e., secular individualist) is considerably smaller, and therein lies the major basis for American family exceptionalism.

16   One thing that makes these categories so prominent in American culture is that they are strongly expressed geographically. As analyzed by demographers at the University of Michigan, the two extremes are reflected in the so-called Red (Republican) and Blue (Democratic) state distinction frequently made in recent national political analysis. (8) The more Progressive Blue states are principally those of the Northeast, the Upper Midwest, and the West Coast, while the more Orthodox Red states are found in the South, the lower Midwest, and the Mountain region of the West. Reflecting their different ideologies, the Blue states tend to have lower marriage and higher cohabitation rates, along with lower fertility, while the Red states are more traditional in their family structure.

17   The ideology and family behavior found in the Blue states resembles that of the other Western nations, although not quite as far down the path of Progressivism. If one were referring only to this part of America, one would not be talking about American exceptionalism. The large Orthodox population of the Red states, however, does give the United States a unique configuration in the modern world. If it were not for this population, we would not be having a "culture war" and we probably would not even be having a national conversation about the weakening of marriage. There is no such conversation about marriage in the Northwestern European nations, despite the fact that the institution of marriage is considerably weaker there than it is here.

18   It is clear that the family structure of America is exceptional in some respects. The question is, are we so exceptional that we can resist the modern trend of marriage and family decline? So far the answer is no—we have been headed down the same path as every other modern, Western society toward ever-increasing secular individualism with its associated family structures. If this trend continues, the family structure of the Red states will come to look more and more like today's Blue states, and the Blue states will look ever more like Europe.

The Prospect for Cultural Change

19   To reverse this trend of marriage and family decline would take a cultural transformation of some kind, and it is interesting to consider and evaluate what this might look like, and what could bring it about. One potential source of change would be a significant expansion in influence and authority of today's orthodox, anti-individualist religions. Much has been written in recent years about the weakening of secularization, pointing out that modernization no longer necessarily means the demise of religion. The evidence for this comes from the newly modernizing countries of the world, however, where orthodox religions have actually been gaining, rather than losing, strength. There is no evidence that anything like this has been happening to date in the Western European and Anglo nations. Quite the opposite; with each passing year these nations—including the United States—are more secular than ever before. The National Cultural Values Survey noted above found that regular churchgoing has dipped below 50 percent and only 36 percent believe "people should live by God's principles," concluding that "America no longer enjoys cultural consensus on God, religion, and what constitutes right and wrong."(9)

20   A powerful indicator of future trends are the beliefs and attitudes of today's young people, which are unmistakably more secular and individualist than those of their elders. A recent study concluded that emerging adults (ages 18–24) in America, compared to their earlier counterparts and their older contemporaries, are more disaffected and disconnected from society, more cynical or negative about people, and have moved in a liberal direction. (10) A Pew Foundation national survey found that 20 percent of today's young people (18–24) say they have no religious affiliation or are atheist or agnostic, nearly double the percentage of the non-religious found in that age group less than 20 years ago. In the same time period the percentage of young people who did *not* agree that they had "old fashioned values about family and marriage" jumped from 17 percent to 31 percent. (11) A study in Britain, starkly pointing up the entrenched nature of this generational shift, found that a child with two religious parents has only a 50 percent chance of being religious, while a child with one religious parent has 25 percent chance of being religious. (12)

21   Another cultural transformation that could move the family in a more traditional direction is widespread immigration. In combination with low birthrates, massive immigration is capable of changing the culture, social experiences, and self-identity of a population—including the ideologies of secularism and individualism. This possibility is beginning to be discussed in Europe, where birthrates in many nations remain well below replacement level and immigration, mostly from orthodox Muslim countries with high birthrates, is high and growing. The percentage of foreign born in many Western European nations is now similar to that in America, around twelve percent, but the birthrates of these groups are typically far higher than the indigenous populations. Projections are that the percentage of people of "foreign origin" may reach as high as one third in some European nations by 2050, and far higher than that in the major cities. (13) What is not known is how these new immigrants ultimately will react to secular individualism and the other cultural beliefs and practices of modern, Western democracies. As many have noted, because of long-standing antipathies between peoples of the Muslim faith and those of Christianity, often violent and going back well more than a millennium, it does seem possible that Europe faces the prospect of a major cultural transformation sometime in the future through immigrants who, rather than assimilate, will pull the culture in a new direction.

22   The immigration situation in the United States, however, is different, and it does not seem as likely that in the foreseeable future immigrant groups will be able to seriously shift our culture in a more traditional direction. The most likely candidate for cultural change, of course, is the growing Hispanic population. The percentage of Hispanics is projected to reach 25 percent of the total population by 2050, when non-Hispanic Whites will make up only a slim majority. (14) But unlike Europe we are already a nation made up of many different immigrant groups; many Hispanics have been here for years, and they share a common religious heritage in Christianity. Thus Hispanics don't pose the same threat of not assimilating to Western culture as do the Muslims. Indeed, to date, Hispanics seem to have assimilated into the American culture of secular individualism more than the reverse. For example, the unwed birth percentage among Hispanics has jumped from 19 percent in 1980 to 48 percent

in 2005 and stands well above the percentage for the non-Hispanic White population (25 percent). Hispanics have the same divorce rate as non-Hispanic Whites, and in recent years their rate of non-marital cohabitation has grown faster than that of any other immigrant group. These trends contradict earlier expectations that Hispanics might bring this nation a new wave of family traditionalism.

23   The prediction of the continued growth of secular individualism within modern cultures rests on some powerful facts. So far in the Western experience, at least, the dominant sociological factors associated with secular individualism are that the higher the educational and income levels of a population, and the more urbanized it is, the greater the degree of secular individualism. Is it likely that any time in the near future educational, income, and urbanization levels in America will drop? They have been increasing inexorably for three centuries, so a turnaround would most likely occur only in the event of some catastrophe, either natural or man-made. Absent such a catastrophe (which certainly cannot be ruled out in today's world), the most likely future scenario is that secular individualism will increasingly dominate the cultures of the West.

24   The best prospects for cultural change, therefore, rest on the possibility that, at some time in the future, new generations of secular individualists themselves will undergo a change of heart. One way this might occur is through the growth of new, non-orthodox religious ideologies that remained compatible with secular individualism but take it in new directions. Unfortunately, the new religious strains that have emerged in recent decades, so-called New Age religions, have been profoundly individualistic. None has shown any interest in preserving marriage and family solidarity. Indeed, they seem part and parcel of the secular individualist movement, albeit with a more "spiritual" bent. The same seems to hold true for today's rapidly growing "green" movement, which itself shows signs of becoming a new quasi-religion in which the environment has replaced God as a focus of almost divine adoration. So far there is little evidence that "pro-green" translates into "pro-marriage" or "pro-family," although it is conceivable that somehow the conservation of nature could become translated into the conservation of the family.

25   Any widely accepted "new morality" that might change family behavior would probably have to be compatible with secular individualism's motivating force— rational self-interest. The self-interest of today's young people still includes the desire to have strong intimate relationships and to want to do best by their children. And there is every reason to believe that these interests will continue into the future because they are, in fact, an intrinsic part of being human. The task that lies ahead, then, is to help young people to see the importance of marriage and strong families as the best way to achieve these interests; to help them realize that a better and more meaningful way of life, both for themselves and for their children, involves a commitment to long-term marriage.

What Can be Done?

26   As a first step, the institution of marriage needs to be promoted by all levels of society, particularly the families, the schools, the churches, the non-profit sector, and the government. The great majority of American high school seniors still want to get

married, with 82 percent of girls and 70 percent of boys recently saying that "having a good marriage and family life" is "extremely important" to them. These percentages, in fact, represent a slight increase from the late 1970s. (15) But as high schoolers reach young adulthood, when the attraction of cohabitation and careers gains strong currency, making the actual commitment to marriage is not easy. Young people need, therefore, to be made continually aware of the many benefits married life brings, both for themselves and for their children. The empirical evidence is now strong and persuasive that a good marriage enhances personal happiness, economic success, health and longevity. This evidence should become a regular part of our educational programs and our public discourse.

27 Yet successful marriage promotion requires more than empirical evidence. Marriage has fallen by the wayside, in part, because it receives less and less social recognition and approval. Any norm of behavior requires for its maintenance the continuing support of the community, including active social pressures to uphold it. When social approval and pressures wither, the norm weakens. Today's young people have been taught through the schools and in their communities a strong message of tolerance for "alternative lifestyles." "Thou shalt not make moral judgments about other people's family behavior" seems to have become a dominant message in our times. The reason for this is completely understandable; children and young people come from ever more diverse family situations which are not of their own doing, and they should be fully accepted and not be penalized. The problem is that this moral message is carried on into adult life, where it is applied not to children and young people but to adults who do have choices about how they shape their lives. In an effort not to judge much less stigmatize any adult life style, we have all too often become virtually silent about the value and importance of marriage. This silence is extremely damaging to the promotion of a pro-marriage culture.

28 The widespread promotion of marriage is directed at only half of the problem, however. Getting people to marry is one thing, helping them to stay married is something else entirely. Helping people to stay married is the main focus of an important set of programs known as marriage education. Typically conducted in group settings rather than counseling situations, marriage education programs focus on developing the knowledge, attitudes and skills needed for making a wise marital choice and having a successful marriage. Although marriage education has been around for decades, it recently has been thrust into the limelight thanks to widespread publicity and government assistance.

29 The importance of marriage education is magnified by the fact that the marital relationship today is so different from what it was in the past. Marriage is now based almost entirely on close friendship and romantic love, mostly stripped of the economic dependencies, legal and religious restrictions, and extended family pressures that have held marriages together for most of human history. Until fairly recent times marriages had little to do with romantic love, sexual passion, or even close friendship; they were functional partnerships in the intense struggle of life. Today, a successful marriage rests almost entirely on how well one gets along, intimately and for the long term, with someone of the opposite sex. The

"relationship knowledge" this requires has never been part of formal education, but there is no reason to believe that it can not effectively be taught to married couples and those about to be married, as well as to younger people as part of the high school curriculum. Indeed, the initial empirical evaluations of marriage education programs conclude that they are both well-received and have generally positive outcomes.

30   Marriage promotion and marriage education are essential steps, but in order fully to rebuild the institution of marriage there would probably have to be a cultural shift of a more fundamental nature. Modern cultures would need to pull back from the now dominant thrust of secular individualism—the excessive pursuit of personal autonomy, immediate gratification, and short-term personal gain—and give greater emphasis to issues of community and social solidarity. This could come about through a growing realization, based on rational self-interest, that our personal happiness and sense of well-being over the long course of life are less affected by the amount of independence, choice, bodily pleasure and wealth we are able to obtain than by the number of stable, long-term and meaningful relationships we have with others. (16) And through a greater recognition of the fact that short-term adult interests can be in conflict with the long-term health and wellbeing of children, and that our children's welfare has everything to do with the future of our nation.

Conclusion

31 America is still the most marrying of Western nations, but nevertheless we are caught up in the prevailing trends of modernity that lead toward an ever-weakening institution of marriage. Marriage rates have been dropping and cohabitation and out-of-wedlock birth rates have been rising, thanks in large part to the growing influence of secular individualism in all modern cultures. The negative effects of this are felt most profoundly by our children, who are growing up in family situations that are less and less optimum from a child-development perspective. As we move in the direction of the weaker family structures of Europe it is important to remember that we lack many of the welfare "safety-nets" found there, and therefore the negative effects of marital decline on children are likely to be heightened in this country.

32   We are not a unified nation in family terms. We have a marriage gap, whereby the college-educated have a stronger marriage culture than the less well-educated. And we have a Red state/Blue state divide, whereby the nation is geographically split up into areas of family traditionalism and non-traditionalism. Yet these divisions remain peripheral to the overall waning of marriage in America.

33   The rebuilding of a stronger marriage culture is possible. In addition to the heavy promotion of marriage built around the self-interest of today's young people, it will probably require a cultural shift of some magnitude, one in which stable, predictable, and long-term relationships with others come to be viewed as the best foundation for adult personalities, childrearing, and family life.

QUESTIONS FOR ANALYSIS AND DISCUSSION

1. In his opening paragraph, Popenoe asks, "Is America still a single nation in family terms, or are we becoming more divided by region and class?" Based on the information in his essay, as well as your own viewpoint, answer his question.
2. Is declaring strong support for marriage discriminatory against people who are not married or who are divorced? Is such a viewpoint tolerant of domestic violence? Explain.
3. How has popular culture influenced the decline of marriage? What about social trends and simply a more tolerant society?
4. What is the state of marriage in European countries, and how does it compare with trends in the United States? What differences exist between family units overseas and in the United States?
5. What is the "red-blue divide"? How does it influence marriage trends? Does it also influence cultural opinion of marriage?
6. According to Popenoe, what is the long-term outlook for marriage? How does your perspective fit into the outlook the author describes?

Five Non-Religious Arguments for Marriage Over Living Together
Dennis Prager

With the long list of celebrities living together and having children out of wedlock, coupled with a divorce rate at almost 50 percent, it would seem as if marriage is becoming passé. At all levels of the economic spectrum, many couples prefer to live together rather than get married, at least for a while. In the next essay, author Dennis Prager gives five reasons why he thinks marriage is preferable to living together.

Prager is a syndicated radio talk show host, columnist, and author noted for his conservative political views and for his study of the consequences of secularism in the twentieth century. He is the author of several books, including *Happiness Is a Serious Problem: A Human Nature Repair Manual* (1999) and *Why the Jews? The Reason for Antisemitism* (with Joseph Telushkin) (2003). Prager formerly wrote for several years for the *Sunday Los Angeles Times's* "Current" section and now writes a weekly column for *Townhall.com*, in which this editorial appeared on October 3, 2006.

BEFORE YOU READ

Many couples move in together without being married first, but eventually marry later. Others never marry. Do you think people should live together before getting married? Should they marry at all? Why or why not?

AS YOU READ

Why do people marry? What values and expectations does marriage carry in our culture? Are they the same values and expectations made of couples who live together? Why or why not?

1   I have always believed that there is no comparing living together with marriage. There are enormous differences between being a "husband" or a "wife" and being a "partner," a "friend" or a "significant other"; between a legal commitment and a voluntary association; between standing before family and community to publicly announce one's commitment to another person on the one hand and simply living together on the other.

2   But attending the weddings of two of my three children this past summer made the differences far clearer and far more significant.

3   First, no matter what you think when living together, your relationship with your significant other changes the moment you marry. You have now made a commitment to each other as husband and wife in front of almost everyone significant in your life. You now see each other in a different and more serious light.

4   Second, words matter. They deeply affect us and others. Living with your "boyfriend" is not the same as living with your "husband." And living with your "girlfriend" or any other title you give her is not the same as making a home with your "wife." Likewise when you introduce that person as your wife or husband to people, you are making a far more important statement of that person's role in your life than you are with any other title.

5   Third, legality matters. Being legally bound to and responsible for another person matters. It is an announcement to him/her and to yourself that you take this relationship with the utmost seriousness. No words of affection or promises of commitment, no matter how sincere, can match the seriousness of legal commitment.

6   Fourth, to better appreciate just how important marriage is to the vast majority of people in your life, consider this: There is no event, no occasion, no moment in your life when so many of the people who matter to you will convene in one place as they will at your wedding. Not the birth of any of your children, not any milestone birthday you may celebrate, not your child's bar-mitzvah or confirmation. The only other time so many of those you care about and who care about you will gather in one place is at your funeral. But by then, unless you die young, nearly all those you love who are older than you will have already died.

7   So this is it. Your wedding will be the greatest gathering of loved ones in your life. There is a reason. It is the biggest moment of your life. No such event will ever happen if you do not have a wedding.

8   Fifth, only with marriage will your man's or your woman's family ever become your family. The two weddings transformed the woman in my son's life into my daughter-in-law and transformed the man in my daughter's life into my son-in-law. And I was instantly transformed from the father of their boyfriend or girlfriend into their father-in-law. This was the most dramatic new realization for me.

I was now related to my children's partners. Their siblings and parents became family. Nothing comparable happens when two people live together without getting married.

9   Many women callers to my radio show have told me that the man in their life sees no reason to marry. "It's only a piece of paper," these men (and now some women) argue.

10   There are two answers to this argument.

11   One is that if in fact "it is only a piece of paper," what exactly is he so afraid of? Why does he fear a mere piece of paper? Either he is lying to himself and to his woman or lying only to her because he knows this piece of paper is far more than "only a piece of paper."

12   The other response is all that is written above. Getting married means I am now your wife, not your live-in; I am now your husband, not your significant other. It means that we get to have a wedding where, before virtually every person alive who means anything to us, we commit ourselves to each other. It means that we have decided to bring all these people we love into our lives. It means we have legal obligations to one another. It means my family becomes yours and yours becomes mine.

13   Thank God my children, ages 30 and 23, decided to marry. Their partners are now my daughter-in-law and son-in-law. They are therefore now mine to love, not merely two people whom my children love.

14   When you realize all that is attainable by marrying and unattainable by living together without marrying, you have to wonder why anyone would voluntarily choose not to marry the person he or she wishes to live with forever.

15   Unless, of course, one of you really isn't planning on forever.

QUESTIONS FOR ANALYSIS AND DISCUSSION ———

1. In your opinion, which of author Dennis Prager's five arguments is the strongest one? the weakest? Explain.
2. Argue the opposite viewpoint; in other words, provide five arguments for living together over getting married.
3. According to Prager, when one partner tells the other that marriage "is only a piece of paper," she or he is either lying or doesn't truly believe that the relationship is in fact "forever." Do you agree with this assertion? Explain.
4. Even though Dennis Prager is vocally opposed to gay marriage, could his essay make an argument for legalizing gay marriage? Explain.
5. If living together with a partner provided the same legal benefits afforded to traditionally married couples, such as health and property insurance, inheritance rights, and retirement benefits, would you still get married?
6. Before you read this editorial, did you have any opinion on this issue? Did the piece change your ideas or give you something to think about that you had not considered before? Was Prager successful in persuading you to his point of view, if you did not already agree with him?

On Not Saying, "I Do"
Dorian Solot

Several of the essays in this chapter lament the decline of marriage as an inevitable, and regrettable, reality. The author of the next reading argues that marriage isn't all it is chalked up to be. In fact, people can exist in meaningful and rewarding relationships without marriage, and children can grow up in nurtured and emotionally stable homes. In the next essay, a personal narrative, Dorian Solot wonders, what is all the fuss about getting married . . . or not?

With partner Marshall Miller, Dorian Solot is cofounder of the Alternatives to Marriage Project, a national nonprofit organization that advocates for equality and fairness for unmarried people. Together, they are the authors of the book *Unmarried to Each Other: The Essential Guide to Living Together as an Unmarried Couple* (2002). They have appeared on NBC News, CNN, and National Public Radio and have been mentioned in *USA Today*, *Time*, *Money*, and many other newspapers, radio, and television programs. This essay first appeared on nerve.com on May 27, 2004.

BEFORE YOU READ

If you decided to live with your significant other, do you think you would feel social pressure to marry after a period of cohabitation? Would your family approve? What are your personal expectations of cohabitation? Explain.

AS YOU READ

The author notes that although living together for a period of time is considered socially acceptable, deciding to maintain such an arrangement with no intention of ever marrying is not. What accounts for this view? If it is okay to live together, why isn't it okay never to get married?

1   I must have missed the day in nursery school when they lined up all the little girls and injected them with the powerful serum that made them dream of wearing a white wedding dress.

2   From that day onward, it seemed, most little girls played bridal dress-up, drew pictures of brides, gazed in magazines at the latest bridal fashions, and eagerly anticipated their prince charming popping the question. More than anything, they dreamed of walking down the aisle and living happily ever after. I dreamed mostly of the cats, dogs, and horses I'd get to adopt when I grew up. When I was old enough to walk around town on my own, I remember my best friend stopping in front of a bridal shop window to point out which dress she'd like to wear someday, and asked me to pick mine. I told her honestly that I didn't like any of them, aware even then that she would probably think I was weird, because that wasn't what girls were supposed to say.

3   In my early twenties, about three years into my relationship with my partner, Marshall, the occasional subtle hints that my family and friends were ready for an engagement announcement became decidedly less subtle. To keep their hopes in check, I announced what had seemed clear to me for a long time: I did not intend to get married. Ever. Be in love, sure. Share my life with this wonderful man, absolutely. But walk down the aisle and exchange rings—the tradition baffles me.

4   I didn't expect my small refusal to matter much to anyone. But I have quickly learned that in a society in which 90% of people get married sometime in their lives, lacking the desire to do so appears in the "barely acceptable" category.

5   Not being married to my partner has meant ending the conversation with a potential landlord after his first three questions: How many people? Are you married? When are you getting married? It's meant paying an extra fee—the unmarried surcharge, you might call it—to be allowed to drive the same rental car. And it's meant having my partner be denied health insurance through my job when he needed it, even though our four years together exceeded the relationship length of my newly-wed coworkers who received joint coverage.

6   It's also meant answering questions that get frustrating. "Do you think you'll change your mind?" is a common one. I want to ask these people, "Do you think you might convert to a new religion? Do you think you might change your mind about the ethics of abortion?" Anything is possible, of course, and I'm not so naïve as to think we all don't change our minds about things over the course of a lifetime. But the frequency with which I'm asked this question makes it less an innocent inquiry about a personal choice, and more a suggestion that says, "Your position is so absurd you can't take it seriously for long."

7   I've lost track of the number of sympathetic strangers who've shared with me their incorrect assumption that as an unmarried woman in a long-term relationship, my partner must suffer from a severe case of commitment phobia. Women in newspaper advice columns and television talk shows are forever strategizing about where to find a man willing to get hitched, and debating whether to leave the guys who won't marry them. Interestingly, though, every survey ever conducted on this subject finds that on average, men are more eager to marry than women are. The National Survey of Families and Households, for example, found that 24% of unmarried 18-35 year old men said they'd like to get married someday, compared to 16 percent of unmarried women the same age.

8   Eventually, frustrated that we couldn't find any group that could provide the support and information we needed, Marshall and I founded the Alternatives to Marriage Project. Judging by the number of emails and phone calls we received after posting a website, we weren't alone. There are growing legions of women who, like me, are not interested in assuming the role of wife. Books like *Marriage Shock: The Transformation of Women into Wives* and *Cutting Loose: Why Women Who End Their Marriages Do So Well* quote scores of women who explain how their relationships changed when they got married. Suddenly, they found themselves more likely to be making breakfast and less likely to be talking candidly about sex. As a result of this kind of research, some made the case for more conscious marriages with fewer gendered assumptions, and I think that's a great goal. But if marriage has that

much power to change people's behavior, I'd rather invest my energy exploring alternatives, not struggling to re-shape an institution that doesn't suit me.

9   To me, the issue isn't whether civil marriage should include same-sex couples. Of course it should; that's a fundamental matter of civil and human rights. The issue is the confusing tangle of meanings in the word "marriage," and how they do and don't correspond to real-life relationships and real people's lives. There's religious marriage, conferred by blessings; civil marriage and the legal protections it brings; and social marriage, the support of communities who give special treatment to couples they perceive to be married. (Having just bought a house in a neighborhood where no one knew us before, it's been fascinating to be treated as a married couple, even though our "marriage" is social, not legal.) On top of that, although the concepts of commitment, monogamy and marriage usually go hand in hand, my work is filled with committed *unmarried* couples. And we've all read the tabloid headlines about *married* ones whose commitments don't last all that long. Among both married and unmarried couples, the vast majority chooses monogamy, while smaller numbers choose polyamory or engage in infidelity. We have only one concept—marriage—that is used to divide the world neatly into two groups, married and not married. The real world is a lot messier than that. Our cultural inability to face that complexity leaves us in a state of collective bafflement about the status and future of marriage (is marriage overvalued? undervalued? having a renaissance? dying out?) and inspires confused debates about same-sex unions. The solution, I believe, is to encourage and support healthy, stable relationships and families in all their forms, instead of linking so many unrelated benefits to the piece of paper we call a marriage license.

10   There are joys to not being married. I love that I am *not* a wife, with all its hidden meanings and baggage. I love the consciousness of my relationship, day after day of "I choose you" that has now lasted eleven years and counting. I take secret pleasure in watching people wrestle silently when I mention "my partner," trying to ascertain my sexual orientation and marital status—as if it mattered. I love reading the headlines as one by one, companies, universities, cities, and states decide to provide equal benefits to the partners of their employees, regardless of marital status. I feel as if my daily life proves to those who say it can't be done—that unmarried relationships will fall apart when times are hard, that we can never achieve true intimacy, that we are doomed to lives of sin, sadness, or "perpetual adolescence"—that maybe the problem is theirs and not mine. There is an amazing diversity of families in this country; I hope one day society will be courageous enough to recognize and validate all of them.

11   I don't know how I failed to acquire a yearning for marriage. Maybe it's because of my feminist, hippie mom, who played *Free to be You and Me* while I was in utero and encouraged me to have goals beyond marrying the handsome prince (and who, by the way, considers my handsome prince her son-in-law—or sometimes, affectionately, her son-outlaw). Perhaps it has to do with too many unhappily married people and the divorces I've seen, too many breezily pledged lifetime vows that lose their meaning long before the lifetimes end. Perhaps it has to do with my friends in same-sex relationships who can't legally marry (unless they live in the

right city or state on the right day of the week), the fact that I already have a food processor, or my academic background in animal behavior, where I learned how few mammals mate for life. Or perhaps it's because I really was absent that day in nursery school.

QUESTIONS FOR ANALYSIS AND DISCUSSION

1. Solot observes that many people live together before getting married. In your opinion, does this arrangement make sense? Is it better to test out a relationship before making a marriage commitment, or does it just make it easier for people to walk away from a relationship when the going gets rough? Would you live together with a sweetheart before making a commitment of marriage? Explain.
2. Solot jokes that she missed the day the little girls were "injected with serum" that makes them obsessed with being brides and getting married. What does she mean? Explain.
3. What is the reaction of friends and family to Solot's decision not to marry? Do you agree that her decision appears in the "barely acceptable" category?
4. Why did the author decide not to get married? What are the benefits she cites about not being married?
5. Before you read this narrative, did you have any opinion on this issue? Did the essay change your ideas or give you something to think about that you had not considered before? Was Solot successful in persuading you to her point of view, if you did not already agree with it?

READING THE VISUAL

Families on Television

In her 1992 book, *The Way We Never Were: American Families and the Nostalgia Trap*, sociologist Stephanie Coontz addresses the influence television has on our images of ideal family life. The problem, explains Coontz, is that such visions "bear a suspicious resemblance to reruns of old television series."

> When I begin teaching a course on family history, I often ask my students to write down ideas that spring to mind when they think of the "traditional family." Their lists always include several images. One is of extended families in which grandparents [were] an integral part of family life. [. . .] In traditional families, my students write—half derisively, half wistfully—men and women [. . .] committed themselves wholly to the marital relationship, experiencing an all-encompassing intimacy that our more crowded modern life seems to preclude.

For over 50 years, television has broadcast into American homes idealized images of American families, families that many of us think were the norm only a few decades ago, and families against which we measure our own. Examine the two photos pictured here of the 1950s family unit of *Leave It to Beaver* and of the modern family in *According to Jim*. How have these programs influenced our cultural expectations of family life? How are the families featured in the programs similar, and how are they different? You may wish to watch at least one episode of each program to assist you in answering the questions that follow.

QUESTIONS FOR ANALYSIS AND DISCUSSION ─────────

1. What influence does television's depiction of family life have on your own personal expectations of family? When you were younger, did you ever wonder why your family wasn't like the ones shown on TV? Did you ever compare your family with the families featured on TV? Explain.

2. What was the family dynamic of *Leave It to Beaver*? What lifestyle did it promote? What expectations, if any, did it create?

3. What is the family dynamic of *According to Jim*? What lifestyle does it promote? Is the family structure different from *Leave It to Beaver*, or essentially the same?

4. How does *Leave It to Beaver* compare with other comedy shows focusing on modern family life, such as CBS's *Two and a Half Men*?

5. In your opinion, what is the "traditional family"? How does your vision of family compare with the families featured on prime time television? Is your vision at all influenced by such programs? Explain.

Marriage and Divorce American Style

E. Mavis Hetherington

The issue of keeping families together for the sake of the children has resurfaced in recent years as policy makers introduce "marriage incentives" and programs designed to keep people married, or encourage unwed parents to tie the knot and stay that way. Children raised in traditional family structures fare better, argue the marriage advocates. And they may be right. But as E. Mavis Hetherington explains in the next essay, a destructive marriage does not make for a happy family and may actually do more harm than good.

Hetherington is emeritus professor in the Department of Psychology at the University of Virginia. The results of her studies are most recently reported in *For Better or For Worse: Divorce Reconsidered* (2002), co-written with John Kelly. This essay, drawn from information she reports in her book, appeared in the April 8, 2002, issue of *The American Prospect.*

BEFORE YOU READ

Is marriage in danger of becoming an obsolete institution? Why do people marry today? Do people marry for different reasons than they did 30, 40, or 50 years ago?

AS YOU READ

Is an intact marriage better than a broken one? Should the happiness of the parents be a factor in maintaining a marriage in which there are children? Should parents stay married for the sake of children? Why or why not?

1   On average, recent studies show parents and children in married families are happier, healthier, wealthier, and better adjusted than those in single-parent households. But these averages conceal wide variations. Before betting the farm on marriage—with a host of new government programs aimed at promoting traditional two-parent families and discouraging divorce—policy makers should take another look at the research. It reveals that there are many kinds of marriage and not all are salutary. Nor are all divorces and single-parent experiences associated with lasting distress. It is not the inevitability of positive or negative responses to marriage or divorce that is striking, but the diversity of them.

2   Men do seem to benefit simply from the state of being married. Married men enjoy better health and longevity and fewer psychological and behavioral problems than single men. But women, studies repeatedly have found, are more sensitive to the emotional quality of the marriage. They benefit from being in a well-functioning marriage, but in troubled marriages they are likely to experience depression, immune-system breakdowns, and other health-related problems.

3   We saw the same thing in the project I directed at the Hetherington Laboratory at the University of Virginia, which followed 1,400 divorced families, including 2,500 kids, over time, some for as long as 30 years, interviewing them, testing them, and observing them at home, at school, and in the community. This was the most comprehensive study of divorce and remarriage ever undertaken; for policy makers, the complexity of the findings is perhaps its most important revelation.

Good Marriages, Bad Marriages

4   By statistical analysis, we identified five broad types of marriage—ranging from "pursuer-distancer" marriages, which we found were the most likely to end in divorce, to disengaged marriages, to operatic marriages, and finally to "cohesive-individuated" marriages and traditional marriages, which had the least risk of instability.

5   To describe them briefly:

> **Pursuer-distancer** marriages are those mismatches in which one spouse, usually the wife, wants to confront and discuss problems and feelings and the other, usually the husband, wants to avoid confrontations and either denies problems or withdraws.
>
> In **disengaged marriages**, couples share few interests, activities, or friends. Conflict is low, but so is affection and sexual satisfaction.
>
> **Operatic marriages** involve couples who like to function at a level of extreme emotional arousal. They are intensely attracted, attached, and volatile, given both to frequent fighting and to passionate lovemaking.
>
> **Cohesive-individuated marriages** are the yuppie and feminist ideal, characterized by equity, respect, warmth, and mutual support, but also by both partners retaining the autonomy to pursue their own goals and to have their own friends.
>
> **Traditional marriages** are those in which the husband is the main income producer and the wife's role is one of nurturance, support, and home and child care. These marriages work well as long as both partners continue to share a traditional view of gender roles.

6   We found that not just the risk of divorce, but also the extent of women's psychological and health troubles, varies according to marriage type—with wives in pursuer-distancer and disengaged marriages experiencing the most problems, those in operatic marriages significantly fewer, and those in cohesive-individuated and traditional marriages the fewest. Like so many other studies, we found that men's responses are less nuanced; the only differentiation among them was that men in pursuer-distancer marriages have more problems than those in the other four types.

7   The issue is not simply the amount of disagreement in the marriage; disagreements, after all, are endemic in close personal relations. It is how people disagree and solve problems—how they interact—that turns out to be closely associated with both the duration of their marriages and the well-being of wives and, to a lesser extent, husbands. Contempt, hostile criticism, belligerence, denial, and withdrawal erode

a marriage. Affection, respect, trust, support, and making the partner feel valued and worthwhile strengthen the relationship.

Good Divorces, Bad Divorces

8   Divorce experiences also are varied. Initially, especially in marriages involving children, divorce is miserable for most couples. In the early years, ex-spouses typically must cope with lingering attachments; with resentment and anger, self-doubts, guilt, depression, and loneliness; with the stress of separation from children or of raising them alone; and with the loss of social networks and, for women, of economic security. Nonetheless, we found that a gradual recovery usually begins by the end of the second year. And by six years after divorce, 80 percent of both men and women have moved on to build reasonably or exceptionally fulfilling lives.

9   Indeed, about 20 percent of the women we observed eventually emerged from divorce enhanced and exhibiting competencies they never would have developed in an unhappy or constraining marriage. They had gone back to school or work to ensure the economic stability of their families, they had built new social networks, and they had become involved and effective parents and socially responsible citizens. Often they had happy second marriages. Divorce had offered them an opportunity to build new and more satisfying relationships and the freedom they needed for personal growth. This was especially true for women moving from a pursuer-distancer or disengaged marriage, or from one in which a contemptuous or belligerent husband undermined their self-esteem and child-rearing practices. Divorced men, we found, are less likely to undergo such remarkable personal growth; still, the vast majority of the men in our study did construct reasonably happy new lives for themselves.

10   As those pressing for government programs to promote marriage will no doubt note, we found that the single most important predictor of a divorced parent's subsequent adjustment is whether he or she has formed a new and mutually supportive intimate relationship. But what should also be noticed is that successful re-partnering takes many forms. We found that about 75 percent of men and 60 percent of women eventually remarry, but an increasing number of adults are opting to cohabit instead—or to remain single and meet their need for intimacy with a dating arrangement, a friendship, or a network of friends or family.

11   There is general agreement among researchers that parents' re-partnering does not do as much for their children. Both young children and adolescents in divorced and remarried families have been found to have, on average, more social, emotional, academic, and behavioral problems than kids in two-parent, non-divorced families. My own research, and that of many other investigators, finds twice as many serious psychological disorders and behavioral problems—such as teenage pregnancy, dropping out of school, substance abuse, unemployment, and marital breakups—among the offspring of divorced parents as among the children of non-divorced families. This is a closer association than between smoking and cancer.

12   However, the troubled youngsters remain a relatively small proportion of the total. In our study, we found that 75 percent to 80 percent of children and

adolescents from divorced families, after a period of initial disruption, are able to cope with the divorce and their new life situation and develop into reasonably or exceptionally well-adjusted individuals. In fact, as we saw with women, some girls eventually emerge from their parents' divorces remarkably competent and responsible. From the divorce experience they also learn how to handle later stresses in their lives.

13   Without ignoring the serious pain and distress experienced by many divorced parents and children, it is important to underscore that substantial research findings confirm the ability of the vast majority to move on successfully.

14   It is also important to recognize that many of the adjustment problems in parents and children—and much of the inept parenting and destructive family relations, which policy makers have attributed to divorce—actually are present before divorce. Being in a dysfunctional family has taken its toll before the breakup occurs.

15   Predicting the aftermath of divorce is complex, and the truth is obscured if one looks only at averages. Differences in experience or personality account for more variation than the averages would suggest. A number of studies have found, for instance, that adults and children who perceived their pre-divorce life as happy and satisfying tend to be more upset by a marital breakup than those who viewed the marriage as contentious, threatening, or unfulfilling. Other studies show that adults and children who are mature, stable, self-regulated, and adaptable are more likely able to cope with the challenges of divorce. Those who are neurotic, antisocial, and impulsive—and who lack a sense of their own efficacy—are likely to have these characteristics exacerbated by the breakup. In other words, the psychologically poor get poorer after a divorce while the rich often get richer.

16   The diversity of American marriages makes it unlikely that any one-size-fits-all policy to promote marriage and prevent divorce will be beneficial. Policy makers are now talking about offering people very brief, untested education and counseling programs, but such approaches rarely have long-lasting effects. And they are generally least successful with the very groups that policy makers are most eager to marry off—single mothers and the poor.

17   In their recent definitive review of the research on family interventions, Phil Cowan, Douglas Powell, and Carolyn Pape Cowan find that the most effective approaches are the most comprehensive ones—those that deal with both parents and children, with family dynamics, and with a family's needs for jobs, education, day care, and/or health care. Beyond that, which interventions work best seems to vary, depending on people's stage of life, the kind of family or ethnic group they are in, and the specific challenges before them.

18   Strengthening and promoting positive family relationships and improving the many settings in which children develop is a laudable goal. However, policies that constrain or encourage people to remain in destructive marriages—or that push uncommitted couples to marry—are likely to do more harm than good. The same is true of marriage incentives and rewards designed to create traditional families with the husband as the economic provider and the wife as homemaker. If our social policies do not recognize the diversity and varied needs of American families, we easily could end up undermining them.

1. What are the benefits of marriage? Are the benefits the same for both men and women? Explain.

2. What are the five broad-types of marriage Hetherington identifies? Which ones are more or less likely to end in divorce? Can you relate to any of the marriages she describes from personal experience? For example, what sorts of marriage did members of your family have? Which one do you think is best, and why?

3. In what ways does divorce adversely affect children long-term? What factors contribute to how a child adjusts to divorce? Explain.

4. Hetherington cautions that many of the adjustment problems experienced by children of divorce, "which policy makers have attributed to divorce—actually are present before divorce. Being in a dysfunctional family has taken its toll before the breakup occurs." What do you think she means by this statement? Explain.

5. What position is Hetherington supporting in this essay? What is her argument? How logical or balanced is her position? Do you agree with her? Why or why not?

READING THE VISUAL

2004 Marriage Trends

The National Marriage Project

Marriage trends in recent decades indicate that Americans have become less likely to marry. Data in 2004 indicate that the marriage rate has steadily declined. Some of this decline may be due to delaying first marriage until older ages. In 1960, the median age for a first marriage for women was 20 and for men was 23. In 2004, the median age jumped to 25 for women and 27 for men. Unmarried cohabitation—a social taboo in the 1960s—is much more common, and may also contribute to the declining marriage rate. This marriage data (Figures 1 and 2) was complied by The National Marriage Project, a nonprofit initiative at Rutgers, the State University of New Jersey, that provides research and analysis on the state of marriage in America, specifically addressing the social, economic, and cultural conditions affecting marriage. These graphs appear in their 2004 report, *The State of Our Unions.*

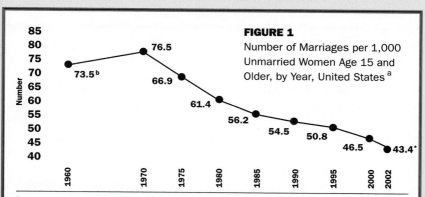

FIGURE 1

Number of Marriages per 1,000 Unmarried Women Age 15 and Older, by Year, United States [a]

[a] We have used the number of marriages per 1,000 unmarried women age 15 and older, rather than the Crude Marriage Rate of marriages per 1,000 population to help avoid the problem of compositional changes in the population; that is, changes which stem merely from there being more or less people in the marriageable ages. Even this more refined measure is somewhat susceptible to compositional changes.

[b] Per 1,000 unmarried women age 14 and older

Source: US Department of the Census, *Statistical Abstract of the United States: 2001*, Page. 87, Table 117; and *Statistical Abstract of the United States: 1986*, Page 79, Table 124.

* Figure for 2002 was obtained using data from the Current Population Surveys, March 2002 Supplement, as well as Births, Marriages, Divorces, and Deaths: Provisional Data for October–December 2002, National Vital Statistics Report 51:10, June 17, 2003, Table 3. (www.cdc.gov/nchs/fastats/pdf/51_10_12_t03.pdf) The CPS, March Supplement, is based on a sample of the US population, rather than an actual count such as those available from the decennial census. See sampling and weighting notes at http://www.bls.census.gov:80/cps/ads/2002/ssampwgt.htm.

FIGURE 2

Percentage of All Persons Age 15 and Older Who Were Married, by Sex and Race, 1960-2003, United States [a]

Year	MALES			FEMALES		
	Total	Blacks	Whites	Total	Blacks	Whites
1960	69.3	60.9	70.2	65.9	59.8	66.6
1970	66.7	56.9	68.0	61.9	54.1	62.8
1980	63.2	48.8	65.0	58.9	44.6	60.7
1990	60.7	45.1	62.8	56.9	40.2	59.1
2000	57.9	42.8	60.0	54.7	36.2	57.4
2003[b]	57.1	42.5	59.3	54.0	36.4	56.6

[a] Includes races other than Black and White.

[b] In 2003, the U.S. Census Bureau expanded its racial categories to permit respondents to identify themselves as belonging to more than one race. This means that racial data computations beginning in 2003 may not be strictly comparable to those of prior years. Source: U.S. Bureau of the Census, Current Population Reports, Series P20-506; *America's Families and Living Arrangements: March 2000* and earlier reports; internet tables (www.census.gov/population/socdemo/hh-fam/tabMS1-1.pdf); and data calculated from the Current Population Surveys, March 2003 Supplement.

QUESTIONS FOR ANALYSIS AND DISCUSSION

1. The National Marriage Project conjectures that the drop in the marriage rate over the last 30 years may be attributed to the older age at which couples enter a first marriage and the increase in cohabitating couples. How much of an impact do you think these two factors have on marriage rates, and why? What other factors might contribute to the decline in marriage?

2. According to the data in Figure 2, the marriage rate for black females actually went up from 2000 to 2003. What might account for this slight increase in the marriage rate? What factors should sociologists investigate to analyze this trend?

3. If you were a sociologist and were presented with the two graphs featured here, what conclusions might you reach based on the data? What projections for the next five years could you make? What other factors in addition to the data should you consider in order to formulate your prediction? Do you think the marriage rate would continue to drop, hold steady, or increase? Explain.

The Decline of Marriage
James Q. Wilson

Recent decades have witnessed a shift in how society views single parenthood. High divorce rates and changing attitudes toward unwed motherhood are partially responsible for this shift. But is this greater acceptance of single parenthood good for children and their parents? In this essay, political science professor James Q. Wilson discusses the decline of marriage in the United States—and its cultural implications as a contributing factor to poverty and unemployment.

Wilson has taught political science at Harvard University, UCLA, and Pepperdine University. He is the author or coauthor of 15 books, most recently *The Marriage Problem* (2002). He has also edited or contributed to books on urban problems, government regulation of business, drugs, crime, and the prevention of delinquency among children. This essay appeared in *City Journal* on February 17, 2002.

BEFORE YOU READ

Is the greater acceptance of single parenthood a good thing? Is it better socially and culturally for both children and parents? What stigmas have traditionally been associated with single parenthood? What has happened to transform social opinion?

AS YOU READ

Evaluate the tone of Wilson's essay. Is he optimistic for the future? Does he provide solutions to the problem he explores?

1   Everyone knows that the rising proportion of women who bear and raise children out of wedlock has greatly weakened the American family system. This phenomenon, once thought limited predominantly to African Americans, now affects whites as well, so much so that the rate at which white children are born to an unmarried mother is now as high as the rate for black children in the mid-1960s, when Daniel Patrick Moynihan issued his famous report on the black family.

> *"For whites the rate is one-fifth; for blacks it is over one-half."*

2   Almost everyone agrees that children in mother-only homes suffer harmful consequences: these youngsters are more likely than those in two-parent families to be suspended from school, have emotional problems, become delinquent, suffer from abuse, and take drugs. Some of these problems may arise from the economic circumstances of these one-parent families, but the best studies show that low income can explain, at most, about half of the differences between single-parent and two-parent families. The rest is explained by a mother living without a husband. And single moms, by virtue of being single, are more likely to be poor than are married moms.

3   Now, not all children born out of wedlock are raised by a single mother. Some are raised by a man and woman who, though living together, are not married; others are raised by a mother who gets married shortly after the birth. Nevertheless, there has been a sharp increase in children who are not only born out of wedlock but are raised without a father. In the United States, the percentage of children living with an unmarried mother has tripled since 1960.

4   Why has this happened? I think there are two possible explanations to consider: money and culture.

5   Money readily comes to mind. If a welfare system pays unmarried mothers enough to have their own apartment, some women will prefer babies to husbands. When government subsidizes something, we get more of it. But for many years, American scholars discounted this possibility. Since the amount of welfare paid per mother had declined in inflation-adjusted terms, and since the amount paid in each state showed no correlation with each state's illegitimacy rate, surely money could not have caused the increase in out-of-wedlock births.

6   There are three arguments against this view. First, what counted was the inflation-adjusted value of all of the benefits an unmarried mother might receive—not only welfare, but also food stamps and Medicaid. By adding these in, welfare kept up with inflation. Second, what counted was not how much money each state paid out, but how much it paid compared to the cost of living in that state. Third, comparing single-parent families and average spending levels neglects the real issue: how attractive is welfare to a low-income unmarried woman in a given locality?

7   When economist Mark Rosenzweig asked this question of women who are part of the national longitudinal survey of youth, he found that a 10 percent increase in welfare benefits made the chances that a poor young woman would have a baby out of wedlock before the age of 22 go up by 12 percent. And this was true for whites as well as blacks. Welfare made a difference.

8   But how big a difference?

9   AFDC began in 1935, but by 1960 only 4 percent of the children getting welfare had a mother who had never been married; the rest had mothers who were widows or had been separated from their husbands. By 1996 that had changed dramatically: now approximately two-thirds of the welfare children had an unmarried mom and hardly any were the offspring of widows.

10   To explain this staggering increase, we must turn to culture. In this context, what I mean by culture is simply that being an unmarried mother and living on welfare has lost its stigma. At one time living on the dole was shameful; now it is much less so.

11   Consider these facts. Women in rural communities who go on welfare leave it much sooner than the same kind of women who take welfare in big cities, and this is true for both whites and blacks and regardless of family size. In a small town, everyone knows who is on welfare, and welfare recipients do not have many friends in the same situation with whom they can associate. But in a big city, welfare recipients are not known to everyone, and each one can easily associate with other women living the same way.

12   American courts have made clear that welfare laws cannot be used to enforce stigma. When Alabama tried in 1960 to deny welfare to an unmarried woman who

was living with a man who was not her husband, the U.S. Supreme Court objected. Immorality, it implied, was an outdated notion. If the state is concerned about immorality, it will have to rehabilitate the women by other means.

13   How did the stigma get weakened by practice and undercut by law, when Americans favor marriage and are skeptical of welfare?

14   Let me suggest that beneath the popular support for marriage there has slowly developed, almost unnoticed, a subversion of it: whereas marriage was once thought to be about a social union, it is now about personal preferences. At one time law and opinion enforced the desirability of marriage without inquiring into what went on in that union; today law and opinion enforce the desirability of individual happiness without worrying too much about maintaining a formal relationship. Marriage was once a sacrament, then it became a contract, and now it is an arrangement. Once religion provided the sacrament, then the law enforced the contract, and now personal preferences define the arrangement.

15   The cultural change that made this happen was the same one that gave us science, technology, freedom, and capitalism: the Enlightenment. The Enlightenment made human reason the measure of all things, throwing off ancient rules if they fell short. What the king once ordered, what bishops once enforced, what tradition once required was to be set aside in the name of scientific knowledge and personal self-discovery.

16   I am a great admirer of the Enlightenment. But it entailed costs. I take great pride in the vast expansion in human freedom that the Enlightenment conferred on so many people, but I also know that the Enlightenment spent little time worrying about those cultural habits that make freedom meaningful. The family was one of these.

17   It was in the world most affected by the Enlightenment that we find both its good and bad legacies. There we encounter both remarkable science and personal self-indulgence. There we find human freedom and high rates of crime. There we find democratic governments and frequent divorces. There we find regimes concerned about the poor and a proliferation of single-parent families.

18   Single-parent families are most common in those nations—England, America, Canada, Australia, France, the Netherlands—where the Enlightenment had its greatest effect. It was in the Enlightened nations that nuclear rather than extended families became common, that individual consent and not clan control was the basis of a marriage contract, and that divorce first became legal.

19   The Enlightenment did not change the family immediately, because everyone took family life for granted. The most important Enlightenment thinkers assumed marriage and denounced divorce. That assumption—and in time that denunciation— slowly lost force, as people slowly experienced the widening of human freedom. The laws, until well into the twentieth century, made it crystal clear that, though a child might be conceived by an unmarried couple, once born it had to have two parents. There was no provision for the state to pay for a single-parent child, and public opinion strongly endorsed that policy.

20   But by the end of the nineteenth century and the early years of the twentieth, policies changed, and then, slowly, opinion changed. Two things precipitated the change: first, a compassionate desire to help needy children and, second, a determination to end the legal burdens under which women suffered.

21   The first was a powerful force, especially since the aid to needy children was designed to help those who had lost their father owing to wars or accidents. Slowly, however, a needy child was redefined to include those of any mother without a husband, and not just any who had become a widow.

22   The emancipation of women was also a desirable process. In America and England, nineteenth-century women already had more rights than those in most of Europe, but when married they still could not easily own property, file for a divorce, or conduct their own affairs. By the 1920s most of these restrictions had ended, and once women got the vote, there was no chance of these limitations ever being reinstated.

23   We should therefore not be surprised that the 20s were an enthusiastic display of unchaperoned dating, provocative dress, and exhibitionist behavior. Had it not been for a timeout imposed by the Great Depression and the Second World War, we would no longer be referring to the 60s as an era of self-indulgence; we would be talking about the legacy of the twenties.

24   The 60s reinstated trends begun half a century earlier, but now without effective opposition. No-fault divorce laws were passed throughout most of the West, the pill and liberalized abortion laws dramatically reduced the chances of unwanted pregnancies, and popular entertainment focused on pleasing the young. As a result, family law lost its moral basis. It was easier to get out of a marriage than a mortgage. This change in culture was made crystal clear by court decisions. At the end of the nineteenth century the Supreme Court referred to marriage as a "sacred obligation." By 1965 the same court described marriage as "an association of two individuals."

25   People still value marriage; but it is only that value—and very little social pressure or legal obligation—that sustains it.

26   But there is another part of the cultural argument, and it goes to the question of why African-Americans have such high rates of mother-only families. When black scholars addressed this question, as did W.E.B. Dubois in 1908, they argued that slavery weakened the black family. When Daniel Patrick Moynihan repeated this argument in 1965, he was denounced for "blaming the victim."

27   An intense scholarly effort to show that slavery did little harm to African-American families followed that denunciation; instead, what really hurt them was migrating to big cities where they encountered racism and oppression.

28   It was an astonishing argument. Slavery, a vast system of organized repression that, for over two centuries, denied to blacks the right to marry, vote, sue, own property, or take an oath; that withheld from them the proceeds of their own labor; that sold them and their children on the auction block; that exposed them to brutal and unjust punishment: all of this misery had little or no effect on family life, but moving as free people to a big city did. To state the argument is to refute it.

29   But since some people take academic nonsense seriously, let me add that we now know that this argument was empirically wrong. The scholars who made it committed some errors. In calculating what percentage of black mothers had husbands in the nineteenth century, they accepted many women's claims that they were widows, when we now know that such claims were often lies, designed to conceal that the respondents had never married. In figuring out what proportion of slaves were married, these scholars focused on large plantations, where the chance of

having a spouse was high, instead of on small ones, where most slaves lived but where the chance of having a spouse was low. On these small farms, only about one-fifth of the slaves lived in a nuclear household.

30   The legacy of this sad history is two-fold. First, generations of slaves grew up without having a family, or without having one that had any social and cultural meaning. Second, black boys grew up aware that their fathers were often absent or were sexually active with other women, giving the boys poor role models for marriage.

31   There remains at least one more puzzle to solve. Culture has shaped how we produce and raise children, but that culture surely had its greatest impact on how educated people think. Yet the problem of weak, single-parent families is greatest among the least educated people. Why should a culture that is so powerfully shaped by upper-middle-class beliefs have so profound an effect on poor people? If white culture has weakened marriage, why should black culture follow suit? I suspect that the answer may be found in Myron Magnet's book, "The Dream and the Nightmare." When the haves remake a culture, the people who pay the price are the have-nots. Let me restate his argument with my own metaphor. Imagine a game of crack-the-whip, in which a line of children, holding hands, starts running in a circle. The first few children have no problem keeping up, but near the end of the line the last few must run so fast that many fall down. Those children who did not begin the turning suffer most from the turn.

32   There are countless examples of our cultural crack-the-whip. Heroin and cocaine use started among elites and then spread down the social scale. When the elites wanted to stop, they could hire doctors and therapists; when the poor wanted to stop, they could not hire anybody. People who practiced contraception endorsed loose sexuality in writing and movies; the poor practice loose sexuality without contraception. Divorce is more common among the affluent than the poor. The latter, who can't afford divorce, deal with unhappy marriages by not getting married in the first place. My only trivial quarrel with Magnet is that I believe these changes began a century ago and even then built on more profound changes that date back centuries.

33   Now you probably expect me to tell you what we can about this, but if you believe, as I do, in the power of culture, you will realize that there is very little one can do. As a University of Chicago professor once put it, if you succeed in explaining why something is so, you have probably succeeded in explaining why it must be so. He implied what is in fact often the case: change is very hard. Moreover, there are many aspects of our culture that no one, least of all I, wants to change.

34   We do not want fewer freedoms or less democracy. Most of us do not want to change any of the gains women have made in establishing their moral and legal standing as independent actors with all of the rights that men once enjoyed alone.

35   We can talk about tighter divorce laws, but it is not easy to design one that both protects people from ending a marriage too quickly with an easy divorce and at the same time makes divorce for a good cause readily available. The right and best way for a culture to restore itself is for it to be rebuilt, not from the top down by government policies, but from the bottom up by personal decisions.

36   On the side of that effort we can find churches—or at least many of them—and the common experience of adults that the essence of marriage is not sex, or money, or even children: it is commitment.

QUESTIONS FOR ANALYSIS AND DISCUSSION ────────

1. What is your opinion of single parenthood? Has society become too accepting of parents who decide to raise children out of wedlock?

2. What cultural and social reasons does Wilson cite for why women in rural communities leave welfare more rapidly than women in urban areas? Do you agree with his analysis?

3. According to Wilson, what factors have contributed to the decline of the American family? Make a list of the social and cultural forces influencing the family.

4. Wilson makes several "bandwagon appeals" in his essay. What is a "bandwagon appeal"? How does it influence the audience? Identify areas of Wilson's essay in which he employs this technique.

5. What role did slavery play in the development of the African-American family structure? Explain.

WRITING ASSIGNMENTS

1. What is the state of marriage in the United States today? In your own words, define what marriage is. Then address the definitions of marriage as described by the authors in this section. Write an essay evaluating the definitions of marriage offered by the authors and comparing these definitions with the American reality of marriage.

2. Select one or two of the articles in this section and write an essay in which you argue for or against its premises. As you formulate your response, pay attention to the author's personal bias, his or her tone, and how the arguments involved are supported. Address these issues in your essay.

3. Several authors express concern regarding single mothers having and raising children alone. What images come to mind when you hear the phrases "single mother" and "single father"? List as many qualities and ideas as you can. How do the two phrases compare? Are they different? How much of that difference has to do with our cultural expectations of men's and women's roles as parents? Explain.

4. Write a personal narrative in which you describe the structure of your family during your childhood, focusing specifically on the role of marriage in your family. Were your parents married? divorced? Do you think the choices they made affected your outlook on marriage? on your life in general? Explain.

5. Read the 2001 policy brief by the Brookings Institution, authored by Sara McLanahan, Irwin Garfinkel, and Ronald B. Mincy, outlining the social science evidence that both children and adults benefit from marriage (http://www .brookings.edu/es/wrb/publications/pb/pb10.pdf). Using this report as your resource, develop a hypothetical government program designed to help welfare families marry and stay married. Explain the reasoning behind your proposals.

GAY MARRIAGE . . . "WE DO?"

The "M" Word
Andrew Sullivan

The issue of homosexual marriage has been hotly argued in recent years, as some states ban and others begin to permit same-sex marriage. Supporters of gay marriage argue that it reduces sexual promiscuity, promotes stronger family units, is healthier for same-sex partners, and legitimizes relationships both socially and legally. Critics of homosexual marriage argue that marriage should be between a man and a woman, and permitting homosexual marriages would render marriage itself meaningless. Is marriage a bond between two loving adults who wish to make a lifelong commitment to each other, regardless of gender? Should it be legal for same-sex couples to marry? Is it a right?

Andrew Sullivan is a senior editor for *The New Republic,* a magazine of cultural and political opinion. He is gay, conservative, and a Roman Catholic. His 1996 book, *Virtually Normal: An Argument About Homosexuality*, argues that the best way to tackle antigay prejudice is to shape public laws and policies extending the same rights and protections to all U.S. citizens, regardless of sexual orientation. His latest book is *Love Undetectable: Notes on Friendship, Sex, and Survival* (1998). The essay reprinted here first appeared in the February 10, 2004, issue of *Time* magazine.

BEFORE YOU READ

Why do people marry? What do they hope to gain by marriage? What does society expect from married couples as compared to unmarried couples?

AS YOU READ

According to Sullivan, why do homosexual couples want to marry—what motivates them? Do heterosexual couples marry for the same reasons as gay couples?

1   What's in a name?

2   Perhaps the best answer is a memory.

3   As a child, I had no idea what homosexuality was. I grew up in a traditional home—Catholic, conservative, middle class. Life was relatively simple: education, work, family. I was brought up to aim high in life, even though my parents hadn't gone to college. But one thing was instilled in me. What matters is not how far you go in life, how much money you make, how big a name you make for yourself. What really matters is family, and the love you have for one another. The most important day of your life was not graduation from college or your first day at work or a raise or even

your first house. The most important day of your life was when you got married. It was on that day that all your friends and all your family got together to celebrate the most important thing in life: your happiness, your ability to make a new home, to form a new but connected family, to find love that puts everything else into perspective.

4   But as I grew older, I found that this was somehow not available to me. I didn't feel the things for girls that my peers did. All the emotions and social rituals and bonding of teenage heterosexual life eluded me. I didn't know why. No one explained it. My emotional bonds to other boys were one-sided; each time I felt myself falling in love, they sensed it, pushed it away. I didn't and couldn't blame them. I got along fine with my buds in a non-emotional context; but something was awry, something not right. I came to know almost instinctively that I would never be a part of my family the way my siblings one day might be. The love I had inside me was unmentionable, anathema-even, in the words of the Church I attended every Sunday, evil. I remember writing in my teenage journal one day: "I'm a professional human being. But what do I do in my private life?"

5   So, like many gay men of my generation, I retreated. I never discussed my real life. I couldn't date girls and so immersed myself in school-work, in the debate team, school plays, anything to give me an excuse not to confront reality. When I looked toward the years ahead, I couldn't see a future. There was just a void. Was I going to be alone my whole life? Would I ever have a "most important day" in my life? It seemed impossible, a negation, an undoing. To be a full part of my family I had to somehow not be me. So like many gay teens, I withdrew, became neurotic, depressed, at times close to suicidal. I shut myself in my room with my books, night after night, while my peers developed the skills needed to form real relationships, and loves. In wounded pride, I even voiced a rejection of family and marriage. It was the only way I could explain my isolation.

6   It took years for me to realize that I was gay, years later to tell others, and more time yet to form any kind of stable emotional bond with another man. Because my sexuality had emerged in solitude—and without any link to the idea of an actual relationship—it was hard later to reconnect sex to love and self-esteem. It still is. But I persevered, each relationship slowly growing longer than the last, learning in my twenties and thirties what my straight friends found out in their teens. But even then, my parents and friends never asked the question they would have asked automatically if I were straight: so when are you going to get married? When is your relationship going to be public? When will we be able to celebrate it and affirm it and support it? In fact, no one—no one—has yet asked me that question.

7   When people talk about "gay marriage," they miss the point. This isn't about gay marriage. It's about marriage. It's about family. It's about love. It isn't about religion. It's about civil marriage licenses—available to atheists as well as believers. These family values are not options for a happy and stable life. They are necessities. Putting gay relationships in some other category—civil unions, domestic partnerships, civil partnerships, whatever—may alleviate real human needs, but, by their very euphemism, by their very separateness, they actually build a wall between gay people and their own families. They put back the barrier many of us have spent a lifetime trying to erase.

8   It's too late for me to undo my own past. But I want above everything else to remember a young kid out there who may even be reading this now. I want to let him know that he doesn't have to choose between himself and his family anymore. I want him to know that his love has dignity, that he does indeed have a future as a full and equal part of the human race. Only marriage will do that. Only marriage can bring him home.

QUESTIONS FOR ANALYSIS AND DISCUSSION

1. How does Sullivan's description of his childhood and his troubled adolescence reach out to his reader? Is his story likely to make his audience more sympathetic? to better understand his point of view? Explain.
2. What does Sullivan's title mean? How does it work with his essay's premise? Why does he call marriage the "M" word?
3. Sullivan says, "When people talk about 'gay marriage,' they miss the point. This isn't about gay marriage." What does he mean? If the issue isn't really about "gay marriage," does it change the point of the argument?
4. Gay couples have been more prominent on television programs over the past few years. What images of gay life has television presented to its viewers? How do the images correspond to Sullivan's claims that many gay men and women just want what marriage affords—"social stability, anchors in relationships, and family and financial security"?
5. How would different audiences receive this argument in favor of gay marriage? For example, would it be as effective in addressing a college audience as it would an older or more conservative audience? What factors could influence the successful reception of Sullivan's essay?

Defining Marriage Down . . . Is No Way to Save It
David Blankenhorn

In the first essay in this section, Andrew Sullivan argues that marriage is a basic human right. He explains that such commitments serve to strengthen the relationship between two committed adults—something marriage is supposed to do. But many people disagree with his view, saying that marriage itself may be a right, but not marriage to someone of the same gender. Marriage, they contend, is a legal agreement between one man and one woman recognized and sanctioned by the government. Gays may pursue their own relationships and lifestyles but should leave marriage alone. In this next essay, conservative David Blankenhorn argues that the institution of marriage has already been seriously weakened culturally by changing social mores. Thus, same-sex marriage would further deinstitutionalize marriage itself, eventually rendering it meaningless.

Blankenhorn is president of the New York-based Institute for American Values, described as a "private, nonpartisan organization devoted to contributing intellectually to the renewal of marriage and family life and the sources of competence, character, and citizenship in the

United States." He is the author of several books, including *Fatherless America* (1995) and *The Future of Marriage* (2007). He has appeared on numerous national television programs, including *Oprah, 20/20, The Today Show*, and *Charlie Rose*. This essay appeared in *The Weekly Standard* on April 2, 2007.

BEFORE YOU READ

In your opinion, should same-sex couples be permitted to marry legally? Are you likely to be swayed by hearing different points of view on the subject? Why or why not?

AS YOU READ

Is marriage a moral "right," or should it be a privilege granted by the state? Does government have a role in defining what marriage "means"? Who determines rights—society, individuals, the government? Who should have the ultimate decision-making authority on what rights are afforded to people?

1   Does permitting same-sex marriage weaken marriage as a social institution? Or does extending to gay and lesbian couples the right to marry have little or no effect on marriage overall? Scholars and commentators have expended much effort trying in vain to wring proof of causation from the data—all the while ignoring the meaning of some simple correlations that the numbers do indubitably show.

2   Much of the disagreement among scholars centers on how to interpret trends in the Netherlands and Scandinavia. Stanley Kurtz has argued that the adoption of gay marriage or same-sex civil unions in those countries has significantly weakened customary marriage, already eroded by easy divorce and stigma-free cohabitation.

3   William Eskridge, a Yale Law School professor, and Darren R. Spedale, an attorney, beg to differ. *In Gay Marriage: For Better or for Worse?*, a book-length reply to Kurtz, they insist that Kurtz does not prove that gay marriage is causing anything in those nations; that Nordic marriage overall appears to be healthier than Kurtz allows; and that even if marriage is declining in that part of the world, "the question remains whether that phenomenon is a lamentable development."

4   Eskridge and Spedale want it both ways. For them, there is no proof that marriage has weakened, but if there were it wouldn't be a problem. For people who care about marriage, this perspective inspires no confidence. Eskridge and Spedale do score one important point, however. Neither Kurtz nor anyone else can scientifically prove that allowing gay marriage causes the institution of marriage to get weaker. Correlation does not imply causation. The relation between two correlated phenomena may be causal, or it may be random, or it may reflect some deeper cause producing both. Even if you could show that every last person in North Carolina eats barbecue, you would not have established that eating barbecue is a result of taking up residence in North Carolina.

5   When it comes to the health of marriage as an institution and the legal status of same-sex unions, there is much to be gained from giving up the search for causation and studying some recurring patterns in the data, as I did for my book *The Future of Marriage*. It turns out that certain clusters of beliefs about and attitudes toward marriage consistently correlate with certain institutional arrangements. The correlations crop up in a large number of countries and recur in data drawn from different surveys of opinion.

6   Take the International Social Survey Programme (ISSP), a collaborative effort of universities in over 40 countries. It interviewed about 50,000 adults in 35 countries in 2002. What is useful for our purposes is that respondents were asked whether they agreed or disagreed with six statements that directly relate to marriage as an institution:

1. Married people are generally happier than unmarried people.
2. People who want children ought to get married.
3. One parent can bring up a child as well as two parents together.
4. It is all right for a couple to live together without intending to get married.
5. Divorce is usually the best solution when a couple can't seem to work out their marriage problems.
6. The main purpose of marriage these days is to have children.

7   Let's stipulate that for statements one, two, and six, an "agree" answer indicates support for traditional marriage as an authoritative institution. Similarly, for statements three, four, and five, let's stipulate that agreement indicates a lack of support, or less support, for traditional marriage.

8   Then divide the countries surveyed into four categories: those that permit same-sex marriage; those that permit same-sex civil unions (but not same-sex marriage); those in which some regions permit same-sex marriage; and those that do not legally recognize same-sex unions.

9   The correlations are strong. Support for marriage is by far the weakest in countries with same-sex marriage. The countries with marriage-like civil unions show significantly more support for marriage. The two countries with only regional recognition of gay marriage (Australia and the United States) do better still on these support-for-marriage measurements, and those without either gay marriage or marriage-like civil unions do best of all.

10   In some instances, the differences are quite large. For example, people in nations with gay marriage are less than half as likely as people in nations without gay unions to say that married people are happier. Perhaps most important, they are significantly less likely to say that people who want children ought to get married (38 percent vs. 60 percent). They are also significantly more likely to say that cohabiting without intending to marry is all right (83 percent vs. 50 percent), and are somewhat more likely to say that divorce is usually the best solution to marital problems. Respondents in the countries with gay marriage are significantly more likely than those in Australia and the United States to say that divorce is usually the best solution.

11   A similar exercise using data from a different survey yields similar results. The World Values Survey, based in Stockholm, Sweden, periodically interviews nationally representative samples of the publics of some 80 countries on six continents—over

100,000 people in all—on a range of issues. It contains three statements directly related to marriage as an institution:

1. A child needs a home with both a father and a mother to grow up happily.
2. It is all right for a woman to want a child but not a stable relationship with a man.
3. Marriage is an outdated institution.

12   Again grouping the countries according to the legal status of same-sex unions, the data from the 1999–2001 wave of interviews yield a clear pattern. Support for marriage as an institution is weakest in those countries with same-sex marriage. Countries with same-sex civil unions show more support, and countries with regional recognition show still more. By significant margins, support for marriage is highest in countries that extend no legal recognition to same-sex unions.

13   So what of it? Granted that these correlations may or may not reflect causation, what exactly can be said about the fact that certain values and attitudes and legal arrangements tend to cluster?

14   Here's an analogy. Find some teenagers who smoke, and you can confidently predict that they are more likely to drink than their nonsmoking peers. Why? Because teen smoking and drinking tend to hang together. What's more, teens who engage in either of these activities are also more likely than nonsmokers or nondrinkers to engage in other risky behaviors, such as skipping school, getting insufficient sleep, and forming friendships with peers who get into trouble.

15   Because these behaviors correlate and tend to reinforce one another, it is virtually impossible for the researcher to pull out any one from the cluster and determine that it alone is causing or is likely to cause some personal or (even harder to measure) social result. All that can be said for sure is that these things go together. To the degree possible, parents hope that their children can avoid all of them, the entire syndrome—drinking, smoking, skipping school, missing sleep, and making friends with other children who get into trouble—in part because each of them increases exposure to the others.

16   It's the same with marriage. Certain trends in values and attitudes tend to cluster with each other and with certain trends in behavior. A rise in unwed childbearing goes hand in hand with a weakening of the belief that people who want to have children should get married. High divorce rates are encountered where the belief in marital permanence is low. More one-parent homes are found where the belief that children need both a father and a mother is weaker. A rise in nonmarital cohabitation is linked at least partly to the belief that marriage as an institution is outmoded. The legal endorsement of gay marriage occurs where the belief prevails that marriage itself should be redefined as a private personal relationship. And all of these marriage-weakening attitudes and behaviors are linked. Around the world, the surveys show, these things go together.

17   Eskridge and Spedale are right. We cannot demonstrate statistically what exactly causes what, or what is likely to have what consequences in the future. But we do see in country after country that these phenomena form a pattern that recurs. They are mutually reinforcing. Socially, an advance for any of them is likely to be an advance for all of them. An individual who tends to accept any one or two of them probably accepts the others as well. And as a political and strategic matter,

anyone who is fighting for any one of them should—almost certainly already does—support all of them, since a victory for any of them clearly coincides with the advance of the others. Which is why, for example, people who have devoted much of their professional lives to attacking marriage as an institution almost always favor gay marriage. These things do go together.

18   Inevitably, the pattern discernible in the statistics is borne out in the statements of the activists. Many of those who most vigorously champion same-sex marriage say that they do so precisely in the hope of dethroning once and for all the traditional "conjugal institution."

19   That phrase comes from Judith Stacey, professor of sociology at New York University and a major expert witness testifying in courts and elsewhere for gay marriage. She views the fight for same-sex marriage as the "vanguard site" for rebuilding family forms. The author of journal articles like "Good Riddance to 'The Family,'" she argues forthrightly that "if we begin to value the meaning and quality of intimate bonds over their customary forms, there are few limits to the kinds of marriage and kinship patterns people might wish to devise."

20   Similarly, David L. Chambers, a law professor at the University of Michigan widely published on family issues, favors gay marriage for itself but also because it would likely "make society receptive to the further evolution of the law." What kind of evolution? He writes, "If the deeply entrenched paradigm we are challenging is the romantically linked man-woman couple, we should respect the similar claims made against the hegemony of the two-person unit and against the romantic foundations of marriage."

21   Examples could be multiplied—the recently deceased Ellen Willis, professor of journalism at NYU and head of its Center for Cultural Reporting and Criticism, expressed the hope that gay marriage would "introduce an implicit revolt against the institution into its very heart, further promoting the democratization and secularization of personal and sexual life"—but they can only illustrate the point already established by the large-scale international comparisons: Empirically speaking, gay marriage goes along with the erosion, not the shoring up, of the institution of marriage.

22   These facts have two implications. First, to the degree that it makes any sense to oppose gay marriage, it makes sense only if one also opposes with equal clarity and intensity the other main trends pushing our society toward postinstitutional marriage. After all, the big idea is not to stop gay marriage. The big idea is to stop the erosion of society's most pro-child institution. Gay marriage is only one facet of the larger threat to the institution.

23   Similarly, it's time to recognize that the beliefs about marriage that correlate with the push for gay marriage do not exist in splendid isolation, unrelated to marriage's overall institutional prospects. Nor do those values have anything to do with strengthening the institution, notwithstanding the much-publicized but undocumented claims to the contrary from those making the "conservative case" for gay marriage.

24   Instead, the deep logic of same-sex marriage is clearly consistent with what scholars call deinstitutionalization—the overturning or weakening of all of the customary forms of marriage, and the dramatic shrinking of marriage's public meaning and institutional authority. Does deinstitutionalization necessarily require gay

marriage? Apparently not. For decades heterosexuals have been doing a fine job on that front all by themselves. But gay marriage clearly presupposes and reinforces deinstitutionalization.

25   By itself, the "conservative case" for gay marriage might be attractive. It would be gratifying to extend the benefits of marriage to same-sex couples—if gay marriage and marriage renewal somehow fit together. But they do not. As individuals and as a society, we can strive to maintain and strengthen marriage as a primary social institution and society's best welfare plan for children (some would say for men and women too). Or we can strive to implement same-sex marriage. But unless we are prepared to tear down with one hand what we are building up with the other, we cannot do both.

QUESTIONS FOR ANALYSIS AND DISCUSSION

1. What does Blankenhorn's title mean? Why does he feel marriage being "defined down" by accepting and legalizing gay marriage? Explain.

2. Blankenhorn notes that while correlation does not necessarily mean causation, we can surmise certain things about gay marriage by analyzing the state of marriage in other countries in which same-sex marriage is legal. What conclusions does he think we can draw from the data? Do you agree with his analysis? Explain.

3. Blankenhorn observes that while some advocates seek same-sex marriage for sincerely good motives, others seek to undermine the institution itself. How does Blankenhorn connect his argument back to this observation? Explain.

4. Respond to Blankenhorn's warning in his conclusion regarding same-sex marriage, "Unless we are prepared to tear down with one hand what we are building up with the other, we cannot do both." Does he make a good point? Why or why not?

5. Blankenhorn states, "The big idea is not to stop gay marriage. The big idea is to stop the erosion of society's most pro-child institution. Gay marriage is only one facet of the larger threat to the institution." Why does he feel that stopping same-sex marriage will prevent the erosion of marriage itself? Explain.

Same-Sex Marriage
Laurie Essig

In 1999, the state of Vermont legalized same-sex marriage. Other states are considering, or have passed, similar legislation. In the next essay, Laurie Essig explains why she isn't running off to Vermont to hold a ceremony with her partner Liza. Not only does she not want a ceremony, she can't understand why anyone would want to be bound by an institution "founded in historical, material and cultural conditions that ensured women's oppression."

Essig is a professor of sociology at Middlebury College. She is the author of *Queer in Russia* (1999). Her commentary has appeared on NPR's "All Things Considered" and in *Legal Affairs*. This essay was published in *Salon* magazine's "Mothers Who Think" section on July 10, 2000.

BEFORE YOU READ ───────────────

Essig observes that many marriages deemed "happy" ones were far from perfect. She asks readers to think about what their parents were like. Think about your parents' relationship. Were they married to each other while you were growing up? single? divorced and married to someone else? Did their relationship influence your view of marriage?

AS YOU READ ───────────────

Essig argues that the institution of marriage is far from "natural and universal." On these grounds, she objects to the institution itself. How does she defend her stance? Does she make a good point?

1   Lately straight relatives and friends have been calling to talk about Vermont and the fact that same-sex "unions" are now legal in that state. They can barely contain their excitement as they ask: "Aren't you just thrilled? You and Liza will go and get married, won't you?"

2   I hate to disappoint them. They so desperately want us to be just like they are, to aspire to nothing more nor less than legal recognition till death do us part. I couch my rejection in subjunctives: "It would be nice if we could be recognized as a family. If we were married, we would save thousands of dollars in insurance bills alone."

3   But the reality is that I don't want to marry Liza (nor she me). In fact, I'm against same-sex marriage for the same reasons I'm against all marriage.

4   Although we like to pretend that marriage is natural and universal, it is an institution founded in historical, material and cultural conditions that ensured women's oppression—and everyone's disappointment. Monogamous, heterosexual marriages were an invention of the Industrial Revolution's emerging middle class. The Victorians created the domestic sphere in which middle class women's labor could be confined and unpaid. At the same time, by infusing the patriarchal family with the romance of monogamy for both parties, the Victorians reduced sexual pleasure to sexual reproduction. All other forms of sex—homosexuality, masturbation, nonreproductive sex—were strictly forbidden.

5   But in the American culture of the '00s, we like to be paid for our labor and we insist on indulging in our pleasures. That's why a truly monogamous and lifelong marriage today is as rare as a Jane Austen book that hasn't been made into a movie.

6   Now don't go getting your wedding dresses in a twist. I don't care if you're married, had a huge wedding, spent $15,000 on a useless dress and let your father

"give you away." I really don't care what personal perversions people partake of in their quest for pleasure.

7   What annoys me is that no one, not even queers, can imagine anything other than marriage as a model for organizing our desires. In the past, we queers have had to beg, cheat, steal and lie in order to create our families. But it's exactly this lack of state and societal recognition that gave us the freedom to organize our lives according to desire rather than convention.

8   Lesbians and gay men have created alliances and households and children together. Lesbians have bought sperm and used it to devious ends, gay men have explored sex as a public spectacle that is democratically available to all—and we have done this while forming intimate, lifelong allegiances with one another. And yes, many gays and lesbians, including me, have mimicked heterosexual marriage as best we could.

9   But why should those of us who have organized our lives in a way that looks a lot like heterosexual marriage be afforded special recognition by the government because of that? What about people who organize their lives in threes, or fours, or ones? What about my friend who is professionally promiscuous, who for ideological and psychological and sexual reasons has refused to ever be paired with anyone? What about my sister who is straight but has never in her 40-odd years seen a reason to participate in marriage? Which group will gain state recognition next? The polygamous? The lifelong celibate?

10   My point is not that we should do away with marriage but that we should do away with favoring some relationships over others with state recognition and privilege. Religions, not the state, should determine what is morally right and desirable in our personal lives. We can choose to be followers of those religions or thumb our noses at them. But the state has no place in my bedroom or family room, or in yours, either.

11   "Ah," but you say, "the state must recognize monogamous couples as more conducive to stable families and therefore better for children." Hello? Have you noticed that a huge number of marriages end in divorce? Even the supposedly "happy" ones aren't necessarily cheery little islands of serenity. What were your parents like?

12   There is absolutely no evidence that monogamous, state-sanctioned couplings are more stable than other sorts of arrangements. Even if there were such evidence, couples should be recognized by the state only when they decide to become parents. Why should anyone get societal privileges, let alone gifts, when he or she marries for the fourth time at age 68 with no intention of ever becoming a parent?

13   Still, as much as I hate to admit it, I am liberal at heart. If gays and lesbians want to get married, then I don't want to stop them. I just want to lay a couple of ground rules:

14   First, do not expect me to be happy. The legalization of gay marriage does not make me feel liberated as much as it makes me feel depressed. It's sort of like getting excited about gays in the military—until I remember that I don't really care about the military as an institution.

15   Second, under absolutely no circumstances should you expect me to give you a gift for such a decision. If you're insane enough to waste money on tacky clothes and bad cake, I'm not going to underwrite your actions with a toaster oven.

QUESTIONS FOR ANALYSIS AND DISCUSSION ─────────

1. How does Essig field inquiries from her friends and family regarding the possibility of nuptials between herself and her partner Liza? Why doesn't she admit her feelings about marriage directly? Explain.
2. Evaluate the author's tone in this essay. Does she seek to engage or antagonize her audience? Explain.
3. Essig argues that if homosexuals are granted the legal right to marry, other alternative lifestyle groups may soon demand legal recognition as well. Does this argument seem valid? Why or why not?
4. In paragraph 10, Essig states that "religions, not the state, should determine what is morally right and desirable in our personal lives." Do you agree with her position? Why or why not?
5. Essig argues that the institution of marriage is far from "natural and universal." On these grounds, she objects to the institution itself. How does she defend her position? What proof does she offer that supports her stance? Explain.
6. A year after she wrote this article, Laurie and Liza were joined in a civil union in Vermont—a decision completely motivated by the fact that they would be "saving thousands of dollars a year in health insurance bills" as a legally joined couple. Two years after their civil union, Laurie and Liza broke up. Read Laurie's description of "My Gay Divorce" in the September 2003 issue of *Legal Affairs* at <http://www.legalaffairs.org/issues/September-October-2003/feature_essig_sepoct03.html>. What do you think of Laurie's decision to undergo a civil union despite her objections described in her original essay? Does her "divorce" reinforce the points she makes in her first essay? Explain.

READING THE VISUAL

Wedding Day

The issue of gay marriage has been hotly argued, as some states ban, and others begin to permit officially, same-sex marriage. The Commonwealth of Massachusetts made headlines at the end of 2003 when its highest court ruled 4 to 3 that same-sex marriage was permissible under its state constitution. Several years earlier, the state of Vermont raised conservative eyebrows when it legally endorsed same-sex civil unions. Yet, despite all the media coverage implying that most people seem to support same-sex marriage, a December 2003 *New York Times* poll reported that 55 percent of Americans supported an amendment to the U.S. Constitution mandating that marriage be between a man and a woman, indicating that the issue is still dividing the country.

Since the court ruling in November 2003, many same-sex couples have filed for civil marriage. In this photo, Massachusetts residents Stuart Wilder Wells IV (left) and Lawton Phillips Bourn exchange rings and vows in their front yard in Rowley on May 17, 2004.

QUESTIONS FOR ANALYSIS AND DISCUSSION

1. What is happening in this photo? How does it present the marriage between the men in the photograph? Consider the background, the way the participants are dressed, etc. How do they all combine to convey a moment captured by the camera?
2. If you were reading a newspaper and saw this photo, would you stop to look at it more closely? Why or why not?
3. What elements of marriage as depicted in this photo meet our traditional expectations of marriage? Explain.

Can This Marriage Be Saved?

Jonathan Rauch

On May 17, 2004, Massachusetts became the first state to legalize same-sex marriage. Other states, such as Connecticut, New Jersey, Vermont, New Hampshire, Maine, Hawaii, Oregon, Washington, and California, permit civil unions of gay couples. Other countries, including the Netherlands, Belgium, and Canada, have similar rights for gay couples. Although Massachusetts has yet to bring the question of gay marriage to a public vote, same-sex marriage will remain legal until at least 2012. In the next essay, Jonathan Rauch considers whether same-sex marriage will ultimately destroy marriage as we know it or, in fact, infuse it with greater stability.

Rauch is a journalist and activist. His writing has appeared in the *The New Republic* magazine and *The Economist*, among many other publications. He is currently a senior writer and columnist for the *National Journal*, a correspondent for *The Atlantic Monthly*, and a writer-in-residence at the Brookings Institution. Rauch is also the author of five books, most recently *Gay Marriage: Why It Is Good for Gays, Good for Straights, and Good for America* (2003). This article was first published by *Reason Magazine* on May 18, 2004.

BEFORE YOU READ

In your opinion, should same-sex couples be permitted to marry legally? Is this a decision, such as in Massachusetts, to be made by the courts, or by popular vote?

AS YOU READ

When does Rauch seem to change his point of view on same-sex marriage? Does this shift confuse readers, or serve to strengthen his argument?

1   In *The Pink Panther Strikes Again*, when Peter Sellers's Inspector Clouseau blunderingly demolishes a grand piano, a horrified onlooker exclaims, "That's a priceless Steinway!" Replies Clouseau: "Not anymore."

2   More than a few Americans now find themselves wondering whether marriage is that piano. On Monday, barring the unexpected, the state of Massachusetts will begin issuing marriage licenses to same-sex couples, under orders from the state's Supreme Court. For the first time, gay marriage will enjoy clear statewide legality. Voters will get the last word in a statewide constitutional referendum, but the earliest that can happen is in 2006.

3   In the United States and the rest of Western civilization, marriage has always been between a man and a woman. As Clouseau said: Not anymore.

4   More than two dozen other states are rushing to write gay-marriage bans into their constitutions. Some of the bans are inspired by panic, or by dislike of homosexuality. But even many people of goodwill toward their gay and lesbian fellow

citizens blanch at redefining society's most basic institution. Gay marriage, to them, seems risky.

5   They have a point. Gay marriage is risky. But not trying gay marriage is riskier.

6   To many of its supporters, gay marriage is a civil-rights issue: Marriage is a right, and every couple should have it. To many of its opponents, gay marriage is a moral issue: Homosexuality is wrong, and society should not condone it. Well, gay marriage is a civil-rights issue and a moral issue, but it is also, perhaps most importantly, a family policy issue. Right now, Americans are deciding the shape of marriage—the basic legal and social framework of family—for years to come. Risk, therefore, is just as relevant as rights or as right and wrong. What, then, is the balance of risks?

7   Begin with what we know for a fact: Something like 3 to 5 percent of the population—all gay and lesbian Americans—are locked out of marriage, which is life's most stabilizing and enriching institution. Even after accounting for differences between the married and unmarried populations, married people are healthier, happier, more prosperous, more secure; they even live longer. To shut millions of Americans off from those benefits is to inflict a very real harm. Moreover, many same-sex couples are raising children: several hundred thousand, at least, and possibly more (there are no firm figures). Presumably, those children would be better off with married parents.

8   So same-sex marriage would benefit gay people and the children they are raising. That much meets with little dispute. But what about the rest of society? Here the debate turns to what economists call "externalities": harms or benefits to society at large that flow from private decisions.

9   Opponents of same-sex marriage insist it will bring grave, perhaps catastrophic, negative externalities that will hurt millions of American families. They have yet to explain, however, precisely how allowing same-sex couples to marry would damage anyone else's marriage or family. More plausible is a second common view, which is that same-sex marriage will have little or no impact on straight families. No-fault divorce changed the terms of marriage for heterosexual couples, which was plainly a big deal. The only thing that same-sex marriage does, by contrast, is to expand by a few percentage points the number of people who are eligible to marry their partner.

10   Less often noticed is a third possibility: positive externalities. Today, a third of all American children are born out of wedlock, cohabitation is soaring, and nearly half of marriages end in divorce. Marriage's problem is not that gay couples want to get married but that straight couples don't want to get married or don't manage to stay married. At long last, gay marriage provides an opportunity to climb back up the slippery slope by reaffirming marriage's status as a norm—not just as a right but as a rite, the gold standard for committed relationships. Gay marriage dramatically affirms that love, sex, and marriage go together—that if you really care, you marry. No exclusions, no excuses.

11   So gay marriage entails potential social benefits as well as potential risks, even apart from the unquestioned benefits for gay couples. And there is a further element, as important as it is overlooked. Banning gay marriage entails its own risks to marriage. And those are not small risks.

12   Because society has an interest in seeing same-sex couples settle down and look after one another, and because gay couples' friends and family care about their

well-being, committed gay couples are winning increasing social support. One way or another, legal support will follow. Banning gay marriage guarantees that the country will busy itself creating gay-inclusive alternatives to marriage (which will be tempting to heterosexuals) and bestowing legal rights and social recognition on cohabitation (which is open to heterosexuals by definition). The result will be to diminish marriage's special status among a plethora of "lifestyle alternatives"—the last thing marriage needs.

13   Moreover, the gay exclusion risks marginalizing marriage by tainting it as discriminatory. A March *Los Angeles Times* poll finds that more than 80 percent of young people (ages 18 to 29) favor anti-discrimination protections for gay people. More than 70 percent believe gays should receive the same kinds of civil-rights protections that are afforded to racial minorities and women. More than half favor gay adoption, three-fourths believe that "a gay person can be a good role model for a child," and more than 70 percent can "accept two men or two women living together like a married couple." Seventy percent describe themselves as sympathetic to the gay community (versus 43 percent of people 65 and older). And three-fourths support gay marriage or civil unions—with the plurality favoring marriage.

14   In other words, America's young are much more hostile to discrimination than to gays or gay marriage. They will increasingly view straights-only marriage the way their parents have come to view men-only clubs: as marginal, anachronistic, even ridiculous. This is not conjecture; it is already beginning. San Francisco regarded its decision to marry gay couples as a protest against discrimination, and Benton County, Ore., recently stopped issuing marriage licenses altogether, on the grounds that it wanted no part of a discriminatory institution.

15   "We are genuinely running the risk of making marriage uncool," Frank Furstenburg, a University of Pennsylvania sociologist, said last month, in an Associated Press article about straight couples who are boycotting marriage to protest discrimination. Today, such couples are rare. But in 10 years? Twenty? So there are risks, large risks, on both sides of the equation. Banning same-sex marriage is no safe harbor. Given that fact, it is irresponsible *not* to try gay marriage, at least if protecting marriage is the goal.

16   Banning same-sex marriage nationally, as President Bush and many conservatives would do, is hardly a conservative approach; it risks putting marriage on the road to cultural irrelevance. On the other hand, national enactment would be an irreversible leap into the unknown. There ought to be a way to try same-sex marriage without betting the whole country one way or the other. And there is. Try gay marriage in a state or two. Say, Massachusetts.

17   Massachusetts is one of only a handful of states where gay marriage can legally happen (most states have enacted pre-emptive bans). Its law prohibits marrying out-of-state gay couples, so the experiment will be local. Massachusetts is gay-friendly, allowing same-sex marriage a fair trial. And it gives the final say to the voters, not judges or politicians or bureaucrats. In short, Massachusetts is the perfect laboratory for an experiment that needs to happen.

18   Starting Monday, and probably for years to come, America will no longer have a uniform national definition of marriage. That is nobody's first choice. Conservatives

wish the issue had never arisen and hope, unrealistically, that a constitutional amendment will put the cork back in the bottle. Many gay-marriage proponents wish, just as unrealistically, that the courts could settle the issue quickly by fiat.

19   But neither a constitutional amendment nor a Supreme Court order could resolve what is, at bottom, a fundamental schism in the social consensus: Older people see same-sex marriage as a contradiction, and younger people see opposite-sex-only marriage as discrimination. Reconciling marriage with homosexuality, equality, and society's needs will be messy, but, as Robert Frost said, the only way out is through. Massachusetts is as good a starting place as the country could have hoped for.

QUESTIONS FOR ANALYSIS AND DISCUSSION

1. Is Rauch's introduction effective in getting his audience's attention? How does he seem to trick his audience about his point of view?
2. According to Rauch, how might banning gay marriage actually do more to destroy the institution of marriage than to keep it sacred?
3. In what ways does Dennis Prager's essay "Five Non-Religious Arguments for Marriage Over Living Together" complement Jonathan Rauch's argument that "straight couples don't want to get married. . . . At long last, gay marriage provides an opportunity to climb back up the slippery slope by reaffirming marriage's status as a norm—not just as a right but as a rite, the gold standard for committed relationships . . . that if you really care, you marry"?
4. Which concrete example does Rauch use to prove his assertion that America's youth accepts the gay community and is hostile to discrimination? Do you know of any other examples either for or against Rauch's claim? Explain.
5. Do you think that in the future same-sex marriage will be repealed, will spread to other states, or will change to civil unions? Explain.

BLOG IT

A really, really, really long post about gay marriage that does not, in the end, support one side or the other

April 02, 2005

http://www.janegalt.net/blog/archives/005244.html

Unlike most libertarians, I don't have an opinion on gay marriage, and I'm not going to have an opinion no matter how much you bait me. However, I had an interesting discussion last night with another libertarian about it, which devolved into an argument about a certain kind of liberal/libertarian argument about gay marriage that I find really unconvincing.

Social conservatives of a more moderate stripe are essentially saying that marriage is an ancient institution, which has been carefully selected for throughout human history. It is the bedrock of our society; if it is destroyed, we will all be much worse off. (See what happened to the inner cities between 1960 and 1990 if you do not believe this.) For some reason, marriage always and everywhere, in every culture we know about, is between a man and a woman; this seems to be an important feature of the institution. We should not go mucking around and changing this extremely important institution, because if we make a bad change, the institution will fall apart.

A very common response to this is essentially to mock this as ridiculous. "Why on earth would it make any difference to me whether gay people are getting married? Why would that change my behavior as a heterosexual?"

To which social conservatives reply that institutions have a number of complex ways in which they fulfill their roles, and one of the very important ways in which the institution of marriage perpetuates itself is by creating a romantic vision of oneself in marriage that is intrinsically tied into expressing one's masculinity or femininity in relation to a person of the opposite sex; stepping into an explicitly gendered role. This may not be true of every single marriage, and indeed undoubtedly it is untrue in some cases. But it is true of the culture-wide institution. By changing the explicitly gendered nature of marriage we might be accidentally cutting away something that turns out to be a crucial underpinning.

To which, again, the other side replies "That's ridiculous! I would never change my willingness to get married based on whether or not gay people were getting married!"

Now, economists hear this sort of argument all the time. "That's ridiculous! I would never start working fewer hours because my taxes went up!" This ignores the fact that you may not be the marginal case. The marginal case may be some consultant who just can't justify sacrificing valuable leisure for a new project when he's only making 60 cents on the dollar. The result will nonetheless be the same: less economic activity. Similarly, you—highly educated, firmly socialized, upper middle class you—may not be the marginal marriage candidate; it may be some high school dropout in Tuscaloosa. That doesn't mean that the institution of marriage won't be weakened in America just the same.

This should not be taken as an endorsement of the idea that gay marriage will weaken the current institution. I can tell a plausible story where it does; I can tell a plausible story where it doesn't. I have no idea which one is true. That is why I have no opinion on gay marriage, and am not planning to develop one. Marriage is a big institution; too big for me to feel I have a successful handle on it.

However, I am bothered by this specific argument, which I have heard over and over from the people I know who favor gay marriage laws. I mean, literally over and over; when they get into arguments, they just repeat it, again and again. "I will get married even if marriage is expanded to include gay people; I cannot imagine anyone up and deciding not to get married because gay people are getting married; therefore, the whole idea is ridiculous and bigoted."

They may well be right. Nonetheless, libertarians should know better. The limits of your imagination are not the limits of reality. Every government program that libertarians have argued against has been defended at its inception with exactly this argument.

Let me take three major legal innovations, one of them general, two specific to marriage.

The first, the general one, is well known to most hard-core libertarians, but let me reprise it anyway. When the income tax was initially being debated, there was a suggestion to put in a mandatory cap; I believe the level was 10 percent.

Don't be ridiculous, the Senator's colleagues told him. Americans would never allow an income tax rate as high as ten percent. They would revolt! It is an outrage to even suggest it!

Many actually fought the cap on the grounds that it would encourage taxes to grow too high, towards the cap. The American people, they asserted, could be well counted on to keep income taxes in the range of a few percentage points.

Oops.

Now, I'm not a tax-crazy libertarian; I don't expect you to be horrified that we have income taxes higher than ten percent, as I'm not. But the point is that the Senators were completely right—at that time. However, the existence of the income tax allowed for a slow creep that eroded the American resistance to income taxation. External changes—from the Great Depression, to the technical ability to manage withholding rather than lump payments, also facilitated the rise, but they could not have without a cultural sea change in feelings about taxation. That "ridiculous" cap would have done a much, much better job holding down tax rates than the culture these Senators erroneously relied upon. Changing the law can, and does, change the culture of the thing regulated.

Another example is welfare. To sketch a brief history of welfare, it emerged in the nineteenth century as "Widows and orphans pensions", which were paid by the state to destitute families whose breadwinner had passed away. They were often not available to blacks; they were never available to unwed mothers. Though public services expanded in the first half of the twentieth century, that mentality was very much the same: public services were about supporting unfortunate families, not unwed mothers. Unwed mothers could not, in most cases, obtain welfare; they were not allowed in public housing (which was supposed to be—and was— a way station for young, struggling families on the way to homeownership, not a permanent abode); they were otherwise discriminated against by social services. The help you could expect from society was a home for wayward girls, in which you would give birth and then put the baby up for adoption.

The description of public housing in the fifties is shocking to anyone who's spent any time in modern public housing. Big item on the agenda at the tenant's meeting: housewives, don't shake your dust cloths out of the windows—other wives don't want your dirt in their apartment! Men, if you wear heavy work boots, please don't walk on the lawns until you can change into lighter shoes, as it damages the grass! (Descriptions taken from the invaluable book, *The Inheritance*, about the transition of the white working class from Democrat to Republican.) Needless to say, if those same housing projects could today find a majority of tenants who reliably dusted, or worked, they would be thrilled. Public housing was, in short, a place full of functioning families.

Now, in the late fifties, a debate began over whether to extend benefits to the unmarried. It was unfair to stigmatize unwed mothers. Why shouldn't they be able to avail themselves of the benefits available to other citizens? The brutal societal prejudice against illegitimacy was old fashioned, bigoted, irrational.

But if you give unmarried mothers money, said the critics, you will get more unmarried mothers.

Ridiculous, said the proponents of the change. Being an unmarried mother is a brutal, thankless task. What kind of idiot would have a baby out of wedlock just because the state was willing to give her paltry welfare benefits?

People do all sorts of idiotic things, said the critics. If you pay for something, you usually get more of it.

C'mon said the activists. That's just silly. I just can't imagine anyone deciding to get pregnant out of wedlock simply because there are welfare benefits available.

Oooops.

Of course, change didn't happen overnight. But the marginal cases did have children out of wedlock, which made it more acceptable for the next marginal case to do so. Meanwhile, women who wanted to get married essentially found themselves in competition for young men with women who were willing to have sex, and bear children, without forcing the men to take any responsibility. This is a pretty attractive proposition for most young men. So despite the fact that the sixties brought us the biggest advance in birth control ever, illegitimacy exploded. In the early 1960s, a black illegitimacy rate of roughly 25 percent caused Daniel Patrick Moynihan to write a tract warning of a crisis in "the negro family" (a tract for which he was eviscerated by many of those selfsame activists.)

By 1990, that rate was over 70 percent. This, despite the fact that the inner city, where the illegitimacy problem was biggest, only accounts for a fraction of the black population. But in that inner city, marriage had been destroyed. It had literally ceased to exist in any meaningful way. Possibly one of the most moving moments in Jason de Parle's absolutely wonderful book, "American Dream," which follows three welfare mothers through welfare reform, is when he reveals that none of these three women, all in their late thirties, had ever been to a wedding.

Marriage matters. It is better for the kids; it is better for the adults raising those kids; and it is better for the childless people in the communities where those kids and adults live. Marriage reduces poverty, improves kids outcomes in all measurable ways, makes men live longer and both spouses happier. Marriage, it turns out, is an incredibly important institution. It also turns out to be a lot more fragile than we thought back then. It looked, to those extremely smart and well-meaning welfare reformers, practically unshakeable; the idea that it could be undone by something as simple as enabling women to have children without husbands, seemed ludicrous. Its cultural underpinnings were far too firm. Why would a woman choose such a hard road? It seemed self-evident that the only unwed mothers claiming benefits would be the ones pushed there by terrible circumstance.

This argument is compelling and logical. I would never become an unwed welfare mother, even if benefits were a great deal higher than they are now. It seems crazy to even suggest that one would bear a child out of wedlock for $567 a month. Indeed, to this day, I find the reformist side much more persuasive than the conservative side, except for one thing, which is that the conservatives turned out to be right. In fact, they turned out to be even more right than they suspected; they were predicting upticks in illegitimacy that were much more modest than what actually occurred—they expected marriage rates to suffer, not collapse.

How did people go so badly wrong? Well, to start with, they fell into the basic fallacy that economists are so well acquainted with: they thought about themselves instead of the marginal case. For another, they completely failed to realize that each additional illegitimate birth would, in effect, slightly destigmatize the next one. They assigned men very little agency, failing to predict that women willing to forgo marriage would essentially become unwelcome competition for women who weren't, and that as the numbers changed, that competition might push the marriage market towards unwelcome outcomes. They failed to foresee the confounding effect that the birth control pill would have on sexual mores.

The third example I'll give is of changes to the marriage laws, specifically the radical relaxation of divorce statutes during the twentieth century.

Divorce, in the nineteenth century, was *unbelievably* hard to get. It took years, was expensive, and required proving that your spouse had abandoned you for an extended period with no financial support; was (if male) not merely discreetly dallying but flagrantly carrying on; or was not just belting you one now and again when you got mouthy, but routinely pummeling you within an inch of your life. After you got divorced, you were a pariah in all but the largest cities. If you were a desperately wronged woman you might change your name, taking your maiden name as your first name and continuing to use your husband's last name to indicate that you expected to continue living as if you were married (i.e. chastely) and expect to have some limited intercourse with your neighbors, though of course you would not be invited to events held in a church, or evening affairs. Financially secure women generally (I am not making this up) moved to Europe; Edith Wharton, who moved to Paris when she got divorced, wrote moving stories about the way divorced women were shunned at home. Men, meanwhile (who were usually the respondents) could expect to see more than half their assets and income settled on their spouse and children.

There were, critics observed, a number of unhappy marriages in which people stuck together. Young people, who shouldn't have gotten married; older people, whose spouses were not physically abusive nor absent, nor flagrantly adulterous, but whose spouse was, for reasons of financial irresponsibility, mental viciousness, or some other major flaw, destroying their life. Why not make divorce easier to get? Rather than requiring people to show that there was an unforgivable, physically visible, cause that the marriage should be dissolved, why not let people who wanted to get divorced agree to do so?

Because if you make divorce easier, said the critics, you will get much more of it, and divorce is bad for society.

That's ridiculous! said the reformers. People stay married because marriage is a bedrock institution of our society, not because of some law! The only people who get divorced will be people who have terrible problems! A few percentage points at most!

Oops. When the law changed, the institution changed. The marginal divorce made the next one easier. Again, the magnitude of the change swamped the dire predictions of the anti-reformist wing; no one could have imagined, in their wildest dreams, a day when half of all marriages ended in divorce.

There were actually two big changes; the first, when divorce laws were amended in most states to make it easier to get a divorce; and the second, when "no fault" divorce allowed one spouse to unilaterally end the marriage. The second change produced another huge surge in the divorce rate, and a nice decline in the incomes of divorced women; it seems advocates had failed to anticipate that removing the leverage of the financially weaker party to hold out for a good settlement would result in men keeping more of their earnings to themselves.

What's more, easy divorce didn't only change the divorce rate; it made drastic changes to the institution of marriage itself. David Brooks makes an argument I find convincing: that the proliferation of the kind of extravagant weddings that used to only be the province of high society (rented venue, extravagant flowers and food, hundreds of guests, a band with dancing, dresses that cost the same as a good used car) is because the event itself doesn't mean nearly as much as it used to, so we have to turn it into a three-ring circus to feel like we're really doing something.

A couple in 1940 (and even more so in 1910) could go to a minister's parlor, or a justice of the peace, and in five minutes totally change their lives. Unless you are a member of certain highly religious subcultures, this is simply no longer true. That is, of course, partly because of the sexual revolution and the emancipation of women; but it is also because you aren't really making a lifetime commitment; you're making a lifetime commitment unless you find something better to do. There is no way, psychologically, to make the latter as big an event as the former, and when you lost that commitment, you lose, on the margin, some willingness to make the marriage work. Again, this doesn't mean I think divorce law should be toughened up; only that changes in law that affect marriage affect the cultural institution, not just the legal practice.

Three laws. Three well-meaning reformers who were genuinely, sincerely incapable of imagining that their changes would wreak such institutional havoc. Three sets of utterly logical and convincing, and wrong arguments about how people would behave after a major change.

So what does this mean? That we shouldn't enact gay marriage because of some sort of social Precautionary Principle.

No. I have no such grand advice.

My only request is that people try to be a leeetle more humble about their ability to imagine the subtle results of big policy changes. The argument that gay marriage will not change the institution of marriage because you can't imagine it changing your personal reaction is pretty arrogant. It imagines, first of all, that your behavior is a guide for the behavior of everyone else in society, when in fact, as you may have noticed, all sorts of different people react to all sorts of different things in all sorts of different ways, which is why we have to have elections and stuff. And second, the unwavering belief that the only reason that marriage, always and everywhere, is a male-female institution (I exclude rare ritual behaviors), is just some sort of bizarre historical coincidence, and that you know better, needs examining. If you think you know why marriage is male-female, and why that's either outdated because of all the ways in which reproduction has lately changed, or was a bad reason to start with, then you are in a good place to advocate reform. If you think that marriage is just that way because our ancestors were all a bunch of repressed bastards with dark Freudian complexes that made them homophobic bigots, I'm a little leery of letting you muck around with it.

Is this post going to convince anyone? I doubt it; everyone but me seems to already know all the answers, so why listen to such a hedging, doubting bore? I myself am trying to draw a very fine line between being humble about making big changes to big social institutions, and telling people (which I am not trying to do) that they can't make those changes because other people have been wrong in the past. In the end, our judgment is all we have; everyone will have to rely on their judgment of whether gay marriage is, on net, a good or a bad idea. All I'm asking for is for people to think more deeply than a quick consultation of their imaginations to make that decision. I realize that this probably falls on the side of supporting the anti-gay-marriage forces, and I'm sorry, but I can't help that. This humility is what I want from liberals when approaching market changes; now I'm asking it from my side too, in approaching social ones. I think the approach is consistent, if not exactly popular.

You Say:

WRITING ASSIGNMENTS

1. The Family Research Council openly opposes homosexuality as "unhealthy, immoral and destructive to individuals, families, and societies." Visit its website at <http://www.frc.org> and read about the council's views on the issue of homosexual marriage. Write an essay in which you address its concerns regarding homosexual marriage's threat to the institution of the American family. Evaluate the council's argument and present your own view for comparison and contrast.

2. Write a letter to a priest, minister, rabbi, or other religious leader. Explain why you think he or she should agree to perform a marriage ceremony celebrating the commitment of two of your best friends—a gay couple. Assume that this leader has not given much thought to the issue of gay marriage. Conversely, you may write a letter against such a marriage. You care deeply about your friends and recognize that your dissent may cause them pain, but your beliefs compel you to advise against a gay union.

3. Gay couples have been more prominent on television and other media in recent years. What images of gay life has television presented to its viewers? How do the images correspond to Andrew Sullivan's claims that gay men and women often live like heterosexual couples? Or do these images try too hard to mimic heterosexual relationships? Write an essay in which you explore the portrayal of gay relationships in the media and how this depiction may or may not influence the public on the issue of gay marriage.

4. Will legalizing gay marriage increase or decrease the problems involved in gaining the social acceptance gay men and women now encounter in America? What benefits might all gay people receive, whether or not they choose to marry? Do you think that a legal change in marriage will help to change the beliefs of people who now disapprove of homosexuality? Why or why not? Explain.

5. Most of the arguments supporting gay marriage note that gay couples are in committed loving relationships and wish to legitimize their relationship with a marriage license. Can you think of other, less idealistic reasons why people marry? Based on these other reasons, including the practical and the shady, could these reasons undermine the movement legalizing homosexual marriage? For example, what if two female heterosexual friends, one employed and the other not, wished to marry for health insurance? Could such alliances be avoided if same-sex marriage were legal? Explain.

CHAPTER 16

Race and Ethnicity

The United States is a union predicated on shared moral values, political and economic self-interest, and a common language. However, it is also a nation of immigrants—people of different races, ethnic identities, religions, and languages. It is a nation whose motto *e pluribus unum* ("one out of many") bespeaks a pride in its multicultural heritage. In this chapter, we explore some of the issues that arise from the diversity of our cultural and ethnic backgrounds.

The first section in this chapter examines the complex ways in which ethnic and racial stereotypes limit our relationships with others and distort how we define ourselves. By definition, stereotypes are misleading assumptions about individuals or groups based on characteristics such as race, ethnic origin, social class, religion, gender, or physical appearance. Sometimes stereotypes can lead one to make assumptions about others that are negative and demeaning. And some can be dangerous—such as the presumption that most Muslims are terrorists. However, it is not only negative stereotypes that can harm us; even stereotypes that attribute positive qualities to certain groups, such as the assumption that Asian Americans are naturally smart, can deny individuals credit for their achievements.

The next section focuses on the ways our multicultural heritage can both unify and divide us. Although the United States has been a multiethnic and multiracial society since its founding, in the last few decades different groups of Americans have reasserted their ethnic and racial identities. And while we may glorify the memory of our own immigrant ancestors, we do not always welcome with open arms new waves of immigrants.

Most of the arguments regarding the issue of immigration focus on illegal aliens circumventing U.S. laws. Some critics argue that immigrants themselves have changed—that the current wave of newcomers is different from ones in the past, that this group refuses to assimilate, threatens the American way of life, and expects free handouts. Immigration advocates counter that all immigrant groups resist integration to a certain extent at first, and then assimilate into mainstream culture. They also contend that immigrants promote diversity, revitalize the workforce, and are

730

good for the economy overall. With such diverse perspectives and positions, the is-sue can be challenging to navigate.

The other section in this chapter addresses the issue of racial profiling, especially as it applies to African Americans and to people of Middle-Eastern descent. When eth-nic stereotyping is used as a law enforcement tool, it is called racial profiling. Each new immigrant group to arrive on America's shores—Irish, Italian, Chinese, German—has experienced some form of racial profiling, usually at the hands of the groups that came before them. As America became more ethnically blended, the profiling of some groups decreased and even disappeared. But racial profiling in America remains an issue for many ethnic groups. Several authors in this section explain that although racial profil-ing may seem to be based on logical premises and patterns of behavior, they feel it is morally wrong under any circumstances. Others argue that racial profiling is a useful tool for law enforcement in the fight against crime and terrorism.

STEREOTYPES: HOW THEY HURT

The Myth of the Latina Woman
Judith Ortiz Cofer

Racial stereotypes are often based on misperceptions and a lack of understanding of another group's cultural heritage. In this essay, Judith Ortiz Cofer explores how racial stereotypes are created by cultural misunderstandings, with often insulting results. She also describes how once stereotypes are established, they can perpetuate degrading popular opinions that, in turn, may damage the self-opinion of an entire group of people.

Ortiz Cofer is Franklin Professor of English and Creative Writing at University of Georgia. A native of Puerto Rico, she moved with her family to the United States when she was a young girl. Educated at both American and British universities, she is the author of many books, including the novel *The Line of the Sun* (1989), for which she was nominated for a Pulitzer Prize, *The Meaning of Consuelo* (2003), and *Call Me Maria* (2004). The following reading appears in her collection of essays, *The Latin Deli* (1993).

BEFORE YOU READ

Consider the ways the media perpetuate cultural stereotypes. Think about how various media, such as television and cinema, promote cultural clichés.

AS YOU READ

Ortiz Cofer comments that certain adjectives are often used to describe indi-viduals from her ethnic background. What is the basis for these adjectives?

What other words can you cite that are used to describe the personalities of women and men from certain ethnic backgrounds?

1   **O**n a bus trip to London from Oxford University where I was earning some grad-uate credits one summer, a young man, obviously fresh from a pub, spotted me and as if struck by inspiration went down on his knees in the aisle. With both hands over his heart he broke into an Irish tenor's rendition of "María" from West Side Story. My politely amused fellow passengers gave his lovely voice the round of gen-tle applause it deserved.

2   Though I was not quite as amused, I managed my version of an English smile: no show of teeth, no extreme contortions of the facial muscles—I was at this time of my life practicing reserve and cool. Oh, that British control, how I coveted it. But María had followed me to London, reminding me of a prime fact of my life: you can leave the Island, master the English language, and travel as far as you can, but if you are a Latina, especially one like me who so obviously belongs to Rita Moreno's gene pool, the Island travels with you.

3   This is sometimes a very good thing—it may win you that extra minute of some-one's attention. But with some people, the same things can make you an island—not so much a tropical paradise as an Alcatraz, a place nobody wants to visit. As a Puerto Rican girl growing up in the United States and wanting like most children to "belong," I resented the stereotype that my Hispanic appearance called forth from many people I met.

4   Our family lived in a large urban center in New Jersey during the sixties, where life was designed as a microcosm of my parents' casas on the island. We spoke in Spanish, we ate Puerto Rican food bought at the bodega, and we practiced strict Catholicism complete with Saturday confession and Sunday mass at a church where our parents were accommodated into a one-hour Spanish mass slot, performed by a Chinese priest trained as a missionary for Latin America.

5   As a girl I was kept under strict surveillance, since virtue and modesty were, by cultural equation, the same as family honor. As a teenager I was instructed on how to behave as a proper señorita. But it was a conflicting message girls got, since the Puerto Rican mothers also encouraged their daughters to look and act like women and to dress in clothes our Anglo friends and their mothers found too "mature" for our age. It was, and is, cultural, yet I often felt humiliated when I appeared at an American friend's party wearing a dress more suitable to a semiformal than to a playroom birthday celebration. At Puerto Rican festivities, neither the music nor the colors we wore could be too loud. I still experience a vague sense of letdown when I'm invited to a "party" and it turns out to be a marathon conversation in hushed tones rather than a fiesta with salsa, laughter, and dancing—the kind of celebration I remember from my childhood.

6   I remember Career Day in our high school, when teachers told us to come dressed as if for a job interview. It quickly became obvious that to the barrio girls, "dressing up" sometimes meant wearing ornate jewelry and clothing that would be more appropriate (by mainstream standards) for the company Christmas party than

as daily office attire. That morning I had agonized in front of my closet, trying to figure out what a "career girl" would wear because, essentially, except for Marlo Thomas on TV, I had no models on which to base my decision. I knew how to dress for school: At the Catholic school I attended we all wore uniforms; I knew how to dress for Sunday mass, and I knew what dresses to wear for parties at my relatives' homes. Though I do not recall the precise details of my Career Day outfit, it must have been a composite of the above choices. But I remember a comment my friend (an Italian-American) made in later years that coalesced my impressions of that day. She said that at the business school she was attending the Puerto Rican girls always stood out for wearing "everything at once." She meant, of course, too much jewelry, too many accessories. On that day at school, we were simply made the negative models by the nuns who were themselves not credible fashion experts to any of us. But it was painfully obvious to me that to the others, in their tailored skirts and silk blouses, we must have seemed "hopeless" and "vulgar." Though I now know that most adolescents feel out of step much of the time, I also know that for the Puerto Rican girls of my generation that sense was intensified. The way our teachers and classmates looked at us that day in school was just a taste of the cultural clash that awaited us in the real world, where prospective employers and men on the street would often misinterpret our tight skirts and jingling bracelets as a come-on.

7   Mixed cultural signals have perpetuated certain stereotypes—for example, that of the Hispanic woman as the "Hot Tamale" or sexual firebrand. It is a one-dimensional view that the media have found easy to promote. In their special vocabulary, advertisers have designated "sizzling" and "smoldering" as the adjectives of choice for describing not only the foods but also the women of Latin America. From conversations in my house I recall hearing about the harassment that Puerto Rican women endured in factories where the "boss men" talked to them as if sexual innuendo was all they understood and, worse, often gave them the choice of submitting to advances or being fired.

8   It is custom, however, not chromosomes, that leads us to choose scarlet over pale pink. As young girls, we were influenced in our decisions about clothes and colors by the women—older sisters and mothers who had grown up on a tropical island where the natural environment was a riot of primary colors, where showing your skin was one way to keep cool as well as to look sexy. Most important of all, on the Island, women perhaps felt freer to dress and move more provocatively, since, in most cases, they were protected by the traditions, mores, and laws of a Spanish/Catholic system of morality and machismo whose main rule was: You may look at my sister, but if you touch her I will kill you. The extended family and church structure could provide a young woman with a circle of safety in her small pueblo on the island; if a man "wronged" a girl, everyone would close in to save her family honor.

9   This is what I have gleaned from my discussions as an adult with older Puerto Rican women. They have told me about dressing in their best party clothes on Saturday nights and going to the town's plaza to promenade with their girlfriends in front of the boys they liked. The males were thus given an opportunity to admire the women and to express their admiration in the form of piropos: erotically charged

street poems they composed on the spot. I have been subjected to a few piropos while visiting the Island, and they can be outrageous, although custom dictates that they must never cross into obscenity. This ritual, as I understand it, also entails a show of studied indifference on the woman's part; if she is "decent," she must not acknowledge the man's impassioned words. So I do understand how things can be lost in translation. When a Puerto Rican girl dressed in her idea of what is attractive meets a man from the mainstream culture who has been trained to react to certain types of clothing as a sexual signal, a clash is likely to take place. The line I first heard based on this aspect of the myth happened when the boy who took me to my first formal dance leaned over to plant a sloppy overeager kiss painfully on my mouth, and when I didn't respond with sufficient passion said in a resentful tone: "I thought you Latin girls were supposed to mature early"—my first instance of being thought of as a fruit or vegetable—I was supposed to ripen, not just grow into womanhood like other girls.

10   It is surprising to some of my professional friends that some people, including those who should know better, still put others "in their place." Though rarer, these incidents are still commonplace in my life. It happened to me most recently during a stay at a very classy metropolitan hotel favored by young professional couples for their weddings. Late one evening after the theater, as I walked toward my room with my new colleague (a woman with whom I was coordinating an arts program), a middle-aged man in a tuxedo, a young girl in satin and lace on his arm, stepped directly into our path. With his champagne glass extended toward me, he exclaimed, "Evita!"

11   Our way blocked, my companion and I listened as the man half-recited, half-bellowed "Don't Cry for Me, Argentina." When he finished, the young girl said: "How about a round of applause for my daddy?" We complied, hoping this would bring the silly spectacle to a close. I was becoming aware that our little group was attracting the attention of the other guests. "Daddy" must have perceived this too, and he once more barred the way as we tried to walk past him. He began to shout-sing a ditty to the tune of "La Bamba"—except the lyrics were about a girl named Maria whose exploits all rhymed with her name and gonorrhea. The girl kept saying "Oh, Daddy" and looking at me with pleading eyes. She wanted me to laugh along with the others. My companion and I stood silently waiting for the man to end his offensive song. When he finished, I looked not at him but at his daughter. I advised her calmly never to ask her father what he had done in the army. Then I walked between them and to my room. My friend complimented me on my cool handling of the situation. I confessed to her that I really had wanted to push the jerk into the swimming pool. I knew that this same man—probably a corporate executive, well educated, even wordly by most standards—would not have been likely to regale a white woman with a dirty song in public. He would perhaps have checked his impulse by assuming that she could be somebody's wife or mother, or at least somebody who might take offense. But to him, I was just an Evita or a María: merely a character in his cartoon-populated universe.

12   Because of my education and my proficiency with the English language, I have acquired many mechanisms for dealing with the anger I experience. This was not

true for my parents, nor is it true for the many Latin women working at menial jobs who must put up with stereotypes about our ethnic group such as: "They make good domestics." This is another facet of the myth of the Latin woman in the United States. Its origin is simple to deduce. Work as domestics, waitressing, and factory jobs are all that's available to women with little English and few skills. The myth of the Hispanic menial has been sustained by the same media phenomenon that made "Mammy" from *Gone with the Wind* America's idea of the black woman for generations; María, the housemaid or counter girl, is now indelibly etched into the national psyche. The big and the little screens have presented us with the picture of the funny Hispanic maid, mispronouncing words and cooking up a spicy storm in a shiny California kitchen.

13   This media-engendered image of the Latina in the United States has been documented by feminist Hispanic scholars, who claim that such portrayals are partially responsible for the denial of opportunities for upward mobility among Latinas in the professions. I have a Chicana friend working on a Ph.D. in philosophy at a major university. She says her doctor still shakes his head in puzzled amazement at all the "big words" she uses. Since I do not wear my diplomas around my neck for all to see, I too have on occasion been sent to that "kitchen," where some think I obviously belong.

14   One such incident that has stayed with me, though I recognize it as a minor offense, happened on the day of my first public poetry reading. It took place in Miami in a boat-restaurant where we were having lunch before the event. I was nervous and excited as I walked in with my notebook in my hand. An older woman motioned me to her table. Thinking (foolish me) that she wanted me to autograph a copy of my brand new slender volume of verse, I went over. She ordered a cup of coffee from me, assuming that I was the waitress. Easy enough to mistake my poems for menus, I suppose. I know that it wasn't an intentional act of cruelty, yet of all the good things that happened that day, I remember that scene most clearly, because it reminded me of what I had to overcome before anyone would take me seriously. In retrospect I understand that my anger gave my reading fire, that I have almost always taken doubts in my abilities as a challenge—and that the result is, most times, a feeling of satisfaction at having won a convert when I see the cold, appraising eyes warm to my words, the body language change, the smile that indicates that I have opened some avenue for communication. That day I read to that woman and her lowered eyes told me that she was embarrassed at her little faux pas, and when I willed her to look up at me, it was my victory, and she graciously allowed me to punish her with my full attention. We shook hands at the end of the reading, and I never saw her again. She has probably forgotten the whole thing but maybe not.

15   Yet I am one of the lucky ones. My parents made it possible for me to acquire a stronger footing in the mainstream culture by giving me the chance at an education. And books and art have saved me from the harsher forms of ethnic and racial prejudice that many of my Hispanic compañeras have had to endure. I travel a lot around the United States, reading from my books of poetry and my novel, and the reception I most often receive is one of positive interest by people who want to know more

about my culture. There are, however, thousands of Latinas without the privilege of an education or the entrée into society that I have. For them life is a struggle against the misconceptions perpetuated by the myth of the Latina as whore, domestic or criminal. We cannot change this by legislating the way people look at us. The transformation, as I see it, has to occur at a much more individual level. My personal goal in my public life is to try to replace the old pervasive stereotypes and myths about Latinas with a much more interesting set of realities. Every time I give a reading, I hope the stories I tell, the dreams and fears I examine in my work, can achieve some universal truth which will get my audience past the particulars of my skin color, my accent, or my clothes.

16   I once wrote a poem in which I called us Latinas "God's brown daughters." This poem is really a prayer of sorts, offered upward, but also, through the human-to-human channel of art, outward. It is a prayer for communication, and for respect. In it, Latin women pray "in Spanish to an Anglo God / with a Jewish heritage," and they are "fervently hoping / that if not omnipotent, / at least He be bilingual."

QUESTIONS FOR ANALYSIS AND DISCUSSION ————

1. How did Ortiz Cofer's cultural background prevent her from "fitting in"? What differences does she describe between Puerto Rican and "white" cultures?
2. How can cultural ideology and history hinder acceptance into "mainstream" corporate and social America? Explain.
3. How have the media promoted the image of the "Latina woman"? Evaluate Ortiz Cofer's analysis of why this stereotyping occurs. Do you agree?
4. What was the "Island system" of morality for Puerto Ricans? How did it both liberate and restrain them? Analyze Ortiz Cofer's connection between the island system of life and the cultural misunderstandings she encountered in urban America.
5. Explain the connection between Ortiz Cofer's poem at the end of her essay and the points she makes earlier. Is this an effective way to end the essay?
6. Why does Ortiz Cofer consider herself to be "one of the lucky ones" (paragraph 15)? Explain.

Fairness for America's Muslims
Omar Ahmad

Sometimes stereotypes can be more than simply insulting; they can interfere with the daily lives of the people victimized by such labels. As Omar Ahmad observes in the next essay, more than 700 violent attacks against Muslims or people who look Muslim occurred in the weeks following September 11. Seven years later, negative stereotypes continue to influence how many Americans view Muslims.

Omar Ahmad is the founder and chair of the Council on American Islamic Relations, the leading Muslim civil rights organization in the United States. This editorial appeared in the November 13, 2004, edition of the *Boston Globe.*

BEFORE YOU READ

Have the terrorist attacks of September 11 and the ensuing conflicts in Afghanistan and Iraq influenced your view of Muslims? If you are Muslim, have you noticed a shift in opinion toward you? Explain.

AS YOU READ

Ahmad notes that non-Muslims who are acquainted with Muslims through work or social connections have a better perception of Islam and are less likely to believe negative stereotypes. How diverse is your own acquaintance with people of different religions and cultures? Do you think that who you know can influence how you think? Why or why not?

1   It is with a combination of hope and fear that nearly seven million Muslim Americans are ending their celebration of Ramadan, a month of daylight fasting, reflection and prayer that concludes with the "eid" feast this weekend. During Ramadan, the world's 1.2 billion Muslims rededicate themselves to two central Islamic values: sharing and tolerance.

2   So it was sobering for me to review a recent poll revealing disturbing levels of intolerance towards Muslims among a random sample of a thousand Americans. The poll was conducted by an independent firm at the request of the Council on American-Islamic relations.

3   Some of the findings were chilling:

- Some 29 percent of Americans strongly or somewhat agree that Muslims teach their children to hate.
- Some 27 percent believe we value life less than other people.
- Some 29 percent believe in a kind of world Muslim conspiracy "to change the American way of life."

With negative stereotypes prevailing among more than a quarter of the American people, there is no wonder that reported hate crimes and discrimination against Muslim Americans increased 70 percent from last year alone.

4   More than 700 violent attacks, including several murders, against us, or those mistaken for us, occurred in the first nine weeks following 9/11. Scores of us were illegally removed from aircraft, sometimes because the flight crew "did not feel comfortable flying with someone named Muhammad."

5   Public leaders made defamatory statements, including the Rev. Jerry Falwell, who opined on "60 Minutes" that our prophet Muhammad was a "terrorist." Louisiana congressman John Cooksey stated on radio that any "guy with a diaper on his head, and a fan belt wrapped around it" should be pulled over by police.

6   The silver lining to the survey was that those with Muslim friends or colleagues had significantly more positive perceptions of Muslims.

7   For this reason, it is imperative for Muslim Americans to overcome our fears and let our friends and colleagues know more about us. As Muslims, we must be proud ambassadors of a faith committed to peace, justice, and mutual respect among peoples.

8   We also ask Muslims and people of other faiths to join more than 700,000 Muslims who have already signed the online petition "Not in the Name of Islam," which rejects violence committed in the name of Islam and unequivocally condemns those who perform un-Islamic acts of terror and cruelty.

9   This year Muslim Americans launched a special "Sharing Ramadan" initiative. Hundreds of mosques across the country opened their doors at the end of the daily fast and invited neighbors to celebrate the evening meal with delicious food from countries all across the globe.

10   However, we Muslims cannot fight anti-Muslim racism by ourselves. We must call upon national and local leaders to speak out against bigotry. We must appeal to legislators to protect Muslim Americans—and indeed all groups—through firm hate-crime legislation. We must encourage the proliferation of interfaith meetings, so that Muslim Americans can share the message of peace and understanding with Christians, Jews, and our neighbors of other faiths.

11   We must ask the media to rethink its sometimes careless and inflammatory depictions of Islam and Muslims. Next time you plan to refer to us, momentarily substitute the word "African Americans" or "Jews" for "Muslims." If you would not make that comment about another group, then don't make it about us.

12   Racial or religious discrimination hurts all Americans. Our nation cherishes certain fundamental principles—among them, the right to live without fear of prejudice and with equal protection of the laws. Like Dr. Martin Luther King, Jr., Muslim Americans also dream of the day when we are judged by the content of our character, and by our contributions to this society, not by our race, religion, or ethnic background.

QUESTIONS FOR ANALYSIS AND DISCUSSION

1. What are the stereotypes that most plague Muslim Americans? What are the roots of these stereotypes? Did they exist before September 11? Explain.

2. What dangers do Muslim Americans face because of ethnic stereotypes? Explain.

3. Ahmad notes that several leaders spoke out against Muslims, including Jerry Falwell, who commented that Muhammad was a "terrorist," and John Cooksey, who warned that any "guy with a diaper on his head, and a fan belt wrapped around it" should be pulled over. What is

your reaction to these comments? How do comments like these serve
to perpetuate stereotypes? Explain.

4. What solutions does Ahmad offer to help dispel religious stereotyping
of Muslims? Evaluate his solution. Do you think his idea will work?
Why or why not?

Hailing While Black
Shelby Steele

Many articles in this section describe how stereotypes create a sense of social and political distrust. But has the high-profile exposure of this issue created an atmosphere in which we have come to expect racism? In the next piece, Shelby Steele explains how even the simple act of hailing a cab in New York City can become fraught with social and political implications.

Shelby Steele is a senior fellow at the Hoover Institution, specializing in the study of race relations, multiculturalism, and affirmative action. In 2006, Steele received the Bradley Prize for his contributions to the study of race in America. He is the author of many books, most recently *White Guilt: How Blacks and Whites Together Destroyed the Promise of the Civil Rights Era* (2006). Steele has written extensively for major publications including the *New York Times* and the *Wall Street Journal*. He is a contributing editor at *Harper's* magazine and has appeared on national current affairs news programs including *Nightline* and *60 Minutes*. This essay appeared in the July 30, 2001, issue of *TIME* magazine.

BEFORE YOU READ ─────────────────────

Have you ever anticipated or expected that you might be mistreated due
to your race, age, or gender? If so, describe the situation and its outcome.

AS YOU READ ─────────────────────

In this essay, Steele presents a black conservative's point of view on racial
profiling and social fairness. Does the fact that Steele is black make his
argument more compelling? Why or why not?

1 In Manhattan recently I attempted something that is thought to be all but impossible for a black man; I tried to hail a cab going uptown toward Harlem after dark. And I'll admit to feeling a new nervousness. This simple action—black man hailing cab—is now a tableau in America's ongoing culture war. If no cab swerves in to pick me up, America is still a racist country, and the entire superstructure of contemporary liberalism is bolstered. If I catch a ride, conservatives can breath easier. So, as I raise my hand and step from the curb, much is at stake.

2   It's all the talk these days of racial profiling that has set off my nerves in this way. Having grown up in the era of segregation, I know I can survive the racial profiling of a cabby. What makes me most nervous is the anxiety that I have wrongly estimated the degree of racism in American life. I am a conservative. But conservatism is a misunderstood identity in blacks that would be much easier to carry in a world where New York City cab drivers stopped for black fares, even after dark.

3   It is easy to believe that racial profiling is a serious problem in America. It fits the American profile, and now politicians have stepped forward to give it credence as a problem. But is it a real problem? Is dark skin a shorthand for criminality in the mind of America's law-enforcement officers? Studies show that we blacks are stopped in numbers higher than our percentage in the population but lower than our documented involvement in crime. If you're trying to measure racism, isn't it better to compare police stops to actual black involvement in crime than to the mere representation of blacks in the population? The elephant in the living room—and the tragedy in black America—is that we commit crimes vastly out of proportion to our numbers in society.

4   But I can already hear "so what?" from those who believe profiling is a serious problem. And I know that the more energetic among them will move numbers and points of reference around like shells in a shill game to show racism. In other words, racial profiling is now an "identity" issue like affirmative action, black reparations or even O. J.'s innocence. It is less a real issue than a coded argument over how much racism exists in society today. We argue these issues fiercely—make a culture war around them—because the moral authority of both the left and right political identities hangs in the balance.

5   Racial profiling is a boon to the left because this political identity justifies its demand for power by estimating racism to be high. The more racism, the more power the left demands for social interventions that go beyond simple fairness under the law. Profiling hurts the right because it makes its fairness-under-the-law position on race seem inadequate, less than moral considering the prevalence of racism. The real debate over racial profiling is not about stops and searches on the New Jersey Turnpike. It is about the degree of racism in America and the distribution of power it justifies.

6   Even as individuals, we Americans cannot define our political and moral identities without making them accountable to an estimate of racism's potency in American life. Our liberalism or conservatism, our faith in government intervention or restraint and our concept of social responsibility on issues from diversity to school reform—all these will be, in part, a response to how bad we think racism is. The politically liberal identity I was born into began to fade as my estimate of American racism declined. I could identify with a wider range of American ideas and possibilities when I thought they were no longer painted by racism. Many whites I know today, who are trying to separate themselves from the shame of America's racist past, will overestimate racism to justify a liberal identity that they hope proves that separateness. First the estimation, then the identity.

7   Recently, after a talk on a college campus, a black girl stood up and told me that she was "frequently" stopped by police while driving in this bucolic and liberal college town. A professor on the same campus told me that blacks there faced an

"unwelcome atmosphere"—unwelcomeness being a newly fashionable estimation at racism's potency on college campuses today. Neither of these people offered supporting facts. But I don't think they were lying so much as "spinning" an estimation of racism that shored up their political identities.

8   We are terrible at discussing our racial problems in America today because we just end up defending our identities and the political power we hope those identities will align us with. On that day in Manhattan I caught the first cab that came along. And I should have been happy just for the convenience of good service. That I also saw this minor event as evidence of something, that I was practicing a kind of political sociology as well as catching a cab—that is the problem.

QUESTIONS FOR ANALYSIS AND DISCUSSION

1. Steele labels himself as "conservative." Do you think that Steele would agree with MacDonald's defense of racial profiling later in this chapter? Why or why not?
2. What is the "elephant in the living room" to which Steele alludes in paragraph 3? How does it relate to the argument in favor of racial profiling?
3. Steele comments that racial profiling has become "an 'identity' issue like affirmative action." In what ways are these issues similar? What is the coded argument that they both veil? Explain.
4. Steele admits that the first available cab stops to pick him up, much to his relief. Do you think he would have written the same essay if the cab had passed him by instead?

Who Is a Whiz-Kid?
Ted Gup

It is easy to spot negative and damaging racial stereotypes that are often the result of intolerance, misunderstanding, and even hate. But what about so-called "good" stereotypes, in which a particular group is dubbed smart, athletic, passionate, or musical? Are stereotypes permissible if they seem positive? How can these "good" stereotypes, in fact, hurt?

Ted Gup is a former writer for the *Washington Post* and *Time* magazine. His work has also appeared in *GQ*, *Smithsonian*, *National Geographic*, *Mother Jones*, and *Sports Illustrated*. He is the author of *Book of Honor* (2000), about CIA operatives. The following article appeared in the April 27, 1997, issue of *Newsweek*.

BEFORE YOU READ

In your experience, do you think society assumes that some races are inherently superior to others? What do you think accounts for such assumptions?

AS YOU READ

Is perpetuating a cultural stereotype acceptable if it promotes positive images? Are all stereotypes unacceptable?

1   Shortly after joining a national magazine some years ago as a writer, I found myself watching in horror as the week's cover story was prepared. The story was about "Asian-American whiz kids," and it featured a series of six student portraits, each face radiating with an intellectual brilliance. Being new to the enterprise, I was at first tentative in my criticism, cautioning that such a story was inherently biased and fueled racial and ethnic stereotypes. My criticism was dismissed. "This is something good we are saying about them," one top editor remarked. I reduced my criticism to writing. "What," I asked, "would be the response if the cover were about 'Jewish whiz kids'? Would anyone really dare to produce such an obviously offensive story?" My memo was ignored. Not long after, the cover appeared on the nation's newsstands, and the criticism began to fly. The editors were taken aback.

2   As a former Fulbright Scholar to China I have long taken a strong interest in the portrayal of Asian-Americans. But my interest went well beyond the academic. Even as the cover was being prepared, I was waiting to adopt my first son from Korea. His name was to be David. He was 5 months old when he arrived. That did not stop even some otherwise sophisticated friends from volunteering that he would no doubt be a good student.

3   Probably a mathematician, they opined, with a tone that uncomfortably straddled jest and prediction. I tried to take it all with good humor, this idea that a 5-month-old who could not yet sit up, speak a word or control his bowels was already destined for academic greatness. Even his major seemed foreordained.

4   Many Asian-Americans seem to walk an uneasy line between taking pride in their remarkable achievements and needing to shake off stereotypes. The jokes abound. There is the apocryphal parent who asks "Where is the other point?" when his or her child scores a 99 on a test. Another familiar refrain has the young Asian-American student enumerating his or her hobbies: "studying, studying and more studying."

5   Several months after David arrived he and I entered a small mom-and-pop convenience store in our neighborhood. The owners were Korean. I noticed that the husband, standing behind the cash register, was eyeing my son. "Is he Korean?" he asked. "Yes," I nodded. He reached out for him and took him into his arms. "He'll be good in math," declared the man. "My God," I muttered. Not him, too!

6   It was preposterous. It was funny. And it was unnerving. Embedded in such elevated expectations were real threats to my son. Suppose, I wondered, he should turn out to be only a mediocre student, or, worse yet, not a student at all. I resented the stereotypes and saw them for what they were, the other side of the coin of racism. It is easy to delude one's self into thinking it harmless to offer racial compliments, but that is an inherent contradiction in terms. Such sweeping descriptives, be they negative or positive,

deny the one thing most precious to all peoples—individuality. These stereotypes are pernicious for two reasons. First, such attributes are relative and tend to pit one race against another. Witness the seething enmity in many inner cities between Korean store owners and their African-American patrons. Stereotypes that hint at superiority in one race implicitly suggest inferiority in another. They are ultimately divisive, and in their most virulent form, even deadly. Who can forget the costs of the Aryan myth?

7 Many stereotypes also place a crushing burden on Asian-Americans. Few would deny that disproportionate numbers of Asian surnames appear each year among the winners of the Westinghouse science prizes or in the ranks of National Merit Scholars. But it might be a reflection of parental influences, personal commitment and cultural predilections, not genetic predisposition. A decade ago, as a Fulbright Lecturer in Beijing, I saw firsthand the staggering hours my Chinese students devoted to their studies. Were my students in the United States to invest similar time in their books I would have every reason to expect similar results.

8 I have often been told that Koreans are the "Jews of Asia," a reference to both their reported skills in business and their inherent intelligence. As a Jew, I cannot help but wince at such descriptions. I remember being one of the very few of my faith in a Midwest boarding school. There were many presumptions weighing on me, most of them grounded in my religion. My own classroom performance almost singlehandedly disabused my teachers of the myth that Jews were academically gifted. I barely made it through. Whether it was a lack of intelligence or simple rebellion against expectation, I do not know. I do know that more than once the fact that I was Jewish was raised as evidence that I could and should be doing better. Expectations based on race, be they raised or lowered, are no less galling.

9 David is now in the first grade. He is already taking math with the second graders and asking me about square roots and percentiles. I think back to the Korean merchant who took him in his arms and pronounced him a math whiz. Was he right? Do Asian-Americans have it easier, endowed with some special strand of DNA? The answer is a resounding no. Especially in our house. My son David has learning disabilities to overcome and what progress he has made is individual in the purest and most heroic sense. No one can or should take that away from him, suggesting he is just another wunderkind belonging to a favored race.

10 A year after my first son arrived, we adopted his brother from Korea. His name is Matthew. Let it be known that Matthew couldn't care less about math. He's a bug man. Slugs and earthworms. I suspect he will never be featured on any cover stories about Asian-American whiz kids, but I will continue to resist anything and anyone who attempts to dictate either his interests or his abilities based on race or place of birth. Bugs are fine by me and should be more than fine by him.

QUESTIONS FOR ANALYSIS AND DISCUSSION

1. When Gup questioned the decision to run a cover story on "Asian-American whiz kids," his editor dismissed his concerns with the comment, "This is something good we are saying about them." What does

this statement say about Gup's editor? Why do you think Gup mentions this comment?

2. What pressures do stereotypes place on children? How can stereotypes affect race relations?

3. How are stereotypes "the other side of the coin of racism"?

4. Analyze Gup's comment that stereotypes contribute to strained relationships between Koreans and blacks in inner cities. Do you agree?

5. What is the "Aryan myth"? What were its costs? Is the myth active today? If so, what is its continued impact?

6. Link some of the opinions and observations on racial stereotypes Gup makes in this article to a personal experience you had with racial stereotypes. How did stereotypes apply to the situation, and how did you handle the incident?

READING THE VISUAL

Chief Wahoo

Chief Wahoo is the official mascot of the Cleveland Indians. The team's history states that their name honors a Native American named Louis Sockalexis, who briefly played for the team when they were known as the Cleveland Spiders. Many Native Americans have disputed this claim, calling it "revisionist history." The image of Chief Wahoo has been bitterly disputed by many Native Americans who consider him a highly racist and unflattering stereotype.

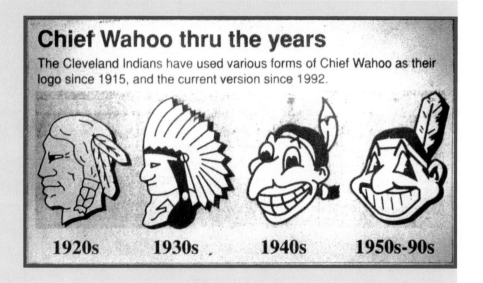

Chief Wahoo thru the years

The Cleveland Indians have used various forms of Chief Wahoo as their logo since 1915, and the current version since 1992.

| 1920s | 1930s | 1940s | 1950s-90s |

QUESTIONS FOR ANALYSIS AND DISCUSSION

1. In what ways could Chief Wahoo be considered offensive to Native Americans? What does his name mean? What image does the mascot project?
2. Could other ethnic groups be presented this way without incident? Why or why not?
3. In your opinion, can the disagreement over the Cleveland Indians' official mascot be resolved? How would you mediate this controversy?

BLOG IT

Is YOUR Mascot a Racial Stereotype?
http://palady.wordpress.com/2007/02/22/is-your-mascot-a-racial-stereotype/

"Chief Illiniwek" of the University of Illinois will perform for the last time tonight. In fact, as I write this, the student who dances as Chief Illiniwek may have already made history as the last person to do so.

From *YahooSports:*

> *The University of Illinois' controversial American Indian mascot was set to perform his last dance, and men who have previously portrayed Chief Illiniwek said they want the tradition to live on in some form.*

> *The mascot, whose fate was decided by school officials last week, will take center stage at Assembly Hall for one last performance during the men's basketball game between Illinois and Michigan on Wednesday night.*

> *Removing the chief frees the university of NCAA sanctions after the organization deemed Illiniwek—portrayed by buckskin-clad students who dance at home football and basketball games and other athletic events—an offensive use of American Indian imagery and barred the school from hosting postseason athletic events.*

I applaud the decision of the University of Illinois to comply with NCAA regulations and join the 21st century in ending the use of a stereotype. Now, it's past time for state and regional high school sports leagues to follow the NCAA's lead and mandate an end to "an offensive use of American Indian imagery."

My daughter's school calls itself, no kidding, the *Redskins.*

I have a lot of problems with this, and have since we first moved here. Let me give you a few examples of what I find offensive: 1) in the sports section of their website (which I won't link to, for privacy reasons) there are "cute" little caricatures of Indians in feathered headdress and buckskin leggings holding basketballs, pretending to be swimming, performing a split and holding pompoms, 2) their mascot is a chief in feathered headdress, 3) there's a tepee on the track/football field!

For one thing, they've mixed up their tribes. The Plains Indians wore the feathered headdress seen on the mascot, not the Susquehannas and/or the Lenni Lenape (Eastern Delaware Nation) which actually lived in my area. Also, the Native tribes of this area lived in *longhouses*, not tepees.

This is important to note because the school is about to celebrate its quasquicentennial (125 years) and thus, was founded about the time of the Indian wars.

Back in the early years of the school, people weren't thinking about ethnic stereo-types, they were busy reading about the Bighorn, Sand Creek and Pine Ridge massacres. (Although, back then, they didn't call them massacres. They were "battles" won or lost by the Army.)

Second, the administrators, boosters, players, etc, don't seem to understand that the word "Redskin" *is* an ethnic slur. One of the most offensive phrases used by this school—and its faculty, students, and alumni—is: "Redskin Pride." Literally, this phrase makes me gag.

Let's be honest. This is a small school district, 95% or so white. There's little native ancestry here, if only because their ancestors wiped out the native popula-tions with their diseases and their wars. These people have a misguided sense of pride if they can use the word "Redskin" as if it were some type of positive attribute—one to which they have no claim.

Over the summer, my mom got into a bit of a verbal tiff with a booster who had the utter audacity to say they weren't demeaning anyone. It was, she said, a way of "honoring" the Native peoples.

Huh?

How utterly stupid. As a person of Native ancestry, I don't feel "honored." I feel in-sulted. My Native ancestors were *not* "Redskins." Those ancestors were of the Bear Clan of the People of the Standing Stone (Oneida Nation) of the Six Nations of the Iroquois.

The Six Nations' Articles of Confederacy—creating the oldest known *participatory* democracy—later inspired the framing of the Constitution of the United States. In fact, the Six Nations' confederation was considered so important to the writing, a delegation of Iroquois were asked to meet with the Continental Congress, and John Hancock was given an Iroquois name: *Karanduawn*, or the Great Tree.

Do you think those whose ancestors were slaves, would feel "honored" if the team was called the "Niggers"? Do you think anyone of Jewish ancestry would feel "honored" if the team was called the "Kikes"? Do you think any of the multi-tudes in this district who came from Irish and Italian immigrants would feel "honored" if the team was the "Micks" or the "Wops"?

Of course not!

Those are *all* derogatory words used to debase another race or belief or ethnic background, and are recognized as such by nearly every sentient being in this country. There is no such recognition for the constant slurs against Native peo-ples used by sports teams across the nation, professional or otherwise.

Let's put it this way, for those still so blind that they continue defending the use of "Redskins" for their high school teams: Would you feel comfortable calling anyone a "Redskin" while you were busy dumping money in a slot machine at a Native-run casino?

Ooh! I saw that! Made you a bit uncomfortable, eh? It's one thing to yell "Go Redskins" at a football game, and quite another to actually use it in a place where the owners are "Redskins."

It's past time for all sports teams to replace names and mascots which represent *"an offensive use of American Indian imagery."*

YOU SAY:

Stereotypes, Positive or Negative, Cloud the Truth

Cathy Hwang

Asians are smart, blacks are great dancers, Irish people are friendly, Latinos are passionate, Jewish people are good with money, and French people are good cooks. All these stereotypes don't seem very harmful; after all, they seem to embody positive traits to which many people aspire. In the next essay, Pomona College junior Cathy Hwang is herself stereotyped in what would seem to be an innocent, even positive way. She explains why stereotyping people, even in ways that may seem inoffensive, is never a good idea.

Cathy Hwang is now a graduate of Pomona College in California. She wrote the following opinion piece for the March 25, 2005, issue of *The Student Life*, a student-written and published news weekly for the Pomona College community.

BEFORE YOU READ ──────────────────────────────

In this editorial, student Cathy Hwang deals with stereotypes attributed to Asians, and most specifically, Taiwanese. Before you read her essay, make a list of your own such stereotypes for Asian students. How could these generalizations harm Asians?

AS YOU READ ──────────────────────────────────

Hwang reacts with "blind anger" when she is asked a question about her ethnicity by a fellow student. Do you think her reaction was justified? What would your reaction be if someone asked you a question about your ethnic background based on a stereotype? Explain.

1 I am a very lazy person. Thus, since I live in Oldenborg, I frequently eat at Oldenborg simply because I am too lazy to trek the four thousand miles to Frank Dining Hall, even on taco day. I often regret this decision after I am resigned to yet another meal of peanut-butter-and-jelly on a day when I could be enjoying guacamole, salsa, and corn tortillas.

2 This past Wednesday, however, I had more reason than just my forgone tacos to hide my head in my hands. I was sitting at the Chinese table, engaged in friendly chatter about the diplomatic state of Taiwan (which is—don't let anybody tell you otherwise—a country, thanks), when a girl two seats to the right asked "I heard Taiwanese people are all really mellow. Is that true? Are all Taiwanese people really mellow?"

3 I nearly gagged on my peanut butter. "Yeah," I managed to choke out. "Just like all Americans are really arrogant."

4   She tossed her head (or I imagine she did, I couldn't really see her because I was blinded by anger), and replied, "Oh, I guess 'mellow' isn't positive."

5   I would like to take this moment to point out that stereotypes are stereotypes, whether they are positive or negative. Furthermore, both "positive stereotypes" and "negative stereotypes" are actually negative, because they lump people into categories and assign some kind of trait to the whole group.

6   For elaboration, let's walk through some so-called "positive stereotypes," and we will discuss (as a group!) why they are actually not positive at all.

7   Consider: "All Americans are rich." "Rich" seems like a pretty positive stereotype, right? If one is rich, one cannot only buy all that they want, they can also use their wealth to alleviate world hunger, finance high school speech and debate teams, make contributions to their favorite political party, or start an orphanage—or whatever pet cause they have that will improve the world. Unfortunately, for the large fraction of Americans who live in poverty (a whopping 12.5%, according to Pomona's very own poverty guru, Professor Michael Steinberger), this is not a stereotype that applies to them. So, when Mr. or Ms. Poor Student travels abroad, he/she may get ripped off by a street hawker who thinks, "I can sell this American a sub-par scarf for twice its worth because the American is rich anyhow." Oops! Not such a positive stereotype after all!

8   Consider: "All Asians are smart," or "All Asians are good at math." These stereotypes are likely to be considered "positive" at a prestigious college. However, for those Asians who aren't academically-inclined, or for those Asians who are slightly mathematically impaired (moi!), such stereotypes put unfair pressure on them to perform simply because they are "Asian." I don't want to be considered "smart" or "good at math" simply because I'm yellow. I want to be considered "smart" if I prove myself, just like everyone else. Furthermore, I don't want to be heaped with unfair expectations—don't tell me that I'm supposed to be good at math, because I might not be.

9   Consider: "All gay guys are hot." I admit—even I was stumped about why this "positive stereotype" might be bad. So, I consulted my good friend Andres Sanchez, a sophomore at Rice, who offered me these sage words: "In my experience as a bi-sexual male, I have found that enormous pressure exists in the gay community to be thin and beautiful. As a result of this pressure to achieve this idealized notion of what a gay man should look like, there is no place for chunky or overweight gay men in the gay community. Larger gay men find themselves being cast as social pariahs, unable to identify with the gay community."

10   So there you have it: three examples of common "positive stereotypes," and why they are bad anyway. In conclusion, I offer this very simple lesson: Don't make stereotypes! Even positive stereotypes are likely to offend and upset the people around you. And, if you really must do so, try to do so in your head, so I don't have to lecture the entire reading public about it.

QUESTIONS FOR ANALYSIS AND DISCUSSION ——————

1. Why does Hwang object to the question posed by her fellow student, "Are all Taiwanese people really mellow?" Explain.

2. Hwang presents the stereotype harbored by some people abroad that Americans are all rich. How can this hurt Americans? What expectations can it create? How can it erode international relationships?

3. Hwang gives three examples of stereotypes she has heard. Before reading this essay, had you heard of the examples she cites? For what other reasons might these "positive" stereotypes be harmful?

4. How compelling is Hwang's argument? Does she indeed "lecture" the public? Is she persuasive? Why or why not.

5. In addition to the stereotype of "mellow," what other stereotypes does Hwang deal with because of her ethnic background? What stereotypes do you face, if any, based on your ethnicity, religion, or gender? Explain.

WRITING ASSIGNMENTS

1. Consider the ways in which Hollywood influences our cultural perspectives of race and ethnicity. Write an essay exploring the influence, however slight, that film and television have had on your own perceptions of race and ethnicity. If you wish, interview other students for their opinions on this issue and address some of their points in your essay.

2. Think about the ways in which the social, intellectual, topographical, and religious histories of an ethnic group can influence the creation of stereotypes. Identify some current stereotypes that are active in American culture. What are the origins of these stereotypes? Write an essay in which you dissect these stereotypes and present ways to dispel them.

3. Write an essay discussing your own family's sense of ethnic or racial identity. What are the origins of some of your family's values, practices, and customs? Have these customs met with prejudice by people who did not understand them? Explain.

READING THE VISUAL

Stereotypes 200 Years Ago

Ethnic stereotypes have existed as long as there have been different groups of people judging one another. Many elements can contribute to a stereotype, including a group's history, generalizations of behavior or custom, and exaggeration of physical or cultural traits. Sociology professor Michael Pickering of Loughborough University observes, "Those who generate and perpetuate stereotypes of others are usually in positions of greater power and status than those who are stereotyped. Stereotypes not only define and place others as inferior, but also implicitly affirm and legitimate those who stereotype in their own position and identity." However, marginalized groups often stereotype groups of people viewed as more powerful. Indeed, it seems as if no single group can escape this practice. This image is taken from *A peep at the world and a picture of some of its inhabitants*, an early nineteenth-century book for children published in London.

4   HOLLAND, AND THE DUTCH.

The Dutch people are natives of Holland, and are a very industrious race.

In most of the towns of Holland, the canals run through the principal streets, with trees planted on each side, which have a very pretty appearance.

The Dutch make the greater part of the small toys that are imported into England and other countries, in the making of which, even the children assist.

CHINA, AND THE CHINESE.   5

It is from China that we obtain tea and silk, and fine muslins.

The Chinese women have very small feet, to procure which, their feet are bandaged while young, by which their growth is prevented.

Chinese children are very obedient to their parents, and respectful to their elders and superiors. The Chinese Empire is the oldest in the world; their own accounts, indeed, go so far back, as to be impossible to be believed.

B 3

http://www.inf.aber.ac.uk/academicliaison/horton/images/apeepattheworldpicture.jpg

RACIAL PROFILING

You Can't Judge a Crook by His Color
Randall Kennedy

Racial profiling is law enforcement's practice of considering race as an indicator of the likelihood of criminal behavior. Based on statistical assumptions, racial profiling presumes that certain groups of people are more likely to commit—or not to commit—certain crimes. The U.S. Supreme Court officially upheld the constitutionality of this practice, as long as race was only one of several factors leading to the detainment or arrest of an individual. In the next article, law professor Randall Kennedy argues that while racial profiling may seem justifiable, it is still morally wrong.

Kennedy is a professor at Harvard Law School, where he teaches courses on the freedom of expression and regulation of race relations. Educated at Princeton, Oxford, and Yale Law School, he is a member of the bar in the District of Columbia and before the U.S. Supreme Court. He is the author of several books, including *Race, Crime, and the Law* (1998), for which he won the 1998 Robert F. Kennedy Book Award. In addition to contributing to many general and scholarly publications, he sits on the editorial boards of *The Nation, Dissent*, and *The American Prospect.* This article first appeared in *The New Republic* in 1999.

BEFORE YOU READ

Do you consider racial profiling justifiable? If so, under what circumstances? If not, why?

AS YOU READ

Evaluate Kennedy's practice of posing questions to his readers and then providing them with the answers. In what ways could this article serve as a class lecture?

1   In Kansas City, a Drug Enforcement Administration officer stops and questions a young man who has just stepped off a flight from Los Angeles. The officer has focused on this man because intelligence reports indicate that black gangs in L.A. are flooding the Kansas City area with illegal drugs. Young, toughly dressed, and appearing nervous, he paid for his ticket in cash, checked no luggage, brought two carry-on bags, and made a beeline for a taxi when he arrived. Oh, and one other thing: The young man is black. When asked why he decided to question this man, the officer declares that he considered race, along with other factors, because doing so helps him allocate limited time and resources efficiently.

2   Should we applaud the officer's conduct? Permit it? Prohibit it? This is not a hypothetical example. Encounters like this take place every day, all over the country,

as police battle street crime, drug trafficking, and illegal immigration. And this particular case study happens to be the real-life scenario presented in a federal lawsuit of the early '90s, *United States* v. *Weaver,* in which the 8th U.S. Circuit Court of Appeals upheld the constitutionality of the officer's action.

3   "Large groups of our citizens," the court declared, "should not be regarded by law enforcement officers as presumptively criminal based upon their race." The court went on to say, however, that "facts are not to be ignored simply because they may be unpleasant." According to the court, the circumstances were such that the young man's race, considered in conjunction with other signals, was a legitimate factor in the decision to approach and ultimately detain him. "We wish it were otherwise," the court maintained, "but we take the facts as they are presented to us, not as we would like them to be." Other courts have agreed that the Constitution does not prohibit police from considering race, as long as they do so for bona fide purposes of law enforcement (not racial harassment) and as long as it is only one of several factors.

4   These decisions have been welcome news to the many law enforcement officials who consider what has come to be known as racial profiling an essential weapon in the war on crime. They maintain that, in areas where young African American males commit a disproportionate number of the street crimes, the cops are justified in scrutinizing that sector of the population more closely than others—just as they are generally justified in scrutinizing men more closely than they do women.

5   As Bernard Parks, chief of the Los Angeles Police Department, explained to Jeffrey Goldberg of *The New York Times Magazine:* "We have an issue of violent crime against jewelry salespeople. . . . The predominant suspects are Colombians. We don't find Mexican Americans, or blacks, or other immigrants. It's a collection of several hundred Colombians who commit this crime. If you see six in a car in front of the Jewelry Mart, and they're waiting and watching people with briefcases, should we play the percentages and follow them? It's common sense."

6   Cops like Parks say that racial profiling is a sensible, statistically based tool. Profiling lowers the cost of obtaining and processing crime information, which in turn lowers the overall cost of doing the business of policing. And the fact that a number of cops who support racial profiling are black, including Parks, buttresses claims that the practice isn't motivated by bigotry. Indeed, these police officers note that racial profiling is race-neutral in that it can be applied to persons of all races, depending on the circumstances. In predominantly black neighborhoods in which white people stick out (as potential drug customers or racist hooligans, for example), whiteness can become part of a profile. In the southwestern United States, where Latinos often traffic in illegal immigrants, apparent Latin American ancestry can become part of a profile.

7   But the defenders of racial profiling are wrong. Ever since the Black and Latino Caucus of the New Jersey Legislature held a series of hearings, complete with testimony from victims of what they claimed was the New Jersey state police force's overly aggressive racial profiling, the air has been thick with public denunciations of the practice.

8   Unfortunately, though, many who condemn racial profiling do so without really thinking the issue through. One common complaint is that using race (say, blackness) as one factor in selecting surveillance targets is fundamentally racist. But selectivity of this sort can be defended on nonracist grounds. "There is nothing more painful to me at this age in my life," Jesse Jackson said in 1993, "than to walk down the street and hear footsteps and start to think about robbery and then look around and see somebody white and feel relieved." Jackson was relieved not because he dislikes black people, but because he estimated that he stood a somewhat greater risk of being robbed by a black person than by a white person. Statistics confirm that African Americans—particularly young black men—commit a dramatically disproportionate share of street crime in the United States. This is a sociological fact, not a figment of a racist media (or police) imagination. In recent years, victims report blacks as perpetrators of around 25 percent of violent crimes, although blacks constitute only about 12 percent of the nation's population.

9   So, if racial profiling isn't bigoted, and if the empirical claim upon which the practice rests is sound, why is it wrong?

10   Racial distinctions are and should be different from other lines of social stratification. That is why, since the civil rights revolution of the 1960s, courts have typically ruled—based on the 14th Amendment's equal protection clause—that mere reasonableness is an insufficient justification for officials to discriminate on racial grounds. In such cases, courts have generally insisted on applying "strict scrutiny"—the most intense level of judicial review—to government actions. Under this tough standard, the use of race in governmental decision making may be upheld only if it serves a compelling government objective and only if it is "narrowly tailored" to advance that objective.

11   A disturbing feature of this debate is that many people, including judges, are suggesting that decisions based on racial distinctions do not constitute unlawful racial discrimination—as long as race is not the only reason a person was treated objectionably. The court that upheld the DEA agent's action at the Kansas City airport, for instance, declined to describe it as racially discriminatory and thus evaded strict scrutiny.

12   But racially discriminatory decisions typically stem from mixed motives. For example, an employer who prefers white candidates to black candidates—except for those black candidates with superior experience and test scores—is engaging in racial discrimination, even though race is not the only factor he considers (since he selects black superstars). In some cases, race is a marginal factor; in others it is the only factor. The distinction may have a bearing on the moral or logical justification, but taking race into account at all means engaging in discrimination.

13   Because both law and morality discourage racial discrimination, proponents should persuade the public that racial profiling is justifiable. Instead, they frequently neglect its costs and minimize the extent to which it adds to the resentment blacks feel toward the law enforcement establishment. When O. J. Simpson was acquitted, many recognized the danger of a large sector of Americans feeling cynical and angry toward the system. Such alienation creates witnesses who fail to cooperate with

police, citizens who view prosecutors as the enemy, lawyers who disdain the rules they have sworn to uphold, and jurors who yearn to get even with a system that has, in their eyes, consistently mistreated them. Racial profiling helps keep this pool of accumulated rage filled to the brim.

14 The courts have not been sufficiently mindful of this risk. In rejecting a 1976 constitutional challenge that accused U.S. Border Patrol officers in California of selecting cars for inspection partly on the basis of drivers' apparent Mexican ancestry, the Supreme Court noted in part that, of the motorists passing the checkpoint, fewer than 1 percent were stopped. It also noted that, of the 820 vehicles inspected during the period in question, roughly 20 percent contained illegal aliens.

15 Justice William J. Brennan dissented, however, saying the Court did not indicate the ancestral makeup of all the persons the Border Patrol stopped. It is likely that many of the innocent people who were questioned were of apparent Mexican ancestry who then had to prove their obedience to the law just because others of the same ethnic background have broken laws in the past.

16 The practice of racial profiling undercuts a good idea that needs more support from both society and the law: Individuals should be judged by public authorities on the basis of their own conduct and not on the basis of racial generalization. Race-dependent policing retards the development of bias-free thinking; indeed, it encourages the opposite.

17 What about the fact that in some communities people associated with a given racial group commit a disproportionately large number of crimes? Our commitment to a just social order should prompt us to end racial profiling even if the generalizations on which the technique is based are supported by empirical evidence. This is not as risky as it may sound. There are actually many contexts in which the law properly enjoins us to forswear playing racial odds even when doing so would advance legitimate goals.

18 For example, public opinion surveys have established that blacks distrust law enforcement more than whites. Thus, it would be rational—and not necessarily racist—for a prosecutor to use ethnic origin as a factor in excluding black potential jurors. Fortunately, the Supreme Court has outlawed racial discrimination of this sort. And because demographics show that in the United States, whites tend to live longer than blacks, it would be perfectly rational for insurers to charge blacks higher life-insurance premiums. Fortunately, the law forbids that, too.

19 The point here is that racial equality, like all good things in life, costs something. Politicians suggest that all Americans need to do in order to attain racial justice is forswear bigotry. But they must also demand equal treatment before the law even when unequal treatment is defensible in the name of nonracist goals—and even when their effort will be costly.

20 Since abandoning racial profiling would make policing more expensive and perhaps less effective, those of us who oppose it must advocate a responsible alternative. Mine is simply to spend more money on other means of enforcement—and then spread the cost on some nonracial basis. One way to do that would be to hire more police officers. Another way would be to subject everyone to closer surveillance. A benefit of the second option would be to acquaint more whites with the burden of police intrusion, which might prompt more of them to insist on limiting police power.

As it stands now, the burden is unfairly placed on minorities—imposing on Mexican Americans, blacks, and others a special kind of tax for the war against illegal immigration, drugs, and other crimes. The racial element of that tax should be repealed.

21   I'm not saying that police should never be able to use race as a guideline. If a young white man with blue hair robs me, the police should certainly be able to use a description of the perpetrator's race. In this situation, though, whiteness is a trait linked to a particular person with respect to a particular incident. It is not a free-floating accusation that hovers over young white men practically all the time—which is the predicament young black men currently face. Nor am I saying that race could never be legitimately relied upon as a signal of increased danger. In an extraordinary circumstance in which plausible alternatives appear to be absent, officials might need to resort to racial profiling. This is a far cry from routine profiling that is subjected to little scrutiny.

22   Now that racial profiling is a hot issue, the prospects for policy change have improved. President Clinton directed federal law enforcement agencies to determine the extent to which their officers focus on individuals on the basis of race. The Customs Service is rethinking its practice of using ethnicity or nationality as a basis for selecting subjects for investigation. The Federal Aviation Administration has been re-evaluating its recommended security procedures; it wants the airlines to combat terrorism with computer profiling, which is purportedly less race-based than random checks by airport personnel. Unfortunately, though, a minefield of complexity lies beneath these options. Unless we understand the complexities, this opportunity will be wasted.

23   To protect ourselves against race-based policing requires no real confrontation with the status quo, because hardly anyone defends police surveillance triggered solely by race. Much of the talk about police "targeting" suspects on the basis of race is, in this sense, misguided and harmful. It diverts attention to a side issue. Another danger is the threat of demagoguery through oversimplification. When politicians talk about "racial profiling," we must insist that they define precisely what they mean. Evasion—putting off hard decisions under the guise of needing more information—is also a danger.

24   Even if routine racial profiling is prohibited, the practice will not cease quickly. An officer who makes a given decision partly on a racial basis is unlikely to acknowledge having done so, and supervisors and judges are loath to reject officers' statements. Nevertheless, it would be helpful for President Clinton to initiate a strict anti-discrimination directive to send a signal to conscientious, law-abiding officers that there are certain criteria they ought not use.

25   To be sure, creating a norm that can't be fully enforced isn't ideal, but it might encourage us all to work toward closing the gap between our laws and the conduct of public authorities. A new rule prohibiting racial profiling might be made to be broken, but it could set a new standard for legitimate government.

QUESTIONS FOR ANALYSIS AND DISCUSSION

1. Kennedy argues that racial profiling is racist. In what ways is it racist? Alternatively, how can it be defended on nonracist grounds? Is it always racist? Explain.

2. A critical reader may argue that Kennedy contradicts himself in some places, such as in paragraph 21 when he follows his argument that racial profiling is wrong with the statement that in "extraordinary circumstances" it may be permissible. Is this indeed a contradiction? Explain.

3. In paragraph 17, Kennedy presents two examples of how the law "properly enjoins us to forswear playing racial odds even when doing so would advance legitimate goals." Do these examples support his argument that all racial profiling should be illegal? Explain.

4. How plausible are the solutions Kennedy offers? For example, he proposes that to end racial profiling, cities should hire more police officers so that the "time-saving" element of racial profiling would no longer be a factor. What issues does he not address that an opponent could use to argue against this solution? What information would you recommend he include to deflect objections? Explain.

5. This essay refers to Jesse Jackson's remark that the negative stereotyping of their own race can influence even blacks. Why do you think Kennedy includes this admission?

6. Evaluate Kennedy's observation that the practice of racial profiling keeps "this pool of accumulated [minority] rage filled to the brim." How does this reaction affect other areas of law enforcement? How can racial profiling backfire in the courtroom and in the streets? Explain.

READING THE VISUAL

Pulling Teeth

American Civil Liberties Union

In October of 2001, as part of a larger campaign to bring attention to the issue of racial profiling in New Jersey, the American Civil Liberties Union ran this advertisement to raise awareness and inform victims of their rights. The ad features Dr. Elmo Randolph, a New Jersey dentist and a plaintiff in a racial profiling case in that state. Randolph, an African-American man, says he had been pulled over approximately 100 times over a five-year period without ever receiving a ticket. In the ad, Dr. Randolph describes his experience with the police, stating that, "The police searched my car and I had to prove to the troopers that being an African-American man in a nice car doesn't mean that I am a drug dealer or car thief." Deborah Jacobs, Executive Director of the ACLU of New Jersey, said of the ad, "We want to send a message to the victims about their rights, and to the state about its obligations." This ad (see next page) ran in the October 29, 2001, edition of the *Newark Star-Ledger*.

QUESTIONS FOR ANALYSIS AND DISCUSSION

1. What words are treated differently within the body text, and why? What is the effect of having certain words in bold or larger typeface than others?

2. How does the headline of the ad connect to the ad's content and message? Explain.

3. In this ad, Elmo Randolph states that he has been pulled over "approximately 100 times without ever receiving a ticket." What is the audience likely to infer from this statement?

4. Consider the photograph used in this ad. How is Dr. Randolph dressed? Where is he sitting? In what environment is he placed? Would this ad be as effective if Randolph were younger? less professionally dressed? Explain.

5. A January 8, 2003, follow-up story in the *New Jersey Star-Ledger* reported that Randolph received a $75,000 settlement for his lawsuit against the state. The story notes, "Randolph said his story began soon after he bought his first BMW. Over the course of a decade, he estimated he was pulled over on North Jersey roads 50 to 100 times." In your opinion, did the ACLU skew the information in its ad? Does it matter if it gets an important point across? Explain.

The Racial Profiling Myth Debunked

Heather MacDonald

In 2001, the issue of racial profiling on the New Jersey Turnpike came to the attention of the nation when the ACLU announced a class action lawsuit demanding an end to the practice by state police. A disproportionate number of minorities were stopped for speeding, as compared to the number of drivers using the turnpike. President Bush announced "Racial profiling is wrong, and we will end it in America." But Heather MacDonald argues that the issue of racial profiling is a "political juggernaut"—a convenient topic for politicians to exploit for attention—to the peril of law enforcement.

Heather MacDonald's writings have appeared in many journals and newspapers, including the *Wall Street Journal, Washington Post, New York Times, The New Republic*, and *Academic Questions*. Her books include *The Burden of Bad Ideas* (2001), a collection of essays, and *Are Cops Racist?* (2003), which investigates the workings of the police and the controversy over racial profiling. This article was printed in the March 27, 2002, issue of *City Journal*.

BEFORE YOU READ

Have you ever been pulled over by a police officer for a traffic violation? What was the experience like? Do you think you were pulled over because you deserved it, or because of your age or race? If you have never been pulled over, what would you expect to happen, and how do you think you would react?

AS YOU READ

Who are the "anti-police" crusaders? What is their crusade? What is their position on racial profiling? Do you think that the new study MacDonald discusses is likely to influence their cause? Why or why not?

1   The anti–racial profiling juggernaut has finally met its nemesis: the truth. According to a new study, black drivers on the New Jersey Turnpike are twice as likely to speed as white drivers, and are even more dominant among drivers breaking 90 miles per hour. This finding demolishes the myth of racial profiling. Precisely for that reason, the Bush Justice Department tried to bury the report so the profiling juggernaut could continue its destructive campaign against law enforcement. What happens next will show whether the politics of racial victimization now trump all other national concerns.

2   Until now, the anti-police crusade that travels under the banner of "ending racial profiling" has traded on ignorance. Its spokesmen went around the country charging

that the police were stopping "too many" minorities for traffic infractions or more serious violations. The reason, explained the anti-cop crowd, was that the police were racist.

3   They can argue that no more. The new turnpike study, commissioned by the New Jersey attorney general, solves one of the most vexing problems in racial profiling analysis: establishing a violator benchmark. To show that the police are stopping "too many" members of a group, you need to know, at a minimum, the rate of lawbreaking among that group—the so-called violator benchmark. Only if the rate of stops or arrests greatly exceeds the rate of criminal behavior should our suspicions be raised. But most of the studies that the ACLU and defense attorneys have proffered to show biased behavior by the police only used crude population measures as the benchmark for comparing police activity—arguing, say, that if 24 percent of speeding stops on a particular stretch of highway were of black drivers, in a city or state where blacks make up 19 percent of the population, the police are over-stopping blacks.

4   Such an analysis is clearly specious, since it fails to say what percentage of speeders are black, but the data required to rebut it were not available. Matthew Zingraff, a criminologist at North Carolina State University, explains why: "Everybody was terrified. Good statisticians were throwing up their hands and saying, 'This is one battle you'll never win. I don't want to be called a racist.'" Even to suggest studying the driving behavior of different racial groups was to demonstrate one's bigotry, as Zingraff himself discovered when he proposed such research in North Carolina and promptly came under attack. Such investigations violate the reigning fiction in anti-racial profiling rhetoric: that all groups commit crime and other infractions at equal rates. It follows from this central fiction that any differences in the rate at which the police interact with certain citizens result only from police bias, not from differences in citizen behavior.

5   Despite the glaring flaws in every racial profiling study heretofore available, the press and the politicians jumped on the anti-profiling bandwagon. How could they lose? They showed their racial sensitivity, and, as for defaming the police without evidence, well, you don't have to worry that the *New York Times* will be on your case if you do.

6   No institution made more destructive use of racial profiling junk science than the Clinton Justice Department. Armed with the shoddy studies, it slapped costly consent decrees on police departments across the country, requiring them to monitor their officers' every interaction with minorities, among other managerial intrusions.

7   No consent decree was more precious to the anti-police agenda than the one slapped on New Jersey. In 1999, then-governor Christine Todd Whitman had declared her state's highway troopers guilty of racial profiling, based on a study of consent searches that would earn an F in a freshmen statistics class. (In a highway consent search, an officer asks a driver for permission to search his car, usually for drugs or weapons.) The study, executed by the New Jersey attorney general, lacked crucial swathes of data on stops, searches, and arrests, and compensated for the lack by mixing data from wildly different time periods. Most fatally, the attorney

general's study lacked any benchmark of the rate at which different racial groups transport illegal drugs on the turnpike. Its conclusion that the New Jersey state troopers were searching "too many" blacks for drugs was therefore meaningless.

8   Hey, no problem! exclaimed the Clinton Justice Department. Here's your consent decree and high-priced federal monitor; we'll expect a lengthy report every three months on your progress in combating your officers' bigotry.

9   Universally decried as racists, New Jersey's troopers started shunning discretionary law-enforcement activity. Consent searches on the turnpike, which totaled 440 in 1999, the year that the anti–racial profiling campaign got in full swing, dropped to an astoundingly low 11 in the six months that ended October 31, 2001. At the height of the drug war in 1988, the troopers filed 7,400 drug charges from the turnpike, most of those from consent searches; in 2000, they filed 370 drug charges, a number that doubtless has been steadily dropping since then. It is unlikely that drug trafficking has dropped on New Jersey's main highway by anything like these percentages.

10   "There's a tremendous demoralizing effect of being guilty until proven innocent," explains trooper union vice president Dave Jones. "Anyone you interact with can claim you've made a race-based stop, and you spend years defending yourself." Arrests by state troopers have also been plummeting since the Whitman–Justice Department racial profiling declaration. Not surprisingly, murder jumped 65 percent in Newark, a major destination of drug traffickers, between 2000 and 2001. In an eerie replay of the eighties' drug battles, Camden is considering inviting the state police back to fight its homicidal drug gangs.

11   But one thing did not change after the much-publicized consent decree: the proportion of blacks stopped on the turnpike for speeding continued to exceed their proportion in the driving population. Man, those troopers must be either really dumb or really racist! thought most observers, including the New Jersey attorney general, who accused the troopers of persistent profiling.

12   Faced with constant calumny for their stop rates, the New Jersey troopers asked the attorney general to do the unthinkable: study speeding behavior on the turnpike. If it turned out that all groups drive the same, as the reigning racial profiling myths hold, then the troopers would accept the consequences.

13   Well, we now know that the troopers were neither dumb nor racist; they were merely doing their jobs. According to the study commissioned by the New Jersey attorney general and leaked first to the *New York Times* and then to the Web, blacks make up 16 percent of the drivers on the turnpike, and 25 percent of the speeders in the 65-mile-per-hour zones, where profiling complaints are most common. (The study counted only those going more than 15 miles per hour over the speed limit as speeders.) Black drivers speed twice as much as white drivers, and speed at reckless levels even more. Blacks are actually stopped less than their speeding behavior would predict—they are 23 percent of those stopped.

14   The devastation wrought by this study to the anti-police agenda is catastrophic. The medieval Vatican could not have been more threatened had Galileo offered photographic proof of the solar system. It turns out that the police stop blacks more for speeding because they speed more. Race has nothing to do with it.

15   This is not a politically acceptable result. And the researchers who conducted the study knew it. Anticipating a huge backlash should they go public with their findings, they checked and rechecked their data. But the results always came out the same.

16   Being scientists, not politicians, they prepared to publish their study this past January, come what may. Not so fast! commanded the now-Bush Justice Department. We have a few questions for you. And the Bush DOJ, manned by the same attorneys who had so eagerly snapped up the laughable New Jersey racial profiling report in 1999, proceeded to pelt the speeding researchers with a series of increasingly desperate objections.

17   The elegant study, designed by the Public Service Research Institute in Maryland, had taken photos with high-speed camera equipment and a radar gun of nearly 40,000 drivers on the turnpike. The researchers then showed the photos to a team of three evaluators, who identified the race of the driver. The evaluators had no idea if the drivers in the photos had been speeding. The photos were then correlated with speeds.

18   The driver identifications are not reliable! whined the Justice Department. The researchers had established a driver's race by agreement among two of the three evaluators. So in response to DOJ's complaint, the researchers reran their analysis, using only photos about which the evaluators had reached unanimous agreement. The speeding ratios came out identically to before.

19   The data are incomplete! shouted the Justice Department next. About one third of the photos had been unreadable, because of windshield glare that interfered with the camera, or the driver's position. Aha! said the federal attorneys. Those unused photos would change your results! But that is a strained argument. The only way that the 12,000 or so unreadable photos would change the study's results would be if windshield glare or a seating position that obstructed the camera disproportionately affected one racial group. Clearly, they do not.

20   Nevertheless, DOJ tried to block the release of the report until its objections were answered. "Based on the questions we have identified, it may well be that the results reported in the draft report are wrong or unreliable," portentously wrote Mark Posner, a Justice lawyer held over from the Clinton era.

21   DOJ's newfound zeal for pseudo-scientific nitpicking is remarkable, given its laissez-faire attitude toward earlier slovenly reports that purported to show racial profiling. Where it gets its new social-science expertise is also a mystery, since according to North Carolina criminologist Matthew Zingraff, "there's not a DOJ attorney who knows a thing about statistical methods and analysis." Equally surprising is Justice's sudden unhappiness with the Public Service Research Institute, since it approved the selection of the institute for an earlier demographic study of the turnpike.

22   The institute proposed a solution to the impasse: Let us submit the study to a peer-reviewed journal or a neutral body like the National Academy of Sciences. If a panel of our scientific peers determines the research to be sound, release the study then. No go, said the Justice Department. That study ain't seeing the light of day.

23   Robert Voas, the study's co-author, is amazed by Justice's intransigence. "I think it's very unfortunate that the politics have gotten in the way of science," he says, choosing his words carefully. "The scientific system has not been allowed to move as it should have in this situation."

24   As DOJ and the New Jersey attorney general stalled, *The Record* of Bergen posted the report on the Web, forcing the state attorney general to release it officially. Now the damage control begins in earnest. Everyone with a stake in the racial profiling myth, from the state attorney general to the ACLU to defense attorneys who have been getting drug dealers out of jail and back on the streets by charging police racism, is trying to minimize the significance of the findings. But they are fighting a rear-guard battle. Waiting in the wings are other racial profiling studies by statisticians who actually understand the benchmark problem: Matthew Zingraff's pioneering traffic research in North Carolina, due out in April, as well as sound studies in Pennsylvania, New York, and Miami. Expect many of the results to support the turnpike data, since circumstantial evidence from traffic fatalities and drunk-driving tests have long suggested different driving behaviors among different racial groups. While racist cops undoubtedly do exist, and undoubtedly they are responsible for isolated instances of racial profiling, the evidence shows that systematic racial profiling by police does not exist.

25   The Bush administration, however desperate to earn racial sensitivity points, should realize that far more than politics is at stake in the poisonous anti–racial profiling agenda. It has strained police-community relations and made it more difficult for the police to protect law-abiding citizens in inner-city neighborhoods. The sooner the truth about policing gets out, the more lives will be saved, and the more communities will be allowed to flourish freed from the yoke of crime.

QUESTIONS FOR ANALYSIS AND DISCUSSION

1. Evaluate the evidence MacDonald uses to support her argument. First, identify facts, statements, and observations she offers as proof to support her argument. Then assess how compelling this proof is in supporting her thesis.
2. In her essay, MacDonald cites statistical data on criminal activity based on race. Review this argument. Based on her information, what conclusions might you draw? What else do you need to know in order to form a crucial assessment on racial profiling by police on the New Jersey Turnpike?
3. In your opinion, if statistical evidence proved that certain racial groups were indeed more likely to engage in criminal activities in certain areas, do you think racial profiling is justifiable? Why or why not? Explain your point of view.
4. Why, according to MacDonald, did the Justice Department attempt to "bury" the new study?
5. How do you think Kennedy would respond to MacDonald's argument that *systematic* racial profiling does not exist?

Are You a Terrorist, or Do You Play One on TV?

Laura Fokkena

Sometimes stereotypes can be more than simply insulting, they can interfere with the daily lives of the people victimized by them. As Laura Fokkena observes in the next essay, Hollywood has long cast people from the Middle East as terrorists. This stereotype wasn't helped by the tragic events of September 11. The perpetuation of the Arab-as-terrorist stereotype has caused Fokkena, who is American, and her husband, who is Egyptian, to face the scrutiny of airport security, to be kept off of flights, and to be eyed with suspicion merely because he resembles the same ethnicity as the Muslim extremists who committed acts of terrorism. As Fokkena explains, for some people, racial profiling, on the street or on the screen, is nothing new.

Laura Fokkena's writing has been published in a variety of newspapers and magazines in the United States and the Middle East, including *HipMama* and *Home Education Magazine*. She is the author of *Wanderlust* (2004), written with Heidi Sandler. This essay first appeared in the November 2002 edition of *PopPolitics*.

BEFORE YOU READ

Think about your own family's sense of ethnic or racial identity. What are the origins of some of your family's values, traditions, and customs? Have these customs ever been questioned by people who did not understand them? What assumptions do you think other people may have about your family?

AS YOU READ

Fokkena notes that immediately following the attacks, many movie studios delayed the release of violent films, especially ones featuring Arabs as the bad guys. In light of the events of September 11, what new obstacles do Arab-Americans face in dispelling the film stereotype Fokkena describes?

1   Several years ago I came home from work one night to find my Egyptian husband and his Jordanian friend up past midnight watching Aladdin. Our daughter—then a toddler and the rightful owner of the video—had gone to bed hours earlier and left the two of them to enjoy their own private cultural studies seminar in our living room.

2   "Oh, God, now the sultan's marrying her off!" cried our Jordanian Friend. "It's barbaric, but hey, it's home," quipped my husband, repeating lyrics from the film while rolling his r's in a baritone imitation of an accent he's never had.

3   I admit it: I purchased Disney crap. In my own defense, I try to avoid all strains of happily-ever-after princess stories. But, other than a few grainy videos that you can order from, say, Syria, Aladdin is one of the rare movies with an Arab heroine available for the 2-to-6-year-old set. And so I had taken my chances with it.

4   My husband preferred to tell my daughter bedtime stories taken straight out of 1,001 Nights, before they'd been contorted at the hands of Hollywood. (Tales of Ali Baba's clever servant Morghana are far more feminist than the big screen version of Aladdin ever was.) For my daughter's sake, I think this is wonderful. But it's also disappointing to see yet another example of unadulterated Middle Eastern literature trapped in Middle Eastern communities, told in whispers to children at bedtime, while the world at large is bombarded with a mammoth distorted Hollywood version replete with hook-nosed villains, limping camels, a manic genie and Jasmine's sultan dad who is (of course) a sexist.

5   While Native Americans, Asian Americans and numerous other ethnic groups have had significant success in battling racist and inaccurate media images of their communities, Muslims and Middle Easterners are just beginning to decry stereotypical portrayals of Arabs and Islam. In April, following another crisis in the West Bank, Edward Said wrote a short piece, published in both the American and Arab press, stressing the importance of media savvy. "We have simply never learned the importance of systematically organizing our political work in this country on a mass level, so that for instance the average American will not immediately think of 'terrorism' when the word 'Palestinian' is pronounced."

6   After Sept. 11, an astonishing number of films and television programs were cancelled, delayed or taken out of production due to unfortunate coincidences between their violent plotlines and, well, reality. It went without saying that all this mad scrambling was for the benefit of a nation momentarily unwilling to see the fun in shoot-em-up action adventures, and that it was not—at least in the case of movies with Middle Eastern characters—indicative of a sudden dose of sensitivity towards anti-Arab stereotyping.

7   But apparently Hollywood has either declared the grieving period over, or has decided that what we need most right now are more escapist fantasies of Americans kicking the asses of aliens and foreigners. A number of films initially pushed back have since been released (some, like *Black Hawk Down* and *Behind Enemy Lines* were actually moved up), and television series that were hastily rewritten to eradicate any terrorist references have now been rewritten again, this time to highlight them.

8   This first became obvious back in March 2002, when CBS was bold enough to broadcast *Executive Decision* (albeit opposite the Oscars). *Executive Decision*, originally released in 1996, is a mediocre thriller that depicts Muslim terrorists hijacking a 747 en route to Washington, D.C. Like most films in its genre, wild-eyed Arabs are foiled by the technological, intellectual and ultimately moral superiority of Americans.

9   *Executive Decision* has since appeared repeatedly on various cable networks, along with *True Lies* (1994), *The Siege* (1998) and *Not Without My Daughter* (1991). NBC's "The West Wing" has written a fictional Arab country into its plotline (and assassinated its defense minister); "Law and Order" opened this year's season with the story of an American convert to Islam who murders a women's rights activist. Islam is treated with varying degrees of nuance in each of these works, but it is always approached as a dilemma to be overcome—one always needs to do something about these troublesome Muslims—rather than folded unproblematically into the

background, the way Josh and Toby's Judaism is presented on "The West Wing," or the way Betty Mahmoody's Christianity is portrayed in *Not Without My Daughter*.

10   According to a recently released report from Human Rights Watch, the federal government received reports of 481 anti-Muslim hate crimes in 2001, 17 times the number it received the year before. It also noted that more than 2,000 cases of harassment were reported to Arab and Muslim organizations. The Bush administration and the Department of Justice have responded on the one hand by condemning hate crimes against the Muslim and Middle Eastern community, and on the other by rounding up Muslims and Middle Easterners for questioning. Most notoriously, the FBI and Justice Department announced last fall their intent to schedule "interviews" with 5,000 men of Arab descent between the ages of 18 and 33. More than 1,000 men were detained indefinitely and incommunicado in the aftermath of Sept. 11, most of them on minor visa charges.

11   Yet racial profiling and ethnic stereotyping are nothing new to Americans of Middle Eastern descent. Hollywood has long used images of bumbling, accented Arabs and Iranians as shorthand for "vile enemy," depicting them as stupid (witness the terrorist lackey in *True Lies* who forgets to put batteries in his camera when making a video to release to the press), yet nevertheless deeply threatening to all that is good and right with America. So ingrained is the image of Arab-as-terrorist that Ray Hanania, an Arab-American satirist, titled his autobiography *I'm Glad I Look Like a Terrorist* ("almost every TV or Hollywood Arab terrorist looks like some uncle or aunt or cousin of mine. The scene where Fred Dryer [of TV's *Hunter*] pounces on a gaggle of terrorists in the movie *Death Before Dishonor* (1987) looks like an assault on a Hanania family reunion").

12   Nowhere is this game of Pin-the-Bomb-Threat-on-the-Muslim more obvious than at the airport. A few years ago I flew out of Cairo with my husband and discovered that F.W.A. (Flying While Arab) is no joke. We landed in Paris with a crying baby and were ushered to the back of the line while the airline attendants processed every other passenger. My husband was unconcerned; he was used to the routine. But I was acutely aware of two things: 1) that the baby was on her last diaper; and 2) that diaper was feeling heavy.

13   Our turn finally came a good three hours later, whereupon we spent another 45 minutes having our carry-on luggage examined and re-examined, answering the same questions again and again, and waiting while security checked and re-checked their computer database. All this over a graduate student from Egypt, married to an American citizen, during a time when world politics were calm enough that Bill Clinton's main preoccupation was rubbing lipstick smudges off his fly.

14   As it happened, most of the French airline workers were on strike that week (imagine that!) so we were sent to an airport hotel for the night and told we could take our connecting flight to D.C. the next day. While the other Americans and Europeans on our flight took the opportunity to spend a free night in Paris, my husband was instructed not to leave the hotel. I suppose the baby and I could have taken our crisp blue passports and gone into the city without him, but the thought of taking advantage of my American citizenship—something I'd just been born into by chance, mind you—while he stayed behind watching bad French television in the hotel lounge was too much to take.

15   Of course, it would be a mistake to assume that the most egregious offenses of racial profiling take place at the airport. The Council on American-Islamic Relations reports that half of the discrimination complaints it received in 2001 were work-related, and there has been a leap in the number of outright hate crimes, including at least three murders, since Sept. 11.

16   The *Atlantic Monthly* featured an essay by Randall Kennedy, a Harvard law professor [in which he] compared racial profiling to its "alter ego," affirmative action. "Supporters of profiling, who are willing to impose what amounts to a racial tax on profiled groups, denounce as betrayals of 'color blindness' programs that require racial diversity," he wrote. "A similar turnabout can be seen on the part of many of those who support affirmative action. Impatient with talk of communal needs in assessing racial profiling, they very often have no difficulty with subordinating the interests of individual white candidates to the purported good of the whole."

17   Kennedy's piece reaches no conclusions—other than to affirm the need for the debate in the first place—but I see no contradiction here. When workers are paid unequally for doing equivalent work, union organizers naturally argue that all workers should be paid what the highest-earning worker is paid, a process called "leveling up." Both the opposition to racial profiling and the support of affirmative action are about leveling up.

18   In both cases, marginalized groups who have suffered from stereotyping and injustice are asking to be considered full-fledged participants in our culture, to be given the same benefit of the doubt that white people have been given for centuries. Membership has its privileges, including job promotions, tenure, the ability to speed in a school zone and get off with a warning, and impromptu nights in Paris cafés. Whether one considers these things rights or luxuries, they are the aspects of citizenship that make one feel both accepted in and loyal to one's community and culture.

19   Some, like Ann Coulter—a columnist so out of touch even *The National Review* fired her—call those who complain about such matters "crazy," "paranoid," "immature nuts" and (my favorite) "ticking time bombs." Though most people would find her language over-the-top, there are many people who agree with the sentiment: that an increase in security, even if it means engaging in racial profiling, is a necessary evil in these dark times.

20   Lori Hope, in a "My Turn" column published in *Newsweek* last spring, worried that in alerting a flight attendant of a suspicious-looking traveler ("He was olive-skinned, black-haired and clean-shaven, with a blanket covering his legs and feet"), she might have "ruined an innocent man's day" when the man was removed from the flight. Nevertheless, she said, "I'm not sure I regret it . . . it's not the same world it was half a lifetime ago."

21   And for her, it probably isn't. But for the thousands of people who have been falsely associated with a handful of extremists for no reason other than their ancestry or their religion, for those who have been targeted not for their crimes but for color of their skin, not a whole lot has changed.

22   The assumption in all these discussions is that getting kicked off a plane is merely a hassle. Granted, no one should be hassled because of their race or ethnicity, but c'mon, be reasonable. This is just a little annoyance we're talking

about, the way watching the mad professor getting chased around by psychotic Libyans in *Back to the Future* is "fun," "just a joke," you know, like someone in blackface. National security is the real issue. Anyone who can't see that must have something to hide.

23   But those who argue that it's an inevitable necessity should look to countries like Egypt, where racial and religious profiling as a manner of combating Islamic extremism is obviously unworkable. Ethnic stereotyping, whether by Hollywood or by the FBI, solidifies the wedge between what we call "mainstream" culture and those who are perceived to be on the outside of it. "Ruining an innocent man's day" isn't the point, just as the hassle of moving to a different seat on the bus wasn't the point for Rosa Parks. Didn't we hammer all this out 40 years ago?

QUESTIONS FOR ANALYSIS AND DISCUSSION ─────

1. Evaluate Fokkena's connection between racial profiling and affirmative action. In what ways are they similar, and how are they different?

2. In what ways has Hollywood promoted the stereotype of Arabs as terrorists? What do you think of this stereotype? Is it art imitating life? Is it unfair? Explain.

3. What does Fokkena allude to in her final sentence? Why does she end her essay with this reference?

4. In paragraph 20, Fokkena refers to an essay written by Lori Hope that appeared in *Newsweek*. Read about the Lawyers Committee for Civil Rights suit <http://www.lccr.com/khan.doc> against the airline that ejected a passenger from the flight on the recommendation of another passenger. Do you think Hope was correct in voicing her concerns? What about the airline? Explain.

5. Fokkena opens her essay with a reference to Disney's *Aladdin,* a movie she purchased because it featured an Arab heroine. Consider the ways Hollywood influences our cultural perspectives of race and ethnicity. Write an essay exploring the influence, however slight, film and television has had on your own perception of race. If you wish, interview other students for their opinions on this issue and address some of their observations in your essay.

WRITING ASSIGNMENTS

1. Look up some of the cases described by Kennedy and evaluate the role racial profiling played in the corresponding legal arguments. Write an analysis of the issue based on your research. Support your analysis with additional information provided by other authors in their essays.

2. Teenagers often complain that they are watched more closely in stores because it is believed they are more likely to be shoplifters. Write an essay in which you consider the validity of other kinds of profiling, such as that based on age, income, or gender. What assumptions of criminal behavior correspond to these

groups? If racial profiling is wrong, is it also wrong to profile on the basis of gender or age? Why or why not?

3. What is the government's official position on racial profiling? Visit the U.S. Department of Justice website and read the "Racial Profiling Fact Sheet" posted online at <http://www.usdoj.gov/opa/pr/2003/June/racial_profiling_fact_sheet.pdf>. Review the entire fact sheet. What exceptions does the government make concerning racial profiling, and why? Identify any areas of the document that you find questionable or particularly compelling and explain why.

4. Visit the ACLU's website on racial equality at <http://www.aclu.org> and review its information on racial profiling. What are the most pressing issues concerning racial profiling today? Select an issue or case described on the ACLU website and research it in greater depth. Write a short essay summarizing the situation or issue and your position on it.

Credits

Text Credits

Omar Ahmad. "Fairness for America's Muslims," from *The Boston Globe*, November 13, 2004. Reprinted with the permission of the author.

Arthur Allen. "Prayer in Prison: Religion as Rehabilitation." Reprinted by permission of the author.

BBC Opinion Poll. "What Do You Think of America?" June 20, 2003. http://news.bbc.co.uk.

David Blankenhorn. "Defining Marriage Down is No Way to Save It," from *Weekly Standard* April 2, 2007. Reprinted with permission from the publisher.

Andrew Braaksma. "Some Lessons I Learned on the Assembly Line," from *Newsweek*, September 12, 2005 © 2005, Newsweek, Inc. All rights reserved. Used by permission.

Mark Bowden. "News Judgment and Jihad," originally published in *The Atlantic Monthly*, December 2004. Copyright © by Mark Bowden. Reprinted by the permission of Dunham Literary as agent for the author.

Stephanie Bower. "What's the Rush?: Speed and Mediocrity in Local TV News." Reprinted by permission of the author.

Joanne K. M. Bratten. " 'In Loco Parentis:' Invasion of Privacy or Moral Information?" University Concourse April 12, 1999 of Franciscan University. Reprinted with permission.

Holly Buchanan. "Blog It: Flip It—Girls Fight Back Against Bad Ads," from marketingtowomenonline blog, October 2007.

Christopher Caldwell. "What a College Education Buys," from The *New York Times*, February 25, 2007. Copyright © by The New York Times Company. Used by permission.

Danise Cavallaro. "Smoking: Offended by the Numbers." Reprinted by permission of the author.

Judith Ortiz Cofer. "The Myth of the Latina Woman," from *The Latin Deli: Prose and Poetry Copyright* © by Judith Ortiz Cofer. Reprinted with permission of the University of Chicago Press.

Amanda Collins. "Bring East Bridgewater Elementary into the World." Reprinted by permission of the author.

Corrina Collins. "BLOG IT: Does Europe Really Hate Us?" *Praesidium Respublicae* (blog) May 14, 2007. Reprinted by permission.

Francis S. Collins. "Science & Spirit," September/October 2007. Reprinted with permission of the Helen Dwight Reid Educational Foundation. Published by Heldref Publications, 1319 Eighteenth St., NW, Washington, DC 20036-1802. Copyright © 2007.

Council on Foreign Relations. "Terrorism and the Media" (Fact-sheet). Reprinted by permission.

Mark Danner. "Words in a Time of War," commencement address delivered to graduates of the Department of Rhetoric at UC Berkeley, May 10, 2007. Reprinted by permission of the author.

Joel Epstein. "Parental Notification: Fact or Fiction?" from *Prevention File*, Vol. 14, No. 2. Reprinted with permission of the publisher.

Laurie Essig. "Same-sex marriage," from *Salon.com*, July 10. 2000. Reprinted by permission of the author.

Susan Faludi and **Karen Lehrman**. "Revisionist Feminism." Copyright © *Slate*. Distributed by United Feature Syndicate, Inc. Reprinted with permission.

Jerry Fensterman. "I See Who Others Choose to Die," from *The Boston Globe*, January 31, 2006. Reprinted by permission of the author's widow, Lisa Bevilaqua.

Robin Fleishman. "Public Policy Proposal: Legalization of Marijuana for Medical Purposes." Reprinted by permission of the author.

Harry Flood. "Manufacturing Desire," from *Adbusters Magazine*, Winter 2000. Reprinted with permission of the author.

Index